Charles E. Merrill Publishing Company
A Bell & Howell Company
Columbus   Toronto   London   Sydney

Buyer Behavior: A Decision-Making Approach

Raymond L. Horton
Lehigh University

To Patricia
Incisive critic, principal advisor, and dedicated wife.

Published by Charles E. Merrill Publishing Company
A Bell & Howell Company
Columbus, Ohio 43216

Production Editor: Gnomi Schrift Gouldin
Cover Design: Tony Faiola
Cover Painting: Sonny Zoback
This book was set in Garamond

Library of Congress Catalog Card Number: 83-62447
International Standard Book Number: 0-675-20105-5

1 2 3 4 5 6 7 8 9—91 90 89 88 87 86 85 84
Printed in the United States of America

Preface

The mass prosperity in the United States that followed World War II ushered in a Consumer Era which was, and continues to be, a truly unique period in the history of the world. The general prosperity that has characterized this period was accompanied by an extraordinary increase in the variety and complexity of available goods and services and heretofore unknown opportunities for buyers to express their individual needs in the marketplace.

From the perspective of marketers, the behavior of buyers in the post-World War II era became more complex and less predictable. Quite suddenly the need for a more precise and detailed understanding of buyer behavior increased dramatically. Fortunately, the theories, methods, and researchers needed to produce this understanding were also becoming increasingly available at this time.

The "demand" for more buyer behavior knowledge resulted in a "supply" of buyer behavior research that has increased at a seemingly exponential rate in the last three decades. During this time much has been learned. Still, the field is very new and to a large extent unsettled. This situation presents many challenges to authors of textbooks on buyer behavior; especially books, such as this one, which attempt to present a review of buyer behavior theory and research that is current, theoretically and methodogically precise, and complete while remaining textbooks rather than research monographs.

This book attempts to meet these challenges in a number of ways. Our analysis of buyer behavior is firmly and directly based upon extensive research. Despite the extensive research base, our review is, of necessity, selective. While it is neither possible nor desirable to entirely avoid questions and controversies, the selection of topics and the depth of coverage has been heavily weighted in favor of knowledge that is well established and of managerial relevance. Finally, in contrast with most consumer and buyer behavior textbooks, this book focuses initially on those aspects of behavior common to all buyers and leaves the discussion of the myriad individual differences among buyers to later chapters. This organizational scheme is intended to keep the reader from initially becoming lost in a sea of individual differences in buying behavior, which tend to vary widely over types of products as well as types of buyers and are rarely organized into general explanatory theories or classification systems.

The theories, concepts, and research findings discussed in this book are organized into seven major sections. Part I provides a general introduction to the field of buyer behavior from several different perspectives. When a buyer recognizes the need to make a purchasing decision, that person will be in one of three decision-making states, generally referred to as routinized response behavior, limited problem solving, and extensive problem solving. The next three parts examine each of these states. The first four parts of the book emphasize the elements of buyers' decision making processes most common to all buyers.

Part V is devoted to a general, and largely illustrative, discussion of the myriad ways in which individual buyers differ in their buying behavior, and the managerial consequences of these differences. Part VI broadens the discussion by examining the special characteristics of buying decisions conducted or experienced on a collective basis by families and organizational buyers. In this section we shall argue that consumer and organizational buying show considerable similarity. For this reason the title chosen for this book is the comprehensive *Buyer Behavior*, rather than the more popular Consumer Behavior or Consumer and Organizational Buying Behavior. Part VII concludes the book with a discussion of how buyer behavior theory and research can facilitate the making of effective and efficient public policy.

ACKNOWLEDGEMENTS

Like all large scale efforts, the writing of this book has benefited from the general knowledge, critical evaluations, and occasionally brilliant insights of a number of persons. Professors Nora Ganim Barnes (Boston College), Joseph Belch (San Diego State University), Edward Riordan (Wayne State University), and Terrell Williams (Utah State University) provided initial reviews that were very useful in rigorously defining the basic concepts which underlie this book. Professors Gary Klein (California State University, Long Beach), Michael K. Mills (University of Southern California), and Charles M. Schaninger (SUNY at Albany) provided insightful reviews and many useful suggestions for revising individual chapters. I am especially indebted to Professor Robert Pitts (University of Mississippi) who served as reviewer and advisor throughout the entire writing of the book. Last, but not least, Professors Robert Eckles (University of Wyoming, Cheyenne) and Carol Scott (UCLA) provided final reviews of the entire manuscript that were of great value in pulling the many diverse themes in the manuscript into a more coordinated and cohesive statement of our current knowledge of buyer behavior.

Among my colleagues at Lehigh University, four deserve special mention. Professors Martin Richter and George Shortess provided expert reviews of the chapters on learning and perception, respectively, and kept me from the common errors that nonexperts frequently make in discussions of these topics. Professor Hugh Daubek, a colleague in marketing, provided a number of general suggestions regarding the strengths and weaknesses of many of my preliminary ideas. I am most indebted to Professor Michael Kolchin who prepared the initial draft of Chapter 16 on Organizational Buying Behavior and who provided consistently detailed and insightful reviews of the initial drafts of many chapters.

Finally, Mrs. Jan Bonge, Mrs. Joyce Chiz, Mrs. Jean Gorman, Ms. Sharon Ruhf, and Mrs. Janice Schaeffer skillfully provided the many secretarial services that intervene between the initial gleam in an author's eyes and the final printed book. I am especially indebted to Mrs. Schaeffer who typed the majority of the manuscript and efficiently and effectively handled the barrage of activities which inevitably arise as the final due date approaches.

Raymond L. Horton
Bath, Pennsylvania

Introduction: The Organization of This Text

One consequence of the mass prosperity that followed World War II is that the behavior of buyers in the United States has become more complex and varied, as have the available goods and services. Thus, marketers have required greater knowledge and deeper understanding of the behavior of buyers, which has led to a dramatic increase in the research on buyer behavior. This book examines the theory and research on buyer behavior and the results of that labor.

Part I opens the text with an overview of buyer behavior. Chapter 1 reviews the development of buyer behavior as an area of study. It discusses the orientation of past research, the characteristics of currently dominant theories, and the research trends that are emerging. Chapter 2 examines four comprehensive models of buyer behavior and their view of buyers' decision-making processes. Variations among buyers' decision making processes in different situations is the subject of Chapter 3.

Parts II–IV are organized around the idea that when a buyer recognizes the need to purchase that buyer will be in *one* of three decision-making states: generally referred to as routinized response behavior, limited problem solving, and extensive problem solving. These three states are distinguished by the buyer's knowledge of the product class and associated brand concepts necessary for efficient and effective decision making.

Part II is devoted to an analysis of the behavior of buyers when their knowledge of the product class and alternative brands within it is sufficient to implement their buying decisions in a routine way. Chapter 4 discusses the characteristics of routinized response behavior. An important consequence of the routinized response behavior of buyers is their tendency toward a high degree of brand loyalty. Developing brand loyalty is a key managerial objective and Chapter 5 is devoted to this topic.

Often, however, buyers will regard their knowledge of the relevant product class as adequate but feel they need more information about the specific brands from which they will make their ultimate choice. This decision-making situation is known as limited problem solving, because the problem is limited to learning about alternative brands. For example, the basic *concept* of many durable goods remains quite stable over long periods of time, while the characteristics of specific brands often change sufficiently that a buyer will need to form new brand concepts *before* a satisfactory purchase can be made. This will require us to deal with how buyers learn a brand concept. To this end, Part III investigates motivation, learning and memory, and attitudes and attitude change.

Occasionally, buyers face the need to evaluate a product with which they are largely or entirely unfamiliar. This decision-making situation is known as extensive problem solving, reflecting the need to learn the characteristics of the basic product class as well as brands within that class. Solar heat, home video recorders, time-sharing resorts, and personal computers are current examples of such new products. New products typically place relatively large information acquisition and evaluation demands upon potential buyers. How buyers cope with these demands is the topic of Part IV.

Because information from other people is so important in extensive problem solving, Part IV begins, in Chapter 9, with an analysis of social influence processes. Chapter 10 addresses the topic of what constitutes a "new" product or innovation and the factors involved in the acceptance of new products. Chapter 11 deals with the very difficult and subtle issues of how perceptions of raw stimuli, such as light or sound waves, are transformed into meaningful information. Although relevant to virtually every aspect of our analysis of buyer behavior, it is precisely under conditions of new and unfamiliar stimuli that the questions addressed in Chapter 11 become most obvious and insistent.

The primary advantage of the organizational scheme of this text is that it allows the reader to focus on what is common to the behavior of all buyers before examining the often bewildering array of specific differences among different types of buyers. However, when a specific company develops marketing *strategies* for a specific product, such differences are critical because it will often be desirable to develop different strategies for different types of buyers. Part V addresses this issue by focusing on the implications of developing so-called segmented marketing strategies. Chapters 12, 13, and 14, respectively, investigate demographic and socioeconomic, value, and social group membership differences among buyers. Collectively, these variables are generally referred to as exogenous variables.

The first fourteen chapters of this text reflect the prevailing perspective of most buyer behavior researchers; that is, they focus on the behavior of the individual buyer. Part VI enhances this perspective by focusing on buyer behavior conducted, or experienced, on a collective basis; specifically, family and organizational buying behavior. Chapter 15 argues that consumer and organizational buying behavior have more in common than might be initially suspected. Thus, the title chosen for this book is the comprehensive *Buyer Behavior* rather than the more popular Consumer Behavior or Consumer and Organizational Buying Behavior. With the exception of the few situations where an explicit distinction is made between organizational *buyers* and ultimate *consumers*, the two terms are used interchangeably. Although the main focus is on collective behavior, the marketing implications of differences among families and organizations is also discussed. In this sense, Chapters 15 and 16 also represent a continuation of the implications of individual differences for the development of segmented marketing strategies.

Throughout this book the primary orientation will be that of a manager trying to understand the behavior of buyers in order to accomplish managerial objectives. Usually there is at least a rough fit between managerial and consumer objectives, for the manager maximizes profits primarily by satisfying consumers. For many reasons, however, the free market mechanism may not work with complete efficiency. Therefore, Part VII, Chapter 17 considers how knowledge of consumer behavior can facilitate public policy in the proper regulation of business practices.

Contents

An Introduction to Buyer Behavior Theory and Research

I

The three chapters of which Part I is comprised are designed to present a broad overview of buyer behavior. Chapter 1 is a brief historical overview of the development of buyer behavior as an area of study. It discusses briefly the major characteristics of the currently dominant information processing approach to the study of buyer behavior, and examines several emerging trends in buyer behavior research. Chapter 2 presents four comprehensive models of buyer behavior. A principle value of such comprehensive models is their overview of the concepts central to the study of buyer behavior and their suggestion of the interrelationships among these concepts. All of these comprehensive models tend to share a common view of the basic nature of buyers' decision-making processes. However, it has become clear in recent years that buyers' decision-making processes are different in different buying situations. Chapter 3 is devoted to the differences in the way buyers approach different types of buying situations.

A Brief History of Buyer Behavior Theory and Research

1

How far back scholarly interest in the buyer or consumer is traced depends on one's perspective and the reasons for such study. Aristotle was keenly interested in man's "consumption" of various forms of leisure and its effect on the individual and society. Similarly, the "invisible hand," which Adam Smith insisted would guide the market to an optimal allocation of resources, was partially based on his observations and presumptions about the behavior of individual buyers.

As a separate and organized area of inquiry, however, consumer behavior is approximately two decades old. The first university courses devoted exclusively to this topic appeared in the mid-1960s; and the first textbook on consumer behavior, by James Engel, David Kollat, and Roger Blackwell, was published in 1968. Soon after, in 1969, the Association for Consumer Research was formed. The *Journal of Consumer Research*, which began in 1974, is the first journal *both* to be exclusively devoted to research on the behavior of the individual consumer and to bring together a large number of academic groups,[1] each of which has some scholarly interest in the consumer. The *Journal of Consumer Research* thus gives explicit recognition to the inherent interdisciplinary nature of consumer behavior research.

Of course, the explosion of interest in the consumer during the 1960s and 1970s did not occur in a vacuum. In fact, systematic interest in, and research into, consumer behavior can be traced back almost a century to the so-called Neoclassical theory of Economic or "Rational" Man that students encounter, often painfully, in their first microeconomics course. The main task of this chapter, therefore, is to briefly trace the history of consumer behavior research and to discuss the current status of consumer behavior theory and research. Due to the broad interdisciplinary nature of consumer behavior, other issues will naturally arise as concepts and methods are borrowed from other academic disciplines.

EVOLVING PERSPECTIVES ON BUYER BEHAVIOR

A complete review of buyer behavior research over the past hundred years would be an enormous undertaking and not especially useful for the present purposes. What is needed, therefore, is a method to extract the essence of the major trends by means of a thread, which runs continuously through past research. Specifically, that thread is the degree to which the consumer has been regarded as rational.

Stated more completely, the argument is that at any point in time, researchers are guided by a specific viewpoint or perspective that includes both assumptions, made explicitly, and presumptions, made implicitly, about the basic nature of

---

[1]Specifically, these groups are
American Anthropological Association
American Association for Public Opinion Research
American Council on Consumer Interests
American Economic Association
American Home Economics Association
American Marketing Association
American Psychological Association (Div. 8 and Div. 23)
American Sociological Association
American Statistical Association
Association for Consumer Research
International Communication Association
The Institute of Management Sciences

consumer behavior. By reconstructing the evolving perspectives in terms of the consumer's presumed rationality, the consumer will be seen to be viewed until quite recently as increasingly *less* rational. In a direct reversal of this trend, the current perspective not only tends to view the consumer as more rational, but also redefines rationality in a way that increases its value in consumer behavior research.

In this overview of research and theory several objectives should be kept carefully in mind. First, all theory is based on a priori assumptions. That is, at any point in time a number of presumptions regarding the behavior of consumers are so widely shared that they are rarely explicitly stated, although most researchers would acknowledge them if asked. Second, and more important, the knowledge of consumer behavior is constantly evolving. The current perspective is different from what it has been and the perspective will change again as knowledge increases. Sensitizing the reader to this truism is, therefore, a major objective of this section. Finally, although the dominant perspective and focus change over time, each perspective discussed has left lasting contributions to the knowledge of consumer behavior.

Economic Rational Man

Although several scholars independently and almost simultaneously developed its foundations, the pure theory of demand is due primarily to Alfred Marshall's synthesis of various distinct economic theories into demand-supply analysis during the late nineteenth century. Our interest, of course, is only on the demand side of the market, with emphasis on how a "rational" consumer decides how much to demand of different products.

The economic analysis of demand proceeds as follows: First, the consumer, it is assumed, derives satisfaction from the consumption of goods, a satisfaction measured in theoretical units of utility. More utility is better. Second, the economist postulates rationality on the part of the consumer. Simply, and somewhat loosely, this means the consumer will try to achieve the maximum utility, or satisfaction, possible given his or her resource limitations: budget, time, etc. More precisely, rational behavior is equivalent to the following statements (Henderson and Quandt 1958, p. 7):

1. for all possible pairs of alternatives A and B the consumer knows whether he prefers A to B or B to A, or whether he is indifferent between them;

2. only one of the three possibilities is true for any pair of alternatives;

3. if the consumer prefers A to B and B to C, he will prefer A to C.

The last statement, referred to as transitivity, means that the consumer's choices are consistent. That is, if a consumer prefers roast beef to pork chops, and pork chops to fish, then that consumer *should* prefer roast beef to fish. To do otherwise would be logically inconsistent and, therefore, not rational.

The preceding statements constitute a complete definition of economic rationality. A major limitation of this definition, however, is that it provides no basis for determining if a specific consumer is behaving rationally: a rational consumer is simply a consumer who maximizes his or her utility or satisfaction. Rationality, as Gary Becker (1962) noted, must be *presumed* because measures of utility are never completely independent and there is no way of empirically separating rational from irrational behavior. Despite this limitation the economic definition of rationality has much value.

Economists developed their models of consumption for the purpose of studying the behavior of markets rather than *individual* consumers. Here, of course, a "law of large numbers" applies where the average consumer, as expressed in the behavior of the market, appears to act rationally even if no single consumer behaves in a strictly rational way. Such a situation is likely to occur if deviations from rational behavior are essentially random thereby canceling one another. When the market behaves as if each consumer is rational, and it usually does, a number of useful predictions can be made: e.g., if a competitor lowers his price sales of my product will fall. By careful statistical analysis it is often possible to develop a demand equation that can predict the magnitude of changes in sales resulting from changing prices (cf. Parsons and Schultz 1976). The reader is referred to Kotler (1965) for an interesting discussion of some other marketing applications of this model.

Second, consumer behavior researchers can, and have, made use of the concept of economic rationality to predict how individual consumers or small aggregations of consumers will behave while making different types of decisions. For example, the rational consumer will search for information regarding brands within a product class until the anticipated costs associated with additional search exceed the expected gains. Such a model of search allows for a large number of interesting hypotheses regarding consumer behavior. For example, the greater the spread of prices in a market, the greater should be consumer search effort. Similarly, two-income families might be expected to be more brand loyal because their time is very valuable and thus the cost of search is higher.

Third, and most relevant to the discussion of evolving perspectives on buyer behavior, the economic definition of rationality provides both a starting point from which buyer behavior research has evolved and a rigorous, formal definition of rationality to serve as a benchmark against which alternative definitions of rationality and alternative models of behavior can be evaluated.

Conspicuous Consumption and Social Motives

The first individuals to closely investigate what have come to be regarded as marketing phenomena were primarily trained as orthodox economists. Generally, these individuals turned their attention to a specific aspect of the demand-supply model and found that model lacking in one or more respects. In terms of the present discussion, the work of Thorstein Veblen is especially important.

Although trained as an economist, Veblen evolved into a radical social thinker. In his *Theory of the Leisure Class*, published in 1899, Veblen developed the concept and social implications of conspicuous consumption. He argued that much consumption is motivated by a desire to impress others with one's position and importance through the extravagant consumption of clothes, jewelry, houses, and similar goods. These goods are conspicuous consumption in the sense that other people can easily observe their use or consumption and vary widely in price, thereby providing the potential for great extravagance. The summer homes built by the wealthy at the turn of the century in Long Island, New York, and Bar Harbor, Maine, are outstanding examples of conspicious consumption. Quaintly called cottages, they typically had more than 25 rooms and employed large staffs of servants even though the home was occupied only a few months of the year.

Since a rational consumer maximizes satisfaction subject to resource limitations, if that consumer derives satisfaction from the adulation or even envy of others, then conspicuous consumption is rational behavior. Economists, however, normally assume that consumers derive satisfaction from the intrinsic, and generally objective, properties of the goods they consume rather than from such social and highly subjective factors as conspicuous consumption.[2] For example, consumers buy houses for shelter and clothes to protect themselves from the elements. The argument that consumers may often be substantially influenced by such subjective, and possibly unquantifiable, factors as the desire for conspicuous consumption is therefore a small attack on the presumed rationality of the buyer. As will be explored in subsequent chapters, however, the recognition of socially determined behavior has been of major importance to an understanding of consumer behavior.

Consumer Behavior in Early Marketing Thought[3]

Shortly after Veblen published his *Theory of the Leisure Class*, marketing courses first appeared in universities such as Michigan, Ohio State, Harvard, and Wisconsin. These courses dealt with what was then known as distributive industries and were primarily offered by professors trained as economists. At the same time, psychologists were becoming interested in the application of psychological principals to advertising, although it would be some time before advertising appeared as a separate course in the business curriculum.[4]

Economists and psychologists brought to their study of marketing the research tools with which they were most familiar, a priori deductive reasoning and laboratory experimentation. It is, therefore, perhaps no surprise that the focus of early marketing research was typically *not* on actual consumers. Rather, those trained as economists continued to base their theories on a priori deductive reasoning; while those trained as psychologists continued to rely primarily on very tightly controlled laboratory experiments, which were far removed from the real world. Even as academicians were trained in marketing, their attention focused only occasionally on narrow aspects of consumer behavior and, even then, their inquiries tended to be based on a priori reasoning or research that did not directly involve the consumer. This can be seen in two examples from the work of M. T. Copeland.

M. T. Copeland was one of the first influential academicians actually to be trained in marketing. His 1923 classification of consumer goods as convenience,

---

[2]While economists assume that consumers are motivated primarily by the intrinsic values of goods, in point of fact, they have no theory of motivation or even, with one notable exception, anything to say about how the specific qualities of goods bring satisfaction to consumers. Lancaster (1971) has been developing an economic theory of demand based on the want-satisfying characteristics of goods. As Howard (1977, pp. 50–51) notes, however, Lancaster has esentially confined his analysis to objective properties of goods, such as distance, weight, and volume.

[3]Much of the material in this section was inspired by Bartels' *The Development of Marketing Thought* (1962). Although aspects of consumer behavior are mentioned in a few places, what most impresses one in reading Bartels' book is how rarely the consumer was the central focus in marketing thought prior to 1960.

[4]According to Bartels the first courses in distribution appeared in 1902 at the universities of Michigan, California, and Illinois (1962, p. 29). The first advertising course cited by Bartels was offered in 1911 at The Ohio State University (p. 31).

shopping, or specialty goods sheds some light on the degree of rationality of consumers presumed during that period. This well-known classification system was partially based on three aspects of consumer behavior: the amount of travel effort the consumer would expend in searching for a good, the amount of comparisons among brands prior to a final purchase decision, and the degree of insistence upon a specific brand. Although Copeland illustrated his system with several anecdotal examples, the system was essentially defined a priori rather than developed through comprehensive empirical research. Furthermore, Copeland's focal point was the development of optimal distribution systems rather than the understanding of consumer behavior per se. Both Copeland's method and perspective were quite common at this time. In terms of the presumed rationality of the consumer, Copeland's system is clearly an extension of the economic rational man concept. That the consumer may decide to compare few brands and may develop a specific brand insistence, however, clearly departs from complete economic rationality.

The second example is taken from Chapter VI of Copeland's 1925 marketing textbook. This chapter presents a lengthy discussion of consumers' buying motives. Table 1.1 lists the motives discussed by Copeland. Although made passe by subsequent research, several aspects of Copeland's discussion of consumers' buying motives are especially relevant to the present discussion. Copeland explains "The purpose of this chapter is to set forth the buying motives which govern the purchases of consumers who buy wares in retail lots" (p. 155). The list of motives, however, was developed from examination of "936 advertisements in current

Table 1.1
Copeland's list of emotional and rational motives

Emotional Motives	Rational Motives
1. Distinctiveness	24. Handiness
2. Emulation	25. Efficiency in Operation or Use
3. Economical Emulation	26. Dependability in Use
4. Pride of Personal Appearance	27. Dependability in Quality
5. Pride in Appearance of Property	28. Reliability of Auxiliary Service
7. Proficiency	29. Durability
8. Expression of Artistic Taste	30. Enhancement of Earnings
9. Happy Selection of Gifts	31. Enhancing Productivity of Property
10. Ambition	32. Economy in Use
11. Romantic Instinct	33. Economy in Purchase
12. Maintaining and Preserving Health	
13. Cleanliness	
14. Proper Care of Children	
15. Satisfaction of the Appetite	
16. Pleasing Sense of Taste	
17. Securing Personal Comfort	
18. Alleviation of Laborious Tasks	
19. Security from Danger	
20. Pleasure of Recreation	
21. Entertainment	
22. Obtaining Opportunity for Greater Leisure	
23. Securing Home Comfort	

Source: Adapted from Melvin Thomas Copeland, *Principles of Merchandising* (Chicago: A.W. Shaw Company, 1925), pp. 178 and 185. Reprinted by Arno Press.

periodicals (chiefly 1923 issues)" (p. 158). As Bartels notes, this procedure was quite common at the time and earlier for "the viewpoint expressed by the authors was that of the manufacturer using advertising. The consumer interest was subordinated" (Bartels 1962, p. 50).

Furthermore, Copeland divided his list of motives into two categories: emotional and rational. The prominence of social motives (emulation, social achievement, etc.) can clearly be seen among the emotional motives. These, of course, are the types of motives upon which conspicuous consumption is based. Almost a third of the list, however, deals with rational motives. In terms of the presumed degree of consumer rationality, one can clearly discern a considerable elaboration of consumer buying motives that are not rational in the traditional economic sense of the word. Copeland's discussion, however, makes clear that emotional motives are less rational than rational motives, rather than irrational.

> When an emotional buying motive is aroused, it stimulates a consumer to action in order to please his personal feelings or to gratify an inherent, instinctive desire. . . . The emotional buying motives are aroused by suggestion, description, or association of ideas, not by a process of reasoning; but in order to arouse a rational buying motive, it is essential to present a careful statement of the reasons for purchase so that the prospective customer may be led to a logical conclusion as to the basis for his action (Copeland 1925, p. 188).

Copeland's discussion of motives was not unusual for the 1920s and 1930s and thus it can be concluded that the presumed rationality of the consumer saw a definite lessening in this period.

Finally, Copeland's list of motives is just that, a list of presumed consumer motives based on Copeland's interpretation of sellers' advertisements. The list is based upon no underlying theory and was developed by research procedures that could fairly be described as informal, if not casual.[5] This perspective on the consumer, including the presumed degree of rationality manifested in buying decisions, continued up to the 1940s, when Freudian theories of psychology began to influence marketers' thinking about the forces that motivate the consumer.

Motivation Research

During the 1940s and 1950s, Freudian psychoanalytic theory began to have a strong impact on how both marketing academics and practitioners viewed the forces that motivate consumer buying. Specifically, the consumer was seen to frequently be guided by motives so deeply repressed that the consumer was not even consciously aware of the true reasons for his or her buying behavior. Research conducted within such a perspective has come to be known as *motivation research*. The salient features of motivation research may be illustrated with a classic study by Mason Haire (1950).

Haire's study involved reasons for not buying instant coffee. He began by noting that when consumers who reported they did not use instant coffee were asked why, most reported "I don't like the flavor" (p. 651). Suspecting that the true reasons were more complex and deeply embedded, Haire decided to use an indirect questioning procedure based on the principle of projection. The essential

---

[5]This statement is not meant as a criticism but as a historical comment on the state of the art. In particular, modern statistical procedures were just beginning to be developed in the 1920s.

idea underlying any projective test is to give the respondent an ambiguous stimulus that must be interpreted. Since the stimulus is ambiguous the person presumably must *project* certain aspects of himself or herself into the stimulus in order to make sense of it.

The ambiguous stimulus used by Haire was two versions of a shopping list consisting of seven items, six of which were common to both lists (1½ lbs. hamburger, 2 loaves Wonder bread, bunch of carrots, 1 can Rumford's Baking Powder, 2 cans Del Monte peaches, 5 lbs. potatoes). The list given to one group of subjects also contained Nescafé Instant Coffee, while the other group's list had 1 lb. Maxwell House Coffee (Drip Grind). The instructions given to subjects were

> Read the shopping list below. Try to project yourself into the situation as far as possible until you can more or less characterize the woman who bought the groceries. Then write a brief description of her personality and character. Wherever possible, indicate what factors influenced your judgment (p. 651).

The results showed a clear tendency for subjects who received the Nescafé list to describe the housewife as lazy, failing to plan household purchases and schedules well, a spendthrift, and not a good wife. Haire also found that subjects reporting such negative descriptions were less likely to be users of instant coffee themselves. Of course, now that instant foods are widely accepted, one might expect that the reactions of subjects today would not show the patterns found by Haire. This has been confirmed in a replication of Haire's study by Webster and von Pechmann (1970).

Clearly, motivation research represents a period in which consumers were thought to show the least amount of rationality in their buying decisions. Just how low a point was reached is well illustrated by the three explanations of consumer behavior based on motivation research that Kotler cited in his well known marketing management text.

1. A man buys a convertible as a substitute "mistress."
2. A woman is very serious when she bakes a cake because unconsciously she is going through the symbolic act of birth.
3. Men want their cigars to be odiferous in order to prove that they (the men) are masculine. (1967, p. 88)

While motivation research produced many interesting and sometimes useful explanations of why consumers purchase or fail to purchase specific goods, it eventually ceased to be a major factor in academic studies of consumer behavior. The reasons for this change are complex and varied. Two basic criticisms, however, were that findings in motivation research studies tended to be very situation specific and different researchers looking at the same problem, and often the same data, frequently reported different conclusions. Fundamentally, motivation research fell out of favor in academic circles because it failed to provide useful generalizations beyond the basic observation that consumers were sometimes motivated by factors that they either could not or would not report directly. This insight, nevertheless, has proved to be of great importance. The method of projection has also been of lasting importance in consumer research although this method is typically *not* used within a Freudian framework to assess deeply repressed motives.

As the problems associated with the projective techniques used in motivation research became evident, researchers searched for more objective research instruments. Among the instruments they found useful were the standard paper and pencil tests of personality. However, their basic presumptions and perspectives on consumer behavior continued to essentially be those associated with motivation research, although this was rarely discussed explicitly.

Although no longer a major focus in academic studies of consumer behavior, motivation research is still conducted extensively and often effectively on a proprietary basis. Much of the strong Freudian orientation of the procedures, however, has been lost.

Perceived Risk

As we have seen, the consumer was increasingly viewed as a less rational individual. A major change in this perspective was initiated by Raymond Bauer in a paper presented to the American Marketing Association in 1960. While acknowledging that consumer behavior might at times conform to the model advocated by motivation researchers, Bauer suggested that consumer behavior might better be viewed as risk taking behavior. Specifically, Bauer argued that

> Consumer behavior involves risk in the sense that any action of a consumer will produce consequences which he cannot anticipate with anything approximating certainty, and some of which at least are likely to be unpleasant. . . . [and that] Consumers characteristically develop decision strategies and ways of reducing risk that enable them to act with relative confidence and ease in situations where their information is inadequate and the consequences of their actions are in some meaningful sense incalculable (1967, pp. 24 and 25).

The viewpoint advocated by Bauer, and the rather substantial amount of research it stimulated, has come to be known as perceived risk. Three aspects of Bauer's argument are crucial in defining the current perspective on consumer behavior taken by the majority of researchers. First, Bauer presented the consumer as a decision maker attempting to choose among alternatives whose consequences are not only uncertain but potentially negative. These decisions, moreover, are often far from trivial. "Unfortunate consumer decisions have cost men frustration and blisters, their self-esteem and the esteem of others, their wives, their jobs, and even their lives" (Bauer 1967, p. 24). Second, he emphasized the use of information in reducing perceived risk to a level where the consumer can make buying decisions "with relative confidence and ease." And, third, especially when contrasted with the prevailing perspective, Bauer's discussion presents the consumer as an individual who attempts, not always successfully, to solve buying problems in a rational way.

CURRENT STATUS OF BUYER BEHAVIOR THEORY AND RESEARCH

Until recently, consumers have increasingly been viewed as less rational in their approach to buying. While the current perspective has reversed this trend, it has also implicitly redefined rationality from the formal definition of economics to one that is more appropriate to the study of individual consumers.

The primary objective in this section is to describe the salient features of the current dominant perspective on consumer behavior. By understanding the assumptions and presumptions which characterize this perspective the reader should be better able to understand why certain research questions and methods are so prominent at this point in time. The reader should also be aware of certain biases inherent in the current perspective. Finally, the current status of attempts to construct comprehensive theories of consumer behavior will be discussed briefly.

Information Processing Approach

The dominant approach to the study of consumer behavior today is generally known as the information processing approach or theory.[6] This perspective, which is historically an extension and deepening of the perceived risk perspective, generally assumes that the consumer is a problem solver who formulates buying problems in terms of a choice among competing alternatives and actively acquires and uses information in an attempt to solve the buying problem in a satisfactory manner. Implicitly, and sometimes explicitly, this approach assumes a relatively high degree of rationality on the part of the consumer.

While most of the traditional consumer behavior topics (motivation, attitude formation and change, and social influence) can be investigated from an information processing perspective, the emphasis of this approach has tended to be more narrowly focused. In a recent review, Kassarjian neatly summarizes the predominate concerns of information processing researchers.

> The central focus of the information processing perspective is on viewing consumers as cognitively active problem solvers and understanding the strategies and plans used in decision making, typically product purchases and choice between brands (Mitchell 1978). Relying heavily on cognitive psychology, the research has revolved around information search, information acquisition, encoding, storage, retrieval, integration, and the processes used in the choice of heuristics, the rule of thumb a consumer might use (1982, p. 630).

Although the information processing approach will figure prominently in the present analysis of buyer behavior, two caveats are appropriate. First, the information processing approach tends to present the consumer as an active decision maker. That is, the consumer recognizes his or her motives, acquires the relevant information, arrives at a buying decision, and finally alters his or her perceptions of the chosen brand in light of the postpurchase experience with the brand. While there are good reasons to believe that consumers do approach some buying decisions in such a systematic, active, decision-making way, there is also good reason to believe that some purchasing behavior involves little, if any, conscious decision making.

The second caveat is that any written discussion of human behavior tends to present that behavior as far more organized and systematic than it actually is. This is especially true of the information processing approach. Rarely, if ever, does the consumer proceed smoothly and without interruption from need recognition, to information acquisition, and ultimately to purchase. More typically, the decision process develops over an extended period of time, the information upon which the decision will be based is frequently ambiguous, and the consumer will make the final brand choice with something less than total confidence that the best possible choice has been made.

---

[6]For a detailed account of one major information processing theory of consumer choice see Bettman (1979).

Environmental Complexity

By viewing buyer behavior in terms of choice alternatives information processing researchers have been forced to consider the nature of those alternatives. This has naturally led to an explicit recognition of the great complexity of the environment in which buying decisions are made. And, of course, that complexity has been increasing rapidly in recent years, as may be seen in a list of some of today's important products: video recorders, microwave ovens, over-the-counter drugs, home computers.

In this vein, Herbert Simon advanced the following interesting hypothesis.

> A man, viewed as a behaving system, is quite simple. The apparent complexity of his behavior over time is largely a reflection of the complexity of the environment in which he finds himself (1969, p. 25).

Although many consumer behavior researchers might take exception to the first part of Simon's hypothesis, agreement is virtually unanimous that much of the behavior of consumers can be at least partially understood in terms of their attempt to cope with an environment that is extraordinarily, and sometimes overwhelmingly, complex.

Limited Cognitive Capabilities

Along with a recognition of the complexity of the environment is a growing recognition that the consumer's ability to process information has rather severe limits. That is, *at any specific point in time*, people appear to be able to deal actively with only a few pieces of information. Most important, this limitation on consumers' information processing or cognitive capabilities is inherent and independent of any unwillingness to actively acquire and process information.

From this perspective, behaviors that may not seem rational become more understandable. Why, for example, do some consumers use price to indicate product quality for certain products when an objective analysis would show little relationship between price and quality for at least some of those products? The answer lies in the fact that a consumer who cannot objectively evaluate a certain product is likely to fall back on some rule of thumb, such as "you get what you pay for," which allows decisions among the alternatives to be made with "relative confidence and ease," to use Bauer's phrase.

Bounded Rationality

As already noted, the dominant current perspective tends to assume a high degree of rationality in consumer buying decisions. Clearly, however, the behaviors that are labeled rational would not meet the formal economic definition of rationality. Frequently, for example, the consumer cannot say whether he or she prefers A to B, B to A, or is indifferent. For example, how many times have you found yourself torn between making use of free time on the computer or going to a football game?

The behavior characterized above as rational is perhaps best described by Simon's concept of bounded rationality (March and Simon 1958): Faced with a complex environment and limited resources (e.g., time, money, cognitive capabilities), consumers attempt to formulate and resolve buying problems in ways that are satisfactory, even if they are not fully optimal. Or to quote Bauer again:

> Consumers characteristically develop decision strategies and ways of reducing risk that enable them to act with relative confidence and ease in situations where their information is inadequate and the consequences of their actions are in some meaningful sense incalculable (1960, p. 25).

Broadening Bauer's focus by replacing "reducing risk" with the more general term behaving produces a good, although very general, description of the orientation and concerns of much of the current consumer behavior research.

Middle Range Theories

One final point will complete this brief survey of the current status of consumer behavior theory and research. The last two decades have seen a number of attempts to construct comprehensive theories of consumer behavior. At the present time, however, there is no generally accepted theory of consumer behavior that can be used to explain all or even most behavior by consumers. Rather, existing comprehensive theories serve more like blueprints to present an overall view of the relevant variables and suggestions as to how these variables may be interrelated. The variables, however, are usually defined in vague terms and the relationships among variables are frequently specified with no greater precision than a change in variable A may give rise to a change in variable B *without* stating whether the change is positive, negative, or dependent on specified circumstances.

The reader should not take the above comments as a criticism of those who attempted to create comprehensive theories nor as an indication that such attempts have no value. In fact, these efforts have great value, as shall be discussed in the next chapter. Rather, these comments reflect the state of the art in consumer behavior theory, a field in which the first fully comprehensive theories are of very recent origin.

Although it is currently fashionable to organize consumer behavior textbooks around what are purported to be comprehensive theories or models, such models tend to be more flowcharts of how topics are organized than theories, as the term is normally used in scientific discussions. Indeed, Harold Kassarjian, a leading consumer behavior scholar, argues that "what is desperately needed at this point is integration (i.e., a comprehensive theory) of the various topics in the field" and that "the field simply does not need another flow chart" (1982, p. 643). Whatever the need, no generally acceptable comprehensive theory of consumer behavior is currently on the horizon, and no attempt will be made to offer a comprehensive theory of consumer behavior to which all of the topics in this book can be directly tied and interrelated.

The Howard-Sheth theory is presented as an organizing scheme to give some cohesion to the analysis of buyer behavior, but for the most part the discussions will center around a variety of what Robertson and Ward (1973) refer to as middle range theories. As shall be seen, the vast majority of buyer behavior research has centered around such middle range theories rather than around comprehensive theories of buyer behavior. Some, but not all, of thse middle range theories can be fitted into the Howard-Sheth theory.

Middle range theories can be distinguished by two characteristics: they are typically less formal than more comprehensive theories and they are limited in scope. That is, they attempt to explain only limited aspects of consumer behavior; e.g., attitude change as a function of postpurchase experience. Within the defined scope, however, the theory should provide a general explanation of the behavior of interest; e.g., the attitude change process should not be limited to a narrow range of products or types of consumers.

The most viable and intensively investigated theories are typically fairly limited in scope. Further, many of the theories overlap *without* competing so directly that only one can be accepted. Thus, the same topic will frequently be approached from mulitple viewpoints and often only general guidelines can be offered as to the circumstances under which each is likely to be most applicable. This, no doubt, will sometimes leave the reader frustrated. It is, however, a fair assessment of the current state of consumer behavior theory and research.

EMERGING TRENDS IN BUYER BEHAVIOR RESEARCH

The information processing approach has now dominated consumer behavior research for more than a decade. This approach has been enormously productive and its dominance seems likely to continue for the foreseeable future. In the last few years, however, a number of researchers have suggested that the information processing approach is not necessarily relevant to or capable of explaining all consumer behaviors (e.g., Olshavsky and Granbois 1979). Other trends are emerging, although none of these trends is currently well developed at either a theoretical or empirical level. While these emerging research trends *can* be interpreted as a challenge to information processing theory *as currently practiced*, the question remains open whether these emerging trends can ultimately be incorporated into a unified theory based upon information processing concepts (cf., Kassarjian 1982).

Low Involvement Processes

The information processing perspective tends to assume, either explicitly or implicitly, that buying decisions are preceded by specific decision-making *processes*, which are in some sense both active and conscious. Put another way, the buyer's level of involvement with the purchase decision is presumed to be sufficient to motivate what might loosely be called *thinking* about a specific purchase decision before making a choice.

Increasingly, it has been recognized that much buyer behavior is characterized by low involvement processes where information is passively accepted, often stored without integration with previously acquired information, and implemented in specific purchase decisions with little, if any, consideration of the merits of alternative choices. Although low involvement processes have been recognized by marketers at least since Krugman's (1965) discussion of how buyers may passively absorb information presented in television advertisements, only recently have low involvement processes been recognized as very general phenomena, which are not restricted to unimportant decisions.

The automobile purchase decision illustrates the generality of low involvement processes. Because of its financial and psychological importance and infrequent purchase, automobiles are frequently cited as an example of a high involvement product where buyers typically engage in a highly active, conscious decision-making process. And yet relatively few buyers consider more than a few automobiles or visit more than a few dealers before purchase. Although many factors are involved, typically, buyers have passively absorbed via low involvement processes a great deal of information about different makes of automobiles and different dealers long before they have even the vaguest intent to consider purchasing an automobile.

Buyers are literally surrounded by information about automobiles. Magazine and television advertisements, news stories about new models and recalls and battles over Japanese imports, conversations with friends and acquaintances, and direct observation of popularity as expressed by ownership are all important sources of information about automobiles that tend to be absorbed via low involvement processes. When the decision-making process begins, the typical buyer finds that he or she knows a great deal more about automobiles than was initially thought. You, for example, can probably describe in some detail the characteristics of a number of automobiles for which you have never attempted to systematically gather information.

Psychologists have extensively investigated low involvement processes. Unfortunately, the intrusion needed to study low involvement processes in a realistic marketing context tends to distort the processes themselves by creating a higher level of involvement on the part of subjects. Thus, most of what is known about low involvement processes has been developed in a tightly controlled laboratory context that is far removed from the everyday context of marketing and involves all of the dangers inherent in borrowing concepts from other disciplines. For this reason, and because low involvement and high involvement processes cannot be neatly separated, low involvement processes shall be discussed as they logically arise under specific topics rather than as a separate chapter.

Motivation and Emotion

A curious, and presumably unintentional, by-product of the dominance of information processing theory is the disappearance of motivation and emotion from the study of consumer behavior. Curious because, as Kassarjian has noted,

> Of all topics, one would think that *motivation* would have been thoroughly explored by this time, and yet it has not been studied much in recent years. Now the trend seems to be turning back to basic motivational aspects and concerns about motivation theory (e.g., Bettman 1979, Fishbein and Ajzen 1975). It simply could be ignored no longer. (1982, p. 642, emphasis in original.)

Holbrook and Hirschman (1982, Hirschman and Holbrook 1982) have explored the research potential of studying motivation and emotion under what they call *hedonic consumption* and *the experiential aspects of consumption*. Their analysis of the role of emotions and feelings in information processing studies of consumer behavior is quite revealing.

> It might be argued that, in the area of affect, the conventional information processing approach has been studying experiential consumption all along.... Fundamentally, however, the information processing perspective emphasizes only one aspect of hedonic response—namely, like or dislike of a particular brand (attitude) or its rank relative to other brands (preference). This attitudinal component represents only a tiny subset of the emotions and feelings of interest of the experiential view.
>
> The full gamut of relevant emotions includes such diverse feelings as love,

hate, fear, joy, boredom, anxiety, pride, anger, disgust, sadness, sympathy, lust, ecstasy, greed, elation, shame, and awe. . . .

Psychological conceptualizations of emotion are still in their seminal stages and, understandably, have not yet cross-pollinated the work of consumer researchers. Yet, it is clear that emotions form an important substrate of consumption and that their systematic investigation is a key requirement for the successful application of the experiential perspective (Holbrook and Hirschman 1982, pp. 136–137).

As Hirschman and Holbrook (1982, pp. 138–139) note, the concept of hedonic consumption supplements and enriches, rather than challenges, traditional information processing theory. Indeed, because the products of principle interest in hedonic research (e.g., leisure, entertainment, art) tend to elicit high levels of interest and involvement, such research may ultimately prove to be highly congenial to an information processing perspective.

Various aspects of hedonic consumption will be considered later under the topic of motivation. The closely related topic of values has also been largely ignored by consumer behavior researchers (Kassarjian 1982, pp. 642–643), and is explored in the context of differences among individual consumers.

Group Behavior

Quite naturally, the information processing approach has emphasized the behavior of the individual consumer. This led to a scarcity of knowledge regarding buying behavior conducted by groups such as business organizations and families (cf. Davis 1977; Sheth 1979; Kassarjian 1982). Sheth, in particular, provides a useful summary of the deficiencies of current research and the need for research on the behavior of groups.

Certain aspects of group behavior fall easily into the information processing approach, e.g., an automobile mechanic telling a friend that a particular car is notoriously unreliable. However, many aspects of group behavior have more to do with relative power, bargaining, and coalition formation than with information processing or decision making that would follow logically from information acquisition and evaluation. Nowhere is this statement truer than in family decision making, where decisions are often made with the objective of group stability rather than making an optimal, or even a "good," purchase.

Later in this text, the topic of group behavior will be considered in the contexts of social influence, social groups, organizational buying behavior, and family buying behavior.

Emerging Trends and the Presumed Rationality of the Consumer

The emerging trends in buyer behavior research extend and deepen the current information processing approach, or at least can be interpreted as such. Efforts to expand the concept and functioning of motivation can almost certainly be seen in this light and probably so can low involvement processes, since information is being processed although by different means and to different consequences. Thus, the emerging research trends continue to characterize the consumer as possessing bounded rationality.

Perhaps the most serious challenge to the presumed rationality of the consumer occurs within group, especially family, buying behavior. Certainly, this area of research requires a number of concepts (e.g., social power, bargaining, coalition formation) that are not currently part of, nor necessarily congenial to, the information processing approach. Moreover, group decision making is sometimes characterized by conflict among group members, which diverts the focus of the decison-making *process* away from the decision itself. However, relatively little is known about conflict resolution by buying groups. Furthermore, there is a fair amount of evidence that groups, including families, do find ways of handling group buying decisions that can be characterized as bounded rationality.

ISSUES IN BORROWING CONCEPTS AND METHODS

This chapter began by noting the inherent interdisciplinary nature of consumer behavior research. Frequently consumer researchers have borrowed concepts and methods from other academic disciplines, such as economics and psychology. Such borrowing has not only been necessary, it has also been very fruitful. However, in borrowing theoretical concepts and research methods from other areas researchers have often failed to *fully* consider their structures and the purposes for which they were developed. This has resulted in much wasted effort and, occasionally, the drawing of improper conclusions.

A full inquiry into issues of borrowing would take us well into what is known as the philosophy of science, which would require a high level of methodological sophistication. Therefore, two examples from the motivation research period will illustrate the problems that may arise in interdisciplinary borrowing: the dubious application of certain concepts and methods borrowed from Freudian psychoanalytic theory; and the clearly inappropriate use of a standard paper and pencil personality test. Our objectives are to call attention to the problems posed by borrowing concepts and methods, and to present several basic questions that should be asked regarding any borrowed concept or theory *before* it is applied to consumer research. More detailed discussions of issues of borrowing may be found in Robertson and Ward (1973, pp. 23–25) and Zaltman, Pinson, and Angelman (1973).

Freudian Theory

The motivation research framework was heavily influenced by concepts and methods originating within Freudian psychoanalytic theory. However, motivation research generally failed to produce findings that could be generalized over different types of products and consumers, save that consumers were sometimes influenced in their buying decisions by motives they either could not or would not reveal when questioned directly. While the reasons for this general failure are undoubtedly complex, it can be argued that motivation researchers borrowed two specific elements from Freudian theory and applied them inappropriately; specifically, the *concept* of the unconscious mind and the *method* of projective testing.

Had motivation researchers more carefully considered other aspects of psychoanalytic theory, they might not have applied the concept of the unconscious mind as freely as they did. Although not specifically a theory of abnormal development, psychoanalysis was developed primarily in a clinical setting where the persons observed were disturbed, sometimes deeply disturbed. Also, psychoanalysis originated in nineteenth century Vienna, a society greatly influenced by Victorian ideas regarding sex. It was, therefore, not surprising that Freud focused much of his attention on society's repression of sexual and elmination needs and the effects such repressions might have on the individual. Clearly the United States, even in the 1950s, was quite different from Victorian Vienna. Interestingly enough, the so-called neo-Freudians (such as Sullivan, Horney, and Fromm), who might have been more easily adapted to consumer behavior research, were almost totally ignored.[7] Finally, the interactions between patient and therapist in which unconscious motives are explored through many different methods, including projection, develop over a period of months or years. In contrast, motivation research studies rarely take more than a few hours of time per subject.

Freudian psychoanalytic theory was developed for a specific purpose, within a specific context; i.e., to understand how the personality develops, with specific interest in how it may fail to develop normally, within the context of the patient-therapist relationship. As we have seen, serious difficulties can arise when concepts and methods, such as those developed in psychoanalytic theory, are applied to consumer behavior.

The Edwards Personal Preference Schedule (EPPS)

Because Freudian theory is complex and controversial and, by the 1950s, had been extended along a number of quite distinct lines by the so-called neo-Freudians, it proved difficult to apply to consumer behavior. In an effort to reduce the inherent ambiguity in the Freudian concept, consumer behavior researchers during the 1960s and early 1970s began to rely extensively on a single paper and pencil personality test, although information was readily available in standard psychology reference works to show how inappropriate the test was for consumer behavior research.

A detailed review of the EPPS can be found in Horton (1974). Because the criticisms of the EPPS are numerous and technically complex, the discussion will focus on the characteristic of the EPPS that most makes it inappropriate for *consumer* personality research—that the personality traits measured by this test are scored *ipsatively* rather than *normatively*, as is done with most personality tests.

Normative tests assess each personality trait individually. A typical normative question would make a statement (such as, "parties are my favorite form of entertainment") and then ask the person to indicate on a five point scale how much the statement describes them. On the basis of responses to this and similar questions, a person would be scored on a specific personality trait, such as need for affiliation. The higher a person's score, the greater is the need for affiliation. The personality trait might then be used to predict such things as the purchases of products used in entertaining. The important point, however, is that when personality traits are measured normatively they can be compared across individual consumers in terms of the strength of a personality trait relative to *other* consumers.

---

[7]Cohen (1967) has developed a personality test, based on Karen Horney's theory of interpersonal orientation, designed specifically for use in consumer research. Noerager (1979), however, indicates that this test, the CAD, has been infrequently used and reports data that casts doubt on its reliability and validity.

A major problem with normative tests is that subjects' responses can be seriously distorted by the social desirability of the alternative answers. For example, a person with a high need for affiliation might believe that other people might view negatively a person who stated that "parties are my favorite form of entertainment" and would, therefore, check a neutral response to the question despite its descriptiveness. This was the problem Edwards tried to overcome by developing the EPPS, and it is the method he chose to deal with the problem of social desirability that makes it inappropriate for consumer personality research.

The EPPS measures fifteen personality needs. Rather than assess each need individually, however, statements for different needs are paired and the respondent is asked to indicate the more self-descriptive statement. For example, a person might be asked to choose whether "parties are my favorite form of entertainment" or "I always want to have the final say in an argument" is more self-descriptive. All pairs of statements had previously been equated by Edwards for social desirability. Depending on which statement a respondent checked as more self-descriptive one point would be tallied for either, say, a need for affiliation or a need for dominance. Personality scales constructed on this basis are referred to as ipsative scales. The crucial point for our discussion is that ipsative scales allow us to compare the relative strength of needs within a person but *not* the relative strength of a single personality need across individuals.

Table 1.2 illustrates the difference between normative and ipsative scales with an extreme example. Subject 1 scores normatively lower on three personality needs than subject 2, but the rank order of the needs within the two subjects is reversed. Thus, from the ipsative scores it *appears* that subject 1 has more of personality need A than subject 2 and just as much of personality need B as subject 2 although normative scores show that this is not true. More specifically, there is no necessary relationship between personality traits measured normatively and the same traits measured ipsatively.

Another way of comparing normative and ipsative scales is to say that normative scales allow us to measure the relative strength of personality traits *among* individuals, while ipsative scales allow us to measure the relative strengths of different personality traits *within* a single individual. Ipsative scales, therefore, are very useful in individual counseling situations, where the goal is to help a person understand the relative strengths of his own personality needs and to relate this understanding to decisions the person must make, such as choosing a career. In

Table 1.2
Comparison of three personality needs measured normatively and ipsatively

Subject	Normative Score *Personality Variable*			Ipsative Score[a] *Personality Variable*		
	A	B	C	A	B	C
1	3	2	1	2	1	0
2	4	5	6	0	1	2

[a]Ipsative scores may be obtained from normative scores by comparing the normative scores for each subject on each independent pair of needs. For subject 1 need A is greater than both needs B and C, while need B is only greater than need C.

Source: Raymond L. Horton, "The Edwards Personal Preference Schedule and Consumer Personality Research," *Journal of Marketing Research*, 11 (August 1974): 336. Reprinted with the kind permission of the American Marketing Association.

fact, this is a frequent use of the EPPS (Horton 1974, p. 336). Furthermore, the EPPS is based on a theory of personality developed by Murray, which argues that fifteen specific personality needs are common to all individuals but that individuals differ in the priority by which each need is to be satisfied. Thus, an ipsative scoring procedure is not only useful for controlling social desirability but is *required* by the theory upon which the EPPS is based.

Since consumer personality research requires comparisons *among* individuals on each personality trait investigated, it is clear that neither the EPPS nor Murray's theoretical system of personality needs are relevant for this use. Despite this, the EPPS was the personality test most frequently used in consumer research for some fifteen years. How did such a situation come about?

The explanation remains somewhat obscure. Kassarjian (1971) attributes the popularity of the EPPS to Evans's (1959) use of the EPPS in his classic study of the personality characteristics of owners of Ford and Chevrolet automobiles. Although Evans's article fails to discuss any of the technical properties of the EPPS as they might relate to consumer research, the simple appearance of the EPPS in a study published in a respected journal seems to have been sufficient to legitimize its use in future studies by other researchers.[8] Thus, once the EPPS appeared in the consumer behavior literature future users of the test could simply cite prior use of the EPPS to justify their use of it. Although the EPPS represents an extreme case of inappropriate borrowing it is not an isolated example.

Principles of Borrowing[9]

So far only some of the problems that can arise in the borrowing of theoretical concepts and research methods have been illustrated. The focus now turns to some more general principles of borrowing and the resulting questions which should be asked.

Underestimation of Complexity

Rarely will the borrower of a concept or method be an expert in the field from which the concept or method emanates. There is, therefore, a natural tendency to focus on basic conclusions *tentatively* reached by the experts in the field without being fully aware of the complexity and controversy that often surrounds any concept or method as to its validity and range of application. Thus, the borrower should actively seek out the complexity and surrounding controversy, which should be *presumed* to exist.

Specific Context, Specific Purpose

All theories and research methods are initially developed in a specific context, for a specific purpose. One of the most important questions regarding any theoretical concept or method is the range of phenomena to which it can be applied. The important point is that this *is* a question. Simply because a concept or method has proved useful once does not mean it can be counted on to do so again, even in a superficially similar situation. Robertson (1971), for example, argued that our

---

[8]In fairness to researchers who have used the EPPS, it should be noted that the test manual makes no mention of the ipsative nature of the test (Horton 1974, p. 336).

[9]This section follows closely the discussion of Robertson and Ward (1973, pp. 24–25).

knowledge of how consumers decide whether or not to adopt new products may be inadequate because much of the research was conducted on farmers' buying decisions. Farming decisions involve substantial cost and require changes in behavior on the part of the consumer; e.g., planting new strains of hybrid seed that, in addition to substantial cost, may involve a different planting time, amount and type of fertilizer, etc. In contrast, most new products represent low costs and little, if any, change in the behavior required of the consumer to use the new products. It is, therefore, arguable that the behavior of consumers regarding typical new product decisions may be quite different from that presumed on the basis of early studies involving major farming and similar new product decisions.

Legitimization

The degree of legitimization attached to any theoretical concept or method should be ascertained. Legitimization refers to how well the concept or method is accepted in the field from which it is borrowed. Legitimization is closely related to the first two principles because those concepts and methods with the greatest degree of legitimization will tend to be less controversial and usually will have been validated in numerous studies, each of which will present a slightly different context. All other things equal, highly legitimized concepts and methods will also tend to be more productive when borrowed.

Justification

Of course, all other things are rarely equal. Thus, the borrower of a concept or method has an obligation to *justify* the use of the borrowed concept or method in the *context* of the specific research problem. That is, the researcher must build a well reasoned argument that the borrowed concept or method can be expected to relate to the phenomenon of interest in a specific way. For example, a convincing argument might be made that the personality trait need for affiliation, as measured by an appropriate test, is positively related to the consumption of snack foods because consumers with a high need for affiliation entertain very frequently. Such an argument would be built by a process of assembling existing facts that suggest such a relationship (e.g., perhaps it is known that persons with a high need for affiliation *do* entertain more although the form of entertainment may not be known) and logical reasoning (e.g., snack foods are a part of many forms of entertainment).

SUMMARY

The development of knowledge about consumer behavior in terms of evolving perspectives has been surveyed in terms of the presumed degree of rationality of the consumer in making purchasing decisions, highlighting some of the major insights made from each perspective. More important, we have tried to make the reader aware of the fact that our knowledge of the buyer is continuously evolving. Subsequent chapters explore what we know about buyer behavior today, and develop a *framework* within which new knowledge may be integrated as it is developed.

Research conducted within an information processing framework not only has its own set of special concerns or questions, but its own set of presumptions.

Principal among these is the presumption that buyer behavior *does* involve a conscious, decision-making choice among alternatives. Of course, every perspective has its own set of special presumptions. Our objective, therefore, is not to use these presumptions to cast doubt on the research conducted within the information processing perspective, but to call attention to the need to view *all* research, whatever its special orientation, with a critical mind. A similar point applies, but with special force, to the application to consumer research of theoretical concepts and methods developed in other disciplines.

Comprehensive Theories and Models of Buyer Behavior

2

Although a number of attempts have been made to construct general or comprehensive theories of buyer behavior, none of these efforts has been widely adopted as a *working* model of buyer behavior. Indeed, John Howard, the originator of a widely noted and respected general theory of buyer behavior, has stated that "It must be freely acknowledged that no current theory of buyer behavior satisfies the end requirements of either the marketer or the researcher" (Howard and Ostlund 1973, p. 3).

Thus, at the level where specific questions regarding buyer behavior are actually formulated and studied, researchers tend to rely on middle range theories rather than on comprehensive theories. Despite the primitive state of existing comprehensive theories of buyer behavior, they do have much value and represent a major step forward in the efforts to better understand buyer behavior.

It is, then, the purpose of this chapter to discuss the value of comprehensive theories of buyer behavior and to review some of the more important efforts to construct such theories. The chapter opens with an introductory-level discussion on the nature and value of theory in general, then focuses briefly on two of the earliest attempts to construct comprehensive theories. Although primarily of historical value, these early theories emphasize the diversity of approaches to the task of constructing comprehensive theories of buyer behavior. The Howard-Sheth theory of buyer behavior will be discussed in greater depth. The chapter concludes with a review of the frequently cited Engle-Kollat-Blackwell theory.

THEORIES, MODELS, AND METHODS

The word theory frequently raises suspicion, and occasionally hostility, among both students and marketing practitioners. Theories, they argue, are too simple, too abstract, too idealized to adequately describe the real world in which marketing decisions are actually made. Despite these widespread suspicions of their practicality, it is also widely recognized that "there is nothing so useful as a good theory."

Why is there such a strong divergence of opinion regarding the value of theory? Part of the reason, of course, is that not all theories are good theories. This is especially likely to be a problem in a new and rapidly developing area, such as buyer behavior. But a major part of the problem is that many people simply do not understand what a theory is and are, therefore, unable to fully appreciate the value of theories.

The Nature of Theory[1]

Theories may be categorized in a great many ways;[2] for example, comprehensive and middle range theories. Theories may also be distinguished by their degree of formality. In a highly formal theory, the various elements that compose the theory

---

[1]The discussion of the nature or character of theory will necessarily be quite brief. For an excellent, in depth evaluation of theory in the study of buyer behavior see Zaltman, Pinson, and Angelman (1973).

[2]For a thorough discussion of the criteria upon which theories of buyer behavior may be distinguished see Howard and Sheth (1969, pp. 15–22) and Zaltman, Pinson, and Angelman (1973, Chaps. 4 and 5).

are defined in great detail and with great precision, as are the interrelationships among these elements. The most formal theories can be stated entirely in mathematical form. Scientists usually prefer formal theories for two reasons. First, they are easier to test than informal theories. Second, they are easier to communicate because the high degree of precision in their specification allows different scientists to be sure they are discussing the same thing. In the early stages of development virtually all areas of study tend to be guided by very informal theories. This is, indeed, true of buyer behavior research.

Whatever their unique properties all theories share certain distinguishing characteristics, the most basic of which is abstraction. Abstraction is frequently cited as a weakness or limitation of theory and, indeed, theories may be *too* abstract. But it is this very abstractness that gives theories their tremendous power to provide insight into the world around us. Good theories select or abstract the *essence* of the behavior under study and organize that essence into a series of interrelated variables that explain *why* the behavior occurs.

The theory of perceived risk can serve as an example to illustrate what we mean by abstraction. The risk concept rests on the notion that consumers may be *harmed* by the products they purchase. This harm can take many forms, of which researchers have considered in depth only a few, such as financial or physical harm. Furthermore, the exact nature and consequences of this harm may be quite different for different consumers considering different products at different times for different purposes, etc.

That buyers could be, and often are, harmed by the products they use was hardly a novel suggestion. It was known prior to Bauer's well known paper, "Consumer Behavior as Risk Taking." Bauer's great insight was to see that all of these many aspects of harm could be organized and systematized under the theoretical concept of perceived risk and that the degree to which consumers perceived risk in choosing among competing brands had specific consequences in terms of both the specific brands they chose and how they arrived at these choices.

Perceived risk then is an *abstraction.* We may discuss perceived risk in a meaningful way without having to state from what the risk stems. It may be physical, financial, psychological, or arise from some source we have not even considered. The exact form of the potential harm that gives rise to the risk is not crucial because all of these potential harms are unified by the fundamental, theoretical, abstract concept of perceived risk.

Perceived risk, however, is an abstraction in an even more basic way. Precisely because it is *perceived*, there is no way in which to *directly* observe and study perceived risk. That is, perceived risk is something that exists *within* the individual buyer and, therefore, can never be *directly* observed. However, the existence of risk can be *inferred* from a buyer's behavior. The simplest *behavior*, of course, is the buyer's verbal report when asked to estimate the risk in a specific buying situation. Note, that even this verbal report is an indirect measure since we must assume that the respondent is both able and willing to accurately report on the perception of risk.

Theory and Method

How is a good theory actually built? The process is relatively simple in principle, although it is often very involved and difficult in practice. To begin, the relevant variables are defined and causal relationships among those variables are specified. Next data are acquired to test the theory. If this empirical test completely supports the theory, little more must be done except to replicate the study to determine if the finding is reliable; that is, not unique to the particular method used in this one study. If the results fail to support the theory, one or more modifications may be necessary. In the extreme, of course, the theory may have to be abandoned as a failure. More often, the theory or the exact method used to test the theory will need to be altered. For example, a relevant variable in the theory may have been missed or the method chosen to measure or manipulate some variable may have been inadequate or incorrect. In practice, this pattern will cycle through a number of iterations where theories are proposed, tested, reformulated and refined, then tested again. It is through such a *process* that sound theories are developed.

A simple example may help to illustrate this interplay between theory and method. As quoted in Chapter 1, Bauer (1960) explained that consumers not only perceive risk in brand choice decisions but develop strategies for dealing with this risk. This implication of a perceived risk theory sounds quite plausible, but is it true? A suitable method must be developed to test the proposition.

Although a great many methods might be developed, for the sake of argument, an experimental method will be used. One way to manipulate perceived risk is by creating two different buying problems. In both, subjects would be faced with the same exact task of selecting one of several brands of a product, none of which they have purchased before. In one situation, however, it would be made known to subjects that all brands perform at a high level (the low risk condition). In the other, subjects would be informed that some of the brands may not be satisfactory (the high risk condition). Presumably, subjects in the high risk situation will be more likely to develop some strategy for dealing with this risk. If we consciously constructed the brands so that some of them are made by well known manufacturers who charge a premium price while the rest are made by unknown manufacturers who charge a much lower price, subjects in the high risk condition might be expected to choose brands made by well known manufacturers, even though this would require paying a higher price. Subjects in the low risk condition would, presumably, not have as strong a need to reduce risk and, therefore, should purchase lower priced brands made by unknown manufacturers more frequently than subjects in the high risk conditon.

In fact, a study has been conducted along these lines (Ring, Shriber, and Horton 1980). The product studied was toothpaste and the subjects were undergraduates. As can be seen in Table 2.1, the results tend to support the hypothesis that subjects in a high risk buying situation are more likely to purchase higher priced brands made by a well known manufacturer. But the support is far from complete. Ten subjects in the high risk condition failed to select the well known brand while eleven subjects in the low risk condition did. Why? Many reasons could be plausibly suggested. Perhaps subjects differ widely in their involvement with toothpaste, and thus the level of risk perceived within the two risk conditions also differs widely. The fact is that we do not know for sure. To ascertain this requires a new study with a revised and extended theory and a different method that provides an appropriate test. In a similar way, this result might not hold up for subjects who are not undergraduates or for products other than toothpaste. Again, new studies are needed, based on different methods. The

Table 2.1
Relationship between risk level and choice
of brands made by known or unknown
manufacturers (number of subjects choosing
known or unknown manufacturer)

Risk	Known	Unknown
High	18	10
Low	11	19

Note: The level of significance is p .02.

Source: Alexander Ring, Mitchell Shriber, and
Raymond L. Horton, "Some Effects of Perceived
Risk on Consumer Information Processing,"
Journal of the Academy of Marketing Science,
(Summer 1980): 8, p. 261.

key point is that if the theories have been carefully refined and adequately tested, something more should be learned about the behavior being studied at each step in the research process.

The Value of Theory

To ask the value of a good theory is to ask what theory does and how buyer behavior researchers and marketing managers are better off with a good theory than without one. Primarily, a theory provides a parsimonious description of the behavior of the buyer. Such a description reveals consistency and regularity in what otherwise appears to be a confusion of unrelated behaviors. When perceived risk is high, for example, some buyers buy higher priced brands, while others show a great reluctance to switch from a satisfactory brand, and still others buy such products only from stores they have come to trust over a period of years. All of this quite diverse behavior can be explained by a simple or parsimonious theory of how buyers handle perceived risk. It is upon such a basic descriptive foundation that we come to *understand* buyer behavior.

A good theory also allows buyer behavior to be predicted. That is, a good theory lends itself to if ... then statements. For example, perceived risk theory suggests that *if* buyers experience, for some reason, a higher level of risk *then* they will tend to engage in specific behaviors designed to reduce that risk. Thus, a buyer who recently moved might travel a longer distance to purchase higher priced, nationally advertised goods because the *familiar* nonbranded goods are no longer available, and therefore, a higher risk is perceived in the buying situation.

Third, theory provides insights into how buyer behavior may be influenced. If, for example, a certain group of buyers is known to perceive a high degree of risk in a particular product, a brand could be priced high and actively promoted as a high priced brand because those buyers will tend to rely on price as an indicator of quality. L'Oreal, for example, has been quite successful at promoting their hair products with this strategy. In a very similar way Detroit is now trying to regain consumers' preferences for their small cars by actively disseminating, via television, recent government studies which show that small American cars are safer than small Japanese cars.

Finally, a good theory provides a framework for integrating a wide range of findings. Such integration is necessary for a full understanding of the buyer as a whole individual as opposed to the isolated glimpses provided by individual studies. While a comprehensive theory would be desirable to completely integrate the analysis of buyer behavior, the present state of the art would make any such attempt at full integration misleading at best. Therefore, a number of middle range theories will serve as vehicles for partial integration of our knowledge of buyer behavior.

From the marketing manager's perspective, then, the principal value of a theory stems from its provision of better understanding, prediction, and ability to influence buyer behavior. Appendix A considers additional ways in which both the researcher and marketing manager may benefit from good buyer behavior theories.

Theories and Models

One final point is the distinction between theories and models. The term model has a much more practical ring than does theory. Indeed, in many areas the term model is reserved for relatively specific, quantitatively specified relationships among a set of variables that have been derived from a more general theory. In the buyer behavior literature, however, the two terms have tended to be used more or less interchangeably; therefore, no attempt shall be made here to sharply distinguish between them.

TWO EARLY EXAMPLES OF COMPREHENSIVE BUYER BEHAVIOR THEORIES

Although neither is widely used today, consideration of two early comprehensive theories of buyer behavior is quite informative. Consideration of earlier theories develops a better appreciation of the roots of the theories in current use and, perhaps more important, impresses upon us the fact that there *are* alternatives to the theories in current use. Just as the earlier theories were displaced by more useful ones, so will the currently accepted theories be displaced as our knowledge of buyer behavior increases.

The Andreason Model

One of the earliest attempts at constructing a comprehensive theory or model of consumer behavior was made by Alan Andreason in 1965. Andreason's model primarily addressed the problem of how a consumer decides whether or not to purchase a new product. Figure 2.1 presents Andreason's model in schematic form. The solid lines in the figure represent direct flows, while the dashed lines represent feedback to previously defined variables.

Information plays a large role in this model. Although not explicitly an information processing model, Andreason gives explicit recognition to the importance of information in consumer decision making and provides a forerunner of the current information processing theories. The heart of the Andreason model is attitudes. Information—in the context of the wants of the consumer, prior purchasing experience, the consumer's personality, and the social norms and expectations

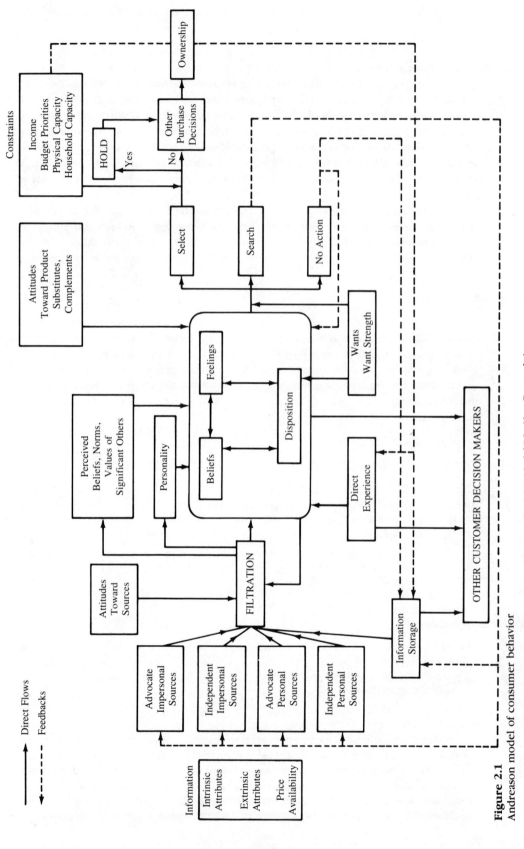

Figure 2.1
Andreason model of consumer behavior

Source: Andreason, Alan R. "Attitudes and Customer Behavior: A Decision Model." In *New Research in Marketing*, figure 4, p. 12. Edited by Lee E. Preston. Berkeley, Calif.: Institute of Business and Economic Research, University of California, 1965.

of significant others—gives rise to attitude. Attitude, which is seen as a predisposition to act toward the attitude object (a particular brand), gives rise to behavior. Thus, behavior may be changed by changing attitudes. And, in Andreason's model, attitudes may be changed in a number of ways. For example, a consumer who changes group affiliation is likely to conform to the new group norms; e.g., an executive, recently named to a top management position, joins a prestigious local country club because it is *expected* of someone in that position.

The Andreason model is not without its limitations. First, it is more or less limited to the development of the initial decision to purchase and has little to say about repeat purchases. Second, it gives extraordinary weight to attitudes at the expense of other variables, which might have been included or more fully developed. Third, the relationships among many of the variables are not very well specified. For example, the filtration box recognizes that information is virtually never stored by the consumer exactly as it was sent by the sender. However, the filtration mechanism itself is left essentially unspecified.

The Nicosia Model

One of the most unique attempts at a comprehensive model of buyer behavior was constructed by Francesco Nicosia (1966). Like the Andreason model, the Nicosia model is primarily concerned with the buying decision for a new product. Nicosia's work, however, was different and unique in several ways. He presented a relatively thorough review of consumer research up to the mid-1960s. More than any other researcher, he emphasized the decision process itself, as opposed to the act of purchase. Furthermore, he cast his model as a computer simulation model. Besides the methodological implications of the formulation, the simulation framework emphasizes the circularity of the relationships involved. In contrast to other models where the flow is essentially in one direction from the earliest recognition of a purchase need to the eventual purchase, the Nicosia model involves an on-going decision process that both precedes and follows the purchase act. The choice of where to start studying the process is quite arbitrary. And finally, the Nicosia model is the only comprehensive model of buyer behavior that explicitly includes the firm.

Figure 2.2 presents a summary description of the Nicosia model in schematic form and a far more detailed description of the model is presented in Figure 2.3. The model itself is divided into four basic fields. Field one focuses on the firm's attempts to communicate with the consumer. The outcome of this process will depend on a complex set of interactions involving both the firm and the consumer. Assuming that the consumer decides that the message is relevant, the consumer will move to field two for a search and evaluation of alternative brand choices. Field three concerns the decision to purchase a specific brand. Finally, field four concerns consumption of the selected brand and the feedbacks through the system; e.g., reevaluation of attitude in light of postpurchase performance.

Individuals who have critically appraised the Nicosia model have generally given the work high marks (e.g., Zaltman, Pinson, and Angelman 1973, pp. 104–111; and Markin 1974, pp. 93–96). The model, however, is not without its limitations or its critics. Like most comprehensive models of buyer behavior, the Nicosia model tends to present all buyer behavior as highly rational. The Nicosia model, however, shows an even stronger tendency in this direction than most other models. A

Field One: From the Source of a Message to the Consumer's Attitude

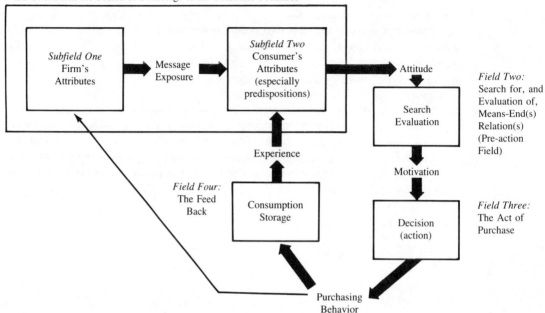

Figure 2.2
A summary description of the Nicosia model

Source: Francesco M. Nicosia, *Consumer Decision Processes,* 156. Englewood Cliffs, N.J.: Prentice-Hall, 1966. Reprinted with permission.

second limitation is that the model has received little empirical testing (e.g., Zaltman et. al. 1973, p. 109) and many of its variables are not satisfactorily defined. Lunn (1974, p. 43), for example, criticizes the definitions of attitude and motivation. Finally, Nicosia attempted to define his model mathematically, which has frequently been criticized as premature (e.g., Ehrenberg, 1968). For all of its limitations, however, the Nicosia model is clearly an important milestone in the study of buyer behavior.

THE HOWARD-SHETH THEORY OF BUYER BEHAVIOR

Although the limitations of the Howard-Sheth theory are now widely recognized and relatively little current buyer behavior research is conducted within the specific framework of this theory, the theory merits our special attention for several reasons. It is historically important; indeed, during the 1970s it seemed that almost every buyer behavior study found it necessary to reference the Howard-Sheth theory. While most comprehensive theories or models of buyer behavior have primarily been summaries of the buyer behavior literature and/or diagrammatic synopses of the organization of material presented in textbooks, the Howard-Sheth theory was developed with the intention of conducting a systematic program of research. In fact, it is the only comprehensive theory of buyer behavior to have been extensively tested or to have been submitted to anything even approximating a comprehensive test of the theory.[3]

Closely related to the first two points is the importance of the Howard-Sheth theory in the development of our knowledge of buyer behavior. Despite its acknowledged limitations, the Howard-Sheth theory is probably still our best comprehensive description of buyer behavior when the buyer's full decision-making processes are aroused; e.g., when considering a new, complex, and important product, such as a solar hot water system. In this capacity, the Howard-Sheth theory provides an excellent introduction to many of the most important buyer behavior concepts and illustrates some of the ways these concepts are interrelated. Many of the insights regarding buyer behavior that can be gleaned from a review of the Howard-Sheth theory will be encountered repeatedly in subsequent discussions of research conducted both within and outside the theory's framework. And, like all good theories, the limitations of the Howard-Sheth theory sharpen our perceptions of what is not known and suggest directions for future research.

Finally, the Howard-Sheth theory is somewhat unique because it is more directly based on reasonably well-developed psychological theories than any other comprehensive theory of buyer behavior. In particular, Zaltman, Pinson, and Angelman note that

> The theory is very deeply rooted in one particular learning theory [Hull's] developed outside marketing, in Osgood's cognitive theory, and in Berlyne's theory of exploratory behavior.
>
> ... [and that] The Howard-Sheth model does bring together relatively confirmed hypotheses from learning theory, cognitive theory, and exploratory behavior theory. These are, of course, highly related areas and students of each area have on occasion assumed the others to be a subpart of their own area. The model also brings together ideas from conflict theory and information processing theory (1973, p. 117).

Recent refinements of the model by Howard (1977) have added a substantial number of information processing concepts to the original model.

Figure 2.4 presents an overview of the Howard-Sheth model. The model consists of five broadly defined components: inputs, perceptual constructs, learning constructs, outputs, and exogenous variables.

Inputs

The stimulus display consists of the information potentially available to buyers. Three broad types of information are specifically recognized. Significative stimuli relate to the object itself. For example, in buying a car significative stimuli would come from kicking the tires, feeling the plushness of the seats, or taking a test drive. Symbolic stimuli represent information about the object of interest that comes from symbols, which indirectly represent the object, rather than the object itself. In buying a car, this could include such things as mass media advertising, *Consumer Reports'* brand evaluations, and newspaper stories. A special type of

---

[3]An appreciation of the complexities involved in trying to provide a comprehensive test of a model as complex as the Howard-Sheth model can be gained by reading Farely and Ring (1970).

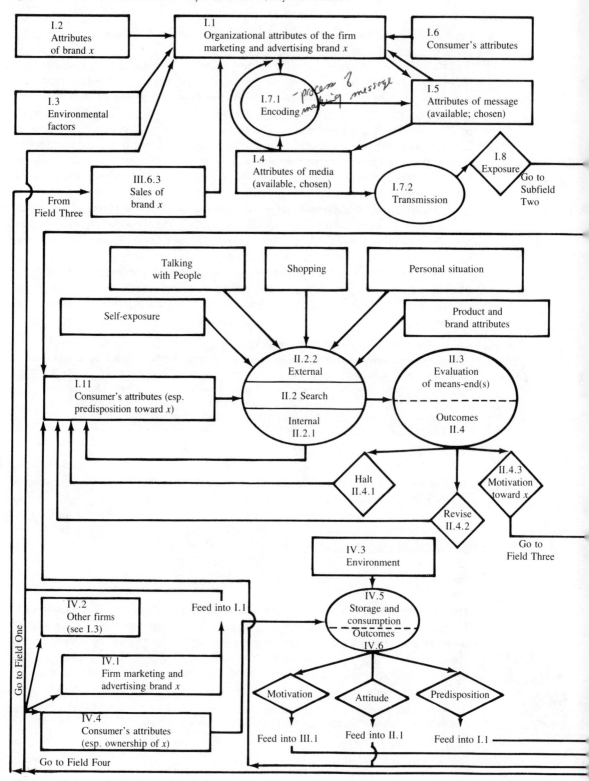

Figure 2.3
The Nicosia model of consumer behavior

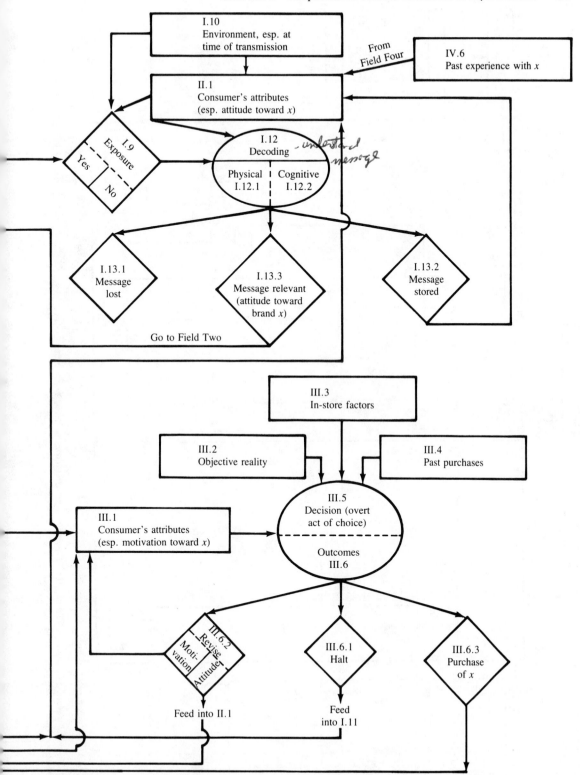

Source: Francesco M. Nicosia, *Consumer Decision Processes.* Englewood Cliffs, N.J.: Prentice-Hall, 1966. Reprinted with permission.

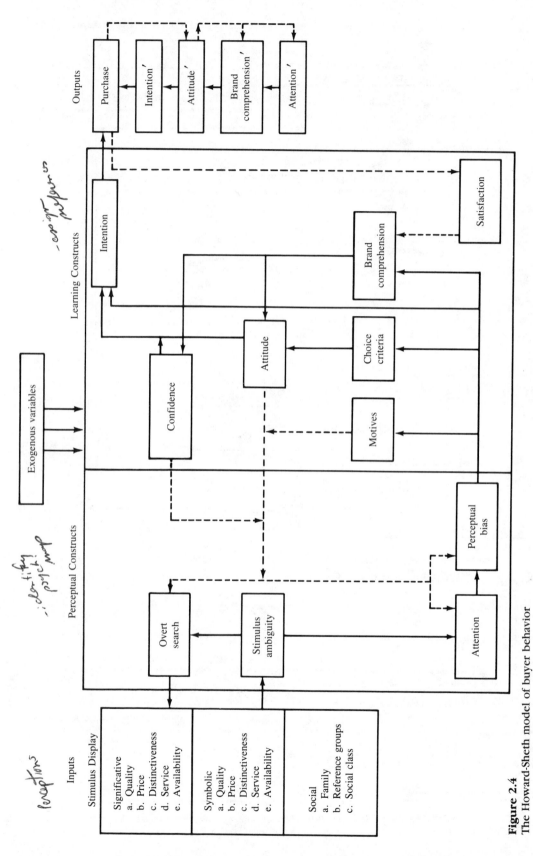

Figure 2.4

The Howard-Sheth model of buyer behavior.

Source: John A Howard and Jagdish N. Sheth, *The Theory of Buyer Behavior*, 30. New York: Wiley & Sons, 1969. Reprinted with permission.

symbolic stimuli, social stimuli, functions differently enough in buying behavior that it merits separate attention.

In subsequent chapters, each of these inputs will be discussed in detail. The general point which needs to be emphasized now is that in a well developed, high level economy, as currently exists in the United States, a great deal of consumer decision making is based on symbolic and social, rather than significative, information. This may seem odd at first. But consider, for example, how many students select a university entirely from reading catalogs and listening to what others have to say about the school. Or how many people decide to see a movie because of a friend's recommendation, a good newspaper review, or an enticing billboard. The primary point is that consumers utilize different types of information quite differently in their decision-making processes.[4]

Perceptual Constructs

Before a buyer can act upon information, the buyer must perceive that information. It is the purpose of the perceptual constructs to explain how the buyer selects, out of the vast amount of information potentially available in the stimulus display, the information upon which the brand choice decision *process* will actually be based.

Two basic mechanisms are involved in this perceptual process: attention and overt search. Attention is passive; that is, for some reason the buyer develops a heightened receptivity to specific types of stimuli. A woman, for example, might need a scarf to complement a particular dress, but the need may not be sufficiently strong or pressing to motivate her to actively search for the scarf. However, should information about an appropriate scarf come accidently within her range of perception, the attention mechanism will allow her to recognize the stimuli as relevant to her needs and she will then acquire that information. Note carefully the expression used is "acquire that information" rather than purchase. The information could be a magazine ad or a chance encounter in which she learns of a store that has "a large selection of scarfs, including two or three that would look just wonderful with your grey wool dress." Even should our hypothetical consumer accidently see the scarf itself, she still must acquire information on the scarf's color, size, etc. to ascertain its relevance to her specific needs.

In contrast to attention, overt search is active. The buyer consciously and actively scans magazine ads, asks friends, reads *Consumer Reports*, or engages in some other activity designed to acquire information relevant to the brand choice decision. Note the dashed lines that link the learning constructs with the perceptual constructs. The dashed lines represent feedback from variables that have already been directly defined by the learning constructs. For example, information from the stimulus display is fed via the perceptual system into the learning construct motives, which in turn "feeds back" into the perceptual system thus altering attention or overt search or both. When feedback exists, the constructs

---

[4]More recently, Howard replaced the very general concept of the stimulus display with the more specific notions of information available, which leads through a variety of perceptual processes to information exposed (information actually acquired by a consumer about a specific brand). Howard also broke the symbolic stimuli into commercial and neutral information. None of these changes, however, has altered Howard and Sheth's basic point regarding the importance of nonsignificative stimuli in the consumer's brand choice decision process. For details see Howard (1977, Chapter 7).

serve both as dependent and independent variables. Such systems are more difficult to deal with quantitatively, but are far more realistic in terms of how the consumer actually makes buying decisions.[5]

The remaining two constructs, stimulus ambiguity and perceptual bias, recognize that the information actually received by the consumer from the stimulus display requires an interpretation process, which presents numerous opportunities for distortion. That is, the consumer must attach "meaning" to the physical stimuli (sight, sound, touch) that emanate from the stimulus display. For example, I slam the door of a new car and it "sounds" solid. I decide, therefore, that this means the car will last many years.

Stimulus ambiguity recognizes that the stimulus itself may not be entirely clear. The stimulus may be physically ambiguous; for example, when I slammed the car door in the showroom, the sound may have been muffled by background music and people talking. The stimulus may also be semantically ambiguous; that is, even though the stimulus is physically clear, its meaning (its semantic properties) may be obscure. For example, I am currently thinking of buying a wood burning stove. Such stoves come in two basic metals: steelplate and castiron. Physically determining which is which is very easy, but what does each mean in terms of such properties as heating efficiency and durability. I do not know because I have not yet learned the semantic meaning to attach to each physical stimulus.

Perceptual bias recognizes that information may be systematically distorted before it is permanently stored by the buyer. Perceptual bias has been frequently criticized as vague. Howard (1977, pp. 230–231) recognized this as a valid criticism of the original Howard-Sheth model and replaced the general idea of perceptual bias with a more specific set of constructs that represent more precisely how information is dealt with by the buyer. Although these changes make the theory more operational, they do not alter the basic point of perceptual bias, that information is rarely stored by the buyer exactly as that information was sent by the sender.

Learning Constructs

The heart of the Howard-Sheth model consists of the learning constructs. To begin, behavior is motivated. In this regard, note how motives feed back to the perceptual system to affect overt search, attention, and perceptual bias. Howard and Sheth argue that motives, in and of themselves, provide no explicit guides to how the

---

[5]Models, such as the Howard-Sheth model, are referred to as nonrecursive. This means that the independent variables that explain a particular dependent variable may in turn be explained by that same dependent variable. This does not happen in recursive models. A simple recursive model might be

$$y = f(x) \qquad (1)$$
$$x = f(z). \qquad (2)$$

Because x is a function of z we may "recursively" substitute z for x in equation (1). In a nonrecursive system, such substitution is not possible. An important consequence of nonrecursiveness is that each equation may not be estimated independently, as in a recursive system, but all of the equations must be estimated simultaneously. The estimation of simultaneous equations is much more complex mathematically and statistically than the estimation of individual equations using simple and multiple regression procedures. Good discussions of simultaneous equation procedures can be found in any good econometrics text. For a thorough, but difficult, treatment of these procedures in a marketing context see Bagozzi (1980).

buyer may satisfy those motives. That is, motives energize behavior but motives do not direct behavior.

Before the buyer can satisfy his or her motives two things must happen. First, the buyer must be able to identify the brand. Brand comprehension serves this function. For example, cars have four wheels while motorcycles have only two wheels. And, until quite recently, American consumers identified luxury automobiles as large automobiles. The automobile manufacturers have had a very difficult task in changing the criteria by which consumers *identify* luxury automobiles so that their downsized versions of luxury automobiles are still identified by potential buyers as luxury automobiles.

Second, the buyer must develop specific criteria for evaluating the extent to which a specific brand satisfies the buyer's motives. These so-called choice criteria are very similar to the identifying criteria in brand comprehension with one major distinction. Brand comprehension is identifying but not evaluative; that is, a buyer may use the characteristics four wheels or luxury automobile to identify and categorize a particular object but may not use either in evaluating one brand against another because the characteristics are not relevant to motives. This evaluative task is handled by choice criteria and attitude.

Compared to its traditional treatment in social psychology, attitude has a very narrow definition here: a buyer's attitude toward a brand is defined as the satisfaction expected from buying the brand and is based directly on the brand's evaluation on the relevant choice criteria. Table 2.2 illustrates this process of attitude formation with a simple numerical example. Whatever the underlying motives, our hypothetical consumer has formed four choice criteria, which will be used to evaluate different brands of automobiles: miles per gallon, repair record, resale value, and safety. Next our consumer assigns ratings, on say a 10 point scale, to each brand on the choice criteria. This is illustrated in Table 2.2 for an arbitrary brand A. Next our consumer must decide how to combine these ratings on the individual choice criteria. The procedure illustrated in Table 2.2 is relatively straightforward. The consumer determines the relative importance or salience of each criterion, multiplies these saliences by the corresponding brand evaluation, and adds these values. The sum, 6.6 in our illustration, is the consumer's attitude toward brand A.

Table 2.2
Illustration of how attitudes are formed via choice criteria

Choice Criteria	Evaluation of Brand A[1]	Salience[2]	Contribution to Attitude
Miles Per Gallon	8	.4	3.2
Repair Record	7	.3	2.1
Resale Value	3	.1	.3
Safety	5	.2	1.0
Overall Attitude			6.6

[1]Rated on a scale, say one to ten, where higher numbers indicate a better evaluation.

[2]The salience of a choice criterion measures its relative importance. In this example, miles per gallon receives 40 percent of the total weight in the overall attitude. By definition, the salience factors total one.

Over the past several decades, a great many studies have examined the degree to which attitudes predict purchase. The correlations between attitudes and purchase have been, generally, disappointingly low. While, of course, there are many possible reasons for the lack of a strong relationship between attitude and purchase, Howard and Sheth suggest that the question itself is improperly framed. They suggest that attitude gives rise to intention rather than invariably giving rise to purchase. Intention represents a plan of action, which may include various contingencies that can inhibit the expression of a favorable attitude in purchase. A man, for example, may have formed a very favorable attitude toward the Datsun 280ZX. He may, however, have a relatively new car and a budget constraint that prohibits him from spending $15,000 or so, which the 280ZX currently costs. He might, therefore, form the following intention or plan. In two years, he expects a major promotion that will include a very large salary increase. Since his present car will be five years old then, he will buy the 280ZX when his promotion comes through. Of course, during the next two years, many things could happen to block or inhibit the purchase. The promotion might not come through. Or by the time the promotion did come, the price of the 280ZX may have risen to the point where he is again priced out of the market. Or, perhaps, he and his wife have a child, in which case a two-seat automobile is no longer practical, whatever his attitude toward the 280ZX.

Notice in Figure 2.4 that intention is influenced by confidence as well as attitude. Confidence recognizes that two buyers can have exactly the same attitude and yet not be equally confident or certain that the satisfaction expected from the purchase and consumption will actually occur. Figure 2.5 illustrates confidence: Two consumers have exactly the same attitude level, 6.6, toward a brand. The high confidence consumer, however, thinks that there is almost no chance that the actual satisfaction achieved from consuming the brand will fall below 5 or above 8, while the low confidence consumer thinks there is a very large chance that this will occur. Confidence plays two quite different roles in the Howard-Sheth theory. At high values confidence *tends* to trigger purchase. At low values confidence *tends* to inhibit purchase and to feed back into the perceptual constructs. The primary effect of this feedback, assuming that the level of motivation is sufficiently high, is to stimulate overt search for information to increase confidence.

The final learning construct, satisfaction, has already been hinted at in the discussion of attitude. Notice from Figure 2.4 that satisfaction is a postpurchase phenomenon. Satisfaction represents the consumer's subjective experience with the brand purchased. This experience is then compared, in the feedback relationships, with the satisfaction that the consumer *expected*, i.e., with attitude. If actual and expected satisfaction are approximately equal then no changes in the system should be expected. If they are different the consumer's attitude toward the brand may change, or the confidence with which that attitude is held or some other construct in the system might be altered in light of the postpurchase experience.

Outputs

All of the perceptual and learning constructs discussed so far are internal to the buyer. They are not directly observable but represent a statement of the forces that are *hypothesized* to underlie the buyer's behavior, and it is for this reason that the perceptual and learning constructs are referred to as hypothetical constructs.

Figure 2.5
Illustration of confidence for
two hypothetical consumers

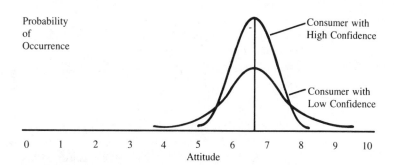

Those who attempt to study the behavior of buyers, however, are forced to rely on what can actually be observed. The hypothetical constructs are of great value because they tell where and what to look for in the way of answers to why buyers behave as they do. Howard and Sheth refer to these potentially observable buyer behaviors as outputs.

Note that, with the exception of purchase, all of the outputs in Figure 2.4 correspond with specific hypothetical constructs, except that the outputs carry a prime. The prime indicates that the output variable is based directly on observable data. For example, in an attitude survey a consumer might be asked to rate her attitude toward a number of brands on a ten point scale. Variables constructed in this way are referred to as intervening variables because they intervene or stand between the hypothetical constructs and the actual behavior of consumers. Appendix A considers the relationships among hypothetical constructs, intervening variables, and data in greater depth.

Exogenous Variables

With the single exception of the inputs from the stimulus display, all of the constructs or variables discussed so far are endogenous variables. The distinguishing feature of endogenous variables is that the model explains how changes in these variables occur. Attitude, for example, changes because of change in brand evaluations on the choice criteria or because of a discrepancy between actual and expected satisfaction.

Exogenous variables, then, are variables that influence the behavior of buyers but for which the model offers no explanation as to how they come into existence or change. For example, the model makes no attempt to explain the stimulus display even though the stimulus display is important in determining the behavior of buyers and elements of the stimulus display, such as prices and point of purchase advertising, frequently change in direct response to the behavior of buyers.

The list of potential exogenous variables that might influence the consumer is almost endless. Religion, sex, race, personality, social class, income, ad infinitum all have been shown to have some impact on various aspects of buyer behavior. Generally, any one study will make use of only one or, at most, a few of these exogeneous variables. The reason that there are so many potential exogenous variables, relative to the limited number of endogenous variables, is that the exogenous variables are literally outside the main model; they are not caught up in the web of interrelationships that define and limit the endogenous variables and we can, therefore, easily add and delete exogenous variables without having to change the model itself.

Learning Stages

Howard and Sheth suggest that the behavior of the buyer can be partially understood in terms of the completeness of the buyer's learning. Specifically, they suggest that buying behavior may be divided into three stages: routinized response behavior, limited problem solving, and extensive problem solving. These three stages of learning are distinguished by how well the buyer has learned the relevant product class concept and associated brand concepts.

In routinized response behavior, this learning is virtually complete, and the buyer's behavior becomes essentially automatic or routine. In limited problem solving, the buyer has a well formed product class concept but the associated brand concepts are not well learned. Before a satisfactory purchase can be made the buyer will have to learn more about the brands from which the final choice will be made. An important aspect of the information acquisition process in limited problem solving is that, because the product class concept is well learned, the buyer knows what information is relevant to the brand choice. In extensive problem solving, the buyer does not even have a well formed product class concept. The lack of a well formed product class concept greatly increases the buyer's information search and brand evaluation tasks. It also presents substantial difficulties for firms trying to communicate with buyers about a new product.

The Brand and Product Class Concepts

So far, the brand and product class concepts have been used without a precise definition. The brand concept is contained in the learning constructs. Specifically, the buyer's concept of a brand is defined by the constructs brand comprehension, attitude, and confidence.

The product class concept is more difficult to define. Howard offers the following definition:

> We may now relate product class to motives. Brands that serve the same motive (or set of motives) for a consumer are, by definition, those brands that make up his or her product class. ... and a product class is a group of brands all judged by the same choice criteria and with the same weight given to each criterion (1977, p. 32).

Thus, brands that compete among themselves to satisfy particular motives are in the same product class.

Obviously, determining to which product class a brand belongs is important to the buyer, the academic researcher, and the marketing manager. Unfortunately, one encounters a great many unresolved conceptual and practical problems in trying to define specific product classes. Perhaps the most troublesome conceptual problem is that different product classes must compete for the buyer's limited resources. How is competition among product classes to be separated from competition among brands within a particular product class. If we observe a consumer trying to decide whether to buy a new washing machine *or* take a week-long vacation we may *believe* the distinction is easy to make. But what if the choice is between a cruiseship tour of the world and a three-month automobile tour of the United States? The fact of the matter is that there is no completely satisfactory resolution to this problem.

Fortunately, a number of procedures are available that help define the degree of competition among a set of brands and the degree to which a set of brands are perceived by consumers as similar. From such empirical data, it is possible to develop tentative conceptions of which brands constitute a product class for specified groups of buyers. A number of such procedures will be presented throughout this book.

Evaluation of the Howard-Sheth Theory

The Howard-Sheth theory has been subjected to extensive empirical testing. In terms of empirical tests of the theory, Holbrook (1974) observed that (1) most studies addressed only a limited portion of the theory, (2) support for the theory has been based largely on two variable (bivariate) relationships even though the theory generally requires more complex tests, (3) no specific aspect of the theory received completely consistent support, and (4) the proportion of the total variance of the data explained by the theory is generally low.

Closely related to Holbrook's fourth point are several methodological issues. Many of the variables in the theory are difficult to measure and the variables actually measured have sometimes born scant resemblance to theoretical specifications of the variables (Taylor and Guttman 1974). Also many exogenous variables need to be explicitly incorporated into the model as endogenous variables. Perhaps the most important and general methodological limitation is that the sheer complexity of the theory makes a truly comprehensive test at this time virtually impossible. Recently, however, Laroche and Howard (1980) showed that the empirical performance of the Howard-Sheth theory can be improved substantially by introducing nonlinear relationships among certain variables. This suggests that one limitation of the original theory was that, despite its apparent complexity, it was *too* simple.

A number of more conceptual criticisms of the Howard-Sheth theory have also been made. One criticism that the Howard-Sheth theory shares with almost all comprehensive theories of buyer behavior is the presumption that buyers engage in a highly organized, very elaborate decision-making *process* which, if successful, *culminates* in a brand purchase decision. There is, however, increasing concern that buyer behavior researchers may have seriously overstated the extent to which purchase decisions are preceded by a true predecision process (cf., Kassarjian 1978, 1982; Olshavsky and Granbois 1979).

Another criticism, raised by Zaltman, Pinson, and Angelman (1973), is that the Howard-Sheth model "seems primarily restricted to frequently purchased items" (p. 115). The authors are not clear about why this is a valid criticism of the model, but it would seem reasonable to presume that it involves the progression of learning about a product class from extensive problem solving to limited problem solving to routinized response behavior. The theory, however, seems quite capable of dealing with behavior that never progresses to the fully routinized stage because of infrequent purchasing needs, e.g., automobiles and major appliances. More serious is the increasing recognition that much buyer behavior does *not* involve the smooth or inevitable progression of the buyer through the stages of learning as postulated in the Howard-Sheth theory.

Another criticism, which is again shared with virtually all comprehensive models of buyer behavior, is that "the model does not cover collective decision-making", e.g., family and organizational buying (Zaltman, Pinson, and Angelman,

1973, p. 115). To understand the importance of this criticism, we need to recall the distinction between endogenous and exogenous variables. It is relatively easy to accommodate variables that reflect collective decision making in any comprehensive model as exogenous variables. Howard and Sheth (1969), for example, use the exogenous variable social and organizational setting to capture certain aspects of collective decision making. Such exogenous variables, however, typically are defined very broadly and, by definition, stand outside the web of interrelationships among the endogenous variables, which are necessary to fully understand the intricacies of buyer behavior.

A basic set of criticisms involves the learning theory base of the Howard-Sheth theory. There are two quite distinct problems. First, the borrowing from learning theory has been more implicit than explicit. Consequences of this are a lack of explicit listing or discussion of the assumptions upon which the Howard-Sheth theory is based and the difficulty of determining precisely what aspects of learning theory are being relied upon to define specific components of the Howard-Sheth model. A second problem is that learning theory has largely been developed in a context (laboratory experimentation, usually with animals) that has little relationship to the context in which buyers normally act.

In attempting a general evaluation of the Howard-Sheth, the question arises, "Does the Howard-Sheth theory *adequately* describe and explain buyer behavior?" Clearly, it does not. But given the primitive state of knowledge, the question is perhaps premature. What can be said for certain is that the Howard-Sheth theory is the only comprehensive theory of buyer behavior that has been developed as part of a systematic and continuing program of empirical research. The theory continues to undergo development and only future results can determine the extent to which the generally recognized limitations of the Howard-Sheth theory will be overcome by future research.

THE ENGEL, KOLLAT, AND BLACKWELL (EKB) MODEL

The Engel, Kollat, and Blackwell, or EKB, model provided the organizational framework for the first true consumer behavior textbook. The text is now in its fourth edition (Engel and Blackwell 1982) and the EKB model has been revised with each edition.

Figure 2.6 presents the EKB model for high involvement decisions. A low involvement version of this model, which involves dropping a number of variables (e.g., external search and yielding/acceptance), and reversing the sequence of alternative evaluation and choice has also been proposed. By now many of the components of the model should be familiar. Note carefully, as the authors acknowledge, the high degree of similarity in the general structures of the EKB and the Howard-Sheth models. Despite this general similarity there are a number of significant differences between the two models.[6] The next few paragraphs will point out several of the more important differences.

Two differences can be recognized in the grouping of variables within the decision process stage. First, the Howard-Sheth model has no construct that di-

---

[6]Engel and Blackwell cast both the EKB model and the Howard-Sheth model in general equation form to facilitate comparisons between the two models. This discussion relies heavily on that material. See Engel and Blackwell (1982, pp. 677–690).

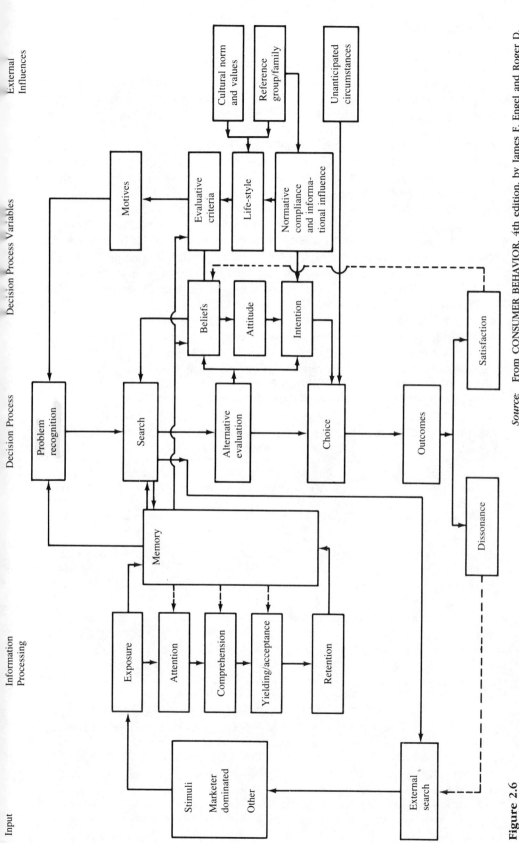

| Input | Information Processing | Decision Process | Decision Process Variables | External Influences |

Figure 2.6
The Engel, Kollat, and Blackwell model of consumer behavior for high involvement decisions

Source: From CONSUMER BEHAVIOR, 4th edition, by James F. Engel and Roger D. Blackwell. Copyright © 1982 by CBS College Publishing. Reprinted by permission of Holt, Rinehart and Winston, CBS College Publishing.

Note: The following variables were deleted in the low involvement version of the EKB model: search, yielding/acceptance, and external search.

rectly corresponds with problem recognition. As Engel, Blackwell, and Kollat (1978, p. 560)[7] note, however, the Howard-Sheth model handles problem recognition indirectly through the arousal function of motives. A second, and major, difference is that the EKB model includes the postpurchase outcome of dissonance as well as satisfaction, which is common to both models. Dissonance occurs when two or more attitudes or attitudes and behavior are contradictory. For example, I dislike a store but buy there because of a special need. Dissonance is an unpleasant psychological state, which gives rise to activities directed toward reducing the dissonance. Precisely how buyers reduce dissonance has substantial implications for buyer behavior, which will be discussed in depth in Chapter 8.

Engel and Blackwell (1982, pp. 688) also argue that "the EKB model is unique in highlighting the decision process and explicitly including the proven relationships of the Fishbein behavioral intentions model under alternative evaluation." Although the first claim is open to debate, certainly the explicit inclusion of the Fishbein model is both unique and important. (The Fishbein model will be examined in some detail during a later discussion of attitudes.)

Finally, variables are contained in the Howard-Sheth model that are not in the EKB model: The two most important are stimulus ambiguity and confidence. Engel and Blackwell (1982, p. 689) state that their model omits these two variables because they see no way to operationalize the former and the latter has not received empirical confirmation. They do note, however, Howard's (1974) argument that confidence has been validated.

A fair evaluation of the EKB model must consider both the purpose for which the model was originally developed and the current state of knowledge of buyer behavior. With regard to purpose Engel and Blackwell note that

> The primary purpose still [in the second edition] was pedagogical, with the result that there was no explicit attempt made to specify quantifiable functional relationships. Although these could have been easily derived from the text itself, it never was our expectation that the model would be tested in the same manner as the Columbia group has done with the Howard model (1982, p. 686).

Engel, Blackwell, and Kollat regard the last two versions of the EKB model as far more testable than the previous two versions. To date, however, the EKB model has not been submitted to empirical testing. Much additional work is needed to develop appropriate empirical tests of the EKB model.[8]

Finally, the state of knowledge of buyer behavior is still quite primitive. Rather than being fully tested and accepted *theories*, the currently available comprehensive models are more like blueprints. They suggest variables and relationships among these variables for empirical testing. They provide a kind of framework for loosely integrating different findings. But like a blueprint they provide little detail. Just as a blueprint may indicate where a wall goes without specifying a type of construction material, so a comprehensive model may indicate that motives are important in understanding buyer behavior without specifying exactly what consti-

---

[7]The comparison of models in the fourth edition of the EKB book is primarily a much condensed version from their third edition. It is for this reason that certain citations are made to this earlier edition.

[8]The additional steps needed to empirically test the theories or models are discussed in some detail in Appendix A.

tutes a motive. Given the high degree of similarity among the available contenders, Engel and Blackwell (1982, p. 690) suggest that the appropriate model to use is perhaps as much a matter of personal taste and preference as anything else.

SUMMARY

A major theme of Chapter 1 was to show that our knowledge of buyer behavior is constantly evolving. In this chapter, the nature of theory was examined, especially as it facilitates and guides the evolutionary process of increasing the knowledge of buyer behavior. A number of comprehensive theories or models of buyer behavior were examined, focusing on the Howard-Sheth model.

As already observed, comprehensive models of buyer behavior have considerable value in identifying important variables and their possible relationships, integrating existing knowledge, and suggesting new hypotheses for empirical testing. However, all of the currently available comprehensive models have serious flaws, which are generally acknowledged, even by the models' originators. Furthermore, an explosion of research in recent years has produced a great deal of new knowledge about buyer behavior that is not easy to assimilate into existing comprehensive theories. Unfortunately, as noted in the last chapter, there is no new comprehensive theory on the horizon that appears capable of providing the necessary integration of old and new research findings. Although the Howard-Sheth model will be used as a vehicle for organizing the majority of the review of buyer behavior theory and research, the fit will often be loose.

Situational Factors

3

As stated in the last chapter, a general criticism of most comprehensive models of buyer behavior is the tendency to presume a high degree of involvement with the purchase decision, which naturally leads the buyer to engage in an active and complex decision-making process that culminates in a purchase. Increasingly, however, it has become clear that not all purchasing decisions are arrived at via such active and complex decision-making processes.

More generally, buyers approach different types of purchasing problems in fundamentally different ways. Understanding these differences is of immense importance both to academic researchers and marketing managers. For example, buyers tend to base their automobile buying decisions on at least a moderate amount of information regarding specific product attributes, such as size and miles per gallon. In contrast, for snow skis or expensive photographic equipment, where product attributes are complex and difficult to relate to desired performance features, buyers tend to base their decisions more on nonproduct information, such as price and the recommendations of salespersons. Clearly different marketing strategies are called for in these two situations *because* buyers approach the two buying decisions in fundamentally different ways. For example, there are significant opportunities to use a high price, relative to competitive brands, to indicate high quality for snow skis and expensive photographic equipment while, with the exception of very expensive automobiles, automobiles are generally promoted on the basis of a low relative price.

It is the purpose of this chapter to identify types of buying situations in which the decision-making processes of consumers are broadly similar within situational categories and fundamentally different among categories. The analysis begins with a brief discussion of what is meant by a buying situation. Next, three different systems for categorizing buying situations are discussed. Each system was developed for a different purpose and focuses on different aspects of buyers' decision-making processes. The three classification systems are then integrated to reveal five basic categories of buying situations. Finally, the managerial implications of this classification system are illustrated in an extended example.

THE CONCEPT OF A BUYING SITUATION

The concept of a buying situation has been used by marketers in at least three different ways. One longstanding use of the term is to identify aspects of the larger economic environment that affect the spending behavior of buyers. For example, when unemployment increases, even people with jobs tend to become more cautious and curtail their spending, especially for expensive durable goods such as automobiles and houses. This use of the buying situation concept is clearly of importance to marketing managers. However, the larger economic environment and its effects on buyers has tended to be of greater concern to economists and social science pollsters than marketing academicians.

Currently, the most common use of a buying situation limits the concept to variables that are not predictable from knowledge of either the person or the choice object (Belk 1975a). For example, research indicates that when products that are normally low involvement goods are purchased as gifts the decision-making process more closely resembles a high involvement decision (Clarke and Belk 1979). This conception of buying situations is especially useful in accounting for variance in buyer behavior studies that would otherwise remain unexplained and possibly obscure the interpretation of the data, and for segmenting markets.

As a practical matter, an infinite number of situational variables might be identified under this second use of the buying situation concept. The relevant situational variables will also vary widely over both products and consumers. For example, a person's evaluation and purchase decision regarding various types and brands of bread may depend upon whether the product is intended for use as toast, a sandwich, stuffing for a turkey. As another example, some consumers make a sharp distinction between cooking wines and drinking wines, while others do not. The reader should have no trouble identifying examples of other situational variables and some of their managerial implications. While this use of situational variables is of considerable interest to the marketing manager, who is interested in developing effective marketing strategies for *specific* products, the sheer number of situational variables makes this use of the buying situation concept inappropriate for the task at hand.

The third use of the concept defines the buying situation in terms of consumer and choice object characteristics, such as self-confidence in judging product attributes and the clarity of relevant product attributes. The resulting classification systems lead to a relatively small number of buying situations that consumers tend to approach with different decision-making processes and to resolve in different ways.

This third conception of buying situations results in theories of situational factors that can be applied to consumer behavior at a high level of generality. The primary managerial value of such theories is not that they provide us with *detailed* answers to specific marketing strategy questions; for clearly they do not. Rather, they help determine which variables are of primary importance in influencing consumers' purchasing decisions. For example, under what conditions is it important that a product be distributed widely instead of at selected outlets. Or under what conditions are consumers likely to be highly influenced by their own personality needs. Knowing such things is very helpful to a manager in structuring the very specific questions which must be asked and answered when developing a marketing strategy for a particular product; e.g., what are the relevant personality needs and how can knowledge of those needs aid in designing an advertising program for a given product.[1]

EXTENSION OF COPELAND'S CLASSIFICATION OF GOODS SYSTEM

Chapter 1 briefly discussed, in an historical context, Copeland's 1923 classification of goods as convenience, shopping, and specialty goods, a system extended by Holbrook and Howard (1976). Figure 3.1 presents the extended system in schematic form.

The four classifications of goods in Figure 3.1 are defined in terms of six basic factors. The first two factors are based on the product characteristics magnitude of purchase and clarity of product characteristics. That is, how costly is the product and how easily visible to the consumer are important product characteristics. The

---

[1]For a more complete discussion of situational factors the reader is referred to Belk (1975a), the comments on Belk's paper by Barker (1975) and Wicker (1975), and Belk's (1975b) reply.

High Clarity
High Specific
  Self-Confidence
Mental Effort during
  Shopping via
  Brand Comparisons

Low Clarity
Low Specific
  Self-Confidence
Mental Effort prior
  to Shopping via
  Information Seeking

	High Clarity / High Specific Self-Confidence	Low Clarity / Low Specific Self-Confidence
Low Magnitude Low Ego Involvement Low Physical Shopping Effort	Convenience Goods	Preference Goods
High Magnitude High Ego Involvement High Physical Shopping Effort	Shopping Goods	Specialty Goods

Figure 3.1.
Holbrook and Howard's revision of Copeland's classification of goods system

Source: Adapted from Morris B. Holbrook and John A. Howard. "Frequently Purchased Nondurable Goods and Services." In *Selected Aspects of Consumer Behavior: A Summary from the Perspective of Different Disciplines,* RANN Program, p. 215. Washington, D.C.: National Science Foundation, 1976.

second two factors are based on the consumer characteristics ego-involvement and specific self-confidence. That is, to what extent is the brand choice of great importance to central values of the consumer, such as the consumer's self-image, and how confident is the consumer in his or her ability to recognize the characteristics of a good brand choice. An important point is that while the magnitude of purchase may cause a purchase to be ego-involving, the two concepts are quite distinct. For example, many consumers view their home and its decor as an extension and expression of themselves; to others it is just a place to live. The third two factors are based on the consumer response variables magnitude of physical shopping effort and timing of mental effort. The last variable refers to whether mental effort in acquiring brand information is expended before or while physically shopping for goods.

The rows of Figure 3.1 are split essentially between nondurable goods (top) and durable goods (bottom). The columns are split between goods for which there is little or no brand insistence (left) and those for which brand insistence is strong (right). The managerial implications of this classification scheme can be defined primarily in terms of distribution and promotion.[2]

Examples of convenience goods would include many household cleaners and canned vegetables. The consumer is willing to exert only a limited physical effort shopping for such goods and is generally unwilling to systematically acquire brand

[2]Assael (1974), in a synthesis of the literature, develops the managerial implications for convenience and shopping goods in considerably more detail. However, he purposefully neglects specialty goods. Preference goods were not a separately recognized product type in 1974. Most of Assael's points will be integrated into subsequent chapters.

information before shopping. Important managerial consequences of this are the need for widespread distribution of the product and effective point of purchase promotions. Physical placement of the brand in retail stores is also very important for convenience goods, as their sales are aided by placement in conspicuous locations, preferably near eye level. Although consumers do not actively seek detailed information on convenience goods, brand name recognition is quite important precisely because the consumer is not highly ego-involved in their purchase. This curious aspect of convenience goods will be investigated in considerable detail when we discuss the third classification system.

Preference goods represent a new category, which was added to Copeland's original system. Holbrook and Howard offer "freeze-dried coffee, feminine hygiene sprays, vegetable-based bacon substitutes, and nutritionally enriched shampoos" (1976, p. 215) as examples of preference goods. Note that, in comparison with convenience goods, the consumer faces a situation where it is difficult to identify important product characteristics and, furthermore, the consumer is not confident of being able to even identify the characteristics of a good brand choice. Therefore, consumers attempt to acquire information on which to develop a brand preference through word of mouth, commercial advertising, and other sources of brand information before physically shopping for the item. The seller thus faces quite a different promotional problem when marketing preference goods, although the need for widespread distribution is similar to that for convenience goods.

Because of the high cost of shopping and specialty goods, the consumer is willing to expend a much greater physical effort than in shopping for convenience and preference goods. That is, the consumer will typically visit more stores at less convenient locations before making a purchase. The consumer is also often more ego-involved in the purchase of these goods, although this effect is likely to be much stronger for specialty goods. The higher level of ego-involvement reinforces the tendency to exert more physical shopping effort before making a brand purchase.

The distinctions between shopping and specialty goods are easily illustrated. Shopping goods would include major appliances, such as room air conditioners. The high clarity of important characteristics for such goods makes consumers feel relatively confident in detecting important product characteristics; e.g., the BTUs, fan speeds, and relative energy efficiency ratings of room air conditioners. While widespread and easily accessible distribution is not crucial for shopping goods, a wide range of alternatives within each store among which consumers can make comparisons, especially with respect to price, is desirable.

Typical specialty goods would include expensive photographic equipment and sophisticated sporting goods, such as high performance downhill skis. In the case of skis, the typical consumer might have great difficulty in knowing how to recognize such an important characteristic as flex, let alone being able to relate flex to performance on a downhill run. These aspects of the buying situation encourage behavior aimed at developing a strong brand preference. Once a brand preference is developed, an otherwise extremely complex and confusing buying problem usually becomes quite manageable. Because of the high level of ego-involvement associated with specialty goods, consumers will often attempt to acquire substantial, detailed, and factual information from a variety of sources before making a final purchase decision. And, an important source of such information is salespeople. This is why people who sell specialty goods typically are the most knowledgeable about the products they sell. It is also why manufacturers of specialty goods prefer exclusive distribution.[3] When brands made by different manufacturers are available, a knowledgable salesperson, by skillful probing of a customer's needs, will often influence that customer to purchase a brand different than the one initially preferred. The salesperson, after all, is typically more interested in satisfying the customer than the manufacturer. And this is especially true for specialty goods, where an initial sale will often give rise to a continuing stream of purchases of supplies and services associated with the initial sale.

The degree to which goods can be unambiguously classified into one of the above four categories is, of course, an empirical rather than a strictly logical question. And, no doubt, different consumers may perceive and approach the same type of good as if it belonged in different categories. Nevertheless, it seems fair to say that most goods will *tend* to fall into only one of the four categories for most consumers. The power of this extension of Copeland's system is, of course, that knowledge of the category to which a good belongs indicates a great deal about the kind of distribution system that will be most effective and the amount, nature, and manner of disseminating information to maximize the effectiveness of the firm's promotional efforts.

BRODY AND CUNNINGHAM'S CLASSIFICATION SYSTEM

Although neither specifically developed as a system for classifying situational effects nor widely cited as such, the second classification scheme sheds considerable light on the problem. As you read this section, note carefully the similarities with the extension of Copeland's system developed by Holbrook and Howard. It is easily seen that the two classification systems view the same basic problem from different perspectives and for quite different purposes. As a consequence, the two systems are essentially complementary rather than competitive.

The immediate purpose of the classification system developed by Brody and Cunningham (1968) was to identify those situations in which personality variables could be expected to predict brand choice. Specifically, they argued that the weak results characteristic of personality research up to 1968 could be at least partially attributed to the *implicit* assumption in most studies that the effects of personality were pervasive, i.e., personality affected consumer behavior regardless of the product being purchased or the circumstances surrounding the purchase. They argued that such an assumption clearly was not correct. In identifying the situations in which personality should be a good predictor of consumer behavior, they also identified three other classes of explanatory variables and the situations in which each of these variables should be related to consumer behavior.

Figure 3.2 presents Brody and Cunningham's system in schematic form. They began by grouping the factors that affect the consumer decision process into the following four groups:

---

[3]The current legal environment makes it very difficult for manufacturers to obtain truly exclusive (i.e., no competing brands) distribution. Unless they are willing to establish their own retail distribution system, most manufacturers must settle for less restrictive distribution generally referred to as selective distribution (i.e., carefully selected distributors).

| | | Specific Self-Confidence (High) Perceived Social Risk | | Specific Self-Confidence (Low) Perceived Social Risk | |
		High	Low	High	Low
Perceived Preference Risk	High	Personal and Social system Variables	Personal System Variables	Risk Reducing Variables	Risk Reducing Variables
	Low	Social System Variables	Exogenous Variables	Risk Reducing Variables	Exogenous Variables

Figure 3.2.
Prediction of the dominant explanatory variables from knowledge of three consumer perceptions

Source: Adapted from Robert P. Brody and Scott M. Cunningham, "Personality Variables and the Consumer Decision Process." *Journal of Marketing Research,* V (February 1968): 52. Reprinted with the kind permission of the American Marketing Association.

(1) personal system variables (e.g., conscious and unconscious needs), (2) social system variables (e.g., membership and reference groups), (3) exogenous variables (e.g., relative price and purchase convenience), and (4) risk-reducing variables (e.g., trusted stores and brands)

Next they argued that

Studying the consumer decision process is further simplified if the relative influence of each variable system is regarded as a function of the person's perception of the choice situation. Three perceptions particularly may act as filters to determine the group of variables with the greatest weight: (a) the perceived performance risk of the decision—to what extent does the person think different brands perform differently in ways that are important, (b) specific self-confidence—how certain is the person that the chosen brand will perform as he expects, and (c) the perceived social risk—to what extent does the person think that other people judge him by his brand decision (1968, p. 51).

Dichotomizing each of the three perceptual filters leads to eight possible combinations. The crucial problem, of course, is to correctly place the four groups of predictor variables into these eight categories. Unfortunately, Brody and Cunningham tended to simply state where each group of explanatory variables belongs without offering a full justification. The following explanation for the placement of the variable groups, therefore, depends heavily on my interpretation.[4]

When the risk of making a poor brand choice is low, due to low performance risk and low social risk,[5] specific self-confidence is not relevant; therefore, the consumer can rely primarily on exogenous variables when making a brand choice. Such a situation is likely to characterize convenience goods. A major reason for this

---

[4]In fairness to Brody and Cunningham, it should be noted that their interest lay almost exclusively in the personal system variables and that their empirical results at least indirectly supported this portion of their classification scheme.

[5]Brody and Cunningham realized that these were not the only risks the consumer might perceive. They did not, however, choose to develop other risks. For details on efforts to further develop the concept of perceived risk, the reader is referred to Bettman (1973), Horton (1976), and Peter and Ryan (1976).

is that the brands have become highly standardized and most of the really bad features of the product have been eliminated or corrected. Thus, exogenous variables, such as price and purchase convenience, are likely to dominate the brand choice under conditions of low performance risk and low social risk.

When a consumer's specific self-confidence is low and a performance or social risk is associated with the choice, the consumer will try to develop methods for reducing this risk. Shoes for young children are a good example of this. Fitting young children is quite difficult. Their feet grow rapidly and their ability to verbalize how the shoes feel is low. Furthermore, the consequences of a poor fit can be quite severe. Thus, many parents come to rely very heavily on one or a few stores that specialize in fitting young children and have a good reputation for knowing how to properly fit them. The existence of such risky situations also explains why consumers sometimes develop strategies for making brand choices that may not *seem* very rational to an observer; for example, selecting a high price brand when an objective analysis would show little association between price and quality for that specific product.

When specific self-confidence is high, the variables that dominate a consumer's brand choice depend on whether performance risk, social risk, or both are high. Having confidence in their ability to make a good brand choice allows consumers to consider more fully such factors as personal needs and social expectations and pressures. When social risk is high, social system variables will tend to dominate. For example, for many upper middle class people locating their homes in prestigious neighborhoods is very important because of social expectations. In a similar way, jeans have almost become an identification badge among many college students.

It is relatively easy to build and empirically support an argument for the placement of exogenous, risk reduction, and social system variables in Brody and Cunningham's classification scheme.[6] It is harder to explain why personal system variables should dominate when both performance risk and specific self-confidence are high. As already noted, Brody and Cunningham stated that this should be true without developing a full explanation for why such a relationship should exist. One possible explanation is that high performance risk means that brands perform differently in ways that are important to consumers. Having high specific self-confidence in their ability to discern these differences allows consumers to closely match brand characteristics to their personal needs.

The data analysis did tend to support Brody and Cunningham's placement of personal system variables. Specifically, they noted that a previous study by Cunningham showed that under conditions of high performance risk and high specific self-confidence, consumers would concentrate their purchases heavily on a favorite brand. Thus, as they restricted their analysis to consumers with increasingly high brand loyalty, personality variables should explain an increasing proportion of brand purchasing behavior, especially for products that presented little social risk. Coffee, they argued, was such a product. With no restrictions on their sample, personality variables explained 3.1 percent of the variance in brand of coffee purchased. This increased to 13 percent when the sample was restricted to families that were at least 40 percent loyal to one brand and increased to 32 percent for

---

[6]Most of this evidence will be cited in subsequent chapters.

families who were 100 percent loyal to one brand. Thus, the results tend to support Brody and Cunningham's theory.

The principal value of Brody and Cunningham's system for classifying buying situations is in forcing a careful consideration of the variables that affect the buying behavior of the consumer. Furthermore, it provides a framework for predicting the types of variables most important in determining consumers' final brand choices. This greatly facilitates the marketing manager's job by providing a partial formulation of the buying problem. From this knowledge, the manager is in a far better position to develop a successful marketing strategy. If risk reducing variables are especially important, the manager will focus on finding ways to reduce this perception of risk through such devices as strong warranties and pricing policies that connote superior quality. L'Oreal, for example, has been very successful in using the high price of their hair products as the central focus in their advertisements. In a similar way, knowing that a particular buying situation presents a high degree of social risk may lead to an advertising strategy aimed at the social prestige associated with owning or using a particular brand, e.g., Schweppes mixers.

Although the system developed by Brody and Cunningham has much value for analyzing buying situations faced by consumers, it has limitations as well. Perhaps the most important of these is that the system has not been systematically developed and empirically tested since Brody and Cunningham first proposed it. Another limitation is that their system is essentially confined to identifying variables that tend to dominate the final brand choice. For example, a buyer may decide to buy a Canon 35mm camera because it is nationally advertised, relatively expensive, and popular; i.e., to rely largely on risk reduction rules. Why the person decided to buy a 35mm camera and how the Canon came to be included in the final choice set are questions that are not addressed by the Brody and Cunningham classification system.

THREE DECISION HIERARCHIES

The two systems for classifying buying situations discussed so far focused on factors that affect the consumer decision process without discussing the process itself. The last system we shall consider argues that consumers will engage in one of three types of buying decision processes depending upon the specific type of buying situation being faced. These different processes have come to be known as hierarchies of effects.

The hierarchies concept can be traced back to an influential paper in which Lavidge and Steiner (1961) suggested that consumers progress sequentially through a set of mental stages that culminates in the purchase of a product. Figure 3.3 presents their conceptualization of this process. Note carefully that the arrows point in one direction only and that there is no feedback that would let a consumer who is, say, uncertain about the strength of his preference for a product return to the knowledge stage to acquire more information about the brands of interest. Because of this and the fact that each stage gives rise to some effect (e.g., developing a liking for a brand), the Lavidge and Steiner model has come to be known as *the* hierarchy of effects.

The hierarchy concept drew much comment, not all of which was favorable. Kristian Palda (1966), in particular, argued that there was virtually no evidence to

Figure 3.3
Lavidge and Steiner's hierarchy of effects model.

Source: Adapted from Robert J. Lavidge and Gary A. Steiner, "A Model for Predictive Measurements of Advertising Effectiveness," *Journal of Marketing,* 25 (October 1961): 61. Reprinted with the kind permission of the American Marketing Association.

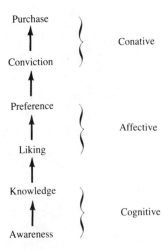

support the hierarchy concept. He did not, however, argue that the idea was necessarily false, only that it had not been empirically supported.[7] The hierarchy concept rested in this state of limbo, being neither supported nor refuted, until the early 1970s when Michael Ray (1973b) synthesized a number of different lines of research into the argument that the consumer decision process required three different hierarchies to be adequately conceptualized. More important, Ray provided empirical support for the existence of three distinct hierarchies and a classification scheme for predicting the conditions under which each would be most likely to occur.

For simplicity, the six stages of the Lavidge and Steiner model can be collapsed into three basic types of psychological processes: cognitive, affective, and conative. The cognitive stage refers to the acquisition of factual information; e.g., President Reagan believes defense spending should be increased. The affective stage refers to how one feels about the object in question given the acquired information; e.g., the fact that the president wants to increase defense spending is good and my affective feeling or liking for the president is positive. Note carefully that no statement has been made regarding the accuracy of the acquired information. Furthermore, all of the cognitions need not be used in making the affective judgment. The conative stage represents the action plan; e.g., I plan to vote for President Reagan in the next election. There are, of course, six different orders in which these three different stages might occur. Ray (1973b) argued, both logically and empirically, that the consumer decision-making process could be adequately represented using only three of these orders. Figure 3.4 presents Ray's classification system in schematic form.

Learning Hierarchy

This hierarchy is essentially the one first proposed by Lavidge and Steiner. In it, the consumer first acquires or learns various cognitions about some object, then makes an affective evaluation of the object based on some portion of those cognitions, and finally develops a plan of action. For example, a consumer might learn that a

[7]Palda's paper is a superb example of methodological criticism in a marketing context.

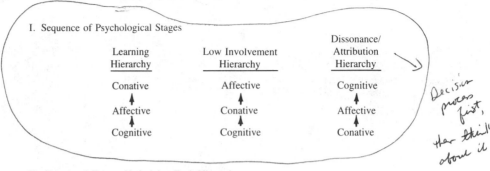

I. Sequence of Psychological Stages

Learning Hierarchy	Low Involvement Hierarchy	Dissonance/ Attribution Hierarchy
Conative	Affective	Cognitive
↑	↑	↑
Affective	Conative	Affective
↑	↑	↑
Cognitive	Cognitive	Conative

Decision process first, then think about it

II. Situational Factors Underlying Each Hierarchy

Situational Factors	Hierarchy		
	Learning	Low-Involvement	Dissonance/ Attribution
Level of Ego-Involvement	High	Low	High
Perceived Differences among Alternatives	Substantial	Similar	Similar
Primary Information Source	Impersonal	Impersonal	Personal
Stage in Life Cycle	Early	Late	Early Maturity

Figure 3.4.
Three consumer decision-making hierarchies.

Source: Partially constructed from Michael L. Ray, "Marketing Communication and the Hierarchy of Effects," working paper, Marketing Science Institute, Cambridge, Mass., 1973.

particular make of automobile gets 30 mpg city, has a resale value after three years equal to 75 percent of the original price of the car, has a sticker price of $7,000, and an excellent overall repair record. If this hypothetical consumer normally keeps a car for a very long time, the three year resale value may not be very relevant to the buying decision. The other information or cognitions, when compared with similar cognitions for other makes of automobiles, may cause our consumer to evaluate this automobile very positively. Our consumer, however, may not be ready to act on her affective evaluation, perhaps because she does not plan to replace her present car for one or two years. The $7,000 price, however, seems reasonable, so the consumer *decides* to purchase this particular make of automobile *when* she next buys a car. This conative *plan* of action, of course, may be substantially altered by subsequent learning and the effects this learning may have on the affective evaluation of the brand.

Research, both developed and cited by Ray, suggests that consumers are likely to follow a learning hierarchy when making decisions about products with which (1) they are highly ego-involved, (2) the differences among alternative brands are not only substantial but also discernable, (3) the product class is in the early stages of its life cycle, and (4) that impersonal sources of communication are primarily involved in the early stages of learning about the product. Stated less formally, there are important differences among the choice alternatives and the consumer feels competent to recognize and evaluate these differences.

Most durable goods (shopping and specialty goods) probably approximate a learning hierarchy fairly closely. In addition, the decision process for most products probably follows something of an approximation to the learning hierarchy when the product class concept is first being developed by the consumer. The Howard and Sheth model, discussed in the last chapter, is in one sense a substantial elaboration of a simple cognitive ⟶ affective ⟶ conative learning model.

Low Involvement Hierarchy

The sequence of stages in this hierarchy is cognitive ⟶ conative ⟶ affective. As in the learning hierarchy, cognitions are acquired first. The manner of acquiring the cognitions, however, is quite different. In the learning hierarchy, largely because of the high level of ego-involvement with the product, the consumer tends to be very conscious of the cognitions as they are acquired. Being conscious of the incoming information and its importance, the consumer tends to evaluate both the source of the information and the information itself as it is acquired. Is the source trustworthy? Does the source have any special expertise in the area? Does the new information seem reasonable, given what is already known about the product? All of this tends to lead to evaluating and integrating new information into the existing attitude toward the product *as the information is received.*

It is primarily the lack of conscious awareness and the lack of constant evaluation of information as it is acquired that makes the low involvement hierarchy so distinctive. These cognitions are, literally, learned in the same way as nonsense words.[8] In fact, the analogy with nonsense words is highly instructive. If a person is asked to memorize a list of nonsense words and then to reproduce that list from memory, the accuracy of recall will be relatively high for words at the beginning or end of the list and relatively low for words in the middle. It was Krugman (1965) who first suggested that this pattern was very similar to that which is observed when subjects are exposed to a series of television commercials and then asked to recall those commercials.

In the low involvement hierarchy, then, information is acquired—perhaps absorbed would be a more descriptive word—without a high level of conscious awareness or active screening as the information is received. Although there is a tendency to forget this information, with sufficient repetition it may become a more or less permanent cognition. For example, even most nonsmokers can complete the slogan "You can take Salem out of the country, but...."

In the low involvement hierarchy, these cognitions tend to exist in isolation. It is not until it is necessary to make a purchasing decision that a consumer will attempt to integrate these cognitions. Because the consumer does not view the product as important and typically has not thought about the purchase decision before a fairly immediate need arises, the consumer typically will purchase a brand even though a strong positive affective judgment has not been made. It is only in the postpurchase use and evaluation that the affective judgment is made.

Products that fall into the low involvement category tend to be in or beyond the maturity stage of the product life cycle. In this stage of the life cycle, most of the problems with the product have been overcome and most of the very desirable features have been copied by all manufacturers. Thus, alternative brands not only

---

[8]Nonsense words consist of three letters arranged consonant-vowel-consonant, e.g., dax, which are meaningless. The use of nonsense words is discussed in most introductory psychology texts.

tend to be quite similar but they also tend to perform at least satisfactorily. For these reasons, the consumer typically faces relatively little risk when choosing a low involvement good despite a lack of well integrated or even extensive cognitions and has no strong affective judgment toward the chosen brand prior to purchase.

Although not considered by Ray, there is a curious aspect of human behavior that throws considerable light both on the consumer decision-making process and the marketing strategy frequently used for low involvement goods. Mere exposure to neutral information, such as a new brand name, seems to produce a positive affective response toward both the information and the object it represents, e.g., the brand name and the product it represents (Zajonc 1980; Zajonc and Markus 1982).

This helps explain why manufacturers of low involvement goods typically follow a marketing strategy that emphasizes widespread distribution, extensive point of purchase promotion, and extensive mass media advertising, which is geared primarily to gaining the audience's attention and making the brand name known. Indeed, there has been much comment on how much of this advertising is silly and even offensive (Greyser and Bauer, 1966; Bauer and Greyser, 1968). Given what we currently know about the consumer decision-making process for low involvement goods, however, this strategy is quite understandable. Knowing that the consumer will make a brand decision on the basis of very limited information, without forming a strong positive affective judgment toward the brand *before* purchase, and that a positive affective response toward the brand will tend to emerge from simple repetition of the brand name, the most important task the marketer faces is to increase consumer awareness of the brand. Silly or even offensive advertisements may accomplish this task. And over time the consumer will tend to forget that awareness emerged from such advertisements. Of course, the selected brand must perform at least satisfactorily. But, for products in the later stages of the life cycle, this is generally not a major problem.

Dissonance/Attribution Hierarchy

This hierarchy reverses the stages of the learning hierarchy: the decision process is conative $\longrightarrow$ affective $\longrightarrow$ cognitive. In the situation presented by this hierarchy the consumer is in some way forced to make a choice quickly, usually on the basis of personal communication. It is only after the choice has been made that the consumer makes an affective judgment based to a large degree on the results of the choice. This is frequently, but by no means always, followed by acquisition of information or cognitions to support the choice made.

The dissonance/attribution hierarchy seems more relevant to services than physical products, and perhaps can be best described with an example.[9] A man,

---

[9]Ray's (1973b) research was based on products. As Ray noted, it was difficult to elicit a dissonance/attribution type of response from subjects in the laboratory experiments he used. In subsequent research, Ray and Dunn (1978) investigated consumer information systems for services. Ray and Dunn found that not only do consumers not want information about services, but in some cases they seem willing to pay to avoid it. While Ray and Dunn suggest this may represent a fourth information avoidance strategy, it seems to be that it may simply be an extreme instance of the dissonance/attribution hierarchy, which abrogates the decision process.

feeling chest pains, is referred by his family physician to a cardiologist The specialist recommends immediate surgery. The hypothetical consumer, fearing there is little time to consider the problem or seek additional advice, *acquiesces* to the surgery. His affective feelings toward the cardiologist will to a large extent depend on the outcome of the surgery and, *perhaps,* what he subsequently learns about the treatment of heart problems in general and the qualifications of his surgeon. The problem, however, is extraordinarily complex, and it would not be surprising if the postoperative heart patient never progressed beyond the point of knowing that he liked the doctor—after all, he's still alive. Although this example is somewhat extreme, it captures fairly well the essence of many situations which involve buying services, where the consumer is forced to rely very heavily on the expertise and recommendations of the service provider.

Buying situations characterized by a dissonance/attribution hierarchy generally occur for goods or services where (1) the consumer is highly ego-involved with the product or service, (2) the differences among alternatives are not easily discernable, although it is often presumed that the differences are large, (3) the product or service is, from the consumer's perspective, in the early maturity stage of its life cycle, and (4) the source of persuasion that initiates action is personal.

The psychological process underlying this hierarchy is known as dissonance. Forced to choose on the basis of limited evidence causes an uncertainty regarding the desirability of the choice, which is known as dissonance. Because dissonance is an unpleasant psychological state, efforts will be made to reduce it. A consumer may do this by developing a more positive affective response toward the product and by acquiring favorable cognitions about the chosen alternative. Thus, the decision-making sequence conative ⟶ affective ⟶ cognitive.

Extensiveness and Nature of Decision Process

A good way to summarize the differences among the three decision hierarchies is in terms of the extensiveness and nature of the process the consumer goes through in making a brand choice. In the learning hierarchy, the consumer is consciously and actively involved in the decision, and the decision process typically requires complex information and often occurs over a long period of time. In the low involvement hierarchy, the consumer's actions in the decision process are typically passive. The information acquired is also usually much less detailed than in the learning hierarchy.

The dissonance/attribution hierarchy is in many ways the most unusual. In this hierarchy, decisions will often be made under great duress. And, it appears, frequently the decision-making process will be interrupted by a decision long before the *process* is completed. Perhaps, this partly explains the great dissatisfaction with services expressed by consumers. Earlier it was suggested that the dissonance/attribution hierarchy seems to primarily characterize decision making for services; however, relatively little is known about the decision process for services. As the United States is becoming primarily a service oriented economy, this lack of knowledge represents a major limitation to the understanding of consumer behavior.

AN INTEGRATED CLASSIFICATION SYSTEM

Earlier it was suggested that the classification systems examined here view the same general problem from different perspectives and for different purposes and are, therefore, complementary systems. Indeed, at a number of points the dimensions that define each system overlap. It is these overlaps that provide much of the rationale for an integrated system. Although speculative, the following integration suggests the potential explanatory power of situational classification schemes.

Table 3.1 presents an analysis of the overlaps of the dimensions that define each classification system. Table 3.2 presents the resulting integration. The checks in Table 3.1 indicate that a dimension is explicitly stated, while an I indicates that a dimension appears to be at least partially implicit in some other dimension, which is referenced by the bracketed number, or in the general discussion regarding the classification system.

Table 3.1
Comparison of dimensions underlying classification systems

| | Classification System | | |
Dimension	Copeland (Extended)	Brody and Cunningham	Decision Hierarchies
1. Magnitude of Purchase	$\checkmark$	I(7)	
2. Level of Ego-Involvement	$\checkmark$	I(7,8)	$\checkmark$
3. Degree of Physical Shopping Effort	$\checkmark$		
4. Clarity of Product Characteristics	$\checkmark$	I(5)	I(9)
5. Specific Self-Confidence	$\checkmark$	$\checkmark$	I(9)
6. Timing of Mental Effort	$\checkmark$		I
7. Perceived Performance Risk	I(1,2)	$\checkmark$	I(9)
8. Perceived Social Risk		$\checkmark$	I(9)
9. Perceived Differences Among Alternatives	I(1)		$\checkmark$
10. Primary Information Source			$\checkmark$
11. Stage in Life Cycle			$\checkmark$

Note: A check indicates the dimension is specifically mentioned. An I denotes a dimension which appears to be implicitly defined. An I followed by a number in brackets denotes that the dimension seems to be at least partially implicit in the dimension number in brackets.

Table 3.2
Integration of classification systems

Classification of Goods (Services)	Hierarchy of Effects	Dominant Explanatory Variables
Convenience	Low Involvement	Exogenous
Preference	Low Involvement	Risk Reduction
Shopping	Learning	Personal and Social
Specialty	Learning	Risk Reduction
(Avoidance)	Dissonance/Attribution	(Chance, Risk Reduction)

Of the thirteen dimensions in the three classification systems, only two overlap directly, level of ego-involvement and specific self-confidence; however, a number of overlaps are implicit. In Copeland's system, "perceived performance risk" would seem to be at least partially implicit in the "magnitude of purchase" and "level of ego-involvement." Similarly, one "perceived difference among alternatives" is the "magnitude of purchase."

In Brody and Cunningham's system, the "magnitude of purchase" and "level of ego-involvement" would seem to be at least partially implicit in the "perceived performance risk." "Perceived social risk" would also seem to be a major reason for a buyer to have a high "level of ego-involvement" with a good or service. Finally, "clarity of product characteristics" would seem to be a major factor in determining the level of a buyer's "specific self-confidence" toward the choice in a specific product class.

The decision hierarchies' "perceived differences among alternatives" seem to implicitly overlap both "perceived performance and social risk." Alternatives may also differ in the "clarity of product characteristics," which, of course, has implications for a buyer's "specific self-confidence." Finally, the very concept of different decision hierarchies would seem to affect the "timing of mental effort."

As can be seen in Table 3.1, the three classification systems fully overlap either explicitly or implicitly in four dimensions: level of ego-involvement, clarity of product characteristics, specific self-confidence, and perceived performance risk. Drawing together the information in Figures 3.1 to 3.4 and Table 3.1, we can now present the rationale for the integrated buying situation classification system in Table 3.2.

Primarily because of the low level of ego-involvement both convenience and preference goods have been identified in the low involvement hierarchy. Although it seems reasonable that goods for which buyers develop a brand preference before physically shopping should call for more of an active decision process and a higher level of involvement than true convenience goods, the argument is that this difference is essentially small, and not substantial enough to place preference goods in the full learning hierarchy. For true convenience goods, exogenous variables (price, ease of purchase, etc.) will be the most important variables explaining purchase because both performance and social risk tend to be very low for these goods. In contrast, performance and social risk tend to be higher for preference goods, while clarity of product characteristics and specific self-confidence are low. Therefore, consumers will tend to rely on risk reduction rules to insure product quality when purchasing preference goods, such as buying only brands made by well known manufacturers or only higher priced brands.

Shopping and specialty goods have been associated with the learning hierarchy. Again, the primary basis for this link lies in the level of ego-involvement associated with these types of goods. For both categories, performance and social risk are likely to be high. However, the consumer will normally have a higher level of specific self-confidence for shopping goods than for specialty goods, e.g., when shopping for a room air conditioner as opposed to a set of high performance skis. Therefore, personal and social system variables are generally associated with shopping goods and risk reduction variables with specialty goods. Note carefully that while risk reduction variables dominate the brand choice for specialty situations, there is no intention to suggest that personal and social system variables are unimportant. Rather, the expectation is that while personal and social system variables are important in initial perception of need and in the selection of alternatives, the final brand choice will be most influenced by risk reduction factors.

The final classification, which is based on the dissonance/attribution hierarchy, has only recently come to be recognized. This category of buying situation is labeled avoidance goods because buyers tend to purchase such goods and services only when circumstances force them to make a decision. Although explanatory variables have not been proposed for this category, it seems likely that chance factors are especially important. For example, many consumers choose a family physician when they get sick or move to a new area, based on recommendations of co-workers and neighbors. What specialists a family uses will depend almost entirely upon referrals by their family physician.

Avoidance goods provide marketers with significant opportunities to devise means of reducing perceived risk and, therefore, to encourage consumers to approach a buying situation they might otherwise avoid. For example, in recent years legal clinics have begun advertising free or low cost initial consultations with a lawyer to counter the perception by many low and middle income consumers that the services of a lawyer are *always* extremely expensive.

MANAGERIAL IMPLICATIONS

The academic researcher is frequently interested in research that helps understand the behavior of buyers, even if the research has few or no immediate implications for managerial decisions. The marketing manager, of course, is primarily interested in knowledge to facilitate decision making. In the present context the question can be phrased in terms of how does placing a particular product or service into one of the five buying situation categories facilitate managerial decision making?

To take a simple example, consider shopping for a new automobile. Clearly, the magnitude of purchase, level of involvement, and physical shopping effort are all high. Although not as obvious, most buyers probably feel that the clarity of important product features and their own specific self-confidence are also high. Therefore, the purchase of an automobile can be identified as a shopping good situation for most buyers. Because of the high level of involvement, the substantial differences among alternatives, and the infrequency of purchase, the automobile is further identified as a learning hierarchy product. Finally, performance risk is high for automobiles and, for many buyers, the social risk may be high as well. When combined with high specific self-confidence, personal and social system variables can be expected to dominate the purchase of automobiles. Whether this analysis is correct, of course, is an empirical question. Nevertheless, the scenario seems to be plausible. Furthermore, placing the product or service into a buying situation category may be limited to one or a few specific market segments.

What precisely is accomplished by placing automobiles, or any other products for that matter, within the buying situation classification system? In broad outline a great deal: First, consumers are known to usually follow a specific set of stages in their decision making, and to generally desire substantial and specific information *before* they make a purchase. Second, something is also known about the required distribution system, including the need for a wide range of alternative choices at different prices. Also a substantial portion of the final decision-making process will occur while the consumer is physically shopping. This has implications for both point of purchase promotion and personal selling. Third, personal needs and, possibly, social pressures and expectations will play a major role in consumers' purchasing decisions.

In detail, of course, much remains to be learned before the firm can implement a complete marketing program. The classification system, however, has provided some help in framing the detailed questions to be asked. For example: Precisely what personal and social needs are consumers trying to satisfy by purchasing an automobile? And, is it possible to identify specific market segments on the basis of differences in personal and social needs?

Similar examples would apply for each of the other types of buying situations. In each case, the process would be identical. categorize the good or service by its salient characteristics, ascribe the general properties of the class to the good or service, and frame the specific questions to be addressed before an effective marketing strategy can be developed. Or, more colloquially, "The answers are easy, it's the questions that are hard." In subsequent chapters, then, a number of additional aspects of buyer behavior theory and research will be considered in order to provide a level of understanding of buyer behavior that will allow the reader to frame the questions a manager must ask in the narrow context of a specific marketing *opportunity*.

SUMMARY

In this chapter, three different systems for classifying buying situations were discussed. Each of the systems examines the same basic problem from a different perspective. For this reason, the systems are essentially complementary rather than competing. A scheme for integrating the three systems was suggested. Because our suggested integration was based solely on a logical analysis of the three classification schemes, the integrated system presented here should be considered a hypothesis rather than a tested theory, although the integration seems sound and useful.

The value of any classification scheme lies in the fact that by knowing to which class a particular product or service belongs, a great deal is known about how consumers will behave when purchasing that product or service and the subsequent implications as to the type of marketing strategy required. By the very nature of situational classification systems, however, this knowledge will be very general. A major task of subsequent chapters is, therefore, to develop insights into the many aspects of consumer behavior that are needed to enhance the very general knowledge provided by situational classification systems and lead to a fully operational marketing strategy for a specific product or service.

Routinized
Response Behavior

II

At this point the reader should have a sense of the origins of the current perspective on buyer behavior, including its inherently interdisciplinary nature, a general grasp of the concepts that are central to the study of buyer behavior, and an appreciation of the fact that the decision processes involved in specific buying situations vary in systematic ways relative to the buyer's perception of the buying situation.

The next three parts of the text are devoted to a detailed examination of the natures and bases of these decision processes. Specifically, the text argues that when a buyer recognizes the need to purchase a specific product, he or she will be in one of three decision-making states: routinized response behavior, limited problem solving, or extensive problem solving. Parts II, III, and IV are devoted to these three decision-making states.

Casual introspection should make it obvious to the reader that most buying decisions are made with relatively little effort or even conscious thought. Part II is devoted to a discussion of buyer behavior when the purchasing decisions can be made in such a routine way. Chapter 4 investigates the characteristics of the decision processes generally referred to as routinized response behavior. As will be seen, buyers in this state typically manifest a high degree of brand loyalty, which is the topic of Chapter 5.

Routinized
Response Behavior

4

The discussion in Chapter 2 of comprehensive models of buying behavior demonstrated that a great many factors may be involved in the buying process. Furthermore, the buying process may require the buyer to gather and evaluate a large amount of information in order to make a satisfactory brand choice. Such a complex decision process can easily consume a substantial amount of time and effort.

Casual observation and personal introspection would suggest that many, and probably most, buying decisions are made rather easily, without any elaborate decision-making process. Furthermore, common sense would suggest that were this not so, the typical buyer would have time for virtually nothing but buying decisions. To function effectively, then, the buyer must ultimately be able to implement most buying decisions in a more or less routine way. When this occurs the buyer's decision making is said to be *routinized response behavior*. An implication of the Chapter 3 discussion of buying situations is that the buyer may reach such routinized behavior in a number of ways. For products characterized by a learning hierarchy, routinized response behavior is the result of an elaborate learning process. For products characterized by other decision hierarchies (i.e., the low involvement and dissonance/attribution hierarchies), highly routinized behavior may develop without any elaborate, *active* learning process although the buyer's incidental learning about the brands purchased and consumed will almost certainly be extensive. While it is reasonable to expect variations in the routinized response patterns developed via these different routes, knowledge is very limited in this regard and, therefore, such fine distinctions cannot be made.

Keep in mind while reading this chapter that although the majority of individual buying decisions are probably made on a routine basis, buying decisions for many product classes rarely, if ever, reach this stage. More specifically, in terms of the Chapter 3 classification of buying situations, routinized response behavior *tends* to be associated with inexpensive, frequently purchased nondurable goods; i.e., convenience and preference goods. For most consumers, buying decisions for shopping and specialty goods typically do not reach a routinized stage of decision making.

What, then, are the characteristics of the buyer's behavior when buying decisions can be implemented on an essentially routine basis? According to Howard (1963, 1977, Howard and Sheth 1969), a buyer goes through three basic stages in learning about a product class and the buyer's behavior will be quite different in each stage. Chapter 4 will begin with a discussion of the stages of buyer learning. The major characteristics of limited and extensive problem solving will be briefly mentioned here. A very important characteristic of buyer behavior that has become routinized is the tendency to make brand choices from a small and relatively stable set of alternative brands. Therefore, the characteristics and managerial importance of this so-called "evoked set" of brands will be taken up next. Routinized response behavior also requires the buyer to have a well formed buying plan to be routinely implemented as the need to purchase arises. The characteristics and managerial implications of these buying plans, or intentions as they are generally called, is the topic of the final section of this chapter.

THREE STAGES OF BUYER LEARNING

Chapter 2 noted that the Howard-Sheth model is a learning model in two quite different senses. First, it is a learning model in the sense that the model is deeply rooted in Hull's psychological theory of learning. Second, Howard and Sheth suggest that the behavior of buyers can be partially understood in terms of how well the buyer has learned the product class concept and the associated concepts for the individual brands that the buyer considers as relevant alternatives within the product class. Specifically, they suggest that buying behavior may be divided into three stages: routinized response behavior (RRB), limited problem solving (LPS), and extensive problem solving (EPS).

In light of the Chapter 2 review of the Howard-Sheth theory, a distinction is needed between the theory that there are three stages of learning and the theory that buyers normally progress *sequentially* through these stages. Several different lines of inquiry suggest the plausibility of a three stage view of learning. What has increasingly come to be doubted is that "normal" buyer behavior is inevitably characterized by an active learning process that progresses sequentially from EPS to LPS to RRB. Thus, while the three stage concept will be used to organize the material in this and the next seven chapters, the adoption of this concept implies commitment neither to the Howard-Sheth theory generally nor to the specific EPS–LPS–RRB progression.

Routinized Response Behavior

In order to implement buying decisions in a routine, almost automatic, way, the buyer must have "fully" learned both the product class concept and the concepts of an acceptable number of alternative brands. The word fully is in quotes because it does *not* mean that the buyer completely understands all aspects of the product class. Rather, fully learned indicates that the buyer knows *enough* to make *acceptable* purchases within the product class without extraordinary effort. For example, a consumer who values clothing very highly may come to know a great deal about the style, quality, and other features of many alternative brands and types of clothing. That same consumer, however, might be able to routinely buy another product, such as frozen vegetables, knowing only that "they taste good."

Developing RRB greatly simplifies the buyer's decision process. To purchase a satisfactory brand, the buyer need only determine a few additional factors such as availability, price, and perhaps whether a special deal is available. Of course, for many product classes, few consumers will develop RRB. As has already been noted, RRB is associated primarily with convenience and preference goods and probably develops only very rarely for shopping and specialty goods.

Limited Problem Solving

In LPS, the buyer has a product class concept that is well learned but inadequate brand concepts, so that further information is required prior to making a satisfactory purchase. This situation is likely to characterize high cost, infrequently purchased durables such as automobiles or refrigerators. For example, a buyer who is thinking of buying a new car for the first time in five years will probably find that the choices considered last time are substantially altered and may, in fact, no longer exist. Despite this, the general criteria by which automobiles are identified and evaluated will probably have changed very little, even if their relative importance has shifted markedly (e.g., miles per gallon may have increased substantially in importance).

In LPS, then, the buyer understands the product class; that is, the buyer has little difficulty recognizing that a specific brand, even a totally new brand, belongs to the product class in question. The buyer also knows the choice criteria relevant to evaluating the brands within the product class.[1] Thus, while LPS requires acquisition of considerable information before a satisfactory brand choice can be made, the buyer at least knows generally the kinds of information required.

LPS raises questions regarding how the buyer learns about the ability of specific brands of a product class to satisfy specific motives. This, of course, leads to questions about the nature of motives, the learning process itself, and the process by which attitudes are formed and changed. Part III is devoted to these topics. This and the next chapter will simply assume that a stable set of attitudes exists, that learning is essentially complete, and that the motives relevant to the product class are being adequately satisfied. All of these conditions are, of course, required for RRB.

Extensive Problem Solving

In EPS, the buyer hasn't even a well formed product class concept, which presents potential difficulties for both the buyer and the seller. The buyer has difficulty evaluating a new brand because there is no established product class concept into which it can be placed. Thus, the buyer is unable to *start* the learning process by ascribing to the new brand the general properties of all brands in an already understood product class. For similar reasons, the seller faces substantial difficulties in conveying information about a new brand to buyers. Furthermore, the seller faces the additional burden of convincing the buyer that the new product class, which is created by a new brand, is relevant to the needs of the buyer.

Quite clearly, EPS presents many obstacles to effective communication between buyer and seller. Furthermore, a buyer whose attention has been attracted to the new brand still faces a very difficult information acquisition task. Without a well developed product class concept, the buyer has few guidelines for judging the relevance of information to make a satisfactory brand choice and for evaluating information once it is acquired. Part IV is devoted to discussion of the decision processes that lead to the acceptance or rejection of a new product and the information acquisition and evaluation processes critical to this decision.

This discussion of RRB assumes that a well established product class concept presently exists and, more important, that the information acquisition process is very limited and quite simple.

Psychological and Economic Perspectives on Stages of Learning

So far the stages of buyer learning have been discussed from the marketer's perspective. Although the division is somewhat arbitrary, the three stage characterization of the buyer's learning process does seem to conform reasonably well with careful empirical observation of buyers. Howard (1977, pp. 13–15) has noted that psychologists, and more recently economists, have both come to three stage views

---

[1]Recall from our discussion in Chapter 2 that a principal way of defining a product class is in terms of choice criteria. That is, brands evaluated by the same choice criteria, in the same exact way, are in the same product class.

Table 4.1
Three perspectives on the stages of consumers' decision processes

	Stage		
Perspective	**1**	**2**	**3**
Marketing Manager	Extensive Problem Solving	Limited Problem Solving	Routinized Response Behavior
Psychologist	Concept Formation	Concept Attainment	Concept Utilization
Economist	Changing Utility Function	Constant Utility Function	Constant Utility Function
		Changing Consumer Technology	Constant Consumer Technology

Source: John A. Howard, *Consumer Behavior: Application of Theory.* (New York: McGraw-Hill, 1977), p. 14. Reprinted with permission.

of selected aspects of human behavior that parallel the marketer's view of buyer behavior quite closely. Table 4.1 presents these three perspectives in schematic form.

A principal issue for cognitive psychologists is how people develop the concepts necessary to function effectively in the world. For example, if you pour a volume of water from one container into a container of different size or shape, very young children will normally report that the amount of water is no longer the same. Eventually, of course, most children learn that the volume of water has not changed and that this would be true whatever the specific liquid. Cognitive psychologists have found that such concepts are generally acquired by a process in which a concept is initially *formed* (conservation of mass), then *attained* for a variety of relevant situations (conservation of mass applies to all liquids) and, with sufficient practice, *utilized* with relatively little conscious thought or effort. These three stages of concept learning closely parallel EPS, LPS, and RRB.

Although marketers have not generally investigated how concepts related to marketing are actually acquired by buyers, a study by Robertson and Rossiter (1974) illustrates the relevance of concept acquisition to marketing. The authors report that the proportion of young children who trust all commercials is negatively, and strongly, related to grade level. This decrease in trust is closely related to an increased understanding by older children that the purpose of commercials is to persuade them to buy things; to the formation, acquisition, and ability to utilize the concept of persuasive intent. Specifically, they report that 52.7 percent, 87.1 percent, and 99.0 percent of first, third, and fifth graders, respectively, understand the persuasive intent of commercials. These data have rather obvious implications for both marketing managers who sell child oriented products and public policy makers.

Recently, some economists, especially Lancaster (1971, 1977), have reformulated economic demand theory in a way that leads to a three stage system, which closely parallels both marketers' and cognitive psychologists' views of human

74 PART II: Routinized Response Behavior

decision processes. This new approach to economic demand theory tends to focus on the characteristics of goods that have motive satisfying properties rather than the goods themselves. Theoretically, each good has associated with it a set of coefficients or numbers to indicate the ability of that good to satisfy specific motives. These coefficients constitute the so-called consumer technology function. The consumer's utility function is related to the choice criteria, which are used to evaluate alternative choices within a product class. Both the technology function and utility function are unique to each consumer.

In what the marketer calls RRB, both the utility and technology functions are constant. Using the economists' terminology, the buyer's tastes and preferences (the utility function) are fixed and the buyer has complete knowledge regarding all alternatives under consideration (the technology function). Under these conditions the amount of the good the buyer will purchase is determined solely by its price. Marketers, of course, consider a number of other factors, such as product availability and special deals. The general principle, however, is the same.

In LPS, the utility function is unchanged but the consumer technology does change. Let us assume, for example, that a buyer considers size, resale value, and status important criteria in purchasing an automobile. The important point is that the buyer is not buying just an automobile but the attributes size, resale value, and status of the automobile. Should a new automobile come on the market that satisfies these criteria more fully than existing automobiles, the *technology* by which the buyer's motives are satisfied will change and that buyer will tend to prefer the new automobile. However, before a final purchase decision is made, the price, and possibly other factors, of the new automobile will still need to be considered.

Finally, in extensive problem solving, the utility function by which goods are evaluated, as well as the specific technology implicit in the choice alternative, is changing. For example, a buyer's tastes and preferences, as reflected in his or her choice criteria, may change. If the buyer no longer considers status and resale value as important criteria in evaluating automobiles but focuses on miles per gallon and repair record, a whole new set of choice alternatives, which in reality constitute a new product class for this buyer, will emerge.

Although a brief review of the three stage views of cognitive psychologists and economists is of value in its own right, its primary importance is that two quite distinct groups of academic researchers, working for quite different purposes under very different perspectives on human behavior, have come to view human stages of learning and decision making in ways that are substantially similar to the marketer's view. This, of course, does not validate the division of buyer learning into EPS, LPS, and RRB stages; however, it does lend considerable credence to the concept. In this regard we should also note that a recent laboratory study by Lehmann, Moore, and Elrod (1982) provided further support for the existence of the LPS and RRB stages of learning. For methodological reasons, the authors did not include the EPS stage in their study.

This brief review provides the background for an in-depth investigation into the nature of RRB. Because so much buying behavior is conducted on a highly routine basis, one might expect that our knowledge of RRB would be relatively large; actually, it is just the reverse. The primary reasons for this lack of knowledge are methodological. The RRB stage is typically reached by a long, broken path in which learning about a product class tends to occur in relatively brief and scattered moments of time that are very difficult to observe: e.g., a television commercial, a brief conversation with a friend, from actually using a product. Furthermore, attempts to observe and measure these learning processes run a very real danger of changing the processes of interest. Despite these problems much is known about the characteristics of RRB.

THE EVOKED SET

The Concept of the Evoked Set

One of the major contributions of Howard and Sheth to the understanding of buyer behavior is the concept of the evoked set, which Howard defines as "the subset of brands that a consumer considers buying out of the set of brands that he or she is aware of in a given product class" (1977, p. 306). Although the buyer may have a partially formed evoked set in other stages of learning, the concept is generally associated with RRB, and is clearly most useful analytically in conjunction with this stage of learning. Primarily this is because in RRB the set of brands in the evoked set is presumably relatively stable for any buyer over relatively long periods of time. This leads to a number of interesting behaviors, such as the development of loyalty to one or more brands.

A major conclusion of buyer behavior research is that the evoked set is small, usually in the range of three to five brands or less. Just how small evoked sets can be is illustrated in a study by Narayana and Markin (1975). They began by breaking the product class into two major subsets: the awareness and unawareness sets. The buyer's awareness set was further divided into three mutually exclusive categories: evoked set, inert set, and inept set. The sets contain those brands that have a positive, neutral, or a negative evaluation, respectively. Table 4.2 presents Narayana and Markin's data on the sizes of these sets for four low cost, frequently purchased nondurable products. The sizes of the evoked sets are quite small, ranging from 1.3 for mouthwash to 3.5 for beer. The latter figure very likely reflects the fact that subjects in Narayana and Markin's study were undergraduate college students. Another striking aspect of the data in Table 4.2 is that, with the exception of beer, the *maximum* size of the evoked set for any one subject was only four brands.

Although the sizes of the evoked sets reported by Narayana and Markin are among the smallest reported in the literature for nondurable goods,[2] results similar to those reported for beer have been found in a number of other studies that investigated different product classes using both students and nonstudents as subjects. Jarvis and Wilcox (1973), for example, found the mean evoked sets for coffee, dishwashing liquid, and table napkins were 4.2, 5.6, and 5.0, respectively.

The few studies that examined the size of the evoked set for durables found them *generally* to be smaller than those found in studies of nondurables. In a survey study of the evoked set for automobiles May and Homans (1977) found a mean evoked set of 1.71. In an experimental study of the evoked set for microwave ovens, Belonax and Mittelstaedt (1978) report evoked set sizes that ranged from 1.79 to 3.09 over six experimental conditions and averaged 2.45 for the entire experiment.

[2]Why the sizes of the evoked sets reported by Narayana and Markin are so small, relative to those reported by others, is unclear. Possible explanations include the use of undergraduates; the few brands available in the small town where the study was conducted; and the specific product classes studied. Also, the research methodology, which appears to be based on a questionnaire, may have tended to elicit only the first one or two brands in the respondents' evoked set.

Table 4.2
Size of awareness, evoked, inert, and inept sets for four product classes

Products	No. of Brands in the Individual Sets		
and Sets	Min.	Max.	Avg.
Toothpaste			
Awareness set	3	11	6.5
Evoked set	1	4	2.0
Inert set	0	8	2.0
Inept set	0	6	2.5
Mouthwash			
Awareness set	1	6	3.5
Evoked set	0	3	1.3
Inert set	0	5	1.2
Inept set	0	3	1.0
Deodorant			
Awareness set	1	11	6.0
Evoked set	0	4	1.6
Inert set	0	8	2.4
Inept set	0	8	2.0
Beer			
Awareness set	3	24	10.6
Evoked set	0	13	3.5
Inert set	0	15	4.7
Inept set	0	18	2.4

Source: Chem L. Narayana and Rom J. Markin, "Consumer Behavior and Product Performance: An Alternative Conceptualization." *Journal of Marketing,* 39 (October 1975): 4. Reprinted with the kind permission of the American Marketing Association.

In an experimental study of the size of the evoked set for automobiles, which reported an average set size of 3.58, Horton (1983a) interprets the available data as follows.

> Although the evidence is limited, the pattern is relatively clear. Evoked set size *tends* to be larger for nondurables than durables. Although initially somewhat perplexing this pattern does have a certain logical consistency with existing consumer research. Presumably, the purchasing task for durables places a much heavier information processing burden on the consumer than does purchasing nondurables. Horton (1983b), for example, presents data for an information processing experiment for automobiles in which subjects acquired two to four times as much information as subjects in similar experiments using nondurables. A small evoked set is one major way consumers can manage this heavier information load.

Further, Horton's (1983a) study found that the size of the evoked set correlates negatively with both the number of attributes of the product class examined by subjects (e.g., miles per gallon) and the subjects' average level of interest in the brands within the evoked set.

A small number of other studies have examined factors that are correlated with the size of the evoked set. Because these studies overlap very little in terms of either the correlates examined or the methodologies employed, it is difficult to draw valid generalizations regarding the factors that affect evoked set size. The general *pattern* of the results, however, tends to support the idea that buyers may be adopting small evoked sets as a strategy for managing complex buying tasks.

One variable correlates with the size of the evoked set in enough studies to warrant a *tentative* judgment that a valid generalization has been found. Three studies (Campbell, 1969; Gronhaug, 1973/74; and Maddox et al., 1978) found that education is positively correlated with the size of the evoked set. The Maddox et al. study is especially interesting because it involves consumers in the United States and Norway, one of the few international studies of buyer behavior. The relationship with education is indirectly supported by Jarvis and Wilcox (1973), who found the size of the evoked set to be positively correlated across product classes, indicating that the size of the evoked set may be partially an individual difference variable. This finding is consistent with the positive relationship between the size of the evoked set and education.

That people with better educations make their brand choice from a larger set of brands is very interesting for it *suggests* that such people may engage in a more extensive brand search and decision-making process. There is a sizeable amount of evidence to support this conjecture, as shall be seen in numerous places throughout this text. Although the direct evidence is limited, there is also good reason to believe that such better educated, and generally higher income, buyers receive better value from their purchasing decisions. More will be said about this point subsequently.

Importance of Evoked Set

The reader may feel that a substantial amount of space has gone into discussing an obvious point. However, the concept of the evoked set, and the tendency for it to be quite small, is only obvious in retrospect. Recognizing that buyers typically make their brand choices from a small set of alternatives leads to several consequences of considerable managerial, as well as academic, importance.

The first consequence is methodological. Most people have had the experience of being asked to evaluate a set of objects; e.g., makes of automobiles or brands of breakfast cereals. The list contains fifteen or twenty items, many of which are unfamiliar to the respondent, who is told that the researchers need a *complete* set of responses. Such instructions typically include a statement to the effect that if you are uncertain about your answer just do the best you can even if you have to guess. There are two primary reasons for this instruction. First, the researchers may be investigating a set of brands for which they know, or believe, that buyers have very little involvement and toward which they have very weak attitudes. The goal in this situation, which is quite appropriate, is to force buyers to express whatever attitudes they might have formed. The second reason is both more common and less appropriate. Many statistical procedures become very difficult or impossible to use when the data are incomplete, especially those based on complex multivariate statistical procedures. However, when respondents are asked to provide information on brands not in their evoked sets, their responses are likely to contain a very large amount of error that can hide or obscure meaningful relationships among variables for the brands in the evoked set. Thus, buyer behavior research that requires questioning respondents about specific brands can often gain much by limiting the questions to those brands that are in each buyer's evoked set.

A second consequence is brand loyalty. Since there is good evidence that the evoked set is usually quite small, one should expect buyers in RRB to exhibit a high degree of brand loyalty. For example, a buyer with three brands in his or her evoked set would exhibit at least one-third loyalty to his or her favorite brand. Furthermore, since the buyer's attitudes toward the three brands will probably not be equal, and for other reasons as well, the loyalty exhibited toward the favorite brand will often be much higher. The phenomena of brand loyalty will be discussed in the next chapter so it shall not be pursued further at this time.

A third consequence concerns the marketing strategy for launching new brands. Because of its very small size, the evoked set permits little expansion to accommodate new brands as they are introduced into the market. Thus, very careful attention must be given to the structure of the market in order to identify brands that may be partially displaced, along with their relevant strengths and weaknesses, when a new product entry is contemplated.

In managerial terms, the target market must be carefully delineated and a detailed market plan constructed for introducing and developing the new brand. This market plan, of course, must consider quite specifically how the new brand is to encroach upon already established brands: e.g., better features, lower price, more aggressive distribution or promotion. Looked at from the individual buyer's perspective, consideration of a new brand places the buyer in the limited problem solving stage of learning. Thus, further discussion of the problem of market entry strategy will be postponed until the examination of limited problem solving in Part III.

INTENTION

The concept of RRB requires some means for storing buying plans to be implemented as each purchasing occasion arises. Of course, both the environment in which buying decisions are implemented and the specific circumstances that give rise to the need for purchase are subject to change. To accommodate such changes, current theories of buyer behavior postulate the existence of permanently stored, flexible buying plans generally referred to as intention (e.g., Howard and Sheth 1969, Howard 1977, Engel et al. 1978, Bettman 1979).

The Concept of Intention

The term intention is used in two different, but related senses. The most common use of the term is as "a propensity to buy." A buyer, for example, might be asked whether his or her chance of buying a new car in the next six months is 1 out of 10, 2 out of 10, and so on to 10 out of 10. The most frequent, and seemingly the most appropriate, use for such measures of intention is for major durables, where there is often a long lead time and many secondary factors to consider prior to purchase; e.g., extra money. Such measures of intention will be discussed in some detail in Chapter 8 in conjunction with attitudes and the attitude-purchase relationship.

The second use of the intention concept is as a plan for implementing purchasing decisions for the product class in question. This plan may allow for contingencies that could cause the buyer to purchase a brand other than his or her favorite brand, possibly one that may not even be in the evoked set. Figure 4.1 illustrates some of the most important aspects of the intention concept with the buying plan of one buyer for purchasing gasoline.[3] The plan begins with what is sometimes referred to as a choice or decision heuristic.[4] The choice heuristic in this case is to buy gas if the tank is "less than one-fourth full." Note carefully that such a rule is quite dependent on the specific person and the circumstances in which the decision is made. For example, the woman whose intention is displayed in Figure 4.1 is the wife of a retired banker, living in New London, New Hampshire, prior to the OPEC oil embargo. A change in any of these factors might alter the decision rule. This, in fact, was a major cause of the all too frequent gas lines of the mid-1970s, as motorists began "topping off" their tanks.

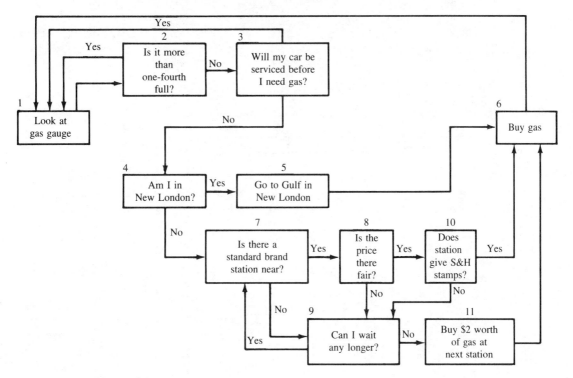

Figure 4.1
Example of intention (buying plan)

Source: John A. Howard and Jagdish N. Sheth, *The Theory of Buyer Behavior,* 134. New York: Wiley & Sons, 1969. Reprinted with permission.

[3]This example of intention was originally published in Howard and Sheth (1969, p. 134). The example was developed by extensive interviewing of one subject. Although they believe this model of intention is accurate, they acknowledge (p. 33) that its ability to predict future behavior, as opposed to describing past behavior, has not been empirically tested. Howard (1973, pp. 62–64) describes this example further, giving additional details about the person whose intention was modeled. More important, Howard states that "Her choice process is not completely idiosyncratic by any means; it is very similar to others that were studied at the same time" (1973, p. 62).

[4]The term heuristic is used in the cognitive psychology and buyer behavior literature to describe rules of thumb that individuals adopt to aid them in making decisions. An example of such a heuristic would be to "buy higher priced brands"; the underlying logic that price and quality tend to be positively related. There is, in fact, considerable evidence that suggests that many buyers use this rule when price is the only available cue to product quality (Gardner, 1977).

Should the tank be less than a quarter full, the plan requires a quick mental check to determine "Will my car be serviced before I need gas?" If the answer is no, a series of rules are implemented to determine which brand, and at which station, to purchase gasoline. If the buyer is in New London the decision is very simple: Go to the Gulf station and buy gas. Why does this rule exist? It may be because the buyer's nephew owns the station, she has all of her servicing work done there, she has a Gulf credit card, or for some other reason. The essential point is the quick and easy way in which this buyer is able to implement her gasoline purchasing decisions.

When our buyer is not at home, the decision process becomes more complex. The rules necessary to implement the decision, however, continue to be well formulated and easy to implement. When not at home our buyer has a preference for any "standard brand." Two additional factors must be considered: (1) if the price is fair and (2) if the station gives S & H stamps. The idea of a fair price is very interesting because there is substantial evidence to suggest that buyers often form lower and upper thresholds within which they consider the asking price of a good acceptable or fair. Prices that are too high are regarded as unwarranted, while prices that are too low cause the buyer to suspect the quality of the good.[5] For this particular buyer, both conditions (a fair price and S & H stamps) must be met before she will buy more than a token amount of gas.

If *any* of the three conditions is not met (a standard brand station, a fair price, or S & H stamps), our buyer will wait if she can. If not, she will "buy $2 worth of gas at next station" and continue to search for an *acceptable* station. An important aspect of this buyer's intention is the inclusion of a contingency that would force her out of her evoked set.

Major Characteristics of Intention

Figure 4.1 has been examined in some depth because it illustrates certain features that seem to be common to most buyer decision making for products characterized by RRB. First, the plan is well formulated and requires the buyer to acquire only a few, easily ascertained facts in order to implement a buying decision. It is largely these features that allow such buying decisions to be implemented routinely. Second, the buying plan need not be simple. Indeed, the plan in Figure 4.1 is one of the simpler examples of intention reported in the literature, and a considerably more complex example will be presented shortly. Third, the criteria are applied in a definite order. A major consequence of this fact, with important managerial implications, is that certain elements of the plan may not be executed under specific conditions. For example, many people buy where they have credit. To inhibit buyers who have forgotten their credit cards from buying elsewhere many department stores allow established customers to charge purchases even if they don't have their charge card, although they usually must produce some identification. Fourth, a brand is dropped from consideration if it fails a single criterion. Clearly understanding what criteria might cause a buyer to drop a brand from consideration has important managerial implications. Fifth, and finally, the decisions at each

---

[5]For evidence supporting the fair price concept, the reader is referred to Gardner (1977, especially pp. 420–422), who also provides a general review of how buyers use price as one piece of information in making brand choices.

stage in the decision process are binary rather than multivalued. That is, the outcome at each decision point in the purchasing plan is a simple yes or no, purchase or don't purchase, or some similar response with only two possible values. In other words each decision point has been simplified to the greatest degree possible.

Decision Net Studies   - SKIP

The model of intention just described is an example of what is generally referred to as a decision net model. The most important characteristics of any decision net model are that the choice alternatives are seen as possessing one or more attributes (e.g., price or use of S & H stamps), which are processed through a sequence of intermediate decisions or nodes that ultimately lead to a final decision. The decision may be to purchase one or more of the alternative choices, abandon the purchasing process, or engage in some other activity such as altering the composition of the evoked set. Decision net models have been developed for a number of different types of buying problems: such as the selection of a stock portfolio (Clarkson 1962; Swinth, Gaumnitz, and Rodriguez 1975), purchase of women's clothing (Alexis, Haines, and Simon, 1968; Haines 1974a, b), purchase of grocery products (Bettman 1970), and home buying (Park et al. 1981; Park and Lutz 1982). Bettman (1979, Chapter 8) provides an excellent review of decision net studies.

In terms of our present discussion, it is important to note that not all decision net models are models of RRB. In fact, an examination of published decision net models uncovers models of decision processes that are more general and flexible than would be expected in a true state of RRB. Remember, however, RRB is the *culmination* of a learning process. Once the buyer is in RRB, many of the elements of the decision process (e.g., rules for forming attitudes toward new brands in an established product class) will be dormant. The full decision net, however, continues to be available whenever the buyer needs or decides to change the composition of his or her evoked set.

Bettman (1970) constructed decision net models for two consumers' choice processes for grocery products. An examination of these models provides additional insights into the concept of intention, as well as an introduction to the procedures used in constructing decision net models. Figures 4.2 and 4.3 present the models constructed by Bettman for consumers C_1 and C_4, respectively. These decision net models were developed by following five housewives as they did their grocery shopping over a six to eight week period. The subjects were encouraged to think aloud as they shopped and their thoughts were recorded on a portable tape recorder. It was from these recordings that the decision net models in Figures 4.2 and 4.3 were developed.[6]

Perhaps the most striking aspect of these two decision net models is their complexity. Part of this complexity is because Bettman was modeling the decision process for a class of products rather than a single product class, as was done in

---

[6]This research procedure is referred to as protocol analysis. Protocol analysis requires substantial verbal skill on the part of subjects. Bettman (1970), for example, was unable to model one consumer because of her inability to verbalize her thoughts. (The other two consumers who were not modeled moved before the project was completed.)

Decision Net

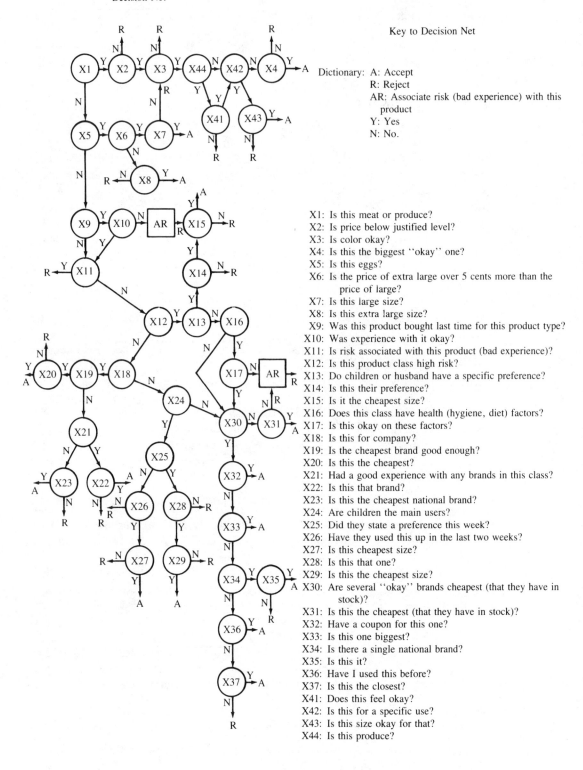

Key to Decision Net

Dictionary: A: Accept
R: Reject
AR: Associate risk (bad experience) with this
product
Y: Yes
N: No.

X1: Is this meat or produce?
X2: Is price below justified level?
X3: Is color okay?
X4: Is this the biggest "okay" one?
X5: Is this eggs?
X6: Is the price of extra large over 5 cents more than the
price of large?
X7: Is this large size?
X8: Is this extra large size?
X9: Was this product bought last time for this product type?
X10: Was experience with it okay?
X11: Is risk associated with this product (bad experience)?
X12: Is this product class high risk?
X13: Do children or husband have a specific preference?
X14: Is this their preference?
X15: Is it the cheapest size?
X16: Does this class have health (hygiene, diet) factors?
X17: Is this okay on these factors?
X18: Is this for company?
X19: Is the cheapest brand good enough?
X20: Is this the cheapest?
X21: Had a good experience with any brands in this class?
X22: Is this that brand?
X23: Is this the cheapest national brand?
X24: Are children the main users?
X25: Did they state a preference this week?
X26: Have they used this up in the last two weeks?
X27: Is this cheapest size?
X28: Is this that one?
X29: Is this the cheapest size?
X30: Are several "okay" brands cheapest (that they have in
stock)?
X31: Is this the cheapest (that they have in stock)?
X32: Have a coupon for this one?
X33: Is this one biggest?
X34: Is there a single national brand?
X35: Is this it?
X36: Have I used this before?
X37: Is this the closest?
X41: Does this feel okay?
X42: Is this for a specific use?
X43: Is this size okay for that?
X44: Is this produce?

most studies. However, most of the single product class studies have found decision nets that are more complex than the net presented in Figure 4.1.

Examining the decision nets in detail reveals that they are quite different. Price, for example, is very important for consumer C_1; at least ten of the 44 nodes in the decision net are concerned with price and eight of those with whether the brand under consideration is cheapest. Price is clearly much less important for consumer C_4. Another difference between the two consumers is the degree to which preferences of others figure prominently in their decisions. Such preferences are very important for consumer C_4 but of little concern for consumer C_1. One final major difference is the much higher degree of risk C_4 perceives in purchasing grocery products in comparison to C_1. Consumer C_4, for example, developed a detailed plan for "legitimizing" her brand choices as a way of coping with this risk (decision nodes $X40$–$X47$). Node $X47$ is especially interesting because it controls the legitimization process in the sense that all decisions for any new brand must ultimately pass through this node, which asks "Had bad experience with other products from this brand?"

An interesting aspect of the two decision nets is the use of various heuristic rules of thumb as decision criteria. Consumer C_1, for example, used the following rule for decisions for deciding which size of eggs to buy: "Is the price of extra large over 5 cents more than the price of large?" Another example for consumer C_1 is the use of color (node X_3) as a cue for judging product quality. This is, apparently, a very common rule of thumb, which accounts for the widespread use of dyes for coloring produce and meat before they are presented to the final consumer for consideration. Oranges, for example, are typically picked green and are often dyed a bright orange before being put on the grocer's shelf. A major controversy grew up in the 1970s over the use of red dye #2 on fresh beef. There was concern that red dye #2 might be a carcinogen. Consumers, however, *expect* high quality beef to have a "healthy" red color and will often refuse to purchase beef which does not have this color. Unless treated with some dying agent beef quickly turns grey without a necessary loss in quality. Although red dye #2 is no longer used, producers continue to color beef red to meet consumer expectations.

An important question, of course, concerns the validity of the decision net models as predictors of future brand purchase decisions, as opposed to merely descriptors of earlier decisions. Although most decision net studies have not gone beyond describing past decisions, Bettman tested his two models. His results were quite encouraging. Specifically, he was able to correctly predict whether a given brand would, or would not, be purchased for 89.7 percent and 87.0 percent of the purchasing decisions for consumers C_1 and C_4, respectively. Recently, in a study of home buying, Park et al. (1981) reported correct predictions for 16 of 21 buyers. In an article apparently based on the same data, Park and Lutz (1982) report that the basic dimensions that defined the decision nets (e.g., price, number of bedrooms) remained relatively stable over the course of the search and decision-making process.

Figure 4.2
Decision net model for consumer C_1

Source: James R. Bettman, "Information Processing Models of Consumer Behavior," *Journal of Marketing Research*, 8 (August 1970): 371. Reprinted with the kind permission of the American Marketing Association.

Decision Net

Key to Decision Net

X1: Is this produce?
X2: Is the color okay?
X3: Is this for a recipe?
X4: Is it small enough?
X5: Is this the right size?
X6: Does it feel okay?
X7: Had experience with this product type?
X8: Is there a convenience type feature?
X9: Does this have that feature?
X10: Can you see the product itself?
X11: Does this have the best color?
X12: Are packages (cans or boxes) damaged?
X13: Does this have least damage?
X14: Is size satisfactory?
X15: Is this the cheapest "okay" one for given size?
X16: Is this high perceived risk?
X17: Had bad experience with this brand?
X18: Is this one legitimized?
X19: Is it the only brand available?
X20: Is it really necessary to have it now?
X21: Does husband have strong preference for brand?
X22: Is this that brand?
X23: Does this product type have a convenience feature?
X24: Does this one have it?
X25: Is there a freshness factor?
X26: Is this factor necessary for this end use?
X27: Is this brand sufficient for this end use?
X28: Does this have that factor?
X29: Was this brand bought last time?
X30: Was last brand liked better than others previously tried?
X31: Are they out of that brand?
X32: Did legitimization of this brand involve trial?
X33: Was this one better than the old one in that trial?
X34: Was this liked better than others previously tried?
X49: Any new brands legitimized since then?
X50: Did this involve trial?
X51: Was the old one better in this trial?

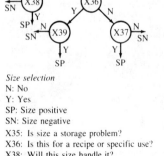

SIZE SELECTION

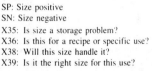

Size selection
N: No
Y: Yes
SP: Size positive
SN: Size negative

X35: Is size a storage problem?
X36: Is this for a recipe or specific use?
X38: Will this size handle it?
X39: Is it the right size for this use?

LEGITIMIZATION

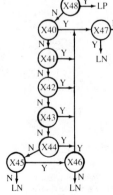

Legitimization
N: No
Y: Yes
LP: Legitimization decision positive
LN: Legitimization decision negative

X40: Has husband mentioned preference?
X41: Hear about it from parents?
X42: Hear about it from friends?
X43: Tried some before (at friends or sample)?
X44: Like other products from same brand?
X45: Seen ads on television?
X46: Familiar company source of ads?
X47: Had bad experience with other products from this brand?
X48: Used it satisfactorily previously?

Evaluating Decision Net Studies

The two decision nets just reviewed, as well as other nets reviewed by Bettman (1979), lend additional support to the concept of intention and to Howard's argument regarding the functioning of intention (e.g., its sequential nature) in buyer decision processes. These nets also show very clearly that buyers develop, and appear to rely heavily on, a variety of decision heuristics, such as judging quality by price or color or generalizing prior experience with one item to all items under the same brand name. It should be quite clear by now that an understanding of buying plans or intention has tremendous potential for facilitating managerial decision making. As an example, consider the implications for branding policy if a large proportion of buyers have a legitimization net similar to C_4. If they do, *and* the firm is certain of uniformly high quality for new product introductions, then a family brands policy in which all items share the same brand name has substantial advantages. Campbells, for example, follows this policy for its soups with the important consequence that it is quite easy to introduce new soups into the market. On the other hand, if uniformly high quality or consumer acceptance cannot be assured, assigning each new item a unique brand name allows it to succeed or fail on its own merits.

Although decision net research supports the concept of intention as a key variable for understanding buyer behavior and holds out the possibility of substantial managerial implications, two cautionary notes are appropriate. First, it is clear from the two decision net models just examined that such models, for a given type of product, *can* be quite different for different buyers. Indeed, in marked contrast to Howard's (1973, p. 62) statement that the Figure 4.1 model of a gasoline purchasing decision was similar among a number of buyers, Bettman in a careful review of decision net studies, found that the limited available literature suggests that most decision net models are highly idiosyncratic (1979, especially Chapter 8). This raises a very interesting and managerially important question. If decision net models describe buyer decision processes with at least a moderate degree of accuracy, and the limited empirical evidence available supports this idea, is it possible to find enough similarity among the decision nets for specific groups of buyers to go beyond the study of individual buyers? Clearly, for the concept of decision nets to be of practical managerial use, the answer will have to be yes.

Unfortunately, at this time we do not know whether it will be possible to develop general decision nets for groups of buyers that will retain a high degree of detail in the network. The goal of most decision net studies has been a detailed description of individual buying processes without any specific attempt to focus on network similarities. Furthermore, because of the extraordinary effort that is required to collect data for constructing decision nets, the total number of nets that have been constructed is small. By focusing on commonalities it may be possible to construct decision nets that explain a large portion of the variance among individual purchasing decisions for specific segments of the market. Perceived risk, for

Figure 4.3
Decision net model for consumer C_4

Note: The size selection net expands node X14. The legitimization net expands node X18.

Source: James R. Bettman, "Information Processing Models of Consumer Behavior," *Journal of Marketing Research,* 8 (August 1970): 272–273. Reprinted with the kind permission of the American Marketing Association.

example, plays a major role in the decision processes of consumers C_1 and C_4. Bettman (1974, 1979) has begun an interesting effort in this direction. He is trying to develop a set of statistics, based on graph theory, for formally analyzing decision nets and grouping buyers who share nets with a high degree of similarity. The methods Bettman is developing are still in the formative stage and remain an intriguing possibility for the future.

The second caution regarding decision net research is methodological. In addition to the difficulty in generalizing the results of this research, this type of research tends to be highly reactive. Reactive means that the subject is aware of being observed and such knowledge may affect his or her behavior. Reactivity is an especially important problem in decision net studies that *ask*, as most of these studies have, the subject to verbally describe his or her thought processes as the decision is made. Such an approach may cause the subject to engage in a much more organized and elaborate decision process than would have occured had the request not been made. Nakanishi in particular, has argued that

> We often find two contradicting patterns in decision-net models. For one thing, the decision-net models published by Bettman (1970), Clarkson (1962), Haines (1969), and others are usually highly complex, containing as many as fifty cues (or decision "nodes") in some cases. Since memorizing the exact sequence of more than a dozen cues would be extremely difficult, it is hard to believe that the subjects in previous studies executed those information-processing rules in predetermined sequence. Yet, despite their apparent complexity, decision-net models do not fully specify the perceptual/cognitive processes associated for each decision node. As Bettman noted, many cues are modeled at such a gross level that there is no knowing why the individual selected one branch or another. In short, decision-net models so far published tend to be too complex for a subject to memorize in their entirety, but are still too oversimplified to explain all of the mental activities accompanying a purchase decision (1974, p. 77).

Nakanishi continues this argument by suggesting that part of the problem with decision net models is that they are conceptualized as a rigid, fixed, basically computerlike program, which simply executes the relevant program. He further argues that, from what we know about human perceptual and information processing mechanisms, people do not operate in such a rigid, inflexible mode. Nakanishi proceeds to develop an alternative, and more flexible, model of human information processing. While interesting, this model has apparently not received empirical testing in a buyer behavior context, thus it shall not be pursued further. For more details on the model and its implications, the reader is referred to Nakanishi (1974) and Bettman (1979, pp. 244–246).

SUMMARY

This chapter investigated the behavior of buyers who have developed or learned the product class and associated brand concepts to a degree where they can implement their buying decisions on a more or less routine basis. Also, buyers were seen to typically make their choices from a very limited number of alternatives, the evoked set, and are capable of developing quite complex buying plans for handling a variety of contingencies, which they may encounter in the marketplace.

In attempting to summarize the implications of decision net research, it seems safe to conclude that, despite some problems and limitations, these studies have been an important source in understanding buyer behavior. The most important implication of these studies, in terms of the chapter's objectives, is the support that decision nets provide for the concept of intention. It appears that the buying plan represented by intention, when the buyer is in RRB, is basically a decision net that has become very well learned and reduced to those elements essential in executing buying decisions for a stable evoked set.

Precisely how adequate decision nets are as descriptions of the behavior of buyers in "real", nonreactive buying situations remains to be established. At this time, decision net studies provide us with our most detailed observations of buyers' decision-making processes. Indeed, from this perspective, much of what is studied in buyer behavior research is in some way related to the concept of a decision net. A number of the attitude models studied in Chapter 8, for example, can be viewed as aspects of a decision net. The difference is that attitude studies normally focus on more general rules than those modeled at the level of the individual buyer in decision net studies. Do not lose sight of the fact, however, that all such "more general" rules are ultimately based on the behavior of individual buyers.

Brand Loyalty

5

The last chapter observed that a logical consequence of a small evoked set is a high degree of brand loyalty. The marketing manager's problem is to establish product, pricing, promotion, and distribution policies that increase the likelihood of loyalty toward the brands for which the manager is responsible. To effectively accomplish this task, the manager must have a clear understanding of what brand loyalty is and why a consumer might become loyal to one or more brands. It is also desirable that the manager have some way of measuring consumers' tendencies to switch from one brand to another.

This chapter examines what it means to say that a buyer is brand loyal, and why a buyer might become loyal to one or more brands. The concluding section introduces the reader to a sophisticated and rapidly developing set of mathematical tools for measuring buyers' brand switching behavior. Of necessity, this discussion avoids the mathematics underlying current brand switching models and focuses on managerial uses. Appendix B discusses the mathematical and statistical bases of three relatively simple brand switching models.

THE CONCEPT OF BRAND LOYALTY

Brand Loyalty and Repeat Purchase Behavior

The last chapter noted that research on the size of the evoked set implies a high degree of brand loyalty (BL). More precisely, what the small size of the evoked set implies is a high degree of repeat purchase behavior (RPB). For a true state of BL to exist, there must be some degree of psychological commitment to the brand. The importance of this distinction becomes readily apparent by considering a buyer who "always buy the cheapest brand." If during the test period one particular brand was always the cheapest, our hypothetical buyer would appear, on the basis of his or her purchase history, to be completely loyal even though this buyer would immediately switch to another brand if its price became lower. As shall be discussed below, much of the literature that has purported to measure BL has in reality measured RPB, and this has created substantial difficulties for anyone trying to draw valid generalizations from the literature.

"Brand" and Other Loyalties

Although research has focused on products, the range of objects toward which a buyer might develop either RPB or BL is considerably larger than this. There is, for example, a considerable literature on RPB and loyalty toward retail stores (cf., Granbois 1977, especially pp. 279–290). Although the choice criteria would be different, the selection of one particular store has a certain similarity to the brand choice decision. Of course, to the retailer, developing store loyalty is critical.

In a similar way, a certain amount of research into RPB and BL concentrated on goods that are unlikely to reach routinized response behavior: e.g., durable goods, such as automobiles. An important aspect of such goods is that the time between purchases is, for most buyers, sufficiently long that the specific "brands," or items being purchased, have changed markedly from one occasion to the next. In such a situation, whatever RPB or "loyalty" is observed is really more toward the brand name than toward the specific brand; that is, loyalty toward the company or a category of products designated by a family brand name such as Chevrolet rather than a specific product.

That RPB or "brand" loyalty may develop at a different level or for a different set of objects than the specific brand is clearly of managerial importance. Indeed, an important goal of management is to develop loyalty toward whatever they are responsible for marketing: a specific brand, a brand or company name, a store name, a political party, or any number of other objects. For the concepts of RPB and BL to be most meaningful, however, the buyer should be essentially in a fully learned, stable buying mode, labeled routinized response behavior in Chapter 4.

Existence of RPB and BL

Ample evidence supports the existence of RPB. Because of the confusion in the literature regarding the distinction between RPB and BL, less evidence supports the existence of BL. There is, however, enough evidence to suggest that much RPB is consistent with the more stringent criteria of BL. Brown (1952), in what is probably the most frequently cited BL study, found degrees of RPB ranging from 54 to 95 percent for a variety of products. He also found degrees of what he termed "undivided loyalty" (i.e., all household purchases went to one brand) ranging from 12 to 73 percent. Many other studies have produced similar results; i.e., relatively high incidences of RPB that vary substantially over product classes (e.g., Cunningham 1956; Farley 1964a). Although imposing the more stringent requirements of true BL reduces the amount of reported loyalty, the degree of BL found is typically still large. Day, for example, reported in a frequently cited study that the

> Loyal segment is often defined as a buyer who devotes at least 50 percent of his product purchase to a single brand. In this study, 108 of 148 buyers would be classified as brand loyal on that basis. However, if loyal buyers were required to have an extremely favorable initial attitude toward the brand as well as buying the brand on a majority of occasions, then the brand loyal segment is reduced to 76 buyers (1969, p. 31).

Day's primary point was the degree to which BL tended to be overstated when a strictly behavioral criterion was used to define BL. However, even when an "extremely favorable" attitude is required, over half of the buyers in the study were defined as BL.

Research into store loyalty has produced very similar results regarding the amount and variance of RPB and loyalty (e.g., Granbois 1976; Newman 1977). In what is perhaps one of the most interesting studies of BL, Guest (1944, 1955, 1964) found that substantial loyalty toward brand names, but not necessarily specific brands, continued over twelve- and twenty-year periods. Thus, there is ample evidence that RPB and BL are real phenomena. And, as shall be discussed below, developing RPB and BL is a most important managerial task. However, such development requires an understanding of the factors that cause RPB and BL. Before attempting any exposition of these causal factors, the current status of RPB and BL research will be briefly assessed, and a managerial perspective developed on the two concepts.

Current Status of RPB and BL Research

As of 1978, according to Jacoby and Chestnut (1978), over 300 articles investigated some aspect of RPB or BL. Despite this vast amount of research, Jacoby and Chestnut found that it was difficult to draw valid conclusions about BL. Part of the difficulty stems from the distinction between an operational definition and a conceptual definition. The most important feature of concepts is that they are abstractions of reality which capture the most important features of that reality. Being abstract and general, they can unify a broad range of phenomena by identifying *important* similarities and ignoring *unimportant* differences. Of course, what is important very much depends both on the subject being studied and the reason for studying it.

In contrast, an operational definition defines a phenomenon in terms of the operations used to measure it. Brown's (1952) concept of "undivided loyalty" can illustrate an operational definition. Specifically, he defined "undivided loyalty" as six consecutive purchases of the same brand. The problem with such an operational definition is that it tends to sidestep the issue of whether the definition is indeed valid. It is, quite literally, what it is.

Without a standard for validation, it is difficult to know upon which studies generalizations can be based. The problem is further complicated by the lack of agreement as to the proper operational definition, or definitions, of BL. As Jacoby and Chestnut (1978, p. 44) show with a very simple example, one can take a given purchase sequence and, by applying different, frequently used operational definitions, come to a variety of inconsistent conclusions regarding the existence or degree of BL. To overcome such problems, they argue for, and provide, a conceptual definition of BL.

A Conceptual Definition of BL

Jacoby and Kyner offer the following conceptual definition of BL.

> Brand loyalty is (1) the biased (i.e., nonrandom) (2) behavioral response (i.e., purchase) (3) expressed over time (4) by some decision-making unit (5) with respect to one or more alternative brands out of a set of such brands, and is (6) a function of psychological (i.e., decision-making, evaluative) processes, (1973, p. 2).

Although not without its critics,[1] this definition of BL appears to be the most satisfactory and informative definition currently available; and therefore, worthwhile to examine in greater detail.

Jacoby and Chestnut argue for the necessity of the first condition by stating:

> More specifically, if BL were a random event, there would be no purpose in making it the object of applied scientific inquiry. Random events, though interesting, defy prediction, modification, and control. Without one or more of the latter three possibilities, there is no justification for expenditures of managerial time (1978, p. 81).

---

[1]The most extensive criticisms of this definition of BL have been made by Tarpey (1974, 1975). In particular, Tarpey argues that the definition is deficient because it does not specify causal mechanisms and that it, in fact, amounts to merely another operational definition. Jacoby (1975) has taken strong exception to this view. He has also noted that his definition of BL has had an influence on the thinking and empirical research of others.

Of the six conditions, this would appear to be the one most subject to challenge. For example, probabilistic models of brand choice have been developed that allow the marketer to draw very interesting conclusions regarding the behavior of a market to a new product's introduction. Such models will be discussed briefly later in this chapter; for the moment it is sufficient to point out that these are primarily models of RPB rather than BL, and that condition one seems unnecessary in light of condition six. The major point here is that there are phenomena, which can be regarded as random, that are worth studying for managerial purposes.

The justification for the second condition (purchase) is that a mere verbal report on preference or intention to buy a particular brand (i.e., a verbal report of bias) is insufficient for defining BL. This is important because many studies that have purported to study BL have, in fact, studied only verbally stated preferences or intentions. For many reasons, which were discussed quite fully in the study of Howard and Sheth's concept of intention, purchase behavior may not reflect the verbally stated preference or intention.

The need to define BL over time is almost self-evident. The term loyalty *implies* a commitment over time. Less evident is the need for the term "some decision-making unit." Although it is not necessary, the tendency is to think of BL in terms of a single individual. Much BL research used panel data in which a single family member, usually the wife, reports purchases for the entire family. This creates a number of problems. For example, the purchaser, user, and decision maker may be different. In such a situation, any attempt to explain BL in terms of purchaser or user characteristics is likely to produce misleading results. Another problem that can arise in these panel studies is a possible serious understatement of the true degree of BL. Imagine a family of four in which each member is a decision maker for the product class in question (e.g., toothpaste), and each person uses only one brand. At the level of the family unit, which is not the decision-making unit, the degree of loyalty toward each of the four brands would be approximately 25 percent each. Thus, it is clearly important to properly identify the decision-making unit in any BL study.

The fifth element in the definition of BL ("with respect to one or more alternative brands") reflects the possibility for an individual to be loyal to more than one brand. In this regard, one of the most important contributions of the concept of the evoked set is that it forces acknowledgment that multibrand loyalty exists. This is very important because most studies of BL have defined loyalty in terms of a single, most preferred or most purchased brand. Recently, the number of studies of BL employing multibrand measures of loyalty has increased. The preponderance of studies, however, continue to employ measures of BL toward a single brand (Jacoby and Chestnut, 1978, p. 83).

The sixth, and last, criterion is that BL is "a function of psychological (i.e., decision-making, evaluative) processes." Such processes need not be elaborate or extensive. The crucial elements are that the person has reasons for acting and develops a commitment toward one or more brands. The reasons for a buyer becoming BL are examined in the next major section of this chapter; however, it is useful to first examine the phenomenon of BL from a somewhat less theoretical and more directly managerial perspective.

A Model of Vulnerability

There are sound reasons for making a key managerial objective the development of loyalty toward a specific brand, a brand name, a store, or some other object. A loyal customer is, by definition, a customer who has a commitment toward the brand. Such a person is often willing to pay a premium price,[2] exert extra effort to purchase the brand should it be out of stock in a particular store or available only in inconvenient locations, and be less subject to competitors' actions, especially price reductions. The more a firm's share of the total market is built upon a base of loyal customers, the more stable is that firm's market share likely to be. Also, market share is linked very directly with profitability. For these reasons, management should pay careful attention to the degree and distribution of loyalty in the market.

Wind (1977) has developed a concept of vulnerability which is useful for assessing the degree and distribution of loyalty in a market. Figure 5.1 presents Wind's vulnerability matrix. The rows and columns of this matrix are based on buyers' purchase patterns and attitudes toward a specific brand: brand i, as viewed from the particular perspective of brand i's manufacturer.

Note carefully that only one of the nine cells of Figure 5.1 is labeled "Loyal" to brand i. Of the remaining eight cells, one is unlikely to be a good target market for brand i, five identify groups of buyers of brand i who are likely to be especially receptive to the efforts of competitors, and two identify groups of buyers of competitive brands who are likely targets for brand i. Wind (1977, pp. 315–317) discusses procedures for measuring the purchase patterns and attitudes that are

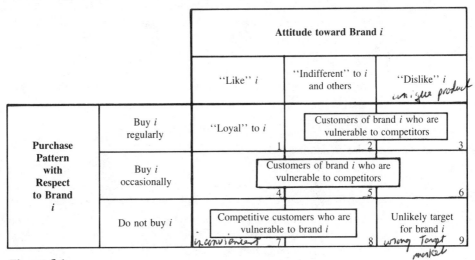

Figure 5.1
The basic vulnerability matrix

Source: Yoram Wind, "Brand Loyalty and Vulnerability." In *Consumer and Industrial Buying Behavior*, edited by Arch G. Woodside, Jagdish N. Sheth, and Peter D. Bennett, 314. New York: Elsevier-North Holland, 1977.

---

[2]In a very innovative study, Pessemier (1959) used resistance to price increases as a means of defining BL. Specifically, Pessemier experimentally increased the price differential between the most preferred brand and other brands over ten consecutive purchase occasions. The longer it took a subject to switch brands, the greater was the presumed degree of BL.

necessary to construct the vulnerability matrix. Measuring the purchase patterns is straightforward; e.g., percent of purchases going to brand *i*. The procedures for measuring attitudes are more complex and shall not be pursued further here. Selected procedures for measuring attitudes, including some suggested by Wind, are presented in Appendix C.

Clearly, the vulnerability matrix provides the manager with useful information. It identifies both loyal customers and those who are unlikely to become so, and therefore not worth the attempt to develop. It also identifies current buyers who are especially likely to switch brands. Knowledge of who these buyers are is the first step in developing them as loyal customers. The manager would then determine what factors would tempt potential customers to switch brands in order to develop appropriate marketing plans to encourage loyalty among those switchers currently buying the firm's product or to encourage switching and loyalty among those now buying a competitor's product. Formulating effective marketing strategies to develop RPB and BL requires an understanding of why a buyer might manifest these behaviors.

EXPLANATIONS OF BRAND LOYALTY AND REPEAT PURCHASE BEHAVIOR

Most studies of BL and RPB have focused on the relationship of these two variables to a wide range of other variables, with some positive results. BL, for example, appears to be related to store loyalty (e.g., Rao 1969; Carman 1970). Far more studies found little or no association among the variables tested. For example, there appears to be almost no association between BL or RPB and a large number of personality, demographic, and socioeconomic variables. Mostly, authors who surveyed the literature found a confusing pattern of mixed and inconclusive results (e.g., Engel, Blackwell, and Kollat, 1978, Chapter 17; Jacoby and Chestnut 1978).

There are many reasons for this confusion. The absence of a conceptual definition of BL and the large number of different and often inconsistent operational definitions of BL and RPB have already been cited. The degree to which BL and RPB vary across different product classes has also been cited. Thus, there is reason to expect studies investigating BL or RPB toward different product classes to often reach different conclusions.

Despite the confusion in the literature, three different general explanations of BL and RPB have been offered that seem of sufficient merit to warrant a brief discussion. However, the reader is warned that, while all three appear quite plausible, the supporting evidence is generally sparse and often implicit rather than explicit. One further point, these three explanations are not necessarily competing; that is, the development of RPB or BL for a specific buyer for a specific product might very well be explained by two or even all three of these theories. More obviously, there is every reason to expect that different theories are likely to be most relevant for different product classes.

Economics of Information

This particular theory, as originally developed by Stigler (1961), was a theory of search for information rather than a theory of BL or RPB. Stigler argued that information was a commodity and, like any commodity, had a value. More specifically,

Stigler, making the standard economic assumption that all alternative brands of a given product class were equivalent or homogeneous, asked: Why do prices vary in the marketplace? His answer was that prices varied only because buyers were ignorant of the actual prices of *all* sellers.

To become informed about prices of different sellers, buyers would have to search for information. Since such search activity was not without cost, the rational buyer would search for price information only up to that point where the incremental gain from price reductions no longer exceeded the incremental or marginal cost of the search. Mathematically, the argument is to search as long as

$$ q \left| \frac{\partial P_{min}}{\partial N} \right| \geq MC_N $$

Although a bit forbidding, this equation is really quite simple. N is the number of searches made; e.g., the number of retailers visited. The term between the vertical bars is the absolute value of the change in the minimum price (P_{min}) as a function of search. For example, if the lowest price of a good after visiting the second retailer was $19.99 and the price offered by the third retailer visited was $17.99 then $\left| \frac{\partial P_{min}}{\partial N} \right|$ would be $2.00. The total gain would depend on the number of units purchased, which is measured by q. If two units are to be purchased, the total savings would be $4.00. MC_N is the marginal cost of the Nth search. If the cost of the third search were greater than or equal to $4.00, the buyer would stop searching. If the cost were less than $4.00, the buyer would continue searching. Figure 5.2 illustrates this example graphically.

Farley (1964b) argued that Stigler's economics of information suggested certain factors that should be correlated with BL. Specifically, he hypothesized that (1) higher income families would search less because the opportunity cost of time should increase as income increases (i.e., MC_N in the equation is positively related to income) and thus would be *more* BL; (2) larger families would tend to search more because they should encounter more financial pressures at any given income level and thus be less BL; and (3) the quantity purchased should be negatively related to BL. Farley also argued that the quantity of a good purchased should be negatively related to the average price paid for the good.

Figure 5.2
Graphic illustration of the economics of information

Note: Four searches will be engaged in because the buyer must determine that the gain no longer exceeds the cost associated with the next search.

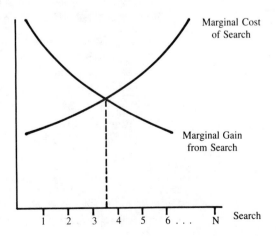

Farley's empirical results supported the hypothesized negative relationship between quantity purchased and average price paid. Contrary to expectation, BL tended to be negatively related to income, and no consistent relationship was found between BL and either quantity purchased or family size. Farley suggested his empirical results might be explained by the fact that the brands within the product classes he studied were *not* homogeneous. In effect, the theory was not given an adequate test. He suggested that the negative relationship between BL and income might be attributable to more efficient information processing, possibly because of better education or experience in higher income families. Further research has given considerable support to this suggestion (e.g., Thorelli, Becker, and Engledow 1975).

The arguments upon which the economics of information explanation of BL is based seem plausible. For the reasons just discussed, Farley's empirical data do not allow an adequate test of the theory.[3] It is, therefore, premature to dismiss it as a viable explanation of why buyers may engage in RPB or become BL. In fact, two different sets of research findings provide preliminary support for an economics of information explanation of RPB and BL.

The first line of evidence concerns search activity. Farley's price data indirectly support the effects of relative costs and gains on the extent of search. As shall be discussed in Chapter 11, a considerable amount of evidence further supports the economics of information arguments regarding the extent of search (Newman 1977). Coupled with the arguments regarding the relationship between store loyalty and brand loyalty, a reasonably strong implicit argument is formed for the economics of information explanation of RPB and BL.

The second line of research suggests a possible relationship between time pressure and BL. Considerable comment has been made on the increasing time pressures on buyers. Kotler (1972), in particular, suggested "Americans are increasingly placing more value on time than on goods" (p. 83). This, of course, would tend to increase the cost of search, reduce search effort, and possibly increase BL. Jacoby, Szybillo, and Berning (1977), in a most interesting review of the literature on time and buyer behavior suggest:

> Another consequence of reduced time may be brand loyalty. For example, data indicate that the longer the interpurchase interval (time between purchases of that item), the higher the probability that consumers will engage in information search prior to making a decision (Bucklin 1965) and the lower the probability of repeat purchase (Kuehn 1962). Working wives generally spend less time grocery shopping, buy more convenience foods, and tend to be more brand loyal than nonworking wives (Carman 1970; Jacoby, Olson, and Kaplan 1970[4]). Roselius (1971) indicated that being brand loyal and purchasing major (national) brands are the two most common strategies that consumers employ to reduce perceived risk of time loss (time, convenience, and effort wasted in getting a product adjusted, repaired, or replaced) (1977, p. 459).

That time pressure may be a source of BL is quite important because of the relatively clear implications for marketing strategy. First, it implies some specific

---

[3]Given our knowledge of the effects of education on buyer behavior, it would be interesting to determine if BL and income are positively related when education level is controlled. Such a test apparently has not been conducted.

[4]This reference is to a proprietary report.

promotional themes; e.g., time is your most valuable commodity, make extra time with brand X for the things you really want to do, etc. Second, it is possible to identify groups of buyers for whom time pressures may be severe. The percentage of working women, for example, has increased dramatically over the past 30 years. Furthermore, while many of these women work because their total family income is low, many others come from relatively high income families. There is, therefore, an identifiable segment of the market whose buying power is far greater than average and who very likely face severe time pressures (Lazer and Smallwood 1977). In this regard, McCall (1977) has gone so far as to suggest that "Convenience may replace price in economic theory" (p. 60).

In summarizing the economics of information of RPB and BL, three points seem especially relevant. First, supporting evidence is preliminary and provides essentially indirect support for the theory rather than direct testing of it. Second, if correct, the theory is unlikely to provide more than a partial explanation for RPB and BL, even within a single product class. Third, by its very nature the economics of information argument is essentially an argument for RPB rather than BL. In fact, Farley's measures of BL were actually measures of RPB, as these two measures are defined in this text. Because, as seen in earlier chapters, buyers tend to have a positive affect or liking of brands in their evoked set, an economics of information explanation of RPB implies a certain degree of commitment and, thus, BL. Such loyalty, however, may not be strong. Despite these caveats, the economics of information explanation does appear to have important implications for marketing management.

Perceived Risk

Somewhat more evidence suggests that high perceived risk can lead to BL. The concept of perceived risk has already been discussed in some depth, so the discussion will not be repeated here, except to quote Bauer's original argument on the possible causes of BL.

> One of our traditional problems is that of brand loyalty. Brand loyalty may involve a number of considerations. In recent years we have heard stressed the compatibility of the brand image with one's self-image, or with the norms of one's reference group. Brand loyalty is also seen as a means of economizing of decision effort by substituting habit for repeated, deliberate, decisions. Without for a moment minimizing such considerations, I would like to reintroduce the old-fashioned concept of "reliability." Much brand loyalty is a device for reducing the risks of consumer decisions. I am told that sugar is one product for which it has traditionally been difficult to develop brand loyalty. But my friend Edward Bursk tells me that when he was a salesman in Lancaster, Pennsylvania, there was a strong loyalty to a particular brand of sugar. The Pennsylvania Dutch housewives of that area are avid and proud bakers and there is more risk involved in making a cake than in sweetening a cup of coffee or a bowl of cereal. Suppose we were to limit ourslves to small ticket items, and to interview a sample of housewives as to the risks—that is, a combination of uncertainty plus seriousness of outcome involved—associated with each category of product. I would predict a strong correlation between degree of risk and brand loyalty (1960, pp. 25–26).

It is clear from the above quote that Bauer is hypothesizing, rather than testing, a relationship between perceived risk and BL. There is, however, a reasonable amount of evidence to support this hypothesized relationship.

The discussion on the economics of information indirectly cited a study by Roselius (1971) that found that being BL and buying major or national brands are the two most common strategies for dealing with the perceived risk of time loss. Not only are these the two most common strategies, they are also perceived as the two most helpful strategies, with BL rated as by far the best strategy. More generally, Roselius surveyed 472 housewives for their perceptions of the effectiveness of eleven different strategies for reducing the following four types of risk:

(1) Time Loss: When some products fail, we waste time, convenience, and effort getting it adjusted, repaired, or replaced.

(2) Hazard Loss: Some products are dangerous to our health or safety when they fail.

(3) Ego Loss: Sometimes when we buy a product that turns out to be defective, we feel foolish, or other people make us feel foolish.

(4) Money Loss: When some products fail, our loss is the money it takes to make the product work properly, or to replace it with a satisfactory product (p. 58).

Posing a number of general purchasing situations, Roselius completed a net favorable percent response[5] for each of the eleven risk reducing strategies for each of the four types of loss. Table 5.1 presents Roselius's findings. As can be seen they strongly support the argument that BL is an effective means for reducing various kinds of risk.

The book edited by Donald Cox (1967) summarizes much of the research on perceived risk up to the mid-1960s. There is considerable data, much of it anecdotal, in this book suggesting a positive relationship between perceived risk and BL. One paper is especially interesting. Cunningham (1967) constructed a measure of perceived brand commitment for three product classes (headache remedies, fabric softener, and dry spaghetti), which was then related to the degree of perceived risk. Cunningham concluded the data "presents one clear conclusion: perceived risk is positively related to perceived brand commitment. Apparently loyalty to one brand is a method of risk reduction" (p. 513).

The research presented so far is based on survey methods. In an interesting experimental study of the development of BL in a risky buying situation, Sheth and Venkatesan (1968) argued that "perceived risk is a necessary condition only for the development of brand loyalty. The sufficient condition is the existence of well-known market brands on which the consumer can rely" (p. 310). This conclusion is further supported by studies which show that buyers who are likely to be more sensitive to or less tolerant of risk are more likely to choose well known (i.e., national) brands (Horton 1979) and that, when the level of risk is systematically increased for a specific buying problem, the likelihood of buying brands made by well known companies increases (Ring, Shriber, and Horton 1980).

The relationship between perceived risk and BL has obvious managerial implications. Clearly, the firm should know what level of risk buyers tend to perceive for the markets in which they compete. A firm, for example, that has a

---

[5]The net favorable percent (NFP) is

$$NFP = \left[\frac{(\text{Number of Favorable Responses}) - (\text{Number of Unfavorable Responses})}{\text{Total Number of Responses}} \right] \times 100$$

Table 5.1
Ranking of risk relievers for four kinds of loss based on responses from all buyers

	KIND OF LOSS							
Response Definition	TIME LOSS		HAZARD LOSS		EGO LOSS		MONEY LOSS	
	NFP*	Reliever	NFP*	Reliever	NFP*	Reliever	NFP*	Reliever
Extremely Favorable	90.2	Brand Loyalty[a]	92.5	Brand Loyalty	96.0	Brand Loyalty	98.0	Brand Loyalty
Very Favorable	44.1	Major Brand[a]	50.6	Major Brand	62.6	Major Brand	65.4	Major Brand
Slightly Favorable	21.5 19.4 16.3	Store Image Shopping Free Sample	34.4	Gov't. Testing	28.3 27.3 27.3	Store Image Free Sample Shopping	29.7 26.8 19.8	Store Image Free Sample Shopping
Neutral	12.9 − 5.4 − 7.4	Word of Mouth Gov't. Testing Endorsements	0.0 − 1.0 − 3.2 −14.0	Word of Mouth Store Image Shopping Private Test	4.0 − 7.0 − 8.1 − 8.1	Word of Mouth Gov't. Testing Endorsements Money Back Guar.	11.9 6.9 − 1.9	Gov't. Testing Word of Mouth Money Back Guar.
Slightly Unfavorable	−20.4	Money Back Guar.	−17.2 −33.3	Free Sample Endorsements	−26.2	Private Test	−12.9 −35.6	Endorsements Private Test
Very Unfavorable	−24.7 −65.6	Private Test Expensive Model[a]	−47.3	Money Back Guar.			−68.2	Expensive Model
Extremely Unfavorable			−79.5	Expensive Model	−75.8	Expensive Model		

*NFP = ((Number of favorable responses—number of unfavorable responses) ÷ total responses) × 100.
[a]A Chi-square analysis indicated that these findings are significant at the .05 level of confidence.

Source: Ted Roselius, "Consumer Rankings of Risk Reduction Methods," *Journal of Marketing,* 35 (January 1971): 59. Reprinted with the kind permission of the American Marketing Association.

national image may want to emphasize the level of risk and how buying a name brand can insure quality. Mixers made by national firms have been advertised on this basis; the message being "A drink is about 75 percent mixer—why take a chance on ruining it with a poor quality mixer". A different strategy would be appropriate for a firm without a national reputation.

In a similar way a detailed knowledge of the risks buyers perceive in buying particular types of products and the strategies they develop to deal with those risks can provide important insights for the development of marketing strategy. The example just given for mixers uses an advertising message based on ego loss. Another example involves time loss. Most firms that manufacture high quality stereos offer reasonable repair warranties. The time it takes to repair a stereo, however, can be frustratingly long. Thus some retailers, particularly small specialized stereo shops, provide loaners should repairs under warranty be needed.

Image Congruence

The final explanation for BL to be considered is image congruence. The basic idea underlying this concept is that buyers have images of themselves, images of many of the products they buy, and tend to purchase brands, or shop at stores, that have images similar to (i.e., congruent with) their self-image.

A study by Dolich (1969) illustrates the image congruence concept. Dolich had subjects rate themselves on a series of bipolar adjectives using a seven point scale. An example would be

the person I am

$$1 \quad 2 \quad 3 \quad 4 \quad 5 \quad 6 \quad 7$$

complex ____ : ____ : __X__ : ____ : ____ : ____ : ____ simple

This particular subject indicates a self-image that tends slightly in the complex direction. The other 21 adjective pairs include good–bad, masculine–feminine, exciting–dull, and sophisticated–unsophisticated, etc. Dolich next asked subjects to rate their most and least preferred brands of four products: beer, cigarettes, bar soap, and toothpaste. He found that the image of the most preferred brand was much more congruent with subjects' self-image than the image of the least preferred brand.

Since the topic of self-image is considered extensively in Chapter 13, where individual differences are discussed, this topic shall not be pursued further here. It is sufficient to say that a number of studies have shown the validity of the concept of image congruence for products (e.g., Birdwell 1968; Grubb and Hupp 1968) and for store patronage (see Granbois 1977, pp. 279–290 for a summary of this literature).[6] As shall be seen in Chapter 8, whether this congruence relationship precedes or follows brand or store choice is open to question. This question, however, does not necessarily affect the validity of image congruence as a basis for developing and maintaining loyalty toward a brand, store, or any other potential choice object.

Image congruence has relatively obvious managerial implications. Recognizing the self-images of their customers and potential customers and how the brands

---

[6]Readers interested in store image will find the winter 1974–1975 issue of the *Journal of Retailing* especially interesting. This issue of the journal was devoted entirely to the topic of store image.

selected or stores patronized help reinforce and communicate those self-images can provide very useful information for developing the firm's marketing strategy. For example, knowing that certain buyers have a fashion conscious, stylish self-image suggests several things to a clothing manufacturer about product design, promotional messages, and distribution.

Gensch (1978) suggests a useful distinction between situations where buyers have relatively objective factors available upon which to base their brand images and situations where this is not possible. Regarding the latter situation, it is well known that for many product classes (e.g., beer, cigarettes), buyers have relatively strong brand preferences and yet cannot identify their favorite brand in blind taste tests. Clearly, in such a situation, promotion can be extremely important in altering the brand image to fit the self-image of a specific target group of buyers. One of the most fascinating examples of such a change in image is Marlboro cigarettes. In the mid-1950s, Marlboro underwent a radical change from a weak selling cigarette with a feminine image to a strong selling national brand with a distinctly masculine image. This change was created with a different and massive mass advertising program, modest product changes that were not emphasized in the ads, and *without* a change in name (for details see Aakers and Myers 1975, pp. 141–145).

Even when images are based upon more objective factors, a knowledge of buyers' brand images can be useful. First, buyers may have acquired incorrect brand images, which keep them from purchasing. Second, it may be possible, and feasible, to alter the product itself as a basis for creating a more favorable brand image. And, third, it reminds the firm of the need to maintain a consistent quality in lines where multiple items carry the same brand name. This is an important reason for creating separate brand names for lines of different quality; e.g., Chevrolet and Cadillac or GE and Hotpoint.

Stop here

STOCHASTIC MODELS OF BRAND LOYALTY, REPEAT PURCHASE BEHAVIOR, AND BRAND SWITCHING

The explanations for RPB and BL that have been considered so far provide the basis for developing specific *deterministic* models of the processes through which buyers make their brand choices, decide to engage in RPB, or become BL. The perceived risk explanation, for example, tells us that the degree of BL developed by the buyer is *determined* by the amount of risk perceived in the product class. The explanation contains no random, probabilistic, or as it is frequently called, stochastic element.

This concluding section will briefly describe two stochastic models of brand switching, both of which are quite complex. Therefore, no attempt will be made to describe them mathematically. Rather, after describing their most important features, focus will shift to the usefulness of these models for managerial decision making. The primary objective in this section is to make the reader aware of the existence of a sophisticated, and rapidly developing, mathematical technology for assessing buyers' brand switching behavior and how that knowledge may be used in the development of more effective marketing strategies. Appendix B describes several relatively simple brand switching models from a more mathematical perspective.

Two Preliminary Points Regarding Stochastic Models of Brand Switching

Before beginning this discussion, two preliminary points need to be made. First, it is generally thought that most stochastic models of brand switching are more descriptions than explanations of buyer behavior. Kalwani and Morrison, in a concluding statement on the first model to be discussed, argue that

> We believe that the Hendry (and other similar) approaches are nothing more than parsimonious *descriptions* of consumer brand switching behavior, albeit very useful and insightful descriptions. Others argue strongly that these approaches constitute a *theory* of switching behavior. We have only focused on the descriptive aspects in this paper, electing to leave the theorizing to some of our stochastic-model-building colleagues (1977, pp. 476–477, emphasis in original).

One of these "stochastic-model-building-colleagues" is Frank Bass, who argued strongly that a full understanding of buyers' brand *choice* processes must include a random or stochastic element (Bass 1974). Although Bass's opinion does not appear to be the prevailing one, he made a cogent argument for this point of view.

Second, most quantitative models of brand switching are models of RPB rather than BL. As shall be seen in the discussion of the second model, however, it is possible to include an element in such models to measure preference for different brands. Although not sufficient for defining a true state of BL, the inclusion of preference measures does represent a step away from strict RPB in the direction of true BL.

Hendry Model

The Hendry model, or system as it is frequently called, is a proprietary system and many of its details have never been publicly revealed.[7] Consequently, its validity has never been publicly tested. Despite its proprietary nature there are a number of reasons for discussing this model. First, it appears to be one of, if not the, most widely used stochastic brand switching models (Howard 1977, p. 245). Second, its properties are such that it is basically appropriate only in situations where most buyers can be assumed to be in RRB and, therefore, provides an opportunity to discuss the characteristics of RRB from a slightly more technical perspective. Third, according to the Hendry Corporation, the model yields a number of significant insights of managerial relevance.

In the terminology used to describe stochastic brand switching models, the Hendry model can be characterized as (1) zero-order, (2) heterogeneous, and (3) aggregate. The first characteristic refers to the fact that it is assumed that the probability of purchasing any particular brand is *not* influenced by any prior purchase. Whatever change occurs in the probability of purchasing each brand is assumed in a zero-order model to be attributable to changes in the environment rather than to buyer experience (buyer learning) from prior purchases. In terms of this chapter, the zero-order assumption is most appropriate when the buyer is in RRB. Second, the Hendry model allows each buyer to have a different set of purchase probabilities for the brands in the buyer's evoked set; this is what is meant by heterogeneous. Such heterogeneity is usually introduced into stochastic

---

[7]A review of the basic Hendry model, which requires more diligence than mathematical skill to follow, can be found in Kalwani and Morrison (1977).

models by assuming that the probability of purchase is distributed according to some distribution. For example, it might be assumed that these probabilities are normally distributed. Since the normal distribution is completely defined by its mean and variance, the researcher would have to estimate these parameters. In practice, distributions that are more flexible than the normal distribution (i.e., capable of assuming a wider range of shapes depending on specific parameter estimates) are used to build stochastic models of brand switching. Third, the Hendry model is an aggregate model because the parameters of the model are estimated from market share data rather than built up from data on individual buyers.

The Hendry model actually consists of two separate components. The first is a procedure for dividing a product class into a set of partitions. Within each partition buyers are assumed to view alternative brands as direct substitutes. As Kalwani and Morrison note

> From a marketing practitioner's viewpoint this is operationally one of the most important concepts underlying the Hendry approach.... A correctly identified preference structure provides the appropriate competitive frame for assessing the relative performance of brands in terms of market share, sales volume, profitability, etc. The preference structure gives an idea of the relative influence of marketing strategies and, thus, helps in the development of strategic marketing plans. In the Hendry system, the structure of partitioning within a product class is determined by analyzing actual consumer brand switching behavior. This is in opposition to the general practice of discovering the structure of partitioning through the judgment of marketing managers and/or consumers' perceptions of the brands (1977, pp. 471–472).

Figure 5.3 illustrates a simple, hypothetical example of two different partitionings of the margarine market. In one case, buyers first decide whether to buy cups or sticks and, only afterward, the specific brand to purchase. Just the opposite occurs in the second partitioning scheme. Knowing which partitioning system is correct has important implications in terms of defining a firm's principal competitors and for such things as the firm's promotion and pricing strategies.

Figure 5.3
Two hypothetical examples of partitioning in the Hendry system

Source: Manohar U. Kalwani and Donald G. Morrison, "A Parsimonious Description of the Hendry System," *Management Science,* 23 (January 1977): 473. Copyright 1977 The Institute of Management Sciences.

I. A Form Primary Market

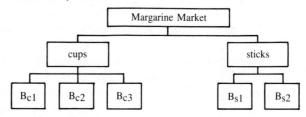

II. A Brand Primary Market

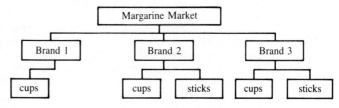

Figure 5.4
Assumed distribution of probability of purchase in Hendry for any brand *i*

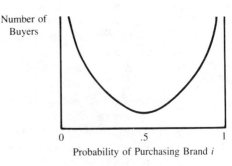

The second component of the Hendry model is the brand switching model. Underlying this model is an assumption that the distribution of the probability of purchase for any specific brand is generally "bath tub" shaped. As can be seen from Figure 5.4 this means that most buyers have a probability of purchasing any specific brand that tends to be closer to 0 or 1 than .5.[8] This distribution, of course, is quite consistent with the small, stable evoked set, which is typical of RRB.

According to the Hendry Corporation, a number of very useful insights may be gained from the Hendry model. One of the most important and interesting of these insights is called "par market share." Par market share is the share of the market that the next brand introduced into the market can expect to achieve, *assuming* the new brand meets normal industry standards of product design, quality, and marketing. It is important to recognize that par market share is a property of the market and not of the brand. That is, some markets are more vulnerable to new brand entries than others. Knowing which markets are vulnerable, before having to engage in expensive product development and test marketing, is obviously of great value to the firm.

The concept of par market share may at first appear unsound. Remember, however, that the Hendry model appears to be most applicable to low cost, frequently purchased, nondurable goods where most buyers are in RRB. Such products are usually in the mature stage of their life cycles and very standardized. This is why the phrase "assuming the new brand meets normal industry standards" is important in defining par market share. According to Ben Butler, Jr., president of the Hendry Corporation, the Hendry model has led to a number of useful general insights regarding the effects of line extensions, including the likelihood that existing brands in a firm's current line will be "cannibalized" by a line extension. In an interview, reported in *Marketing News*, he listed some of his findings. These are displayed in Figure 5.5. The Hendry model is also purportedly able to help the firm assess the effects of pricing, advertising, and distribution decisions. However, very little information about these additional capabilities of the Hendry model is publicly available.

---

[8]An important implication of the Hendry model is that the market share for any new brand will *tend* to come from buyers at the trough of the probability of purchase distribution; i.e., from buyers whose probability of purchase is closer to .5 than 1 or 0. Recently, this idea has been challenged. In particular, Blattberg, Buesing, and Sen (1980) present data to suggest that a new national brand should be targeted at buyers who are loyal to existing national brands and private labels, as well as to the brand switching segment of the market.

Figure 5.5
Some principles on the effects of line extensions developed from the Hendry system

Source: Interview with Ben Butler, Jr., president of the Hendry Corporation in "Hendry System Gives Marketers Handle on Buyers Prior to New Brand Introduction." *Marketing News* (8 September 1978): 5. Reprinted with the kind permission of the American Marketing Association.

- The larger the brand share of a company's existing product(s), the greater will be the share of market obtained by the line extension product.

- The greater the degree to which competing brands share customers with each other, as reflected in consumer switching levels, the greater the percentage of incremental volume for a new line extension—and also the greater the percentage of cannibalism resulting.

- Absolute incremental volume expressed in share points gained by the brand increases as the brand share approaches 50 percent and decreases as brand share exceeds 50 percent.

- Absolute incremental volume for the *next* line extension, expressed in share points gained by the brand, decreases as the number of line extensions of a brand increases.

- The lower the existing brand's share, the greater the percentage incremental volume and the percentage increase in brand volume for the next line extension.

- The lower the brand share, the greater the *relative* loss in volume resulting from a line deletion. The higher the brand share (up to 50 percent share) the greater the *absolute* volume loss from line deletion.

- The greater the degree by which the brand share exceeds 50 percent share, the smaller the absolute volume loss from a line deletion.

"In the past," Butler said, "there have been many new product successes—some of which were spectacular and for which marketing executives deserved much credit. There have, however, also been many failures, due not to properties of the product but to properties of the market.

ASSESSOR

Currently being developed by researchers at M. I. T. (Silk and Urban 1978),[9] ASSESSOR is a brand switching model designed specifically to provide management with information on potential new product offerings *before* expensive market testing is conducted. More specifically

> ASSESSOR is a set of measurement procedures and models to aid management in evaluating new packaged goods before test marketing when a positioning strategy has been developed and executed to the point where the product, packaging, and advertising copy are available and an introductory marketing plan (price, promotion, and advertising) has been formulated. Given these inputs, the system is intended to:
>
> 1. Predict the new brand's equilibrium or long run market share.
>
> 2. Estimate the sources of the new brand's share—"cannibalization" of the firm's existing brand(s) and "draw" from competitors' brands.

[9]A somewhat less technical discussion of ASSESSOR, and several related models, can be found in Urban and Hauser (1980, Chapter 14).

3. Produce actionable diagnostic information for product improvement and the development of advertising copy and other creative materials.

4. Permit low cost screening of selected elements of alternative marketing plans (advertising, price, and package design) (Silk and Urban 1978, p. 173).

ASSESSOR may be contrasted with the Hendry model on a number of dimensions. First, the development of ASSESSOR has been more publicly visible; hence, much more is known about its details. Second, ASSESSOR is a disaggregated model; that is, the basic input data comes from individual buyers in contrast to Hendry, where the input data is market shares. Third, the brand switching portion of ASSESSOR is based on a first-order Markov process[10] rather than a zero-order probabilistic process. An important consequence of this is that new learning may occur from trial to trial; which, of course, would seem to be appropriate when a new brand is introduced to buyers.

Figure 5.6 presents the structure of the ASSESSOR system in flowchart form. The management input requires decisions regarding product specification, packaging, pricing, promotion, etc.; that is, the product and its marketing plan need to be well specified. The positioning strategy refers to management's perceptions of the brands with which the new brand is likely or intended to compete. Consumer input data are collected in a simulated shopping environment and in subsequent telephone interviews in which subjects are given an opportunity to repurchase the new brand. Table 5.2 presents the consumer data acquisition procedures in more detail.

At the heart of the ASSESSOR system are two separate models: one models buyer preferences while the other models trial and repeat purchase; both yield estimates of market share. While agreement between the two market share estimates does not *prove* that the estimates are correct, it increases confidence in the outputs of the ASSESSOR system.

Figure 5.6
Structure of the ASSESSOR system

Source: Alvin J. Silk and Glen L. Urban, "Pre-Test-Market Evaluation of New Packaged Goods: A Model and Measurement Methodology." *Journal of Marketing Research* 15 (May 1978): 173. Reprinted with the kind permission of the American Marketing Association.

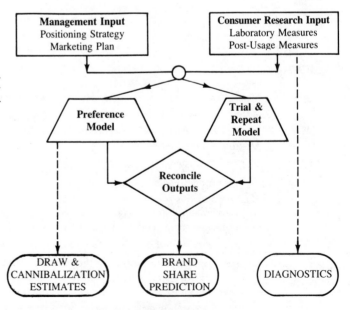

[10]An example of a first-order Markov brand switching model is described in Appendix B.

Table 5.2
Research design and measurement procedures for ASSESSOR system

Design	Procedure	Measurement
O_1	Respondent screening and recruitment (personal interview)	Criteria for target group identification (e.g., product class usage)
O_2	Premeasurement for established brands (self-administered questionnaire)	Composition of "relevant set" of established brands, attribute weights and ratings, and preferences
X_1	Exposure to advertising for established brands *and* new brand	
$[O_3]$	Measurement of reactions to the advertising materials (self-administered questionnaire)	Optional, e.g., likability and believability ratings of advertising materials
X_2	Simulated shopping trip and exposure to display of new and established brands	
O_4	Purchase opportunity (choice recorded by research personnel)	Brand(s) purchased
X_3	Home use/consumption of new brand	
O_5	Post-usage measurement (telephone interview)	New brand usage rate, satisfaction ratings, and repeat purchase propensity: attribute ratings and preferences for "relevant set" of established brands plus the new brand

O = Measurement.
X = Advertising or product exposure.

Source: Alvin J. Silk and Glen L. Urban, "Pre-Test-Market Evaluation of New Packaged Goods: A Model and Measurement Methology." *Journal of Marketing Research* 15 (May 1978): 174. Reprinted with the kind permission of the American Marketing Association.

The preference model is based on research that relates preferences to the probability of choice. Estimates of the market shares of existing brands can be made from stated preferences for these brands. If the model is appropriate the estimates should agree approximately with known market shares. Adding the preference data for the new brand allows estimating the market share for the new brand, as well as estimating the degree to which share will be "drawn" from competitors and "cannibalize" existing brands in the firm's current product line.

The trial and repeat model is based upon a widely used scheme for predicting the market share of a new brand. In equation form this model, which is originally due to Parfitt and Collins (1968), can be stated as

$$M(t) = TS$$

where $M(t)$ is market share for brand t, T is the proportion of buyers in the target market who ultimately try brand t, and S is the proportion of triers who continue to purchase brand t. For example, if 50 percent of the market tries brand t and 30 percent of triers continue purchasing, then brand t's ultimate share of the market is 15 percent; i.e., $.50 \times .30$.

Silk and Urban proceed to model T and S in detail. Estimates of T are based on such factors as the creation of brand awareness through advertising, the extent of product availability in retail outlets, and brand exposure through such things as free samples. S is modeled directly from purchase and repurchase data collected in the buyer study. Once the trial and repeat purchase model is constructed, management is in a position to estimate the effects of changing specific elements in the marketing plan. For example, one might ask what the effect on market share would be if awareness were increased 10 percent by additional advertising; or, what if distribution could be increased from 65 percent to 80 percent of the market. ASSESSOR provides a means for addressing these questions.

As Silk and Urban acknowledge (1978, p. 187) "No tightly controlled tests of the present system's predictive accuracy has been performed." Despite this, the initial results of ASSESSOR are very encouraging. Table 5.3 presents data for nine different new brand introductions where estimates from ASSESSOR and test market evaluations are both available. The tests are listed chronologically. Except for the first test (deodorant) the agreement between the two models (preference and trial-repeat purchase) and between predicted and observed market shares is quite close. These data clearly suggest the potential value of the ASSESSOR model for managerial decisions regarding new product introductions.

The Value of Quantitative Models

Although we have described the Hendry and ASSESSOR models only at a verbal level, the potential value of these and similar quantitative models as aids for managerial decision making should be obvious. The Hendry model provides a formal, mathematically specified procedure for defining a product class and its internal structure; i.e., its preference structure. Hendry also provides a mechanism for identifying *markets* that are potentially receptive to new brand introductions. ASSESSOR provides a mechanism for testing a *specific new brand* and its contemplated marketing plan before test marketing. Both of these models provide valuable managerial insights, which should aid marketing managers in making more effective and profitable decisions.

Must quantitative brand switching models be explanatory to be useful? Although brand switching behavior is frequently modeled as a probabilistic process no one seriously intends to suggest that real buyers actually go through the mental equivalent of flipping a coin in making their brand choices. Such probabilistic models can be *useful* as long as the description of buyer brand switching behavior is consistent with such a model. This could occur, for example, if the large number of variables that *explain* the brand choice decision vary across buyers and over purchase occasions in such a way that the brand choice itself begins to "look like" a probabilistic process. This was the reason for taking issue earlier with Jacoby and Chestnut's assertion that random events were not worth the expenditure of managerial time necessary to study such events. Both Hendry and ASSESSOR suggest the value of modeling random events. Appendix B considers several additional brand switching models from a more mathematical perspective.

SUMMARY

The existence of a small evoked set implies a high degree of RPB. The chapter argues that much RPB reflects true BL and that understanding the factors that

Table 5.3
Predicted and observed market shares in the application of ASSESSOR to nine new packaged goods

Product	Timing of pre-test in relation to test market		Difference in share predictions of preference and trial-repeat models[a]	Market share (%)		Deviation[b]
	Concurrent	Before		Predicted	Observed	
Deodorant	✓		+7.3	13.3	10.4	+2.9
Antacid	✓		−0.9	9.6	10.5	−0.9
Laundry ingredient	✓		+0.1	1.8	1.8[c] / 2.0	−0.1
Household cleanser		✓	−0.4	12.0	12.5	−0.5
Shampoo		✓	+0.7	3.0	3.2	−0.2
Dishwashing ingredient		✓	−0.2	9.3	8.5	+0.8
Pain reliever		✓	+1.0	3.0	2.0	+1.0
Fruit drink		✓	−0.2	4.9	5.0	−0.1
Cereal		✓	+0.1	6.0	4.4	+1.6
Average (Absolute)			1.2	7.0	6.5	0.9

[a]Market share prediction obtained from the preference model minus that obtained from the trial-repeat model.

[b]Predicted minus observed market shares.

[c]Shares observed in two test market cities. The "observed" share used to calculate the "deviation" for this product was the mean of these two figures.

Source: Alvin J. Silk and Glen L. Urban, "Pre-Test-Market Evaluation of New Packaged Goods: A Model and Measurement Methodology," *Journal of Marketing Research*, 15 (May 1978): 188. Reprinted with the kind permission of the American Marketing Association.

cause BL has important implications for marketing decision making. In particular, it is argued that building loyalty among customers is a key marketing task.

The discussion of quantitative models of brand switching shows how such models can facilitate managerial decision making. A particular concern of many of these models is the prediction of the success, usually expressed in terms of market share, of new brand introductions into an established product class. For the buyer to consider such a new brand requires a shift from RRB to limited problem solving.

While quantitative brand switching models provide insights into the process and outcome of limited problem solving, they provide little insight into why or how a buyer comes to actually develop a new brand concept for an existing product class. Understanding the process through which buyers form new brand concepts requires an understanding of motivation, the learning process itself, and attitude formation and change. It is to these topics that Part III is devoted.

Limited
Problem Solving

III

As seen in Part II, the essence of routinized response behavior is stability. In particular, routinized response behavior is characterized by choice from a small, stable evoked set of brands via a well defined, stable plan (intention) for implementing purchase decisions routinely in a changing environment. The next two parts consider the behavior of buyers faced with purchasing tasks that cannot be decided routinely.

Part III discusses a number of topics that are particularly relevant to decision-making processes faced by buyers when the basic product class concept is well understood but additional information and evaluation of brands within the product class is necessary before a final decision can be made. This type of buying problem is referred to as limited problem solving (LPS) because new learning is largely limited to brands within the product class and new learning about the basic nature of the product class itself is not required. Consequently, while buyers need additional information, they generally know what kinds of information are needed, where such information can be acquired, and how to evaluate the information once it is found. That is, in LPS buyers have well developed cognitive frameworks for acquiring and evaluating new brand information.

The information acquisition and evaluation that occurs in LPS is directed toward the satisfaction of buyers' motives. Thus, what buyers must learn in LPS is the motive satisfying capacities of brands within a product class. Attitude toward a specific brand is one of the most important results of this learning. Indeed, building favorable attitudes among buyers is generally regarded as one of the marketing manager's principal objectives.

As noted in Part II, limited problem solving is most likely to occur for infrequently purchased durable goods such as automobiles, refrigerators, and cameras. Under such circumstances buyers' efforts to learn the motive satisfying properties of brands within a product class may be viewed most clearly and unambiguously. The topics of motivation, learning, and attitudes, however, are also relevant to routinized response behavior and extensive problem solving.

In routinized response behavior only the results of learning are observed. Nevertheless, the marketing manager who desires to entice customers of competitive brands, protect products from competitive assaults, or introduce a new brand into an established market will find the topics discussed in Part III of considerable value in the development of effective marketing strategies. The same point applies to extensive problem solving. Here, however, both the buyer and marketing manager must grapple with an *additional* set of problems that arises from the buyer's lack of understanding of the basic nature of the new and unfamiliar product class.

Motivation

6

When a person is observed engaging in an action, such as buying designer jeans, the inclination is to ask *why* this action was taken. One answer is to say that the action, or behavior, occurs because the person is *motivated* to do it. Perhaps, our hypothetical buyer is motivated by a need for the social status obtained by wearing designer jeans; or, perhaps there is some other reason for this particular action. Theories of motivation are designed to provide explanations as to why buyers behave as they do. The important insights into buyer behavior they provide can lead to more effective managerial decisions.

After a brief discussion of the concept of a motive, the majority of the chapter is devoted to examining a number of different theories of motivation. Problems and marketing opportunities can arise when a buying decision puts two or more motives in conflict and these are considered next. Finally, two motives are used with sufficient frequency by marketers to require special consideration: eros (romantic love) and fear.

As noted in Chapter 1, Harold Kassarjian observed that motivation "has not been studied much in recent years" (1982, p. 642). Despite this observation, the concept of motivation has been and continues to be of central concern to marketers. Most research on motivation, however, has been conducted by psychologists with marketers drawing indirect inferences regarding the implications for marketing strategy. The discussion in the remainder of this chapter directly reflects this state of the art of motivation theory in the study of buyer behavior.

THE CONCEPT OF A MOTIVE[1]

Motives Energize and Direct Behavior

The motive concept is concerned with the reasons that behavior occurs. Traditionally, motivation has been thought of as consisting of two components: first, the vigor or energy associated with the behavior; and second, the direction of the behavior. In the designer jeans example, one might ask what level of energy is put into the behavior (e.g., does the buyer make a special trip for this purchase), and why does the purchase of designer jeans satisfy a social status motive better than some other behavior that might convey social status.

Motives Are Unobservable

It must be remembered that motives are internal states of the buyer and are, even in principle, unobservable. One can, to be sure, observe behavior and infer a relevant motive; e.g., many people say designer jeans have social status value and, therefore, a person buying designer jeans may be thought at least partially to be trying to satisfy a social status motive. Based on this knowledge, a very successful advertising campaign for designer jeans may be built on a theme of social approval. All of this may suggest, quite properly, that social status motivation is present and can be satisfied (at least partially) by purchasing designer jeans. But, while the

---

[1]For a full psychological treatment of the concept of a motive, see any text on motivation theory. A particularly good and current motivation text is Petri (1981).

indicators of motives may be observed, the motives are never seen directly. An inferential process is always at work.

The point is that one must be very careful and always alert to the possibility that the nature of the motive may not have been correctly inferred. Our buyer of designer jeans, for example, may be motivated not by a motive for social status but rather by a motive to belong; a different interpretation of the same behavior with other obvious implications for promotion. Thus, a sensitivity to the problem of inference *and* careful research are required before the marketing plan is implemented.

Learned Motives

A second point can be introduced by recalling the roll of motives in the Howard-Sheth theory of buyer behavior. Specifically, they argue that motives energize, but do not direct, behavior. The directing function has been assigned to the construct choice criteria. The separation of these functions is partially semantic. It does, however, call attention to the fact that some theories and theorists, mostly older ones, have tried to confine the study of motivation to the energizing of behavior, leaving the question of direction to learning theorists.

Many theories of motivation, however, deal with motives that are not directly biologically based but are learned. The inclusion of theories of motivation that are *not* directly based on biological needs requires the acknowledgement that motives are not immutable but are, rather, constantly evolving through complex individual learning and social conditioning processes.

Multiple Motives

A third point concerns the tendency to speak of single motives. It may be true that a single motive dominates the final brand choice decision. Rarely, however, will a purchase be addressed to a single motive. To return to the example of designer jeans, our buyer's final brand choice may well be determined by social status motives. But there is also very likely a need for protection from the elements and a need for peer approval, among other possible motives, for this particular purchase.

Unconscious Motives

A fourth point concerns unconscious motives. The concept of the unconscious is largely attributable to Freud and, as Hall and Lindzey (1968) noted, psychoanalytic theory developed in a patient-therapist environment without a strong experimental research tradition that could provide an objective basis for validating the concept of unconscious motives. Although intuitively appealing, the idea of unconscious motivation has not proven especially productive for the development of buyer behavior theory and research.

Despite these problems the question of the existence of unconscious motives raises a very important point. Specifically, a person's unwillingness to reveal a motive must be sharply distinguished from his or her inability to do so. A person buying designer jeans, for example, may be fulfilling some *deeply repressed* sexual fantasy while giving an interviewer a rather different description of the motives underlying the purchase. On the other hand, this buyer may be quite aware of the sexual significance of the purchase but be unwilling to reveal the true motives publicly.

Another significant point regarding unconscious motivation is that the distinction between conscious and unconscious is becoming increasingly less clear. As Hall and Lindzey (1968, p. 259) note, in his earlier writings Freud spoke of the unconscious and conscious minds as regions of the brain. In his later writings, the conscious and unconscious became more psychological and less physiological. Interestingly, as we learn more about the physiology of the brain (e.g., Hansen 1981), it becomes increasingly likely that what has been called consciousness represents brain activities that are accessible to the speech center of the brain *and* that areas of the brain not readily accessible to the speech center can also affect behavior. This provocative topic will return in the discussion of attention and search in Chapter 11.

Competing and Complementary Theories

The fifth, and final, point concerns the degree to which the different theories of motivation presented in this chapter are competing or complementary. Many of the theories *are* in conflict to such a degree that one cannot be accepted as correct for explaining a particular behavior without rejecting other theories. There is, however, no single, generally accepted theory of motivation. Indeed, it is not clear that there *must* be a *single* true theory of motivation. It is quite possible that different types of behavior may require different motivational theories for their explanation. Therefore, in the pages that follow, a number of motivational theories will be examined from the perspective of how knowledge of each can contribute to the understanding of buyer behavior and the development of effective marketing strategies.

INSTINCT THEORIES

Early Instinct "Theories"

Instinct theories are among the oldest systematic theories of motivation. As originally developed, instinct "theories" often amounted to little more than naming an observed behavior. McDougall (1908, 1932), for example, identified a large, and changing, number of instincts including food-seeking, disgust, sex, fear, and curiosity. Clearly, many of these "instincts" amount to simple labeling of observed behavior. Holt (1931, p. 4) scathingly describes this practice, which was previously warned about, as follows: "Thus everything is explained with the facility of magic—word magic".

Modern Conceptions of Instinct

Recently, scientists known as ethologists (e.g., Lorenz 1952; Tinbergen 1951) have resurrected the concept of instincts and subjected theories of instinctual behavior to rigorous scientific testing. Common examples of instinctive animal behaviors are the migratory flights of birds and the spawning behavior of salmon. Kimble describes instinctive behavior in the following way.

> Instinctive behavior is defined as an unlearned, relatively stereotyped act or
> series of acts ... which is tied to some specific environmental stimulus.... The

energy (psychologically, drive) for instinctive behavior is thought of as existing in the nervous system as *action specific energy.* Instinctive behavior is elicited by a highly specific stimulus, or releaser, which initiates the action of a neurological *innate releasing mechanism.* Except in the presence of a releaser, the action specific energy is held in check or blocked, so that the instinctive act ordinarily occurs only to the biologically appropriate stimulus (1968, p. 425).

Instinctual Behavior in Humans

The phrase "biologically appropriate stimulus" in the preceding quote is quite important. Instincts presumably develop because they have survival value for the species. Given the proper releasing mechanism, the behavior will *automatically* occur unless something specifically blocks it. For example, a sizeable literature on the *bonding* of mothers (and more recently fathers) to their infants suggests that certain attributes of newborns elicit instinctual reactions to the infant (Klaus and Kennell 1976), reactions that clearly have survival value. Such bonding may contribute to the normally positive response that adults typically display toward any infant; an idea with obvious implications for advertising.

Other behaviors that have been suggested to have an instinctual base include smiling (Berlyne 1968) and aggression and defense of a personal space or territory (Lorenz 1966). Whether these, and other, behaviors are truly instinctual is controversial. This is due both to the existence of contradictory evidence and to the enormous difficulty of creating (with human subjects) conditions where opportunities for learned behavior can be controlled or eliminated. From a marketing viewpoint, of course, the question of whether motives such as aggression are instinctual or learned is of less importance than the fact that appeals to these motives can be quite effective. As an example, consider the strong themes of territoriality implicit or explicit in the marketing of fences.

Although the importance of truly instinctual human behavior is quite controversial, there is little doubt that behaviors that have frequently been regarded as instinctual can be influenced by learning (Kimble 1968). Human behavior is, of course, greatly influenced by learning and the theories of motivation that involve learning make use of that influence. It is to these theories that the text now turns.

DRIVE THEORIES

The Drive Concept

Instinctual behavior is characterized by a genetically programmed pattern of behavior. Certain migratory animals, for example, are able to return to the spot of their birth, even when raised without contact with other members of their species, a procedure which would seem to preclude learning the way home. Drive theories, in comparison, postulate an internal source of energy that quite literally, *drives* the organism to action. The action or behavior that will satisfy the drive, however, is *not* genetically programmed but must be learned.

Berkowitz summarizes the traditional view of drive as follows:

> ... From the time the term "drive" was first introuced into psychology in 1918 by Woodworth, the concept has referred to an internal excitement which presumably impelled the organism to action. The stimulation was supposedly the result of deprivations which produced either lack of tissue substances necessary for survival (as in the case of hunger) or an excess of other substances (as in sex). Whatever the specific nature of the deprivation, the tissue requirements gave rise to peripheral stimulation, such as stomach contractions, which then automatically drove the behavior until objects could be found which would satisfy the tissue needs (1969, p. 59).

Note the phrase "until objects could be found." A hungry or sexually deprived organism must *learn* what objects will satisfy those specific motives and which behaviors are necessary to obtain those objects.

The drive theory of motivation and learning theory would appear to be intimately related. This is indeed the case, as shall be seen in detail in the next chapter's examination of learning theory. In anticipation of that discussion it need only be said that drive is an aversive state, which the organism seeks to reduce; that reduction of drive is pleasurable or rewarding; and that it is this rewarding effect which produces learning. The immediate problem, however, is to understand the nature of the factors that are capable of producing drive or acquiring drive properties; therefore, a full discussion of learning theory must be sidestepped for now although acknowledging its role, especially in what are referred to as secondary motives.

Primary Motives

Primary motives are those that arise directly from the biological needs of the organism. Such motives are presumably necessary for survival of the organism. Organisms incapable of satisfying primary motives simply cannot survive and the species perishes. The list of primary motives has varied over time and by researcher; but hunger, sex, thirst, and pain avoidance are those most commonly cited.[2] Because primary motives are so primitive and basic, their immediate value to marketers in a high level economy, such as the United States, is limited. That is, behavior arising from the thirst motive may explain very little about how to market COKE to teenagers or other target groups of buyers.

Secondary Motives

The motives that are variously described as secondary, learned, or acquired are of considerably more interest to marketing than primary motives per se. The list of secondary motives could be almost as long as one might care to make it; but examples that have been frequently researched include fear, achievement, and affiliation. All secondary motives share one important property: they acquire their ability to motivate or drive behavior by being linked to primary drives.

Fear can serve as an example of how a secondary motive is acquired. How does a person come to fear the word fire. Presumably the word fire would not elicit any particular behavior, such as preparing to run, from a person who had

---

[2] Many introductory psychology texts discuss the physiological basis of primary motives. For a particularly good elementary discussion see Wrightsman and Sanford (1975, pp. 287–301).

never heard the word. (It may help to think of being warned about a fire by someone using a foreign language.) If such a naive person hears the word fire (a neutral stimulus) and immediately thereafter experiences the pain of a burn from that fire (a primary motive), the word fire may become capable of eliciting certain behaviors, such as preparing to run. Thus, the word fire has come to be capable of driving or motivating behavior because of its association with the primary motive pain.

In principle, virtually any secondary motive can be acquired by linking it with a primary motive. In this way, it is possible for people to acquire motives for achievement, affiliation, status, power, ad infinitum. Two points regarding such secondary motives are very important. First, over time a secondary motive can become autonomous from the primary motive from which the secondary motive first derived its drive power. Second, the level of drive that a secondary motive has can be very strong. Both points can be illustrated by the motivating effects of grades on most students. Clearly, grades are not a primary motive. Indeed, most parents use a variety of devices such as punishments and rewards to get their children to achieve high grades. Long after such primary rewards have been withdrawn, however, grades continue to have a strong influence on behavior. (Many of you, I am sure, have spent an "all-nighter" in a frantic attempt to improve your course grade enough to push it over into the next higher grade category with the *only* immediate reward being the higher grade itself.)

One final point regarding the distinction between primary and secondary motives needs to be made. Specifically, once a secondary motive has been well established it may become the basis for another secondary motive. As an example, consider fear. Fear, as has already been discussed, is a secondary motive based on the primary motive of pain avoidance. There is good evidence (Berkowitz 1969) that fear is the basis upon which a large number of other secondary motives are based; e.g., striving for wealth. Schachter (1959), for example, experimentally increased the level of anxiety (fear) in subjects by leading them to believe electric shocks would be given later, although, in fact, they never were given. As a result, his anxious subjects showed an increased desire to be with other people (affiliation motive). This affiliation motive had presumably been learned because it can reduce the secondary motive, fear.

Uses and Limitations of the Drive Concept

There is little doubt that an understanding of primary and secondary drives can contribute to our understanding of human behavior. And, from the few examples cited here, it should be quite clear that understanding the drive concept is very important to a proper understanding of buyer behavior. Think, for example, of the number of products that are promoted with a strong and explicit affiliation theme and an implicit fear of rejection if the viewer does not purchase the advertised product.

Despite their many contributions to the understanding of human behavior, drive theories are not without their problems and limitations. In general, the problems are of two types. First, behaviors have been observed that contradict the drive theory predictions. A rat, for example, will tend to run a maze faster if it is given a small piece of cheese (the reward at the end of the maze) despite the fact that it does *not* appear possible for the hunger drive to have increased. Second, much evidence, accumulated in recent years, has found that organisms will often go out of their way to seek external stimulation. The reader, no doubt, has experienced the very unpleasant feelings that arise from having too little to do; e.g., being completely alone on a rainy day. Various theories have been proposed for dealing with these problems and it is to these theories that the chapter now turns.

INCENTIVE THEORIES

To understand more fully the problems with drive theories that incentive theories attempt to solve, recall Berkowitz's description of primary drive as a tissue deprivation "which then automatically drove the behavior until objects could be found which would satisfy the tissue needs." That is, except for extreme deprivation, a deprived organism should be more active than one not so deprived. Both casual observation and careful experimental studies, however, show that this expected differential activity level often does not occur. Food deprivation studies with rats, for example, show that deprived and nondeprived rats have the same activity level when food is not present. However, when food is introduced the reaction of the deprived animals is greater than the nondeprived animals; a finding that is consistent with drive theory. There is, however, an additional problem, as noted earlier. A rat, or other animal, in a laboratory setting will often work harder for a reward if it is first given a sample of the reward; a finding which drive theories have some difficulty assimilating.

The Concept of an Incentive

Incentive theorists have postulated two concepts for dealing with the problems mentioned earlier. The first is called the sensitization-invigoration mechanism (SIM). The function of the SIM is to explain the energizing or invigorating effect on behavior of selective sensitization to specific stimuli. How many times, for example, have you *suddenly* found yourself made hungry by the presence or smell of food, perhaps only a picture of food; or, how often have you been sexually aroused by the *sight* of a potential partner. In both instances there are specific physiological mechanisms at work. What the SIM posits is that these physiological mechanisms do not *drive* the organism but rather *sensitize* it to specific types of stimuli, e.g., food or a potential sexual partner. Berger and Lambert (1968, p. 102) suggest that "This [SIM] effect is probably an innate one, but one that can be modified by learning."

The second construct posited by incentive theorists is known as the anticipation-invigoration mechanism (AIM). The AIM construct postulates that the organism is energized or invigorated by previously learned expectations of reward. The anticipation of reward, for example, is why a rat runs faster in a maze when given a sample of cheese at the start of the task. Incentive theories assume that the organism knows the consequences of its behavior, that the organism has goals.

One important difference between drive and incentive theories is their focus on internal and external factors in motivation. Drive theories focus on the internal (primary and secondary) needs of the individual. In contrast, incentive theories focus on the ability of external stimulus to affect behavior. Note carefully that incentive theories do *not* posit an absence of internal motivation. Rather they focus on the degree to which this presumed latent internal motivation can be energized and directed by specific external stimuli.

Buyer Behavior Implications

This focus on external stimuli is clearly of importance for marketing because, while marketers have little ability to control primary or even secondary drives, they do have control over some of the stimuli that influence buyer behavior. These stimuli, of course, are the traditional marketing mix variables: product, price, promotion, and distribution. People, for example, may have hunger needs that can be satisfied by cereal. But it takes careful product testing to determine the best product characteristics (the stimuli) to serve a specific market segment. In a similar way, retailers of high fashion, high price women's clothing typically go to considerable effort and expense to create an environment that will cause the buyer to *anticipate* the excitement and the social superiority that can come from wearing designer clothes. The reader should be able to think of many additional examples of how marketing mix variables can be used explicitly as stimuli to elicit buyer anticipations of the rewards (or avoidance of punishment) that can be experienced by purchasing the seller's good or service.

AROUSAL THEORIES ˉ *NOT TOO impT.*

Stimulus Seeking Behavior

A second major challenge to traditional drive theories of motivation comes from the abundant evidence, from both casual observation and careful laboratory research, that organisms often go out of their way to seek stimulation. Laboratory research, for example, shows that monkeys will work hard and learn just for an opportunity to view novel objects; e.g., to watch a toy train run. Also, rats that have learned both a simple and a complex maze often prefer a complex maze if given a choice. A third example involves what is called spontaneous alteration. In studies with rats it has been found that

> Many of them, after being rewarded for turning right will turn left the next time. These rats will develop a pattern of alteration in which they will go first right and then left. Each time this alteration occurs, *they are going toward the goal with less attraction in terms of recency of reward.* This phenomena has also been observed in humans (Schultz 1964). (Faison 1977, p. 173, emphasis added).

Each of these examples is clearly incompatible with a pure drive theory of motivation and suggests that the organism being studied is going out of its way to seek stimulation.[3]

In a similar way, many everyday examples of human behavior may be seen where the people act in ways that are clearly stimulating rather than drive reducing. Consider mountain climbing, going to a movie, a "Sunday" drive, reading the

---

[3]For a full discussion of these and other examples the reader is referred to Berkowitz (1968, especially pp. 108–113), Bourne and Ekstrand (1979, Chapter 7, especially pp. 255–257), and Faison (1977).

comics, or playing cards, to name but a few examples An even more dramatic example of stimulus seeking behavior comes from a December 27, 1971 report in *Time Magazine*. Over a period of three years, a group of bored volunteer firemen set, and then fought, some 40 fires because "we'd hang around the station on the night shift without a thing to do. We just wanted to get the red light flashing and the bells clanging" (cited in Bourne and Ekstrand 1979, p. 257). One final example illustrates just how strong the need for stimulation can be. In carefully controlled laboratory studies, generally referred to as sensory-deprivation experiments, human subjects were placed in an environment in which all sources of stimulation (e.g., sound, touch) are reduced to the absolute minimum possible. The subjects were instructed to remain as long as they could. A classic study by Bexton, Heron, and Scott (1954) found that few subjects could tolerate such conditions for very long. Many reported bizarre experiences, such as hallucinations, and virtually all reported that the environment was unpleasant despite the $25 daily pay to remain in the sensory deprived environment—a very high rate of pay in the early 1950s.

The Concept of Arousal

As the above examples make abundantly clear, organisms *often* seek stimulation. But it is equally clear that organisms *often* seek to reduce stimulation, to reduce drive. One way to resolve these seemingly contradictory data is to postulate that organisms seek to maintain an intermediate level of stimulation. This line of thinking, known as arousal or activation theory, represents a major extension of earlier theories of motivation.

A number of somewhat different arousal theories have been proposed; e.g., Berlyne (1960, 1963, 1968), Fiske and Maddi (1961), Hunt (1963), and Maddi (1968). Berlyne's theory, which is by far the best known and most frequently referenced arousal theory in the buyer behavior literature, will be used to illustrate the basic concepts. Figure 6.1 graphically presents some of the major ideas of Berlyne's theory.

Arousal is basically envisioned as a variable that measures the level of activation of the organism;[4] that is, how awake, alert, or activated is the organism. Arousal is generally conceived of as ranging on a continuum from extremely low (e.g., in deep sleep) to extremely high (e.g., in strong rage). For this reason arousal has been regarded by some theorists as a kind of general drive.

Stimuli are conceived of as having properties, called collative properties, that can cause arousal: e.g., novelty, surprisingness, change, ambiguity, incongruity, blurredness, and power to induce uncertainty (Berlyne 1963, p. 290). These properties are called collative because they must be collated or compared with what is already known by the individual. Because of the collative properties, the amount of

---

[4]Much of this research has been conducted at the physiological level of the central nervous system. In a seminal study, Olds and Milner (1954) demonstrated that rats would learn to press a bar, and would bar press thousands of times, to receive an electric stimulus to a specific area of the brain. Interestingly, rats strive equally hard to avoid having another specific area of the brain electrically stimulated. These brain centers, for obvious reasons, have come to be known as pleasure and pain centers. As the physiological aspects of arousal theory are enormously complex and controversial we shall not pursue them further; the interested reader is referred to Petri (1981, especially Chapter 3) for further details. Fortunately, as Berkowitz (1968) has argued, we can apply the insights gained from arousal theory without subscribing to any specific physiological mechanisms.

Figure 6.1
Relationship between arousal and arousal potential of a stimulus

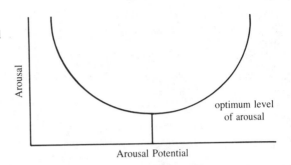

information contained in a stimulus is low and this causes uncertainty, which arouses the individual. As can be seen in Figure 6.1, arousal theory postulates that the organism seeks to maintain an optimal level of arousal and thus prefers stimuli with an intermediate level of arousal potential.

Many factors can affect the organism's preferred level of arousal. Among these are time of day, the specific stimulus, and differences among individuals. It is also known that small ups and downs in the level of arousal tend to be pleasurable. Berlyne calls these sought after changes "arousal jags." It is the pleasure associated with such jags that gives rise to a search for stimuli which are "moderately uncertain, novel, complex, surprising, or changing" (Berkowitz 1968, p. 111).

The preceding brief discussion has certainly not done justice to the richness of arousal theory. It is, however, sufficient for the immediate purpose of understanding the nature of buyer motivation. Berkowitz (1968, p. 104) places the usefulness of the arousal concept in perspective by stating that "the arousal notion is a helpful working concept for psychologists. A host of observations can be summarized using just a few words." The arousal concept is also very helpful for explaining a host of observations on buyer behavior.

Buyer Behavior Implications

Although working from a different perspective than arousal theory, Maloney (1962) argued that to be effective for promoting *new brands* the advertising message must elicit curiosity about the new product. Maloney further argues that this curiosity can be aroused by advertisements that create in the buyer a moderate amount of nonbelief and a low to medium amount of uncertainty. That is, curiosity can be aroused via the collative properties of advertisements.

The earliest effort to explicitly use arousal theory to explain buyer behavior was made by Howard and Sheth (1969). They based their theory of search behavior directly on arousal theory. Figure 6.2 displays their theory of search graphically. Note the similarity to Figure 6.1. The curve, except for the portion to the extreme right, is identical to Figure 6.1. Stimulus ambiguity appears in place of arousal potential because in the Howard-Sheth theory stimulus ambiguity is a major source of arousal. A stimulus may be ambiguous for many reasons; e.g., physical blurredness (a fuzzy TV picture), novelty (bean sprouts in salads), or incongruity (why would they call their car a bug?). It should be evident that these reasons for ambiguity correspond to the collative properties of a stimulus and cause arousal in the manner specified by Berlyne's theory. Stimulus ambiguity and arousal affect buyer search behavior in the following way.

Figure 6.2
Howard and Sheth's arousal-stimulus ambiguity theory
of search

Source: John A. Howard and Jagdish N. Sheth, *The Theory of Buyer Behavior.* New York: Wiley & Sons, 1969, p. 161. Reprinted with permission.

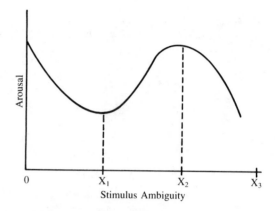

From 0 to X_1 (in Figure 6.2), the level of ambiguity is so low that the buyer is bored and is, therefore, aroused to search for ways to complicate the choice environment. In such circumstances, an individual might be tempted to try an unknown brand or even purchase from a new product class; e.g., buying a new brand of cereal just to try a new taste. Think, for example, of the number of advertisements that begin "Tired of the same old ..." From X_1 to X_2 ambiguity is moderately high and the buyer is aroused to search for information to simplify the choice; e.g., acquiring information on a number of brands of automobiles before making a final choice. If arousal becomes too high, to the right of X_2, distortions of the normal search process may occur. The buyer, for example, may attempt to avoid or postpone the purchase. Howard and Sheth (1969, Chapter 5) present substantial evidence consistent with the theory of search summarized in Figure 6.2. A particularly interesting implication of their arousal based search theory concerns brand loyalty.

> ... we postulate that a buyer may repeatedly pass through a cycle of loyalty and disloyalty. He tries a brand, likes it and becomes loyal. After a period of consuming it either he becomes bored or his aspiration level rises and he looks around for another brand. Executives in the detergent industry report that they observe this happening among consumers of detergent (Howard and Sheth, 1969, p. 166).

Indeed, a number of researchers (cf., McAlister 1982) have noted that two distinct phases of brand switching can be distinguished when subjects are asked to make repeated choices from a set of previously unfamiliar brands. The first stage is characterized by information seeking. This corresponds to the range X_1–X_2 in Figure 6.2. The second stage is characterized by "variety-seeking." This corresponds to the range 0–X, in Figure 6.2.

Recently, McAlister (1982) proposed and tested a so-called *dynamic attribute satiation* model of variety-seeking. This model views the consumption process as giving rise to inventories of product attributes (e.g., caffeine), which cumulate over time. It is presumed that these inventories yield diminishing marginal utility and deplete over time. As a consumer satiates on a specific product attribute (e.g., caffeine), the probability of change increases (e.g., consuming a noncaffeine beverage such as 7-Up). McAlister concludes that the dynamic attribute satiation model "reproduces preferences and predicts choices better than a model that does not consider past choices" (p. 147).

Hansen (1972) made arousal a key component of his "cognitive theory" of buyer behavior. Hansen relies heavily on the notion of an optimal level of arousal as is evidenced by his description of the effect of perceived risk on the buyer.

> Just as it is unwise to purchase a new product if it will be unsatisfactory, it may be unwise *not* to buy a new product if it will be better than the one presently used. That is, there is a possible risk of not obtaining the advantages inherent in a new product that really is superior. This formulation conforms to arousal theory as the quest for an intermediate level of arousal [that] will secure a strategy that balances the two counteracting "risks" (Hansen 1972, pp. 89–90, emphasis in original).

This notion of preferring an intermediate level of risk is consistent with a sizeable amount of research in psychology suggesting that many people prefer tasks of moderate difficulty and modest risk to extreme tasks (Berkowitz 1968). People do not always want to avoid all effort and all risk, although they appear to require some incremental reward for the extra effort or risk. Think, for example, of the many advertisements that state that the product is a *little* more difficult to use, expensive, . . . —but well worth it.

A large number of other examples could be cited in which arousal theory has been used to explain, or provide a framework for studying, buyer behavior. It is, for example, well known that frequent repetition of an advertisement leads to boredom and less effectiveness, which can be overcome by varying the components of the advertisement slightly while leaving the key elements of the message intact (Aakers and Myers 1975, p. 524). Faison (1977, p. 174) argues that this result is what one would expect from arousal theory. Recently, Hirschman (1980) proposed a model using arousal concepts for studying the processes by which buyers come to accept new products.

As the preceding examples suggest, the arousal theory of motivation provides a powerful mechanism for understanding a wide range of buyer behaviors. A single theoretical framework can be used to explain why buyers seek the novelty provided by new products and the variation of switching their purchases among a familiar set of brands; why buyers sometimes seek information to reduce the uncertainty of buying, seek information to enrich and complicate the brand choice problem, and, if arousal is too high, fail to engage in "normal search and purchase behavior"; and why it is important to vary the precise format of an advertisement when frequently repeating the same basic message. Clearly arousal theory has the potential for greatly increasing our understanding of buyer behavior.

The careful reader, however, may have noted that all of the preceding marketing examples refer to behavior that is *consistent with* arousal theory. For many reasons, buyer behavior research has not employed direct measures of arousal; however, two seem especially important. First, much of the equipment needed to measure arousal is quite sophisticated and most buyer behavior researchers have neither ready access to the equipment nor the expertise to use such equipment properly. Second, direct measures of arousal can create a highly unusual environment, which may seriously affect the behavior in question. Imagine, for example, watching commercials being flashed on a screen while you sit in a chair with electrodes attached to your scalp.

Recently, Kroeber-Riel (1979), using a physiological measure of arousal, presented evidence suggesting a positive relationship between level of arousal and recall of an advertisement. Ryan (1980), however, criticized this research on both conceptual and methodological grounds (see Kroeher-Riel 1980 for a rejoinder). Thus, while arousal theory provides a powerful theoretical device for understanding buyer behavior, it remains to be seen whether direct measures of arousal can be fruitfully employed in buyer behavior research. The prospect, however, is both intriguing and exciting.

COGNITIVE THEORIES

Cognitive Effects on Motivation

The theories of motivation considered so far are built upon "drive-like" mechanisms. Instinct, drive, incentive, and arousal theories do contain substantial and important differences in their conceptions of how behavior is energized and directed. What they share is, in a very general sense, a view of the individual being *pushed* by internal factors into behavior. In recent years, increasing attention has been paid to the effects of cognitions on motivation and behavior. Cognitive theories emphasize the rational, information acquisition and processing, decision-making aspects of motivation. In such theories, the individual is seen as a purposeful organism engaging in what in everyday parlance would be called thinking.

The idea that cognitive factors can affect motivation has already been touched upon in the discussion of the anticipation-invigoration mechanism (AIM) postulated to exist by incentive theorists. In this view, the organism anticipates the reward from the goal; e.g., from eating the food. Quite literally the organism "thinks" about the potential rewards and this cognitive activity increases its level of motivation. Incentive theorists, however, have traditionally focused their attention on the incentive properties of potential stimuli and have not developed the cognitive implications of their theory.

Another line of research, known as labeling of emotions, shows very clearly how cognitions can affect motivation and behavior. The question raised by this research is how do we know what emotion we are experiencing; i.e., what label do we assign to a particular emotion. For example, subjectively there is a large difference between the emotions labeled anger and fear. There is also a large difference in the behaviors of an individual when angered and when afraid. Physiological research, however, has failed to find clear-cut differences between these two emotional states (Berkowitz 1968, p. 104).

The classic research on the labeling of emotions has been done by Schacter (1964, Schacter and Singer 1962). The basic idea is that the full emotional experience is composed of two parts: a physiological arousal and a cognitive label. Because both normally occur together, we are generally not aware of the two separate components. Schacter and Singer (1962) tested this theory by chemically inducing a state of arousal in subjects. Through instructions to the subjects and cues provided by a confederate of the experimenters, who acted either euphoric or angry, Schacter and Singer created conditions that they argued should lead subjects to *label* the *same physiological arousal* as anger, euphoria, or make them unable to label the emotion at all. The results supported their theory.[5]

---

[5]Experiments such as this raise difficult ethical issues regarding potential harm to the subjects and informed consent of subjects. Professional societies and most universities now have formal standards and review committees to supervise such research.

Marketing managers make use of this labeling phenomenon when they create events, such as carnival sale days, to display their wares. The food, music, crowds, etc. of such events heighten buyer arousal, which the manager hopes will be labeled by potential buyers as arising from the product. Such effects are presumably quite subtle and the participants in the events would not be expected to be consciously aware of such a labeling process. The general idea, however, is quite consistent with what is known about the labeling of emotions.

A large number of cognitive theories of motivation have been proposed.[6] Two of the most important to the study of buyer behavior are cognitive dissonance and attribution theory. Since these theories shall be discussed extensively in subsequent chapters, in the context of specific types of buyer behavior research, they will not be pursued further here. Instead, Maslow's hierarchy of needs theory will illustrate a cognitively based theory of motivation, as well as certain other aspects of motivation.

Maslow's "Hierarchy of Needs" *– SKIP*

Maslow (1973a, 1973b) proposed a theory of motivation in which motives are arranged in a hierarchial order with the individual ultimately striving for self-actualization. Figure 6.3 presents Maslow's hierarchy of needs in schematic form.

The first level consists of the physiological needs, such as hunger and thirst. The second level consists of safety needs. The idea of a hierarchy can be illustrated by a starving man. Such a person will most likely give safety very little concern, relative to a well-fed person, in his quest for food. Note that safety is not an irrelevant need; it merely becomes much less important when more basic physiological needs are not being satisfied.

The third level consists of the need for love or belongingness; that is, the need to love and be loved, to belong to one or more larger groups. Such needs can be satisfied in a large number of ways; e.g., marriage, social clubs. Maslow has suggested that frustration of these needs leads to serious behavioral problems and that this is the most common basis for behavioral problems in our society (Petri 1981, p. 303)—an observation particularly important to marketing. Note the large number of products which are promoted with a belongingness theme: e.g., "Join the Pepsi generation."

The next level of needs are for esteem; for a positive, high evaluation of oneself *both* from oneself *and* from others. Although Maslow argued that the belongingness needs usually were satisfied first, he did suggest that for some individuals the esteem needs had a higher priority than the belongingness needs. The need for esteem leads one to strive for achievement, confidence, success, reputation, and status; all of which form the basis for marketing many products. Lincoln Continental and Chivas Regal scotch, for example, are marketed largely by appealing to esteem needs.

The first four levels of needs are associated with deprivations of various types.

---

[6]A full treatment of cognitive theories of motivation can be found in Petri (1981, Chapters 9–12).

Although speculative, Bettman (1979, Chapter 3) proposed a theory of consumer choice behavior incorporating a cognitive theory of motivation that includes mechanisms for scanning the environment for information relevant to achieving the buyer's goals and interrupt mechanisms for switching a buyer from one activity to another.

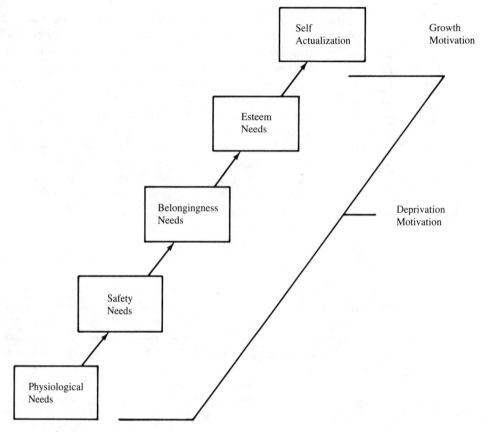

Figure 6.3
Maslow's hierarchy of needs

The final level, the need for self-actualization, is concerned with the growth of the individual, which means the need to be all one can be, to maximally use one's talents. Maslow suggested that relatively few individuals, perhaps 1 percent, could be classified as truly self-actualizing, and that such persons would be normally 60 years of age or older, as self-actualization takes considerable time.

Maslow's hierarchy of needs theory of motivation has a number of implications for our understanding of buyer behavior. First, it reminds us that multiple motives are often at work in a specific behavior. A person buying a gourmet food, for example, may want to impress his or her friends but probably also considers that he or she will be hungry and the food tastes good. Second, the hierarchy concept alerts us to the fact that individuals can move up, and down, the hierarchy in terms of the priority of the various categories of needs. For example, contemporary society has largely moved beyond a high priority for physiological and safety needs. With the rise in crime, however, certain individuals, especially the elderly living in large cities, have found the need for safety dominating their lives as well as their buying behavior. Third, the hierarchy concept has implications for differentiating groups of buyers according to the priority they assign different categories of needs. Foreign travel, for example, is largely an upper middle and upper class phenomenon. This is true even when income differences among different social classes are taken into account. One explanation for this observation is that, in contrast to lower social class groups where safety and belongingness needs are of relatively greater importance, foreign travel enhances one's sense of self-esteem and possibly one's sense of self-actualization through its broadening effects. Finally, as the above examples suggest, Maslow's hierarchy of needs concept provides a method of identifying needs to form the basis for successful marketing programs.

Goal Directed Behavior

Fundamentally, what cognitive theories require is the recognition that much behavior is goal directed. The individual is able to form long-term goals; e.g., develop a successful career, buy a house, and direct his or her behavior to achieve those goals. Despite frequent and, sometimes lengthy, interruptions individuals are able to work toward their goals even though they may take years to achieve. Markin (1977, p. 45) neatly captures the spirit of this argument by stating that "Thus, instead of arguing that behavior is caused by drives that push, we assert that behavior is caused by goals which pull." The importance of this for marketing is that goods and services can play a role both in achieving one's goals and in communicating that one's goals have been reached. Understanding this provides an important framework for conducting marketing research (i.e., assessing buyer goals and how the firm's products relate to those goals) and for constructing the firm's marketing program.

SOCIAL MOTIVATION

No discussion of motivation would be complete without some mention of social factors as a source of motivation. Since two chapters are devoted to a full discussion of the effects of social factors on buyer behavior, the present discussion shall not be lengthy. Rather, several examples of social effects on motivation will be presented to illustrate that such effects can be both subtle and powerful.

The first example concerns what are generally called social facilitation effects (Zajonc 1965). Recognition of such effects extends back to the beginning of this century, when it was first noted that athletes typically performed better when competing against other athletes as opposed to a clock; that is, the presence of others seems to *facilitate* the behavior. It has even been observed that the mere presence of others as observers, but not performers, facilitates behavior. This effect, called the audience effect, has been observed in even so lowly an animal as the cockroach.

The second example comes from the psychological literature on verbal conditioning and illustrates just how subtle the effects of social factors can be. In a very simple verbal conditioning experiment, the experimenter picks a particular type of word (e.g., proper nouns) and reinforces the use of that type of word by reacting in a way that presumably connotes social approval (e.g., saying good or O.K.) every time the subject utters a proper noun. With such conditioning subjects tend to significantly increase their use of words that are reinforced with social approval. Thus, it is possible to influence human behavior with nothing more tangible than an intermittent word of approval, such as good or O.K.

The final example illustrates just how powerful social factors can be in motivating behavior. The classic research in this area was performed by Asch

Figure 6.4
Asch experiment on social influence

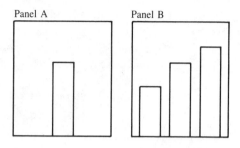

(1952). The question Asch asked was: Would a subject agree with an opinion expressed by others if that opinion was patently incorrect? Given the standard line length in panel A of Figure 6.4, subjects are asked to select the line in panel B that most closely matches the length of the line in panel A. Seven to nine "subjects" participate in this task. Unknown to the *true* subject, who is always the last to respond, all the other participants are confederates of the experimenter. After a few warm-up sessions, where everyone replies with the correct answer, the confederates begin to respond with a uniformly wrong choice. Imagine yourself in this situation. Seven or eight seemingly normal people say that the left line in panel B is closest to the standard in panel A. What would *you* do? Over twelve experimental trials, some 80 percent of the subjects conformed to the patently incorrect opinion at least once.

The objectives in this section have been to introduce the idea of social effects on motivation and to give the reader some appreciation as to just how subtle and powerful such effects can be. Subsequent chapters will analyze in detail the effects of social factors on buyer behavior and their implications for marketing managers.

MOTIVE CONFLICT

As noted in the beginning of this chapter, multiple motives are frequently involved in a single purchase. Furthermore, these multiple motives are often in conflict when a buyer considers a purchase. Specifically, three types of conflict have been recognized: approach-approach, approach-avoidance, and avoidance-avoidance.

Approach-Approach   *skip*

This type of conflict occurs when two alternatives have positive value but only one can be acquired, or approached in the psychologist's terminology. In a high level economy, as exists in the United States, buyers are frequently torn between alternatives, none of which are truly necessary; e.g., buying a new car or taking a European vacation. "But now—pay later" plans are clearly geared to resolving such motive conflict. Another promotional ploy frequently used by manufacturers of expensive, big-ticket items whose prices tend to be at the low end of the line is to compare a higher priced competitive brand with their brand *and* a number of desirable alternatives. For example, an advertisement might ask a buyer whether he or she would prefer automobile A *or* automobile B *and* a European vacation?

Approach-Avoidance

This is the classic type of conflict that has been studied so extensively in psychology. The object the organism desires has both positive and negative features. In laboratory studies, for example, an animal might press a bar which gives both food and an electric shock. The behavior of the organism will be governed by relative strengths of the tendency to approach and the tendency to avoid the desired object.

Buying decisions regarding many expensive, infrequently purchased, durable goods seem to put buyers into an approach-avoidance conflict. They want the new car or new stereo system, but when they think of the cost, the difficulty and expense of correcting a bad purchase, etc., they hesitate and sometimes abandon the contemplated purchase entirely. According to Myers and Reynolds (1967) "Some observers feel that many consumers enter into a state of virtual panic before making the final decision on an expensive item" (p. 85). Successful salespeople become skillful at identifying signs of approach-avoidance conflict and in developing methods to resolve such conflict. Warranties, guarantees to refund the price difference should the buyer find the same brand at a lower price within some number of days, and many similar devices are used to help the buyer resolve the approach-avoidance conflict in favor of approach.

Avoidance-Avoidance

In this type of conflict the individual faces two undesirable alternatives. A voter, for example, may feel neither candidate is very good. Such a person can either vote for the lesser of two evils or not vote at all. Such a situation, of course, presents an ideal opportunity for a third candidate; i.e., an opportunity to introduce a superior product. Urban commuters are often faced with similar choices. They may drive, fight traffic, and pay what they regard as an exhorbitant parking fee *or* they can take what they believe is inconvenient, unclean, unsafe mass transit.

Avoidance-avoidance conflicts can be dealt with in a number of ways. First, people's beliefs may be mistaken. Thus, it may be possible to correct these beliefs, at least partially, through promotion. New York City, for example, has actively promoted the fact that there are safe, convenient ways to reach the city and that one can easily drive in *and* find a place to park on the weekend. Second, avoidance-avoidance conflicts typically present significant opportunities for new or improved products. Reserved lanes for buses and express buses to the suburbs during rush hours are examples of this. Third, it may be necessary to admit that no choice is entirely satisfactory but that the recommended choice is the best alternative. Many medical diagnostic and treatment procedures (e.g., for cancer) fall into this category.

TWO MOTIVES OF SPECIAL IMPORTANCE TO MARKETING

This chapter has surveyed a large number of theories of motivation. It has also discussed, and illustrated through brief examples, how a knowledge of motivation theories can contribute to the knowledge of buyer behavior. In subsequent chapters, it shall, on occasion, be necessary to refer explicity to motivational concepts. Of necessity, the motive concept shall remain largely implicit in subsequent discussions; i.e., implicit in the very fundamental sense that all behavior is believed to be motivated. Before leaving the discussion of motivation theory, however, discussion is needed on the marketing implications of two types of motives frequently used by marketers: eros and fear.

Eros

Kotler (1980) begins his chapter on the firm's product decisions with a famous quote by Charles Revson, of Revlon Cosmetics, that "In the factory we make cosmetics, and in the drugstore we sell hope." Kotler's main point is that the buyer is buying not a physical product but, rather, the motive satisfying properties of the physical product. The quote also suggests the extent to which sex is used as a motivational theme in marketing.

We are, of course, sexual beings and it is, therefore, not surprising that sexual themes can provide a powerful basis for motivating behavior. Subsequent chapters will deal with such questions as the portrayal of women, and men, as sex objects and the use of nudity in advertising. The present discussion focuses on a culturally determined (i.e., learned) motive that is both subtle and pervasive. This motive, called eros, has been described by novelist Francine du Plessix Gray[7] as

> . . . the notion that sexual union between men and women who believe that they are passionately in love, a union achieved by free choice and legalized by marriage, tends to offer a life of perpetual bliss and is the most desirable human bond available on earth (1978, p. 190).

As Gray notes, the concept of romantic love is a largely western phenomena, which until quite recently has been confined to the middle class. In terminology used here, the motive of romantic love is a learned motive. Although romantic love can involve a longing for the beloved, it can also exist in a context where the "beloved" plays only a minor role. That is, one can be in love with love; a very strongly narcissistic situation with strong arousal potential and with obvious potential for promoting certain goods and services; e.g., Harlequin Romances.

The importance of eros in marketing is almost self-evident. To return to Charles Revson's phrase "in the drugstore we sell hope." Hope, that is, for a *perfect* romantic union, if only the buyer will use the advertised product. The appeal to eros is fundamental to many other industries; e.g., perfume and cologne, health and exercise spas, romantic fiction novels. Even such a "practical" thing as an automobile is often marketed with a strong appeal to eros. As one sports car ad notes "You not only get the car, you get the girl."

Despite the importance of eros as a motive upon which many marketing programs are built, surprisingly little academic research has been done on this motive. There is a small amount of research, which will be reviewed in subsequent chapters, on sex role portrayals, physical attractiveness of models, and the effects of nudity. This research, however, concerns only very narrow aspects of what has been labeled eros. Why this state of affairs exists is difficult to say. Part of the reason may be the very pervasiveness of commercial appeals to eros. A more

---

[7]Much of the inspiration for this section is drawn from Francine du Plessix Gray's 1978 commencement address at Barnard College. Gray's theme is friendship, especially friendship among women. Her address is especially interesting to persons with an interest in buyer behavior because of her analysis of friendship vis a vis eros or romantic love. In particular, she notes that the concept of romantic love has been extensively exploited commercially.

important reason may be that, at least in the Western world, the concept of romantic love is so basic that attempts to study it amount to an attempt to study the whole individual at once, a procedure more suited to the novel than to scientific research. Indeed, the reader may learn much of very practical value to the practicing marketing manager from the study of romantic novels, such as Madame Bovary.

Fear

The discussion of drive theories of motivation used fear to illustrate how a secondary motive is acquired. Fear, of course, is frequently used as the basis for marketing programs. Life and health insurance, anti-smoking, personal hygiene products, to name only a few products, rely heavily on fear and the ability of the advertised good or service to remove the threat to motivate the buyer.

There is a large psychological literature, and a modest marketing literature, on the effects of fear appeals on attitudes and behavior. The empirical data is mixed, some studies find a positive and others a negative relationship between level of fear appeal and changes in attitude and behavior (Ray and Wilkie 1970; Sternthal and Craig 1974). Ray and Wilkie suggested that the contradictory findings may be reconciled by postulating a nonlinear relationship between level of fear and changes in attitudes and behavior. Figure 6.5 presents Ray and Wilkie's theory.

According to Ray and Wilkie, two things happen as the level of the fear appeal increases. First, the attention getting value of the message increases, which facilitates acceptance of the message's recommendations. For example, a highway safety message might contain full color pictures of particularly gruesome accidents with the very pointed message that this could have been you. Second, high levels of fear tend to cause the receiver to deny or distort the message, which has an inhibiting effect on acceptance of the message's recommendations. For example, the thought of a gruesome death may be so threatening that the person attempts to reduce the fear by denying or distorting the message. One way to do this would be to argue that the victims were at least partially responsible for the accident, perhaps they

Figure 6.5
Ray and Wilkie's reconciliation of contradictory fear appeal research findings
*The word nonmonotonic means that through part of its range the curve may be rising while through other parts it may be falling.
Source: Michael L. Ray and William L. Wilkie, "Fear: The Potential of an Appeal Neglected by Marketing." *Journal of Marketing,* 34 (January 1970): 56. Reprinted with the kind permission of the American Marketing Association.

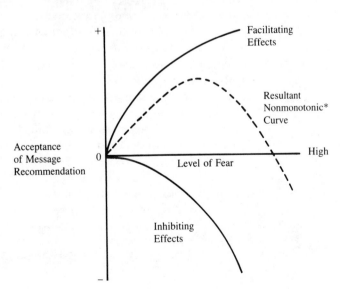

were drunk, and since our hypothetical message receiver is a careful and sober driver this could not happen to him. In fact, ample evidence supports this scenario (Ray and Wilkie 1970).

As can be seen in Figure 6.5, Ray and Wilkie postulate that the sum of the facilitating and inhibiting effects of fear give rise to an inverted U relationship with an intermediate level of fear having the greatest impact on acceptance of the message's recommendations. This may account for the frequent failure of messages that employ very high levels of fear; e.g., smoking and cancer. The important conclusion, of course, is that the marketer must find an optimal level of fear: high enough to get the individual's attention but not so high as to cause distortion or denial of the message.

A number of individual differences have been found in the optimal level of fear. According to Ray and Wilkie

> High fear appeals have worked best with people who are low in anxiety and high in self-esteem, who exhibit coping behavior, who normally find the topic or category of low relevance, and who normally see themselves as having low vulnerability to the threat in the fear message (1970, p. 59).

Such individual differences suggest the possibility of defining specific target markets that can be appealed to with different promotional strategies including differences in the level of fear. For example, anti-smoking campaigns aimed at nonsmokers could presumably employ a greater level of fear than campaigns aimed at smokers. Another example would be a campaign to raise money for the Multiple Sclerosis Society. Since MS is almost exclusively confined to young adults, much higher levels of fear (the threat being to others rather than to oneself) might be used in messages targeted to middle age and older adults.

Research on fear has produced other findings with potential implications for marketing management. There is evidence to suggest that a high fear appeal is most effective when the message is delivered by a highly credible source (Sternthal and Craig 1974). In the case of an anti-smoking campaign, a highly credible source might be the director of cancer research at the National Institute of Health. It has also been found that fear is most likely to produce compliance with recommended actions when the actions are perceived to be effective and the recommended action is outlined specifically (Sternthal and Craig 1974).

Fear appeals appear to provide a powerful means for motivating buyer behavior. Implementing the findings of research on fear presents certain problems. The inverted U relationship postulated by Ray and Wilkie, while capable of integrating a number of contradictory findings, has been challenged by Sternthal and Craig (1974). They found it to be an essentially post hoc explanation, appealing but inadequately documented. A recent study by Burnett and Oliver (1979), however, provides some empirical support for Ray and Wilkie's hypothesis. Another problem is that most research on fear has used physical threats of one kind or another, while much of marketing's use of fear is based on social approval or disapproval. One study, which looked at social approval, found that social approval, and especially social disapproval, were effective in changing attitudes. This effect was enhanced when the message was delivered by a high credibility source (Sternthal and Craig 1974).

In summary, sufficient research evidence indicates that fear appeals can provide a successful basis for motivating buyer behavior. Careful research in each specific application will be required to determine the optimal level of fear for each target audience the marketer is attempting to reach and influence.

SUMMARY

The preceding pages have introduced the reader to a number of different theories of motivation. As the discussion and examples have indicated, each theory can provide significant insights into why buyers behave as they do and, thereby, provide the marketing manager with a more rational basis for designing effective marketing programs. Indeed, a thorough understanding of buyer motives lies at the heart of the modern marketing concept, for it is by developing total marketing programs that satisfy buyers more completely and efficiently than those of competitors that the modern marketing manager maximizes corporate profits.

Learning and
Memory

7

The previous chapter's discussion of motivation noted that it is not possible to completely separate motivation and learning. Motivation explains the reasons for behavior but, except for truly instinctual behavior, learning must occur before the individual can determine, other than randomly, which specific behavior will satisfy specific motives. Furthermore, as seen in our discussion of secondary motives, learning may produce entirely new motives. Thus, the topics of motivation and learning are highly interrelated.

The purpose of this chapter is to complete the discussion of motivation by examining how buyers learn ways to satisfy their motives. This chapter begins with an overview of the relevance of theories of learning to managerial decision making. This is followed by a review of basic learning concepts and terminology and then an examination of four theories of learning. These theories are more complementary than competing. In fact, learning theorists now recognize that most learning situations cannot be fully understood without employing concepts from two or more of the traditional theories of learning. Also, learning theories overlap in their recognition of certain principles of learning. Several of these principles, which have special relevance to marketing, will be discussed. A special application of learning principles, behavior modification, will be explored in terms of how the marketing manager can manipulate the environment in which buying occurs to influence the buyer. Finally, learning implies some means for storing what has been learned. Thus, the chapter concludes with a brief inquiry into the nature of memory and its implications for understanding buyer behavior.

MANAGERIAL RELEVANCE OF THEORIES OF LEARNING

In a very important way, the thrust of this chapter is quite different from both the current mainstream of buyer behavior research and from most of the other chapters in this book. Emphasis in recent years has tended to be on variables that are internal to the buyer such as perceived risk, self-confidence, motivation, intention to buy, and attitudes. Knowledge of such internal variables can be enormously useful to the marketing manager as well as the academic researcher. Such knowledge, however, typically yields insights into why buyers behave as they do without *explicitly* determining how specific managerial actions can lead to specific buyer responses.

With the conspicuous exception of cognitive theories, learning theories are developed in terms of variables such as stimuli and responses, which are external to the buyer and directly observable. More important, managerial decision variables (product, price, promotion, and distribution) can be directly translated into learning theory concepts. For this reason, theories of learning provide an important vehicle for *directly* linking buyer behavior to managerial decision making.

Before beginning a discussion of learning theory, it should be noted that the current state of buyer behavior literature on learning theory closely parallels that of motivation; that is, while learning theory concepts are crucial to an understanding of buyer behavior relatively little buyer behavior research has been conducted within the specific framework of any learning theory. Thus, the discussion will draw heavily from psychological sources. Fortunately, the relevance of learning theories to managerial decision making is now widely recognized (cf. Nord and

Peter 1980; Rothschild and Gaidis 1981; Nord and Peter 1982) and it is likely that buyer behavior research based directly on learning theory concepts will increase in the future.

BASIC CONCEPTS AND TERMINOLOGY

The discussion of theories of learning will be facilitated by a brief review of some of the basic concepts and terms that will be referred to repeatedly in this chapter.[1]

Learning

Learning refers to a relatively permanent change in behavior caused by experience and practice. This definition specifically excludes instinctual behavior. It also excludes behavior that occurs through more or less accidental movements. Finally, the behavior in the definition need not be overt. Unobservable behavior, such as memorizing a brand name, is a part of learning. Of course, an observer can determine if learning has occurred only by observing some overt behavior, such as the ability to recall a brand name.

Stimulus

A stimulus is any event capable of activating an organism. A stimulus may be either internal (for example, hunger) or external (for example, an advertisement).

Response

A response is any behavior elicited by a stimulus. Responses commonly used in laboratory studies of animals are bar pressing (e.g., rats) and pecking (e.g., pigeons). The range of responses of interest in human behavior is roughly identical with the totality of human behavior. It should be noted again that the response of interest need not be directly observable.

Reinforcer

A reinforcer is any stimulus that increases the likelihood of a response that it follows. A positive reinforcer increases the likelihood of the response it follows. A negative reinforcer also increases the likelihood of the response when the response causes cessation of a negative situation. Positive and negative reinforcers are both important to marketers. Positive reinforcers are more obvious, e.g., food that tastes good and satisfies hunger or an automobile that is extremely reliable and fuel-efficient. Negative reinforcers, however, can be equally important. For example, over-the-counter drugs are promoted to relieve aches and pains of one kind or another. To the extent that the recommended drug does relieve the ache or pain, the use of that drug will be negatively reinforced.

---

[1]The terminology, concepts, and principles presented in this chapter are highly standardized and, therefore, no specific citations to the literature will be made for them. For an excellent introduction to learning theory from a psychological perspective, the reader is referred to Bourne and Ekstrand (1979, especially pp. 114–234 and 358–363). For a more advanced, but fairly readable, discussion see Hill (1977).

Punishment

Punishment is an aversive stimulus whose administration is contingent upon the occurrence of undesired behavior. The effect of punishment is to decrease a response with which it is associated. Although conceptually distinct from negative reinforcement the two concepts are frequently confused, partially because punishment and negative reinforcement frequently occur together and both involve aversive stimuli.

To illustrate the difference between negative reinforcement and punishment, consider the following marketing example. A salesperson is selling encyclopedias door-to-door. Of the many responses a potential buyer might make, the two of most immediate concern to the salesperson are the decision to purchase or the decision not to purchase the encyclopedia. Let us suppose that the buyer is not responding to the positive inducements put forward by the salesperson. In such circumstances, the salesperson might try to embarrass the potential buyer by suggesting that the family's children are being deprived of a valuable and necessary educational resource. This suggestion, and its implied condemnation, punishes the response not to purchase. It also serves as a potential negative reinforcer for the response to purchase, i.e., the implied condemnation will be removed *if* the person buys the encyclopedia.

If administered properly, such combinations of punishment and negative reinforcers can be quite effective in producing the desired response. Of course, a salesperson employing such negative inducements runs the danger of producing responses other than a decision to purchase or not to purchase; e.g., throwing the salesperon out of the house.

Reward

The term reward is often used synonymously for reinforcers and punishment. A positive reinforcer, or the removal of a negative reinforcer, is presumed to be a positive reward because both *increase* the likelihood of a particular response. Similarly, punishment is presumed to be a negative reward because it decreases the likelihood of a particular response. Psychologists generally prefer the greater precision of the terms reinforcer and punishment to reward. The reason for this greater precision is that while a specific response may be reinforced or punished only an individual, as a whole person, may be rewarded.

Cues

A cue is a stimulus that controls a response through a process known as discrimination. A classic example of a cue is the use of punishment to stop a child from using profanity. If the punishment is administered only by the parents, punishment occurs only when the parents are present *and* the child uses profanity. Here the presence of the parents becomes a discriminative stimulus, or cue, and the child learns not to use profanity when they are present. To the extent that the use of profanity is rewarded in other situations (for example, it may elicit peer-approval), profanity will tend to be used in the absence of the parents.

It is hard to overstate the importance of cues in the behavior of buyers. The heuristic decision rules discussed in previous chapters illustrate the use of cues in buyer behavior. For example, when a buyer uses the color of a piece of meat or an orange as a guide to its quality, color is a cue that the buyer believes is related to whether the purchase and consumption of the product will be positive or negative. Using price as an indicator of quality provides another illustration of the use of cues. Perhaps the brand name is the most important example of a cue in marketing. A brand name, which the buyer has come to know and trust, provides for many buyers a satisfactory basis, a cue, to purchase a product never tried before and which may even be an entirely new product (Jacoby, Szybillo, and Busato-Schach 1977). Birds Eye and Campbells, for example, have quite successfully used their brand names in this way. With this introduction to basic learning concepts and terminology completed, we are now prepared to discuss theories of learning.

CONTIGUITY THEORIES OF LEARNING

Pavlov's Classical Conditioning

- couple stimulus of response

Probably the best known experimental demonstration of learning is Russian psychologist Ivan Pavlov's conditioning of a dog to salivate upon hearing a bell ring. The procedure used by Pavlov, classical conditioning, falls within the general class of learning theories known as contiguity theories. Figure 7.1 illustrates schematically Pavlov's classical conditioning experiment.

Any classical conditioning experiment begins with an already well established relationship between a stimulus and a response. Becase this relationship exists prior to the conditioning process, the stimulus and response are referred to as unconditioned. In Pavlov's experiment, the unconditioned stimulus (UCS) is food and the unconditioned response (UCR) is salivation. The specific UCS and UCR employed in a classical conditioning procedure are not critical. It is only necessary that the relationship between them be well established. In the immediate case, this means that the dog, when presented with the food, will begin to salivate.

The conditioning experiment itself proceeds as follows. Immediately before the food is presented to the dog, a bell is rung. The ringing of the bell is called a conditioned stimulus (CS) because, without new learning, it will not give rise to salivation. Over a number of trials the bell is rung, the food is immediately presented to the dog, and the dog salivates. After a number of trials, the dog will salivate when the bell is rung even if no food is presented; that is, the dog has come to be conditioned to the ringing of the bell. For reasons to be elaborated on, the response to the bell is referred to as a conditioned response (CR), although it appears superficially to be identical to the UCR.

Figure 7.1
Pavlov's classical conditioning of salivation in a dog.

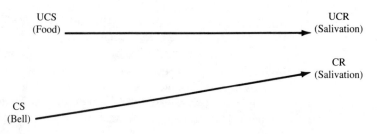

The Effects of Conditioning

Two points are crucial to a proper understanding of the effects of conditioning. First, what has been learned is the relationship between the CS and the UCS. The dog *associates* the ringing of the bell with the subsequent presentation of food. In learning theory terms, what has been learned is a stimulus-stimulus or S-S relationship. Although the reinforcing effect of food is important to this learning, the learning itself is confined to the association of the ringing of the bell and the appearance of food.

The second point concerns the distinction between the UCR and the CR. In Pavlov's experiment both responses are salivation. Despite their superficial similarity, the exact responses are frequently different. The dog, for example, may salivate less and for a shorter period of time to the ringing of the bell (CS) when presented alone than to the food (UCS) when presented alone. Furthermore, over a number of trials the tendency to salivate when the bell is rung will decrease and eventually stop if the food is no longer presented; a phenomenon known as extinction. For these reasons it is considered theoretically and practically important to distinguish between an organism's response to an UCS and its response to a CS.

The difference between the CR and UCR in human behavior can be illustrated by recalling an example from the last chapter: How the word fire comes to have motivating properties. A physical fire (UCS) will give rise to a complex UCR that may include such responses as screaming, orientating oneself to the source of the fire and possible escape routes, preparing to run, running. The word fire (CS), however, will generally elicit only a subset of these responses. The CR to the word fire may include trying to locate the source of the fire and possible escape routes and preparing to run but, most likely, it will not include screaming, running, and the full terror normally elicited by an actual fire. In psychological terms, the various elements of the UCR are not equally conditionable. The CS will tend to elicit the most easily conditioned elements first. The stronger the CS, the more less conditionable elements of the UCR are likely to be elicited. The response to the word fire uttered in a calm voice, for example, is likely to be quite different from the response to "Fire!" shouted in panic and terror.

The importance to marketing of the distinction between the UCR and the CR is clearly seen in the distinction between a brand name (CS) and the actual item itself (UCS). The brand name Triumph, for example, may elicit anticipation of excitement, but that excitement is likely to be quite weak compared to actually driving and owning the car. It may, however, be sufficiently strong to motivate a person to consider buying a Triumph and, perhaps, going to a dealer for a test drive.

The Law of Contiguity

Pavlov's experiment demonstrates what has come to be called the law of contiguity, which states that things that occur in close proximity in time and space, things that are contiguous, come to be associated. In Pavlov's experiment the dog comes to associate the ringing of the bell with food because the food is contiguous with the ringing of the bell.

As Wingfield and Byrnes (1981) note, the most important characteristic of any association is its strength. The more frequently the two elements of an association occur together, the stronger will be the association between them and the more likely a person is to recall one element of the association from the presence of the other.

The importance of the strength of association is well illustrated by the fact that most individuals find it extremely difficult to reproduce the letters of the alphabet in any order other than alphabetically (Wingfield and Byrnes 1981, p. 13). To take a marketing example, one might ask, "What does one do with orange juice?" That is, with what is orange juice associated? A breakfast drink? Or, possibly, a mixer for vodka? This narrow range of associations is something orange juice growers have gone to considerable effort and expense to expand by suggesting a much wider range of uses (i.e., associations) for orange juice; e.g., as an afternoon refresher.

Implications for Buyer Behavior

Contiguity learning plays an important role in the behavior of buyers. In particular, attitudes and brand and store images, which are a specific type of attitude, are formed to a large degree on the basis of contiguity learning. Consider two specific examples.

The first example concerns brand images. To be specific, consider the image of Rolls Royce. When you think of Rolls Royce, what images come to your mind, with what things is this brand name associated. While your image may not correspond precisely with mine, I suspect that it includes high quality, expense, luxury, and very successful people. If asked to explain how you formed your image of Rolls Royce, using the terminology of learning theory, you might say that your experiences over many years associate all of these things with the name Rolls Royce because they have been contiguous in your experiences. Indeed, the name Rolls Royce has become virtually synonymous with high quality. For example, because of their high quality, Beechcraft airplanes are frequently referred to as "the Rolls Royce of the Air."

The second example involves the learning of social attitudes; specifically, how sex roles and stereotypes are learned. This controversial topic has been selected for several reasons. First, it illustrates the principle of contiguity very effectively. Second, it illustrates how marketing makes use of attitudes that are formed in the larger society outside the specific context of marketing. Third, traditional sex roles and stereotypes are receiving increasing attention and appear to be undergoing change. Such changes in social attitudes can have substantial impacts on the effectiveness of specific marketing practices and this example further sensitizes us to the need to be alert to such possible social changes.

It is self-evident that there are stereotypes of what it means to be male or female and ascribed roles or activities that are considered to be distinctly masculine or feminine.[2] Indeed, research shows that children three- or four-years-old not

---

[2]A role is a set of activities expected of an individual. An important distinction is the difference between an earned role and an ascribed role. A professor, for example, is expected to make assignments, determine grades, etc. The right to perform this role is earned through a variety of activities such as education and joining a university faculty, activities which the individual must choose to engage in. An ascribed role is assigned to an individual because the individual has specific attributes. One of the most important and pervasive types of ascribed role in our society is a sex role. To the extent that such ascribed and expected sex roles are rigidly specified, they become stereotypes. The concept of roles will be explored more fully in Chapter 9 in a discussion of social group influences on buyer behavior.

only know whether they are boys or girls but also a great deal about what is considered proper behavior for boys or girls; e.g., boys are aggressive, girls are not (Stone and Church 1979). The factors that produce such learning are pervasive in our society and extend well beyond contiguity learning. Contiguity, however, is an important part of such learning.

The ascribed sex roles and sex stereotypes are literally everywhere. For example, Courtney and Lockeretz (1971), in an analysis of the portrayal of women in advertising in general audience magazines, found four major stereotypes: (1) a woman's place is in the home; (2) women don't make important decisions; (3) women are dependent on men; and (4) men regard women primarily as sex objects. Just how pervasive such stereotypes are in our society is revealed by content analyses of children's textbooks that show "that while male characters are dominant, active, make decisions, take risks, and have fun, females are subordinate, passive, dependent, play it safe, complain, and are the butt of jokes" (Zimbardo, 1979, p. 82). In short, the many elements of what are portrayed as actual, and presumably appropriate, roles for males and females occur with great frequency and high contiguity.

Ascribed sex roles and sex stereotypes are important in the formulation of marketing strategy for many products. Cosmetics and clothing, for example, are frequently marketed on the basis of how use of the product will make one more feminine or more masculine. Other products are marketed on the basis of how use of that product will allow people to more successfully fulfill their sex role obligations. Wisk detergent (Oh, those dirty rings!), for example, makes quite obvious use of this type of appeal. One final example is the sex of off-screen announcers in television commercials. The off-screen announcer is the unseen person who typically summarizes the message's key point (e.g., Wisk ends ring-around-the-collar) or gives the command to buy the product. Such off-screen announcers are predominately male, even for products marketed to women. Although the reasons for the predominant use of male off-screen announcers are not entirely clear, a major part of the explanation is very likely that because the male has traditionally been stereotyped as more decisive, dominant, etc., than the female, the male voice carries more authority and credibility than the female voice.

There is every reason to believe that major differences in ascribed sex roles and stereotypes of men and women will continue for the forseeable future and that these differences will contain important marketing implications. It appears equally likely that certain major changes in the content and especially the rigidity of ascribed sex roles and stereotypes have been set in motion. Precisely how far these changes will go and what their exact content will be remains to be seen. From research accumulated to date it is clear that these changes will change many marketing practices. Lundstrom and Sciglimpaglia (1977), for example, have shown that many, but not all, women are turned off by advertising that portrays women in traditional roles. And, as the actual roles change, marketing practices will need to change to accommodate them. McCall (1977), for example, discussed in some detail the marketing implications of the increasing number of "workwives" to use her phrase.[3] Some of these changes are obvious; e.g., the "workwife" shops more

[3]For more information on the marketing implications of a number of demographic and socioeconomic changes involving women the reader is referred to the special July 1977 issue of the *Journal of Marketing*, which was largely devoted to this topic.

often at night. Others may be surprising; e.g., the "workwife" buys less expensive dresses than the nonworking wife (p. 57).

As the above examples suggest, what marketers frequently attempt to do is to tap buyers into a network of previously learned associations that will increase the perceived positive attributes of their brand. This procedure is referred to as respondent conditioning; respondents are behaviors that follow specific stimuli and are controlled by those stimuli. For example, sellers make heavy use of respondent conditioning in such ways as associating their products with excitement, glamour, youth, etc. Domestic automobile manufacturers, in their battle with Japanese imports, have made use of respondent conditioning by incorporating patriotic symbols, such as the American flag, in their promotions. To the extent that the buyer is patriotic, considering buying a domestic car may give rise to a response of patriotic feelings. The positive reinforcement from feeling patriotic may provide an incremental reward that will lead to the actual purchase of a domestic automobile.

Although complete control over the stimuli that may become associated with the seller's product is not possible, a substantial amount of control is often possible. Advertising presents perhaps the most obvious illustrations of how sellers try to associate their products with special perceptions and emotions. Another, less obvious illustration concerns Christmas carols. Nord and Peter (1980, p. 38) suggest that the effect of such music, when played in stores, may be to give rise to what might be labeled Christmas spirit, and that these emotions may be incompatible with "sales resistance," thereby, increasing the likelihood of purchase.

Many stimuli, of course, are largely beyond the control of the marketer. The people that use the products, the uses to which the products are put, and a host of similar variables are largely beyond the control of the firm. Many stimuli, however, are with effort at least partially controllable. Examples include the surroundings in which the firm's products are displayed and the manner in which customers are treated by salespeople.

By now it should be apparent that the specific stimuli which became associated with a product can have a powerful effect on the success of the product in the marketplace. Careful association of a product with desired stimuli where control is possible and assessment of the associations that buyers have actually made through procedures such as image analysis, give the marketer a powerful means for creating an environment in which buyers' responses will lead to profits for the firm.

REINFORCEMENT THEORIES OF LEARNING

Using the terminology of psychological learning theorists, contiguity learning is characterized as S-S learning; that is, the contiguity learning task is to learn which stimulus elements tend to be associated in time and space. Another question one might ask is how does an individual come to learn to make a particular response when presented with a specific stimulus. In learning theory shorthand, how is the stimulus-response or S-R relationship learned. Reinforcement theories of learning provide one answer.

A Simple Example of Reinforcement Learning

Figure 7.2 presents a simple example of how learning occurs through positive reinforcement. In an experimental study involving rats, the stimulus might be

Figure 7.2.
A simple example of reinforcement learning

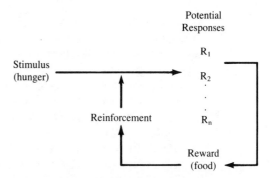

hunger. The rat in Figure 7.2, for example, may have been deprived of food for twelve hours. The rat is placed in a device called a Skinner box (named after the well-known behaviorist B. F. Skinner). This box contains a lever that, if pressed, releases a pellet of food into a tray where it can be consumed by the rat. The rat is unconstrained and free to make any number of responses (represented by R_1, R_2, ... R_n). Eventually, the rat will press the level (response R_2) and will be rewarded with a food pellet. The food will positively reinforce the probability that the rat will press the lever the next time it is placed in the Skinner box when hungry. Because the response (pushing the lever) is the instrument by which the rat obtains a reward, this type of learning is frequently referred to as instrumental conditioning.

The experiment in Figure 7.2 could just as easily have been run using negative reinforcement. For example, a mild, but aversive, electric shock could be administered through the floor of the Skinner box. Pressing the lever would turn off the electric shock. With sufficient practice the rat will learn to make this response.

Lever pressing can be stopped, extinguished in learning theory terms, by either not reinforcing the response or by punishing the response through some means, such as shocking the rat *after* it presses the lever. Furthermore, if pressing the lever *sometimes* gives food and *sometimes* gives a shock and a cue is available to tell the rat which will occur when the lever is pressed, the rat will learn to use this cue. For example, if a small light bulb in the box is turned on when pressing the lever gives food but turned off when the same response gives shock, the rat will quickly learn to press the lever only when the light is on.

The Effects of Reinforcement

The basic idea of reinforcement is deceptively simple. Reinforcement strengthens the bond between stimulus and response. This is why instrumental conditioning is often called stimulus-response theory.

The idea of reinforcement is described as deceptively simple because the myriad effects of different types of reinforcement are so complex that entire careers have been devoted to the study of the effects of reinforcement.[4] For example, learning depends greatly on the *schedule* of reinforcement. If reinforce-

---

[4]An appreciation of the full richness and complexity of the concept of reinforcement can be gotten from a reading of most introductory psychology texts, e.g., Bourne and Ekstrand (1979). Skinner (1971) discussed in detail how reinforcement and punishment are and can be used to control virtually all aspects of human behavior. Skinner's ideas are both thought provoking and controversial.

ment is delivered after every correct response (continuous reinforcement), the correct response is learned very rapidly but the response also extinguishes very quickly once reinforcement is terminated. In contrast, if reinforcement is delivered after some, but not all, correct responses (partial reinforcement) initial learning will be slower but the behavior will be much more resistant to extinction.[5] Part of the great fascination that slot machines hold for many people seems to be due to the intermittent delivery of the reinforcement (the payout). In a similar vein, Myers and Reynolds (1967, p. 54) suggest that the reason it is often extremely difficult to change brand images is that such images are frequently learned on the basis of partial reinforcement, e.g., a few intermittent good or bad experiences with a brand.

Implications for Buyer Behavior

The most basic implication of reinforcement theories of learning is that, all other things equal, responses that are reinforced are more likely to be repeated in the presence of the stimulus condition present when the response was made, while responses that are punished are less likely to be repeated. Thorndike, based on his animal laboratory studies at the turn of this century, called this phenomenon the *law of effect*. The law of effect states that

> If a stimulus was followed by a response and then by a *satisfier,* the stimulus-response connection was strengthened. If, however, a stimulus was followed by a response and then by an *annoyer*, the stimulus-response connection was weakened. Thus satisfying and annoying effects of responses determined whether the stimulus-response connections would be stamped in or stamped out. (Hill, 1977, p. 54)

The basic concept expressed by the law of effect, the stamping in or out of stimulus-response connections, is just as relevant to the buyer considering which of several brands of cereal to buy as to the rat in a Skinner box. For example, the idea of stamping in or stamping out S-R connections is implicit in most quantitative models of brand switching and loyalty. In fact, most of these models assume that the purchase of a particular brand on one occasion *increases* the likelihood that the same brand will be purchased again. In learning theory terms, this corresponds to an assumption that purchase of the product is a reinforcing (i.e., satisfactory) and not a punishing (i.e., unsatisfactory) experience. As discussed in Chapter 5, this is most likely to be true of products that are in the maturity phase of the product life cycle, which is one reason why the most successful applications of quantitative brand switching models tend to be made for such products.

Thorndike's law of effect has been modernized by the more precise terminology of reinforcement theory. The reason for presenting this law here is its use of terms such as *satisfier* and *annoyer*, terms that a buyer might use to describe his or her own buying experiences. Reinforcement tends to be pleasurable and satisfying, while punishment is unpleasant and dissatisfying. The buyer will tend to purchase and, more important, repurchase brands that are satisfying and avoid brands that are not satisfying or dissatisfying. Indeed, when the idea is put in these terms, reinforcement could be used as an operational definition of the modern marketing concept; i.e., *the creation of profits through the satisfaction of buyers.*

---

[5]A number of different types of partial reinforcement schedules, each with different effects on learning, have been identified. For details see Kimble (1968, pp. 160–164 and 188–192).

Most of the ways that firms attempt to satisfy their customers and reinforce them for buying their products are fairly straightforward, although not necessarily easy to achieve. The marketing oriented firm will attempt to develop its products, set prices, promote, and distribute its products (i.e., to establish its total marketing program) upon a firm foundation of knowledge of buyers' needs, which is established *before* the marketing program is implemented. Successful firms will be the ones that sufficiently satisfy their customers to reinforce repeat purchases. How this satisfaction is delivered is considered in detail in the introductory marketing course and in specialized courses in product design and management, pricing, promotion, and distribution. This chapter will only present several examples to illustrate the somewhat more subtle ways in which the marketing manger can use reinforcement conditioning techniques to create an environment in which buyers will tend to make the response desired by the manager.

The first example concerns the use of partial reinforcement. As noted earlier, partial reinforcement schedules produce learning that is slower but far more resistant to extinction than learning produced under a continuous reinforcement schedule. This finding has been well established in laboratory studies where the choice alternatives are strictly limited and controlled by the experimenter. As Rothschild and Gaidis (1981, p. 72) note, the marketing environment typically consists of many alternative choices and, therefore, the marketer must normally provide continuous reinforcement or the buyer will switch to products that do so. Despite this, situations arise where partial reinforcement can be quite effective (Peter and Nord 1982, p. 105).

An example of the use of partial reinforcement is Deslauries and Everett's (1977) study of the effects of reinforcement, in the form of tokens, for riding the bus delivered on either a *variable ratio* or a continuous reinforcement schedule. On a ratio reinforcement schedule, the reinforcer is delivered after every so many responses; every third response in the Deslauries and Everett study. On a *variable* ratio schedule this number is an average; whether a reinforcer is delivered after any particular response is determined randomly. Deslauries and Everett found that the two schedules were equally effective in producing bus ridership. The cost of the variable ratio schedule, however, was only about one-third the cost of the continuous reinforcement schedule.

In assessing the applicability of Deslauries and Everett's findings to other situations, it is important to note that the competitive alternatives contain only one bus company. More important, the tokens used as positive reinforcers were *incremental* to whatever reinforcement was provided by the bus ride itself. If the basic product or service is good, if it is positively reinforcing and delivered on a continuous schedule, incremental reinforcement delivered on a ratio schedule can be used quite effectively by the firm.

A good example of what is in essence a variable ratio reinforcement schedule is Hickory Farms' periodic placement of sample trays of cheese throughout their stores, so anyone who wanders through can try one or more samples. This encourages the person who happens to be near a Hickory Farms store, but not specifically shopping for cheese, to stop by just to sample new cheeses. The increased store traffic can be an important part of sales.

A subtle use of reinforcement involves the phenomenon known as shaping. A Skinner box is a very limited and simple environment, and a rat placed in it will soon press the lever that releases the food pellet. In more varied and complex environments, however, there is no assurance that the correct response will ever be made.

Shaping is a procedure to reinforce behavior that is *similar* to or an element of the desired response. Over time, closer and closer approximations to the desired response are required for the response to be reinforced. With shaping procedures, it is possible to condition responses that have a low probability of spontaneous occurrence or are sufficiently complex that the correct response is unlikely to occur before the individual gives up for lack of reinforcement. A common, although largely unconscious, use of shaping techniques in academic settings occurs when students are required to perform at increasingly higher levels to achieve the same grade.

Peter and Nord offer the following example of shaping

> ... suppose a car dealer wants to shape an automobile purchase. Free coffee and donuts are offered and given to anyone who comes to the dealership. Five dollars cash is offered and given to any licensed driver who will test drive a car. A $500 rebate is offered and given to anyone who purchases a car (1982, p. 106).

What has been done here is to break the complex process of buying an automobile into a series of simpler steps. Each step is reinforced with the objective of gradually "shaping" the buyer's responses toward the desired behavior, purchasing an automobile.

The final example of the marketing implications of reinforcement theory concerns typical marketing practices involving incentives such as free samples, cents-off coupons, and other premiums to launch new products. As Rothschild and Gaidis (1981) note, sellers typically offer large incentives for a short time and then terminate the incentives abruptly. This results in a sharp decline in the amount of reinforcement, and the response of buying the new brand is quickly extinguished. Rothschild and Gaidis argue that the desired response is more likely to be maintained if the amount of the reinforcement is gradually reduced. They also show that this scenario is consistent with studies of the effects of incentives on buyers conducted by Prentice (1975), Scott (1977), and Dodson, Tybout, and Sternthal (1978).[6]

COGNITIVE THEORIES OF LEARNING

Contiguity and reinforcement theories of learning are frequently referred to collectively as behavioristic learning theories. As Markin (1974) notes the basic question of interest to the behaviorist is "What has the subject learned to do?" (p. 239). Cognitive theorists, in contrast, emphasize the information processing and problem solving aspects of behavior along with the cognitive structures, such as attitudes and goals, which are an inherent component of cognitive learning. Markin, one of the earliest and most articulate advocates of a cognitive approach to buyer behavior, describes the perspective of the cognitive learning theorist in the following way.

> The cognitivist, on the other hand, would be inclined to ask, "How has the subject learned to perceive the situation?" The cognitivist is interested in examining a learning situation in terms of such factors as motivation, the perceived goals,

---

[6]Rothschild and Gaidis present this example as an illustration of shaping. Recently, Peter and Nord (1982) pointed out that this is actually an example of changing the contingencies of reinforcement rather than shaping.

the aspiration level, the overall nature of the situation, and the beliefs, values, and personality of the subject—in short, the entire range of the subject's psychological field. The cognitivist, as opposed to the behaviorist, contends that consumers do not respond simply to stimuli but instead act on beliefs, express attitudes, and strive towards goals. The cognitivist is thus concerned with this entire range of conscious experience and not just objective behavior (1974, p. 239).

The Nature of Cognitive Learning Theories

Many cognitive theories of learning have been developed (see Petri 1981, Chapters 9–12 for an excellent review). What all of these theories share, despite their many differences, is a view of the individual engaging in a variety of behaviors that, in everyday language, would be called "thinking." In this view the individual behaves because he or she has *reasons* for behaving. Given the reasons, the individual must think of ways (i.e., behaviors) of accomplishing the tasks necessary to satisfy the reasons. This viewpoint lies behind Markin's statement, which was discussed briefly in the last chapter, that "Thus, instead of arguing that behavior is caused by drives that push, we assert that behavior is caused by goals which pull" (1977, p. 45).

In recent years cognitive approaches to motivation and learning have played an increasingly important role in buyer behavior theory and research (see, for example, Kassarjian 1973; Bettman 1979). Indeed, most of this book can be regarded as a presentation of ideas that reflect a cognitive approach to behavior. Therefore, only a single, highly applied example will be used to illustrate the concepts and types of research questions that are involved in cognitive theories of learning.

An Example of Cognitive Effects on Learning

This example, from Carey et al. (1976), concerns an experiment to use positive reinforcement to increase sales for a small, independent jewelry store. The researchers divided the store's customers into three groups: a group which received a phone call thanking them for being customers; a group that received the same message *plus* an opportunity to buy in-stock diamonds at 20 percent off; and a third control group that was not contacted. The researchers reported that total sales increased 27 percent over the same month in the previous year, despite the fact that year-to-date sales were down 25 percent, and virtually all of the increase came from the two groups contacted by phone, the two positively reinforced groups. Although sales fell somewhat in the second month following the test, suggesting some borrowing from future sales, sales recovered in the third month and continued at a rate above the pre-test period, indicating that the attempt to increase sales through a careful administration of positive reinforcement was successful.

The researchers also found that the increase in sales differed substantially in the two experimental groups with 70 percent of the increase coming from customers who received only the phone call and 30 percent coming from customers who received both a phone call *and* an offer to buy diamonds at 20 percent off. Since the amount of positive reinforcement would seem to be greater in the second group, it would appear that something *in addition to* positive reinforcement has occurred.

To see what this something might be, put yourself in the position of a person who has just received a call from the jewelry store thanking you for being a customer. What would be your first reaction after hanging up the telephone? Probably, it would be to *think*, "I wonder why they called?" If you received the thank you *and* the offer to buy diamonds at a discount, you would very likely attribute the call to a normal, although somewhat unique, promotion for the store. Your interest in buying jewelry might be stimulated but your basic image of the store would most likely not change since promotion is an expected business practice. On the other hand, what if you received *only* a thank you. This is not only unusual but also not what most people would expect from a profit-making business. To what might this unusual behavior be attributed? The authors note that many people who received only a thank-you call came into the store "... commenting about 'that nice person who called' saying they had never had a call like that before ... [and that] Many wanted to meet the person who called" (p. 99). Apparently, the simple thank-you call led these consumers to engage in a cognitive evaluation process that indicated that the jewelry store had a genuine concern and appreciation of their customers.

SOCIAL LEARNING THEORIES

Social Factors in Learning

The fourth, and final, type of learning theory we shall consider are referred to collectively as social learning theories. A number of different social learning theories have been proposed (Hill 1977; Petri 1981). To varying degrees, all social learning theories draw heavily upon concepts already discussed in conjunction with contiguity, reinforcement, and cognitive theories of learning. Social learning theories are distinctive because of their emphasis upon social conditions in learning. Of particular importance to buyer behavior is the phenomenon known as modeling.

Modeling Through Observational Learning

According to Bandura (1969, 1971, 1977), who is most responsible for the concept of modeling, a great deal of our learning occurs through simple observation of the behavior of others. Unlike other theories, social learning theories emphasize the fact that learning can occur, with or without direct reinforcement of the observer, by simple observation of the model being reinforced. This process is referred to as vicarious reinforcement. Research suggests that vicarious reinforcement affects behavior in the same way as reinforcers that are directly experienced, but with less intensity (Atkin 1976, p. 514).

Bandura argues that observational learning has a number of significant advantages to the individual in comparison with other types of learning. First, by observing competent models the individual can avoid costly mistakes associated with trial and error learning. An example of this is the learning of brand and store preferences by new residents of an area (Andreasen and Durkson 1968, Sheth 1968). Second, many novel forms of behavior would seem to be best, and possibly only, learned through observation. Consider, for example, learning to use solar, as opposed to conventional, energy for heating or learning how to use a programmable calculator.[7] Third, the time necessary to learn the behavior can be shortened. Imagine, for example, how long it would take a buyer to learn how to use almost any new product if the buyer could learn only through direct experience. Finally, some behaviors are so dangerous that trial and error learning would be extremely detrimental to the individual. Consider, for example, the great emphasis on safety in recent years. Attempts to teach safety rely heavily on models demonstrating correct and incorrect behavior.

Three distinct types of learning through the observation of models have been distinguished (Hill 1977, pp. 239–241). First is the learning of entirely new responses such as how to properly and safely operate a power tool or a hot iron. Second is the inhibition or the disinhibition of a response. Inhibition refers to stopping a response. Many advertisements aimed at getting people not to smoke illustrate attempts to inhibit a response through modeling. Disinhibition refers to the case where a person has learned to make a response in some situations but not in other situations, and observation of the model elicits the response. Many large cities, for examples, have attempted to entice back individuals who no longer use the inner city for relaxation and entertainment through the use of models demonstrating the fun, as well as ease of access and safety, that can be found in the inner city. Third, observation of models can elicit an already well-learned response. This is the use of modeling most frequently made by marketers. The model is shown enjoying the benefits of the good or service with the hope that this will entice the observer to make the same response.

Bandura has suggested that learning via modeling is governed by four interrelated processes: attention, retention, motoric reproduction, and reinforcement and motivation. To be effective the model must first get the attention of the observer. Research shows that observers are most likely to attend to models they have frequently observed in the past. Also, some models seem to be particularly strong attractors. Television is a good example of such a model (Petri 1981, p. 202). Retention, of course, implies memory, which is our last topic for this chapter. Motoric reproduction processes mean that the individual must be capable of making the required response. An important consequence of this, for novel responses, is that the observer's first responses are likely to be only rough approximations of the model's behaviors; for example, a person's first attempt to serve a tennis ball after having observed a model demonstrate the proper method. With sufficient practice the observer's serve may become as good, or even better, than the model's. Finally, even if a response has been well learned through observation, it will normally take some form of motivation or reinforcement to get the observer to actually make the response. As noted earlier, a great deal of television advertising is aimed at providing the motivation necessary to elicit already learned responses.

Implications for Buyer Behavior

Research shows quite clearly that learning can occur through the observation of competent models. Casual observation, (i.e., observational learning) reveals abundant buyer behavior examples of this type of learning. Television advertising

---

[7]In the case of a programmable calculator the model of correct behavior could be the instruction book. Such books typically illustrate correct use of the machine through a large number of examples which the user is encouraged to follow, i.e., to model.

employing models is perhaps the clearest example of observational learning. Any instruction manual that relies heavily on step by step examples, however, is also a model in the sense that the term is used by social learning theorists. Modeling will also be encountered in the discussion of the *socialization* process through which parents teach their children how to become buyers in Chapter 15.

Despite the great importance of modeling as a source of learning buyer behavior researchers have made very little *explicit* use of observational learning concepts. Ray (1973a, pp. 76–79), citing examples from psychological and mass media research, suggests that observational learning research has great potential for understanding buyer behavior. Markin and Narayana (1976) express a similar sentiment when they note that many of today's most successful products, Pepsi-Cola, Nyquil, Crest, and Head and Shoulders, are promoted largely with a strategy of frequent advertisements showing models receiving positive reinforcement for using the products. Furthermore, as Nord and Peter note (1980, pp. 40–41), observational learning presents one of the few instances where punishment may be readily used to reduce the frequency of unwanted behaviors of a potential or present buyer. Examples they cite are smoking, drinking, overeating, wasting energy, polluting and littering, and using a competitor's product.

Atkin (1976), in one of the few observational learning studies conducted on buyer behavior, produced evidence of the effectiveness of modeling in television advertising to elicit desired behavior from children. Atkin's research is especially valuable because it examines the attention, retention, and motivation subprocesses associated with observational learning in detail and provides empirical support for each. It is to be hoped that more use will be made of observational learning concepts in the future by buyer behavior researchers.

LEARNING PRINCIPLES OF SPECIAL RELEVANCE TO MARKETING

This study of learning theories has shown that learning can occur in a number of different ways. Each of the four types of theories, as we have seen, is particularly relevant to certain types of learning situations. All learning theories, however, recognize certain learning principles. The purpose of this section is to review a number of principles developed by learning theorists that are especially relevant to the study of buyer behavior and to managerial decision making.

Stimulus Generalization

Stimulus generalization can be illustrated by Pavlov's classical conditioning of a dog to salivate upon hearing a bell ring. A natural extension of Pavlov's experiment is to determine the response of the dog to a bell of a different tone. It turns out that the animal will tend to produce the conditional response as a direct function of the similarity of the tone of the new bell to the tone of the bell to which the animal was originally conditioned. This procedure demonstrates the fact that the dog has *generalized* the stimulus (ringing bell) beyond the specific bell to which it was conditioned. The phenomenon of stimulus generalization has been demonstrated for a wide range of stimuli and is as relevant to human behavior as it is to animal behavior.

Stimulus generalization is of great importance to marketing. For example, evidence suggests that buyers learn about a new brand by ascribing the properties of the most similar known brand to the new brand (Howard 1977). Stefflre (1968) made use of a variant of this concept to predict how buyers will respond to a new product. Specifically, he argues that new products tend to elicit the responses of old products to the extent to which the new and old products are similar.

The use of family brand names, such as Campbells, illustrates another use of the stimulus generalization concept. Because of the high quality reputation that Campbells enjoys, they are able to introduce new products to the market with great ease, as buyers tend to generalize their experiences, presumably satisfactory experiences, with other Campbells' products to the new product.

When buyers' experiences are positive the phenomenon of stimulus generalization can greatly facilitate a company's efforts to introduce new products onto the market. The phenomenon, however, works equally well in reverse and a few bad experiences can seriously damage a firm's marketing program. This happened a few years ago when a number of food poisoning cases were traced to Bon Vivant's vichyssoise soup with disastrous effects on all the firm's soups.

Stimulus Discrimination

The process of learning to discriminate one stimulus from another similar stimulus is known as stimulus discrimination. This process, which is essentially the opposite of stimulus generalization, is based upon the existence of discriminative stimuli or cues. In Pavlov's experiment, for example, if food follows only the ringing of a bell of a specific tone, the dog will quickly come to learn to use the tone of the bell as a cue and will tend to salivate only when a bell of the proper tone is rung.

It should be readily apparent that stimulus generalization and stimulus discrimination are intimately related learning phenomena. The organism's first response to a novel stimulus is, as was previously discussed, normally very close to the response the organism would make to the most similar familiar stimulus. It is only after this generalization and with subsequent learning of appropriate cues, that the organism comes to discriminate the new stimulus from similar old stimuli and respond uniquely to the new stimulus.

Howard (1977; Howard and Sheth 1969) suggested that this process of stimulus generalization, followed by stimulus discrimination, is essential to the eventual success of a new product. The reason for this is that the buyer's first response to a new product is to ask to what is it most similar. Having made this identification, the buyer then ascribes the properties of the known product to the new product; i.e., generalizes the stimulus. For the new product to become successful, however, it will generally be necessary for the buyer to come to perceive unique characteristics of the new product that discriminate it from the older product with which it was originally grouped. The uniqueness may be no more than offering essentially the same product at a lower price. It may, however, involve a number of factors, many of which will be presented in the discussion of the diffusion of innovations in Chapter 10.

There is good reason to believe that the failure of many new products is largely attributable to a lack of stimulus generalization or subsequent stimulus discrimination. If unable to identify a new product as being of a certain type, then the buyer must quite literally build entirely new brand and product class concepts. This is a formidable task, and exceptionally strong motivation is required to induce the buyer to undertake the necessary search for and evaluation of relevant information. In such circumstances, the buyer's response will most likely be to refuse to consider the new product. This difficulty of stimulus generalization is very likely at least partially responsible for the very slow acceptance that solar energy has received. The need for stimulus discrimination is more obvious but no less important. Quite simply, if there is no net positive benefit, the buyer has little reason to buy the new brand.

Data compiled by Davidson (1976) on the relative performance and price and on differences in distinctiveness for 50 successful and 50 unsuccessful products, illustrates just how important positive discrimination is to successful introduction of a new product. This is presented in Table 7.1. Note, in part I of the table, that of the successful products almost half were characterized by a "significantly better performance" at a "higher price." Part II of the table reveals that too great a distinctiveness from competitive products can be detrimental. This can occur because the new product cannot be generalized and, therefore, most buyers simply choose to ignore it.

Table 7.1
Differences in performance, price, and distinctiveness for 50 successful and 50 unsuccessful products

Part I. Differences in performance

Difference from competitor	Of 50 successes (by percent)	Of 50 failures (by percent)
Significantly better performance, higher price	44	8
Marginally better performance, higher price	6	12
Better performance, same price	24	0
Same performance, lower price	8	0
Same performance, same price	16	30
Same performance, higher price	2	30
Worse performance, same or higher price	0	20
Total	100	100

Part II. Differences in distinctiveness

Degree of difference	Of 50 successes (by percent)	Of 50 failures (by percent)
Dramatically different	20	8
Very different	48	22
Marginally different	12	38
Similar	20	32
Total	100	100

Source: J. Hugh Davidson, "Why Most New Consumer Brands Fail." *Harvard Business Review*, 54 (March–April 1976): 119, 120. Copyright © 1976 by the President and Fellows of Harvard College; all rights reserved. Reprinted by permission of the Harvard Business Review.

Repetition and Forgetting

That learning increases with repetition and that forgetting occurs over time are among the earliest and most durable findings of learning research. In fact, research shows that both initial acquisition and subsequent forgetting of a response tend to follow an exponential pattern (Ray 1973a). Such exponential learning and forgetting curves are clearly seen in Figure 7.3, which presents recall data for advertising delivered under two different schedules. Zielske (1959) sent one group of women an advertisement for a product every week for thirteen consecutive weeks. Another group of women received the same thirteen advertisements once every four weeks over a 52 week period. Such spacing of material to be learned is referred to as massed and distributed practice, respectively. Brand recall was assessed for both groups via telephone interviews conducted over all 52 weeks of the year during which the study was conducted. Both exponential acquisition and forgetting are clearly evident for the group that received thirteen consecutive advertisements but none thereafter. Only the acquisition portion of the curve is evident for the group that received the thirteen advertisements distributed evenly over the 52 weeks. An important marketing implication of the Zielske study is that, other things equal, massed advertising is best for highly seasonal products (e.g., chocolate Easter bunnies), while distributed advertising is best for products without a strong seasonal sales pattern (e.g., many personal care products).

Another important learning principle related to forgetting is known as Jost's Law: If two habits are of equal strength, but different ages, the newer one will tend to be forgotten more rapidly than the older one. Jost's law is a direct consequence of exponential forgetting (Ray 1973a, p. 88) and partially explains why older brands require less advertising than newer brands and why the earliest brands on the market have an advantage over brands introduced later (Myers and Reynolds 1967, p. 57).

Figure 7.3.
Advertising illustration of exponential acquisition and exponential forgetting

Source: H. A. Zielske, "The Remembering and Forgetting of Advertising." *Journal of Marketing*, 23 (January, 1959): 240.

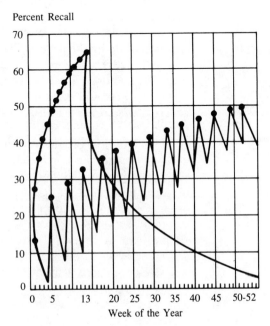

We might also recall the mere exposure hypothesis, discussed in Chapter 3, that repetition of a stimulus leads to a positive evaluation of that stimulus. Sawyer (1977) examined the marketing implications of the mere exposure hypothesis and concluded that there is abundant evidence "that repetition is effective in increasing brand preference and purchase intention, especially for little-known new brands" (p. 241).

Extinction

Extinction occurs when a response is no longer reinforced or when punishment follows the response. Conceptually, extinction is quite different from forgetting. That is, one may remember quite clearly that a particular response was, at an earlier time, reinforced but is now not reinforced or is punished. This could happen, for example, when a food product is reformulated or when an automobile manufacturer makes a design change. Although conceptually distinct from extinction, forgetting is a major cause of extinction. The reason for this is that if a person forgets a response, that response will not be made and, therefore, the response cannot be reinforced. In this way, forgetting leads to extinction through lack of reinforcement. To counter this, many sellers make heavy use of so-called *reminder* advertising. Reminder advertising, as the name suggests, is primarily aimed at keeping the buyer from forgetting rather than creating new learning.

The principle of extinction is most directly applicable to the brand choice decision. Whether extinction occurs depends on a number of factors. Generally, it will be harder to extinguish a response (1) the greater is the degree of reinforcement in the initial learning, (2) the greater is the number of occasions on which the response has been reinforced, (3) the greater is the importance of the response to the individual (i.e., the level of involvement with the product class), and (4) the lesser is the potential reinforcement available from alternative responses. All of the above effects are quite evident in the common observation that it is extremely difficult, but not impossible, to dislodge a dominant brand from the market.

An interesting application of the principle of extinction in the public policy area was made by the Federal Trade Commission when it required Listerine to run corrective advertising to counter Listerine's long-standing claim that Listerine helps stop colds. According to *Advertising Age*, the reason for this decision was that "The FTC said it believed it had ample evidence to demonstrate that the effects of Listerine advertising will carry over into future consumer buying decisions unless corrective advertising is implemented" (13 September 1976, p. 124).

Our last example of the principle of extinction in a marketing context concerns one-sided versus two-sided persuasive messages. A one-sided message presents only positive arguments. A two-sided message contains both positive *and* negative arguments. Of course, the negative arguments are minor relative to the positive arguments. Typical examples of two-sided arguments would be L'Oreal's mention of its higher price or Listerine's claim that their product "has the taste people hate twice a day." A great deal of research has shown that a one-sided argument, when presented alone, produces more initial attitude change than a two-sided argument. It is, however, much easier to extinguish a one-sided than a two-sided argument. The explanation for this finding has been labeled the "inoculation hypothesis." The inoculation hypothesis is based on a medical analogy. Just as a weakened exposure to a disease can arouse the individual's physical defenses against the disease, a weakened dose of the expected counter arguments from competitors (the negative arguments) can arouse the individual's psychological defenses to defend his or her beliefs (Ray 1973a, pp. 96–97). Because counter arguments can be expected in many competitive situations, two-sided arguments have become increasingly popular among advertisers. This is quite interesting because until fairly recently one of the strongest rules in advertising was "Never mention anything negative about your product." The prohibition is good advice in some circumstances, but not when counter arguments can be expected and not when the product in question *does* have some negative features that are small relative to its positive features.

BEHAVIOR MODIFICATION — NOT TO Big ON

The final learning theory topic, behavior modification, provides an opportunity both to reinforce the managerial importance of learning theory and to introduce a special use of learning theory concepts that does not fit neatly into any of the previously discussed learning theories. Behavior modification theory is an outgrowth of various learning theories that focuses on how the environment in which behavior occurs affects that behavior. A number of different theories of behavior modification have been developed (e.g., Bandura 1969, 1978; Skinner 1953, 1969; Staats 1975). All, however, share one central concept: behavior can be changed by changing the environment in which the behavior occurs.

Peter and Nord describe behavior modification in the following way:

> It [behavior modification] is a response-reinforcement model that focuses on changing the probabilities and/or frequencies of behavior by manipulating stimuli that appear *after* a response has occurred (1982, p. 103, emphasis in original).

Peter and Nord also state that

> Basically, the BMP (behavior modification perspective) views the role of marketing as influencing, modifying and controlling consumer behavior in order to achieve organizational objectives. It views consumer behavior as being controlled by the environment rather than by inferred, internal psychological processes such as needs, awareness, knowledge, attitudes, etc. In short, the BMP views marketing as a technology that seeks more effective solutions to practical problems rather than as a science that seeks better theories and explanations of internal events (O'Shaughnessy and Ryan 1979), (p. 102).

The essence of behavior modification is well illustrated by our previous Hickory Farms example. A buyer wandering through Hickory Farms (response) is rewarded with one or more free cheese samples (reinforcement). This reinforcement should increase the probability or frequency that the buyer will engage in the behavior (wandering through Hickory Farms) in the future.

With the exception of cognitive theories, the theories of learning previously discussed can all be treated from a behavior modification perspective. What a strict behavior modification perspective does is drop reference to any presumed internal state, such as drive, need, or motive. For this reason our examples of the use of behavior modification techniques will be confined to a use not previously discussed, known as ecological design.

Ecological Design

The term ecological design recognizes that the larger environment or ecology in which behavior occurs is, to a large extent, manmade and that the environment in which behavior occurs can strongly affect behavior. A study by Milliman (1982) provides us with a formal demonstration of the effects of ecological design on buyer behavior. The study investigated the effects of programmed background music on in-store shopping behavior. The experimental treatments were no music, music with a slow tempo, and music with a fast tempo. Milliman found no significant differences between no music and music with a slow tempo. Significant and strong differences were found between the slow and fast tempos. The rate of flow of in-store traffic was almost 15 percent slower with slow tempo. Most important, however, was the fact that gross daily sales averaged $16,740.23 with the slow tempo music but only $12,112.85 with the fast tempo music.

Although the Milliman study is one of the few formal studies of ecological design that has appeared in the buyer behavior literature, informal examples abound. Stores tend to place items that buyers are likely to purchase without making a special shopping trip, items loosely referred to as impulse goods, in high traffic areas to maximize exposure to potential buyers. In contrast, furniture is typically located in more out-of-the-way locations, since people rarely pick up a chair or a sofa "on the way home." In a very similar way shopping malls, and the location of each store within a shopping mall, are designed to affect buyer behavior in specific ways. For example, it is common practice to locate major department stores, so-called anchors, at opposite ends of a mall to maximize the flow of traffic in front of the smaller stores in between.

Any number of additional examples of the use of ecological design for behavior modification could be easily cited. The crucial point, of course, is that the design of the environment in which buyer behavior occurs is, to a larger extent than is often realized, under the control of the marketing manager.

Situational Effects

An obviously important questions is: Under what types of situations are behavior modification techniques most appropriate? Although definitive data appear to be lacking, Rothschild and Gaidis (1981) tentatively advance an explanation that is sufficiently plausible to deserve careful attention. They suggest that behavior modification techniques are likely to be most applicable to buying situations of low involvement. For buying situations that arouse a high level of involvement, cognitive approaches which emphasize variables that are internal to the buyer are likely to be more relevant. Even in high involvement situations, however, behavior modification techniques continue to be relevant (Peter and Nord 1982).

The argument that Rothschild and Gaidis advance should be somewhat familiar, since it follows quite closely the discussion of low involvement buying situations in Chapter 3. By definition, a low involvement buying situation is one in which there are few reasons for becoming actively involved in an extensive decision-making process. This is further reinforced by the fact that most products that can be classed as low involvement are low cost goods in the mature phase of their life cycles. Thus, almost any choice is likely to be at least minimally satisfactory. Furthermore, the risks associated with an unsatisfactory choice are typically small.

Consequently, in a low involvement buying situation, the buyer is likely to be strongly influenced by such things as high brand recognition, immediate availability, and special incentives; all of which variables may be used quite explicity for behavior modification.

In contrast, when faced with a high involvement buying situation the buyer has strong reasons for *thinking* about the purchase. In such situations, the buyer can be expected to engage in a variety of cognitive activities such as gathering information, making explicit brand comparisons, and planning a future purchase, which may involve a number of contingencies. Although behavior modification techniques continue to be relevant in such high involvement situations, an understanding of the internal cognitive activities of the buyer is far more important than in low involvement buying situations.

MEMORY

In the beginning of this chapter, learning was defined as "a relatively permanent change in behavior caused by experience and practice." This definition of learning clearly implies a more or less permanent means for storing what has been learned. Memory provides this means of storage.

It is only recently that buyer behavior researchers have given much attention to the concept of memory (e.g., Bettman 1979; Johnson and Russo 1978; Olson 1979). A major reason for the increasing interest in memory is the recognition that an internal memory search for information relevant to a purchasing problem is almost surely likely to be the buyer's *first* response and that an understanding of memory is essential to a full understanding of buyer behavior (Bettman 1979, pp. 107–110; Newman 1977).

Despite the obvious importance of memory to buyer behavior very little research has been devoted explicitly to memory in a buyer behavior context. Psychologists, however, have had a long-standing interest in memory and produced a voluminous literature on the topic.[8] Psychological work on memory has typically been conducted under carefully controlled laboratory conditions and, for purposes of control, tended to rely heavily on memorization of material that has no inherent meaning for subjects, e.g., memorizing lists of nonsense words or sequences of numbers. Because of this, one must be cautious about the transferability of psychological work on memory to a buyer behavior context. However, psychological research on memory provides insights that are potentially very useful in understanding buyer behavior.

Memory Functions

Memory serves two basic functions. First, it provides a series of temporary stores in which raw information, such as sound or light waves, is *processed.* Processing involves a number of complex activities: such as examining the information for meaning, integrating new and old information, and placing relevant information in permanent storage. The processing function of memory is considered in depth in

---

[8]For a recent, and excellent, discussion of psychological research on memory see Wingfield and Byrnes (1981).

Chapter 11 under the topic of perception. The second function of memory is as a permanent store of information. As will be seen, long-term memory (LTM) has a number of characteristics with important implications for understanding buyer behavior.

Characteristics of LTM

The most striking characteristic of LTM is its capacity. As a practical matter, there appears to be no limit on how much information can be stored in LTM. A second characteristic of LTM concerns what is stored. There is now general agreement that what is stored are concepts and relationships among those concepts (Wingfield and Byrnes 1981). These concepts include such things as objects, attributes of objects, higher level abstractions, rules for processing information, events, attributes of events, etc. A buyer, for example, may remember that he bought a television (event), that the television was a Sony (object), and that the Sony was both high priced and of high quality (attributes). From this experience a buyer might conclude that all Sony products are high quality (abstraction) and, unless there is contradictory information, products with higher prices should be judged as being of higher quality (processing rule).

A third characteristic of LTM concerns the way information is organized. Here it is necessary to make a distinction between episodic and semantic memory (Tulving 1972). Episodic memory concerns the memorization of episodes or events. For example, I remember that I bought a Sony television set on Saturday, October 18, 1983 to watch a football game—my team lost. Episodic memory is characterized by simple perceptual descriptions of events that are organized in terms of their relationship in time and space. To see how episodic memory works, think how you go about finding your car keys when you have "forgotten" where you left them. Your search might proceed something like this: The last time I drove the car was Saturday, it was raining on Saturday, I had my raincoat on, the keys are in the pocket of my raincoat. Marketing makes use of episodic memory whenever a promotion urges the buyer to *recall* that special moment: your wedding day or your first new car, and all the special feelings you had back then. Bell Telephone, for example, uses such an approach by urging people to recall special moments with friends and family and to renew those feelings with a long-distance telephone call.

In contrast to episodic memory, semantic memory is not organized by simple time and space coordinates. Rather, the organization of semantic memory is abstract, conceptual, and complex. Some of the relationships among the elements in semantic memory can be illustrated with an example from Collins and Quillian (1969), which is reproduced in Figure 7.4 This model is referred to as a network model of memory. The network consists of units (the stored concepts), pointers (the interconnections among the units), and properties (the attributes of the units). For example, the *units* canary and bird are related by the arrow which *points* from canary to bird, indicating that canary is a type of bird. Note carefully, that the organization is hierarchical and that exceptions to the rule are stored directly with the concept to which the exception applies. For example, an ostrich is a bird and birds have the *property* of flight; ostriches, however, do not fly.

One of the principle types of empirical support for the network model of memory comes from reaction times to questions that require information from two

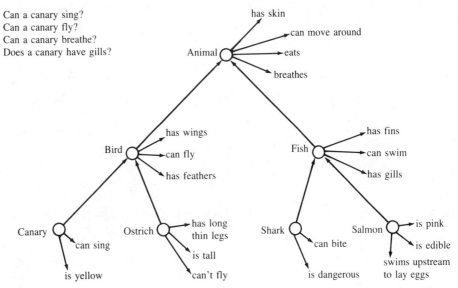

Can a canary sing?
Can a canary fly?
Can a canary breathe?
Does a canary have gills?

Figure 7.4.
A network model of semantic memory

Source: A. M. Collins and M. R. Quillian, "Retrieval Time from Semantic Memory." *Journal of Verbal Learning and Verbal Behavior,* 8 (1969): 241.

points in the memory hierarchy. Collins and Quillian (1969) asked subjects to respond true or false to questions such as "A canary can sing?" "A canary can breathe?" "A canary has gills?" Note in Figure 7.4 that the answers to these three questions require information that is stored in increasingly distant points in the semantic memory hierarchy. As expected, Collins and Quillian found that the time it took subjects to answer questions was positively related to the distance between the required pieces of information.

LTM and the Brand Concept

From a marketing perspective, one of the most important concepts stored in memory is buyers' concepts of seller's brands. Just as a network memory for the general class of objects animals can be constructed, as in Figure 7.4, so can such models of a buyer's brand concept and its relationship to other concepts in the buyer's memory.

Figure 7.5 illustrates a portion of a hypothetical buyer's memory network for the general concept food. This network contains much information of value to the marketing manager. For one thing, it can tell the manager something about whether, and under what circumstances, a product and brand will be used. Soybeans, for example, are identified as an animal food and, therefore, would not be considered for purchase. Similarly, orange juice is regarded as a breakfast food but not a snack food. As we have noted previously, this is a restriction that orange growers have attempted to overcome in recent years. From our current perspective, this effort represents an attempt to reorganize buyers' memories so that orange juice appears under other consumption situations, such as snacks. If successful, the effect of such a memory reorganization is that when the buyer thinks of a snack drink, he or she thinks of orange juice as an alternative.

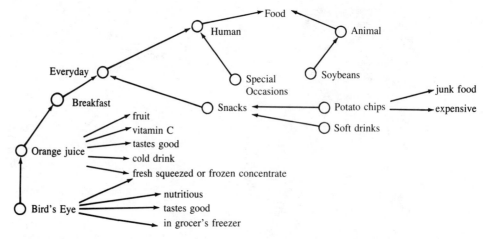

Figure 7.5.
An illustration of a hypothetical buyer's memory network for the general concept food

The memory network can also tell the manager something about how the buyer identifies and evaluates a brand. Birds Eye, for example, is a type of orange juice and, therefore, shares the general properties of all brands of orange juice. The buyer expects to find Birds Eye in the grocer's freezer section and evaluates Birds Eye orange juice as being both nutritious and good tasting.

A particularly interesting point is that our hypothetical buyer identifies orange juice as coming in only two forms: fresh squeezed or frozen concentrate. Thus, this particular buyer would not look in the dairy case for bottled orange juice. The implication of this is quite general. One of the things frequently stored in memory is the location of the object in question. When that object is placed in an unusual or unexpected location the marketer must go to special efforts to inform the buyer of this fact. Pillsbury, for example, includes the statement "look for them in your grocer's dairy case" in their advertisements for Crescent Dinner Rolls since, otherwise, the buyer might tend to look for them where the other bread products are stored.

SUMMARY

This chapter examined four different learning theories. Each theory is especially relevant to specific kinds of learning situations. Of course, most learning situations will be found, upon close examination, to require concepts from more than one learning theory. Furthermore, all learning theories recognize certain basic principles, such as stimulus generalization and stimulus discrimination. Proper application of these learning principles can be extremely useful to the marketing manager as a guide for formulating effective marketing programs.

A most important outgrowth of traditional learning theories is behavior modification theory. Behavior modification is not an alternative to traditional learning theories; rather, it is an application of these traditional theories. It is explicitly constructed on the premise that behavior may be changed by changing the environment in which the behavior occurs. Of course, every time the marketing manager implements a product, price, promotion, or distribution decision, he or she is consciously altering the environment in which buying decisions are made. This is done with the expectation that the changed environment will cause buyers to change their behavior in ways which will be beneficial to the firm. Behavior modification theory provides an explicit framework that can be used, especially in low involvement buying situations, to make these managerial decisions more effectively.

Our final topic was memory. From a marketing viewpoint, the most important characteristics of long-term memory are the concepts that have been stored and the organization in memory of those concepts. Much of what marketing managers attempt to do, in fact, can be phrased in terms of placing specific concepts (e.g., creating new or altering existing brand images) in buyers' memories or in rearranging existing concepts (e.g., suggesting alternative uses for established brands).

Attitudes and
Attitude Change

8

The previous two chapters discussed the nature of motives and how buyers learn to satisfy their motives, including a brief review of the nature of memory that focused on the organization of the concepts stored in long term memory. This chapter continues the discussion of memory by considering in depth the nature of a very special type of stored concept, known as an attitude. An attitude is generally defined as "a learned predisposition to respond in a consistently favorable or unfavorable manner in respect to a given object" (Fishbein and Ajzen 1975, p. 6).

From the preceding definition, it is obvious that a knowledge of buyers' attitudes toward a seller's and competitors' brands can be immensely useful to the marketer. Indeed, there is good evidence that attitudes are closely related to such things as brand purchased (e.g., Achenbaum 1966, 1972) and market share (e.g., Assael and Day 1968). Thus, it is in the interest of marketers to know the attitudes of buyers toward their brand and competitive brands and to attempt to create favorable attitudes toward their brands.

The purpose of this chapter then, is to explore the nature of attitudes and to show how an understanding of attitudes can help the marketing manager create more effective marketing programs by either adapting to existing buyer attitudes or by creating strategies to change existing buyer attitudes. Indeed, in the following discussion, the reader should keep carefully in mind that adapting to and attempting to change buyer attitudes are both viable strategies. Furthermore, it is generally easier, although not necessarily more profitable, to adapt to existing attitudes than to try to change those attitudes.

The discussion begins by reviewing the concept of an attitude, followed by the examination of a very special class of attitude models known as multiattribute models. Multiattribute models have special properties that make them potentially very useful to both academic buyer behavior researchers and to marketing managers. Three additional theories of attitudes are examined because they throw further light on the nature of attitudes and the strategies most effective in changing existing attitudes. Finally, the relationships among attitudes, intentions, and behavior will be considered; particularly, the strength of the attitude-intention and attitude-behavior relationships and the controversial question of whether attitudes cause behavior. An elementary discussion of two recently developed and highly sophisticated procedures for measuring attitudes is presented in Appendix C.

THE CONCEPT OF AN ATTITUDE

Although most of this chapter is devoted to specific theories of attitude structure and attitude change, the attitude concept must first be described in terms of characteristics of attitudes that are generally applicable within the context of any specific attitude theory.

Allport's Definition of Attitude

The classic definition of an attitude was published by Gordon Allport in 1935; Allport's definition is still widely accepted and quoted. According to Allport, an attitude consists of at least the following aspects: (1) *it is a mental and neural state* (2) *of readiness to respond,* (3) *organized* (4) *through experience* (5) *exerting a directive and/or dynamic influence on behavior.* This definition is important because, besides being widely accepted, it also touches on most of the important theoretical issues that arise in the study of attitudes.

As a *mental and neural state* attitudes are not, even in principle, observable. In the terminology of psychologists, attitude is a mediating construct that stands between environmental antecedents and behavioral consequents. In other words, stimuli such as the product, advertising, and brand evaluations by other people (environmental antecedents) cause the buyer to form an attitude toward each brand (mediating construct) and these attitudes will be factors in determining which brand is purchased (behavioral consequent).

That attitude is a neural, as well as mental, state suggests the possibility of direct physiological measures of attitudes. Indeed, there was some early enthusiasm for physiological measures such as galvanic skin response (e.g., Cook and Selltiz 1964) and pupil dilation (e.g., Hess 1965). However, interest in physiological measures of attitudes declined (Day 1973) as it became clear that while physiological measures may give some indication of the strength of an attitude they cannot tell whether the attitude is positive or negative (McGuire 1969, p. 143).

The status of attitude as a mediating construct is also reflected by the description of it as a state *of readiness to respond.* This phrase also reminds us that attitudes and behavior *are* different. Furthermore, there are, as discussed in detail in Chapters 2 and 4, many reasons why a person may fail to express his or her attitudes in overt behavior.

Of crucial importance is the idea that an attitude is *organized.* To see the importance of this recall the discussion, in Chapter 3, of the different ways in which buyers acquire and evaluate information for products characterized by a "learning" hierarchy as opposed to a "low involvement" hierarchy of decision making. For products in the learning hierarchy, the buyer tends to actively seek out and evaluate information as it is received. The buyer also attempts to compare this new information with what is already known and, if the information is determined to be credible, to integrate the new information into the buyer's existing attitude toward the product. In marked contrast, for low involvement products, the buyer will passively receive information. With sufficient repetition the new information will become part of the buyer's long-term memory store. However, this new information will tend to exist in isolation, to exist in an unorganized form.

There is virtually unanimous agreement that attitudes are acquired *through experience*; that is, attitudes are learned. Somewhat more controversial is the characterization of attitudes as *exerting a directive and/or dynamic influence on behavior.* That attitudes direct behavior is generally accepted (McGuire 1969, pp. 147–149); however, there is some disagreement as to the nature of the directive process. Learning theorists view attitudes as altering the probabilities that specific responses will be made. Perceptual theorists argue that attitudes direct behavior by altering the individual's perception of the attitude object. The classic example of the perceptual view of attitudes involves politicians. A person who initially views politicians very poorly may, through some means such as a strong positive statement from someone the person highly respects, change his or her attitude and come to see politicians more as statesmen than as ward heelers. As McGuire (1969, pp. 265–268) notes, the weight of the evidence seems to favor the perceptual theorists. However, McGuire (1969, p. 268) also notes that the two conceptions of the directive nature of attitudes are essentially complementary rather than competing.

The question of whether attitudes have a dynamic influence on behavior can be restated as "do attitudes affect the level of the energy of behavior?" This argument has already been discussed under the topic of cognitive theories of motivation. Cognitive theorists consider cognitions an important source of motivation for behavior. Attitudes, of course, are a special type of cognition. The buyer has an attitude toward a brand; the more positive the attitude, the greater will be the level of motivation (i.e., energy) and the greater will be the total energy spent on acquiring and consuming the good. Although not without its critics in psychology, buyer behavior researchers have largely accepted the cognitivist's view that attitudes have a dynamic influence on behavior (Bettman 1979).

Attitude Structure

Many attempts have been made to divide the attitude concept into finer components and to determine the structure of those components. Broadly, these efforts fall into two categories: cognitive-affective-conative structure and means-end analysis. The first, and older, category is the cognitive-affective-conative structure (Bagozzi et al. 1979). This view of the structure of attitudes can be traced back as far as classic Greece. It holds that the human condition can be resolved into three basic existential states: knowing, feeling, and doing. Without using the term attitude, these three components of attitude appeared in the Chapter 3 discussion of the learning, low involvement, and dissonance/attribution decision-making hierarchies. An important implication of the existence of these three different hierarchies is that the processes by which attitudes are acquired can be quite different in different situations. The text will return to this point in the discussion of the direction of causality in the attitude-behavior relationship, later in this chapter.

The second, and more recent, category of conceptions of attitude structure is generally known as means-end analysis. In this view, objects are conceived of as having attributes that vary in value to the individual. Quite literally, the attributes of the object constitute the means by which the individual's goals (the end) are to be achieved. The individual's attitude in this view is an expression of the ability of the attitude object to satisfy the individual's goals. This view of the structure of attitudes has found wide acceptance in buyer behavior research in the form of multiattribute models of attitude.

Dimensions of Attitude

All attitudes, whatever their structure, can be characterized as varying on certain dimensions. Scott (1968), in a thorough review of the psychological literature on attitude measurement, identified eleven possible dimensions, six of which are especially relevant to the study of buyer behavior.

The most obvious dimension of an attitude is its direction; i.e., whether it is favorable or unfavorable. A less obvious aspect of the direction dimension concerns the "neutral" point. Imagine an attitude scale which runs from -3 (very unfavorable) to $+3$ (very favorable). What interpretation should be given to a response of zero? The possibilities include: I'm not aware of the thing I'm being asked about; I'm aware of it, but it is of no interest to me; I'm aware of it, interested, and my attitude toward the thing is neither favorable nor unfavorable, it is neutral. The question of the interpretation of the neutral point is very important to buyer behavior researchers because buyer attitudes toward brands are frequently quite weak. Fortunately, there are methods, which are discussed in most marketing research texts, for distinguishing among these different interpretations of the midpoint of an attitude scale.

The second dimension of an attitude is its magnitude; that is, the degree of favorableness or unfavorableness. An important conclusion from attitude research is that the difficulty of changing attitudes tends to be directly related to the so-called extremity of the attitude. (An extreme attitude is either very favorable *or* very unfavorable.) As already noted, many, but by no means all, brand attitudes are weak (low on extremity) and, therefore, easier to change than more extreme attitudes. This fact is of obvious importance to marketers.

The third dimension of an attitude is its ambivalence. Although attitudes tend to be thought of as varying on a *single* dimension that runs from very favorable to very unfavorable, a closer inspection will normally reveal that this aggregate affective judgment is based on a number of more specific attributes of the object in question. One may, for example, have a favorable evaluation of an automobile's style, fuel efficiency, and front seating comfort but have an unfavorable evaluation of its repair record and rear seating comfort. Ambivalent attitudes are presumably held with low confidence, and, therefore, are less stable and more subject to change than unambivalent attitudes (e.g., Howard and Sheth 1969; Howard 1977).

A fourth dimension of an attitude is its centrality. The centrality of an attitude reflects the importance of the attitude to the person. For example, a buyer might think of himself or herself as an athlete. This buyer's attitudes toward various brands of sporting equipment might be quite important, or central to such a buyer. Everything else equal, attitudes that are high in centrality should be harder to change than attitudes that are low in centrality.

The fifth dimension of an attitude is its embeddedness, which means to how many other attitudes is the attitude in question related and how strong are these relationships. For example, a buyer might have a favorable attitude toward Chevrolet. This attitude could be more or less unrelated to any other attitude. It could, however, be closely related to other attitudes, such as being patritotic. In our present example, our buyer might feel that in buying a Chevrolet, he or she would not only be getting a good car but would be supporting America. All other things equal, the difficulty of changing an attitude is directly related to its embeddedness.

The sixth, and final, dimension of an attitude is its affective salience. This dimension is particularly relevant to the cognitive-affective-conative view of attitude structure. The term affective salience refers to the extent to which an attitude is dominated by the affective component. The basic idea of affective salience is well-illustrated by Abelson's (1963) concept of "hot" cognitions. Some cognitions (e.g., "women make just as good workers as men") are hot in the sense that they carry a lot of feeling or affect. Other cognitions (e.g., "Kraft makes an excellent Swiss cheese") are cool in the sense that they carry little affect. Indeed, in a provocative article titled "Feeling and Thinking: Preferences Need No Inferences," Zajonc (1980) suggested that our first reactions to many things (presumably including the things we buy) are affective and that affect can develop without a previously established cognitive base.[1] An important implication of the affective

---

[1]That one may develop strong feelings or affect without first developing a relevant set of cognitions may seem strange. Consider, however, your own reactions to meeting a person for the first time. If you are like most people, your first reaction will be affective; i.e., you will tend to either like or dislike the person.

salience dimension is as a reminder that the extent to which attitudes rest upon a firm and large cognitive base is a matter of degree.

An issue closely related to affective salience is whether rational (cognitive) *or* emotional (affective) advertising appeals are more effective. The problem with this question is the way it is framed; the question implies that advertising appeals can be placed on a single dimension that runs from highly rational to highly emotional. However, cognitions and affect are two separate dimensions and, properly stated, the question should ask for the optimal combination of rational and emotional appeals in an advertisement. Cox (1967b, p. 116) argues that the optimal appeal is both highly rational *and* highly emotional.

A full understanding of attitudes requires information on all of the preceding six dimensions. Most empirical studies of attitudes, however, attempt to assess only the first two dimensions, direction and magnitude (Scott 1968). A marketer who intends to change buyer attitudes is well advised to consider all six attitude dimensions before attempting to create a marketing program designed to change existing buyer attitudes.

MULTIATTRIBUTE MODELS OF ATTITUDE

This section will discuss the properties of an important class of attitude models known as multiattribute models. Although a number of different models have been proposed, all multiattribute attitude models share certain basic properties. These properties can be illustrated by recalling the example used in Chapter 2 to illustrate the attitude concept in the Howard-Sheth theory of buyer behavior. For convenience that example is reproduced here as Table 8.1.

The attitude object in Table 8.1 is a specific automobile. The buyer considers four choice criteria to be relevant to judging automobiles. In more general terms, these choice criteria are the attributes to be used to judge the object in question. The buyer must evaluate the automobile on each attribute and combine the evaluations into an overall attitude toward the automobile. In this example, each attribute evaluation is weighted by its relative salience or importance and the sum

Table 8.1
Illustration of a multiattribute attitude

Choice Criteria (Attributes)	Evaluation of Brand A[1]	Salience[2]	Contribution to Attitude
Miles per Gallon	8	.4	3.2
Repair Record	7	.3	2.1
Resale Value	3	.1	.3
Safety	5	.2	1.0
Overall Attitude			6.6

Note carefully that the attitude illustrated in this example is for a single buyer toward a single brand.

[1]Rated on some scale, say 1 to 10, where higher numbers indicate a better evaluation.

[2]The salience of an attribute measures its relative importance. In this example, miles per gallon receives 40 percent of the total weight in the overall attitude. By definition, the salience factors sum to one.

of these weighted evaluations yield the final attitude. As shall be seen subsequently, much of the research on multiattribute models concerns how the attributes are to be conceptualized and how individual attribute evaluations are combined to form attitude.

Multiattribute models have found widespread acceptance among both academic marketers and marketing managers. Lutz and Bettman (1977, p. 137) attribute this acceptance to four factors. First, multiattribute models provide more than just a procedure for measuring attitudes; they also provide a powerful means for diagnosing marketing problems and developing solutions to those problems. The second factor is the intuitive appeal of multiattribute models. Marketers typically think of goods and services in terms of their need or motive satisfying properties. The attributes of the object are the *means* through which the buyer's motives are satisfied, which is why multiattribute models are regarded as possessing a means-ends structure. The third factor is research pragmatics. Multiattribute data are relatively easy to collect and analyze. Fourth, and finally, multiattribute models developed out of specific psychological theories in which the formation of buyers' attitudes is tied to more basic psychological processes.

The Rosenberg Model

The Rosenberg (1956) model developed out of cognitive consistency theory. Algebraically, Rosenberg's model of attitude takes the form

$$A_o = \sum_{i=1}^{N} (VI_i) (PI_i)$$

where
A_o is the overall attitude toward object o
VI_i is the importance of value i
PI_i is the perceived instrumentality of object o in obtaining value i
N   is the number of values.

An example of a value relevant to personal care products would be "keeping in good health" (Mazis, Ahtola, and Klippel 1975). Value importance is measured on a 21-point scale ranging from "gives me maximum satisfaction" to "gives me maximum dissatisfaction." Perceived instrumentality is measured on an 11-point scale ranging from "the condition is completely attained through a given action" to "the condition is completely blocked through undertaking the given action." Finally, Rosenberg specified that the importance of each value is to be multiplied by the perceived instrumentality of the object in attaining each value and summed over all values.

In essence, the Rosenberg model states that people form attitudes, which direct their behavior, in ways that satisfy (i.e., are consistent with) their values. In a buyer behavior context, the buyer's attitude expresses his or her expectation that relevant values can be attained through certain products; which is why multiattribute models, such as the Rosenberg model, are also known as expectancy-value models.

A number of attempts have been made to apply the Rosenberg model to buyer attitudes (e.g., Hansen 1969; Sheth and Talarzk 1972; Mazis, Ahtola, and Klippel 1975). However, as Lutz and Bettman (1977) note, most of these efforts involved some type of alteration that makes them somewhat different from the original

Rosenberg model and from each other. These alterations are largely of two types: substitution of product attributes for the deeper values called for by the original Rosenberg model, and substitution of a measure of attribute importance for the satisfaction-dissatisfaction measure. Multiattribute models in which both of these modifications have been made are known as adequacy-importance models. Most multiattribute models employed in buyer behavior studies have been adequacy-importance models.

The Rosenberg model, in either its orginal or modified form, has been sufficiently successful to suggest that under the proper circumstances the model can provide a useful description of buyer attitudes. In particular, it would seem reasonable to suggest that the Rosenberg model is most applicable where use of a product is closely related to personal values.

The Fishbein Model

A second multiattribute attitude model has been developed by Fishbein (1967). The Fishbein model is based on behavioral learning theory and has been very widely applied by both marketing academics and practitioners. Algebraically, Fishbein's model of attitude takes the form

$$A_o = \sum_{i=1}^{N} B_i a_i$$

where
A_o is the overall attitude toward object o
B_i is the belief that object o possesses some attribute i
a_i is the evaluation of the goodness or badness of attribute i
N is the number of beliefs.

Both beliefs and evaluations are measured on 5-point scales anchored by bipolar adjectives; e.g., probable–improbable for beliefs and good–bad for evaluations. Like the Rosenberg model, beliefs are multiplied by evaluations and summed over all beliefs.

Although the Rosenberg and Fishbein models appear quite similar, they contain important differences. The most important difference is that Rosenberg's model is developed in terms of personal values, which may be difficult to relate directly to products, while Fishbein's beliefs can easily be formulated in terms of beliefs about product attributes. Although less drastic, it is also likely that the evaluation of an attitude object in terms of satisfaction–dissatisfaction (Rosenberg) is somewhat different than evaluation of the same object in terms of good–bad (Fishbein). Despite their differences, both models are expectancy value, means-ends models of attitude that view the attitude object as the means for satisfying ends.

The Fishbein model, and a number of variations of the basic Fishbein model, have been widely investigated by buyer behavior researchers. Although a great many controversies and technical issues remain to be resolved,[2] the Fishbein

---

[2]Excellent discussions of the controversies and issues surrounding multiattribute models, including the Fishbein model, can be found in Wilkie and Pessemier (1973) and Lutz and Bettman (1977).

model has received sufficient empirical support to earn it an important place in buyer behavior research both as a theory for explaining buyer attitudes and as a research tool for helping the manager formulate marketing strategy.

The Extended Fishbein Model

Fishbein (1967; Fishbein and Ajzen 1975) developed a significant extension of his original attitude model. The extension involves two separate changes in the original model. First, attitude toward the object (symbolized by A_o) is replaced with attitude toward the *act* involving the object (symbolized by A_{act}). Although this change may seem minor, it represents a major change in thinking about how attitude should be conceptualized. Specifically, it recognizes that one may have a very favorable attitude toward an object and yet believe that expressing that attitude in behavior (in an act) is undesirable. For example, a buyer might have a very favorable attitude toward a Triumph Spitfire and yet have a negative attitude toward the *act* of buying a Triumph Spitfire for any number of reasons such as size, reliability, and difficulty and expense of repairs.

From the buyer's point of view, the difference between A_o and A_{act} is in the frame of reference from which his or her statements or attitude are expressed. A_{act} puts the buyer in a much less abstract frame of reference than does A_o. That is, when queried about his or her attitude toward buying the product, the buyer is required to frame his or her responses in terms of the total consequences of engaging in the act. To continue the Triumph example, nothing is inherently inconsistent about A_o being positive and A_{act} being negative. In the abstract, the contemplated fun and excitement associated with a Triumph may be very appealing. In the concrete, where the buyer may be financially constrained to one automobile and have a job that frequently involves transporting clients, the prospect of actually owning a Triumph may be considerably less appealing.[3]

The second change in the original Fishbein model involves the addition of two variables representing the norms governing the act in question and the person's motivation to comply with those norms. Norms are socially sanctioned standards of behavior. Norms governing the purchase of a Triumph, for example, might be "sport cars are for young people" and "Americans should buy American-made cars." A buyer may, of course, recognize the existence of a norm and decide not to comply, which is why motivation to comply must be included in the model.

Algebraically, the extended Fishbein model takes the form

$$B \approx BI = (A_{act})w_1 + \left(\sum_{j=1}^{k} NB_i \times MC_j\right)w_2$$

where

B	is overt behavior
BI	is behavioral intention
A_{act}	is the attitude toward taking a specific action
NB	is normative beliefs
MC	is motivation to comply with the normative beliefs

[3]It is interesting to note the relationship between A_o and A_{act} in comparison with the Howard-Sheth theory of buyer behavior. A_o is quite similar to Howard and Sheths' hypothetical construct attitude. A_{act} merges elements of intention, particularly inhibitors, into A_o by changing the respondent's frame of reference. One potentially undesirable consequence of the extended Fishbein model is that the important role of inhibitors may not be explictly recognized.

k   is the number of normative beliefs

w_1,w_2 are weights reflecting the relative importance of the two components that must be statistically estimated via regression analysis.

The term A_{act} is defined in the same way as A_o; i.e.,

$$A_{act} = \sum_{i=1}^{N} B_i a_i$$

except that the questions used to measure the beliefs and the evaluations of those beliefs are stated in terms of the act of buying the brand. Note the symbol $\approx$ which stands for "is approximately equal to." What this means is that the extended Fishbein model is a model of behavioral intention and not behavior per se. This is because unanticipated events can block the expression of behavioral intentions in action.

Procedures for measuring the beliefs and evaluations of the beliefs upon which A_{act} is based are similar to the procedures used in the original Fishbein model, except that the frame of reference is changed to the act of buying the brand. Similar procedures are used to measure beliefs regarding norms and the buyer's motivation to comply with those norms,[4] e.g.,

I believe most of my friends and acquaintances believe
that Americans should buy American-made cars.

True _____ _____ _____ _____ _____ False

and

I intend to buy an American-made car.

Probable _____ _____ _____ _____ _____ _____ Improbable.

The extended Fishbein model has received extensive empirical testing over a number of different product classes (Ryan and Bonfield 1975). In general, the extended model performed better than the original model. The extended model also proved moderately successful in predicting both behavioral intentions and behavior. The predictive power of the model has, not unexpectedly, proved to be somewhat less in buyer behavior applications than in more tightly controlled psychological studies (Ryan and Bonfield 1975, 1980).

It has also been found that the correlation between BI and B tends to be high when the BI and B measures occur close together in time (e.g., Wilson, Mathews, and Harvey 1975) but the correlations drop considerably as the time increases between measurement of BI and B (e.g., Bonfield 1974). This, of course, is to be expected, since the lengthening time provides increasing opportunities for unanticipated factors to arise that block the completion of the intended behavior. The most appropriate overall evaluation of the extended Fishbein model is that the model is currently useful to both the academic and the marketing practitioner, but that it will require further development in the specific context of buyer behavior research (Ryan and Bonfield 1975, 1980; Ryan 1977; Miniard and Cohen 1979).

Compositional Rules

Despite major differences, the Rosenberg, Fishbein, and extended Fishbein models share a common view of how beliefs and evaluation of those beliefs should be

[4]For a more detailed description of these measurement procedures see Fishbein and Ajzen (1975).

combined to form attitude. Each model proposes that beliefs are multiplied by evaluations and summed over beliefs to yield attitude. Buyer behavior researchers have examined this proposition in some detail and concluded that attitude formation does not always follow this particular "compositional rule." A large number of different compositional rules have been investigated; but because this literature is quite technical and the specific merits of each rule largely unsettled only two broad classes of compositional rules, compensatory and noncompensatory, will be discussed here.[5]

Table 8.2 illustrates the so-called "weighted linear compensatory" composi-

Table 8.2
Illustration of weighted linear compensatory model

Part I. Belief Evaluations

| | | | Brand | | |
Attribute	A	B	C	D	E
Miles per Gallon	9	5	8	7	7
Repair Record	7	6	7	4	6
Resale Value	7	2	8	5	5
Safety	3	8	3	5	6
Style	4	7	6	6	6

Part II. Attribute Importance Weights for Two Buyers

| | Importance Weights | |
Attribute	Buyer I	Buyer II
Miles per Gallon	.40	.30
Repair Record	.30	.20
Resale Value	.10	.05
Safety	.10	.30
Style	.10	.15

Part III. Attitudes Toward Five Brands

| | Attitude[1] | |
Brand	Buyer I	Buyer II
A	7.10	5.95
B	5.50	8.65
C	7.00	6.00
D	5.60	5.55
E	6.30	6.25

Note: This example assumes that the two hypothetical buyers share the same beliefs regarding the attributes of each brand. It also assumes that higher belief ratings are desirable.

[1]Attitude is formed by multiplying beliefs by importance weights and summing across attributes. For example, the attitude of buyer I toward brand A is .40 (9) + .30 (7) + .1 (7) + .1 (3) + .1 (4) = 7.10.

[5]A good discussion, from an essentially nonmathematical perspective, and references to the literature concerning different compositional rules can be found in Bettman (1979, especially Chapter 7).

tional rule for two hypothetical buyers, who are assumed to have the same beliefs but different importance weights. The importance weights are multiplied by the corresponding beliefs and these weighted beliefs are then summed across beliefs to yield attitude.[6] The model is called a linear model because the weighted beliefs are added to form attitude. It is called a compensatory model because a deficiency on one attribute can be *compensated for* by another attribute. For example, if buyer I's belief about miles per gallon for brand A were 8 instead of 9 then attitude toward brand A would fall from 7.1 to 6.7 (i.e., by .4 × 1). However, this fall could be compensated for by increasing the belief in safety for brand A from 3 to 7 (i.e., .1 × 4). Note that buyers I and II have different attitudes toward the five brands, because they apply different weights to the beliefs they share. In a similar way, two buyers could share the same attribute saliencies but have different attitudes because of different beliefs. Note also that the Rosenberg, Fishbein, and extended Fishbein models are weighted linear compensatory models.

A noncompensatory model does not allow a deficiency on one attribute to be compensated for by another attribute. Using the belief data in Table 8.2, Table 8.3 illustrates the basic idea of a noncompensatory model using the so-called conjunctive rule. The conjunctive rule states that the buyer has a minimum cutoff value for each attribute and that failure of a brand to pass even one cutoff value renders that brand unacceptable. As can be seen from Tables 8.2 and 8.3 only brands C and E are acceptable. Brand A is unacceptable on the style attribute, brand B fails to pass the miles per gallon and resale attributes, and brand D fails the repair record test.

An important aspect of the conjunctive rule, which is shared by most noncompensatory models, is that while the rule yields a group of acceptable brands it does not assign numerical values to attitudes for each acceptable brand. This raises the question of how, and even if, specific attitudes are formed for brands that are judged acceptable. A particularly interesting idea is that buyers may sometimes engage in what are called "phased decision strategies" (Wright and Barbour 1977), in which

Table 8.3
Illustration of noncompensatory conjunctive model using belief data

Attribute	Minimum Cutoff Value
Miles per Gallon	7
Repair Record	6
Resale Value	5
Safety	2
Style	5

Acceptable Brands: C, E.
Unacceptable Brands: A, B, D

[6]Note, from the earlier discussion, that multiattribute models differ in how they define the weights that are muliplied by the beliefs. The Rosenberg model defines the weights as perceived instrumentalities of an object in attaining values, while the Fishbein model defines the weights as the goodness or badness of an attribute. Consumer behavior researchers have frequently defined the belief weights as the relative importance of the beliefs to the buyer in evaluating a brand, i.e., as attribute saliencies.

there is a first phase to eliminate unacceptable alternatives and a second phase to make more detailed evaluations of each alternative and comparisons among alternatives. This suggestion is quite consistent with what is currently known about buyers' capacities and willingness to acquire and process brand information.

For the weighted linear compensatory model two additional issues regarding the compositional rules have been raised. The first issue is whether it is necessary to weight the beliefs. Research to date suggests that, in the context of buyer behavior research, dropping the weights from the model does not seriously reduce the ability of multiattribute models to predict attitudes (Lutz and Bettman 1977). In fact, unweighted linear compensatory models generally compare favorably with any alternative formulation of the basic multiattribute model in the ability to predict attitudes. Despite this conclusion, a full understanding of how buyers form brand attitudes requires inclusion of weights to the extent that the weights are psychologically meaningful. Furthermore, as shall be discussed subsequently, the weights may be of considerable value to the marketing manager in deciding on a strategy for changing buyer attitudes.

The second issue is known as the additive-averaging controversy. The question raised here is whether the weighted beliefs are added together or averaged over all beliefs to form attitude. The importance of this issue is clearly seen when considering the effect of adding a new belief component to attitude. If the new weighted belief is positive *and* added to the previously existing attitude, the attitude must become more positive. If an averaging model is appropriate, however, the direction of the attitude change will depend upon the value of the new belief relative to the average of the previous weighted beliefs; i.e., relative to the old attitude. In particular, a sufficiently low belief rating can reduce the overall attitude when a new belief is added to an existing attitude.

Most buyer behavior studies have used an additive version of the multiattribute model. Fishbein and Ajzen (1975, pp. 235–255) examined the literature regarding the additive-averaging controversy in detail and concluded that the additive model is most appropriate for the types of situations for which the Fishbein model is typically used. Bettman, Capon, and Lutz (1975a, b), however, suggest that averaging across attributes may be more common than adding across attributes. Of course, it is not necessary that all buyers use one rule or the other, and it is quite possible that the rule used may be both product and attribute specific.

It is possible that whether adding or averaging is appropriate depends upon whether a new belief augments or redefines the attitude object in question. For example, consider a buyer who has formed a very favorable attitude toward a new automobile that he or she is considering buying. Now consider the differences between two potential additional beliefs regarding the automobile: (1) the automobile comes with an AM radio that is not of particularly high quality, and (2) the overall repair record of the automobile is below average. In the first instance the automobile has been augmented to become an automobile *with* an AM radio. In the second, the automobile has been redefined as an *unreliable* automobile. An additive rule would seem most appropriate for the radio belief, while an averaging rule would seem most appropriate for the reliability belief. Whether this scenario is correct remains to be seen. The important point here is that it is quite likely that whether beliefs are added or averaged may depend very much on the specific buying situation.

Choosing a Multiattribute Model

Many different multiattribute models have been proposed and empirical support can be found for each of the major versions of the multiattribute model examined. Which model should the practitioner use? The best advice at this time would seem to be to consider carefully the motives the buyer is attempting to satisfy in purchasing a particular product. If the buyer is attempting to express or support important values, the Rosenberg model may be especially appropriate. If social norms and pressures are especially prominent the extended Fishbein model may be more appropriate. Building a multiattribute model for a specific product re-quires careful analysis of the buyers' motives, insight and intuition, and *careful empirical testing.*

Changing Buyer Attitudes

One of the most important reasons for studying attitudes is to gain insights into how attitudes may be changed. Multiattribute models are especially useful for developing attitude change strategies because they tend to focus directly upon attributes that may be changed by appropriate managerial decisions. For example, government crash tests may show a particular automobile to be especially safe. If, however, multiattribute studies showed that buyers believed the safety of the automobile to be only average, the marketer might attempt to change this percep-tion through its promotional activities.

In any multiattribute model based on weighted beliefs, the overall attitude may be changed in one of three ways: by changing beliefs; by changing the weights of different weights; or by adding one or more new weighted beliefs. Limited research suggests that changing attitudes by changing beliefs may be the most feasible strategy (Lutz 1975, Olson and Dover 1976). All three strategies, however, would seem to have merit under certain circumstances. For example, where the evaluation of the goodness or badness of attributes is largely a matter of personal taste, as in fashion, a strategy aimed at changing the evaluative weights may be quite successful; e.g., this year short skirts are *in* fashion. Changing circumstances may also require or make desirable the addition of new beliefs. For example, most automobile buyers did not seem to consider gasoline mileage before the 1973 oil embargo. By the early 1980s, however, the change in buyers' attitudes toward high mileage automobiles had become a major problem for American automobile manufacturers.

The automobile example brings up a final point regarding attitude change strategies. There is a tendency to think of these strategies primarily in terms of promotion. However, the firm's product, pricing, and distribution decisions may be equally or even more important in changing attitudes. If quality is difficult to judge directly, a price increase may be desirable. Or, if service is important and the firm's distributors are not service oriented, some change in the channel may be necessary. And, of course, one must always take a hard look at the product itself. Even a successful, high quality product may become competitively deficient through the introduction of new products or from changes in the larger environment.

ALTERNATIVE CONCEPTIONS OF ATTITUDE

In recent years, the buyer behavior literature on attitude has been dominated by research on multiattribute models. There are, however, a number of other theories of attitude structure and change. This section focuses on three of these theories: functional, social judgment, and cognitive dissonance. Although the three theories are not entirely compatible either among themselves or with the multiattribute approach, they basically focus on different aspects of the processes of attitude formation and attitude change. Thus, study of the alternative attitude theories enriches our total understanding of the role of attitudes in buyer behavior.

Functional Approach

The functional approach to the study of attitudes is most closely associated with Daniel Katz (1960). More than any other attitude theory, the functional approach directly ties attitudes to the motives that presumably underlie them. The essence of the functional approach is that attitudes help the individual better satisfy his or her motives; that is, the *function* of attitudes is to facilitate motive satisfaction.

Katz postulated four attitude functions: utilitarian, knowledge, value-expressive, and ego-defensive. He also argued that the same attitude could be held by two individuals for quite different reasons. For example, a positive attitude could be held toward Marlboro cigarettes because they taste good (utilitarian function) or because the buyer is attempting to bolster a threatened sense of masculinity (ego-defensive function). Furthermore, he argued that in order to develop effective attitude change strategies it was necessary to know what function a specific attitude was serving.

The utilitarian function of attitudes is to serve as a summary store of experiences. Positive attitudes develop toward objects and actions that have been reinforced while negative attitudes develop toward objects and actions that have been punished. The utilitarian function of attitudes is to aid the individual in making choices that will lead to desired ends. The utilitarian function is especially evident when the buyer is in the routinized response behavior stage of learning. Indeed, it is the existence of well developed attitudes toward brands in the evoked set that allows brand choices to be made routinely.

The proper strategy to change attitudes that serve a utilitarian function is to alter the buyer's expectation of the rewards associated with the product. Product performance appeals such as EPA mileage estimates, cavity prevention ability, and nutritional value attempt to alter buyer attitudes through advertising targeted at the utilitarian function. Because utilitarian attitudes are developed through direct experience, it has been suggested that they are difficult to change through simple verbal appeals (Day 1973). This suggests that the marketer will need to find ways to induce the buyer to try the product to change a utilitarian attitude.

The similarity between utilitarian attitudes and behavioral learning theory should be readily apparent. Indeed, this is the case and the behavioral learning principles that were discussed in the last chapter provide an important set of tools for changing attitudes that serve a utilitarian function. There is also a link between utilitarian attitudes and multiattribute models; especially the Fishbein model, which was developed directly out of behavioral learning theory. Because utilitarian attitudes are likely to be based directly upon product attributes, it has been suggested that multiattribute models may be useful for studying utilitarian attitudes (Lutz 1979).

The second function of attitudes is the knowledge function. Attitudes serving the knowledge function help the individual better understand and categorize the world. Two different interpretations of the knowledge function are possible (McGuire, 1969). The first interpretation is that increased knowledge allows the individual to adapt better to the world in which he or she lives. In this sense, the knowledge function is a special case of the utilitarian function. However, it is not presumed that the attitude has been directly reinforced except to the extent that the individual believes that the attitude may be of use in the future. For example, a person might acquire the knowledge that Harvard has an excellent MBA program and, therefore, develop a positive attitude toward the Harvard MBA program even though that person has no plans to obtain an MBA degree or use the attitude in any other way. Of course, the attitude is available should a need for it arise; e.g., hiring an MBA.

The second interpretation posits a need to know that drives the individual to acquire knowledge. The basis for this motive was discussed in Chapter 6 under the heading arousal theories of motivation. Under conditions, which were generally labeled boredom in Chapter 6, buyers will actively seek out new information and be especially receptive to new product introductions. By providing new and novel products and promotions the marketer is able to provide buyers with a means for satisfying their need to know; i.e., with a means for changing old attitudes and creating new attitudes.

Examples of appeals based on the knowledge function are numerous. New products, and the programs used to promote them, clearly belong in this category. So-called institutional advertising where a company or even an industry rather than a product is being promoted also are largely targeted at the knowledge function. GE, for example, boasts that "Progress is our most important product."

The third attitude function is the value-expressive function. Value-expressive attitudes give the individual a means for positively expressing his or her central values and self-image. A woman, for example, may think of herself as sophisticated, elegant, and socially adept. Any number of products (automobiles, furniture, clothing, beverages, etc.) can be used to give expression to these values and components of self-image.

Marketers, of course, make heavy use of value-expressive attitudes in developing market segmentation programs, designing products compatible with the values and self-images of buyers in each segment, and developing appropriate promotion and distribution strategies. For example, in recent years a whole industry has grown up around the home do-it-yourselfer who takes great pride in his or her creativity and self-reliance. Many specialized magazines appeal directly to value-expressive attitudes.

In general, marketers have little influence on buyers' values and self-images. Marketers can change value-expressive attitudes by showing how their product fulfills the value-expressive function for buyers with specific values and self-images. Promotion, of course, plays a major role in this process. The marketer, however, should not discount the other elements of the marketing mix. The same piece of jewelry, for example, will project a quite different image if it is sold by Tiffany's rather than at a discount jewelry firm. Marketers also need to monitor how changes in the larger environment affect buyer values that are relevant to their business.

With skyrocketing energy prices, the value of thriftiness has become more widespread. Buyers have also become more concerned about health in recent years; a change that has had major impact on such industries as food and sporting goods.

The fourth, and final, function of attitudes is the ego-defensive function. Ego-defensive attitudes protect the individual from internal fears and anxieties and from external threats. Clear examples of the use of ego-defensive attitudes by marketers are somewhat scarce. The shopping list study by Haire (1950), discussed in Chapter 1, can be interpreted as housewives holding negative attitudes toward instant coffee because it threatened their homemaker role. One way marketers attempted to deal with such ego-defensive attitudes was by showing how use of instant foods could actually enhance the homemaker role; e.g., by making time for you to do things *with* your family.

The idea that two people may hold the same attitude for quite different reasons is seen quite clearly in the distinction between the value-expressive and ego-defensive functions. For example, one man might hold a positive attitude toward Marlboro cigarettes because it expresses a value of masculinity while another man might express the same attitude as a way of defending against a lack of masculine identity. Indeed, Lutz (1979) suggested that the clearest appeals to ego-defensive attitudes can be found in areas involving sex appeals and issues of masculinity/femininity. In each case, a threat to the ego is suggested and the advertised product is shown to eliminate, or at least reduce, the threat. Lutz (1979) also suggests that ego-defensive attitudes are especially important to marketers because they are extremely strong or potent relative to other attitude functions.

A casual inspection of current advertisement suggests that marketing practitioners apply Katz's functional concept at least implicitly. Examples of explicit use of the functional approach to attitudes in marketing are extremely scarce. Day (1973, p. 343) attributes this situation to the lack of explicit procedures for measuring the function of attitudes. Recently, Locander and Spivey (1978) developed a procedure for measuring attitude functions and provided empirical support regarding the validity of their approach. Lutz (1979) suggested a procedure for assessing the degree to which an attitude is serving different functions through multiattribute measurement procedures. Lutz also outlines a procedure for using the functional approach as a basis for developing advertising programs. Although promising, Lutz's approach has not yet been subjected to empirical testing.

Social Judgment

The social judgment concept of attitudes and the processes by which attitudes change can be introduced by a simple psychophysical experiment. A subject is asked to place one hand in a bucket of hot water and the other hand in a bucket of cold water. After a few minutes the subject is asked to plunge both hands into a third bucket of water of moderate temperature. When asked the temperature of the water in the third bucket the subject will report that it feels *both* hot *and* cold, hot to the hand previously in cold water and cold to the hand previously in hot water.

This experiment is labeled psychophysical because it requires a psychological response (the perception of temperature) to a physical stimulus (water temperature). What the experiment shows is that the judgment will depend very much upon the reference point from which the judgment is made. Such reference points are generally known as psychological anchors. There is a large literature that shows psychological judgments to depend very much on the anchors that the person uses to render those judgments.

Social judgments theory grows out of a very fruitful collaborative effort by Muzafer Sherif and Carl Hovland as part of the Yale attitude and communication research program (Sherif and Hovland 1961; Sherif, Sherif, and Nebergall 1965). What social judgment theory does is apply certain concepts and findings from psychophysics to the study of attitudes.[7] Because social judgment theory is framed explicitly in terms of the effects of persuasive communications on attitude change, it is especially relevant to marketing.

Figure 8.1 illustrates the social judgment concept of attitude structure. A number of different positions may be taken with respect to any attitude object. Whatever position a particular person holds that person will likely find a number of mildly different or discrepant positions acceptable. For example, a person might say that a particular automobile is a "great looking car" but agree that "good, but not exactly great, looking" is a reasonable or acceptable evaluation. Such acceptable positions are said to fall within the latitude of acceptance. If a statement is too discrepant with the person's attitude, however, the person will reject the statement as unacceptable. For example, the evaluation "that car is really ugly" would probably be rejected as unacceptable. Such unacceptable positions are said to fall within the latitude of rejection. Separating the latitudes of acceptance and rejection is the latitude of noncommitment. As can be seen in Figure 8.1, three regions are associated with extreme attitudes and five regions associated with moderate attitudes.

An essential assumption of social judgment theory is that, when a person receives a message regarding an attitude that the person holds, a judgment process is elicited; specifically, a judgment regarding the similarity of the position advocated by the message to the person's present attitude. A large number of factors can distort this judgment process, such as an extreme anchor to which the judgment is made, ambiguity in the message, limited experience with the attitude object, situational effects, and strong involvement with the attitude object (Kiesler, Collins,

Figure 8.1
Latitudes of acceptance, rejection, and non-commitment by individuals with extreme and moderate attitudes

LA = Latitude of acceptance
LNC = Latitude of noncommitment
LR = Latitude of rejection

 [1]This example assumes an extremely unfavorable attitude. For an extremely favorable attitude the order of the three latitudes would be reversed.

Part I. Latitudes for Extreme Attitude[1]

Part II. Latitudes for Moderate Attitude

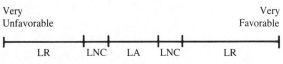

 [7]There is a vast literature on attitude measurement techniques that stem directly from psychophysics. For an excellent introduction see Torgerson (1958).

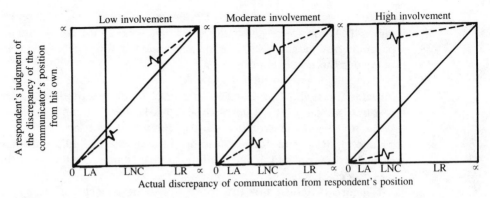

Figure 8.2
Theoretically predicted distortions in judgments of the communicator's position and shifts in the latitudes of noncommitment and rejection under three levels of involvement

LA   = Latitude of acceptance
LNC = Latitude of noncommitment
LR   = Latitude of rejection
————— Unbiased "correct" judgment
– – – – – Theoretically predicted judgment

Source: Charles A. Kiesler, Barry E. Collins, and Norman Miller, *Attitude Change.* New York: Wiley & Sons, 1969, p. 247. Reprinted with permission.

and Miller 1969, p. 246). However, research on social judgment theory has largely focused on the effects of involvement.

Figure 8.2 graphically illustrates the attitude change process. The horizontal axis in each graph is the actual discrepancy between the position advocated by a communication and the position held by an individual. The vertical axis in each graph is the person's judgment of the discrepancy between the advocated and held positions. The three graphs are drawn to reflect predictions of social judgment theory regarding the effects of involvement on the magnitude of the distortion of the judgment. As can be seen in Figure 8.2, one important effect on high involvement is that the size of the latitude of rejection increases. Although Sherif and Hovland originally hypothesized that high involvement should narrow the latitude of acceptance, research has not supported this hypothesis (Kiesler, Collins, and Miller 1969, p. 246).

If the communication falls within the latitude of acceptance, the message will tend to be judged *less* discrepant from the person's attitude than it really is and the person will tend to *assimilate* the communication into his or her attitude. This assimilation effect will tend to cause the person's attitude to change in the direction advocated by the communication. As can be seen in Figure 8.2, the degree of the judgment distortion increases with increasing involvement. According to social judgment theory the maximum amount of attitude change occurs near the boundary between the latitude of acceptance and the latitude of noncommitment.

If the communication falls within the latitude of rejection there will be a tendency for the message to be judged *more* discrepant from the person's attitude than it really is and the person will tend to *contrast* the communication with his or her attitude. This contrast effect will tend to reinforce the person's present attitude and may even cause the attitude to change in the opposite direction from that advocated by the communication. The effects of involvement are the same as those when the message is in the latitude of acceptance. Finally, the transition from assimilation to contrast effects occurs within the latitude of noncommitment.

Predictions regarding attitude change have been largely supported in empirical studies (Kiesler, Collins, and Miller 1969, p. 299). The implications for marketing managers are readily apparent. The design of persuasive communications, which will produce the maximum possible amount of attitude change, requires knowledge of the location of the boundaries of the latitudes of acceptance, noncommitment, and rejection. Of course, the boundaries will tend to be different for different buyers. Thus, an important task is to group buyers with similar boundaries into segments for which different persuasive communications can be developed. Another important implication of social judgment theory is that to change attitudes beyond the latitude of acceptance requires a series of messages. As attitudes change, the boundaries of the latitude of acceptance should also change, making buyers more likely to accept messages they previously would have rejected.

Despite important implications for the study of buyer behavior and for the development of marketing policy few applications of social judgment theory appear in the marketing literature. Recently, Newman and Dolich (1979) have attempted to use social judgment theory as a basis for predicting attitude change toward a Pinto automobile resulting from a demonstration ride. Mitchell (1979), however, raises serious objections to this use of social judgment theory on both methodological and theoretical grounds. This lack of interest in social judgment theory is unfortunate for, as Day (1973) noted, social judgment theory may ultimately prove more relevant to the marketing context than the apparently competitive and more widely accepted theory of cognitive dissonance.

Cognitive Dissonance

The final theory of attitudes to be considered is cognitive dissonance theory. Cognitive dissonance theory was initially developed by Festinger (1957) and is a member of a larger class of theories known as consistency theories.[8] Like all consistency theories, cognitive dissonance theory is concerned with the relationships among different cognitions. Some of these cognitions may be about behavior; e.g., I smoke cigarettes. When two, or more, cognitions imply the obverse of another cognition, a state which Festinger called dissonance is said to exist. For example, the cognitions "I smoke," "Smoking causes lung cancer," and "Good health is important to me" would be dissonant.[9] Dissonance is presumed to be a negative motivational state that causes the individual to engage in behaviors to reduce the level of dissonance.

[8]Cognitive dissonance theory is the only consistency theory that has been extensively studied in a buyer behavior context. For an introduction to other consistency theories of attitude, and suggested implications for marketing, see Calder (1981).

[9]It is common to speak of two cognitions as being dissonant or not dissonant. However, as Kiesler, Collins and Miller (1969, pp. 196–197) note, it is always necessary to include at least one more cognition which relates at least two cognitions. Thus, when "Smoking causes lung cancer" and "I smoke" are said to be dissonant a link is presumed between these cognitions; e.g., "Good health is important to me." To put the matter more specifically, dissonance is produced only when a set of cognitions have psychological implications for one another. For example, "I love tennis," "I love my wife," and "My wife does not like tennis" would not produce dissonance because there are no necessary psychological implications among these three cognitions.

The basic concepts of cognitive dissonance theory are nicely demonstrated in an experiment by Cohen (1962). In 1959, the New Haven, Connecticut, police quelled a disturbance at Yale University. The police action produced very negative attitudes toward the New Haven police among the Yale undergraduates. Using the minimum possible pressure, subjects (Yale undergraduates) were induced to write an essay entitled "Why the New Haven Police Actions Were Justified." The experimental variable was the amount subjects were paid to write the essay: specifically, $.50, $1.00, $5.00, or $10.00. Subsequently, the subjects were asked to rate the extent to which the police actions were justified on a 31-point scale ranging from "not at all justified" to "completely justified." The question in the experiment was the relationship of the rate of payment to the reported degree of justification; i.e., to the attitude.

From a reinforcement theory perspective one might expect subjects receiving larger payments (i.e., larger reinforcement) to express more positive attitudes. However, the results of this, and many other similar, experiments are just the reverse of this expectation. The dissonance theory explanation of this result is as follows. The cognition of writing the essay in favor of the New Haven police actions is discrepant from the negative attitude toward the police held by the subjects. This discrepancy is psychologically uncomfortable and gives rise to dissonance. In some sense, the subject will ask "Why did I write that essay?" Subjects who received a large payment (e.g., $10.00) have a logical explanation in the high rate of payment. What about the subject who received only $.50? Fifty cents is very little payment for writing a counter-attitudinal essay. Thus, these subjects must look elsewhere for an explanation of the discrepancy between attitude and behavior. One way to resolve the discrepancy, and hence reduce the dissonance, is to change attitude. To the extent that a subject cannot explain the attitude-behavior discrepancy in terms of factors such as rate of payment, alternative methods of dissonance reduction, such as attitude change, will be invoked. For example, in the Cohen experiment subjects who received only $.50 might reduce dissonance by thinking "As unfortunate as the police action was, it was necessary; after all we do live in a society governed by law. I guess my attitude toward the police is really more favorable than I first thought."

The above experiment is an example of the "forced compliance paradigm." In this paradigm each subject is "forced" to engage in the behavior desired by the experimenter. This prevents self-selection; i.e., subjects with a positive attitude toward the police writing an essay in favor of the police and those with a negative attitude writing an unfavorable essay. The danger in this procedure is that if the pressure to comply is too great the subject can reduce dissonance with the cognition "I was forced to write an essay that is contrary to my attitude." In this case no attitude change would occur. This is why it is necessary to use the "minimum possible pressure" to achieve compliance with the desired behavior.

Cognitive dissonance theory is also relevant to situations where a person must choose one of several alternatives. For example, a buyer may be considering several makes of automobile. Each alternative will generally present a mix of desirable and undesirable attributes; e.g., high gas mileage but poor acceleration or sports car with no rear seat. From the available choices the buyer presumably makes the most desirable choice. However, to the extent that one automobile is not totally superior on all attributes, the buyer is always in the position of accepting a choice with undesirable features and rejecting choices with desirable attributes. This situation should produce dissonance and one should expect to find new car buyers engaging in dissonance reducing behaviors *after* commiting themselves to the purchase; e.g., reading advertisements for the automobile they have just bought. Furthermore, the strength of these dissonance reducing behaviors should be expected to relate directly to the level of dissonance produced by the choice situation.

Dissonance theory makes some interesting predictions regarding the level of dissonance as a function of the choice alternatives. First, the greater is the importance of the choice to an individual, the greater the dissonance produced by the choice process. Second, the *closer* is the relative attractiveness of the chosen and rejected alternatives, the greater the dissonance. For example, a student who *really* wants to attend an Ivy League school should experience more dissonance if the choice is made among Harvard, Yale, and Princeton rather than among Princeton and several non-Ivy League schools. Third, the more similar are the alternatives, the less the dissonance. For example, there should be less dissonance when choosing between two or more automobiles than when choosing between an automobile and remodeling the kitchen (leaving aside any question of husband-wife conflict). In general, the research evidence supports these predictions (Kiesler, Collins, and Miller 1969, p. 205).

Despite the support received by dissonance theory, it is easy to cite both careful research and casual observations which are inconsistent with dissonance theory predictions. Zajonc (1960), for example, cites the centuries-old popularity of magicians as an experience that should be dissonance producing and thus avoided as a contrary example. This raises the important question of under what conditions dissonance can be expected to arise.

As already noted in the forced compliance paradigm, if the subject feels he or she has been pressured into a counter-attitudinal behavior dissonance is not likely to arise. Thus, the person must see the discrepant behavior or belief as being voluntary (Brehm and Cohen 1962). There is also good evidence to suggest that the person must be committed to the cognitions in question for dissonance to arise (Brehm and Cohen 1962; Kiesler, Collins, and Miller 1969). Dissonance is likely to be especially strong where a person has publicly committed himself or herself to dissonant cognitions. For example, a person who has always taken a strong public position on being patriotic but who has recently bought a foreign-made automobile might be expected to experience a great deal of dissonance because of the public nature of the commitment to these cognitions. Finally, it has been suggested that an important source of dissonance is violation of strong expectations, particularly expectations about one's self-image (Aronson 1968, 1969; Bramel, 1968; Collins 1969). For example, a man who views his masculinity in terms of a strong body but realizes that his body is deteriorating with advancing age and overindulgence in food would be likely to experience dissonance.

Cognitive dissonance theory has a number of interesting implications for the development of marketing strategy (Cummings and Venkatesan 1976). First, it may be possible to create dissonance by providing information to buyers that is discrepant with their existing cognitions or that brings other discrepant existing cognitions into a dissonant relationship. For example, a buyer who believes that a company makes high quality products because it is small, family-owned and -operated, and has been in business for a long time might be informed that the company was recently acquired by a conglomerate that changed most management personnel.

Or, in a campaign aimed at buyers who are union members, it might be pointed out that buying nonunion-made products is inconsistent with their status as union workers. Both of these examples have the potential for arousing dissonance and in both cases dissonance can be reduced by a change in attitude.

Another interesting implication of dissonance theory is that the act of choosing one of several alternatives should set in motion a process of reevaluation of the choice alternatives in which the chosen item tends to be reevaluated more favorably relative to the rejected items. Research has generally supported this implication of dissonance theory (Calder 1981, pp. 265–266). Sellers can facilitate the reevaluation process by providing supportive information. This is one reason why many manufacturers include with their product a congratulatory message which compliments the buyer on his or her selection and carefully explains the high quality of the product even though the message can only be read *after* the product has been purchased.

As part of this reevaluation of choice alternatives process one might expect that information supportive of the choice would be preferred, and possibly actively sought, and information not supportive of the choice would be avoided. This is one area where the predictions from dissonance theory have faired rather poorly (Freedman and Sears 1965). On the whole, the evidence favors seeking supportive information over avoiding nonsupportive information (Kiesler, Collins, and Miller 1969). For example, Ehrlich et al. (1957) found that *after* purchasing a new car, buyers were more likely to read ads for the chosen car than for other cars. Contrary to dissonance theory, however, they also found that buyers were more likely to read ads for the rejected cars as opposed to cars that were not considered at all. One explanation for this finding is that dissonant information may be useful information in defending a choice. For example, by knowing that the car purchased has a worse-than-average record a buyer is better able to defend his or her purchase as the best choice. It may be that the record is better-than-average in the class of cars which are sports cars selling under $9,000.

The importance of commitment in the dissonance arousal process has an interesting implication for the "introductory low price" strategy for introducing a new product. While the low price should attract buyers to the extent that the price is low (the extreme case would be a free sample), the buyer's commitment to the product is low and hence the buying situation is less capable of arousing dissonance. For example, a buyer might be induced to try a new product even though satisfactory alternatives exist in the product class. This could produce dissonance; e.g., "Why did I buy that new brand when my old brand is perfectly satisfactory." The buyer who received a large discount could reduce the dissonance with the cognition "it was cheap." This would not be possible if something near full price had been paid. In such a situation, dissonance could be reduced by deciding "it really is a superior product." Thus, too steep a discount may actually be counterproductive to the long-term success of a new product. Doob et al. (1969) provide data to support this idea.

One final point regarding dissonance reduction needs to be made. Although most research has focused on attitude change as the way to reduce dissonance, dissonance may be reduced in other ways. First, an individual might downgrade the importance of the area; e.g., "In the total scheme of life, how important is it that I bought an automobile which is a lemon." Second, one or more cognitive elements may be added that reduce the dissonance without changing the attitude.

For example, the cognitions "I own a sports car" and "Sports cars are mechanically unreliable" would presumably be less dissonant when combined with the cognitions "I have another reliable car" and "Money is not a major problem for me." Third, one may resolve dissonance by derogating the source of the communication. This is why celebrities who make a substantial part of their income from product endorsements are often extremely careful about the quality of the products they endorse.

The possibility that a person may derogate the source of a message rather than change their attitude provides a means for reconciling an important conflict in the predictions made by social judgment theory and cognitive dissonance theory regarding the relationship between the amount of discrepancy in a communication and the amount of attitude change. Specifically, dissonance theory predicts that attitude change should increase with increasing discrepancy of a message from a person's current position, while social judgment theory predicts that at some point beyond the latitude of acceptance attitude change will cease to occur and may even change in the opposite direction. One way of reconciling these two predictions is by noting that, as discrepancy increases, there will be a tendency to resolve dissonance by derogating the source rather than changing attitude (Kiesler, Collins, and Miller 1969, pp. 292–297). This effect seems to be most pronounced for low credibility sources. Since marketing communicators are often perceived to be low in credibility the implication is that a message that is too discrepant may lead to derogation of the source rather than attitude change. The clear implication for marketers is to be extremely careful and wary about using promotional messages that are very discrepant from the attitudes currently held by their target audiences.

THE RELATIONSHIPS AMONG ATTITUDE, INTENTION, AND BEHAVIOR

There is little doubt among either marketing practitioners or academic researchers that attitude is a most important concept for understanding buying behavior. The reader, however, may feel somewhat overwhelmed by what seems to be a maze of contradictory evidence regarding the relationship of attitude to other buyer behavior variables. This is especially true of the attitude-behavior relationship. At different points in this and prior chapters, it has been suggested that the attitude-behavior relationship is *both* weak and strong and that attitudes may *both* cause and be caused by behavior. There is, not surprisingly, merit to all of these statements. It is now time to try to place these evidently contradictory statements into some kind of systematic framework. This discussion will include the concept of intention because of its important mediating role in the attitude-behavior relationship.

The Attitude-Intention Relationship

As noted in Chapter 4, the concept of intention has been used in two different, but related, ways in the buyer behavior literature. First, intention is used in the rather broad sense of a "buying plan," as was discussed thoroughly in Chapter 4. Second, intention is used in the more specific and limited sense of a likelihood or probability of purchase. For example, a person might be asked whether the chances of his buying a new car in the next six months are 0 out of 10, 1 out of 10, or 10 out of 10. It is this second use of the intention concept that will be focused on here.

Fishbein and Ajzen (1975, Chapter 7) examined in detail the factors, including attitudes, that affect the formation of intentions. They concluded that the correlations between attitudes and intentions are low; i.e., the relationship is very weak. The reason for this is that, while a positive attitude may be a necessary condition for the formation of an intention to purchase, it is only one of a number of factors that lead to intention. More specifically, a number of factors may block the expression of a favorable attitude in behavior, and therefore, in the expression of an intention to behave. Chapters 2 and 4 discussed these factors under the headings of confidence and inhibitors to purchase.

Another factor that affects the attitude-intention relationship is the degree of specificity of the intention variable. In particular, Fishbein and Ajzen (1975, p. 292) note that intention can vary in specificity on four dimensions: behavior, target object, situation, and time. For example, a buyer may intend to buy a car (behavior), which is a new Oldsmobile Cutlass (target object), from Faulkner Olds (situation or place in which the behavior is to occur), next week (time). Fishbein and Ajzen (1975, p. 297) argue that the attitude-intention relationship weakens as the level of specificity of intention increases. As support they offer their own 1974 study of the correlations between five measures of attitude toward religion and intention to perform 100 specific religious behaviors; e.g., praying before meals. These attitude-intention correlations ranged from .16 to .20. However, when an aggregate (and, therefore, much less specific) index of intention was constructed from the 100 possible religious behaviors the correlations improved dramatically to a range of .60 to .75. The point, of course, is that there are many ways in which a religious attitude may be expressed and that one should not necessarily expect to find a strong relationship between attitude toward religion and any one specific religious behavior.

The Intention-Behavior Relationship

In marked contrast to the attitude-intention relationship, there is much evidence to support the existence of a strong relationship between intention and behavior (Fishbein and Ajzen 1975, Chapter 8). Perhaps the best known studies of the intention-behavior relationship come from the Survey Research Center at the University of Michigan. In *The Powerful Consumer*, Katona (1960), former director of the center, reported that among those reporting that they intended to purchase a new car 63 percent did so within one year, while only 29 percent of those not intending to purchase a new car did so. These figures have been found in a sufficient number of studies that Assael (1981, p. 171) concluded that average purchase rates for intenders and nonintenders are approximately 60 percent and 30 percent, respectively.

That intention and behavior tend to be strongly related should not be surprising. As Fishbein and Ajzen (1975, p. 369) note, for many, and probably most, behaviors the simplest and most efficient way to determine if a person intends to perform the behavior is to ask. More specifically, they suggest that the following three factors are positively related to the strength of the intention-behavior relationship: (1) the degree to which intention and behavior are measured at the same level of specificity, (2) the stability of the intention, and (3) the degree to which the behavior in question is under the control of the individual (p. 369). As shall be discussed shortly, this last factor is very important, because some behaviors are largely controlled by factors other than attitude and intention.

Figure 8.3
Relationship between brand attitude and brand usage

**Attitude Ratings for all
Nineteen Brands Studied**

% Using
58

23

6

2   1   0

Excellent   Very Good   Good   Fair   Not so Good   Poor

Source: Alvin A. Achenbaum, "Advertising Doesn't Manipulate Consumers." *Journal of Advertising Research* 12 (April, 1972): 7. Reprinted with permission.

The Magnitude of the Attitude-Behavior Relationship

As already noted, many examples can be cited of a failure to find even a modest relationship between attitude and behavior. Although perhaps less numerous, many examples of moderate to strong attitude-behavior relationships can also be cited. Among the marketing examples of moderate to strong attitude-behavior relationships are the use of private label products (Myers 1967), use of trading stamps (Udel 1965), and a large number of goods and services (cf., Ryan and Bonfield 1975).

Just how important a favorable attitude is to the success of a product is shown in a study of nineteen brands by Achenbaum (1972). The results of Achenbaum's study are displayed in Figure 8.3. As attitude becomes less positive the percent of respondents using the brand drops off extremely rapidly. In fact, based on his experience with the Grey Advertising Agency, Achenbaum drew a very strong conclusion regarding the attitude-behavior relationship in the context o

> In our own work, we have found in every study we have done—and there has not been a single exception—that there is a very direct relationship between attitudes and useage behavior ... the more favorable the attitude, the higher the incidence of useage; the less favorable the attitude, the lower the incidence of useage (1966, p. 112).

Achenbaum (1966) also showed that a positive change in attitude can produce a large gain in market share. Assael and Day (1968) also reported data to support this relationship between attitude and market share.

The factors that govern the strength of the attitude-behavior relationship are essentially the same as those governing the strength of the attitude-intention and intention-behavior relationships. Strong relationships are likely to emerge only when attitudes and behavior are measured at the same level of specificity (Fishbein and Ajzen 1975; Bagozzi and Burnkrant 1979). For example, a buyer may have a strong positive attitude toward mass transit. There are, however, a number of ways in which this attitude might be expressed in behavior: commuting by bus, subway, or train; car pooling; etc. Without further specification, there is no logical reason why this general attitude should be related to any specific behavior. One might more reasonably expect a positive attitude toward mass transit to be related to use of *some* form of mass transit *assuming it is a feasible choice for a buyer.* Of course, if our interest is confined to a specific form of mass transit, the questions should be phrased in terms of attitude toward using that specific form of mass transit.

A recent study of the attitude-behavior relationship for major appliances by Day and Deutscher (1982) suggests that the source of an attitude may have important implications for the strength of the attitude-behavior relationship. Although purchasing a major appliance is generally a high involvement decision, Day and Deutscher argue that "Attitudes towards brands of major appliances appear to be formed mainly through the process of learning without involvement" (p. 197). However, these attitudes are not likely to be strong or even well-organized and, therefore, are likely to change as the decision-making process proceeds once a need to purchase a specific major appliance is recognized. An important exception to this pattern occurs for manufacturers who follow" a full-line, national brand support advertising strategy" (p. 198). The authors suggest that the stronger attitude-behavior relationship observed for such brands arises from the fact that attitudes for such brands arise to a large extent from *direct experience* with other appliances in the manufacturer's line.

As noted repeatedly, there are any number of reasons why a favorable attitude toward an object may not be expressed in behavior. In the case of durable goods, for example, if a person owns a brand with a large number of years left on its life expectancy, there is little likelihood of a new purchase occurring whatever the person's attitudes toward brands currently on the market. Of course, a buyer may very well express an intention to purchase a specific brand on the next purchase occasion. However, as we know, the longer the time that elapses between the expression of attitude and intention and the behavior in question, the less likely is the behavior to occur.

Finally, there is the very important question of whether the behavior is under attitudinal control. Many behaviors are not. For example, a buyer may have a very strong positive attitude toward Honda automobiles. However, if that buyer's employer imposes strong sanctions against employees who drive foreign cars, it is unlikely that this buyer will purchase a Honda. This, of course, is why Fishbein incorporated variables measuring social norms and intention to comply with those norms in his extended model. On the basis of research on the relevance of the extended Fishbein model to buyer behavior, purchasing behavior appears to be largely, although not exclusively, under attitudinal control (Ryan and Bonfield 1975).

The Direction of Causality in the Attitude-Behavior Relationship

There is little doubt that buyers tend to have positive attitudes toward the brands they use. Furthermore, as we have seen, market studies show strong correlations between buyer attitudes and market share. All of this suggests that successful brands are normally *associated* with positive attitudes. The association between attitudes and behaviors, however, still leaves unanswered the question of the direction of the causal relationship between attitudes and behavior.

It is possible to identify four basic causal relationships between attitudes and behaviors: (1) no causal relationship exists, (2) attitudes cause behaviors, (3) behaviors cause attitudes, and (4) causation is reciprocal between attitudes and behaviors. As Kahle and Berman (1979, p. 315) note, each of these positions has a contemporary advocate. However, because it is possible to marshall substantial support for each position, it seems more appropriate to try to identify the situations in which each of the four basic relationships is likely to hold rather than defend any one type of relationship as the true relationship.

As previously suggested, there are numerous explanations for the failure to find a relationship between attitudes and behaviors. First, attitudes can change over time and any number of events can block the expression of a favorable attitude in behavior. Thus, we might reasonably expect to find a weak, or even no, relationship between attitudes and behaviors when a lengthy time gap separates the attitude measurement and the occurrence of the behavior.

Second, there is the problem of the level of specificity of attitudes and behaviors and the recently recognized, important distinction between an attitude toward an object and an attitude toward an action involving an object. For example, just because a person has a very positive attitude toward good health, that person will not necessarily buy health foods or exercise regularly. A positive attitude toward good health can be expressed in many other ways; e.g., consuming less animal fat and more fiber, regular medical checkups, contributing to the American Cancer Society. If our interest is limited to health foods then our questions should be framed in terms of buying and consuming health foods. If our interest is less specific, we may want to investigate how different individuals express in behavior their attitudes toward good health.

Finally, the behavior may not be under attitudinal control. Explicit recognition of this factor is an important contribution of the extended Fishbein model. In a related vein, Bettman (1979, pp. 209–210) suggested that certain brand choice rules are consistent with brand choice without a previously formed attitude; e.g., buy the cheapest brand. However, in this case it seems likely that a positive attitude would tend to develop *after* purchase.

Data have been previously cited to support the theory that attitudes cause behavior. Kahle and Berman (1979), using recently developed analytical techniques, which have the ability to determine the direction of causal relationships from field data and are known variously as cross-logged correlations, confirmatory factor analysis, and causal modeling, provided clear evidence that attitudes do cause behavior for the four issues they investigated. The issues investigated were Jimmy Carter's presidential candidacy, Gerald Ford's candidacy, drinking, and religion. For most people, these are likely to be high involvement issues. They also seem to fall into the categories of buying situations labeled learning hierarchy situations (i.e., shopping and specialty buying situations) and it seems reasonable to suggest that in such buying situations attitudes do form prior to and cause behavior. This, of course, assumes that the behavior in question is under attitudinal control.

In recent years, both theories and empirical data have been developed to suggest that, under certain circumstances, behavior can lead to the formation of attitudes and to attitude change. Cognitive dissonance theory provides a clear illustration of how behaviors can change attitudes. Of course, as was discussed previously, the situation must be capable of arousing dissonance and of leading to the reduction of dissonance through attitude change instead of some other means, such as derogating the source. Also, as was discussed in Chapter 2, an attitude can be viewed as representing an expected level of satisfaction. Should the actual level of satisfaction be different from the expected level, attitudes may change. Of course, the discrepancy between expected and actual satisfaction can be resolved in ways other than attitude change; e.g., by attributing the discrepancy to factors that are essentially random and beyond the control of the manufacturer.

In terms of the discussion of buying situations in Chapter 3, behaviors would be expected to cause attitudes in those situations labeled the low involvement hierarchy (i.e., convenience and preference situations) and the dissonance/attribution hierarchy (i.e., avoidance situations). The reasons for the causal relationship flowing from behaviors to attitudes are somewhat different for the two hierarchies. In the dissonance/attribution hierarchy, the buyer is forced to make a choice *before* the information upon which an attitude could be based is available. In the low involvement hierarchy, the information that might form an attitude exists in unorganized form because of the lack of importance of the choice. In this case, the positive attitude is likely to develop directly out of experience with the product.

Bem (1972) developed a special theory of attribution that provides some support for the above assertions about the circumstances under which behaviors may precede and cause attitudes. Specifically, Bem's theory of self-perception argues that behavior and its effects constitute the major cues from which an actor makes causal attributions. For example, when asked about his or her attitude toward peanut butter, a buyer might say, "Well I eat a lot of peanut butter, I guess I really like it." That is, the buyer infers an attitude from his or her own behavior. In an interesting refutation of a number of criticisms of self-perception theory, Bem (1968) noted that his theory assumes that the person is not aware of his or her initial position. Bem and McConnell (1970) subsequently provided empirical data to support this assumption. In a buyer behavior context, this assumption suggests that perception theory should be especially relevant to low-involvement buying situations.

An outgrowth of self-perception theory, which has some interesting implications for marketing, is known as the foot-in-the-door technique. The basic idea here is that by obtaining compliance with a small request, by getting a foot in the door, it will be easier to obtain compliance with a larger subsequent request. Self-perception theory explains this prediction in the following way. When the larger request is made, the person will reflect back on his previous behavior. This will provide a basis for forming a positive attitude toward the larger request and thus increase the likelihood of obtaining compliance with the larger request. Scott (1977) has tested the foot-in-the-door technique using requests to help in the ecology cause. She found that making a small request dramatically increased the likelihood of obtaining compliance with a larger request when contrasted with a control group from whom only the second larger request was made. Among the possible marketing applications of the foot-in-the-door technique are charitable giving, gaining participation in any type of social or political cause, and increasing the response rate in marketing research studies.

Finally, there is the possibility of a reciprocal relationship between attitudes and behaviors (Kelman 1974; McGuire 1976). This seems especially likely to characterize low involvement and avoidance buying situations, where behaviors lead to attitudes, which in turn lead to new behaviors.

SUMMARY

The concept of an attitude is extremely important for anyone who wishes to understand or influence buyer behavior. Like all such important concepts, it is characterized by many dimensions and is subject to many theoretical interpretations. While most empirical studies focus on the magnitude of the evaluative dimension of attitude, attitudes do vary on a number of other dimensions, such as centrality and embeddedness. A full and proper understanding of buyer attitudes cannot ignore these dimensions of the attitude concept.

In recent years, buyer behavior research has tended to focus on multiattribute models of attitude. The study of multiattribute attitude models has provided a number of significant insights into the role of attitudes in buyer behavior and has proved especially valuable to marketing managers because multiattribute models can be formulated in terms of attributes that are under the control of the manager.

As has been seen, a number of other conceptualizations of attitudes exist. These alternatives are more complementary than competitive with multiattribute models and, thus, enrich our total understanding of attitudes. The functional approach directs our attention to the motives that attitudes serve and to the need to understand the motivational basis for attitudes as a prerequisite for developing effective attitude change strategies.

In a similar way, social judgment theory suggests the very reasonable idea that people do not hold rigid, numerically precise attitudes but, rather, regard as reasonable or acceptable a range of opinions on any given topic. Social judgment theory also provides an explicit theory as to how buyers incorporate new persuasive communications into previously existing attitudes. Finally, social judgment theory *explicity* incorporates the level of involvement in the attitude change process. This is important because, as suggested at numerous points, the level of involvement is an important variable in determining how buyers act in different buying situations.

As discussed in this chapter and earlier, the long-standing assumption regarding the attitude-behavior relationship is that attitudes cause behavior. Cognitive disonance theory provides us with one theoretical explanation of how behavior may cause attitudes. This possibility was explored in some detail in a subsequent section of the chapter. The discussion of cognitive dissonance theory also suggested that dissonance may be resolved in ways other than attitude change. This is clearly of importance to marketers, who are typically perceived to be low credibility sources.

The discussion of the relationships among attitudes, intentions, and behaviors can be summarized as follows. A positive attitude is generally a necessary condition for a successful product, but it is not sufficient. Any number of factors can block the expression of a favorable attitude in behavior. Furthermore, it appears that behavior can occur without a previously formed, strong attitude. The evidence suggests, however, that if a positive attitude does not develop out of the behavior that behavior will be discontinued.

Extensive Problem
Solving

IV

Part III examined a number of topics that are particularly germane to the decision-making processes of buyers faced with purchasing problems in which the basic product class concept is well understood but a final decision cannot be made without additional information and evaluation of brands within the product class. Part IV continues the discussion of buyers' decision-making processes by focusing on the situation in which buyers do not have a well formed product class concept. Such a situation, of course, exists whenever a buyer becomes aware of a radically new product, such as home computers or passive solar heat systems. The decision-making processes involved in such purchasing situations are referred to generally as extensive problem solving (EPS).

It is important to a proper understanding of EPS to recognize that the label refers to the difficulty of making a satisfactory decision and not to the amount of effort expended during the decision-making process per se. For example, a person who buys a new car every five or six years will probably collect and evaluate a considerable amount of information on new cars from a variety of sources before making a final purchase decision. Even though this decision process may involve a considerable amount of effort and occur over a lengthy period of time, it is generally not an EPS situation because the buyer generally understands what kinds of information are required, where to find such information, and how to evaluate the information received. That is, even though the decision may be complex it is well structured in the sense that the buyer generally understands what is required to make a purchasing decision that has a high probability of being satisfactory.

In contrast, EPS presents the buyer with an unstructured problem, where even which questions to ask are frequently unknown. The problem, of course, is that the buyer does not have a well formed concept of the product class. This means that the buyer will have to spend considerable effort developing a concept of the basic product class before an effective evaluation of alternative brands can be conducted. It also generally means that the perceived risk of a poor brand choice will be high. As a consequence of these characteristics, once buyers recognize that they face an EPS situation they are very likely to abandon the decision-making process. Thus, a critical task in the marketing of goods and services that require EPS is to induce buyers to engage in and complete the decision-making process.

The heart of Part IV is Chapter 10, where the processes through which buyers decide whether or not to adopt a new product are considered. Because it is well known that personal sources of information play a large, and frequently critical, role in new product adoption decisions, Part IV begins with a general discussion of social influence processes. Chapter 11 probes more deeply into the nature of perception and how raw perceptions (e.g., sound waves) are transformed into meaningful information. Although Chapters 9 and 11 are also relevant to limited problem solving and routinized response behavior they have been placed in Part IV because it is in the context of EPS that they become most obvious and important.

As you read Part IV, keep in mind that the topics discussed in previous chapters—especially motives, learning, and attitudes—continue to be relevant to buyers' decision-making processes. What distinguishes EPS from limited problem solving is that in EPS the question of what constitutes a good choice is uncertain because the evaluative criteria for defining a good choice are uncertain.

Social Influence
Processes

9

Although the focus of previous chapters has been on the individual buyer, it is necessary to recognize that buyers exist within and are often influenced by a larger social environment. Sometimes this social influence has been explicitly recognized, as during the discussion of the social sources of motivation in Chapter 6 and the influence of social norms on attitudes in the last chapter. More often, however, the role of social influence has been left implicit.

It is the task of this chapter to explicitly develop the concept of a social group and the processes through which social groups influence buyers. The benefits of this analysis are twofold. First, this analysis will extend our general understanding of buyer behavior. Second, an understanding of the processes through which social influence operates can provide the marketer with concepts from which more effective marketing strategies can be constructed. As shall be seen in the next chapter, such concepts are especially important in the development of effective marketing strategies for new products.

This chapter begins with a discussion of the concept of a social group, followed by a review of the processes through which social influence operates, and concludes with a discussion of factors that affect the relevance of social influence. This is quite important because the relevance of social groups varies widely across product classes.

THE SOCIAL GROUP CONCEPT

The concept of a social group is a familiar one. We are all members of many social groups. Family, classmates, friendship cliques, special interest clubs, business associates, religious congregations, political parties, and neighbors are all everyday examples of social groups. Of special interest to marketers are so-called reference groups. A reference group is a group to which a person "refers" for evaluation standards when making judgments or decisions. Virtually every social group is a potential reference group for *some* buyers for *some* buying decisions. The emphasis, obviously, is on the word some. Most social groups influence only a very small range of behaviors and many behaviors (e.g., what brand of oil to use) are largely unaffected by social influence.

Despite its familiarity the concept of a reference group is difficult to define. Sherif, in a widely cited definition, defines a reference group as "those groups to which the individual relates himself as a part or to which he aspires to relate himself psychologically" (1953, p. 206). As this definition makes clear, the individual ultimately defines both the composition of the group and the criteria by which that individual relates to the group. The group itself, of course, plays an important role in this process and the individual is not unconstrained in how he or she defines and relates to the group. Nevertheless, two members of a group may define and relate to the group quite differently.

Stafford and Cocanougher (1977) have suggested that the lack of clear conceptual and operational definitions of the reference group concept accounts for the paucity of marketing studies on reference groups after a brief flurry of interest between 1965 and 1970. Recently, Sheth (1979) drew attention to need for more research on group behavior and gave specific suggestions for needed research. Sheth's suggestions are very appropriate because, despite the "fuzziness," reference groups are clearly of great importance to buyer behavior. In the next few pages, the discussion turns to a number of characteristics of groups that have relevance to buyer behavior.[1]

Types of Groups

Groups may be classified in many different ways. One very useful classification is in terms of membership status. Groups to which an individual actually belongs are called affiliative groups. Affiliative groups may be further broken down as to whether they are primary or secondary. Primary groups are typically small and involve face-to-face contact; e.g., family, friendship cliques, work groups. Secondary groups are typically larger and often involve little face-to-face contact; e.g., social class, political parties. Groups to which an individual does not belong but desires to join are referred to as aspiration groups. Finally, disassociative groups are groups to which an individual does not want to belong or to be associated with by other persons.

Group Functions

A number of writers have examined the functions that reference groups perform for individuals (e.g., Kelley 1952; Shibutani 1955). The two most widely recognized functions of groups are the normative function and the comparison function. The normative function involves the setting of standards for beliefs, attitudes, and behavior. Norms frequently have major implications for buying behavior as the reader may recall from the discussion of the extended Fishbein model of attitudes in Chapter 8. The wise, young, automobile executive, for example, does not own a Toyota and certainly doesn't drive it to work.

Norms vary considerably in their explicitness. At one extreme, they are explicitly codified as laws and company indoctrination manuals, etc. More often, however, norms are generally understood without being explicitly stated. This is a principal reason for the substantial difficulties in ascertaining "correct" behavior encountered by persons who aspire to higher status groups. Sometimes norms may be generally recognized without being explicitly discussed. Zaltman and Wallendorf (1979) provide two interesting examples. The first is reciprocity of purchasing among business firms, which while generally recognized is illegal if explicitly discussed. The second concerns the automobile brand preferences of faculty. As Zaltman and Wallendorf note, one is hard pressed to find a Cadillac on a faculty parking lot even though the lot may contain a number of comparably priced cars.

Social groups enforce their norms by applying sanctions to violators. Generally, these sanctions involve some degree of ridicule or ostracism. Marketers frequently attempt to motivate buyers by suggesting that sanctions may be applied to them if they don't use the advertised product. Personal hygiene products, for example, are

---

[1]Our review of group characteristics is highly selective, this reflects both our purposes and the fact that the concept of a social group has not been highly developed in the context of buyer behavior. The reader interested in more information on basic research on social groups might begin with the excellent review contained in the *Handbook of Social Psychology,* edited by Lindzey and Aronson (1969). Also of interest is the critical review of the reference group concept both generally and as it is employed by buyer behavior researchers by Stafford and Cocanougher (1977). Although their analysis is of necessity somewhat speculative, Zaltman and Wallendorf (1979, especially Chapters 4–8) provide an interesting and useful sociological perspective on buyer behavior.

largely promoted with the threat of ridicule or ostracism from the group if the sponsor's product is not used. Another frequent ploy is the buyer who thought he or she was being smart by buying a less expensive "bargain brand" only to be left feeling embarrassed and foolish in front of family or friends when the bargain brand performs poorly. Next time, of course, the buyer will *really* be smart and buy the sponsor's brand.

The second function of social groups is a comparison function. The essence of this function is that individuals use reference groups to make comparative judgments regarding their beliefs, attitudes, values, abilities, social position, etc. An excellent example of the comparison function is work by Coleman (1960) and Peters (1970) on the relationship between relative income and certain attributes of a family's primary automobile.

The relative income argument states that people judge the adequacy of their incomes *relative* to a group of similar others rather than in absolute terms. A person is said to be over-privileged or under-privileged to the extent that the person's income is higher or lower than the reference group. Large, luxury cars tend to be purchased by over-privileged buyers while small, economy cars tend to be purchased by under-privileged buyers. Recently, Schaninger (1981) provided further support for the relative income hypothesis for automobiles, television sets, use of certain types of makeup, and higher priced dresses.

Festinger (1954) developed a theory of social comparison that is especially relevant to the influence of informal social groups in situations where objective standards are not available or relevant. Jones and Gerard (1967), in an extension of Festinger's theory, suggest that people tend to choose for comparison an individual or group that is similar to them on important attributes, a so-called "co-oriented peer." They further argue that two different types of comparison are possible: reflected appraisal and comparative appraisal. Reflected appraisal is "any evaluation of the self that is inferred from the behavior of other persons during interaction with them" (p. 717). Comparative appraisal is the "evaluation of one's own relative standing with respect to an attitude, belief, ability, or emotion by observing the behavior of appropriate reference persons" (p. 709). While reflected appraisal requires face-to-face interaction, comparative appraisal can operate at a distance. Moschis (1976) provided evidence that both reflected and comparative appraisal can affect buyers' seeking of information from co-oriented peers, perceptions of source credibility, and product choice. The findings regarding source credibility are especially interesting because they suggest that under certain conditions it may be more desirable to use spokespeople who are similar to the target audience rather than the more commonly used "expert."

Roles and Role Relationships

An important concept for understanding social behavior is the idea of a role. "Role, a term borrowed directly from the theater, is a metaphor intended to denote that conduct adheres to certain 'parts' (or positions) rather than to the players who recite them" (Sarbin and Allen 1969, p. 489). You, for example, occupy the role of "student" and perform the many behaviors, such as writing papers and taking tests, that are expected of those who occupy the role.

Of course, there is more flexibility in the performance of a role in real life than typically occurs in the theater. Nevertheless, other persons have many, often quite specific, expectations in terms of the attributes and the behavior of a person in a specific role. To see this, examine the role relationships presented in Table 9.1. The barber–customer role relationship, for example, involves a number of expectations regarding the service to be rendered, payment for that service, and tipping. In a similar way, the good dinner guest will bring the host or hostess a small gift, while the good host or hostess will provide a satisfying meal and pleasant company. Although these roles are informal, they are well understood in terms of expected behavior. Sometimes, of course, role relationships are highly formalized; e.g., judge–defense attorney, assembly worker–foreman.

The role concept has rather obvious implications for buyer behavior. The buyer–seller relationship, for example, can be construed in terms of roles and role relationships. Similarly, the distinctions among decision makers, purchasers, users, gatekeepers, and opinion leaders can all be analyzed in terms of roles and role relationships. Despite the emphasis on the exchange relationship as the essence of marketing (cf., Bagozzi 1975a, 1975b) and the ease with which many buyer behaviors can be understood in terms of role behavior, there is virtually no empirical research on buyer roles (Zaltman and Wallendorf 1979, Chapter 7). Nevertheless, a number of managerial implications can be drawn from the role concept.

Kernan, Dommermuth, and Sommers (1970) developed the idea of a role-related product cluster. A role-related product cluster is a set of products that are considered either functionally or symbolically necessary to properly fulfill a given role. The elegant hostess, for example, will surround herself with the china, crystal, and furnishings that are functionally and symbolically necessary to fulfill that role. Another interesting example of a role-related product is the attache case that is standard executive equipment even if it contains no more than a newspaper and lunch. The implication is clear and frequently drawn for potential buyers by marketers: if you want to play the role, you *must* have the proper tools and symbols.

Individuals typically occupy a great many different roles at any one time and, over the course of a lifetime, roles change. This leads us to the ideas of role conflict and role transition. Role conflict is a common experience of everyday life. The existence and recognition of role conflicts creates a number of significant opportunities for marketers to create goods and services to reduce such conflicts. Speed reading, for example, is promoted to students as a means for reducing the time needed to satisfactorily perform the "student" role thus leaving one more time for other, presumably more pleasurable, roles. Similarly, many labor saving devices for the home are sold on the basis of allowing one to perform "homemaker" and "handyman" roles more efficiently, thereby leaving more time for other roles such as spouse and parent.

Transitions in roles are important to marketers because they are frequently accompanied by extensive acquisitions of new goods and services. They are also frequently marked by considerable uncertainty precisely because the role is new and unfamiliar. For example, the college senior taking his or her first job will generally require a new wardrobe. Precisely what clothes go with the new role is often difficult to determine. This is especially a problem for women since their options are greater and their superiors, largely men, are more likely to judge a woman by her appearance.

Many other role transitions permit or require the acquisition of goods and

Table 9.1
Examples of role relationships

1. barber—customer
2. judge—defense lawyer
3. abortionist—client
4. dean—college president
5. bridegroom—bride
6. bishop—priest
7. host—dinner guest
8. dancer—conductor
9. company president—private secretary
10. police chief—district attorney
11. social worker—supervisor
12. father—son (age 12)
13. screen star—autograph seeker
14. newspaper vendor—buyer
15. guard—convict
16. surgeon—head nurse
17. school superintendent—member/Bd. of Ed.
18. grandfather—grandson (age 12)
19. football coach—player
20. writer—editor
21. company president—union president
22. ward leader—voter
23. hospital administrator—benefactor
24. boyfriend (age 16)—girlfriend (age 15)
25. rabbi—minister
26. stripper—customer
27. assembly worker—foreman
28. policeman—speeder
29. psychiatrist—patient
30. elementary school teacher—student
31. aunt—nephew
32. kibitzer—card player
33. artist—model
34. typist—typist (same office)
35. social worker—unwed mother
36. husband—wife
37. best friend—best friend (same sex)
38. company president—member/Bd. of Dir.
39. combat soldier—enemy soldier
40. dentist—patient
41. professor—undergraduate student
42. father—son (age 22)
43. confessor—penitent
44. movie customer—usher
45. conductor—musician
46. office boy—typist
47. general practitioner—surgeon
48. boxer—manager
49. real estate salesman—buyer
50. policeman—reporter
51. social worker—slum teenage boy
52. chemist—laboratory technician
53. boyfriend (age 23)—girlfriend (age 22)
54. bridge player—partner
55. farmer—farmhand
56. company president—pool typist
57. army private—army private
58. surgeon—X-ray technician
59. professor—graduate student
60. uncle—nephew
61. minister—member of congregation
62. caddy—golfer
63. actor—director
64. company president—vice-president
65. mayor—local industrialist
66. social worker—prospective adoptive parents
67. prostitute—customer
68. bookie—customer
69. supermarket cashier—customer
70. politician—newspaper interviewer
71. general practitioner—drug salesman
72. housemother—student
73. brother (age 16)—brother (age 12)
74. priest—altar boy
75. boy scout—scout master
76. performer—accompanist
77. company president—bank president
78. judge—district attorney
79. resident surgeon—dietitian
80. school superintendent—high sch. prin.
81. mother—son (age 12)
82. star—supporting actor
83. sculptor—gallery owner
84. landlord—tenant
85. interrogator—captive
86. nurse—nurse's aide
87. dean—professor
88. prostitute—procurer
89. minister—church elder
90. quarterback—center
91. jazzman—audience member
92. assembly line worker—shop steward
93. head of state—head of state
94. surgeon—surgeon
95. high school teacher—high sch. teacher
96. sister (age 16)—brother (age 12)
97. bartender—customer
98. actor—agent
99. drug store mgr.—mfgrs.' representative
100. acquaintance—acquaintance

Source: Gerald Maxwell and Jerald Hage, "The Organization of Role Relationships: A Systematic Description." *American Sociological Review*, 35 (October 1970): 900. Reprinted with permission.

services. Becoming a parent, changing jobs (especially if it involves a major upward move), and retiring all have this potential. Perhaps the single greatest buying binge caused by a role transition is occasioned by a woman's first marriage. In addition to all of the goods and services associated with the wedding and honeymoon, many home-related products will be necessary. Indeed, according to *Modern Bride*, market research "shows the bride-to-be spends more money, in a shorter period of time, than ever again in her life" (cited in Zaltman and Wallendorf 1979, p. 167). Fortunately for the marketer, the lucrative bride-to-be market is easily reached through such vehicles as bridal registries and magazines like *Modern Bride*.

Other Attributes of Reference Groups

Many additional attributes may be used to describe reference groups. There is, for example, some evidence that the strength of the forces on members to remain in the group, so-called cohesiveness, is positively related to the *similarity* of brand choice among group members (e.g., Witt 1969). A study by Stafford (1966) suggests that informal group leaders can influence choice behavior.

Unfortunately, these findings are based on very limited evidence and it is possible to find nonsupportive or contradictory examples. Hansen (1970a), for example, found no support for an effect attributable to cohesiveness, while Ford and Ellis (1980) recently provided a direct refutation of Stafford's (1966) leadership study. Clearly, more research is necessary to sort out the attributes of social groups that are related to buyer behavior and to determine the conditions under which these attributes will actually influence specific buyer behaviors.[2]

SOCIAL POWER AND SOCIAL INFLUENCE PROCESSES

Everyday observation and a considerable amount of psychological and buyer behavior research leaves no doubt about the importance of social influence. This section examines the various processes through which social influence operates. As Burnkrant and Cousineau (1975) note, there have been extremely few social influence studies of the specific processes through which social influence affects buyer behavior.[3] Thus, the discussion will be based primarily on psychological research and theoretical marketing discussions of social influence processes.

Social Power

"Social power is defined as the potential influence of some influencing agent, O, over some person, P. Influence is defined as a change in cognition, attitude, behavior, or emotion of P which can be attributed to O" (Collins and Raven 1969, p. 160). Six different types of social power have generally been recognized:

[2]Although not written from a buyer behavior perspective, the review article on "Group Structure: Attraction, Coalitions, Communication, and Power" (Collins and Raven 1969) is a rich source of ideas regarding the influence of social groups and potential hypotheses as to how this influence may affect buyer behavior.

[3]Notable exceptions are studies by Cohen and Golden (1972), Burnkrant and Cousineau (1975), and Calder and Burnkrant (1977).

coercive, reward, referent, expert, legitimate, and informational. Social power may operate either positively (when exercised by affiliative or aspiration groups) or negatively (when exercised by disassociative groups) (Collins and Raven 1969, pp. 166–168).

Coercive and reward power are based on the ability of the influencer to dispense or withhold rewards and punishments. Thus, the influencing agent must be able to observe the relevant behavior. Coercive and reward power were extensively discussed in Chapter 7 in conjunction with the reinforcement model of learning.

Referent power exists when the individual uses members of reference groups as a point of comparison for self-evaluation. As discussed previously in conjunction with the comparison function of reference groups, referent power is especially likely to operate when objective reality is not readily discernable and the individual must look to others to define a "social reality." Unlike coercive and reward power, referent power does not require surveillance by the influencing agent.

Another type of power that does not require surveillance is expert power. An expert is a person or agency that is perceived to have special knowledge or ability. Marketers make extensive use of expert power to influence potential buyers to purchase their goods and services. Perhaps the best example of expert power is the American Dental Association's endorsement of Crest toothpaste. Marketers are also attempting to use expert power when they employ well known athletes as spokespeople for their sports equipment or in such statements as "Researchers at a leading university. . . ."

Legitimate power derives from generally recognized powers that are associated with specific roles. Parents, teachers, policemen, and physicians all have well recognized powers accorded to them by virtue of the roles they occupy. Legitimate power may arise from other sources of power, especially expert power. In a marketing context, one can see legitimate power exercised by information sources that have legitimated themselves in the eyes of the public; e.g., *Consumer Reports, Good Housekeeping, Parents' Magazine*. Another example is prescription drugs, which are consumed under doctor's orders, often with virtually no knowledge of what is being consumed.

The final source of power, informational power, has not been widely recognized by marketers (cf., Burnkrant and Cousineau 1975). "The most important characteristic of informational influence is that it is socially independent of the source" (Collins and Raven 1969, p. 166). That is, the effect of the information on the receiver would be the same irrespective of the specific source of the information. Burnkrant and Cousineau (1975), for example, recently suggested that the knowledge that other persons are using a particular product provides the individual with *information* that suggests that the product is probably a good one.

Social Influence Processes

Most discussions of social influence processes recognize, and often incorporate, Kelman's (1961) distinctions among the compliance, identification, and internalization processes of social influence. Bauer (1967, 1970), for example, related Kelman's system of social influence to source effects as they operate in what he refers to as problem solving and psychosocial "games." Figure 9.1 presents Bauer's ideas schematically. In a related effort, Burnkrant and Cousineau (1975) brought to-

Figure 9.1
Problem solving and psychosocial games

The Game	Components		Type of Attitude Change
Problem Solving Psychosocial	Competence Power	Trust Likability	Internalization Compliance Identification

Source: Raymond A. Bauer, "Source Effect and Persuasibility: A New Look," in D. F. Cox (ed.), *Risk Taking and Information Handling in Consumer Behavior.* Boston: Division of Research, Harvard University, Graduate School of Business Administration, 1967, p. 563.

Figure 9.2
Social influence processes

Influence	Process	Goal Orientation	Behavioral Implications
Informational Normative	Internalization Identification	Knowledge Self Maintenance or Enrichment	Accept ◀— X* Associate ◀— X —▶ Dissociate
	Compliance	External Reward	Conform

* X represents the individual's initial position.

Source: Robert E. Burnkrant and Alain Cousineau, "Informational and Normative Social Influence in Buyer Behavior." *Journal of Consumer Research*, 2 (December 1975): 207.

gether a number of ideas involving the distinction between informational and normative influence processes (Deutsch and Gerard 1955), attributions made on the basis of product evaluations by other persons (Kelley 1967), and the notion of a problem solving game as these concepts relate to Kelman's system of social influence processes. Burnkrant and Cousineau's analysis is presented schematically in Figure 9.2

The compliance influence process is based on reward and coercive power. It also involves externally defined norms governing behavior. While the individual may conform his or her behavior, this behavioral change is unlikely to be accompanied by a corresponding change in beliefs and attitudes. Compliance induced behavior will normally be continued only as long as surveillance is maintained. Purchasing behavior induced by compliance involves the buyer in a type of psychosocial "game" that can have relatively little to do with the intrinsic attributes of the good or service being purchased.

Compliance processes are frequently involved in purchasing decisions. Occasionally, compliance necessitates the purchase of a specific brand. Your purchase of this book, for example, is presumably in *compliance* with instructions from the instructor of your course. Compliance with specific "suggestions" is also common in the purchase of repair services. This occurs because the need is often very pressing (e.g., no hot water) and the inability of the buyer to make an independent decision. Much more frequently, however, compliance tends to define relatively broad boundaries of acceptable and unacceptable purchasing behavior. Clothing and housing, for example, are especially subject to this type of influence.

A considerably different type of psychosocial game is involved in social influence based on identification. Identification influence processes are based on the desire to develop a satisfying role relationship with another person or persons. Such role relationships tend to enhance and enrich the individual's self-image. Likability of the source plays a key role in the identification influence process. As in compliance induced behavior, intrinsic product attributes are frequently of limited importance in purchasing decisions based upon identification influence processes. However, to the extent that the desired role relationship is obtained attitude, as well as behavior, may be expected to change. Surveillance, of course, is not necessary to maintain the desired behavior.

Like compliance, identification involves group defined norms. In this case, the norms specify the requirements for participation in particular role relationships. The idea of role-related product clusters is directly related to identification influence processes. The person who wants to be attractive to the opposite sex, for example, should use a sex appeal toothpaste, a dandruff shampoo, a strong and long lasting deodorant, and drive a sportscar. In a similar way, the fast-track young executive and the society hostess will acquire the accoutrements necessary to the roles they wish to play.

The third influence process, internalization, involves a quite different type of "game." This game is based on the need to solve a specific buying problem. Intrinsic product attributes are critical to the decision and the individual desires relevant and accurate information. Desired characteristics of the sources of information are competence (i.e., expert power) and trust. That is, the sources should be highly credible. Under these conditions, the individual will tend to accept and internalize the acquired information with consequent changes in behavior, attitudes, and beliefs.

Marketers suffer from a general perception of being low credibility sources because they have a strong vested interest in the purchasing decision. For this reason, marketers rely on a variety of means to enhance their credibility. Hiring "expert" spokespeople is probably the most common strategy. Certain celebrities, Arthur Godfrey is one of the best known examples, have acquired reputations for being very careful about the products they endorse. In the long run, however, credibility in the minds of consumers is best established by making good products and standing behind them should they fail to perform properly.[4]

One final point regarding social influence processes needs to be made. Although it is common to discuss the three processes separately, they probably all occur to some degree in an actual purchasing decision. For example, the buyer must comply with the general social mandate to purchase and wear clothes. Most buyers also probably desire to "look good" in the clothes they wear, although this will mean different things to different people and vary in strength considerably across individuals. And, no doubt, most buyers, most of the time, desire to purchase clothes that solve problems involving warmth, comfort, durability, ease of care, and so forth.

---

[4]A personal experience illustrates this point very effectively. Some years ago, we had a Kitchen Aid garbage disposal that, somehow, managed to drive a bone through the housing of the disposal. Although the disposal was out of warranty and even though I made no request for a free replacement, the distributor gave us a new disposal because the problem "just shouldn't have happened." We have had an extremely good image of Kitchen Aid ever since.

FACTORS AFFECTING THE RELEVANCE OF SOCIAL INFLUENCE

Research shows that social influence is a relevant factor in the purchase of many goods and services; e.g., men's suits (Venkatesan 1966), automobiles, cigarettes, beer, drugs (Bourne 1957), cook-in-bag frozen foods and coffee (Witt and Bruce 1972). On the other hand, research also includes many results where social influence is not related to purchasing behavior; e.g., laundry detergent, dust-and-wax furniture spray (Witt and Bruce 1972), and bread (Ford and Ellis 1980). This raises an important question: Under what conditions is social influence likely to affect buyer behavior? The answer is of two different types depending upon whether the influence process is informative or normative.

Informative Influence

Social influence frequently occurs without any special desire or intent on the part of the influencer. Buyers learn much about the existence and characteristics of many goods and services simply by observing other persons. Even more important is what Riesman (1950) called the "taste exchange" process. People frequently exchange information in social gatherings about clothing, automobiles, restaurants, movies, vacation spots, medicines, sports equipment, beauty products, ad infinitum, as a matter of general interest without any intention or desire to influence the other person. Listeners, of course, retain much of this information and undoubtedly incorporate some of it in their buying decisions.

Of course, the social visibility and the tendency to exchange product and brand information varies considerably across product classes. Nevertheless, it is probably true that informative social influence is to some degree relevant to most goods and services. Thus, most firms should attempt to monitor interpersonal communication regarding their products and, to the extent possible, incorporate interpersonal influence into their marketing strategies. This important topic will be discussed further in Chapter 10 in conjunction with the diffusion of innovations.

Normative Influence

In normative influence, the influencer is providing standards for product evaluation in addition to product information. Robertson (1971, pp. 191–192) suggested that personal influence is especially likely to operate under conditions of high social visibility, high complexity, high perceived risk, and low testability (i.e., ability to try the product without making a major commitment to it).[5] Recently, Ford and Ellis (1980) provided further support for Robertson's guidelines.

In considering normative influence, it is important to keep in mind that over time norms change both in their content and rigidity. For example, less than twenty years ago anything other than a white dress shirt or a clean-shaven face would have been inconceivable for an executive. Of course, acceptable standards of dress and personal grooming for executives continue to exist. They have, however, changed and become less rigid. In a similar way, there have been definite changes in the symbols of status over the last several decades. Automobiles, for

---

[5]Although Robertson does not use the term normative, it is clear from the context that he is referring to what we have called normative influence as opposed to influence that is purely informational.

example, have decreased in importance as status symbols while second homes have become more important. Such social norms are frequently of great importance to marketers, and marketers are well advised to keep abreast of the strategy implications of changing social norms.

Reference Group Influence Over Product Class and Brand Choices

A final, and very important, point regarding the relevance of social influence is whether the influence is directed toward the product class choice, the brand choice, or both. This distinction was originally developed by Bourne (1957) who argued that reference group influence is a function of two forms of product conspicuousness. The first is exclusiveness. If virtually everyone owns the product then it is not conspicuous in this sense. Thus, reference group influence over product class choice is likely to be strong for luxury goods and weak for necessities. The second form of conspicuousness is whether the good is consumed publicly or privately. For the brand choice to be subject to reference group influence the good must be publicly consumed in such a way that the brand is readily identified.

Recently, Bearden and Etzel (1982) extended and empirically tested the social influence categorization scheme originally suggested by Bourne. Figure 9.3 presents their hypotheses in schematic form along with examples of each of the four types of products identified. A mail survey of 800 members of a statewide (South Carolina) consumer panel produced general support for the hypotheses. A particularly interesting finding was that the strength of reference group influence was "consistently greater for brand choices as opposed to product choice decisions. This suggests a greater role for appeals based on reference groups in stimulating selective demand" (Bearden and Etzel 1982, p. 192).

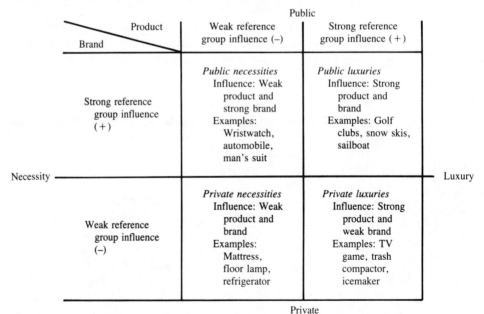

Figure 9.3
Reference group influence over product class and brand choice decisions

Source: William O. Bearden and Michael J. Etzel, "Reference Group Influence on Product and Brand Purchase Decisions." *Journal of Consumer Research*, 9 (September 1982): 185.

SUMMARY

This chapter examined the processes through which social groups influence individual buyers. These processes were seen to be both numerous and complex. In many buying situations, there are group pressures of varying strength to limit choice alternatives. Although these pressures may occasionally dictate a specific brand or brands, it is probably more common that they define broad categories of acceptable and unacceptable choices.

Historically, marketers emphasized the normative aspects of social influence. The recent recognition of informational influence via such means as casual observation and "taste exchange" is another example of the increasing recognition that much buyer behavior is characterized by low involvement decision processes. This is not to deny that direct and highly conscious influence attempts occur and frequently succeed. Rather, what must be recognized is that social influence is pervasive, often subtle, and is a factor in most buying decisions, irrespective of whether an elaborate, prepurchase decision-making process is involved.

Diffusion of Innovations

10

This chapter addresses the central issues concerning extensive problem solving (EPS) by focusing on buyer's decision-making processes concerning whether or not to adopt a new product. In the research literature, the topic under discussion in this chapter is known as the diffusion of innovations. Diffusion is defined as "(1) the adoption (2) of new products and services (3) over time (4) by consumers (5) within social systems (6) as encouraged by marketing activities" (Robertson, 1971, p. 32). The new products and services in the definition are generally known as innovations. Since EPS can require substantial effort on the part of buyers, one might suspect that getting an innovation adopted by buyers is often a difficult task. In fact, by almost any standard used, most new products are commercial failures. Indeed, this high failure rate is one of the principle reasons for research into the processes that govern the adoption and diffusion of innovations.

The chapter begins with a brief review of the product life cycle and its important implication that the firm has little choice but to innovate despite the steep odds against success. The chapter next considers what is meant by saying that a product is "new." This will lead to a discussion of the processes by which a single buyer or buying unit decides whether to adopt an innovation and the factors that facilitate or inhibit the adoption process. The special characteristics of buyers who are first to adopt an innovation are considered here. Such individuals serve as important sources of information for later adopters, which leads naturally into a general discussion of how information about innovations is disseminated to potential adopters. It is known that personal, as opposed to impersonal, information sources are especially important when buyers are considering purchase of an innovation. Therefore, some ways in which the firm may explicitly incorporate personal influence into its marketing strategy are discussed. Finally, the chapter briefly discusses some quantitative models that have been used to predict the rate at which an innovation will diffuse.

THE NEED TO INNOVATE

The Product Life Cycle

As already noted, most new products are failures. Given this situation, one might be tempted to ask: Why innovate at all? Some of the reasons for innovating have already been discussed. For example, as known from learning theory as well as from market experience, the first firm onto the market tends to enjoy a substantial competitive advantage. More fundamentally, a phenomenon, which has come to be known as the product life cycle, shows us that in the long run an industry has no choice but to innovate if it is to survive.

The product life cycle describes how sales and profits tend to vary over time. Figure 10.1 graphically displays the competitive dynamics of the product life cycle. During the period immediately following introduction of a new product, sales tend to be low and profits negative. If the product is to be successful, it will next enter a growth period in which sales increase rapidly. Because demand tends to be greater than supply through most of the growth period, profits are likely to be at their highest level. High profits, of course, tend to attract competitors. The entry of new competitors signals the onset of the maturity period. When this happens increasing competition will tend to force down total industry profits even though total sales

Figure 10.1
Profitability and the product life cycle

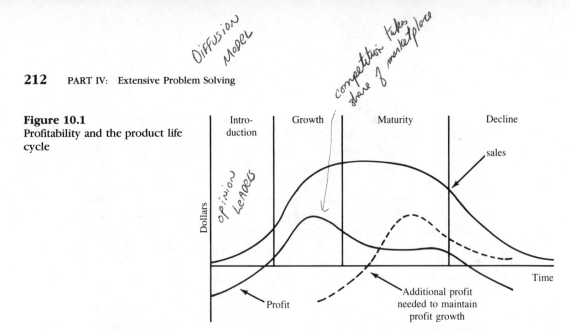

may be rising. If the industry is to maintain or increase its total profitability, new *and* successful products must be introduced during or before the maturity period. Finally, forces, internal and external to the industry, will cause demand to decline and profits to be further reduced and possibly turn to losses.[1]

The Likelihood and Cost of New Product Failures

The product life cycle depicted in Figure 10.1 assumes that the product is successful; however, as already noted, most new products are not successful. A frequently cited study by the consulting firm Booz, Allen & Hamilton (Management of New Products 1968) suggests just how serious this problem is. According to the report, less than 5 percent of all new product ideas ever become commercially successful. More important, even after eliminating the many new product ideas that fail to pass preliminary tests, approximately 40 percent of the new products placed on the market are not commercially successful.

The magnitude of resources expended on unsuccessful products is huge. According to the Booz, Allen & Hamilton (1968) study, some 70 percent of all product development expenditures are made on unsuccessful products. At the national level, this translates into billions of dollars of unproductive expenditures. At the level of the individual company, losses that are counted in the tens of millions are not unusual (e.g., Angelus 1969, Danzig 1971).

A Managerial Dilemma

From the data presented above, it is clear that the decision to innovate presents management with something of a dilemma. At the level of the industry, the need to innovate is inescapable. While at the level of the firm it is possible to successfully adopt a follow-the-leader strategy, the rewards to the successful innovator are enticingly large. Unfortunately, the likelihood and the cost of failure are also large. Clearly, any knowledge that increases the likelihood of identifying, developing, and commercially introducing to the market successful new products is of enormous

---

[1]It is important to note that Figure 10.1 is a highly idealized description of the life cycle that may be experienced by any specific product form. Although research has shown that the product life cycle is generally valid, exceptions do exist (e.g., Polli and Cook 1969).

value. The remainder of this chapter will consider research on buyer behavior to facilitate the introduction of new products to the market.[2]

DEFINITIONS OF NEWNESS

It is sometimes said that a product is "new" if a potential buyer is not aware of it. While this may be true, such a definition is not very helpful at either a conceptual or operational level. More important, it fails to recognize that the "newness" of an innovation is a matter of degree. This section considers three different, but related, ways in which the newness of an innovation can be defined.

Cognitive

The newness of an innovation can be defined in terms of the additional information that a buyer needs in order to make a satisfactory brand choice. This cognitive conception of the degree of newness, which is attributable to Howard and Sheth (1969, Chapter 8), postulates the following three categories of innovations in increasing order of newness: minor, normal, and major. In the case of major innovations

> ... the buyer has no place "to put them", he has no well-defined product class concept. One implication of this is that he must learn a set of words to identify, describe, and think about the brand. Words for talking about the brand become especially important because of the influence that other people may exert on the buyer, provided, of course, that he talks to them about it. (Howard and Sheth 1969, p. 280).

Good examples of major innovations are home computers, active solar heating systems, and windmill electric generation systems.

Normal and minor innovations place fewer information demands upon buyers. In the case of a normal innovation, the buyer knows to which product class the innovation belongs but needs additional information to properly identify and evaluate the new product. Good examples of normal innovations are electric cars and video recorders. In the case of a minor innovation, the new product is very similar to existing brands with which the buyer is familiar and the buyer needs to know little more than that the new brand exists to make a satisfactory brand choice. In terms of sheer numbers, most innovations fall into the category of minor innovations (Robertson 1971, p. 11).

The reader has probably noted that the descriptions of major, normal, and minor innovations parallel, respectively, the definitions of extensive problem solving, limited problem solving, and routinized response behavior. This is indeed the case. Like the stages of decision making, the three categories of newness are somewhat arbitrarily defined categories along a continuum of newness. Furthermore, because the decision-making task increases in difficulty with the increasing newness of the innovation, the likelihood of buyers adopting a given new product is, all other things equal, inversely related to its degree of newness.

---

[2]There is a sizeable literature that is relevant to the development of new products but is outside the boundaries of this discussion. For an excellent introduction to this literature, see Urban and Hauser (1980).

Consumption Behavior

A second way to define the degree of newness of a product is to ask how much the buyer would have to change his or her behavior in order to successfully use or consume the innovation. Robertson (1967) has suggested that this continuum of change in consumption behavior can be divided into three broad categories, which he labels continuous, dynamically continuous, and discontinuous. A continuous innovation requires little or no change in use behavior. Most innovations fall into this category; e.g., yearly automobile style changes, adding fluoride to toothpaste. A discontinuous innovation requires a very large change in consumption behavior; e.g., home computers, health maintenance organizations. A dynamically continuous innovation requires some intermediate change in use behavior. A good example of a dynamically continuous innovation is time-of-day pricing for electricity, which requires alteration of the timing and sequencing of such things as heating hot water, bathing, and washing clothes.

The relationship between the required change in use behavior and the likelihood of commercial success for an innovation is the same as the relationship between success and the cognitive definition of newness. That is, all other things equal, the degree of newness is negatively related to the likelihood of commercial success. Despite this similarity, it is important to recognize that the cognitive and use behavior definitions of the newness of an innovation are conceptually distinct. Although major innovations probably tend toward the discontinuous end of the use behavior continuum, this is not required. For example, although passive solar heating would seem to be a major innovation in terms of its cognitive demands, it is almost by definition a continuous innovation; i.e., the heat of the sun is passively absorbed to reduce the "load" on traditional heating sources.

Legal

Finally, there is little question that marketers have a tendency to use the word new somewhat loosely. As a consequence, the Federal Trade Commission (1967) advised that the word "new" may be used "only when (the product) is either entirely new or has been changed in a functionally significant and substantial respect. A product may not be called 'new' when only the package has been altered or some other change made which is functionally insignificant or insubstantial" (p. 1). The FTC advisory opinion also limits the use of the word new to six months after the product enters full distribution.

THE ADOPTION PROCESS

All other things equal, market success and the newness of an innovation, as defined above, are inversely related. Of course, all other things rarely are equal. In fact, much is known that can increase the likelihood of success of an innovation; that is, the likelihood of an innovation being adopted. Adoption refers to the process by which a buyer or buying unit comes to a decision about using an innovation. Most of the findings cited in this section are based on research into innovations that tend to be major or discontinuous or both. Although diffusion research findings may be at least partially transferable to innovations presenting lesser degrees of newness, the clarity and consistency of diffusion research results tends to be greatest for products that are truly new. Also, it is important to keep in mind as the adoption process is discussed that for numerous reasons the process may not be successfully completed.

Adoption

Conceptually, adoption represents a commitment to the continued use of a new product. This definition, of course, parallels the earlier discussion of repeat purchase behavior and brand loyalty. Indeed, in the context of the diffusion of innovations, much of the discussion in Chapter 5 could be reconstructed here as an analysis of what it means to say that a buyer has "adopted" a product. In a similar way, the concept of adoption is not limited to brands of a product class. In the case of a truly new durable good, for example, it is probably more accurate to think of a person adopting the services provided by the new class of goods rather than a specific brand. The adoption concept can also be applied to a wide range of services, political causes, and ideas. For example, the *idea* of government responsibility for the disadvantaged has been actively promoted by politicians loosely identified as liberals for over half a century, and that idea has been widely *adopted* by the American public.

Before beginning discussion of the adoption process, it is appropriate to briefly consider what Rogers (1976, pp. 229–231) considers to be a strong pro-innovation bias. Implicit in most diffusion research is the assumption that innovation is "good" and that nonadoption represents some type of individual or social failure. Many innovations, however, are harmful both to individual adopters and to society at large; e.g., illegal drugs. Other innovations may be good for individual adopters but harmful to society; e.g., nonreturnable plastic bottles. Realistically, most innovations are good for some people and bad for others. A good example of this is solar hot water systems. The desirability of solar hot water system depends on many factors including geography and life style. The truth is that a solar hot water system is not desirable for everyone, as many early adopters found much to their dismay. Finally, from the perspective of the individual company, it is often desirable to slow down the adoption rate until the company can prepare its own entry into the market. For these reasons, it is important to consider factors that inhibit, as well as those that facilitate, adoption.

A "Typical" Adoption Process Model

Over the years, a number of different models describing the adoption process have been proposed (cf., Robertson 1971, especially Chapter 3). All of these models represent elaborations and variations on the learning hierarchy of decision making, which was discussed thoroughly in Chapter 3. The assumption that buyers go through a learning hierarchy type of decision process before arriving at an adoption decision is probably reasonable for major and discontinuous innovations. The reader should keep in mind, however, that all of these adoption process models are idealized or theoretical reconstructions of the process that an individual goes through. More specifically, substantial variations should be expected among buyers in such things as the time it takes to go through each stage, possible skipping of stages, and the *exact* sequencing of stages in the adoption process.

Figure 10.2
Adoption process model

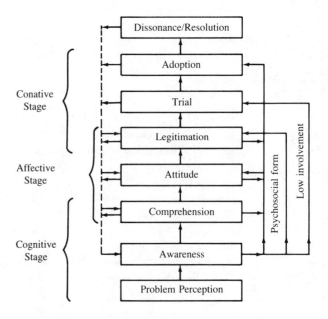

Figure 10.2 presents a synthesis of several adoption process models. The solid arrows, in the center and right side, represent upward flows from one stage to a higher stage. The dashed lines, on the left side, represent feedbacks from one stage to an earlier stage. The process begins with the perception that a "problem" exists. Sometimes the problem is obvious; e.g., diseases for which there is no known cure. Often, however, the problem will not be at all obvious. This is frequently the situation when an innovation represents an improved method for accomplishing some task. For example, the tasks performed by so-called personal computers (e.g., budgeting, tax preparation, entertainment) are all tasks that people continuously perform but that can be performed by a computer in a very different, and presumably better, way. More broadly, the question raised by problem perception is that of motivation, to which the material presented in Chapter 6 is directly applicable.

Of course, before the buyer can begin to solve a perceived problem there must be awareness that a potential solution exists in the form of one or more new products. In the full learning hierarchy, the buyer next develops a comprehension of what the new product is and forms an attitude toward that product. The processes involved in comprehension and attitude formation are the same as those discussed extensively in previous chapters. The major differences are that, because the product is new, the processes of comprehension and attitude formation are more difficult and more likely to be abandoned before completion.

The next stage in the adoption process is the legitimization of the new product. The concept of legitimization is very close to aspects of confidence and intention in the Howard and Sheth theory of buyer behavior. Specifically, the potential adopter needs to become convinced that adopting the innovation is the appropriate course of action to take. A number of ways in which a new product may become legitimized has already been considered. For example, Chapter 4 (Figure 4.4) examined the decision act of a housewife who used the question "Had bad experience with other products from this brand?" as a basis for deciding the legitimacy of a contemplated purchase of a new product. In a similar way, a buyer may use any number of different types of information as a basis for legitimizing a new product; e.g., price, reputation of manufacturer or reseller, warranty. For major and discontinuous innovations, it is well known that personal sources of information are especially important in the legitimization process (Robertson 1971, especially Chapters 7 and 8).

Assuming that the innovation is legitimized, the next step in the adoption process is trial. The exact nature of the trial stage depends very much upon the characteristics of the innovation in question. For an inexpensive nondurable, the trial stage will generally involve purchase and use of the product. For expensive durables, the buyer will frequently attempt to sample the product; e.g., take a test ride in an automobile or try out a friend's microwave oven. Of course, frequently a satisfactory trial is either very difficult or impossible to obtain. In the context of discussions of the adoption process, the importance of the trial stage is that it represents only a tentative commitment to the product.

The result of a satisfactory trial is adoption. Adoption, as already noted, represents a commitment to the continued use of an innovation. Defining adoption conceptually is not difficult. Empirically, however, it is often difficult to determine when, and if, adoption has occured. In the case of inexpensive, frequently purchased products a buyer may "try" a new product several times before coming to a final adoption decision. For example, with a new food product the buyer may need several trials to get used to a new taste and see if family and friends like the new food. In the case of durables, of course, purchase requirements are often such that trial and adoption cannot be separated on any basis other than asking people if they would buy the product again. As known from earlier discussions, a number of forces might *bias* a buyer's response to such a question toward a positive response.

The final stage is dissonance or, more accurately, dissonance reduction. The discussion of cognitive dissonance theory in Chapter 8, including ways a seller might help a buyer reduce dissonance, is relevant to this concluding stage of the adoption process. Two additional points, however, are relevant. First, to the extent that a buyer must commit himself or herself to a product (e.g., a trial purchase), dissonance may occur after the trial stage as well as after the adoption stage. Second, because dissonance only occurs under special circumstances, some writers (e.g., Campbell 1966; Zaltman and Wallendorf 1979) prefer the more general term resolution stage. Whatever this stage is called, it is the period in which the buyer makes whatever cognitive or behavioral adjustments are necessary as a consequence of the adoption decision.

So far the stages in the adoption process have been discussed sequentially. Of course, for many reasons, a buyer may decide to return to an earlier stage. For example, a buyer who has had an unsuccessful trial of a new food product may return to the comprehension stage to find out if the food was properly prepared or served with appropriate accompanying dishes. The dashed, feedback arrows on the left-hand side of Figure 10.2 recognize this possibility of feedback from one stage to an earlier stage.

The arrows on the right-hand side of Figure 10.2 recognize that certain stages may be skipped entirely by some buyers and for some products. In the low involvement form of the adoption process, the buyer skips directly from awareness to trial. Nakanishi (1968 cited in Robertson 1971) found that this process is characteristic of the adoption of new grocery products. More specifically, because of low unit prices, ease of trial, and the low commitment to the decision, buyers tend to integrate the comprehension, attitude, and legitimation stages into a more comprehensive trial stage, in which all of these activities occur together. The psychosocial form of the adoption process is most likely to occur where the opinions of socially significant other individuals are especially important to the adoption decision. In this case, the buyer will tend to skip directly from awareness to legitimation to determine if there is social support for the contemplated purchase. For example, when considering the purchase of high fashion clothes, others' opinions regarding the desirability of a new style may be *the* critical factor in the adoption process.

Attributes of Innovations Which Facilitate Adoption

This chapter began with a discussion of the concept of newness and a statement that, in the sense of being a major or discontinuous innovation, the newer is the innovation, the less likely it will be adopted. This idea will be expanded on here by discussing in more detail specific attributes of innovations that are related to the likelihood of adoption.[3] The importance of this discussion is indicated by research by Ostlund (1974), which found that buyers' perceptions of the attributes of an innovation were the most important variables in predicting adoption.

Table 10.1 presents a summary of the principal innovation attributes or characteristics that are related to adoption. These attributes are based on respondents' perceptions of the innovation. Note that the number of studies (in the far right column) varies considerably for different attributes and that all other numbers in the table are stated as percentages. With the exception of complexity, the relationships between the product attributes and the likelihood of adoption are all positive.

The attributes relative advantage, fulfillment of felt needs, immediacy of benefit, and availability form a cluster of closely related attributes. Relative advantage is the degree to which the innovation is superior to available alternatives. The telephone, for example, was vastly superior to alternative methods of communication. Fulfillment of felt needs is basically a motivational variable. The more important the motive or need and the greater the perception that the innovation will satisfy that need, the more likely is adoption. Furthermore, the more immediate the benefit, in the form of motive satisfaction, from adopting the innovation the more likely is adoption. Closely related to immediacy of benefit is the availability of the innovation. Obviously, the innovation must be available before its benefits can be enjoyed.

Compatibility represents the degree to which the innovation is consistent, or compatible, with existing patterns of thinking and behavior. This, of course, is another way of stating that major innovations (thinking) and discontinuous innovations (behaving) are less likely, all other things equal, to be adopted than innovations that represent lesser degrees of newness. The concept of compatibility is well illustrated by Saxon Graham's (1956) classic study of the rate of adoption for five innovations by six social classes. Canasta was readily accepted by members of the upper class but not by members of lower social classes. Graham explained this finding by noting that active (as opposed to passive) recreation, general participa-

---

[3]This section relies heavily on analyses of diffusion research conducted by the Diffusion Documents Center at Michigan State University. The center systematically codes the findings of diffusion studies and enters this information into a computer system for subsequent retrieval and analysis. For a description of this system, see Rogers and Stanfield (1968).

Table 10.1
Attributes of innovations related to likelihood of adoption

Characteristics of the Innovation	Number of Generalizations with Each Type of Relationship to Innovativeness (Percent)					Total Number of Generali- zations
	Positive	None	Nega- tive	Condi- tional	Total	
1. Relative advantage	79	15	3	3	100	66
2. Compatibility	86	14	0	0	100	50
3. Fulfillment of felt needs	92	4	4	0	100	27
4. Complexity	19	37	44	0	100	16
5. Divisibility	43	43	14	0	100	14
6. Communicability	75	25	0	0	100	8
7. Availability	56	22	17	5	100	18
8. Immediacy of benefit	57	29	14	0	100	7

Source: Adapted from Everett M. Rogers and J. David Stanfield "Adoption and Diffusion of New Products: Emerging Generalizations and Hypotheses." In *Applications of the Sciences in Marketing Management*, edited by F. M. Bass, C. W. King, and E. A. Pessemier, 243. New York: Wiley & Sons, 1968.

tion in card playing, and more frequent gathering with friends are all characteristics of the upper class, which made canasta a very compatible innovation. In contrast, television was much more readily accepted by members of the lower social class despite the high cost of this innovation. The other three innovations (supermarkets, Blue Cross, and Medical Service) showed no consistent differences in adoption across social classes.

We have already discussed the concept of divisibility in conjunction with the trial stage of the adoption process. Divisibility is a measure of the degree to which an innovation may be "divided" into small units for trial on a limited basis. This division can occur in a number of ways; e.g., trial sizes, demonstration models, or trial period during which the product may be returned. A highly divisible product requires little commitment on the part of the buyer and implies little risk. Looked at from a slightly different perspective, there is also evidence that given a choice of sizes buyers tend to purchase smaller quantities than usual when they purchase a new product (Shoemaker and Shoaf 1975).

Communicability is a measure of the ease with which information about an innovation is transmitted from one individual to another. Innovations that are used in a social setting (e.g., television, games) by their very nature invite conversation. Other innovations, for a variety of reasons, are frequent topics of conversation; e.g., new movies, solar energy. In contrast, many innovations are not the subject of conversation because of such factors as privacy of use, lack of general interest in the product class, and social inhibitions. A good example of this is feminine hygiene products.

Complex innovations place an extra burden on the individual because they require teaching the potential adopter how to use the product, as well as conveying what the product is and what benefits result from adopting the product. While there is a modest negative relationship between the complexity of an innovation and the likelihood of adoption, the results are less clear-cut than for most of the other attributes. Probably the most reasonable interpretation of the data is that, all other things equal, complexity is negatively related to adoption. Of course, all other things rarely are equal, and often a high relative advantage can be obtained only at a cost of some increase in complexity. It must be recognized that the innovation attributes listed in Table 10.1 are generally *not* independent. Thus, while it may be desirable to develop an innovation that has a high relative advantage, low complexity, high communicability and so on, this will normally not be possible. The skillful marketer, however, will take care not to create an innovation that places *needless* burdens on buyers and, where such burdens cannot be avoided, will try to develop means for helping buyers through the adoption process.

INNOVATIVENESS

Individuals who are among the first to adopt an innovation are said to be innovative. Innovative buyers are important to the firm for many reasons. First, sales to such buyers provide the first critical indications of the likelihood of the innovation's success. Second, getting the innovation out where other potential adopters can see it is an important factor to market success. Third, innovative buyers are important sources of information for less innovative buyers. Fourth, earlier adopters are less likely than later adopters to abandon use of the innovation (Rogers and Shoemaker 1971). This section discusses the special characteristics of individuals who are high in innovativeness. The next section discusses how information, both personal and impersonal, is transmitted to and among potential adopters.

Adopter Categories

Innovativeness is normally defined in terms of time of adoption.[4] How innovativeness is distributed among buyers can be determined by plotting the number of adopters by time period in which the adoption occurred. Although idealized, it has been found that this distribution *tends* to be normal (Rogers and Shoemaker 1971). Figure 10.3 presents this idealized adoption curve. Because the total time necessary for an innovation to diffuse varies widely among innovations, the horizontal axis is defined in terms of the average time to adoption ($\bar{x}$) and the number of standard deviations from this average (sd).

As can be seen in Figure 10.3, five categories of adopters are recognized in terms of the number of standard deviations from the average time of adoption. Although the groups are defined somewhat arbitrarily, research showed that each adopter group has a distinct profile of demographic, socioeconomic, and personality characteristics. Figure 10.4 presents a verbal summary of some of the most important of these characteristics for each category of adopters.

---

[4]This conception of innovativeness has a number of problems. First, it is essentially an operational definition. Second, it confounds a number of circumstantial factors with the behavioral trait innovativeness. For example, it has been suggested that those who are first to adopt may be those who first receive information about the innovation or those with an immediate need for the innovation. Despite these caveats, there is sufficient agreement among a number of studies to suggest that time of adoption is a meaningful, although clearly not optimal, measure of innovativeness. For a detailed critique of the innovativeness concept, see Midgley and Dowling (1978).

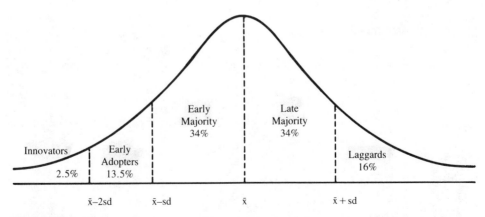

Figure 10.3
Adopter categorization on the basis of innovativeness

The innovativeness dimension, as measured by the time at which an individual adopts an innovation or innovations, is continuous. However, this variable may be partitioned into five adopter categories by laying off standard deviations from the average time of adoption.

Source: Reprinted with permission of Macmillan Publishing Company from *The Communication of Innovations* by Everett M. Rogers and F. Floyd Shoemaker. Copyright © 1971 by The Free Press, a Division of Macmillan Publishing Company.

Correlates of Innovativeness

Innovators and early adopters are clearly of importance to the success of a new product. For this reason it is important that the marketer be able to identify and reach individuals high in innovativeness. A number of characteristics, or correlates as they are frequently called, of individuals high in innovativeness have been identified in summaries of diffusion research findings prepared by Rogers and Stanfield (1968). Tables 10.2 to 10.4 present these summaries. The reader should note that these findings are based largely on major and discontinuous innovations. Research on innovations with lesser degrees of newness tends to produce less definitive results.

Table 10.2
Social characteristics variables related to innovativeness

Social Character- istics of the Unit of Adoption	Number of Generalizations with Each Type of Relationship to Innovativeness (percent)					Total Number of Generali- zations
	Positive	None	Nega- tive	Condi- tional	Total	
1. Education	75	16	5	4	100	193
2. Literacy	70	22	4	4	100	27
3. Income	80	11	6	3	100	112
4. Level of living	83	10	2	5	100	40
5. Age	32	40	18	10	100	158

Source: Everett M. Rogers and J. David Stanfield, "Adoption and Diffusion of New Products: Emerging Generalizations and Hypotheses." In *Applications of the Sciences in Marketing Management,* edited by F. M. Bass, C. W. King, and E. A. Pessemier, 240. New York: Wiley & Sons, 1968. Reprinted with permission.

Innovators: Venturesome

Observers have noted that venturesomeness is almost an obsession with innovators. They are eager to try new ideas. This interest leads them out of a local circle of peers and into more cosmopolite social relationships. Communication patterns and friendships among a clique of innovators are common, even though the geographical distance between the innovators may be great. Being an innovator has several prerequisites. These include control of substantial financial resources to absorb the possible loss due to an unprofitable innovation and the ability to understand and apply complex technical knowledge.

The salient value of the innovator is venturesomeness. He desires the hazardous, the rash, the daring, and the risky. The innovator also must be willing to accept an occasional setback when one of the new ideas he adopts proves unsuccessful.

Early Adopters: Respectable

Early adopters are a more integrated part of the local system than are innovators. Whereas innovators are cosmopolites, early adopters are localites. This adopter category, more than any other, has the greatest degree of opinion leadership in most social systems. Potential adopters look to early adopters for advice and information about the innovation. The early adopter is considered by many as "the man to check with" before using a new idea. This adopter category is generally sought by change agents to be a local missionary for speeding the diffusion process. Because early adopters are not too far ahead of the average individual in innovativeness, they serve as a role model for many other members of a social system. The early adopter is respected by his peers. He is the embodiment of successful and discrete use of new ideas. And the early adopter knows that he must continue to earn this esteem of his colleagues if his position in the social structure is to be maintained.

Early Majority: Deliberate

The early majority adopt new ideas just before the average member of a social system. The early majority interact frequently with their peers, but leadership positions are rarely held by them. The early majority's unique position between the very early and the relatively late to adopt makes them an important link in the diffusion process.

The early majority may deliberate for some time before completely adopting a new idea. Their innovation-decision is relatively longer than that of the innovator and the early adopter. "Be not the last to lay the old aside, nor the first by which the new is tried," might be the motto of the early majority. They follow with deliberate willingness in adopting innovations, but seldom lead.

Late Majority: Skeptical

The late majority adopt new ideas just after the average member of a social system. Adoption may be both an economic necessity and the answer to increasing social pressures. Innovations are approached with a skeptical and cautious air, and the late majority do not adopt until most others in their social system have done so. The weight of system norms must definitely favor the innovation before the late majority are convinced. They can be persuaded of the utility of new ideas, but the pressure of peers is necessary to motivate adoption.

Laggards: Traditional

Laggards are the last to adopt an innovation. They possess almost no opinion leadership. They are the most localite in their outlook of all adopter categories; many are near isolates. The point of reference for the laggard is the past. Decisions are usually made in terms of what has been done in previous generations. This individual interacts primarily with others who have traditional values. When laggards finally adopt an innovation, it may already have been superseded by another more recent idea which the innovators are already using. Laggards tend to be frankly suspicious of innovations, innovators, and change agents. Their tradition direction slows the innovation-decision process to a crawl. Adoption lags far behind knowledge of the idea. Alienation from a too-fast-moving world is apparent in much of the laggard's outlook. While most individuals in a social system are looking to the road of change ahead, the laggard has his attention fixed on the rear-view mirror.

Figure 10.4
Profiles of adopter categories

Source: Reprinted with permission of Macmillan Publishing Company from *The Communication of Innovations* by Everett M. Rogers and F. Floyd Shoemaker. Copyright © 1971 by The Free Press, a Division of Macmillan Publishing Company.

Table 10.3
Attitudinal-type variables related to innovativeness

Attitudinal-Type Characteristics of the Unit of Adoption	Number of Generalizations with Each Type of Relationship to Innovativeness (percent)					Total Number of Generalizations
	Positive	None	Nega-tive	Condi-tional	Total	
1. Knowledge-ability	79	17	1	3	100	66
2. General attitude toward change	74	14	8	4	100	159
3. Achievement motivation	65	23	0	12	100	17
4. Educational aspirations	83	9	4	4	100	23
5. Business orientation	60	20	20	0	100	5
6. Satisfaction with life	29	28	43	0	100	7
7. Empathy	75	0	25	0	100	4
8. Mental rigidity	21	25	50	4	100	24

Source: Everett M. Rogers and J. David Stanfield, "Adoption and Diffusion of New Products: Emerging Generalizations and Hypotheses." In *Applications of the Sciences in Marketing Management,* edited by F. M. Bass, C. W. King, and E. A. Pessemier, 241. New York: Wiley & Sons. Reprinted with permission.

Table 10.2 shows that innovativeness is positively correlated with education, literacy, income, and general level or standard of living. This suggests that more innovative individuals are more able to afford the risks inherent in innovation. Research also suggests that more innovative buyers tend to perceive less risk in an innovation than do less innovative buyers (e.g., Lambert 1972). The positive correlation of innovativeness with education and income is another example of a conclusion discussed previously; higher income, better educated buyers seem more able to acquire and process information and tend to get more for their purchasing dollar.[5] The relationship between innovativeness and age tends to be negative. The pattern, however, is much less clear than for the other variables listed in Table 10.2. Thus, it is reasonable to conclude that the relationship between innovativeness and age varies markedly by product category.

Table 10.3 presents a summary of diffusion research findings for eight attitudinal-type variables. High innovativeness is associated with a high level of awareness of the outside world (knowledgeability), a general receptiveness to new ideas (general attitude toward change), upward social mobility, high achievement motivation, high educational aspirations (especially for one's children), dissatisfaction with life, and low mental rigidity. This profile of the innovative buyer is both extended and

[5]The reader may object that this statement is a reflection of the pro-innovation bias discussed earlier. The fact, however, is that the vast majority of diffusion research has been conducted on innovations that are positive, or at least neutral, in their impact at both the individual and social level. Clearly negative innovations have largely been ignored in diffusion research.

Table 10.4
Social relationships of the unit of adoption to the social system as related to innovativeness

Social Relationship of the Unit of Adoption to the Social System	Number of Generalizations with Each Type of Relationship to Innovativeness (percent)					Total Number of Generalizations
	Positive	None	Negative	Conditional	Total	
1. Cosmopoliteness	81	11	3	5	100	73
2. Mass media exposure	86	12	0	2	100	49
3. Contact with change agencies	92	7	0	1	100	136
4. Deviancy from norms of the social system	54	14	28	4	100	28
5. Group participation	79	10	6	5	100	156
6. Interpersonal communication exposure	70	15	15	0	100	40
7. Opinion leadership	64	22	7	7	100	14

Source: Everett M. Rogers and J. David Stanfield, "Adoption and Diffusion of New Products: Emerging Generalizations and Hypotheses." In *Applications of the Sciences in Marketing Management*, edited by F. M. Bass, C. W. King, and E. A. Pessemier, 242. New York: Wiley & Sons, 1968. Reprinted with permission.

reinforced by personality research that shows that innovativeness is associated with high venturesomeness (Robertson and Kennedy 1968), low dogmatism (Ehrlich and Lee 1969, Jacoby 1971), and inner directedness (Donnelly 1970, Donnelly and Ivancevich 1974). The inner-directed person is guided in his or her decisions by internal values, as opposed to the opinions of other persons, to a greater extent than so-called other-directed persons. The person low in dogmatism is less threatened by change than someone high in dogmatism. Clearly, the innovative buyer is a person who is oriented toward change.

Table 10.4 presents a summary of diffusion research involving the relationship of innovators to the larger social system. Persons high in innovativeness tend to have a cosmopolitan, as opposed to provincial, outlook and tend to participate in group activities to a greater degree than persons low in innovativeness. Higher innovativeness is also associated with higher levels of interpersonal communication and greater contact with information sources such as the mass media and change agencies, who have a formal responsibility for promoting change. The classic example of a change agent is the county agricultural extension agent. Advertising agencies are another example of a change agent. Interestingly, while innovators are an important source of information for individuals who have not yet adopted an innovation—i.e., innovativeness is positively related to opinion leadership—innovators are also more likely to deviate from established social norms than later adopters.

The last point regarding deviancy from group norms requires us to make a sharp distinction between true innovators and early adopters; both of whom are high in innovativeness. True innovators tend to be less tied into their local social environments than early adopters. They also tend to have more contacts with more groups, which are often geographically dispersed, than early adopters. Thus, true innovators tend to be less tied to any one social group while at the same time being exposed to more social groups than early adopters. For this reason, innovators are more likely to deviate from group norms. On the other hand, because they are more supportive of group norms, early adopters are more likely to be opinion leaders than true innovators.

The Generality of Innovativeness

The correlates of innovativeness present a relatively clear portrait of the innovative person: well educated, exposed to diverse sources of information, oriented toward change, and with sufficient financial resources to absorb the costs of inevitable failures. This consistent profile of characteristics raises the important question of the degree to which innovativeness is a general personality characteristic. That is, is there a tendency for certain buyers to be innovators or early adopters over a wide range of unrelated products.

Research in sociology, especially rural sociology where acceptance of farming innovations have been extensively studied, suggests that innovativeness is a relatively general trait (Rogers and Shoemaker 1971). Most marketing studies, however, have come to the conclusion that innovativeness tends to be limited to individual products or groups of highly similar products (e.g., Arndt 1968; Robertson and Myers 1969; Robertson 1971, pp. 110–112). The most likely explanation for this contradiction is that research in sociology has been largely confined to major and discontinuous innovations while marketing research has largely focused on products possessing lesser degrees of newness.

THE FLOW OF INFORMATION ABOUT INNOVATIONS

Before a potential adopter can adopt a new product, he or she must become aware of the innovation. As seen in the last section, especially Table 10.4, a notable characteristic of innovators and early adopters is their relatively high exposure to personal and impersonal sources of information. This section discusses what is known about how information about innovations is distributed to potential adopters. Particular attention will be paid to that form of interpersonal communication known as word-of-mouth (W-O-M) communication.

The Two-Step Hypothesis

The first models of the effects of the mass media, which coincided with the rapid growth of radio in the 1930s, conceived of the mass media as having relatively strong and immediate effects on an atomized[6] audience (Zaltman and Stiff 1973, p. 435). Studies of voting behavior in the 1940s by Lazarfeld and his associates (summarized in Katz and Lazarfeld 1955) produced a different model of the effects

---

[6]The term atomized is applied to social structures where each member exists as an isolated "atom" with no strong connections to any other members of that social structure.

Figure 10.5
The two-step hypothesis

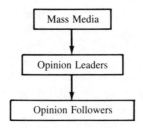

of the mass media, which has come to be known as the two-step hypothesis. Figure 10.5 presents this hypothesis in schematic form.

According to the two-step hypothesis information flows first from the mass media to individuals known as opinion leaders and, then, from these opinion leaders to individuals known as opinion followers, who are not connected directly to the mass media. Although much evidence is consistent with the two-step hypothesis, subsequent research showed that the relationships between the mass media and the interpersonal W-O-M communication network, and within the W-O-M network itself, are far more complex than the two-step hypothesis suggests.

A Multi-Step Model of Information Flows

Figure 10.6 presents a more realistic multi-step extension of the two-step hypothesis that summarizes much of what is known about information flows regarding innovations. First, note the dashed line that flows from the mass media to followers. This reflects the common sense, as well as research supported, idea that individuals designated as opinion followers are directly exposed to the mass media. The line is dashed because opinion followers are not as extensively or intensely linked to the mass media as opinion leaders.

In addition to being more exposed to the mass media, research indicates that opinion leaders are more likely to use objective information than followers, who are more likely to use personal information sources (Katz and Lazarfeld 1955; Summers 1970; Armstrong and Feldman 1976). Furthermore, one of the distinguishing characteristics of innovators, who are also important information sources, is their greater exposure to special interest media, especially specialized magazines (Summers 1972). Male fashion innovators, for example, tend to be frequent readers of *Esquire* and *Gentlemen's Quarterly* (Darden and Reynolds 1974). This greater exposure to specialized information sources is very important because it provides an efficient means of communicating with opinion leaders. It also lessens the problems of identifying opinion leaders since they tend to be self-selecting in terms of the mass media to which they expose themselves.

Figure 10.6
A multi-step flow model of information transmission

Source: From Henry Assael, *Consumer Behavior and Marketing Action* (Boston: Kent Publishing Company, 1981), p. 373. © 1981 by Wadsworth, Inc. Reprinted by permission of Kent Publishing, a division of Wadsworth, Inc.

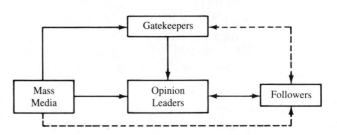

A second extension of the two-step hypothesis is indicated by the double headed arrow linking opinion leaders and followers. This recognizes that information flows from followers to leaders as well as in the reverse direction. Summers (1971), for example, found that for one-third of the cases studied, opinion leaders were *asked* for their opinions. Closely related to this point is a wide range of research which shows that individuals who are typically identified in diffusion research studies as opinion leaders are well integrated into their social groups and generally socially active (Rogers and Agarwala-Rogers 1976; Reynolds and Darden 1972). Furthermore, it has generally been concluded that opinion leaders and followers tend to be very similar in terms of socioeconomic, demographic, and attitudinal variables (e.g., Katz and Lazarfeld 1955; Myers and Robertson 1972).

A third extension of the two-step hypothesis is the recognition of individuals known as gatekeepers. A gatekeeper is a person who controls the flow of information within a social system. Gatekeepers are frequently different from both innovators and opinion leaders. Publisher's representatives, who call on faculty to present their latest textbooks, are a good example of the gatekeeper concept; so are disc jockeys, who control the flow of information about which new releases to play. Gatekeepers are especially important in family and organizational buying. For example, children frequently serve a gatekeeper function for candy and toys. Company purchasing agents are perhaps the clearest examples of gatekeepers in organizational buying.

Strength in Weak Ties

An important principle regarding W-O-M communication about innovations ties together a number of points just raised and summarizes much of what is known about information flows within and between social groups. This principle, which has come to be known as the strength in weak ties, states that "The informational strength of dyadic communication relationships is *inversely* related to the degree of homophily (and the strength of the attraction) between the source and the receiver" (Rogers 1976, p. 233, emphasis added). The principle of strength in weak ties was discovered almost simultaneously through analyses of W-O-M communication networks by Liu and Duff (1972) and Granovetter (1973).

Simply stated, the principle of strength in weak ties recognizes that social groups are typically made up of individuals who have highly similar characteristics. This is what is meant by homophily. Among these characteristics are beliefs and norms regarding behavior. These characteristics tend to produce strong attraction among group members and strong cohesion within the group as a whole. Since major and discontinuous innovations imply change, such innovations are frequently perceived by group members as a threat to the stability of the group and, therefore, tend to be resisted. The consequence of this is that "an innovation is diffused to a larger number of individuals and traverses a greater social distance when passed through weak ties rather than strong ones" (Rogers 1976, p. 233).

The principle of strength in weak ties raises an important distinction between true innovators and early adopters. Innovators tend to be more cosmopolitan and less likely to be closely tied to local social groups than early adopters. One implication of this is that weak ties are likely to be especially characteristic of that first 2–3 percent of adopters, who are labeled innovators. In terms of the multistep information model presented in Figure 10.6 this suggests that innovators are more likely to serve as gatekeepers, while early adopters are more likely to serve as opinion leaders within their social groups.

Characteristics and Generality of Opinion Leaders

As seen previously, innovativeness and opinion leadership are positively correlated. Thus, opinion leaders tend to reflect the characteristics of innovative individuals. However, partially because opinion leaders are less likely to be early adopters than true innovators, the characteristics of opinion leaders are less sharply defined than are the characteristics of innovators. Perhaps the most distinguishing characteristic of opinion leaders is their high level of social integration. In marked contrast to innovators, research has shown that opinion leaders are *more* likely to adhere to group norms than the average group member (Robertson 1971, p. 177). In a very real sense opinion leaders hold their position within the group precisely because they so strongly embody the standards and values of the group.

An important issue concerning opinion leadership is the degree to which it is a general personality trait. That is, is a person who is an opinion leader for one product category likely to be an opinion leader for a wide range of other product categories? There is general agreement that the answer to this question is no, *unless* the product categories are closely related. For example, a person is much more likely to be an opinion leader for women's clothing fashion *and* cosmetics and personal grooming aids than for cosmetics and personal grooming aids *and* large appliances (King and Summers 1970). This very plausible idea is reinforced by research that shows that the overlap in opinion leadership across product categories tends to correspond closely with the overlap in interest among the same categories (e.g., Montgomery and Silk 1971).

Is Opinion "Leadership" a Misnomer?

The conception of what is meant by opinion leadership has come a long way from the two-step hypothesis and its implications of an unsolicited, unidirection flow of information from knowledgeable opinion leaders to largely passive and ignorant opinion followers. W-O-M communication is clearly a complex phenomenon. For many reasons, some of which were previously discussed, there has been an increasing tendency to temper and reinterpret what is meant by opinion "leadership."

Certainly, there is no implication that the opinion leader is either the formal or informal leader of the group. Rather, the opinion leader tends to be someone who is recognized by others as knowledgeable about and interested in a particular product category. Furthermore, although more formal exchanges of information do occur, much of the exchange of information about innovations between "leaders" and "followers" tends to occur in casual, product specific conversations. For example, in a study of W-O-M communication about Maxim coffee (then a new product), Belk (1971) found that almost 80 percent of conversations about Maxim occurred in a situation involving food and that approximately a third of the conversations occurred while Maxim was being consumed.

Belk's findings are further supported by Summers' (1971) study of W-O-M communication for four products, which found that almost two-thirds of the conversations occurred between only two people as opposed to a larger group. Summers noted that this dyadic pattern of communication "suggests a casual passing on of product information rather than 'lecturing' by transmitters" (p. 433). It should be noted, however, that the percent of dyadic communication ranged from a high of 77 percent to a low of 54 percent, and that none of the products represented major or discontinuous innovations. This pattern suggests moderate variability in the degree of casualness of information transmission across product categories and raises the possibility that casual transmission may be most characteristic of minor or continuous innovations. Of course, such innovations are of very frequent concern to marketers.

INCORPORATING PERSONAL INFLUENCE IN THE FIRM'S MARKETING STRATEGY

Personal influence can be of enormous importance to the eventual success or failure of a new product as well as to the continued success of established products. Arndt (1967), for example, found that of those individuals who received favorable W-O-M communication about a new food product, 54 percent adopted the new product; while only 18 percent of those who received unfavorable W-O-M became adopters. It is also well established that as buyers progress from the early stages of the adoption process (i.e., awareness, comprehension) to later stages (i.e., attitude, legitimation, trial) the importance of information from the mass media tends to lessen, while the importance of interpersonal sources of information tends to rise. And, as already mentioned, less innovative individuals tend to rely more heavily upon interpersonal sources of information than do more innovative persons.

For many reasons it *may* be desirable for the firm to incorporate personal influence into its marketing strategy. The word may is emphasized because the importance of W-O-M communication varies substantially by product category; e.g., different innovations will have different levels of communicability. Thus, the first task facing the firm is to determine if W-O-M communication is sufficiently important to be explicitly incorporated into its marketing strategy. Assuming that it is, this section will explore some ways in which the firm may stimulate W-O-M communication networks to produce a more extensive and favorable flow of information about its innovation among potential adopters.

Monitoring Interpersonal Communications

If the firm is to successfully incorporate interpersonal influence into its marketing strategy, it will need information about what people are saying to each other about the product. The techniques needed to gather such information are essentially the standard marketing research procedures that the firm uses to gather other types of market information. The difference is one of focus. In addition to determining what people think and feel about the product, it is important to know what they are *saying* to each other about the product.

Knowledge of interpersonal communications can be of great value to the firm in terms of understanding buyers' extent and accuracy of knowledge about product attributes, the uses to which buyers have put the product (some of which may be unexpected), and problems and disadvantages encountered. The extent to which these topics are the subject of interpersonal communication is probably a good measure of involvement with and importance of the new product, since people are most likely to talk about important things or things causing them concern. Continuous monitoring of the interpersonal communication network can also alert the firm to problems in time to do something about them.

Direct Communication With Opinion Leaders

The most straightforward method of attempting to stimulate interpersonal communication is direct communication with opinion leaders. This presumes that the firm is able to identify the opinion leaders. Probably, the most frequently used technique for identifying opinion leaders is self-designation, in which respondents are asked questions such as the number of times other people ask them for their opinions about a given topic or the extent to which they think they influence other people. Unfortunately, the self-designation technique is plagued with problems (cf., Zaltman and Stiff 1973). In particular, it has been suggested, self-designation may be as much or more a measure of self-esteem as opinion leadership. Despite these criticisms, Yavas and Riecken (1982) recently demonstrated the reliability of a simple self-designating opinion leadership scale, originally developed by King and Summers (1970).

Where smaller numbers of individuals are potential adopters, opinion leaders may be identified through using sociometric techniques. For example, a number of sociometric studies were conducted on information flows among physicians (e.g., Menzel and Katz 1956). Respondents in a sociometric study are asked to identify those individuals to whom they go for advice about an innovation. The result is a sociogram of the W-O-M communication network; a hypothetical example of which is given in Figure 10.7. Let us assume that the individuals in Figure 10.7 are physicians communicating about a new prescription drug. Doctors 6 and 8 are clearly crucial links. Doctor 8 receives information from respondent 2 who, for example, might be a medical researcher. Information flows from one group of doctors to the other group through doctor 4 who is a gatekeeper but not an opinion leader. Finally, doctors 13 and 14 are isolates who do not interact with any other doctor in the sociogram.

There are a number of other methods for identifying and communicating with opinion leaders. We know that innovators are important sources of information for opinion leaders and that they can be opinion leaders themselves. Often innovators can be located through such means as purchase records, warranty registrations, and mail-in rebates. Also, because it reflects interest in the product category, individuals who respond to contests or offers for additional product information

Figure 10.7
A simple sociogram of interpersonal communication among fourteen physicians

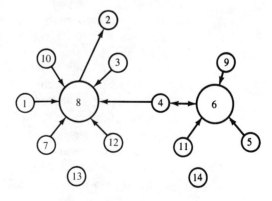

are likely to be opinion leaders (Assael 1981, p. 384). And, there is the previously mentioned possibility of reaching opinion leaders through the specialized media that opinion leaders tend to expose themselves to because of their special interests. Virtually every hobby and interest has one, and often more, magazines devoted to it. In addition to fairly well-known publications, such as *Golf Digest* and *Stereo Review*, there are many highly specialized magazines, which are almost totally unknown outside of quite limited groups; e.g., *Flying Physician*. Because of the high level of interest, and often equally high level of knowledge, of readers of specialized magazines, advertising messages can present far more extensive and technically detailed copy than is possible in media targeted at more general audiences.

Creating Opinion Leaders

It is sometimes said that to create an "expert" one need only ask a person for his or her opinion. A manifestation of this observation is the common practice among firms that maintain consumer panels of replacing panel members every year or so. This is done to counteract the tendency of more experienced panel members to begin reporting "objective" opinions on how an "average" consumer might evaluate a product rather than their own opinions. This "problem" in consumer panel studies suggests the possibility of creating opinion leaders through strategies such as soliciting their opinions.

Mancuso (1969) reported on an effort to create opinion leaders for rock-and-roll records by recruiting high school social leaders (e.g., class presidents, secretaries, sports captains, and cheerleaders) for a record evaluation panel. Panel members were told they had been selected because as leaders they should be better able to identify potential hits than their classmates. They were also encouraged to discuss their choices of potential hits with others. Mancuso reported (unfortunately without detailed supporting data) that several records reached the "top ten" charts in test cities but failed to reach the "top ten" in control cities, where no panels had been established.

Marketers have developed a number of other techniques for creating opinion leaders and stimulating W-O-M communication. Automobile companies have provided carefully selected individuals with complimentary new cars for limited periods of time. They are especially likely to do this when a new car involves major design changes (for example, the Mustang) or major technical changes (for example, an unsuccessful turbine powered car developed by Chrysler in the 1960s). In a similar way, swimming pool manufacturers often attempt to get strategically located families (e.g., in the middle of a block) to purchase by offering those families very low promotional prices.[7] Party plans used by firms such as Tupperware are another way of creating opinion leaders and stimulating W-O-M communication. Many other examples could be cited. In all cases, the firm's objectives include getting the product out where potential adopters can see it, creating a point in the W-O-M network through which the firm can channel information, and stimulating (what they hope is favorable) W-O-M communication.

---

[7]The "special promotional price" has been used unethically often enough that it is worth mentioning that many firms do use this device as a legitimate promotional tool.

Stimulating W-O-M Communication

Another strategy is to attempt to stimulate W-O-M communication without necessarily creating opinion leaders. The classic means of doing this is the so-called teaser ad. Teaser ads attempt to create curiosity and uncertainty. Ford, for example, verbally extolled the Mustang for months, while keeping the car itself carefully under wraps until its scheduled introduction date. Trouble cologne ran ads asking "Are you looking for Trouble" and stating "Trouble is coming soon" without any further information or brand identification. In a local example, signs recently began appearing on billboards stating that "Jerry Lipsky is a Lover." Several weeks later readers were informed on those same billboards that "Jerry Lipsky just loves to sell Chevrolets".

Other strategies for stimulating W-O-M include creating ads that are sufficiently humorous to become a topic of conversation and suggesting that the person ask a friend about the product. Volkswagen, for example, was very successful by poking fun at its "beetle." For some time, Firestone used the theme "Ask a friend about Firestone." In all of these techniques, the objective is to arouse buyer interest and curiosity to a level that stimulates interpersonal communication. This strategy, of course, implies that the resulting W-O-M will be favorable. The firm, therefore, should have good reason to believe the resulting W-O-M will be favorable as well as a system for monitoring interpersonal communications.

Simulating W-O-M Communication

Closely related to stimulating W-O-M communication is the strategy of simulating favorable W-O-M communication. Testimonials, celebrity endorsements, "man-on-the-street" interviews are designed to simulate W-O-M communication. The effectiveness of such techniques depends to a large degree on the extent to which the simulated W-O-M is seen as unsolicited. In the case of celebrity endorsements, it is generally desirable that the celebrity have some relationship to the product.

Coping with Negative W-O-M Communication

Because it is such a powerful factor in buyers' purchasing decisions, negative W-O-M communication is something that must be effectively dealt with when it occurs. Sometimes negative W-O-M communication can occur suddenly with devastating impact on the firm, as happened when untrue rumors began spreading in the late 1970s that Bubble Yum caused cancer and contained spider eggs. Sometimes negative W-O-M communication grows slowly and is not noticed by the firm until the negative information has taken on a durable quality through long-term exposure. The American automobile industry, for example, seems to be suffering partially from a long time developing impression that the quality of its cars are inferior to those of many foreign competitors.

The best strategy for coping with negative W-O-M communication depends on a number of factors, such as whether the information is true and the nature of the product. Bubble Yum, for example, hired private detectives to track down the source of the rumor and ran full-page ads in 30 newspapers with the message "Someone is Telling Your Kids Very Bad Lies About A Very Good Gum" (*Wall Street Journal*, 24 March 1977). If there is at least some truth to the negative information more fundamental changes may be required. The American automobile industry, for example, seems to be taking the image of poor quality quite seriously. In addition to promotional messages such as Ford's "Quality is Job 1," a number of more substantial changes in the way automobiles are produced are being made; e.g., using robots for such critical jobs as welding, which machines can perform better than humans.

Finally, there is the strategy of getting into and out of the market before negative W-O-M communication becomes a serious impediment to sales. This may be the firm's only alternative when the product is highly perishable. Katz and Lazarfeld (1955), in what has become the classic example of this situation, suggest that when a movie is bad distributors rely on a strategy of massive promotion to get as many potential viewers into the theater as quickly as possible, before people can begin telling each other how bad the movie is. On the other hand, if a movie is very good distributors are more likely to use a strategy of slow and selective distribution that maximizes the effect of interpersonal communication. Despite the continued success of this strategy for movie distributors, it is a strategy that can raise serious ethical problems and can, outside of special circumstances such as seem to characterize the movie industry, seriously damage the reputation of the firm.[8]

MODELING THE DIFFUSION PROCESS

Although social processes are often intimately involved, the adoption decision is ultimately the decision of individual buyers or buying units. From the perspective of the firm, a critical question is to what extent and how rapidly will the market for the innovation develop. That is, how rapidly will adoption spread or *diffuse* across a defined population of potential adopters. The phrase defined population of potential adopters is, of course, critical, since the concept of adoption is only meaningful when applied to individuals for whom the innovation is relevant.

Knowing to what extent and how rapidly the market for a new product will develop is important for planning marketing strategy as well as for predicting the ultimate success of a new product. For example, it is known that availability of an innovation facilitates adoption (see Table 10.1). This requires an adequate distribution plan. In a similar way, pricing strategy can depend very much on how rapidly the market is expected to develop. For example, if it is difficult for competitors to enter the market and the market is expected to develop slowly, a so-called skim pricing strategy (in which a high initial price is gradually reduced over time) is often desirable. In contrast, if competitive entry is easy and especially if the market is expected to develop rapidly, a so-called penetration pricing strategy (in which a low initial price is established to preempt competition and solidly establish the firm in the market) may be desirable.

Given the importance of the rate of diffusion of an innovation, it should come as no surprise that substantial effort has been devoted to developing quantitative models of the diffusion process. This section will introduce the reader to such

---

[8]In particular, the movie industry involves a situation when quality judgments are highly subjective. Even if most people find a movie "bad," many others will enjoy it. Also a distinction should be made between a product that is inferior in the sense of being below average quality and one that is defective. There is a market for inferior, but not defective, products. The question is not if, but how, such inferior products should be marketed.

models.[9] Because of the variety and complexity of diffusion models, the discussion is limited to acquainting the reader with the characteristics and capabilities of some of the more important diffusion models. The reader desiring a more detailed discussion of diffusion models might begin by consulting Kotler (1971, Chapter 17), Urban and Hauser (1980), and the references cited in this section.

Penetration Models

One of the earliest types of diffusion models begins with the assumption that there is a potential market that will be "penetrated" over time. In recent years, a number of such models have been constructed that are capable of incorporating the effects of marketer controlled variables; e.g., price, promotion, distribution (cf., Mahajan and Muller 1979). These models tend to be more sophisticated than can be adequately discussed here. Therefore, this presentation is limited to an early model developed by Fourt and Woodlock (1960) in which time is the only independent variable. Note carefully that the dependent variable is first purchase. Subsequently, so-called trial/repeat models, which consider more than one purchase occasion, will be briefly discussed.

Fourt and Woodlock based their model on observations of new grocery products that showed (1) market penetration (i.e., number of households purchasing a new product at least once) rising until it reached some upper limit, and (2) successive increments in penetration decreasing over time. Figure 10.8 illustrates this pattern of market penetration.

The formula for the *increment* in market penetration in any given time period is

$$Q_t = r\overline{Q}(1 - r)^{t-1}$$

where

Q_t is increment in market penetration at time period t

$\overline{Q}$ is potential sales as a percentage of all buyers

r   is the rate of penetration

t   is time period

Figure 10.8
Fourt and Woodlock penetration model

Source: Louis A. Fourt and Joseph W. Woodlock, "Early Prediction of Market Success for New Grocery Products." *Journal of Marketing,* 25 (October 1960): 33. Reprinted with the kind permission of the American Marketing Association.

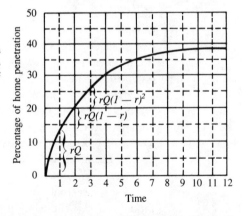

[9]The reader will probably notice a certain similarity between the quantitative models discussed here and those discussed in Chapter 5 under the heading "Stochastic Models of Brand Loyalty, . . .". The difference is that the previously discussed models are most appropriate to the introduction of a new brand into a well-defined, generally stable market and tend to focus on market shares rather than the growth of the entire market. In contrast, the models discussed here are more appropriate to situations where the market is less well-defined, less stable, and growing; i.e., to new and dynamic markets. The distinction, however, is essentially a matter of degree and emphasis.

The model assumes that sales potential is constant and that time periods are of equal duration. To see how the formula works, assume that $\overline{Q} = .5$ and $r = .3$; then,

$$Q_1 = .3 \times .5(1 - .3)^{1-1} = .150$$
$$Q_2 = .3 \times .5(1 - .3)^{2-1} = .105$$
$$Q_3 = .3 \times .5(1 - .3)^{3-1} = .074$$

In other words, in every time period 15 percent of the *untapped* potential market will be penetrated; i.e., $r \times \overline{Q} = .3 \times .5$. Of course, as the market is penetrated, the size of the untapped potential market is shrinking. This is why $\overline{Q}$ must be adjusted downward by $(1 - r)^{t-1}$. For example, in the second time period 15 percent of the market has already been tapped leaving only 35 percent untapped; i.e., $.5(1 - .3)^1 = .5 \times .7 = .35$.

The Fourt and Woodlock model requires the estimation of only two parameters: potential sales as a percent of all buyers ($\overline{Q}_t$) and rate of penetration (r). The rate of penetration is estimated from early sales results, while the potential market is estimated from market studies or managerial judgment. Given these two parameters, constructing the market penetration curve is a simple matter of calculation.

The Fourt and Woodlock model has been successfully used to model the diffusion of such things as grocery products (Fourt and Woodlock 1960) and store patronage (Kelly 1967). That is, this model has been most successful with innovations that are of only moderate newness and have short time intervals between purchase occasions. Innovations that present greater degrees of newness have been successfully modeled with S-shaped growth curves, in which sales rise slowly at first then begin to rise rapidly and finally flatten out (Kotler 1971, pp. 527–530). This pattern, of course, describes the pattern of the product life cycle. An S-shaped penetration curve is also consistent with the normal distribution of adopter categories.[10] Although the mathematics are more complex, the principles involved are the same as those discussed for the Fourt and Woodlock model.

Epidemiological Models

Another type of diffusion model is based upon medical models of the spread of communicable diseases. The analogy is quite direct. One person or a small group of people (the innovators) is initially infected and spreads the disease (the innovation) through personal contact (by W-O-M communication). The epidemic spreads, or diffuses, until all who are susceptible have been infected.

Bass (1969) proposed and tested an epidemiological model for the diffusion of consumer durables. Because of the long time intervals between purchase occasions, the dependent variable in the Bass model measures only the first purchase. Mathematically,

$$P(t) = p(0) + \frac{q}{m}Y(t)$$

where

is the key, must define who your Target market is

---

[10]This statement does not mean that the normal distribution is always best for modeling an S-shaped diffusion pattern. For alternatives and details, see Kotler (1971, Chapter 17).

P(t)   is the probability of purchase at time t given no previous purchase (i.e., probability of first purchase at time t)

p(0)   is the initial probability of trial

Y(t)   is the total number of people who have ever purchased

m   is the number of potential buyers

q   is a parameter measuring the rate of diffusion

The term p(0) captures the tendency to innovate; i.e., to try the product without interpersonal influence. The term $\frac{q}{m}$ is a constant that reflects a social interaction effect, which grows with Y(t). That is, the more people who have accepted the innovation the greater is the pressure to accept on those who have not yet adopted the innovation. This latter effect is sometimes called an imitation effect. Since the probability of purchase in time period t is defined in terms of potential buyers who have not previously purchased the product, sales in time period t is equal to

$$S(t) = [m - Y(t)] P(t)$$
where
S(t)   is sales in time period t

As first purchases grow, the term [m − Y(t)] falls reflecting the shrinking size of the untapped portion of the total market. Thus, first purchases tend to rise over time first from innovators but increasingly from the subsequent effects of W-O-M communication until the untapped market becomes sufficiently small that first time buyers begin to decline. This pattern is precisely what one might expect for relatively expensive, infrequently purchased, high risk durable goods. The Bass model has been successfully applied to a wide range of durable goods and innovative services (e.g., Bass 1969; Nevers 1972). An example, for clothes dryers, is given in Figure 10.9. Recently, Tigert and Farivar (1981) applied the Bass model, with mixed but encouraging results, to a high technology product (optical scanning equipment for supermarkets).

Deterministic Model   -SKIP

A deterministic model is built on the premise that a response is predictable from one or more antecedent conditions. For example, a deterministic model of the diffusion process would incorporate variables such as characteristics of the innova-

Figure 10.9
Actual and predicted sales by Bass first purchase diffusion model for clothes dryers

Source: Reprinted by permission of Frank M. Bass, "A New Product Growth Model for Consumer Durables," *Management Science,* 15 (January 1969): 224. Copyright 1969 The Institute of Management Sciences.

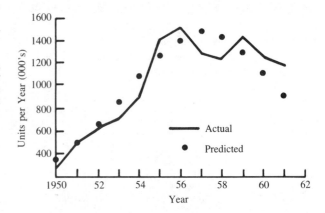

tion and W-O-M communication in predicting the spread of adoption across a defined population of potential adopters. The majority of deterministic models of the diffusion process have been based on variations of the adoption process discussed earlier (see Figure 10.2). These models are often large and complex.

Urban (1970; Urban and Karash 1971), for example, developed a model, known as SPRINTER, based upon the decision-making sequence: awareness, intent, search, trial, repeat purchase. In this model awareness depends on advertising spending level, intent depends on advertising appeal effectiveness, and availability of the product in the market depends on distribution. Advanced versions of SPRINTER are capable of incorporating the effects of additional variables such as samples, coupons, middleman deals, number of sales calls, price, advertising, and W-O-M communication (Urban and Karash 1971, p. 64). Kotler (1971, pp. 536–552) discusses a number of other adoption process models of diffusion.

Deterministic models of diffusion will be illustrated by a model recently proposed and tested by Midgley (1976). This model is especially noteworthy because of its inclusion of *negative* W-O-M communication. Figure 10.10 presents the model schematically. The model recognizes four categories of adopters. Potential adopters have not yet adopted the new product. Active adopters have adopted the innovation and provide favorable W-O-M communication to others. Active rejectors have purchased the innovation once, rejected it, and provide negative W-O-M communication to others. Passive adopters have adopted the innovation but provide no W-O-M communication.

The heart of the model is four mechanisms that provide pathways through which potential adopters may move from one state, or adopter category, to another: influence of active adopters, influence of marketing activities, influence of active rejectors, influence of other state change mechanisms. The first three mechanisms should be self-explanatory. The fourth refers to such nonpersonal,

Figure 10.10
A schematic representation of the Midgley diffusion model

Source: David F. Midgley, "A Simple Mathematical Model of Innovative Behavior." *Journal of Consumer Research*, 3 (June 1976): 33. Reprinted with permission.

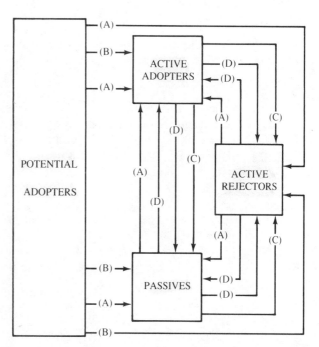

nonmarketing information sources as news reports, government reports, and *Consumer Reports*. The arrows represent the direction of movement. For example, it is hypothesized that potential adopters are initially moved into another adopter category by either active adopters or marketing activities (arrows labeled A or B in Figure 10.10). Note that it is only possible to move *out* of the potential adopter category.

The mathematical formulation of the Midgley model is well beyond the level of this discussion. Figure 10.11 presents graphical output of the model for two products: one successful and one unsuccessful. Note the rapid growth of active rejectors for the unsuccessful product. In addition to predicting the degree of market penetration and likelihood of long-term success, examination of the estimated parameters of the model can provide very useful information. For example, marketing activities can lead potential adopters into any of the three adopter categories. The relative size of these flows is obviously important information for marketing managers. Similarly, the effects of the other change mechanisms can provide useful information on the effects of such things as favorable or unfavorable product evaluations by, for example, government agencies or *Consumer Reports*. Although the Midgley model has not been extensively tested to date, preliminary empirical tests are encouraging (for details, see Midgley 1976).

Stochastic Models

Stochastic models model the diffusion process in probabilistic terms. A number of stochastic models have been developed (e.g., Massey 1969; Eskin and Malec 1976; Herniter and Cook 1978). Mathematically, stochastic models tend to be quite complex. For this and other reasons stochastic models have not been widely accepted despite their analytical usefulness (Urban and Hauser 1980, p. 431).

Trial/Repeat Models

The diffusion models discussed so far are all so-called first purchase models, in which the dependent variable is defined in terms of whether the innovation has been purchased *at least* once. As a practical matter, first purchase models are adequate for modeling the diffusion of goods and services, primarily durable goods, with long time intervals between purchase occasions. For goods and services that are frequently purchased, it is desirable to separate trial from adoption. Since the distinction between trial and adoption is a matter of degree, so-called trial/repeat models typically operationalize this distinction in terms of the number of repeat purchases made by a buying unit.

The importance of trial/repeat models is rooted in the fact that the long-term success of frequently purchased products is closely tied to the rate of repeat purchase.[11] Research also shows that the likelihood of purchasing a brand tends to increase with the number of repeat purchases. For example, in a test of their repeat purchase model Fourt and Woodlock estimated the probability of the first repeat at .485 while the probability of the fifth repeat was .797. Trial/repeat models are

---

[11]The quantity purchased on each purchase occasion is also important to the success of a new product. Relatively few diffusion models incorporate the quantity of the product purchased. An exception is the DEMON model (Learner 1968).

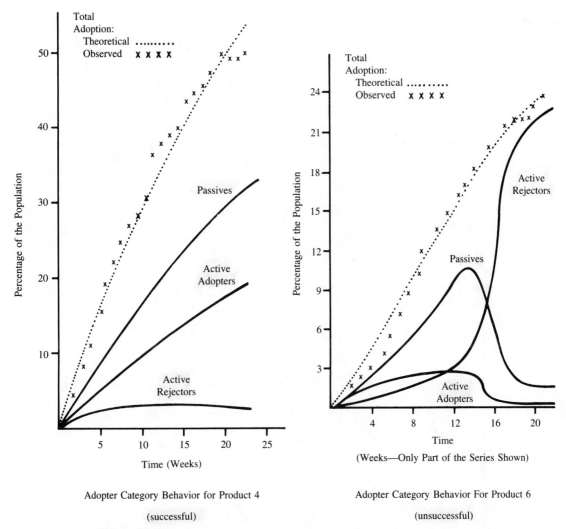

Adopter Category Behavior for Product 4 (successful)

Adopter Category Behavior For Product 6 (unsuccessful)

Figure 10.11
Illustration of application of Midgley diffusion model to one successful and one unsuccessful innovation

Source: David F. Midgley, "A Simple Mathematical Model of Innovative Behavior." *Journal of Consumer Research*, 3 (June 1976): 37. Reprinted with permission.

particularly important for early identification of the potentially disastrous situation in which sales are rising rapidly in the short-run from a marketing program that is bringing in large numbers of one-time purchasers but not creating repeat buyers.

The basic concepts upon which trial/repeat models are constructed are the same as those already illustrated for first purchase models. The mathematics, however, are generally more complex. The reader desiring more information on trial/repeat models of diffusion might begin by consulting Kotler (1971, pp. 552–560) and Urban and Hauser (1980).

SUMMARY

Both the risks and potential rewards of innovation are large. As seen in this chapter, much is known about the processes that buyers go through in making an adoption decision, which can be used by the firm to increase the likelihood of a positive decision. We have also seen that personal sources of information play a large role in the adoption decision, especially for major and discontinuous innovations. While not a wholly controllable variable W-O-M communication is not beyond the influence of the firm. Finally, the last two decades have seen a rapid increase in quantitative models for predicting the rate of diffusion of innovations.

Perception and Meaning

11

The environment in which buying decisions are made is extremely complex. This complexity is most obvious in buying situations that require extensive problem solving. Although less obvious, buying situations that require limited problem solving or even routinized response behavior also present buyers with an extremely rich array of stimuli upon which to base their buying decisions. It is only because the required behavior has been well learned that the environment appears to be quite simple.

Indeed, perceptual psychologists have emphasized that the world is literally a "buzz" of *potential* stimuli. If people were not highly selective as to which of these stimuli they consciously attended they would, quite literally, be immobilized by a kaleidoscope of meaningless and overwhelming stimulation. Of course, people are highly selective about the stimuli to which they consciously attend. More important, this selectivity occurs at all levels of information acquisition, evaluation, retention, and recall.

This selective attention by buyers has been largely implicit in the discussions in earlier chapters. This chapter will discuss the processes through which stimuli are acquired and given meaning. A full understanding of these so-called *perceptual* processes provides important insights into buyer behavior that both extend our knowledge generally and facilitate the development of effective marketing strategies.

The discussion begins with a review of some basic concepts and terminology. Next, the factors that affect the stimuli to which buyers attend are considered at some length; followed by a review of some well established principles of perception that have important implications for marketers. Implicit in these principles is the establishment of meaning through comparison, contrast, and integration with previous perceptions stored in long-term memory. This leads to a discussion of the processes through which buyers *infer* the meaning of stimuli. The chapter concludes with a discussion of factors that affect the amount and type of information actively sought by buyers through external search.

SOME BASIC CONCEPTS AND TERMINOLOGY

Objective and Subjective Reality

Our experiences with the world external to our mental and physical selves appear to be immediate, direct, and veridical. Veridical means that our perceptions of the external objective world are genuine and not illusory. A slightly more sophisticated way to state this point is to say that, from the individual's perspective, each person seems to *experience* the external world directly rather than to *construct* a subjective reality from external objective data. For example, as you read these pages your subjective reality is one of directly experiencing the meaning in the words and sentences. Of course, what you are directly experiencing is *only* the pattern of light and dark visual images on your retina. In a similar way we hear "words" when all that we can *directly* experience is sound waves.

The point that needs to be made clearly is that our subjective reality, the reality from which decisions are made, *is* different from reality as it objectively exists. Furthermore, our subjective reality is constructed not only from the sensory stimuli we directly experience but also includes such things as expectations and motives. What is truly remarkable is that our perceptual processes typically work

Figure 11.1
Relationship among four types of
concepts used in perception and how
these concepts apply to a real-life
example

Source: From PSYCHOLOGY, 3rd
edition, by Lyle E. Bourne, Jr., and Bruce
K. Ekstrand. Copyright © 1976, 1979 by
Holt, Rinehart and Winston, CBS College
Publishing.

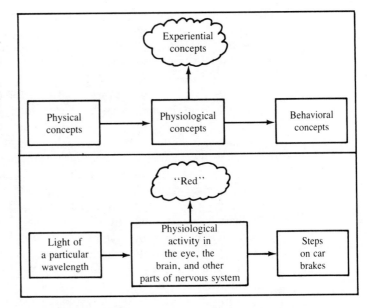

so efficiently and effectively that we are unaware of the process of constructing a
subjective reality or even that what we are experiencing is a subjective representation of the world and not the world itself.

Perception

Perception may be defined as "the process by which the brain constructs an
internal representation of the outside world" (Bourne and Ekstrand 1979, p. 67).
Four types of concepts are involved in perceptual phenomena: physical, physiological,
experiential, and behavioral. Figure 11.1 illustrates the relationships among these
four types of concepts using the extremely simple example of a driver's reactions
to a stop light.

Note the irregular boundary around the experiential concepts. This indicates
that experiential concepts are, even in principle, unobservable. We may observe a
light of given wavelength, measure a change in neural activity, and observe a driver
breaking for a traffic light. From this we may conclude that the driver has seen a
"Red" light. However reasonable, this conclusion must remain an inference from
observables; it can never be an observable itself. This, of course, is a relationship
encountered in numerous earlier discussions of buyer behavior concepts such as
brand loyalty and attitudes.

Meaning and Communication[1]

From a marketing perspective, the most important perceptions are those that arise
from activities generally labeled communication. Communication is a process

---

[1]For a more extensive discussion of meaning as it exists and is conveyed by language, see
Rubenstein (1973). A more general reference on meaning, especially in the context of persuasive
communications, is Bettinghaus (1973).

through which meanings are exchanged among individuals. Because each individual lives in a personal, subjective world, it should be clear that "meaning" exists only within the individual. This raises two important questions: What is the nature of meaning? And, how is meaning transmitted from one person to another?

To begin, meaning exists in the *pattern* of relationships among objects, ideas, and the signs that are used as mental stores for experience. For example, certain cloud configurations imply possible turbulent air conditions. This is an example of an object-object relationship. Communication among individuals is exceedingly slow and often difficult when restricted to object-object form. By developing signs to represent previous experiences, great advantages in terms of speed, accuracy, flexibility, and creativity can be achieved, For example, to the experienced pilot the sign "nimbostratus" conveys very quickly and accurately the nature of the object, a type of rain cloud, that may be encountered. Perhaps most important, signs allow us to develop sign-sign relationships that provide the basis for abstract and creative thought. For example, we can use the sign "motives" as the logical basis upon which "attitudes" (another sign) are constructed through a variety of other hypothetical constructs each of which is identified by a specific sign; e.g., attributes, dissonance.

Language provides the most obvious example of signs and sign systems. However, a number of paralinguistic and nonverbal sign systems also exist. Paralinguistic sign systems are intermediate between verbal and nonverbal systems. They include such things as voice tone, rate of speech, sighs, and utterances such as "um" (Bettinghaus 1973). Nonverbal sign systems is a catchall category, which includes such things as body posture and color perception. For example, leaning forward generally indicates interest.[2] Similarly, red is a "warm" color, which is why hot foods are typically packaged in colors from the red end of the spectrum.

The above ideas have been neatly summarized in a diagram by Wilbur Schramm, presented in Figure 11.2. The terms source and destination are used by communication researchers to designate the sender and receiver of a communication,

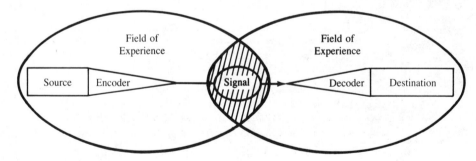

Figure 11.2
Communication and fields of experience

Source: Wilbur Schramm, "How Communication Works." In *The Process and Effects of Mass Communication*, edited by Wilbur Schramm, 6. Urbana, Ill.: University of Illinois Press, 1955. Reprinted with permission.

[2]Erving Goffman wrote a marvelous little book called *Gender Advertisements*, which illustrates how sex roles are communicated through nonverbal means. Women, for example, are frequently shown under male protection. The reverse rarely occurs. In a similar way, females are frequently shown using their fingers and hands to trace, caress, or just barely touch—the feminine touch. In contrast, males are more likely to grasp, manipulate, or hold (1979, p. 16).

respectively. Since thoughts cannot be transmitted directly, meaning can be exchanged between a sender and receiver only through sign systems. The processes of transforming thoughts into signs by the sender and transforming signs back into thoughts by the receiver are referred to as encoding and decoding, respectively. The accuracy of the exchange of thoughts depends, among other things, on the degree to which sender and receiver attach the same meanings to specific signs. Since both the encoding and decoding processes occur within each person's so-called field of experience, thought or meaning can be communicated only to the extent that the sender's and receiver's fields of experience overlap.

The extent to which the sender and receiver attach the same meaning to a sign is always a matter of degree. Sometimes the discrepancies are substantial. Ricks, Fu, and Arpan (1974) in a serious, but very entertaining book, *International Business Blunders*, provide a number of relevant examples. Colgate-Palmolive, for example, introduced its Cue toothpaste into French-speaking countries without realizing that "Cue" was a pornographic word in French (p. 12). Pepsi's well known slogan "Come Alive with Pepsi" translates to "come alive out of the grave" in German (p. 11). Nonverbal signs can also convey different meanings than those intended. For example, Ricks, Fu, and Arpan (1974) cite the case of a manufacturer of water recreation products whose international emblem was green—the symbol of danger and disease in Malaysia (pp. 14–15).

Of course, the communication process as represented in Figure 11.2 is highly simplified. Typically, multiple encodings and decodings will occur in developing and transmitting a message. The so-called "source" of a message is also often complex and ambiguous. Consider, for example, a TV ad featuring Bob Hope as a spokesman for Texaco. Who is the receiver likely to perceive as the source of the message: Bob Hope, Texaco, or the TV network. There is good reason to believe that a receiver's interpretation of such an ad may depend very much on the perceived source of the communication. We also know that the circumstances under which promotional messages are received are often far from ideal; e.g., a TV ad in a noisy room, a glance at a billboard from a fast-moving car. All of these factors point to one basic conclusion: There are many reasons why a receiver may attach different meanings to a communication than those intended by the sender. This is why careful pretesting and posttesting of marketing communications is so important to an effective marketing program.

ATTENTION AND MEANING[3]

Earlier the world was described as "literally a 'buzz' of potential stimuli." Even when the stimuli are restricted to those relevant to purchase and consumption behavior, this description loses none of its relevance. For example, Bauer and Greyser (1968), in *Advertising in America*, suggest that buyers are potentially exposed to some 1,600 advertisements daily. Buyers must, and do, select only a small portion of these stimuli for conscious attention. Bauer and Greyser suggest that buyers attend to perhaps 5 percent of these advertisements; i.e., to approximately 80 advertisements per day. Other studies with different numbers of poten-

---

[3]This section relies heavily on a recent summary and interpretation of the extensive literature on attention and its relationship to memory by Wingfield and Byrnes (1981, especially Chapter 6).

tial exposures and actual attention could be cited (e.g., Britt, Adams, and Miller 1972). The basic findings of all such studies, however, are very consistent: buyers are highly selective in the stimuli to which they consciously attend.

Marketers have an obvious interest in getting buyers to attend to their messages and to delivering their messages in such a form that the intended meaning is received. This section will address these problems through a discussion of the phenomenon of attention or, more precisely, selective attention. Attention is a complex phenomenon and the section is, of necessity, somewhat lengthy. Since almost no research on the psychological mechanisms underlying attention has been conducted by buyer behavior researchers, the discussion will depend largely on studies by psychologists. The last part of the section draws out in some detail the implications for buyer behavior from what is known about attention. As shall be seen, the phenomenon of selective attention ties together a number of ideas regarding buyer behavior previously discussed.

Sensation and Sensory Memory

To appreciate the phenomenon of selective attention and the problems that selective attention presents to perceptual researchers, it is necessary to briefly discuss a type of information store known as sensory memory. Whenever a neural receptor cell is struck by an appropriate stimulus of sufficient magnitude, there is a change in neural activity known as sensation. For example, light striking a rod or cone in the eye or sound waves striking the eardrum give rise to sensations. Since these sensations occur over a finite period of time, they constitute a type of memory known generally as sensory memory.

Sensory memory has three important characteristics (Wingfield and Byrnes 1981, p. 149). First, it has an extremely large capacity. Literally millions of neural cells may be firing at the same time or in "parallel." Second, sensory memory stores information in raw form; i.e., without meaning. For example, the letter A is stored in sensory memory as a visual pattern of lines rather than as the alphabetic symbol "A." Third, the duration of any sensation in sensory memory is extremely brief, e.g., a fraction of a second for visual sensory memory.

If the information in sensory memory is not picked up by other mechanisms and further processed, that information is lost forever. The processes involved in the "pick up" of information from sensory memory constitute the phenomenon generally known as selective attention. Research on selective attention presents perceptual theorists with a number of perplexing problems that are collectively known as the "cocktail party problem."

The Cocktail Party Problem

When we enter an on-going party, our first impression is usually a "buzz" of meaningless stimuli; e.g., music, everyone talking at once. Nevertheless, we normally do not find it difficult to focus on a single conversation. Although generally aware of other conversations, we normally are not able to report the content or even the topic of those other conversations. If asked why, we would probably say that we were not paying attention. This suggests that our capacity to pay attention is quite limited. Indeed, once we *choose* a specific conversation for attention our commitment to that conversation, or "channel"[4] of information, seems almost absolute.

However, if someone in another conversation, the so-called "unattended" channel, speaks our name we are very likely to become aware of it. Thus, the paradox of the cocktail party problem and the paradox of attention generally. If we are not attending to these "unattended" channels, how can we "hear" our own name? And, if we are attending to them, why can't we report any detail of these conversations (Wingfield and Byrnes 1981, p. 193)? Before attempting to resolve this paradox, the concept of attention must be defined in more specific terms.

The Concept of Attention

Attention has been defined in a number of different, but related, ways. It can be defined in terms of arousal, a topic discussed previously as a theory of motivation. When aroused we are alert, more fully aware of our immediate surroundings, and ready for any unexpected stimuli. All of the variables discussed in Chapter 6 that affect the level of arousal also affect the level of attention; e.g., novelty, surprisingness, change, ambiguity, incongruity, blurredness, power to induce uncertainty.

Another way to define attention is in terms of Neisser's (1967) distinction between preattentive and focal attention processes. Neisser took the term "focal attention" from psychoanalytic theory to indicate focusing attention fully on a single object in order to "perceive it or understand it from many sides, as clearly as possible" (Schachter 1959, cited in Wingfield and Byrnes 1981, p. 190). In Neisser's view, focal attention is extremely limited in terms of the stimuli to which it can simultaneously attend, and it operates only after preattentive processes have scanned the environment and located the object for focal attention (Neisser 1967, 1975).

Wingfield and Byrnes (1981, pp. 190–191) present a very useful analogy for understanding the idea of scanning and interrupt perceptual mechanisms. Imagine yourself looking for a specific book in a dark room. Your only source of illumination is a special flashlight that allows you to adjust the width or "focus" of the light beam. Of course, the wider the focus the weaker is the illumination. Under these conditions, a good search strategy would be to set the beam width at its widest setting and "scan" the room to locate objects that are books. Other objects would probably be identified no further than "not books." Having located the books, you presumably would narrow the light beam and "focus" on each book, one at a time, until you found the specific book of interest. Of course, an actual search would generally consist of a series of scan, interrupt, focus, scan, etc. sequences.

Two Theories of Attention

According to Wingfield and Byrnes (1981, pp. 193–194), the large number of specific models of attention that exist can generally be sorted into either of two

---

[4]The idea of a channel of information is easily illustrated by stereo sound. The normal stereo has two channels of sound; i.e., the left speaker and the right speaker. Because the two channels are closely related by the "meaning" of their information, stereo tends to be experienced as a single channel, although we can separate the channels if so instructed. In everyday experiences, we can separate channels in a number of ways; for example, different conversations can be separated by the physical location of the source of the sound.

categories: time-sharing or capacity models. Both models are based on analogies with digital computers. Time-sharing models postulate a system of limited capacity through which information from sensory memory must pass *before* it can be processed for "meaning." More specifically, time-sharing models generally assume that only one channel of meaningful information can be processed at a time. What appears to be simultaneous processing of information from different channels is merely very rapid shifting among channels. The memory stores model, discussed in Chapter 7, postulates that information is transmitted from sensory to short-term to long-term memory and provides the basis for an important class of attention models known as filter models. Such models postulate a filter mechanism between sensory and short-term memory, which "filters out" irrelevant information, allowing only relevant information to filter through into short-term memory for a semantic analysis for meaning and possible storage in long-term memory. The Howard-Sheth model of buyer behavior (1969, especially as revised by Howard 1977) assumes this type of attentional mechanism.

One problem with time-sharing models is that research on attention frequently found evidence to suggest that information from two or more channels is being simultaneously processed for meaning. This led to the more recent formulation of a number of so-called capacity models, which assume that there is some limited capacity for attention that may be allocated to a number of information channels simultaneously (e.g., Kahneman 1973). How much capacity is required depends on a number of factors, such as the demands of the task and the level of processing desired.

Task Demands and Skilled vs. Unskilled Performances

What capacity models suggest is that attention can be explained to a large degree in terms of task demands *and* previously acquired skills for performing a specific task. The following example illustrates the relationships among task demands, performance skills, and amount of attentional effort required for a specific task.

The reader has probably had the experience of driving along a familiar route and suddenly realizing that several blocks have been traveled without any trace of the experience in memory. During the "missing period," you may have been daydreaming, considering how to deal with a personal or business problem, or even considering an important purchase. Such experiences are common and the unremembered distances are almost always traveled safely. This suggests that information is being processed and affecting behavior even though there is no conscious awareness of the process. More important, should an unusual stimulus present itself (e.g., an ambulance siren or another car approaching from a side street) *attention* will normally focus on this stimulus and competing activities will cease.

Norman and Bobrow (1975), in an effort to reconcile a number of different models of attention, made an interesting analysis of task demands and performance skills that provide both an explanation of the driving example and a useful way of analyzing buying tasks. Specifically, tasks may be analyzed in terms of resource and data limitations. Resource limitations refer to the attentional effort the individual is willing to devote to a task. A task is said to be *resource limited* if an individual can improve his or her performance simply by devoting more effort to the task; i.e., by trying harder. Two types of data limitations may be recognized. A task is said to be *signal data-limited* when performance is limited by the quality of the signal itself. A task is said to be *memory data-limited* when performance is limited by the lack of necessary information in long-term memory. As the reader may have noticed, the distinction between signal and memory data-limitations parallels the distinction between sensory and semantic ambiguity in the Howard-Sheth model of buyer behavior. The idea of resource limitations may have also reminded the reader of the important distinction between the low involvement and learning decision-making hierarchies.

In the driving example, the route is familiar and the driver is presumably highly skilled in performing the task. This requires very little attentional capacity, which is why the driver is able to simultaneously engage in one or more additional tasks. However, an unexpected or unfamiliar task requires a larger amount of attentional capacity, which is why in an emergency attention becomes narrowly focused and activities that would compete for attentional resources cease. Indeed, if the task requirements exceed available attentional resources, task performance is likely to decrease.

Cognitive Schema

The distinction between skilled and unskilled performances is an important one. Anyone who has mastered a complex skill (e.g., playing a musical instrument) can recall how much thought and attention every move initially demanded and how awkward and poor was the resulting performance. Indeed, highly skilled performances are seemingly made with relatively little effort. Why?

The answer seems to reside to a large degree in the fact that the stimuli involved in a highly skilled performance have a great deal of "meaning" for the performer.[5] For a musician, the relevant stimuli might be the motion of the conductor's baton and the relative positions and pressures of the fingers on the instrument that instruct the musician *both* in the next response and the next piece of information that should be forthcoming. For a buyer considering the purchase of a familiar vegetable, the relevant stimuli might include color, softness, and smell.

Neisser (1975) uses the concept of cognitive schemas and, what he calls, the perceptual cycle to explain many of the phenomena so far discussed as a part of selective attention. Figure 11.3 presents the perceptual cycle in diagrammatic form. As a cycle, the starting point is arbitrary; indeed, it *is* wherever the perceiver is at the moment. For our purposes, however, it is most appropriate to begin with the concept of a cognitive schema. According to Neisser (1975)

---

[5]Psychological research on problem solving has shown that it is easier for subjects to solve problems constructed from meaningful elements as opposed to formally identical problems constructed from more abstract elements (e.g., Wason and Johnson-Laird 1972). Perhaps one of the most interesting examples of the effects of meaning comes from studies of memorization of chess positions. Chess masters, after observing chess positions from actual games for five seconds, can almost perfectly reproduce the positions of the pieces on the board. Less skilled performers come nowhere near this level. What is most interesting, however, is that chess masters' recall is not significantly different from less skilled players when the pieces are *randomly* distributed on the board (Simon and Gilmartin 1973; Chase and Simon 1973). This suggests that it is the meaning of the positions of the chess pieces, rather than greater skill in memorization per se, that accounts for the superior performance of chess masters.

Figure 11.3
The perceptual cycle

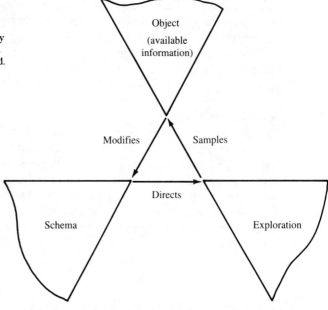

A schema is that portion of the entire perceptual cycle which is internal to the perceiver, modifiable by experience, and somehow specific to what is being perceived. The schema accepts information as it becomes available at sensory surfaces and is changed by that information; it directs movements and exploratory activities that make more information available, by which it is further modified (p. 54).

Schema can be best understood as expectations: expectations about the structure of the world, expectations about the form in which information about the world will be forthcoming, and expectations that are themselves modifiable by experience. Thus, schemas constitute extremely flexible, and modifiable, *plans* for exploring and learning about the world. As Neisser points out this conception of schemas implies that there could never be a time when we were totally without at least some type of elementary schema. Neisser (1975, pp. 63–70) illustrates this idea with research that shows that infants only a few minutes old often move their eyes in the *direction* of a sound, even though they are unable to move their heads at this age. The basis for this "performance" is the time-difference of sound reaching each ear. This suggests a type of schema that is somehow genetically endowed. The infant's performance on this "task" is very unskilled, as indicated by the fact that the exact location of the source of the sound is not identified with a high degree of precision. It is, however, sufficient to begin learning additional things about locating the sources of sound and the objects that make sounds; i.e., *for developing new and more sophisticated schema.*

Resolving the Cocktail Party Problem

Among the most important and powerful of cognitive schemas is a person's self-image. Information relevant to this schema presumably carries a large amount of meaning. Put another way, recognition of such information—especially one's own name—is a highly skilled performance. Thus, it should require little attentional capacity and should be processed for meaning at a low level of depth, in the sense of depth of processing theories. It is these remarkable properties of our own perceptual system that allow us to recognize our own names, spoken in an "unattended" channel, even as we are engrossed in a different conversation.

Buyer Behavior Implications

One very important implication of the preceding discussion is that perception is *not* primarily a matter of filtering out irrelevant stimuli. Rather, perception is an active, goal directed process in which a person selects specific stimuli for attention. Schema play a critical role in this process because they give meaning to stimuli that would otherwise carry no meaning for a person. Indeed, Neisser (1975, p. 80) asserts that perceivers can pick up *only* information for which they have schema.

As a buyer behavior example, consider the increasing emphasis on "natural" foods in recent years. The distinction, usually in terms of amount of processing or the presence of chemical additives, between "natural" and "not natural" foods required appropriate cognitive schemas. Until recently such schemas did not exist for most buyers. Many marketers have in recent years successfully exploited the concept of natural foods by producing foods that meet buyers' concepts or schemas of what constitutes a natural food and by providing information that helps other buyers develop appropriate natural food schemas.

To say that perception is an active process does not imply a physical search for information in even such a limited way as turning one's head. Indeed, we know that a great deal of information is acquired in quite casual, passive, even largely unconscious ways. As an example, consider something that you have never purchased, actively considered, or even personally experienced; e.g., a personal computer, a sailboat, a "dish" antenna for directly receiving satellite transmissions. Try to think of everything you know about this object—it is probably a great deal—and try to think of when, where, and how you acquired that information, it is probably extremely limited.

Such passive learning typically occurs under conditions of low involvement and is variously referred to as low involvement, latent, environmental, and incidental learning. Among the many reasons or motives for such learning are curiosity and the desire for general information that may be useful at some unspecified future date. As will be suggested later in this chapter, the large amount of information that is often acquired passively may partially account for the small amount of active search for brand information typically reported by buyers.

The importance of passive learning also suggests one reason why it is often desirable for sellers to provide potential buyers with a relatively continuous stream of information about the company and its product and service offerings. If buyers have relevant schema, they will tend to acquire such information. When the need to purchase arises they will, quite literally, tend to know a great deal more about a product than they might have believed until the need to purchase forced them to think about what they do know. Such passively acquired information will not necessarily cause a buyer to purchase a specific brand, but will tend to be a critical factor in determining which brands are considered for purchase.

The discussion of cognitive schemas may have reminded the reader of the concept of decision nets discussed in Chapter 4. In concluding that earlier discussion, criticisms of the decision net concept made by Nakanishi (1974) were briefly

Name:	Restaurant			
Props:	Tables		**Roles:**	Customer
	Menu			Waiter
	Food			Cook
	Bill			Cashier
	Money			Owner
	Tip			
Entry Conditions:	Customer is hungry.		**Results:**	Customer has less money.
	Customer has money.			Owner has more money.
				Customer is not hungry.

Scene 1: *Entering*
Customer enters restaurant.
Customer looks for table.
Customer decides where to sit.
Customer goes to table.
Customer sits down.

Scene 2: *Ordering*
Customer picks up menu.
Customer looks at menu.
Customer decides on food.
Customer signals waitress.
Waitress comes to table.
Customer orders food.
Waitress goes to cook.
Waitress gives food order to cook.
Cook prepares food.

Scene 3: *Eating*
Cook gives food to waitress.
Waitress brings food to customer.
Customer eats food.

Scene 4: *Exiting*
Waitress writes bill.
Waitress goes over to customer.
Waitress gives bill to customer.
Customer gives tip to waitress.
Customer goes to cashier.
Customer gives money to cashier.
Customer leaves restaurant.

Figure 11.4
Schema for going to a restaurant.

Source: G. H. Bower, J. B. Black and T. S. Turner, "Scripts in Memory for Text." *Cognitive Psychology*, 11 (April 1979): 179. Reprinted with permission.

quoted. Of particular interest here is Nakanishi's conclusion that "Many of the difficulties, it seems, stem from the conception of decision nets as fixed programs rigidly followed by the subject during a purchase decision, much in the same manner as electronic computers execute their programs" (p. 77). Cognitive schema, because they are composed of expectations and plans for acquiring relevant information, are far more flexible than decision nets. As an example, Figure 11.4 presents a schema for going to a restaurant, which illustrates quite clearly the less rigid structure of cognitive schema.

Figure 11.4 has several interesting characteristics. First, the schema is quite general. It could easily be applied to most restaurants. Second, it includes expectations about activities that are normally not observed. Third, it illustrates what Bettman (1979) refers to as an external memory. The external memory in Figure 11.4 is the menu. A part of the buyer's schema is that the menu is *where* to find out about the specific foods available and their prices. Bettman has suggested that buyers may *choose* to rely on such an external memory rather than attempt to memorize detailed brand information. This suggests that such things as package information and point-of-purchase displays can be important devices for buyers to "store" information with high efficiency and low effort. Knowing what types of information and in what formats this information is desired by buyers in external memory can be very useful to the marketer.

Several important implications for understanding buyer behavior follow from the recognition that buyers' product class and brand concepts constitute a type of cognitive schema. The critical problem of product postioning depends, among other things, on understanding buyers' product class and brand concepts. This is especially important when introducing a new brand because buyers will not have a brand concept for the new brand. What they will tend to do, *if their attention is captured*, is to try to fit the new brand into an existing schema. If this can be done, it will provide buyers with an initial understanding of what the new brand is and what needs it can satisfy. It will also define the brands with which the new brand will compete. By understanding the relevant product class and brand concepts, the marketer is often able to influence the position of a brand in the market.

Seven Up, for example, was quite successful in promoting their product as a high quality mixer. This gave them a position in the soft drink market that was safely distant from the competitive "wars" characteristic of the "cola" segment of the market; wars that could easily have swamped a smaller competitor. As their market strength grew, Seven Up attempted to reposition their brand in more direct competition with colas. The resulting "Uncola" campaign, which was quite successful, was essentially based on a contrast between two well established schemas—one for Seven Up, the other for colas—that had the effect of broadening the uses for Seven Up beyond those of a mixer; e.g., as a soft drink to be consumed by itself. The important point to understand is that the "Uncola" campaign would have been meaningless without well established schemas for the two different types of soft drinks.

If buyers have well developed schemas for the product class in question, it may be desirable to design marketing communications with a planned degree of ambiguity. The classic illustration of this idea is Ford's initial introduction of the Mustang. Ford's problem was where to position the car in the automobile market: as a sportscar, a personal car, a car for the young at heart, etc. Ford, quite successfully, chose to leave the market position ambiguous in their promotional messages. This ambiguity allowed buyers to "interpret" the Mustang in several different ways, according to the preferences of each buyer. The success of this campaign rested upon the existence of well established cognitive schemas for different types of cars and the fact that the Mustang had characteristics that allowed it to be identified with more than a single type of automobile.

The concept of cognitive schemas also has implications for how marketers should attempt to gain buyers' attention. Table 11.1 lists a number of factors that have been found useful in gaining attention. These factors overlap, to a large extent, the factors discussed in Chapter 6 that create arousal. This is not surprising since, as we have seen, one way to *define* the concept of attention is in terms of arousal.

Table 11.1
Some well established methods for getting buyers' attention

Method	Effect
Size	Larger advertisements attract greater attention
Movement	Objects in motion, or apparent motion, tend to attract attention
Intensity	Loud noises, strong smells, bright lights, vibrant colors and similar intense stimuli tend to attract attention
Novelty	Unfamiliar stimuli tend to attract greater attention
Contrast	Stimuli which are markedly different from their surroundings, e.g., a black and white TV advertisement, tend to attract attention
Suddenness	Stimuli which appear suddenly, especially if intense, tend to attract attention
Position	Certain positions, e.g., upper half of a newspaper or eye level on a supermarket shelf, tend to attract attention
Multiple Sensory Messages	Messages which affect more than one sense, e.g., television, scratch and sniff magazine ads, tend to attract attention

Source: Adapted from M. Wayne DeLozier, *The Marketing Communication Process.* New York: McGraw-Hill, 1976, pp. 34–42. Reprinted with permission.

When buyers have well developed concepts of the product class and brands of interest, the principal problem of the marketer *is* to get the buyer's attention. Because the relevant schemas are highly developed and the performances involved in tracking the advertisements are highly skilled, buyers can attend to the messages with minimal allocation of attentional capacity. Indeed, under these circumstances it is possible to meaningfully communicate with buyers, even when their initial attention is attracted in ways that might be described as irrelevant, or outrageous, or even in ways that could be perceived as offensive or insulting. This occurs because, if the marketer can get the buyer's attention, even a small amount of meaningful information (e.g., a brand name) tends to tap the buyer into a larger store of information in long-term memory. The effect of this is to reinforce the prominence of that schema and to associate the marketer's goods with that schema. Of course, there is always the possibility that the method chosen to gain the buyer's attention may result in a negative association. Experience, however, suggests that this is less of a problem than it might initially appear.

When buyers do not have well developed product class and brand concepts, the methods used to get attention should directly communicate meaning. Simple, direct, and unambiguous messages targeted at buyers' motives are especially important. For example, although buyers may not have well developed schemas for personal computers, they do understand budgeting, financial record keeping, taxes, and similar tasks for which a personal computer might be useful. By their very newness, such products tend to elicit at least a moderate degree of interest; thus, making the techniques used to gain buyers' attention for familiar, low involvement products less necessary.

One final point, which has been alluded to already, is that the psychological experience of perception is a holistic phenomena. That is, we tend to perceive the world in relatively large chunks that are inherently meaningful. Indeed, in the absence of specific stimuli that *should be* present, we tend to fill in the missing information, often without being consciously aware of having done so. For example, a car that is low to the ground and sleek is typically perceived as fast and powerful. Or, in the previously discussed restaurant schema, the diner need not actually see the food prepared to *presume* that this activity is occurring in the kitchen. Indeed, the diner might be both surprised and shocked to find out that the food was fully prepared, shipped frozen, and microwaved just prior to serving, a practice that (unfortunately) occurs even in some better restaurants. The next two sections will expand on these, and related ideas, in a discussion of some basic principles of perception and the drawing of inferences from perceptual data.

PRINCIPLES OF PERCEPTION

During the last century psychologists developed a large number of principles regarding perception. Particularly important to the study of buyer behavior is the work of those known as Gestalt psychologists, who argue that perception is more than a process of assembling basic sensations. The word gestalt means structure or pattern. Gestalt psychologists emphasize the organization, patterning, and wholeness in nature and argue that human behavior can be understood only in terms of responses to the whole rather than as a summation of individual units of sensation. Perhaps the clearest example of the idea of a gestalt comes from music. Listeners have no difficulty in recognizing the commonality of a single composition played in two different keys despite the fact that the individual sensations are entirely different. This section discusses a number of principles of perception that are especially important for understanding buyer behavior and for developing marketing strategy.

Thresholds

The human ear can generally detect sounds only within the range of 20–20,000 cycles per second. In a similar way there are *absolute* thresholds below or above which stimuli cannot be perceived. The major importance of absolute thresholds stems from the fact that these thresholds can vary considerably across individuals. For example, taste sensitivity declines steadily with age. Infants, in particular, are extremely sensitive to taste because they have far more functioning taste buds than older individuals. In fact, infants even have taste buds on the insides of their cheeks (Wrightsman and Sanford 1975, p. 266). This is one reason why infants and young children frequently reject foods that adults tend to like. This accounts for the tendency to prefer certain types of foods to vary substantially as a function of age. It also helps explain the importance of age as a market segmentation variable for many food products.

A different type of threshold is known as a *differential* threshold and is defined in terms of the just noticeable difference, or jnd. The jnd is the amount by which a stimulus must change before a perceiver can detect that a change has occurred. A particularly important formulation of the jnd is Weber's Law, which can be formally stated as

$$\frac{\Delta I}{I} = K$$

where I is the intensity of some stimulus, ΔI is the change in intensity of that stimulus, and K is a constant. That is, the jnd is a constant percentage. For example, the value of K for lifted weights is 1/53 or approximately a 2 percent difference (Boring, et. al. 1935. p. 199).[6] Thus, the greater the intensity of the stimulus the larger will be the change needed for detection. Weber's Law has been well documented for such stimuli as pitch, brightness, weight, loudness, and smell.

Weber's Law suggests rather immediate applications to marketing, especially in the area of pricing. The research support for Weber's Law in this application, however, is mixed (Monroe 1973). Among the possible reasons for these mixed results is the fact that "price" is not a simple and well-defined stimulus compared with the stimuli (e.g., pitch and brightness) used to validate Weber's Law in psychology. Despite this caveat, there is sufficient positive evidence (e.g., Gabor, Granger, and Sowter 1971; Monroe 1971) to support Weber's Law as a useful analytical tool for marketers within *a specific marketing context*. The last phrase is important because research suggests that the jnd constant K varies for different product classes (Cooper 1970 a,b). Thus, it is necessary to investigate the sensitivity of buyers to price changes *within* specific product classes.

Price, of course, can be changed indirectly as well as directly. For example, over a 23-year period the weight of the Hershey chocolate bar has changed fourteen times while the price has changed only three times (*Wall Street Journal*, 17 February 1977). Most buyers were apparently unaware of these changes. In a very similar way, newspapers and magazines often change the number of pages per issue, while manufacturers of canned and packaged foods, and a variety of other products change the size of their containers apparently without most buyers becoming aware of the change.

One final illustration of the concept of the jnd concerns the use of different types of oils in making candy. According to Gilden (1976) one company found that tasters cannot tell the difference between chocolate made with cocoa butter and vegetable oil. Under such circumstances producers may substitute one oil for another, based upon relative costs, without buyers becoming aware of the change in the product. This practice is apparently widespread as can be seen from the number of products whose ingredients lists contain the phrase "and one or more of the following types of oil...." In principle, this application of the jnd can be applied to any product that is composed of two or more substitutable ingredients. Of course, careful research is necessary to identify the limits of the jnd.

Closure

Closure is the tendency to complete an incomplete stimulus. Figure 11.5 presents several simple examples of closure. The objects in Figure 11.5 are easily recognized as a triangle, circle, and horse despite the incomplete lines of the drawings. The perceiver tends to fill in, or close, the stimulus to make it complete. Of course, closure requires a relevant schema that can supply the necessary information to make closure possible.

---

[6]Like all laws, Weber's Law tends to break down at the extremes. For example, the value of K for lifted weights in this example was established at a base of 300 grams. More importantly in laboratory studies where the value of K has been established for a variety of stimuli, each with its own K value, judgments of the jnd are made with both stimuli simultaneously or very close together in time. Most marketing applications of Weber's Law involve longer time intervals between stimuli.

Figure 11.5
Illustrations of closure

One of the most interesting and frequently cited marketing applications of the closure principle concerns an advertising campaign for Salem cigarettes, which began with promotion of the now well recognized slogan

> You can take Salem out of the country but—
> You can't take the country out of Salem

and a bell ringing between the two parts of the slogan. Subsequently, advertisements were run using only the first part of the slogan and the bell. The listener, expecting the second part of the slogan to follow, was left with an incomplete stimulus and tended to close the message by silently repeating the concluding phrase of the slogan. Such closure is especially important because it requires *active* participation by the listener, and it is a well established principle of learning theory that learning occurs best under conditions of active participation.

A number of other examples of the closure principle could be sighted. The Kellogg company, for example, used the closure principle in a series of billboard advertisements in which the last "g" was cut off by the right boundary of the billboard (Myers and Reynolds 1967, p. 21). In a particularly interesting public service advertisement, Smokey the Bear is shown with the message "Repeat after me, 'Only you . . .'."

Effective use of the closure principle requires that one caveat must always be kept clearly in mind. Receivers of an incomplete message must have the information, the schema, necessary to complete the message. If not, they may ignore the message or even have a negative reaction; e.g., frustration because of their inability to complete the message. This calls for careful pretesting whenever the principle of closure is considered as the basis for a marketing communication.

Context

The idea of context is well illustrated by the following example. A company informed its employees of a 10 percent reduction in pay via individual letters signed by the company president. Unexpectedly, the reaction of the employees to the letter was one of amusement. This was because the letters had been delivered—unintentionally—on April Fool's Day (Myers and Reynolds 1967, p. 22).

Context is of critical importance to successful marketing communication. Runyon (1980, p. 327), for example, cites the very successful Clairol "Does she—or doesn't she" hair coloring campaign, where an attractive young woman is shown with a child cuddled up to her. Take the child out of the picture and the entire meaning of the advertisement changes.

Two areas where the effects of context are particularly evident are cigarette and beer advertisements. The Marlboro man, for example, is always shown in "macho" activities and surroundings. Virginia Slims appeals to the "modern" woman through advertisements that place her present social situation in historial context with the slogan "You've come a long way, baby." In a similar way one can tell quite easily from such contextual factors as cars, houses, clothes, games, etc., what segment of the market Michelob beer is attempting to reach.

Proximity

Another important principle of perception is known as proximity. Objects or events that exist in close proximity to one another are often perceived to be related. This idea is closely related to a learning principle, the law of contiguity, which was discussed extensively in Chapter 7. Marketers make use of the perceptual principle of proximity when they show their products in situations that are happy, intimate, luxurious, etc., in the hope that buyers will associate their product with these situations.

Figure-Ground

Figure 11.6 presents a classic example of the figure-ground concept. Depending on one's focus, Figure 11.6 takes on the appearance of either a vase *or* two opposing faces. When one perceives the vase the white portion of the stimulus appears to be in front with the dark portion behind it. Just the reverse occurs when the two faces are seen.

The concept of the figure-ground relationship has important implications for marketers. Specifically, marketers want their products to be perceived as the figure and not as the ground. Marketers use a variety of devices, such as a soft or fuzzy focus of the desired background and the emphasizing of the brand name or slogan, to insure that the intended elements of an advertisement become the figure and not the ground.

The devices that marketers frequently use to attempt to capture a buyer's attention can be analyzed in terms of figure-ground relationships. For example, sex and humor are frequently used, often successfully, to capture buyers' attention. However, the results of research on sex (e.g., Steadman 1969, Peterson and Kerin 1977, Horton, Leib and Hewitt 1982) and humor (e.g., Sternthal and Craig 1973) in advertising show decidedly mixed results in terms of message comprehension

Figure 11.6
Illustration of figure-ground relationship

and attitude change. Among the possible explanations for these results is that the product and the main message often become the ground and the sexual or humorous device used to attract attention becomes the figure.

Perceptual Vigilance and Defense

The final principles of perception to be discussed here are known as perceptual vigilance and defense (Postman, Bruner, and McGinnies 1948). Simply stated, perception is motivated. Buyers are especially likely to perceive stimuli of high interest; i.e., to be vigilant for such information. Conversely, stimuli likely to arouse fear or anxiety are likely to be screened out or distorted; i.e., to be defended against. The concepts of perceptual vigilance and defense have, of course, been extensively discussed in previous chapters and so will not be pursued further here.

DERIVING INFERENCES FROM PERCEPTUAL DATA

Perceptual data, in and of itself, cannot tell the buyer whether a contemplated purchase will be satisfying. To make such a determination requires another step. Specifically, an inference from perceptual data, much of which is stored in long-term memory, is required. Of course, this idea is not entirely new. Inference making was discussed earlier in the contexts of buying heuristics and decision nets. This section will reinforce and extend the earlier discussions through a brief examination of the phenomena of perceptual categorization, cue "values," and inferences of causal attributions.

Perceptual Categorization

Previous sections noted the importance of the category, the market position, into which buyers place a brand. Bruner (1957) described this categorization process in terms of the following four stages: primitive categorization, cue search, confirmation check, and confirmation completion. Primitive categorization is an initial step in which an object is isolated and identified at a gross level; e.g., as food. This is followed by a cue search in which the object is examined for specific features to provide a basis for more precise categorical placement; e.g., a product made with eggs. In the next stage the search for information becomes much more selective and is focused on information that will confirm the categorization; e.g., although the cholesterol has been removed it's still made from real eggs. And finally, once the individual is satisfied that the object has been properly identified, the categorization confirmation process is completed and the search for additional information largely ceases.

Knowing what cues buyers use to infer brand characteristics and competitive categorization is of obvious importance to the marketing manager. Frequently, the cues used by buyers seem almost obvious in retrospect. Color is an important cue in judging the richness of ice cream, while odor and suds are important cues for judging the cleaning power of cleansers (Cox 1962). Despite this retrospective obviousness, it typically takes careful research to determine which cues buyers are using and how they are using them. Sometimes the results are surprising. Politz, for example, found that car buyers valued acceleration. However, acceleration is very difficult to "feel" at the rate it is experienced in an automobile. After some research, Politz concluded that drivers used the softness of the accelerator as a surrogate for acceleration; i.e., cars with soft accelerators have fast acceleration (cited in Howard 1977, p. 123).

Unfortunately, marketers sometimes put on the market products which contain cues that communicate a message different from the intended message. Runyon (1980, pp. 322–323) cites a particularly interesting example of unintended cues with Starch-Eze, a product made by Monsanto Chemical Company. Among its differences from traditional starches, Starch-Eze was designed to be used only in every tenth washing or so. Using it in every washing would, to use Runyon's graphic phrase, "turn a soft piece of fabric into a suit of armor" (p. 323). Many users of Starch-Eze categorized the brand as a traditional starch, used it in every wash with clearly unsatisfactory results, and the product failed in the marketplace. Although the unique characteristics of Starch-Eze were clearly spelled out, the brand name conveyed the message that Starch-Eze was an easy to use starch.[7]

Finally, as discussed previously, marketers frequently add essentially irrelevant cues to their products because they know that buyers use those cues in specific ways. Food, in particular, is frequently altered through such devices as dyes (e.g., oranges, meat) and waxing (e.g., cucumbers) because it is known that buyers use such cues as a basis for inferring qualities such as freshness. The use of irrelevant cues is not limited to food products. For example, toilet tissue is judged by many buyers by its softness. This is why some manufacturers use a special process to blow air into the tissue as it is rolled to create an increased sensation of softness when the package is squeezed (*Consumer Reports*, April 1977, pp. 466–468).

Predictive and Confidence Value of a Cue

The preceding examples of cues used by buyers fit into a pattern that recurs throughout the discussions in this book. Buyers frequently, but by no means always, use cues that have little relationship to the product qualities being inferred from the cue. For example, price, as noted on several occasions, is often used to infer product quality. Yet in a study of the price-quality relationship from data in *Consumer Reports* for 48 product categories in the years 1958–1967, Morris and Bronson (1969) concluded that "the study indicates that price and quality do correlate, but at a level so low as to lack practical significance" (p. 33). Why then do so many buyers persist in using price, and similar cues, to infer product attributes such as quality?

Cox (1962) argued that the answer lies partially in distinguishing between the predictive value and confidence value of a cue. Cox defines predictive value as "a measure of the probability with which a cue seems associated with (i.e., predicts) a specific product attribute" (p. 416). Cues, however, can be defined on another dimension, which Cox called the cue's confidence value and defined as "a measure of how certain the consumer is that the cue is what she thinks it is" (p. 416). Cox illustrates the distinction between the predictive value and confidence value of a

---

[7]This example suggests that many buyers subscribe to the rule "if all else fails read the directions." Although there is probably some truth to this rule, there is also reason to believe that the buyers of Starch-Eze may have believed they were using a regular starch and, therefore, did not need to read the instructions for proper use of the product.

cue with an example of an audiophile and a suburban housewife who are attempting to judge the quality of a stereo amplifier. Both might share the belief that the specific internal components used to construct the amplifier have high predictive value. The housewife, in marked contrast to the audiophile, would probably have little confidence in her ability to judge the quality of the internal components.

Based on the results of a study designed to test the distinction between the predictive and the confidence value of a cue, Cox concluded that everything else equal, consumers prefer cues with higher predictive validity. However, confidence value exercises a type of veto in the sense that a buyer must be relatively sure of what a cue is before he or she can use it. Thus, buyers are frequently in a position where the only cues they have confidence in are cues of relatively low predictive value.

Attribution Theory

Inferences regarding categorization of a brand and cue value address the question of "what is it?" Another type of inference concerns cause and effect relations, and addresses the questions of why: "Why did I buy brand X?" "Why did I give to charity Y?" "Why is this salesman telling me something negative about this product?" That is, to what *cause* should I attribute an *effect*. Such questions fall under a class of theories generally referred to as attribution theory.

In recent years, attribution theory has been frequently used as a basis for predicting and explaining buyer behavior. In fact, as the reader may recall, attribution theory was briefly referred to as a possible explanation for certain learning and attitude-behavior phenomena. In the case of learning, it was suggested that receiving a telephone call from a jewelry store simply saying thank-you for being a customer would tend to elicit a response such as "I wonder *why* they did that—they didn't even ask me to buy anything." In the case of attitudes, Bem's self-perception theory, a type of attribution theory, was discussed as one explanation of why attitudes might follow, rather than precede, behavior. This section will discuss attribution theory more fully.

Three attribution theories are generally recognized: person-perception (Heider 1944, 1958; Jones and Davis 1965), self-perception (Bem 1965, 1967, 1972), and object and generalized perception (Kelley 1967, 1971, 1973). Mizerski, Golden, and Kernan (1979) provided an extensive review of these attribution theories including their application to buyer behavior. Table 11.2 presents their summarization of the key elements of each theory.

In his theory of person-perception, Heider proposed that people act as "naive psychologists," who attempt to understand the behavior of other people by determining the causes for their behavior. In particular, Heider focused on the degree to which a person is perceived to be personally responsible for a behavior. These ideas were extended and given a form suitable for analysis of buyer behavior by Jones and Davis (1965) who emphasized the effects of actions, rather than the actions themselves, and the commonality and desirability of the effects. Attributions are most likely to be based on actions and effects that are both uncommon and undesirable. For example, when an advertiser admits to an undesirable product attribute, a buyer may attribute this admission to honesty because such admissions are both uncommon and undesirable in the sense that the admission might jeopardize a sale.

Table 11.2
Comparison of major paradigms of attribution theory

Dimension	Contributors			
	Heider (1944, 1958)	**Jones and Davis** (1965)	**Bem** (1965, 1967, 1972)	**Kelley** (1967, 1971, 1973)
Major contribution	Originator of modern attribution theory	Made Heider's attribution theory amenable to empirical test	Extended attribution theory to self-perception	Extended attribution theory to object and generalized perception
Data used for making attributions	Others' actions or knowledge of others' actions	Perceived effects of others' actions	One's own behavior	Actions or effects of actions (events)
Treatment of others' perceptions or attributions	Implicit	Implicit	None	Explicit—specifically develops paradigm to reflect the processing of information from others
Attributable causes of action				
Personal	Intention, exertion ability	Intention/knowledge, ability/possibility of action (i.e., "can")	"Tact" responses	Intention
Environmental	Task difficulty	Situation and role	"Mand" responses	Entities, modalities, persons
Basis for attribution	Naive analysis of action, using levels of personal responsibility	Commonality and desirability of effects	Perceived freedom of choice, salience of initial attitude[1]	Covariance; causal schemata
Output of attribution	Judgment of extent actor is personally responsible for action	Intention and underlying disposition of the actor	Perception of personal or environmental causality	Cause of an action or effect
Major focus	Person-perception	Person-perception	Self-perception	Object and general perception

[1]Often operationalized through investigator inference

Source: Richard W. Mizerski, Linda L. Golden, and Jerome B. Kernan. "The Attribution Process in Consumer Decision Making." *Journal of Consumer Research*, 6 (September 1979): 124. Reprinted with permission.

An important extension of person-perception is provided by Bem, who argues that the processes underlying self-perception are very similar to those governing perception of other people.[8] An important aspect of Bem's theory is the distinction between "tact" and "mand" responses. A "mand" (as in demand) response is under control of a strong reward or threat, which a "tact" response is not. Mand responses tend to be *attributed* to environmental factors (e.g., it was so cheap, I had to buy it) while tact responses tend to be *attributed* to personal factors (e.g., I must like brand X because I always buy it). Bem's theory, as previously discussed in Chapter 8, is primarily relevant to low involvement situations where buyers are unlikely to form well-structured brand attitudes before purchase.

The most general attribution theory, which in principle is capable of incorporating the other two theories (Mizerski, Golden, and Kernan 1979, p. 127), was developed by Kelley and is referred to as object and generalized perception. Kelley's theory proposes two different principles of *covariation* and *configuration or causal schema*, which are appropriate to multiple-observation and single-observation situations, respectively. The principle of causal schema is also closely related to Neisser's concept of cognitive schema which was discussed extensively earlier.

The following four criteria are used in the covariation principle to determine if the observed effect is an inherent property of the entity in question.

1. Distinctiveness—the effect is attributed to the entity if it uniquely occurs when the entity is present and does not occur in its absence.

2. Consistency over time—each time the entity is present, the individual's reaction must be the same, or nearly so.

3. Consistency over modality—the reaction must be consistent even though the mode of interaction with the entity varies.

4. Consensus—actions or their effects are perceived the same way by all observers (Mizerski, Golden, and Kernan 1979, pp. 126–127).

For example, in inferring how smoothly a car runs (the effect) on brand A gasoline (the entity), a buyer may observe that the car misses and knocks (also effects) only when brand A is used (distinctiveness), that this has happened over multiple fill-ups (consistency ever time), in city and highway driving (consistency over modality), and that passengers agree with the buyer's observations (consensus).

Kelley (1967) suggested that the four criteria upon which the covariation principle is based can be combined to form an index of attributional validity that is analogous to the F-statistic in the analysis of variance.[9] Specifically,

$$\text{Naive F/attribution index} = \frac{\text{distinctiveness}}{\text{consistency over time/modality, consensus.}}$$

The hypothesis being tested by the naive F is that the observed association of a possible cause and effect is a random occurrence and not indicative of a true cause-effect relationship. The criteria in the naive F are scaled in such a way that

---

[8]The assumption that self-perception and perception of others is very similar has been strongly challenged by other researchers (cf., Fishbein and Ajzen 1975).

[9]Readers unfamiliar with the F-statistic and the analysis of variance need only note that the F-statistic is used to determine the probability of an event occurring.

greater distinctiveness, consistency, and consensus increase the value of the naive F and, therefore, lower the probability that the observed cause-effect relationship is merely a random observation. At some point, the value of the naive F will become large enough that the observer will draw an inference that the observed variables are in fact causally related. Although the concept of the naive F is useful it should not be interpreted too literally. More specifically, the naive F concept implies that observers are behaving "as if" they were testing a hypothesis. There is no implication that they are conducting a formal test of a statistical hypothesis.

Attribution theory forms the basis for a relatively large and rapidly growing portion of the buyer behavior literature. Mizerski, Golden, and Kernan (1979), for example, cite over 40 such studies. Among the topics to which attribution theory has been applied are product dissatisfaction (e.g., Landon and Emery 1975, Valle and Wallendorf 1977), advertiser credibility (e.g., Settle and Golden 1974, Dholakia and Sternthal 1977), the effects of physical attractiveness of models in print advertisements (e.g., Baker and Churchill 1977), preference for different information sources as a function of type of product (e.g., Settle 1972), interpersonal influence (e.g., Calder and Burnkrant 1977), energy conservation (Allen 1982), and the so-called foot-in-the-door technique previously discussed in Chapter 7 (e.g., Reingen and Kernan 1977, 1979; Scott 1977; Tybout 1978).

In all of the above applications, the research concerns the inferences about the causes that subjects will attribute to different types of observed effects. In controlled experiments, researchers usually attempt to carefully limit the attributions that subjects can be expected to make. In applied settings, the range of potential causes is probably considerably larger. Thus, successful application of attribution theory requires an understanding of the causal schema buyers are likely to apply in specific situations and the factors, in the form of observed effects, that determine which causal schema will be selected to explain the observed effect. What theories of attribution provide the marketer is an explicit framework for thinking about how buyers draw causal inferences. Despite the appeal and potential usefulness of attribution theory, a caveat is necessary. Attribution processes as they occur in buyer behavior appear to be very complex and, at this time, the factors that cause specific attributions to be made in particular circumstances are not well understood.

EXTERNAL SEARCH[10]

The final topic considered in this chapter is known as external search. This is normally used to designate information acquisition activities that are active and goal directed. That is, external search is directed by the need to solve a specific buying problem. Specifically excluded from this definition are a variety of means by which buyers acquire information, which were previously discussed under such topics as low involvement, latent, incidental, environmental, and passive learning. Internal memory search is also excluded from the definition of external search.

There is a vast literature on external search. The present examination will examine three specific aspects of this literature: First, the amount of external

---

[10]An excellent review of the external search literature can be found in Newman (1977). This section relies heavily on Newman's review.

search activity that precedes purchase; second, factors found to be associated with the amount of external search, so-called correlates of external search; and third, factors that influence buyers' preferences for specific sources of information.

Amount of External Search

A large, and relatively old, literature attempted to quantify the amount of external search engaged in by buyers prior to purchase. The most frequently used measure of amount of external search is the number of retail stores visited (e.g., Bucklin 1966; Claxton, Fry and Portis 1974, Newman and Lockeman 1975; Newman and Staelin 1972). Other measures include the number of information sources consulted (e.g., Katona and Mueller 1955; Newman and Staelin 1973), the number of different types of information consulted (e.g., Katona and Mueller 1955; Olshavsky 1973), the number of choice alternatives considered (e.g., Katona and Mueller 1955; Dommermuth 1965; Newman and Staelin 1972), and the time duration of the purchase decision (e.g., Ferber 1955; Katona and Mueller 1955; Newman and Staelin 1971). Finally, a few attempts have been made to construct indices of total search (e.g., Katona and Mueller 1955; Newman and Staelin 1972; Claxton, Fry, and Portis 1974).

Whatever criterion one chooses to judge the amount of external information search, one conclusion emerges. For most buyers external search is very limited. Data from a study by Dommermuth (1965), reproduced in Table 11.3, illustrates this conclusion very effectively. As can be seen from the table, 36 percent of the buyers considered only one brand of refrigerator *and* visited only one store before making their purchase. Refrigerators, of course, are a relatively expensive purchase. For a less expensive product, electric irons, the corresponding figure rises to a relatively dramatic 62 percent. Similar figures could be cited from other studies.

Based on three studies that span twenty years and that developed general indices of total external search in major durables (Katona and Mueller 1955; Newman and Staelin 1972; Claxton, Fry and Portis 1974), Hawkins, Coney, and Best (1980, pp. 418–420) suggest that buyers may be categorized into three general classes in terms of the total external search they engage in prior to purchasing a major durable good (e.g., an automobile or a refrigerator). Nonsearchers, who comprise some 60 percent of all buyers, engage in little or no external search prior to purchase. Information searchers, about 30 percent of all buyers, are generally characterized as "thorough and balanced" in the sense that they tend to collect data from a moderate number of sources (about three) and visit a moderate number of stores (about four) prior to purchase. Finally, extended information searchers, about 10 percent of all buyers, tend to acquire a large amount of information before making a purchase. As Hawkins, Coney, and Best note, the extent of external search tends to be much less for less expensive goods.

Although the amount of external information search tends to be small, it is also clear that there are substantial differences among buyers. An inquiry into the characteristics of high information seeking individuals reveals a familiar pattern. Information seekers represent a socioeconomic/educational elite. They are generally better educated, wealthier, and tend to be exposed to a wide range of information sources, although they tend to watch less television (e.g., Thorelli, Becker, and Engledow 1975; McEwen 1978). The study by McEwen is particularly interesting because of the finding that individuals who tend to use toll-free 800

Table 11.3
Dommermuth's shopping matrix

I. Refrigerators

Number of Brands Examined	Number of Retail Outlets Shopped				
	1	2	3	4	5
1	36*	4			
2	3	6	2	1	1
3	3	3	5	5	1
4		2	3	3	3
5 or more			5	5	8

II. Electric Irons

Number of Brands Examined	Number of Retail Outlets Shopped				
	1	2	3	4	5
1	62*	2	1		
2	11	3	1	1	
3	5	1	3	1	
4	4		1	1	1
5 or more		1	1		

*Percent of respondents

Source: Adapted from William P. Dommermuth "The Shopping Matrix and Marketing Strategy." *Journal of Marketing Research*, 2 (May 1965): 128. Reprinted with the kind permission of the American Marketing Association.

numbers as a source of buying information have essentially the same socio-economic/educational profile as users of more frequently studied sources of information. This similarity is particularly interesting because the use of toll-free numbers would not seem to require the high level communication skills or physical transportation to information sources that are logical explanations for the greater information seeking on the part of higher income, better educated buyers. This point will be considered further in the discussion of correlates of external search.

Some researchers take the lack of extensive external search by the majority of buyers prior to purchase of even such major items as automobiles as indicative of a frequent lack of a decision-making process that precedes purchase.[11] Undoubtedly, there is some truth to this notion, especially for low involvement products. However, there are a number of reasons for believing that research on external search may understate the degree of decision making by buyers. First, for many reasons, including such things as previous product experience and passive learning, the

[11]Regarding this point the reader is referred to the exchange of articles between Olshavsky and Granbois (1979, 1980) and Ursic (1980).

buyer is likely to know a great deal about a number of choice alternatives at the time that a need to purchase is recognized. Second, as Bettman (1979, Chapter 5) explicitly recognized, a buyer's first response is likely to be an *internal* search of memory, which may produce sufficient information for making a satisfactory brand choice decision. As Bettman also notes, virtually nothing is known about such internal memory searches by buyers. Third, measures of external search tend to be quite limited and there is reason to believe that reported studies of external search probably understate the total amount of such search (cf., Newman 1977, p. 93).[12] Fourth, as will be discussed in the next section, research on correlates of external search suggests that buyers at least implicitly consider the tradeoffs between the costs and the benefits of external search.

Although the data on the amount of external search present certain difficulties in interpretation, two general conclusions of managerial importance seem warranted. First, a portion of the market tends to acquire substantial amounts of information via external search prior to purchase. The importance of this part of the market is greater than its numbers might suggest because external search is positively correlated with income. As an example of how a marketer might appeal to such information seeking individuals, the French automobile manufacturer Puegot has been quite successful with a recent advertising campaign featuring two-page advertisements containing extensive factual information about the Peugot automobile and the company's manufacturing and testing procedures.

The second conclusion follows directly from the fact that a large number of buyers apparently visit very few stores and consider very few brands between the time that search is initiated and a final purchase is made. This suggests that the set of alternatives, for both brands and stores, from which the final choice will be made is often largely determined at the outset of the search process. To be sure, other factors such as price and point-of-purchase promotion affect the final decision, and the search process itself may alter the composition of the choice alternatives. Nevertheless, the data on external search clearly suggest that a major goal for marketers should be to create what can be called top-of-the-mind awareness; i.e., the brands that immediately come to mind when the need to purchase from a specific product class is first recognized.

Correlates of External Search

Most researchers who examined the amount of external search were equally, or more, concerned with investigating the variables associated or correlated with the amount of external search. Although the list of such correlates is large (cf, Newman 1977), the general findings are relatively easy to summarize.

First, and most important, is the sheer complexity of the available data. For many variables it is possible to find examples of negative, zero, positive, and even nonlinear correlations with amount of external search. For example, although the majority of research found a negative correlation between product experience and external search, some studies found essentially no relationship (e.g., Bennett and Mandell 1969; Claxton, Fry, and Portis 1974), while a study of home buying by Hempel (1969) found that buyers sought more information for their second, as

---

[12]Olshavsky and Granbois (1979, p. 94), however, argued that external search may be overstated.

Table 11.4

Hypothesized direction of belief-search relationships, bivariate correlation coefficients, and multiple regression coefficients for 27 market-related beliefs

Belief	Hypothesized direction	Bivariate correlation	Multiple regression coefficient (β)
Attribute surrogates or signals			
Brand:			
S1 The same brands tend to be the best year after year	−[a]	−.08	.02
Store:			
S2 Just because a store sells good merchandise in one product area, there is little reason to believe that it also sells good merchandise in other product categories	+	.18[b]	.05
Price:			
S3 To sell at prices lower than the competition, a manufacturer must sacrifice quality	−	−.15[b]	−.01
S4 Usually, I pay for unnecessary extras when I purchase the highest priced product	+	.06	−.01
S5 The price of a product tells me little about its quality	+	.14[b]	.15
Advertising:			
S6 Heavily advertised brands are almost always good products[d]	−	−.11	−.01
S7 Heavily advertised products are generally priced significantly higher than less advertised products of comparable quality[d]	−	.03	.16[b]
Salesperson:			
S8 Most store salesmen are well-informed about the products they sell	−	−.30[c]	−.13
Market share:			
S9 The best brands are usually the ones that sell the most[d]	−	−.27[c]	−.07
S10 High volume stores have lower prices[d]	−	.01	.01
Foreign manufacture:			
S11 Foreign made products give me similar quality for less money than American made products[d]	−	−.09	−.08
Ability to judge			
J12 I am a poor judge when it comes to evaluating products which are mechanical or technical in nature	−	−.34[c]	−.19[b]
J13 In general, I am quite capable when it comes to distinguishing good brands from bad ones	+	.11	−.07
J14 Generally speaking, I am not a particularly knowledgeable shopper	−	−.26[c]	−.20[b]
Benefits of search			
B15 When important purchases are made quickly, they are usually regretted	+	.36[c]	.28[c]
B16 Today's color television sets rarely need repair or servicing[d]	−	−.08	−.05

B17	Extensive shopping makes it harder rather than easier for a person to make the choice	−	$-.31^c$	$-.14$
B18	Television dealers in this city do not compete aggressively against each other	−	$-.14^b$	$-.05$
B19	I need to look at all the available choices if I am to tell which is the best one	+	$.27^c$	$.14$
Variance of offerings				
VO20	In most product categories, there are one or two brands which are noticeably superior to all others	−	$.06$	$.15$
VO21	Competition among appliance manufacturers tends to keep the prices of different brands about the same	−	$-.24^c$	$-.10$
VO22	Almost any feature that I would want on an appliance is usually available in most brands	−	$-.12^b$	$.05$
Variance in sources of supply				
VS23	Smaller stores tend to charge more for the same brand than do larger stores[d]	−	$-.11$	$-.10$
VS24	Local, independently owned stores give you better and more personalized service than do larger department or chain stores[d]	−	$-.18^c$	$-.22^c$
VS25	When it comes to credit, I can do better by shopping at local stores specializing in one type of product than at large department stores[d]	−	$-.05$	$-.01$
Not classified				
26	It is not difficult to obtain repair service for foreign made products[d]	−	$-.09$	$-.05$
27	I have a civic duty to support local business by shopping at locally-owned stores[d]	−	$-.21^c$	$-.09$

[a]Strength of belief endorsement was measured on a five-point scale where 1 = strongly disagree and 5 = strongly agree. A negative associatic was hypothesized between belief S1 and extent of search; as extent of agreement increased (e.g., higher score), extent of search was expected to decrease.

[b]Significant at the .05 level.

[c]Significant at the .01 level.

[d]Belief classified as "alternative limiting."

Source: Calvin P. Duncan and Richard W. Olshavsky "External Search: The Role of Consumer Beliefs." *Journal of Marketing Research*, 14 (February 1982): 34. Reprinted with the kind permission of the American Marketing Association.

opposed to first and third, home purchases. All of this suggests that quite complex forces act upon the buyer in determining the amount of external search.

Second, and more encouraging for those who believe in a buyer who attempts to act rationally, the general pattern of the data is consistent with the idea that buyers engage in external search when the benefits outweigh the costs of search (cf, Newman 1977). For example, the amount of external search has been found to be positively correlated with price level and price difference among sellers (e.g., Bucklin 1966; Dommermuth 1965; Newman and Staelin 1972); the importance of style and appearance (e.g., Claxton, Fry, and Portis 1974; Dommermuth and Cundiff 1967; Newman and Staelin 1972); the number, location, and geographical proximity among retail stores (e.g., Nelson 1974; Cort and Dominguez 1977); and, as previously mentioned, with lack of product experience.

Third, the amount of external search has been related to a number of personality/self-concept and situational variables. The amount of external search has been found to be positively related to the enjoyment derived from shopping (Katona and Mueller 1955), perception of oneself as a deliberative buyer (Kelly 1968), dependency on others for information (Newman and Staelin 1972), and open-mindedness and self-confidence (Green 1966). Among situational variables, perhaps the most important finding is that external search for major durables is negatively correlated with urgency of purchase (e.g., Claxton, Fry, and Portis 1974; Katona and Mueller 1955; Newman and Staelin 1972). One implication of this finding is the need for a large stock and quick delivery for goods that are frequently bought under serious time pressure; e.g., when the refrigerator stops and the ice cream is running across the kitchen floor.

Fourth, and particularly important, is the fact that multivariate analyses of external search typically are capable of explaining only a small proportion of the variance in the amount of external search. For example, Bucklin (1969) was able to explain only 24 percent of the variance in external data using a data base that included 100 variables. In another study, Newman and Staelin (1972) explained 16 percent of the variance of external search using a data base that included 29 variables.

Although research findings show a certain consistency regarding external search, especially with regard to the implication of a consideration of the costs versus benefits, the research findings are extraordinarily complex and incomplete. Recently, Duncan and Olshavsky (1982) suggested that researchers should extend their investigations to include buyers' beliefs about the marketplace and their ability to benefit from external search.

Investigating external search behavior for purchase of a color television, Duncan and Olshavsky found that they could explain approximately 50 percent of the variance in search from 27 beliefs about the marketplace. Table 11.4 presents the beliefs and the correlations between each belief and the amount of external search. Particularly interesting are beliefs that Duncan and Olshavsky refer to as alternative limiting; e.g., "heavily advertised brands are almost always good products." This emphasis on beliefs puts the focus of external search research directly on the buying problem *as perceived by the buyer*. The buyer's perceptions, of course, are connected with reality and thus tend to reflect important characteristics of the market that affect external search; e.g., the number of directly competitive stores in a specific local market.

Preferred Information Sources

The final aspect of external search to be considered concerns the factors that influence the sources of information that buyers prefer when facing specific types of buying problems. One of the clearest conclusions from the external search literature is that buyers rarely rely on a single source of information. Thus, different information sources are complementary rather than competing.

There has also been a great deal of research, some of which was cited in the last chapter, on factors that influence the preference for mass media vs. personal sources of information. Mass media were found to be especially important in the early stages of the decision process, where the buyer is primarily becoming aware of and informed about possible alternative choices (e.g., Katona and Mueller 1955; Berning and Jacoby 1974). As the buyer nears the point of decision, there is a tendency for personal sources of information to become more important. Finally, as was discussed extensively in the previous chapter, there is a tendency for buyers to prefer personal sources of information for new and high involvement products.

There has also been some research on the effect of product characteristics on preferred sources of information. In an experimental study based on attribution theory, Settle (1972) examined the relative preferences for four different sources of information as a function of the complexity, social visibility, durability, and multipurposeness (i.e., number of different uses for the product) of different pairs of products. Twelve product pairs were selected so that each pair contrasted on one product characteristic and was essentially identical on the other three characteristics. For example, stereo tuner and living room chair were contrasted on complexity, while skirt and pajamas were contrasted on social visibility. For complex and socially visible products, the preferred sources of information were a conversation with an expert and a conversation with a close friend, respectively. For durable and multipurpose products the preferred sources of information were personal experience over a long period of time and over a wide variety of uses, respectively. In evaluating Settle's results it should be kept in mind that the preferences are relative and there is no implication that the "preferred" source is the only source from which information will be acquired.

There has also been some research on preferred media. Television appears to be an important source of information where appearance factors, such as style and design, are important (Houston 1979). There is also reason to believe that television is an important source of information in low involvement buying situations. In contrast, it has been suggested that print media may be more important in high involvement purchasing decisions (Krugman 1979; Rothschild 1979). Finally, there is reason to believe that salespersons may be important sources of information in complex, high involvement decisions. For example, Claxton and Anderson (1980) found that buyers preferred to rely on salespersons, rather than energy use labels, when evaluating major durables.

SUMMARY

This chapter investigated the perceptual processes through which buyers acquire and give meaning to stimuli. Buyers are highly selective in the stimuli to which they attend. This selectivity is based upon active, goal directed mechanisms that allow the buyer to select "relevant" information from a virtually infinite pool of potential stimuli. Motivation, experience, and cognitive schema play critical roles both in terms of determining which stimuli are selected for attention and in the meaning that the attended stimuli are inferred to possess.

The perceptual processes through which buyers acquire information were seen to be both complex and subtle. Typically, buyers acquire information from a wide range of sources. More important, much of this information acquisition occurs outside the narrow boundaries of external search for information to solve specific buying problems. Indeed, there is good reason to believe that much of this information acquisition occurs in the context of well developed cognitive schemas and highly skilled performances, which require no more conscious attention than does driving an extremely familiar route. Conversely, the special demands that innovations place upon buyers can be understood in terms of the lack of well developed schemas and largely unskilled performances in the acquisition and evaluation of brand information.

Finally, knowledge of perceptual processes provides important managerial insights. By understanding the processes through which buyers select and give meaning to stimuli, the marketer is better able to communicate effectively with buyers.

Exogenous Variables: Individual Differences Among Buyers

V

The first eleven chapters of this book focused on the fundamental processes that underlie buying behavior and that are common to all buyers. On occasion, reference was made to ways in which buyers with specific characteristics differ in their buying behavior. However, the purpose in these earlier discussions was primarily either to illustrate a general idea (e.g., systematic changes in taste perception as a function of age), or to discuss the special roles certain types of individuals play in buyers' decision processes (e.g., innovators and opinion leaders). Part V turns to the many ways in which individual buyers differ and the implications these differences have for marketing strategy.

Collectively, the individual difference variables discussed in Part V are referred to as exogenous variables. As the reader may recall from the discussion of the Howard-Sheth model in Chapter 2, exogenous variables are those that influence the behavior of buyers but for which a theory or model offers no explanation as to how they come into existence or change. Sometimes exogenous variables are absolutely fixed for each individual; e.g., sex, race, cultural heritage. Frequently, however, a variable is treated as exogenous although it might be treated as endogenous (i.e., changes in the variable might be explained by the model). For example, buyer behavior researchers virtually always treat income as an exogenous variable. However, it is clear that buying decisions can influence income via a variety of mechanisms, such as upward career mobility and greater opportunities to marry a high income person. Such influences may be ignored for many valid reasons: e.g., the need to limit the number of endogenous variables to a manageable set, the presumption that the magnitude of the influence is minor or the presumption that the influence is so complex and subtle as to preclude its incorporation into the web of interrelationships among the endogenous variables.

How exogenous variables influence buyer behavior can be illustrated by considering how a person's sex might influence the automobile buying decision. Men and women both develop choice criteria to guide their information search and evaluation and final choice of an automobile. The specific content of these choice criteria, however, tends to vary systematically with a person's sex. In particular, men tend to be more concerned with mechanical features and exterior styling of an automobile, while women are more concerned with color and interior styling. In a similar way, there are probably a number of specific differences between men and women in the exact motives that are satisfied by automobile ownership, in the level of confidence with which the final decision is made, etc.

The study of individual differences is important for three fundamental reasons. First, an understanding of individual differences can enrich the general understanding of buyer behavior. Second, sophisticated marketing-oriented firms generally find that it is more effective and profitable to develop specific marketing programs targeted to different segments of the market rather than to attempt to serve the entire market with a single marketing program. Third, trends in individual difference variables provide an important basis for projecting market trends and developing strategic marketing plans for exploiting these future trends.

Since each person can be characterized by a large number of variables—age, income, sex, self-confidence, ad infinitum—*and* each of these variables may have different implications for different products, the number of ways in which individual differences may impact upon firms' marketing strategies is as a practical matter infinite. Clearly, it is not possible to assess the implication of individual difference variables comprehensively. What can be done is to familiarize the reader with a number of the most frequently and successfully utilized individual difference variables, illustrate how these variables have been used in firms' marketing strategies and, where possible, discuss expected future trends and the implications these trends may have for buyer behavior. The reader is warned, however, that the projection and interpretation of such trends is extremely risky. Careful monitoring of trends that are important to the firm is always required.

Chapter 12 discusses a number of demographic and socioeconomic differences among buyers and the implications these differences have for marketers. The variables discussed here are relatively "hard" in the sense that they are well defined and easily measured. Chapter 13 focuses on more subjective, but no less important, value, personality, and lifestyle differences among buyers. Chapter 14 concludes the analysis of exogenous variables by discussing the marketing implications of buyers' membership in different social groups based on cultural, subcultural, and social class differences.

In considering the material presented in the next three chapters, it must be recognized that individual difference variables rarely cause a buyer to buy a specific brand and frequently do not even require purchase from any specific product class. Rather, individual difference variables represent forces that impel the individual in certain directions, tend to open certain options, and tend to close other options. Knowledge of individual differences among buyers provides the marketer a firmer basis on which to build total marketing strategies tailored to the specific requirements of each segment of the market, thereby increasing the likelihood of success in the marketplace.

Individual Differences: Demographic and Socioeconomic Variables

12

Demographic and socioeconomic variables are among the oldest and most frequently used variables for analyzing markets. Among the many uses of these variables, one of the most important is for dividing the total market into more homogeneous segments that can be approached with unique strategies, precisely tailored to the characteristics of each segment. Because the use of individual difference variables is so closely linked with the segmentation of markets, this chapter begins with a brief review of the market segmentation concept. The remainder of the chapter is devoted to discussions of the marketing implications of a number of the most important and most frequently used demographic and socioeconomic differences among buyers.

MARKET SEGMENTATION[1]

The concept of market segmentation is widely regarded as one of the most fundamental and important concepts of modern marketing (Wind 1978). The importance of the segmentation concept rests on two basic facts. First, all buyers do not respond in the same way to any specific combination of product, price, promotion, and distribution; i.e., markets are heterogeneous. Second, in a high level economy, such as exists in the United States and other developed nations today, production *capacity* is typically sufficient to supply in *the long run* more of any particular good or service than is demanded. This situation intensifies competition among firms in an industry and forces each firm to consider buyers' needs and desires far more carefully than would be necessary if demand exceeded long-run supply.[2]

It is important to be very clear about what market segmentation is and what it is not. In particular, segmentation is more than "mere variety" (Reynolds 1965). The fact that a firm produces more than one version of a product and prices, promotes, and distributes that product in more than one way is *not* necessarily indicative of a true segmentation program. To quote from Wendell Smith's (1956) original discussion of the segmentation concept:

> Segmentation is based upon developments on the demand side of the market and represents a rational and more precise adjustment of product and marketing effort to consumer or user requirements. In the language of the economist, segmentation is *disaggregative* in its effects and tends to bring about recognition of several demand schedules where only one was recognized before (p. 5, emphasis in original).

---

[1]The discussion of market segmentation is necessarily brief. Virtually all introductory marketing textbooks discuss the concept of market segmentation in considerable detail. For a critical evaluation of the status of segmentation theory and research, the reader is referred to the special section of the *Journal of Marketing Research* (August 1978).

[2]Long-term excess demand is relatively common in most undeveloped and developing nations. This is one reason why sophisticated marketing systems are largely absent in such countries. In the developed nations, excess demand does occur but it is more frequently of a short-term nature. This situation requires that the excess demand be temporarily discouraged without permanently alienating potential customers while supply is increased to match demand. This need to occasionally *demarket* goods in the short run, however, reinforces the general principle that *potential* capacity typically exceeds demand. For an interesting discussion of the concept of demarketing, the reader is referred to Kotler and Levy (1971).

The next few pages will briefly discuss the following four requirements for a successful market segmentation program: heterogeneous demand functions, identifiable and measurable submarkets, the ability to access identified submarkets, and substantial size for each market segment.

Heterogeneous Demand Functions

The *sine qua non* of any market segmentation program is the existence of heterogeneous demand functions among buyers. Heterogeneous demand functions mean that buyers respond differently to one or more elements of the firm's marketing mix (i.e., product, price, promotion, and distribution). For example, some buyers prefer small, fuel efficient cars while others prefer large luxury cars. Or, to recall the discussion of motivation in Chapter 6, strong fear appeals will tend to be more effective with persons who do not see the threat as especially relevant while milder fear appeals will tend to be more effective with those for whom the threat is more relevant.

From the firm's perspective, the importance of heterogeneous demand is that the firm's profits will be greater if the firm's marketing mix decisions are made separately for each group of buyers with *homogeneous demand functions* than if these decisions are made on the basis of the aggregate of the individual demand functions. This conclusion, however, requires that the firm's costs not be increased by segmentation and that the firm has the ability to effectively implement its segmented marketing mix decisions. Both of these caveats will be addressed shortly.

Price Discrimination

The classic example of market segmentation is the price discriminator who sells the same good or service to different groups of buyers at different prices. In this situation, the optimal pricing policy is based upon the elasticity of demand in each market segment, with prices being higher in the less elastic segment and lower in the more elastic segment than they would be if a single profit maximizing price were set on the basis of a single aggregate demand function. Profits will also be higher under a segmentation program if the cost function remains constant.[3]

One of the most familiar examples of price discrimination is airfares, where the same seat may be sold under a large number of specific fare schedules that frequently differ by a factor of two or more. This seeming chaos of airfares springs from two basic factors. First, potential air travelers vary greatly in their sensitivity to price. The least price sensitive segment of the market tends to be business travelers, who are traveling for specific business purposes, for short periods of time, and are usually not paying their own fares. Other segments (e.g., retirees, students, vacationers, spouses of business travelers) are typically more price sensitive. Second, the cost of flying an airplane full is not much greater than flying it empty. This cost structure provides a strong incentive to fill any vacant seat with a paying passenger, even if that passenger is only willing to pay a modest fraction of the "full" fare.

---

[3]Although the proof of these assertions is not difficult, a knowledge of calculus is required. For a more formal discussion of price discrimination, see any good intermediate level microeconomics text (e.g., Henderson and Quandt 1958, especially pp. 170–172).

The problem, of course, is to set up the fare schedules in such a way that the segments are properly separated. This is why, for example, so-called "super saver" fares often require a Saturday to intervene between departure and return dates. Business travelers, the least price sensitive segment, are much less likely than other, more price sensitive, travelers to stay over a weekend. In a similar way, the "get one ticket at half-price when you buy one ticket at full-price" offer is designed to encourage the business traveler to bring his or her spouse along on a business trip. Other types of special fares are similarly constructed to appeal to specific types of individuals with specific price sensitivities and patterns of travel.[4]

Situations where what is obviously the same good or service are offered to different groups of buyers at different prices are not limited to high priced items, such as air travel. For example, the same theater seat may cost different amounts depending upon one's age, the time of day, or the day of week. Similarly, many restaurants and retailers give senior citizen discounts that are frequently limited to purchases made during normally slow business hours.[5]

Other Bases for Discrimination

Much more common than offering the same good to different segments is the situation in which some product changes are made. Sometimes these changes are limited to the brand name. For example, many national brands are also sold under store or generic labels. Sometimes product changes are real but modest. For example, several models of Plymouth and Dodge automobiles are almost identical except for minor design features. Also, it is quite common for "deluxe" or "luxury" versions of a product to be offered at prices far in excess of that justified solely by their incremental costs. This is because the buyers of such goods tend to be less price sensitive than buyers of standard lines. Often, of course, firms offer different market segments versions of a product that are quite different. Sears, for example, offers two different quality lines of hand tools at two different price levels. Similarly, manufacturers of small appliances frequently offer both regular and professional lines. Such prestige lines are targeted at buyers who typically use the product intensively and have a high level of involvement with the product class.

In summary, an effective market segmentation strategy requires the existence of heterogeneous demand functions and logically begins with a careful analysis of the exact nature of each identifiable type of demand function. The result will be a set of marketing mix decisions, each of which is specifically tailored to the needs of its market segment. However, before the firm can determine whether it can and should implement such a segmented marketing strategy, several additional issues must be resolved.

[4]It should be noted that in the last few years airfare structures have become truly chaotic as a result of the competition that accompanied federal deregulation of the airline industry. This situation, however, should rectify itself as a more stable competitive structure is established in the newly deregulated environment.

[5]One potential problem with selling the same good at different prices is that those paying a higher price may very much resent that fact. This is especially a problem for the airlines since it is not uncommon for business travelers to be *sandwiched* between two "Super Saver" travelers, who may be paying only half as much. In an effort to retain the goodwill of full-fare passengers, some airlines have instituted a special "business traveler" class with amenities such as being seated next to a vacant seat when one is available.

Identifiable and Measurable Submarkets

To implement a market segmentation strategy it is necessary to determine to which market segments individual buyers belong. For example, the heaviest consumers of beer are young males. This segment of the market can be readily identified, and the size of the segment estimated, because both age and sex are variables that are easily measured and for which good statistics are readily available.

In contrast, many variables that might be used to identify market segments are very difficult to measure. For example, a marketer who knew that high anxiety individuals were a particularly good potential segment for a new extra-strength pain reliever would still face a very difficult problem in trying to measure this trait. Fortunately, it is often possible to use a surrogate variable. For example, high anxiety persons might *tend* to have a specific profile of more measurable variables such as age, education, income, and occupation. Also, some market segments tend to be self-identifying through such things as magazine subscriptions and professional association memberships.

Accessibility

Another requirement for an effective segmentation strategy is the ability to efficiently reach, or access, identified market segments. Efficiency requires that the method of access be cost effective. Among other factors, cost effectiveness depends upon the total cost of a message, the total audience reached by that message, and the portion of that total audience in the market segment. In many instances, it will be possible to reach targeted buyers in a highly efficient manner; e.g., skiers through ski magazines, young mothers through *Parents Magazine* or afternoon soap operas.

Sometimes, however, it will be necessary to turn to more general media and let buyers self-select according to their interest in the good or service. Although this strategy typically involves wasted coverage, it still may prove cost effective. Where the general media are used to access different segments with different marketing programs, careful attention must be paid to the possibility of negative effects from messages intended for one segment reaching other segments. For example, recently General Motors offered especially attractive trade-in allowances for late model GM cars. When received by the owner of a similar non-GM car, this message may have produced a negative reaction. Such a possible negative effect may account for the relatively short life of this particular promotion.

Substantiality

Earlier it was noted that profits under a segmentation program are greater than they would be otherwise *if* the cost function remains constant. Typically, however, a segmentation strategy increases costs. Thus, an effective segmentation strategy must generate enough additional revenue to more than cover the additional costs. This is the final criterion of substantiality.

DEMOGRAPHIC AND SOCIOECONOMIC VARIABLES

Demographic and socioeconomic variables describe the size, distribution, structural characteristics (e.g., age, sex, race), and rate of change of populations (Stockwell

1976). These individual differences provide important bases for explaining and predicting buyer behavior and, consequently, form important bases for constructing market segments. Sometimes the relationship between a specific behavior and a demographic or socioeconomic variable is quite direct. Baby food sales, for example, depend closely on the number of babies born each year. More often demographic and socioeconomic variables serve as surrogates for more basic forces. For example, a great many buying behaviors are closely related to age (e.g., purchase of first home) although it is clear that age per se is not a causal variable. Even though it is obviously a surrogate, a variable may still be the best basis for identifying market segments for such reasons as availability and ease of use.

In the United States, and most other developed countries, readily available demographic and socioeconomic data are both extensive and, generally, relatively accurate. Much of this data is collected by government (particularly the Bureau of the Census) and is available at no, or only nominal, cost. Even when desired data are not available in published form, they may be obtainable. The Census Bureau, for example, will prepare special data analyses on a cost basis as long as the results are sufficiently aggregated to maintain confidentiality of individual respondents.

In fact, much of the data collected by the Census Bureau are now available to the public in the form of computer tapes. Some private firms have made enterprising use of these data. Metromedia Mail, for example, matches telephone directory information with census information on a number of demographic and socioeconomic variables. From this data base, clients can be supplied with names, addresses, and telephone numbers of individuals selected from small, relatively homogeneous, locations identified by such characteristics as age of head of household, income, home ownership, presence of minor children, and a number of other demographic and socioeconomic variables. A large number of other firms offer specialized services for accessing markets with special characteristics.

Demographic and socioeconomic data are also useful for predicting market trends. Forecasting, of course, is always risky. Nevertheless, many important trends can be predicted with reasonable accuracy some years into the future. For example, all the individuals who will be in the 65–85 age bracket twenty years from now have already been born. Furthermore, barring some unforeseen disaster, age specific death rates are sufficiently stable to allow quite accurate prediction of the number of persons in this age group twenty years into the future. On the other hand, the fertility rate—the average number of children produced per woman during her lifetime—has proved very unstable and extremely difficult to predict.

The remainder of this section discusses a number of the most generally used and useful demographic and socioeconomic variables, and some expected trends in these variables that have important implications for marketers. The reader is reminded that this review is highly selective and primarily illustrative of the relevance of demographic and socioeconomic variables to buyer behavior.

Age and Sex Distribution

As of 1980, the total population of the United States was just over 226-million. Of the many ways in which this total population may be characterized, none is more basic than its age and sex distribution. Table 12.1 presents relevant data for the years 1960, 1970, and 1980. A number of features of the age and sex distribution are immediately obvious and have important marketing implications, e.g., the post

Table 12.1

Age and sex distribution of population of the United States for the years 1960, 1970, and 1980 (in thousands, except as indicated)

Year, Sex, and Race	Total, all years	Under 5 years	5–9 years	10–14 years	15–19 years	20–24 years	25–29 years	30–34 years	35–39 years	40–44 years	45—49 years	50–54 years	55–59 years	60–64 years	65 years and over	Median age (yr.)
1960, total[1]	179,323	20,321	18,692	16,773	13,219	10,801	10,869	11,949	12,481	11,600	10,879	9,606	8,430	7,142	16,560	29.5
Male	88,331	10,330	9,504	8,524	6,634	5,272	5,333	5,846	6,080	5,676	5,358	4,735	4,127	3,409	7,503	28.7
Female	90,992	9,991	9,187	8,249	6,586	5,528	5,536	6,103	6,402	5,924	5,522	4,871	4,303	3,733	9,056	30.3
1970, total[1][2]	203,235	17,163	19,969	20,804	19,084	16,383	13,486	11,437	11,113	11,988	12,124	11,111	9,979	8,623	19,972	28.0
Male	98,926	8,750	10,175	10,598	9,641	7,925	6,626	5,599	5,416	5,823	5,855	5,351	4,769	4,030	8,367	26.8
Female	104,309	8,413	9,794	10,206	9,443	8,458	6,859	5,838	5,697	6,166	6,269	5,759	5,210	4,593	11,605	29.3
1980, total[1]	226,505	16,344	16,697	18,241	21,162	21,313	19,518	17,558	13,963	11,668	11,088	11,709	11,614	10,086	25,544	30.0
Male	110,032	8,360	8,538	9,315	10,752	10,660	9,703	8,676	6,860	5,708	5,388	5,620	5,481	4,669	10,303	28.8
Female	116,473	7,984	8,159	8,926	10,410	10,652	9,814	8,882	7,103	5,961	5,701	6,089	6,133	5,416	15,242	31.3
Percent																
1960	100.0	11.3	10.4	9.4	7.4	6.0	6.1	6.7	7.0	6.5	6.1	5.4	4.7	4.0	9.2	(x)
1970	100.0	8.4	9.8	10.2	9.4	8.1	6.6	5.6	5.5	5.9	6.0	5.5	4.9	4.2	9.8	(x)
1980, total	100.0	7.2	7.4	8.1	9.3	9.4	8.6	7.8	6.2	5.2	4.9	5.2	5.1	4.5	11.3	(x)
Male	100.0	7.6	7.8	8.5	9.8	9.7	8.8	7.9	6.2	5.2	4.9	5.1	5.0	4.2	9.4	(x)
Female	100.0	6.9	7.0	7.7	8.9	9.1	8.4	7.6	6.1	5.1	4.9	5.2	5.3	4.7	13.1	(x)

X Not applicable.

[1] Includes other races, not shown separately.

[2] The 1970 population count is 203,302,031: the difference of 66,733 is due to errors found after tabulations were completed

Source: U.S. Bureau of the Census, *Census of Population: 1960 and 1970,* vol. 1; and *1980 Census of Population,* Supplementary Reports, series PC 80–51–1.

World War II baby boom, the dramatic fall in the birthrate that began around 1960, the greater longevity of women that results in a very high proportion of the elderly being women.

Sex

Sex is obviously an important segmentation variable for many products. A great many products are almost entirely consumed by only one sex; e.g., lipstick, hunting rifles, cigars, and earrings. Many other products are consumed very unequally by males and females even though both sexes use the product; e.g., beer, baseball equipment, romantic novels. Frequently, there are subtle, but important, differences in values, motives, and attitudes between the sexes that affect the way a specific product is marketed to males and females. For example, automobile advertisements targeted at men are more likely to focus on performance and exterior styling, while advertisements targeted at women are more likely to focus on interior styling and comfort. Finally, it should be noted that the relaxing of sex role stereotypes in recent years has been accompanied by changes in product consumption; e.g., women wearing masculine style clothing, men using hair sprays. It is worth noting, however, that the use of masculine products by females is still generally much more socially acceptable than the use of feminine products by males.

Age

Age is even more important than sex as a segmentation variable. The reason for this is that age is moderately to highly correlated with a large number of other variables which are related to buying behavior. The presence and age of children, home ownership, income, tastes and preferences, health and physical stamina, are all examples of variables that can be systematically, although imperfectly, related to age. Thus, age can serve as an easily measured surrogate for a wide range of more fundamental variables that influence buying behavior.

In considering the effects of age on buyer behavior, a distinction needs to be made between effects associated with age per se and effects associated with specific age cohorts. An age cohort is a group of persons born within a specific and limited time period. Cohort effects arise from the fact that individuals born at approximately the same time share a wide range of experiences that uniquely affect their behavior; e.g., savings habits of persons who experienced the Great Depression and are strongly motivated by the need for economic security. Such cohort effects will not necessarily be repeated by different age cohorts as they pass through specific age categories. We shall discuss cohort effects further in the next chapter on values.

Many effects associated with age will tend to be experienced by all individuals as they pass through specific ages. For example, health and mobility problems of the elderly and the consequent need for specialized living arrangements face all age cohorts eventually. A particularly interesting example of the use of age to segment the market comes from Helena Rubinstein, which has five lines of cosmetics targeted at specific age groups with different skin care needs:

> Bio Clear is the line for teenagers to treat acne. Fresh Cover speaks to the woman in her mid-twenties with the line 'it lets your skin breathe.' Skin Dew is aimed at the woman in her early thirties who is looking for protection from aging.

Ultra Feminine is for the middle aged woman, providing moisturizing, and the latest, Madame Rubinstein, just out this fall, is positioned for the over-fifty woman, offering sebum replacement. (*Product Marketing*, November 1977, p. 32)

Fertility

It is readily apparent from Table 12.1 that the rate of growth of the population has periodically undergone dramatic changes. The changes come from two sources: changes in the birthrate, or fertility rate as it is called by demographers, and net immigration. Immigration will be briefly discussed in the next section. The fertility rate is defined as the average number of children born per woman over her reproductive lifetime. Although historical fertility rates can be calculated, at any given time, the fertility rate can only be estimated because it is defined in terms of future expectations about child bearing.

Predicting the fertility rate has proven to be extremely difficult.[6] Indeed, the baby boom following World War II was largely unexpected. Furthermore, although the long-term trend is clearly down, there have been dramatic short-term fluctuations in the fertility rate. For example, in the past 30 years the fertility rate ranged from a high of 3.8 (in the late 1950s) to a low of 1.7 (in the mid-1970s). As a benchmark, a fertility rate of 2.11 is required for a stable population. Currently, the trend is up (about 1.9) although no one can be certain how long this trend will continue or how high it will go.

Table 12.2 illustrates how even small changes in the fertility rate can have a major impact on the rate of population growth. The relevance of this point is quite critical at present because of the large number of baby boom women who are now in, but not through, their childbearing years. It is quite apparent from existing data that these women are marrying and having children at a later age. However, the total number of children this cohort of baby boom will have is still very much in doubt.

Table 12.2
The effect of fertility rate on population growth

	Fertility Rate			
	1.7		**2.1**	
	number of people	% increase	number of people	% increase
1980	220.7	3.4	222.2	4.1
1985	228.9	3.7	232.9	4.8
1990	236.3	3.2	243.5	4.4
1995	242.0	2.4	252.8	3.8
2000	245.9	1.6	260.4	3.0

Source: U.S. Bureau of the Census, *Current Population Reports,* Series P-25, No. 704, "Projections of the Population of the United States: 1977 to 2050." Washington, D.C.: U.S. Government Printing Office, 1977.

[6]For an interesting review of a number of theories of fertility, see Bagozzi and Van Loo (1978).

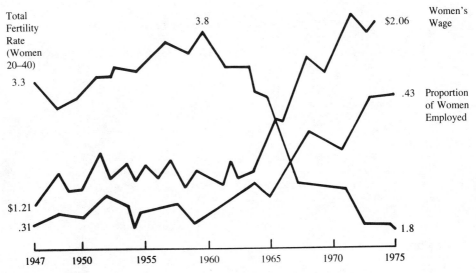

Figure 12.1
Fertility, women's income, and women's employment

*in constant 1964 dollars

Source: W. Butz and M. Ward, "Baby Boom and Baby Bust: A New View." *American Demographics,* 1 (September 1979):14. Reprinted with permission.

Figure 12.1 presents one set of provocative data showing a rather close negative relationship between fertility and both women's wages and work force participation. This suggests that the extremely low fertility rate of recent years may be permanent. On the other hand, the popular media suggests a great interest in childbearing and childrearing on the part of young women, as is readily apparent from any magazine rack. Although only time can tell for certain, my own guess is that the fertility rate will continue to increase modestly as the baby boom generation of women approach their biological time limits on childbearing.

Table 12.3 presents historical data and population projections, by age group, to the year 2000 assuming a moderate fertility rate of 2.11. Note the rather dramatic changes that are expected to occur in certain age groups; e.g., 18–24, as well as the rather substantial increase in the average age of the population. This aging of the population is responsible for a number of important trends, such as the use of older models in advertisements and the rapidly increasing number of products being targeted at older persons; e.g., the Madame Rubinstein line of cosmetics mentioned previously.

Note also in both Table 12.2 and 12.3 that the population will continue to grow even at a fertility rate as low as 1.7. The reason for this is the very high proportion of women currently in their prime childbearing years. Closely related to this is another interesting phenomenon. Although the fertility rate is at a historic low, the number of women having children is close to a historic high. As can be seen from the data in Table 12.4, the number of first births is up, second births are relatively constant, while third and higher order births are down dramatically. What these data suggest is that the sale of products more dependent on the number of families with children than the absolute number of children (e.g., baby furniture and clothes) should hold up very well. In contrast, sales of goods and services that

Table 12.3
Estimates and projections of the population by age: 1950–2000

	Total, all ages (000)	Percent of population in various age categories									Median age
		Under 5	5–13	14–17	18–24	25–34	35–44	45–54	55–64	65 and over	
Estimates											
1950	152,271	10.8	14.7	5.5	10.6	15.8	14.2	11.5	8.8	8.1	30.2
1955	165,931	11.1	16.8	5.6	9.0	14.6	13.8	11.4	8.8	8.8	30.2
1960	180,671	11.3	18.2	6.2	8.9	12.7	13.4	11.4	8.6	9.2	29.4
1965	194,303	10.2	18.4	7.3	10.4	11.6	12.6	11.2	8.8	9.5	28.1
1970	204,878	8.4	17.9	7.8	12.0	12.3	11.3	11.4	9.1	9.8	27.9
1975	213,540	7.4	15.7	7.9	12.9	14.5	10.7	11.1	9.3	10.5	28.8
Projections											
1980	222,159	7.2	13.6	7.1	13.3	16.3	11.6	10.2	9.5	11.2	30.2
1985	232,880	8.1	12.5	6.2	12.0	17.1	13.5	9.6	9.3	11.7	31.5
1990	243,513	8.0	13.4	5.2	10.3	16.9	15.0	10.4	8.5	12.2	32.8
1995	252,750	7.4	14.0	5.6	9.2	15.1	15.9	12.2	8.1	12.4	34.2
2000	260,378	6.9	13.5	6.2	9.5	13.2	15.9	13.8	8.9	12.2	35.5

Source: U.S. Bureau of the Census, *Current Population Reports,* Series P-25, No. 704, "Projections of the Population of the United States: 1977–2050." Washington, D.C.: U.S. Government Printing Office, 1977.

Table 12.4
Births by birth order (thousands)

Year	First Child	Second Child	Third Child	Fourth Child and Over
1945	961	763	446	688
1946	1,291	935	487	699
1947	1,574	1,019	524	700
1948	1,343	1,047	545	701
1949	1,235	1,093	584	737
1950	1,140	1,097	630	764
1951	1,195	1,116	666	826
1952	1,169	1,122	733	889
1953	1,150	1,120	753	942
1954	1,160	1,119	785	1,014
1955	1,138	1,104	800	1,063
1956	1,166	1,109	821	1,122
1957	1,180	1,111	838	1,179
1958	1,140	1,085	826	1,203
1959	1,124	1,066	821	1,232
1960	1,122	1,053	820	1,263
1961	1,132	1,032	813	1,292
1962	1,118	1,002	782	1,265
1963	1,131	987	752	1,228
1964	1,167	965	721	1,175
1965	1,159	911	647	1,043

Table 12.4 continued

Year	First Child	Second Child	Third Child	Fourth Child and Over
1966	1,226	888	585	908
1967	1,238	908	560	815
1968	1,312	919	539	731
1969	1,365	973	560	703
1970	1,450	1,025	579	677
1971	1,396	1,007	544	610
1972	1,329	956	473	500
1973	1,307	956	445	430
1974	1,336	995	442	387
1975	1,337	997	446	364
1976	1,325	1,004	456	347
1977	1,387	1,065	492	324

Source: U.S. Department of Health and Human Services, *Vital Statistics of the United States, vol. 1—Natality."* Washington, D.C.: U.S. Government Printing Office.

depend primarily on the number of children (e.g., baby food and pediatric services) can expect serious erosion of their markets.

Note the rather sharp increase in 1977 for first, second, and third births. Although it is dangerous to project a trend in population growth on the basis of a single year, the upsurge in births is noteworthy in light of the question of the ultimate fertility of baby boom women.

Net Immigration

The second major source of population increase is net immigration. Since the United States has little out migration, net immigration is very close to total immigration. Since much of this immigration is illegal, estimates of total immigration are difficult to make. During the 1970s, legal immigration varied by year but ran in the vicinity of 400,000 per year. Illegal immigration may have tripled this figure. Although the exact numbers are not available, it is clear that immigration accounts for a large portion of population growth. Table 12.5 presents historical immigration data. Table 12.6 presents a detailed comparison of country of origin for the years 1965 and 1978. Both total immigration and place of origin have fluctuated dramatically over time.

Immigration is important to marketers for reasons that go well beyond increasing the size of the total population. First, by virtue of coming from a different cultural environment, immigrants typically have many distinct buying needs and preferences. These are most evident in areas such as food, clothing, and home furnishings. Second, new immigrants tend to cluster geographically; e.g., Cubans in the Miami area, Puerto Ricans in the New York City area, and Mexicans in the Southwest. This geographic clustering greatly facilitates accessing these market segments, a fact especially important to small businesses. Third, many immigrants manage to establish permanent communities that maintain many of the "old country" ways even as they are absorbed into the mainstream of American life. Good examples of such immigrant communities are "Little Havana" in Miami and

Table 12.5
Total immigration to the United States, 1820–1978 (From 1820 to 1867, figures represent alien passengers arrived; from 1868 through 1891 and 1895 through 1897, immigrant aliens arrived; from 1892 through 1894 and 1898 to the present time, immigrant aliens admitted)

Year	Number of persons	Year	Number of persons	Year	Number of persons	Year	Number of persons
1820–1978	48,664,965						
1820	8,385						
1821–1830	143,439	1861–1970	2,314,824	1901–1910	8,795,386	1941–1950	1,035,039
1821	9,127	1861	91,918	1901	487,918	1941	51,776
1822	6,911	1862	91,985	1902	648,743	1942	28,781
1823	6,354	1863	176,282	1903	857,046	1943	23,725
1824	7,912	1864	193,418	1904	812,870	1944	28,551
1825	10,199	1865	248,120	1905	1,026,499	1945	38,119
1826	10,837	1866	318,568	1906	1,100,735	1946	108,721
1827	18,875	1867	315,722	1907	1,285,349	1947	147,292
1828	27,382	1868	138,840	1908	782,870	1948	170,570
1829	22,520	1869	352,768	1909	751,786	1949	188,317
1830	23,322	1870	387,203	1910	1,041,570	1950	249,187
1831–1840	599,125	1871–1880	2,812,191	1911–1920	5,735,811	1951–1960	2,515,479
1831	22,633	1871	321,350	1911	878,587	1951	205,717
1832	60,482	1872	404,806	1912	838,172	1952	265,520
1833	58,640	1873	459,803	1913	1,197,892	1953	170,434
1834	65,365	1874	313,339	1914	1,218,480	1954	208,177
1835	45,374	1875	227,498	1915	326,700	1955	237,790
1836	76,242	1876	169,986	1916	298,826	1956	321,625
1837	79,340	1877	141,857	1917	295,403	1957	326,867
1838	38,914	1878	138,469	1918	110,618	1958	253,265
1839	68,069	1879	177,826	1919	141,132	1959	260,686
1840	84,066	1880	457,257	1920	430,001	1960	265,398

Source: U.S. Department of Justice, *1978 Statistical Yearbook of the Immigration and Naturalization Service.* Washington, D.C.: U.S. Government Printing Office, 1978.

From 1869 to 1976, the data is for fiscal years ended June 30. Prior to fiscal year 1869, the periods covered are as follows: from 1820–1831 and 1843–1849, the years ended on September 30—1843

the many East European groups (e.g., Poles, Czechs) in midwestern cities such as Chicago and Milwaukee.

One aspect of immigration will be pursued in some depth in Chapter 14's discussion of the Hispanic subculture.

Geographic Distribution and Rate of Population Growth

Table 12.7 gives data on population size and rate of growth for major geographic sections of the United States for the years 1970 and 1980. Both size and growth rate vary widely by region. These differences have some important implications for marketers; the broadest of these implications is simply that growth in business opportunities is closely related to population growth. There are also, of course, major differences in buying patterns that are directly related to the imperatives of life in specific climates. The shift of population to the Sunbelt, for example, can be expected to have a positive effect on the sale of air conditioners and a negative effect on the sale of snowblowers.

Table 12.5 continued

Year	Number of persons	Year	Number of persons	Year	Number of persons	Year	Number of persons
1841–1850	*1,713,251*	1881–1890	*5,246,613*	1921–1930	*4,107,209*	1961–1970	*3,321,677*
1841	80,289	1881	669,431	1921	805,228	1961	271,344
1842	104,565	1882	788,992	1922	309,556	1962	283,763
1843	52,496	1883	603,322	1923	522,919	1963	306,260
1844	78,615	1884	518,592	1924	706,896	1964	292,248
1845	114,371	1885	395,346	1925	294,314	1965	296,697
1846	154,416	1886	334,203	1926	304,488	1966	323,040
1847	234,968	1887	490,109	1927	335,175	1967	361,972
1848	226,527	1888	546,889	1928	307,255	1968	454,448
1849	297,024	1889	444,427	1929	279,678	1969	358,579
1850	369,980	1890	455,302	1930	241,700	1970	373,326
1851–1860	*2,598,214*	1891–1900	*3,687,564*	1931–1940	*528,431*		
1851	379,466	1891	560,319	1931	97,139	1971	370,478
1852	371,603	1892	579,663	1932	35,576	1972	384,685
1853	368,645	1893	439,730	1933	23,068	1973	400,063
1854	427,833	1894	285,631	1934	29,470	1974	394,861
1855	200,877	1895	258,536	1935	34,956	1975	386,194
1856	200,436	1896	343,267	1936	36,329	1976	398,613
1857	251,306	1897	230,832	1937	50,244	1976	103,676
1858	123,126	1898	229,299	1938	67,895	1977	462,315
1859	121,282	1899	311,715	1939	82,998	1978	601,442
1860	153,640	1900	448,572	1940	70,736		

covers nine months; from 1832–1842 and 1850–1867, the years ended on December 31—1832 and 1850 covers fifteen months. For 1868, the periods ended on June 30 and covers six months. The transition quarter (TQ) for 1976 covers the three-month period, July–September 1976. Beginning October 1, 1976, the fiscal years ended on September 30.

Regional differences in buying patterns extend well beyond those that can be explained by climatic differences. Indeed, according to a 1975 lifestyle survey by Needham, Harper, and Steers, there are strong regional differences in the use and ownership of many products. Tables 12.8 and 12.9 present selected data from the Needham, Harper and Steers study.

The importance of geographic distribution is not limited to regions of the country. There are also many differences among urban, suburban, and rural residents. Table 12.10 provides illustrative data. Note particularly the relatively large differences for clothes dryers, dishwashers, and home food freezers.

Households

One of the most important demographic trends of the past two decades, and a trend expected to continue through the 1980s, is an increase in the number of households that far exceeds the increase in total population. Among the many reasons for this trend are later age at first marriage, divorce, and the tendency of

Table 12.6
Immigrants admitted by country or region of birth fiscal years ended September 30, 1978 and June 30, 1965

Country of birth	Number		Percent change
	1978	1965	
All countries	601,442	296,697	+ 202.8
Europe	73,198	113,426	− 35.3
Austria	467	1,680	− 72.2
Belgium	439	1,005	− 56.3
Czechoslovakia	744	1,894	− 60.7
Denmark	409	1,384	− 70.4
France	1,844	4,039	− 54.3
Germany	6,739	24,045	− 72.0
Greece	7,035	3,002	+ 134.3
Hungary	941	1,574	− 40.2
Ireland	1,180	5,463	− 78.4
Italy	7,415	10,821	− 31.5
Netherlands	1,153	3,085	− 62.6
Norway	423	2,256	− 81.3
Poland	5,050	8,465	− 40.3
Portugal	10,445	2,005	+ 420.9
Romania	2,037	1,644	+ 23.9
Spain	2,297	2,200	+ 4.4
Sweden	638	2,411	− 73.5
Switzerland	706	1,984	− 64.4
U.S.S.R.	5,161	1,853	+ 178.5
United Kingdom	14,245	27,358	− 47.9
Yugoslavia	2,621	2,818	− 7.0
Other Europe	1,209	2,438	− 50.4
Asia	249,776	20,683	+ 1,107.6
China and Taiwan	21,315	4,057	+ 425.4
Hong Kong	5,158	712	+ 624.4
India	20,753	582	+ 3,465.8
Iran	5,861	804	+ 629.0
Japan	4,010	3,180	+ 26.1
Korea	29,288	2,165	+ 1,252.8
Pakistan	3,876	187	+ 1,972.7
Philippines	37,216	3,130	+ 1,089.0
Thailand	3,574	214	+ 94.0
Vietnam	88,543	226	+ 39,078.3
Other Asia	30,182	5,426	+ 456.2
North America	220,778	126,729	+ 74.2
Canada	16,863	38,327	− 56.0
Mexico	92,367	37,969	+ 143.3
West Indies	91,361	37,583	+ 143.1
Cuba	29,754	19,760	+ 50.6
Dominican Republic	19,458	9,504	+ 104.7
Haiti	6,470	3,609	+ 79.3
Jamaica	19,265	1,837	+ 928.7
Trindad and Tobago	5,973	485	+ 1,131.5
Other West Indies	10,441	2,388	+ 337.2
Other North America	20,187	12,850	+ 57.1

Source: U.S. Department of Justice, *1978 Statistical Yearbook of the Immigration and Naturalization Service.* Washington, D.C.: U.S. Government Printing Office, 1978.

Table 12.6 continued

| Country of birth | Number | | Percent change |
	1978	1965	
South America	41,764	30,962	+ 34.9
Argentina	3,732	6,124	− 39.1
Brazil	1,923	2,869	− 33.0
Colombia	11,032	10,885	+ 1.4
Other South America	25,077	11,084	+ 126.2
Africa	11,524	3,383	+ 240.6
Oceania	4,402	1,512	+ 191.1
Other countries	−	4	−

Table 12.7
Population and rate of population growth for states and major regions of the United States for the years 1970–1980

| Region, division and state | Population | | Percent change April 1, 1970 to April 1, 1980 |
	April 1, 1980 (census)	April 1, 1970[1] (census)	
United States	**226,504,825**	**203,302,031**	**11.4**
Northeast	*49,136,667*	*49,060,514*	*0.2*
New England	12,348,493	11,847,245	4.2
Middle Alantic	36,788,174	37,213,269	−1.1
North Central	*58,853,804*	*56,590,294*	*4.0*
East North Central	41,669,738	40,262,747	3.5
West North Central	17,184,066	16,327,547	5.2
South	*75,349,155*	*62,812,980*	*20.0*
South Atlantic	36,943,139	30,678,826	20.4
East South Central	14,662,882	12,808,077	14.5
West South Central	23,743,134	19,326,077	22.9
West	*43,165,199*	*34,838,243*	*23.9*
Mountain	11,368,330	8,289,901	37.1
Pacific	31,796,869	26,548,342	19.8
New England:			
Maine	1,124,660	993,722	13.2
New Hampshire	920,610	737,681	24.8
Vermont	511,456	444,732	15.0
Massachusetts	5,737,037	5,689,170	0.8
Rhode Island	947,154	949,723	−0.3
Connecticut	3,107,576	3,032,217	2.5
Middle Atlantic:			
New York	17,557,288	18,241,391	−3.8
New Jersey	7,364,158	7,171,112	2.7
Pennsylvania	11,866,728	11,800,766	0.6

[1]Includes revisions to 1970 census counts.

Source: U.S. Bureau of the Census, *1980 Census of Population and Housing,* Advance Reports. PHC 80-v-1 (April 1981): *Current Population Reports,* Series p-25. No. 911 (April 1982).

Table 12.7 continued

Region, division and state	Population April 1, 1980 (census)	Population April 1, 1970[1] (census)	Percent change April 1, 1970 to April 1, 1980
East North Central:			
Ohio	10,797,419	10,657,423	1.3
Indiana	5,490,179	5,195,392	5.7
Illinois	11,418,461	11,110,285	2.8
Michigan	9,258,344	8,881,826	4.2
Wisconsin	4,705,335	4,417,821	6.5
West North Central:			
Minnesota	4,077,148	3,806,103	7.1
Iowa	2,913,387	2,825,368	3.1
Missouri	4,917,444	4,677,623	5.1
North Dakota	652,695	617,792	5.6
South Dakota	690,178	666,257	3.6
Nebraska	1,570,006	1,485,333	5.7
Kansas	2,363,208	2,249,071	5.1
South Atlantic:			
Delaware	595,225	548,104	8.6
Maryland	4,216,446	3,923,897	7.5
District of Columbia	637,651	756,668	−15.7
Virginia	5,346,279	4,651,448	14.9
West Virginia	1,949,644	1,744,237	11.8
North Carolina	5,874,429	5,084,411	15.5
South Carolina	3,119,208	2,590,713	20.4
Georgia	5,464,265	4,587,930	19.1
Florida	9,739,992	6,791,418	43.4
East South Central:			
Kentucky	3,661,433	3,220,711	13.7
Tennessee	4,590,750	3,926,018	16.9
Alabama	3,890,061	3,444,354	12.9
Mississippi	2,520,638	2,216,994	13.7
West South Central:			
Arkansas	2,285,513	1,923,322	18.8
Louisiana	4,203,972	3,644,637	15.3
Oklahoma	3,025,266	2,559,463	18.2
Texas	14,228,383	11,198,655	27.1
Mountain:			
Montana	786,690	694,409	13,3
Idaho	943,935	713,015	32.4
Wyoming	470,816	332,416	41.6
Colorado	2,888,834	2,209,596	30.7
New Mexico	1,299,968	1,017,055	27.8
Arizona	2,717,866	1,775,399	53.1
Utah	1,461,037	1,059,273	37.9
Nevada	799,184	488,738	63.5
Pacific:			
Washington	4,130,163	3,413,244	21.0
Oregon	2,632,663	2,091,533	25.9
California	23,668,562	19,971,069	18.5
Alaska	400,481	302,583	32.4
Hawaii	965,000	769,913	25.3

[1]Includes revisions to 1970 census counts.

Table 12.8
Regional consumption differences

Product	Percentage reporting using once a week or more					
	Total	East	South	Mid-west	West	South-west
Regular chewing gum	26	17	40	30	24	26
Mouthwash	51	48	62	47	40	54
Men's cologne	61	58	72	61	55	71
Shaving cream in a can	55	55	54	55	45	54
Toothpaste	88	89	92	89	90	82
Regular coffee (nondecaffeinated)	62	59	63	58	72	66
Instant coffee (nondecaffeinated)	36	40	33	36	31	24
Hot tea	29	44	14	30	30	24
Iced tea (summer)	69	73	84	69	52	76
Regular soft drinks	53	46	67	53	35	63
Artificial sweetener	18	19	30	19	11	21
Nondairy powdered creamer (Coffee-mate, Cremora, etc.)	23	23	33	23	20	15
Potato chips	35	21	48	41	26	43
Fresh sausage	18	15	30	15	11	22
Bologna	33	30	23	36	31	28
Cottage cheese	32	27	17	41	40	30
Yogurt	5	9	2	4	11	3
Vitamin tablets	35	36	21	36	44	35
Domestic wine	14	15	5	16	28	8
Blended whiskey	11	16	4	13	13	7
Scotch	7	12	5	7	8	2

Source: Needham, Harper & Steers, "1975 Life Style Survey." Reprinted with permission.

Table 12.9
Regional differences in appliance ownership

Product	Percentage owning					
	Total	East	South	Mid-west	West	South-west
Automatic dishwasher	43	44	42	42	56	56
Garbage disposal	28	11	8	35	50	44
Freezer	58	48	68	62	58	60
Water softener	13	6	1	21	14	9
Room air conditioner	41	45	45	42	28	37
Color TV set	77	79	65	83	83	77

Source: Needham, Harper & Steers, "1975 Life Style Survey." Reprinted with permission.

older persons to continue living alone rather than moving in with their children. Table 12.11 presents data on the growth in the number of households and changes in the number of persons per household. The magnitude of this increase is indicated by the fact that while the population increased by 11.4 percent between 1970 and 1980, the number of households increased by 26.7 percent.

The importance of the rate of growth of households lies in the fact that the consumption of many products is more a function of the number of households than of the total population. Large and small appliances, household cleaning products, home furnishings, gardening equipment, and a host of other products are all examples of products whose rate of purchase depends primarily upon the rapidly increasing number of households.

The fact that the number of households has been growing more rapidly than total population means that average household size has been falling. For example, the average household contained 3.33 people in 1960 but only 2.75 people in 1980. In fact, almost one-fourth of all households today contain only one person. This decrease in household size has a number of marketing implications, which range from the need for smaller houses to single serving sizes of prepackaged foods.

Income

Markets are, by definition, a function of both people and money. Although it is true that persons or families with equal incomes often have quite different buying patterns, it is also true that the purchase of many goods and services are closely correlated with income. Figure 12.2 illustrates the differential sensitivity of a wide range of products to increasing income. Note carefully that the minimum increase in any product category is approximately 23 percent and ranges upwards to over 100 percent. In many cases (e.g., floor coverings) these differences reflect primarily the purchase of higher quality and more expensive items rather than a simple increase in quantity.

Table 12.12 presents historical data on median real family income growth (measured in 1979 dollars). Between 1950 and 1970, real family income grew by over 80 percent. Since the early 1970s, however, real income has been relatively constant, increasing by a scant 6.7 percent between 1970 and 1979 and with real income in 1979 being slightly below its peak value in 1973. Whether real income will remain static is a major question at this time.[7] The relatively upbeat forecasts of the mid- and late-1970s have largely been replaced by more pessimistic forecasts. For example, *Sales and Marketing Management* magazine (October 26, 1981) recently forecast a slightly less than 16 percent increase in real income between 1980 and 1990.

The American economic machine clearly stumbled in the 1970s and early 1980s. This economic stagnation, however, occurred at a very high level. In 1979 median family income was $19,961. Mean family income was even higher at $22,376. This discrepancy reflects the fact that the income distribution is positively skewed. Table 12.13 presents detailed data on the distribution of income for both families and households of unrelated individuals for the year 1979. It is immediately apparent from Table 12.13 that the traditional income pyramid has been considerably flattened.

---

[7]The first two years of the 1980s have not been encouraging. The United States has been locked in the worst economic slump of the post-World War II period, with unemployment hovering around 9 percent. Largely because of widespread unemployment median real family income dropped by 5.5 percent in 1980 and dropped another 3.5 percent in 1981. Families that did not experience unemployment, however, experienced small income gains.

Table 12.10
Urban, suburban, and rural differences in ownership of selected durable goods

Durable	Urban	Suburban	Rural
Washing machine	60.0	77.0	77.9
Clothes dryer	39.6	61.6	55.0
Dishwasher	23.5	38.5	21.2
Refrigerator	98.4	99.1	99.2
Home food freezer	20.3	33.9	47.0
Kitchen range	97.8	98.8	98.8
Any TV	95.6	97.7	96.3
Color TV	56.1	69.4	57.0
Room air conditioning	33.1	32.2	30.1
Central air conditioner	17.3	23.4	14.5

*Urban is defined as the central city in a metropolitan area: suburban is the remainder of the metropolitan area and *rural* is a nonmetropolitan area.

Source: H. Axel (ed.), *A Guide to Consumer Markets 1976–1977.* New York: The Conference Board, 1977, p. 192. Reprinted with permission.

Table 12.11
Number of households: 1950–1980 (In millions, except percent as of March. Based on Current Population Survey. See also *Historical Statistics, Colonial Times to 1970,* series A. 335–349)

Size of Household	1950[1,2]	1955[2]	1960[2]	1965[2]	1970[2]	1975	1976	1977	1978	1979	1980
Total	43.5	47.8	52.6	57.3	62.9	71.1	72.9	74.1	76.0	77.3	79.1
1 person	4.7	5.2	6.9	8.6	10.7	13.9	15.0	15.6	16.7	17.2	17.8
Male	1.8	1.7	2.3	2.9	3.5	4.9	5.4	5.5	6.4	6.5	6.8
Female	3.0	3.5	4.6	5.7	7.2	9.0	9.6	9.9	10.4	10.7	11.0
2 persons	12.5	13.6	14.6	16.1	18.1	21.8	22.3	22.8	23.3	23.9	24.7
3 persons	9.8	9.7	9.9	10.2	10.9	12.4	12.5	12.8	13.0	13.4	13.8
4 persons	7.7	9.1	9.3	9.2	9.9	11.1	11.4	11.6	12.0	12.3	12.5
5 persons	4.4	5.3	6.1	6.3	6.5	6.4	6.3	6.3	6.4	6.2	6.0
6 persons	2.2	2.6	3.0	3.3	3.5	3.1	3.0	2.9	2.7	2.6	2.5
7 or more	2.1	2.3	2.9	3.5	3.2	2.5	2.4	2.3	1.9	1.8	1.7
Percentage total:											
1 person	10.9	10.9	13.1	15.0	17.0	19.6	20.6	20.9	22.0	22.2	22.5
2 persons	28.8	28.5	27.8	28.1	28.8	30.6	30.6	30.7	30.7	30.9	31.3
3 persons	22.6	20.4	18.9	17.9	17.3	17.4	17.2	17.3	17.2	17.3	17.5
4 persons	17.8	18.9	17.6	16.1	15.8	15.6	15.7	15.7	15.7	15.9	15.8
5 persons	10.0	11.1	11.5	11.0	10.4	9.0	8.6	8.5	8.4	8.0	7.6
6 persons	5.1	5.4	5.7	5.8	5.6	4.3	4.1	3.9	3.6	3.3	3.2
7 or more	4.9	4.9	5.4	6.1	5.1	3.5	3.2	3.1	2.5	2.3	2.2

[1]Covers related persons only, therefore not strictly comparable with later years.
[2]Data were not revised using population controls from subsequent census.

Source: U.S. Bureau of the Census

Given the well publicized economic problems of the 1970s, it may be surprising that incomes increased at all. Among the many ways in which Americans attempted to maintain their affluent lifestyles during the 1970s, none is more important than the increased participation of women in the labor force. Tables

The Classes of Spending
Percent change in expenditures as household income increases*

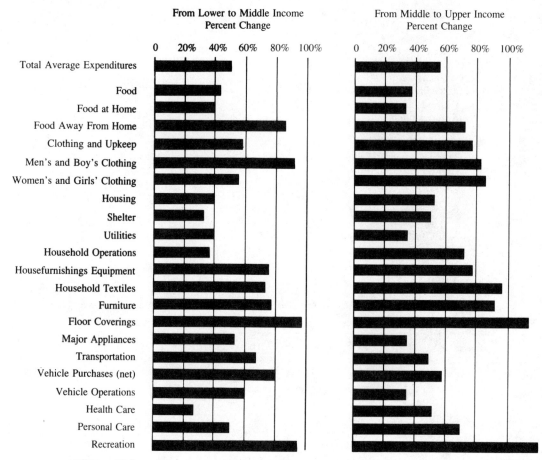

Figure 12.2
Responsiveness of 21 product classes to increases in income

Source: Fabian Linden, "Downstairs, Upstairs." *Across the Board,* XIV (October 1977):59. Reprinted with permission.

 *This chart shows the percent increase in spending for selected goods and services as household income increases. For example, as we move from the middle to the upper income brackets, total household expenditures for consumption rise by somewhat over 55%. Total spending for food, however, by about 35%, while outlays for recreation more than double. As defined in this presentation, "lower income" includes households in the $5,000–$10,000 earning bracket; "middle income" in the $10,000–20,000 bracket; and "upper income" in the $20,000-and-over bracket. All data are based on a survey by the Bureau of Labor Statistics on consumer expenditures in the year 1973.

12.14 and 12.15 present relevant data. Note in Table 12.15 the especially large increase of married women with young children in the labor force. In 1979, the median percentage contribution of working wives to total family income was 26.1 percent. Particularly interesting is the fact that labor force participation of wives is a nonlinear function of husband's income as can be seen in Table 12.16. This data suggests the importance of a wife's earnings to the maintenance of a middle class lifestyle.

The two income family trend has a number of important implications. *Sales and Marketing Management* magazine (October 26, 1981) estimated, for example, that the median income of two income families will increase almost twice as fast (22.4 percent) during the 1980s as the median income of all families (13.4 percent). This trend, when combined with such other trends as the tendency to have fewer children and to begin childbearing at a later age, will tend to produce important market segments with unique characteristics and lifestyles. For example, there is a rapidly growing segment of the market that is young, without children, and very affluent. This segment is a prime target for everything from expensive restaurants to luxury cars. For example, Cadillac has begun to pursue this market segment with an advertising campaign that shows a young, career oriented, upwardly mobile executive entering his Cadillac while the announcer intones "Haven't you promised yourself a Cadillac long enough?" (Gray 1978).

One final point regarding the implications of changing income level and distribution needs to be made. Despite the emphasis on buyers with above average incomes, lower income groups will continue to offer important opportunities to

Table 12.12
Median family income in 1950 to 1979 in constant (1979) dollars and percent change

| Year | Median family income | | Year | Median family income | |
	In current dollars	In 1979 dollars		In current dollars	In 1979 dollars
1979	$19,661	$19,661	Percent Change—Con.		
1978	17,640	19,626			
1977	16,009	19,176	1970 to 1979—Con.		
1976	14,958	19,073	1976 to 1977	*7.0	0.5
1975	13,719	18,502	1975 to 1976	*9.0	*3.1
			1974ʳ to 1975	*6.3	*−2.6
1974ʳ	12,902	18,990	1973 to 1974	*6.5	*−4.0
1974	12,836	18,893	1972 to 1973	*8.4	*2.1
1973	12,051	19,684	1971 to 1972	*8.1	*4.6
1972	11,116	19,287	1970 to 1971	*4.2	−0.1
1971	10,285	18,433			
			1960 to 1970	*75.6	*33.9
1970	9,867	18,444	1965 to 1970	*41.8	*15.2
1965	6,957	16,005	1960 to 1965	*23.8	*16.2
1960	5,620	13,774	1950 to 1960	*69.3	*37.6
1955	4,418	11,976	1955 to 1960	*27.2	*15.0
1950	3,319	10,008	1950 to 1955	*33.1	*19.7
Percent Change			Annual Average Percent Change		
1970 to 1979	*99.3	*6.6	1970 to 1979	*7.9	*0.7
1978 to 1979	*11.5	0.1	1960 to 1970	*5.8	*3.0
1977 to 1978	*10.2	*2.3	1950 to 1960	*5.5	*3.3

ʳBased on revised methodology.

Note: An asterisk (*) preceding percent change indicates statistically significant change at the 95-percent confidence level.

Source: U.S. Bureau of the Census, *Current Population Reports,* Series P-60, No. 129, "Money Income of Families and Persons in the United States: 1979." Washington, D.C.; U.S. Government Printing Office, p. 2.

Table 12.13
Income distribution for families and unrelated individuals for the year 1979 (families and unrelated individuals as of March 1980)

Total money income	Families and unrelated individuals		Families		Unrelated individuals	
	Number (thousands)	Percent distribution	Number (thousands)	Percent distribution	Number (thousands)	Percent distribution
Total	84,011	100.0	58,426	100.0	25,585	100.0
Under $2,500	4,101	4.9	1,266	2.2	2,835	11.1
$2,500 to $4,999	8,709	10.4	2,782	4.8	5,927	23.2
$5,000 to $7,499	7,777	9.3	3,771	6.5	4,006	15.7
$7,500 to $9,999	7,154	8.5	4,127	7.1	3,027	11.8
$10,000 to $12,499	7,746	9.2	4,860	8.3	2,886	11.3
$12,500 to $14,999	5,964	7.1	4,257	7.3	1,707	6.7
$15,000 to $17,499	6,063	7.2	4,414	7.6	1,649	6.4
$17,500 to $19,999	5,297	6.3	4,322	7.4	975	3.8
$20,000 to $22,499	5,371	6.4	4,542	7.8	829	3.2
$22,500 to $24,999	4,331	5.2	3,846	6.6	486	1.9
$25,000 to $27,499	4,076	4.9	3,710	6.3	365	1.4
$27,500 to $29,999	3,205	3.8	2,999	5.1	206	0.8
$30,000 to $32,499	2,802	3.3	2,636	4.5	166	0.6
$32,500 to $34,999	1,941	2.3	1,865	3.2	75	0.3
$35,000 to $37,499	1,767	2.1	1,683	2.9	84	0.3
$37,500 to $39,999	1,228	1.5	1,164	2.0	64	0.3
$40,000 to $44,999	2,046	2.4	1,954	3.3	92	0.4
$45,000 to $49,999	1,255	1.5	1,199	2.1	56	0.2
$50,000 to $59,999	1,422	1.7	1,366	2.3	56	0.2
$60,000 to $74,999	922	1.1	882	1.5	40	0.2
$75,000 and over	836	1.0	781	1.3	55	0.2
Median income	$15,229	(x)	$19,661	(x)	$7,521	(x)
Standard error	$78	(x)	$92	(x)	$79	(x)
Mean income	$18,546	(x)	$22,376	(x)	$9,798	(x)
Standard error	$71	(x)	$90	(x)	$75	(x)

(x) Not applicable.

Source: U.S. Bureau of the Census, *Current Population Reports,* Series P-60, No. 129, "Money Income of Families and Persons in the United States: 1979." Washington, D.C.: U.S. Government Printing Office, p.2.

Table 12.14

Marital status of women in the civilian labor force: 1940–1980

[Persons 14 year old and over through 1965; 16 years old and over thereafter. As of March except as indicated. Prior to 1960, excludes Alaska and Hawaii. Figures for 1940 based on complete census revised for compatability with intercensal series. Later data based on Current Population Survey, see text, p. 1. Beginning 1955, figures not strictly comparable with previous years as a result of introduction into estimating procedure of 1950 census data through 1960, and of 1960 census data beginning 1965. See also *Historical Statistics Colonial Times to 1970*, series D 49–62]

Year	Female Labor Force (1,000)					Percent Distribution Female Labor Force			Female Labor Force as Percent of Female Population				
	Total	Single	Married total	Married, husband present	Widowed or divorced	Single	Married	Widowed or divorced	Total	Single	Married total	Married, husband present	Widowed or divorced
1940	13,840	6,710	5,040	[1]4,200	2,090	48.5	36.4	15.1	27.4	48.1	16.7	14.7	32.0
1944[1]	18,449	7,542	8,433	6,226	2,474	40.9	45.7	13.4	35.0	58.6	25.6	21.7	35.7
1947[1]	16,323	8,181	7,545	6,676	2,597	37.9	46.2	15.9	29.8	51.2	21.4	20.0	34.6
1950	17,795	5,621	9,273	8,550	2,901	31.6	52.1	16.3	31.4	50.5	24.8	23.8	36.0
1955[1]	20,154	5,087	11,839	10,423	3,227	25.2	58.7	16.0	33.5	46.4	29.4	27.7	36.0
1960	22,519	5,401	13,485	12,253	3,629	24.0	59.9	16.1	34.8	44.1	31.7	30.5	37.1
1965	25,952	5,912	16,154	14,708	3,886	22.8	62.2	15.0	36.7	40.5	35.7	34.7	35.7
1968	28,778	6,358	18,234	16,821	4,187	22.1	63.4	14.6	40.7	51.3	39.1	38.3	35.8
1969	29,898	6,501	19,100	17,595	4,297	21.7	63.9	14.4	41.6	51.2	40.4	39.6	35.8
1970	31,233	6,965	19,799	18,377	4,469	22.3	63.4	14.3	42.6	53.0	41.4	40.8	36.2
1971	31,681	7,187	19,986	18,530	4,508	22.7	63.1	14.2	42.5	52.7	41.4	40.8	35.7
1972	32,939	7,477	20,749	19,249	4,713	22.7	63.0	14.3	43.6	54.9	42.1	41.5	37.2
1973	33,904	7,739	21,343	19,821	4,822	22.8	63.0	14.2	44.1	55.8	42.8	42.2	36.7
1974	35,320	8,230	22,009	20,367	5,081	23.3	62.3	14.4	45.2	57.2	43.8	43.0	37.8
1975	36,496	8,433	22,796	21,143	5,266	23.1	62.5	14.4	45.9	56.8	45.0	44.4	37.7
1976	37,817	9,083	23,355	21,544	5,379	24.0	61.8	14.2	46.8	58.9	45.8	45.0	37.3
1977	39,374	9,470	24,092	22,377	5,812	24.1	61.3	14.8	48.0	58.9	47.1	46.6	39.0
1978	40,971	10,222	24,591	22,789	6,152	24.9	60.0	15.0	49.1	60.5	48.1	47.6	40.0
1979	42,971	11,006	25,640	23,832	6,325	25.6	59.7	14.7	50.7	62.7	50.0	49.4	40.0
1980	43,963	10,911	26,347	24,466	6,706	24.8	59.9	15.3	51.1	61.2	50.7	50.2	41.1

[1] As of April

Source: U.S. Bureau of the Census, *Current Population Reports*, Series P-50 and U.S. Bureau of Labor Statistics, *Special Labor Force Reports*. Washington, D.C.: U.S. Government Printing Office.

Table 12.15
Marital status of women in labor force: 1960–1980 (in millions, except rate. As of March. Based on Current Population Survey)

Item	In Labor Force				Participation Rate[1]				Unemployment Rate[2]			
	1960	1970	1975	1980	1960	1970	1975	1980	1960	1970	1975	1980
Married, husband present, total	12.3	18.4	21.1	24.5	30.5	40.8	44.4	50.2	5.4	4.8	8.5	5.2
No children under 18	5.7	8.2	9.7	11.0	34.7	42.2	43.9	46.1	4.8	3.2	7.0	4.5
Children 6–17 yr. only	4.1	6.3	7.0	8.4	39.0	49.2	52.3	61.8	4.9	4.7	7.2	4.3
Children under 6 yr.	2.5	3.9	4.4	5.1	18.6	30.3	36.6	45.0	7.8	7.8	13.9	8.0
Separated, total	(NA)	1.4	1.6	1.9	(NA)	52.3	54.8	59.4	(NA)	6.9	14.8	9.7
No children under 18	(NA)	.7	.7	.9	(NA)	52.3	56.4	58.7	(NA)	4.2	10.4	8.2
Children 6–17 yr. only	(NA)	.4	.5	.6	(NA)	60.6	59.0	66.4	(NA)	5.9	12.9	10.3
Children under 6 yr.	(NA)	.3	.4	.4	(NA)	45.4	49.1	51.8	(NA)	13.3	23.7	12.0
Divorced, total	(NA)	1.9	2.9	4.3	(NA)	70.9	72.1	74.5	(NA)	5.2	8.4	6.3
No children under 18	(NA)	1.1	1.5	2.3	(NA)	67.7	69.9	71.4	(NA)	4.7	7.2	4.5
Children 6–17 yr. only	(NA)	.6	.9	1.6	(NA)	82.4	80.1	82.3	(NA)	6.5	9.1	6.5
Children under 6 yr.	(NA)	.3	.4	.5	(NA)	63.3	65.6	68.0	(NA)	5.2	10.4	13.2

NA   Not available.
[1]Percent of women in each specific category in the labor force.
[2]Unemployed as a percent of civilian labor force in specified group.

Source: U.S. Bureau of Labor Statistics, *Special Labor Force Reports.* Washington, D.C.; U.S. Government Printing Office.

Table 12.16
Labor force participation of wives by income of husband in 1979

Income of Husband	Labor Participation Rates of Wives
<3,000	41.2%
3,000 < 5,000	35.5
5,000 < 7,000	38.8
7,000 < 10,000	49.3
10,000 < 13,000	55.3
13,000 < 15,000	58.4
15,000 < 20,000	56.7
20,000 < 25,000	51.1
25,000 < 35,000	47.5
35,000 < 50,000	39.5
> 50,000	32.1

Source: U.S. Bureau of Labor Statistics, *Marital and Family Characteristics of the Labor Force,* March 1979, Special Labor Force Report 237. Washington, D.C.: U.S. Government Printing Office.

marketers. Although their average incomes are low, the total purchasing power of low income buyers is large. More important, the low income segment of the market has special characteristics and special needs. Specifically, minorities, the elderly, and female headed households are disproportionately represented among

Table 12.17
Educational attainment of individuals age 25 and over: 1965–1980

	1965	1970	1975	1980	1985
Educational attainment	100.0%	100.0%	100.0%	100.0%	100.0%
Elementary or less	33.0	27.8	21.9	18.3	14.4
Some high school	18.0	17.0	15.6	16.3	15.4
High school graduate	30.7	34.0	36.2	37.9	38.9
Some college	8.8	10.3	12.4	12.5	13.7
College graduate	9.4	11.1	13.9	15.0	17.5

Source: Fabian Linden, "From Here to 1985." *Across the Board,* XIV (June): 24. Reprinted with permission.

the lowest income groups. Among the many special needs of these groups are low cost medial care, easily digestible foods, and low cost and readily accessible child day care facilities.

Education

As Table 12.17 shows, the number of years of formal education of Americans increased substantially in recent years. Associated with increased education are more professional and white-collar employment, higher income, and changing tastes and preferences. As we know, better educated, higher income buyers tend to be more sophisticated shoppers, who demand and get better value for their money. They also are more interested in a wide range of products such as art, classical music, literature, and foreign travel.

Despite this general increase, a large number of Americans have too little education to function effectively in a complex society. As Table 12.17 indicates, in 1985 it is estimated that approximately 30 percent of adults over 25 years of age will not have a high school education. Indeed, according to a recent MacNeil-Lehrer report some 25-million Americans are totally illiterate while another 35-million are unable to read a newspaper article. These tasks are probably no more difficult than reading a product test report, an ingredients list, or a product warranty, and suggest the magnitude of the problems faced both by undereducated buyers and by sellers who attempt to communicate effectively with such buyers.

Complex Measures

So far, this chapter has discussed a number of demographic and socioeconomic variables individually. It is possible to build from these variables more complex measures that provide additional insights into behavior of buyers. The most familiar examples of such complex measures are social class—which is constructed from variables such as occupation, education, *source* of income, and place of residence—and the family life cycle—which is constructed from variables such as age, marital status, and presence and age of children. Since social class and the family life cycle are discussed in later chapters, they will not be pursued further here. The purpose here is simply to point out that there is frequently much merit in the construction of complex measures of individual differences.

SUMMARY

This chapter discussed some of the marketing implications of a number of demographic and socioeconomic variables. The review has been highly selective and it must be emphasized that the surface of available demographic and socioeconomic data has barely been scratched. Furthermore, much of this data is available in great detail for very small geographic areas. For example, the 1979 Census Bureau report "Money Income of Families and Persons in the United States" is 321 pages of extremely detailed statistics on the income of persons classified in a large number of different ways. Recently, the Bureau of the Census began publishing a very useful comprehensive "Subject Index to Current Population Reports" (Series P-23).

Perhaps the most appropriate note to conclude this chapter is one with which Part V began. Demographic variables rarely cause a buyer to buy a specific brand and frequently do not even require purchase from any specific product class. Rather, these variables represent forces that impel the individual in certain directions and tend to open certain options and to close others. Knowledge of demographic and socioeconomic differences among buyers provides the marketer a firmer basis upon which to build total marketing strategies tailored to the specific requirements of each segment of the market, thereby increasing the likelihood of success in the marketplace.

Individual Differences: Values, Personality, and Lifestyles

13

This chapter continues the discussion of the marketing implications of individual differences among buyers by focusing on the more subjective, but no less important, differences in values, personality, and lifestyles among buyers.

VALUES

Demographic and socioeconomic variables are clearly important both for explaining buyer behavior and for segmenting markets. Frequently, however, these variables provide a shallow explanation. A much richer and deeper understanding of buyer behavior can be obtained by examining the values buyers hold and how these values affect behavior. Americans, for example, are very materialistic and frequently use material objects to express who and what they are.

Values are clearly important to buyer behavior.[1] It is, therefore, surprising how little marketing research has been devoted to the explicit study of values and their implications for buyer behavior. As Henry notes "The notion of a causal relationship (between values and buyer behavior) seems to be based on intuitive assumptions not supported to any great extent by empirical evidence" (1976, p. 121). Despite this lack of research, the topic of values is of sufficient importance that it demands our attention even if that attention must be somewhat speculative. Fortunately, there are enough positive results to convince us of the importance of values to buyer behavior. Furthermore, although their research is not aimed at rigorously establishing the existence of a causal relationship between values and buyer behavior, some consulting firms do conduct value research. The marketing research firm of Yankelovich, Skelly and White is particularly active in such research. At the end of this section, a general value-based segmentation scheme developed by SRI International will be discussed.

The Concept of Values

According to Rokeach (1968, p.124), the concept of values has three distinct meanings. First, value is used by some writers as a sociological concept whereby a natural object is given a socially defined meaning. Second, value is used by others synonymously with attitude. Third, and this includes Rokeach, values are conceived of as similar to attitudes but more basic and stable. Furthermore, values frequently underlie and support more specific attitudes.

As Rokeach is one of the principle researchers of values and as his ideas have been very influential, it is worth quoting at length his conception of what constitutes a value.

> I consider a value to be a type of belief, centrally located within one's total belief system, about how one ought or ought not to behave, or about some end-state of existence worth or not worth attaining. Values are thus abstract ideals, positive or negative, not tied to any specific attitude object or situation, representing a person's beliefs about ideal modes of conduct and ideal terminal goals—what Lovejoy calls generalized adjectival and terminal values. Some exam-

---

[1]A recent, and excellent, source of information on value research is the volume edited by Rokeach (1979). In addition to discussions of basic concepts, this book has specific papers on topics such as values and smoking behavior and the effects of the mass media on values.

ples of ideal modes of conduct are to seek truth and beauty, to be clean and orderly, to behave with sincerity, justice, reason, compassion, humility, respect, honor, and loyalty. Some examples of ideal goals or end-states are security, happiness, freedom, equality, ecstasy, fame, power, and states of grace and salvation. A person's values, like all beliefs, may be consciously conceived or unconsciously held, and must be inferred from what a person says or does.

An adult probably has tens or hundreds of thousands of beliefs, thousands of attitudes, but only dozens of values. A *value system* is a hierarchial organization—a rank ordering—of ideals or values in terms of importance. To one person truth, beauty, and freedom may be at the top of the list, and thrift, order, and cleanliness at the bottom; to another person, the order may be reversed . . . (p. 124, emphasis in original).

In the following discussion, the term value will be used in Rokeach's preferred sense. In considering the relevance of values to buyer behavior, it is important to keep certain points in mind. First, values are broad, fundamental beliefs that are not tied to specific situations or objects, although they frequently support such specific beliefs. Second, different individuals frequently share a common, dominant, or *core* set of values but attach different priorities to those values and/or must seek to satisfy their values in different environments with different available resources. (Sturdivant 1973). These differences among groups can give rise to far more differences in buying behavior than can be accounted for solely by values that are unique to each group. Third, and closely related to the second point, since core values are widely shared, these values are worth studying, even though further analysis will typically be required to determine precisely how these values will be expressed in the purchasing behavior of specific groups of buyers.

The Relevance of Values to Buyer Behavior

A number of buyer behavior phenomena closely related to values have already been discussed; two of the most important of which were the value-expressive function of attitudes and the image congruence explanation for many brand and store choice decisions. In fact, although typically discussed separately and employed somewhat differently in research, these two concepts are closely related by their emphasis on how buyers attempt to satisfy their values through the purchase of selected goods and services.

Howard (1977, pp. 92–95) suggested that values are the underlying basis for the choice criteria that guide choice behavior. Howard's analysis requires a distinction to be made between what Rokeach (1973) calls terminal values and instrumental values. Table 13.1 lists eighteen terminal and eighteen instrumental values that Rokeach systematically developed. Terminal values are related to states of being while instrumental values are related to doing. Together, terminal and instrumental values form a type of means-end chain similar to that discussed in conjunction with multiattribute models of attitude.

Howard illustrates the relationships among terminal and instrumental values and choice criteria with the following example. A buyer may have as terminal values a comfortable life and family security. One way to achieve these end-states is by developing the instrumental value of being logical in making purchasing decisions. Thus, when buying gasoline this buyer might use the choice criterion of mileage, since this is a logical criterion that contributes to the ultimately desired end-states of a comfortable life and family security.

Table 13.1
Terminal and instrumental values

Terminal value	r*	Instrumental value	r
A comfortable life (a prosperous life)	.70	Ambitious (hard-working, aspiring)	.70
An exciting life (a stimulating, active life)	.73	Broadminded (open-minded)	.57
A sense of accomplishment (lasting contribution)	.51	Capable (competent, effective)	.51
A world at peace (free of war and conflict)	.67	Cheerful (lighthearted, joyful)	.65
A world of beauty (beauty of nature and the arts)	.66	Clean (neat, tidy)	.66
Equality (brotherhood, equal opportunity for all)	.71	Courageous (standing up for your beliefs)	.52
Family security (taking care of loved ones)	.64	Forgiving (willing to pardon others)	.62
Freedom (independence, free choice)	.61	Helpful (working for the welfare of others)	.66
Happiness (contentedness)	.62	Honest (sincere, truthful)	.62
Inner harmony (freedom from inner conflict)	.65	Imaginative (daring, creative)	.69
Mature love (sexual and spiritual intimacy)	.68	Independent (self-reliant, self-sufficient)	.60
National security (protection from attack)	.67	Intellectual (intelligent, reflective)	.67
Pleasure (an enjoyable, leisurely life)	.57	Logical (consistent, rational)	.57
Salvation (saved, eternal life)	.88	Loving (affectionate, tender)	.65
Self-respect (self-esteem)	.58	Obedient (dutiful, respectful)	.53
Social recognition (respect, admiration)	.65	Polite (courteous, well-mannered)	.53
True friendship (close companionship)	.59	Responsible (dependable, reliable)	.45
Wisdom (a mature understanding of life)	.60	Self-controlled (restrained, self-disciplined)	.52

*Numbers are test-retest correlation coefficients.

Source: Reprinted with permission of Macmillan Publishing Company from *The Nature of Human Values* by Milton Rokeach. Copyright © 1973 by The Free Press, a Division of Macmillan Publishing Company.

A particularly interesting use of the distinction between terminal and instrumental values was suggested by Howard (1977, pp. 96–102). Specifically, he proposed a two levels of choice model, in which terminal values are first used to select among product classes and then instrumental values are used to choose among brands. Howard cited an unpublished dissertation by Boote (1975), which investigated brand choice for nine major household appliances, to support this model.

Despite the need for further development and testing this two levels of choice model is potentially very useful, because in a high level economy many of the most important and difficult choices are made among product classes rather than among brands of a specific product class. For example, a family might be attempting to select from among a set of product classes that includes a new car, recarpeting the house, a European vacation, a new washer and dryer, and saving for their child's college education, only a portion of which are feasible at any given time.

Finally, two points need to be made regarding the specificity of the relationship between values and buyer behavior. First, there are typically many ways in which a value may be satisfied. This, of course, is a restatement of the point made in the last chapter that individual difference variables rarely require the purchase of any specific brand or even product class. Second, the meaning of a value in a specific buying situation may be quite different for buyers in different circumstances. Both points are well illustrated in a study by Henry (1976). Using a scale developed by Kluckhohn and Strodtbeck (1961), Henry related the four value dimensions presented in Table 13.2 to type, but not brand, of automobile owned (i.e., full size, intermediate, compact, subcompact, and sports). Henry also found that the exact relationship between values and type of automobile owned depended upon the *number* of automobiles owned.

Core American Values

Values widely shared by members of a culture are referred to as dominant or core values. Core values are important to marketers for three reasons. First, products aimed at the mass market of necessity must appeal to core values. Second, core values suggest promotional themes for existing products and frequently suggest entirely new products. Third, even people from different cultural backgrounds will typically be continuously exposed to and influenced by the core values of a culture. This is especially likely to be true in countries, such as the United States, with highly developed mass communication systems. In fact, some researchers have suggested that the importance of differences in value systems among social groups is considerably exaggerated and that differences in buying behavior among groups are as much or more a reflection of the exigencies of their condition; e.g., low income, low education, urban location (cf., Sturdivant 1973). For example, the options for expressing a status value are quite different for high and low income buyers.

Table 13.2
Kluckhorn and Strodtbeck values orientation matrix

Value dimension	Alternatives		
Man's relation to nature	Subjugated by	In harmony with	Mastery over
Time dimension	Past	Present	Future
Personal activity	Being	Being-in-becoming	Doing
Man's relation to others	Lineal	Collateral	Individualistic

Source: Walter A. Henry "Cultural Values Do Correlate with Consumer Behavior." *Journal of Marketing Research*, 13 (May 1976): 122. Reprinted with the kind permission of the American Marketing Association.

Schiffman and Kanuk (1978, p. 359) constructed a list of core American values that are especially relevant for buyer behavior. Their list, which includes examples of the relevance of each value to buyer behavior, is presented in Table 13.3. Examine the list closely. Note that Schiffman and Kanuk's suggestions regarding relevance are *not* brand, or even product class, specific.

Table 13.3
American core values

Value	General features	Relevance to consumer behavior
Achievement and success	Hard work is good; success flows from hard work	Acts as a justification for acquisition of goods ("You deserve it")
Activity	Keeping busy is healthy and natural	Stimulates interest in products that save time and enhance leisure-time activities
Efficiency and practicality	Admiration of things that solve problems (e.g., save time and effort)	Stimulates purchase of products that function well and save time
Progress	People can improve themselves; tomorrow should be better	Stimulates desire for new products that fulfill unsatisfied needs; acceptance of products that claim to be "new" or "improved"
Material comfort	"The good life"	Fosters acceptance of convenience and luxury products that make life more enjoyable
Individualism	Being one's self (e.g., self-reliance, self-interest, and self-esteem)	Stimulates acceptance of customized or unique products that enable a person to "express his own personality"
Freedom	Freedom of choice	Fosters interest in wide product lines and differentiated products
External conformity	Uniformity of observable behavior; desire to be accepted	Stimulates interest in products that are used or owned by others in the same social group
Humanitarianism	Caring for others, particularly the underdog	Stimulates patronage of firms that compete with market leaders.
Youthfulness	A state of mind that stresses being young at heart or appearing young	Stimulates acceptance of products that provide the illusion of maintaining or fostering youth

Source: Leon G. Schiffman, Leslie Lazur Kanuk, CONSUMER BEHAVIOR, 2nd ed., © 1983, p. 420. Reprinted by permission of Prentice-Hall, Inc., Englewood Cliffs, N.J.

The core value achievement and success will be used to illustrate how a marketer might use core values in building a marketing program. First, this core value can be satisfied by many product classes; e.g., cars, houses, clothing. Second, although most individuals will tend to acknowledge achievement and success as a core value, people will vary markedly in the priority they attach to this particular value. Thus, the marketer must identify those individuals who attach a high priority to achievement and success *and* who believe, or can be convinced to believe, that the seller's product expresses that particular value. Third, the marketer must determine whether the purchase of the product is feasible for the identified segment.

To return to an earlier example, several years ago Cadillac recognized the emergence of a segment of the market that was young, affluent, career oriented, and valued highly achievement and success. They appealed to this segment with a series of promotions built around the theme "Haven't you promised yourself a Cadillac long enough?" Recently, Cadillac introduced a new, fuel efficient, lower priced model, the Cimarron, in a further attempt to develop this young, affluent market segment. The Cimarron, with a 1983 list price of just over $12,000, is a far more feasible choice for this market segment than other models of Cadillac, which generally carry a $20,000+ pricetag.

Sources of Values and Value Changes

The sources of values are many. Family, religion, schools, the mass media, peers, and major life experiences such as wars, depressions, marriage, and the birth of children are all sources of values. Changes in values are produced by forces that affect the sources of values. Within American society perhaps the most fundamental of these forces is technology. Indeed, that the pace of technology has been rapidly changing the structure and values of American society, both positively and negatively, has been part of the conventional wisdom at least since the publication of Alvin Toffler's *Future Shock* (1970).

There is probably no better example of how changing technology has affected society than the electronic broadcast media, especially television (cf., Comstock 1978). Television, in particular, has diffused the core values of society to all social groups and, perhaps just as important, exposed all Americans to alternative value systems. The effect of this diffusion has been a greater tendency of minority groups to pursue, if not fully accept, the core values of the mainstream American culture and a simultaneous tendency for members of the mainstream to be more cognizant of and influenced by alternative value systems.

One of the most dramatic examples of how television can reshape institutions and alter values is the nonviolent civil rights marches of the late 1950s and early 1960s. The televised news coverage of these marches with their frequent graphic pictures of passive marchers being hosed, beaten with clubs, and attacked by guard dogs was partially responsible for a major change in public attitudes toward segregation. The civil rights movement, however, produced more than some fundamental institutional changes in the treatment of Blacks. Basic values, especially for younger Americans, shifted considerably away from materialism, competition, and judging persons by performance standards toward more nonmaterialistic, cooperative, and egalitarian values.

Perhaps the most important fact regarding television is that it has become a pervasive aspect of modern life. Indeed, it is difficult for persons born after 1950 to appreciate what fundamental *changes* in American life have been produced by television. Television entertains us, informs us, even babysits our children. Indeed, many children now spend as much or more time in front of the TV as they do in school. This has given rise to increasing concern that television is becoming a major source of childrens' values. This concern is especially evident in the debates regarding violence on television (cf., Comstock 1978) and the promotion of "junk foods" on television programs aimed at children (cf., FTC Staff Report on Television Advertising to Children, February 1978).

Changing American Values

American values have and are continuing to undergo major changes. There are two ways in which to attempt to systematically assess these changes: first, by looking across generations; second, by attempting to assess how forces that are believed to affect values are changing and predict the consequent changes in values over time. Both methods are difficult to implement, speculative, and frequently very productive in their insights into how markets are changing and for developing new marketing strategies to successfully serve these changing markets.

When looking across generations, we are to some extent looking across time and seeing the effects of the unique aspects of different time periods. We are also, of course, observing differences attributable to the aging process itself and so must be careful not to confuse the two sources of differences. Despite this caveat there are sufficient differences among generations that different labels are frequently applied to each generation. Engel and Blackwell (1982, pp. 202–205), for example, divide buyers into three generational cohorts that experienced quite different environments during their formative years.

The first cohort, pre-World War II consumers, spent their formative years during the Great Depression and experienced the continued traumas and deprivations of WW II as young adults. As a result this generation formed strong and deeply held values toward "job security, patriotism, and the acquisition of material goods" (Engel and Blackwell 1982, p. 203).

The second cohort, the interpersonal generation of the 1950s and 1960s, spent their formative years during one of the world's greatest economic expansions; a period in which the United States became a culture of mass affluence and the "poor" became a distinct minority. This affluence gave rise to a de-emphasis on material concerns and, especially when coupled with the civil rights movement, which was itself partially a result of the increasing affluence that largely bypassed Black Americans, led to a heightened interpersonal awareness and concern.

The third cohort, somewhat derisively labeled the Me generation by Engel and Blackwell and many other writers, spent their formative years during the Vietnam War and the stalling of the American economic miracle that began in the early 1970s. The values of this generation increasingly center around self. Everything from the election of President Reagan and the consequent de-emphasis on social spending to the increasing prominence of businesses such as health spas, personal counseling, and wilderness travel to the rapidly increasing divorce rate have been attributed to the emphasis on self of the Me generation.

A study by Vinson and Munson (1976) illustrates the effects of value differences among generations on buyer behavior. Using Rokeach's list of terminal and instrumental values, previously displayed in Table 13.1, and importance ratings of twenty automobile attributes, Vinson and Munson found highly significant differences between students and their parents in the profiles of both their values and automobile attribute importance ratings. Students emphasized aesthetic and socially observable attributes such as styling, prestige, and luxury interior, while parents emphasized functional attributes such as quality of warranty, service required, and handling. Vinson and Munson note that "The mean importance ratings of the automobile attributes ... appear logically consistent with the value data" (p. 316).[2]

Forecasts of future values typically involve an assessment of past and present values, an examination of historical trends in value changes, an analysis of how variables believed to affect values are changing, and an analysis of how these forces will combine to affect future values. Of course, a number of variables that are likely to affect the values of Americans have already been discussed. More working women, more women pursuing careers rather than temporary jobs, smaller families, rising affluence, increasingly sophisticated communications technology, increasing size and complexity of society, and the substantial distrust of big business and big government can all be expected to affect values.

Hawkins, Coney, and Best (1980, pp. 96–105) provided a frankly speculative but nevertheless useful analysis of changing American values. Their list of core values includes eighteen values divided into three major categories. Each is assessed as to its traditional, current, and emerging position.

The first category of values is labeled control values. "Control refers to the extent to which a person feels unrestricted in his or her choices of actions" (Hawkins, Coney, and Best 1980, p.98). In addition to changes in specific directions such as toward a more collective sense of social responsibility and a greater emphasis and respect for age, there is a major trend toward a greater diversity in actions or roles that are socially acceptable. For example, being "older" no longer has the stigma once associated with it. This has opened a wide range of market opportunities such as cosmetics that are frankly addressed to "mature" women and living communities that exclude "young" people. Similarly, the movement away from an almost totally masculine value orientation has made it permissable and often desirable to promote products with advertisements showing men doing traditionally feminine activities; e.g., changing an infant, doing housework, grocery shopping.

Directional values "help to determine which way people will go in life" (Hawkins, Coney, and Best 1980, p. 100). Among the factors which are largely responsible for changes in directional values are affluence, better education, an increasingly complex society that makes the well-being of individuals increasingly interdependent, and an increasing recognition of our resource limits and the need to protect our natural environment. Increasing leisure and an emphasis on a more active, healthful life will affect not only the amount but the type of activities that fill Americans' leisure time. Particularly likely to benefit from these trends are

---

[2]The few marketing studies of values have been correlational. That is, they show concurrent differences in values and buyer behavior among nonexperimentally defined subject groups. Although difficult, especially in a buyer behavior context, it is possible to systematically manipulate values through a process of self-confrontation which leads to self-dissatisfaction and value change (cf., Rokeach 1979).

sporting equipment and clothing, "how to" books, "do-it-yourself" stores, and firms providing active experiences, such as white water canoeing. The increasing recognition and admiration of nature will have impact on a wide range of products designed to use natural resources effectively and to create a natural living environment. The interest in biodegradable products and packaging, natural foods, and rural living can all be partially attributed to an increasing admiration of nature.

Finally, feeling values relate to the "relative degree of pleasure or pleasantness evoked from a situation or activity" (Hawkins, Coney, and Best 1980, p. 103). The authors indicate that no clear trends are evident regarding this category of values. Americans are expected to remain child oriented, demand immediate gratification of needs, continue to emphasize sensual gratification, appreciate humor, continue to move away from a romantic emphasis on heroes and underdogs, and continue to value highly personal cleanliness. Each of these values has important marketing implications. As they are relatively straightforward and as relevant examples have previously been given, it will be left to the reader to supply examples of the marketing implications of feeling values.

A General Value-Based Market Segmentation System

So far the value systems presented have either been general value systems developed outside the context of buyer behavior, e.g., Rokeach's value system, or value systems applied to a specific product class, e.g., Boote (1975), Henry (1976). Recently, as part of SRI International's Values and Lifestyles Program, Mitchell (1978) developed a general nine segment consumer typology based directly on consumer values. The typology includes the values and lifestyles, demographics, buying patterns, and population and buying power estimates for 1978 and 1988. Table 13.4 presents a summary of the typology. The labels have been chosen to be highly descriptive of the basic values of each segment. Mitchell's typology is an extremely rich source of interesting, and potentially useful, information on the marketing implications of values. In the next few pages, some of the key points of this typology will be briefly discussed.[3]

Need-Driven Consumers

Need-driven consumers are driven in their buying behavior by the exigencies of their conditions. Survivors live in or close to poverty, are frequently unemployed, have a fatalistic outlook, tend to purchase erratically depending on cash on hand, and are responsive to marketing schemes that reduce the need for immediate cash. Sustainers have low, but above poverty level, incomes and tend to focus on sustaining their positions and not losing ground. Sustainers are cautious, risk avoiding buyers who place great emphasis on anything that suggests a guarantee; e.g., a written warranty, national brand, popularity or high price of the product. Mitchell estimates that between 1978 and 1988 need-driven consumers will drop from 16 percent to 12 percent of the population, while their total real personal consumption expenditures will remain virtually unchanged at approximately $45 billion.

---

[3]The discussion in this section relies very heavily on Mitchell (1978); no further citations to Mitchell will be made except for direct quotations.

Outer-Directed Consumers

Outer-directed consumers represent middle America and form the heart of the mass market. Mitchell estimates that in 1978 outer-directed consumers made up 70 percent of the population and controlled 81 percent of personal consumption expenditures. The term outer-directed is derived from the concept of the "other directed" individual made famous by Riesman (1950) in *The Lonely Crowd.* Outer-directed consumers are characterized by a concern for what other people think, or what they believe they think, that is frequently more important than their own inner satisfaction.

The most fundamental way in which the three outer-directed segments can be differentiated is in terms of the outer forces that drive them. Belongers are low to middle income, not upwardly mobile, tradition oriented individuals who tend to be joiners and are guided in their behavior by the need for acceptance by their social groups. Belongers are particularly susceptible to ethnic, religious, and patriotic appeals. They also tend to be unreceptive to change; making a virtue out of sameness and emphasizing old-fashionedness, reliability, and dependability.

In terms of their buying power, achievers are by far the most important segment of the market. In 1978, achievers were estimated to comprise 28 percent of the population and control 45 percent of the total personal consumption expenditures. Achievers, as the name implies, are orientated to success. Indeed they are frequently driven by the need for success. Achievers want, and can afford, the best. They are oriented to new ideas and products, especially technological innovations. Achievers construct worlds and lifestyles for themselves that reflect their central drive for success and convey to others that they are indeed successful.

Emulators represent a transition between belongers and achievers. Relatively young, with good incomes, and upwardly mobile, emulators aspire to higher stations in life. Frequently, they choose achievers to emulate. As emulators, they tend to follow, rather than lead, styles and frequently push fads and fashions to extremes just as they are dying out among those they seek to emulate. Mitchell catches the spirit of the emulator segment by suggesting that "an Emulator may spend handsomely for a gourmet meal in a well-known restaurant while dining at home on TV dinners; or he may have an interior decorator do his office while his apartment gets only the most cursory attention" (p. 7).

Mitchell estimates that between 1978 and 1988 outer-directed consumers will fall from 70 percent to 62 percent of the population while their real personal consumption expenditures will rise approximately 13 percent from $890-billion to $1,007-billion. More detailed figures for the three segments are given in Table 13.4.

Inner-Directed Consumers

The term inner-directed is also taken from *The Lonely Crowd* (Riesman 1950). Inner-directed consumers are driven chiefly to satisfy their own wants and pleasures irrespective of the social norms of others. Inner-directed consumers constitute by far the fastest growing segment of the market both in numbers and purchasing power. Mitchell estimates that between 1978 and 1988 the number of inner-directed consumers will almost double, growing from 14 percent to 26 percent of the population, while their control over real personal consumption expenditures will increase by a staggering 262 percent from $159-billion to $418-billion. Spotting and tracking trends in these inner-directed segments, however, will not be

Table 13.4
A general value based segmentation system

Percentage of Population	Consumer Type	Values and Lifestyles	Demographics	Buying Patterns	Spending Power
Need-Driven Consumers					
6	*Survivors*	Struggle for survival Distrustful Socially misfitted Ruled by appetites	Poverty-level income Little education Many minority members Live in city slums	Price dominant Focused on basics Buy for immediate needs	$13 billion
10	*Sustainers*	Concern with safety, security Insecure, compulsive Dependent, following Want law and order	Low-income Low education Much unemployment Live in country as well as cities	Price important Want warranty Cautious buyers	$32 billion
Outer-Directed Consumers					
32	*Belongers*	Conforming, conventional Unexperimental Traditional, formal Nostalgic	Low to middle income Low to average education Blue collar jobs Tend toward noncity living	Family Home Fads Middle and lower mass markets	$280 billion
10	*Emulators*	Ambitious, show-off Status conscious Upwardly mobile Macho, competitive	Good to excellent income Youngish Highly urban Traditionally male, but changing	Conspicuous consumption "In" items Imitative Popular fashion	$120 billion

28	*Achievers*	Achievement, success, fame Materialism Leadership, efficiency Comfort	Excellent incomes Leaders in business, politics, etc. Good education Suburban and city living	Give evidence of success Top of the line Luxury and gift markets "New and improved" products	$500 billion

Inner-Directed Consumers

3	*I-Am-Me*	Fiercely individualistic Dramatic, impulsive Experimental Volatile	Young Many single Student or starting job Affluent backgrounds	Display one's taste Experimental fads Source of far-out fads Clique buying	$25 billion
5	*Experiential*	Drive to direct experience Active, participative Person-centered Artistic	Bimodal incomes Mostly under 40 Many young families Good education	Process over product Vigorous, outdoor sports "Making" home pursuits Crafts and introspection	$56 billion
4	*Societally Conscious*	Societal responsibility Simple living Smallness of scale Inner growth	Bimodal low and high incomes Excellent education Diverse ages and places of residence Largely white	Conservation emphasis Simplicity Frugality Environmental concerns	$50 billion
2	*Integrated*	Psychological maturity Sense of fittingness Tolerant, self-actualizing World perspective	Good to excellent incomes Bimodal in age Excellent education Diverse jobs and residential patterns	Varied self-expression Esthetically oriented Ecologically aware One-of-a-kind items	$28 billion

Source: Assembled from data presented in Arnold Mitchell, *Consumer Values: A Typology.* Menlo Park, Calif.: SRI International, 1978.

easy because these segments, almost by definition, tend to be highly individualistic and fragmented in their buying behavior.

The four types of inner-directed consumers can be distinguished in terms of the inner wants and pleasures which drive them. The I-am-me segment is driven by an almost childlike insistence on satisfying their own whims. These whims will be diverse ranging from extreme fads in clothing and furniture to jazzy cars. The I-am-me segment tends to be transitory with individuals quickly moving through to one of the other inner-directed segments. Consequently, it is not expected to show much growth.

The experiential segment "avidly seeks direct experience, intense personal relationships, deep involvement, and a rich inner life" (p. 10). They prefer process over product. Ownership of products, per se, is not highly valued. It is the experience that counts. Experientials will tend to be interested in a wide range of products that allow them to directly and intensively experience life; e.g., sky diving, home winemaking, gardening, furniture building. Strong growth is expected in this segment with the number of experientials more than doubling and their spending power almost tripling.

The societally conscious segment defines itself. "Philosophically the Societally Conscious consumer supports products that are functional, healthful, nonpolluting, durable, repairable, recyclable or made from renewable raw materials, energy-cheap to produce, authentic, esthetically pleasing" (p. 12). Many of these consumers have developed a lifestyle of voluntary simplicity.[4] Mitchell suggests that perhaps one-third are very consistent in following the above criteria in their buying decisions and the remainder apply the criteria inconsistently across product classes. He also notes that societal concerns are not limited to this segment although they are especially prominent in this group. As can be seen from Table 13.4, the societally conscious segment of the market is estimated to be growing even more rapidly than the experiential segment, both in terms of numbers and spending power.

The final segment, integrated consumers, ". . . live in accord with an inner sense of what is fitting, self-fulfilling, releasing, balanced" (p. 13). They are difficult to sell to ". . . because many of their prime interests fall outside the marketplace and because they will not often buy for 'show' reasons" (p. 13). They are likely, however, to be motivated by appeals as to how their decisions affect others, insist on top quality for the products they are involved with, and be active givers of products they admire. "Ultimately, the consumption patterns of Integrated consumers are likely to set the standard for Inner-Directed people, just as the styles of Achievement buyers form the template for Emulators" (p. 13). Although growing, Mitchell suggests that this segment is likely to remain small.

Alternative Scenarios

The projections cited here regarding the numbers of persons and the spending power of each market segment were made under what Mitchell calls a "best guess" scenario. This scenario foresees a continued turbulent social environment with its consequent internal strains and contradictions, demographic changes that result

---

[4]Leonard-Barton (1981) provides an interesting historical perspective on the concept of voluntary simplicity lifestyles. She also discusses the development of a scale to measure voluntary simplicity and the implications for energy conservation.

Table 13.5
Alternative futures value forecasts

Description	Best Guess Mixed bag—business almost as usual	Prosperity Booming free-enterprise success	Recession/ Depression Dismal economic picture	Transformation Massive shift in values toward inner direction
Need-Driven Population (%)	12	10	20	15
Outer-Directed Population (%)	62	78	74	54
Inner-Directed Population (%)	26	12	6	31
Average Annual Growth in Real GNP, 1978–1988 (%)	3	5	1	2
Gross National Product (trillions of 1975 dollars)	2.30	2.90	1.82	2.05
Personal Consumption Expenditures (trillions of 1975 dollars)	1.47	1.85	1.16	1.31
Unemployment Rate (%)	5	3	15	2
Population Aged 18 or Over	180	180	180	180
Total Population	240	250	232	238

Source: Arnold Mitchell, *Consumer Values: A Typology.* Menlo Park, Calif.: SRI International, 1978, p. 26.

from a lowered birth rate and higher immigration, and economic growth that is lower than the 1960s but better than the first half of the 1970s. Mitchell also made projections under three alternative scenarios: (1) a prosperity future with a booming economy and successful application of technology to societal problems, (2) a recession/depression future, and (3) a transformation future in which there is a massive increase in the number of consumers adopting the values of societally conscious consumers.

Table 13.5 presents a broad summary of these four futures. Examine this table closely. Note that the four scenarios differ considerably for all variables except population aged 18 or over. The numbers within any one scenario are also highly interdependent. For example, the prosperity future is marked by a decrease in the percentage of both need-driven and inner-directed consumers. This pattern reflects the fact that the prosperity future is based upon the successful adoption of achiever values by large numbers of individuals, with a consequent decrease, especially, in the number of societally conscious consumers. Indeed, the prosperity future forecasts a rise in achievers from 28 percent to 37 percent of the population, while the transformation future foresees a drop to 21 percent. Finally, note that subsequent events have tended to fall somewhere between the best guess and recession/depression futures. This is one reason why the inclusion of alternative scenarios is desirable in any forecast.

PERSONALITY

Closely related to both attitudes and values is personality. Although the three concepts do have important distinctions in their theoretical formulations and research uses, the boundaries among attitudes, personality, and values are not sharply defined. No generally accepted definition of personality exists, but different theories of personality are united by "the concept of consistent responses to the world of stimuli surrounding the individual" and reflect the fact that "[m]an does tend to be consistent in coping with his environment" (Kassarjian 1971, p. 409). In terms of its relationship to attitudes and values, personality is generally conceived to be intermediate both in its stability and its pervasiveness of effects on behavior.

As discussed briefly in Chapter 1, personality research using objective measures of personality grew out of a reaction to the problems of motivation research, particularly the lack of consistency. Although there are some exceptions, generally the results of personality research have been poor. This poor performance can be attributed in part to four general criticisms of the majority of personality research:

1. Personality traits do not have a pervasive influence on consumer behavior but rather are situation bound (Brody and Cunningham 1968; Engel, Kollat, and Blackwell 1969).

2. The specific personality tests used must be carefully justified in the context of the research hypotheses (Cohen 1967; Horton 1973a, b; Kassarjian 1971).

3. Specific brand choice and brand loyalty, the most frequently used dependent variables in consumer personality research, are often inappropriate dependent variables as there is usually no theoretical or empirical reason for expecting personality to be causally related to either of these dependent variables (Horton 1973a, b).

4. The panel-diary research methods used in most personality studies do not allow the researcher to control, or even specify, the stimulus presented to subjects and thus the stimulus condition of each observation is generally unique (Horton 1973 a, b; Massy, Frank, and Lodahl 1968). (Horton 1979, p. 233).

In recent years, researchers have come to recognize and cope with the above criticisms of personality research. They have also largely turned their attention away from personality studies. Among the many reasons for this change, two are especially important. First, a number of alternative theories and research methods became available, especially in the 1970s, that promised to be more successful and to provide a richer and deeper understanding of buyer behavior. Second, positive results from personality research frequently proved difficult to interpret and void of clear managerial implications. For example, in one study it was found that brand loyalty to Chase and Sanborn or Folgers coffee could be distinguished on the basis of seven personality traits for the female head of household (exhibition, autonomy, dependence, dominance, endurance, heterosexuality, and aggression) and six personality traits for the male head of household (analysis, dependence, depreciation, assistance, heterosexuality, and consistency) (Brody and Cunningham 1968). It is not at all clear how one would translate these findings into a marketing strategy or how one could identify and access the defined market segments.

Despite important criticisms, personality research is not without value. Previous chapters cited several personality studies that contribute to the understanding of a number of aspects of buyer behavior. Recently, personality studies have appeared that provide a careful justification for the personality variables studied, stronger relationships with selected buyer behavior, and more interpretable results. Horton (1979), for example, related the personality variables self-confidence and anxiety to a preference for nationally branded, higher priced products. In a particularly interesting study, Schaninger and Sciglimpaglia (1981) related several cognitive personality traits (e.g., need for clarity, self-esteem, anxiety) to acquisition of information (number of alternatives and number of attributes examined). This research also found relationships with several demographic variables, which should facilitate managerial applications.

Perhaps one of the best examples of personality research with relatively clear managerial implications comes from an early personality study by Kassarjian (1965). Kassarjian provided subjects with a number of magazine advertisements constructed to have an inner-directed or an outer-directed appeal, as described in Figure 13.1. Kassarjian found that subjects with inner-directed personalities preferred inner-directed appeals, while those with outer-directed personalities preferred outer-directed appeals. Kassarjian's research is particularly important because it relates quite directly to our previous discussion of Mitchell's value-based segmentation scheme. It also reinforces the point made at the beginning of this section, that the boundary between values and personality is not well defined.[5]

LIFESTYLE RESEARCH

The individual difference variables discussed in this chapter tend to affect buyer behavior in broad, nonspecific ways. The anxious buyer, for example, can cope with his or her anxiety in many ways; e.g., buying name brand goods, goods with excellent guarantees, or buying tranquilizers. More generally, demographic, socioeconomic, value, and personality variables are only indirectly tied to buyer behavior (Wells and Cosmas 1977, p. 300). Building on these more general concepts lifestyle research attempts to recast these concepts in forms directly relevant to buyer behavior.

Wells and Cosmas (1977, pp. 299–301) provide an interesting historical perspective on the lifestyle concept noting its use in literature, sociology, psychology and, relatively recently, marketing. In marketing, lifestyle research grew largely out of efforts to give more precision and managerial relevance to motivation and personality research. Although a lifestyle study is relatively easy to identify, there is no generally accepted operational definition of the lifestyle concept (Wells and Cosmas 1977, pp. 311–312). This lack of an operational definition has given lifestyle research an ad hoc nature, which makes it difficult to draw valid generalizations across different lifestyle studies (cf., Lastovicka 1982). Therefore, this text will confine itself to a general discussion and illustration of the nature of lifestyle research.

Lifestyle Questions

Lifestyle questions are frequently referred to as *AIO*: activities, interests, and opinions. AIO questions are of two types: general lifestyle and product specific. Examples of general AIO questions are

> Exercise is crucial to good health.
> A woman's place is in the home.
> I will probably have more money next year than I have now.
> People should not need the government to help them.
> Children are the most important thing in a marriage.

[5]This comment does not imply that either Mitchell or Kassarjian used the inner/outer directed concept incorrectly; rather they are using the same general concept differently.

Figure 13.1
Advertising appeals to inner- and other-directed personality types

Product	Inner-directed appeal		Other-directed appeal	
	Slogan	Illustration	Slogan	Illustration
Telephone company	just dial—its so easy, fast, and dependable	Attractive girl holding telephone and staring into space	The personal touch for every occasion	Five separate pictures of young ladies in a variety of situations talking on the telephone
High-fidelity turntable	Accurate, dependable, quality high fidelity equipment	Record player, AM-FM radio in quality cabinet	In selecting components use the latest high fidelity equipment	Turntable in foreground with homemade but attractive cabinet in back
Ralph's Market	Ralph's—Known for the finest quality at the right price	Food presented on extremely expensive silver serving piece	Ralph's—The supermarket with the greatest choice	Paper plates, supper napkins, many types of food in a buffet setting
Sea & Ski	For proper sun protection —Sea & Ski	Beach scene with three unrelated couples	For a desirable vacation glow—Sea & Ski	Two men and three women water skiing from the same boat
IBM Typewriter	You save time and money when you buy IBM typewriters	Typist in foreground with boss giving orders in background	Your IBM Typewriter is part of the team in progressive management	Typewriter in foreground Man and woman in background smiling and looking at some papers
Bayer Aspirin	Don't spoil your leisure time—Bayer Aspirin	Man working in "do it yourself" workshop	Don't spoil your leisure time—Bayer Aspirin	Two men holding drinks, talking at cocktail party
Kodak	For a lasting record	Man photographing London Bridge	Share your experiences with friends at home	Man photographing women in front of building. European travel posters in foreground
Fairchild's Restaurant	The height of sophistication	Waiter in tuxedo	Good food, reasonable price, gay atmosphere	People being served in fancy restaurant
Oregon Chamber of Commerce	Oregon, a must for those who appreciate natural beauty	Single man fishing for trout	Make new friends—enjoy carefree, "crowded with fun" weeks at Oregon.	Four people camping at a lake. Two power boats in foreground.

Product				
Community organization	Take an active part in community life—do your part for your country.	Older man in foreground. Seven men sitting around a table in background.	Knowing what is going on—join a community project, etc.	Seven men in a room drinking in background. Man holding papers in foreground.
Books	Improve yourself. Read and learn.	Dozen books including: "My Life in Court," "The Outline of History," "The Valiant Years," "Conversations with Stalin."	Improve yourself; be confident in any crowd.	Illustrations of 11 books including: "Lose Weight and Live," "Women and Fatigue," "Ship of Fools," etc.
New house	A house that makes others stop, timeless, superb construction, designed apart	Suburban house	Contemporary style, nice neighborhood, close to schools	Suburban house
Tennis shoes	Heels reinforced, arch support—the built-in heels for sportsmen	Girl standing on deck of ship	Feel happier, comfortable in fashion	Girl dressed in tennis attire
Swedish glass	You make your party unique with Swedish glass	Formal dining table set with wine glasses	You entertain in style when you serve on Swedish glass	Canapes, potato chips and dips on a counter
Umbrella	The smart sophisticated umbrella, timeless and attractive	Man and woman walking in rain, arm in arm	The choice of popular young women—in all color ranges and sizes	Four women carrying different umbrellas
Chrysler	Excellent craftsmanship, best materials—made to last a lifetime	Chrysler auto—no background	The modern, up-to-date car for active people	Chrysler auto parked in front of nightclub
Swiss watches	The watch that is dependable	Watch pictured on wrist of man	The watch that is dependable	Watches in foreground. Two boys and a girl drinking in background
Anthony Squire Clothes	Feel smart and look smart	Young man walking in hallway	Clothing for the rising young executive	Young man and older man talking
Columbia Record Club	Select your favorite Columbia record	Illustrations of 18 albums ranging from popular to classical music	Share happy moments listening and dancing to recorded music	Two men and two women listening to records

Source: Harold H. Kassarjian, "Social Character and Differential Preference for Mass Communication." *Journal of Marketing Research*, 2 (May 1965): 149–150. Reprinted with the kind permission of the American Marketing Association.

Figure 13.1 continued

Product	Inner-directed appeal		Other-directed appeal	
	Slogan	Illustration	Slogan	Illustration
All-State Insurance	For the finishing touch—All-State Insurance	Young man fixing motor on car	For the finishing touch—All-State Insurance	Father and son washing family car
Squibb Toothbrush Co.	For the busy man on the go. Squibb's Electric Toothbrush	Man with pleasant smile	For a natural friendly smile—Squibb's Electric Toothbrush	Man and woman smiling
Tishman Realty Co.	Maximum efficiency with a minimum of upkeep in a modern office. Tishman Realty Co.	Secretary working hard at desk	Happy employees and pleasant working conditions in a modern office. Tishman Reality Co.	Two men in an office
Horton and Converse Vitamins	For individual all around development—Horton and Converse Vitamins	Six separate illustrations of individual sports	For outstanding achievement in your group	Illustrations of basketball, golf and bowling
RCA Television	RCA Television	Man watching television	RCA Television	Two men and two women watching television
School bonds	Your child needs the best education there is. Vote yes on school bonds	Children and teacher in classroom	Your child wants to be part of it. Vote Yes on school bonds	Four illustrations of children in school and playground
Metropolitan Life Insurance Co.	Leave some time for relaxation. Metropolitan Life Insurance Co.	Man watching television	Leave some time for relaxation. Metropolitan Life Insurance Co.	Two couples at cocktail party
Body by Fisher	Body by Fisher	Car parked at lake. Couple in foreground	Body by Fisher	Car parked in front of house. Guests being greeted by hostess

Examples of specific AIO questions are

> I jog at least three times a week.
> I do almost all my baking from scratch.
> I frequently use a bank credit card.
> I always vote Republican.
> Children should develop a musical talent.

Note carefully that each specific AIO question is potentially relevant to a general AIO question. For example, joggers may jog because "exercise is crucial to good health."

In addition to AIO questions, which are also referred to as psychographics, lifestyle studies frequently collect a wide range of other data; e.g., demographic, socioeconomic, self-image. Such data are useful in developing a more detailed understanding of buyers and for developing effective market segmentation plans. Indeed, the word "detailed" is appropriate, for as Wells and Cosmas (1977) note, "Most life-style questionnaires have been very large. Many have run more than 20 pages and have included hundreds of questions" (p. 312). Such length imposes substantial burdens on both respondents (who must answer the questions) and researchers (who must analyze and then interpret the responses). In designing lifestyle questionnaires, researchers need to consider carefully the rationale for each question to counter the strong bias into AIO studies to ask everything that conceivably might be relevant to the topic.

Uses of Lifestyle Research

Literally hundreds of academic lifestyle studies exist, and the number of commercial studies is undoubtedly much higher. One major use of lifestyle data is to profile different groups of buyers. The objective in such research is to develop a deeper understanding of existing segments of the market. Table 13.6 presents an example of profiles of male bank credit card users and nonusers from a study by Plummer (1971). One can easily see that the profiles are quite distinct and provide useful insights into who uses these cards, and how and why they use their cards. Plummer also collected demographic and socioeconomic data, which further identifies the two groups, and performed a similar analysis on female users and nonusers. The profiles of males and females were, as the reader probably suspects, quite distinct.

A second use of lifestyle data is in the development of market segments. The objective of the analysis is to group subjects into relatively homogeneous segments (usually using cluster analysis or Q-type factor analysis). There are a number of ways in which this type of analysis can be conducted. A study by Pernica (1974) can serve as an example of a typical analysis. AIO data on automobiles and driving were collected. An analysis revealed four segments. An examination of the profiles of these four segments, including data not specifically related to automobiles that was *not* used to form the segments, led to the following characterizations of the four segments:

> *Speed Enthusiasts.* These were young, well-educated motorists with great interest in cars (car buffs). They looked for power in the product, which they equated with performance and speed.

Table 13.6
Lifestyle profiles of users and nonusers of bank credit cards

#	Statement	Card Users Definite and General Agreement	Noncard Users Definite and General Agreement
8.	I enjoy going to concerts.	25%	17%
10.	A woman's place is in the home.	27	41
17.	In my job I tell people what to do.	53	21
18.	I am a good cook.	36	26
23.	My greatest achievements are ahead of me.	56	42
24.	I buy many things with a charge or credit card.	39	22
29.	We will probably move once in the next five years.	46	37
39.	Five years from now the family income will probably be a lot higher than it is now.	71	60
42.	Good grooming is a sign of self-respect.	52	71
53.	There is too much advertising on TV today.	59	70
70.	Women wear too much make-up today.	43	51
74.	My job requires a lot of selling ability.	51	37
77.	I like to pay cash for everything I buy.	26	67
86.	Television is a primary source of our entertainment.	25	40
94.	Investing in the stock market is too risky for most families.	47	56
109.	To buy anything other than a house or car on credit is unwise.	29	47
117.	Young people have too many privileges today.	52	64
112.	I love the outdoors.	54	76
126.	There is too much emphasis on sex today.	52	64
130.	There are day people and there are night people; I am a day person.	58	69
135.	I expect to be a top executive in the next ten years.	44	27
152.	I am or have been president of a society or club.	51	36
174.	I would like to have my boss' job.	42	33
175.	A party wouldn't be a party without liquor.	29	17
177.	I would rather live in or near a big city than in or near a small town.	46	34
183.	I often bet money at the races.	18	8
184.	I like to think I'm a bit of a swinger.	38	26
194.	I stay home most evenings.	62	71
198.	Advertising can't sell me anything I don't want.	55	68
200.	I often have a cocktail before dinner.	36	20
202.	I like ballet.	26	16
209.	When I must choose between the two, I usually dress for fashion, not comfort.	19	10
214.	Liquor is a curse on American life.	34	49
217.	Movies should be censored.	41	57
218.	I read one or more business magazines regularly.	34	18

Note: All differences are significant above the .05 level based on Chi-square tests of significance.

Source: Joseph T. Plummer, "Life Style Patterns and Commercial Bank Credit Card Usage." *Journal of Marketing,* 35 (April 1971): 38. Reprinted with the kind permission of the American Marketing Association.

Table 13.6 continued

#	Statement	Card Users Definite and General Agreement	Noncard Users Definite and General Agreement
230.	I am active in two or more service organizations.	28	17
248.	I do more things socially than most of my friends.	19	10
269.	We often serve wine with dinner.	30	16
272.	I buy at least three suits a year.	25	11
273.	Playboy is one of my favorite magazines.	25	16
275.	I spend too much time talking on the telephone.	31	17
282.	It is good to have charge accounts.	33	21
283.	Hippies should be drafted.	48	61
286.	When I think of bad health, I think of doctor bills.	31	46
290.	My days seem to follow a definite routine.	47	58

Note: All differences are significant above the .05 level based on Chi-square tests of significance.

Power Drivers. These tended to be modern middle class Americans who looked for power in the product to give them control and confidence in driving.

Apprehensive Motorists. These were typically older and women. They were less concerned with power and were apprehensive about the workings of a car. They looked primarily for good service which would give them assurance of safety, dependability, and confidence in driving.

Pragmatists. These tended to be older with lower education and income. For them, a car was just a means of transportation, and a service station just a filling station. They did not go for power or styling frills, and considered economy of driving as the major criterion in brand choice (Pernica 1974, p. 310).

The descriptions of the four segments have relatively obvious implications for product design, promotion, and pricing.

Although profiling existing market segments and developing new markets are probably the most frequent uses of lifestyle research, lifestyle data have been employed in a variety of other uses. First, lifestyle analysis has been used for crosscultural comparisons. Douglas and Urban (1977), for example, used lifestyle analysis to examine the feasibility of using the same segmentation strategies in different cultures (America, France, United Kingdom). Second, lifestyle research has been used to study media use in the same way it has been applied to products (Michaels 1973, Darden and Perreault 1975). This information is extremely useful for both the media and potential advertisers. Third, lifestyle analyses enrich our understanding of demographic variables and other familiar concepts. Reynolds and Darden (1972) and Darden and Perreault (1976), for example, considerably enriched our understanding of outshoppers—persons who tend to shop outside the normal trading boundaries of where they reside—by adding lifestyle concepts to what is already known about such individuals. Finally, lifestyle analysis has been applied to public policy issues. Ahmed and Jackson (1979), for example, used lifestyle concepts to study welfare policies in Canada.

Limitations of the Lifestyle Concept

At the beginning of this section, the "ad hoc" nature of most lifestyle research was noted. The typical lifestyle study starts with the topic of interest and "brainstorming" for relevant lifestyle traits. Examples of lifestyle traits are "compulsive housekeeper" (Burns and Harrison 1979), "service-quality consciousness" (Teel, Bearden, and Durand 1979), "first-class traveler" (Darden and Perreault 1975). These traits are operationalized in a number of AIO and other questions believed to provide useful information.

As a recent review of the literature makes clear, researchers have had no difficulty generating lifestyle traits and questions. Indeed, Lastovicka (1982) found over 100 lifestyle traits in fourteen separate studies with relatively little overlap of traits among the studies. More seriously, Lastovicka found relatively little attention given to the critical question of the reliability and validity of lifestyle traits and questions. In fact, the fourteen studies reviewed were the only ones located by Lastovicka that had attempted to formally assess reliability and/or validity, and in only four of these studies were these issues of primary interest.

Despite the limitations of the lifestyle concept noted above, there is little doubt that lifestyle research can be and has been very useful, especially to marketing managers. In recent years academic marketing researchers have become much more sensitized to the need for measures whose reliability and validity are rigorously established. There is little doubt that in the future lifestyle concepts will be exposed to such treatment. Lastovicka's review, which contains an illustrative validity study, gives good direction for such work.

SUMMARY

This and the previous chapter discussed a relatively large number of variables that are useful for classifying individual buyers. Although broad generalizations regarding individual difference variables are largely lacking, there is no doubt that such measures are extremely useful in the context of specific marketing problems. Clearly, individual difference variables can provide important managerial insights into the design, pricing, promotion, and distribution of goods and services. Indeed, without these variables sophisticated market segmentation strategies would be impossible.

Culture, Subculture, and Social Class

14

The last two chapters discussed how marketing can develop sophisticated market segmentation strategies based upon demographic, socioeconomic, and value system differences among buyers. This chapter continues the discussion of segmentation strategies with discussions of the marketing implications of cultural, subcultural, and social class differences among buyers.

CULTURE

The Concept of a Culture

The broadest of social groups is referred to as a culture. The concept of a culture has been defined in numerous ways. A definition by Kroeber and Kluckhohn, however, is particularly relevant to our purposes:

> Culture consists of patterns, explicit and implicit, of and for behavior, acquired and transmitted by symbols constituting the distinctive achievement of human groups, including their embodiment in artifacts; the essential core of culture consists of traditional (i.e., historically derived and selected) ideas and especially their attached *values*; culture systems may, on the one hand, be considered as products of action, on the other as conditioning elements of future action (1952, p. 181, emphasis added).

The word values in the above definition has been emphasized because the discussion of core values in the last chapter is central to defining the character of the American culture.

The concept of a culture may be applied at many levels and, at the boundary, it is often difficult to determine where one culture begins and another ends. It is, for example, common to speak of Eastern and Western cultures. At another level, however, it is also common to speak of American, French, German, and British cultures. The relatively clear distinction between Eastern and Western cultures reflects the historical physical and social separation of these two cultures, which has only recently begun to be penetrated. In contrast, the many Western cultures have had extensive physical and social contact, all too often in the form of wars, for centuries. Although there are many important differences among Western cultures these differences are nowhere as fundamental as the split between East and West.

Although it is common, and frequently appropriate, to divide cultures along national boundaries, such divisions can be misleading. Nowhere is this clearer than in Africa where European colonialists created national boundaries with virtually no regard to the fundamental tribal divisions of African society.

Despite an inherent vagueness, the concept of cultural differences among buyers is of immense importance to marketers.

Marketing Implications of Culture

The vast differences among cultures in terms of demographics, socioeconomics, values, languages, and the physical and social infrastructure that supports each makes the importance of cultural variables to the development of effective marketing strategy self-evident. It is quite easy to cite innumerable examples of how cultural differences have affected, often adversely, firms' marketing strategies.

International Business Blunders (Ricks, Fu, and Arpan 1974) is an especially rich source of such examples, some of which have been previously cited.

One of the most interesting examples of how cultural differences can impact upon a firm's marketing strategy is Ricks, Fu, and Arpan's, (1974, pp. 20–22) description of Simmons' attempt to build and market beds in Japan. On the production side everything went quite smoothly. On the marketing side, however, Simmons ran into cultural barriers at almost every turn. To begin with, very few Japanese sleep on beds; most sleep on a type of floor pallet called a *futon.* This gave Simmons both a small initial market and a formidable task in convincing Japanese buyers to change their sleeping habits. Also, after rigorously screening and training a sales force, Simmons learned that none of their salesmen had ever slept on a bed and, therefore, could not attest to the quality and comfort of the product they were selling. In addition, Simmons found a range of other cultural factors that they had not anticipated, did not understand, and which caused them serious problems. Among these problems were an intricate caste system that seriously limited the clients a salesman could call upon, language differences among castes, and the baffling Japanese distribution system, which depends as much upon an intricate system of favors and obligations as it does on profits.

It would be easy to continue citing cultural factors as they have affected specific firms' marketing strategies. This, however, would not extend our general understanding of buyer behavior. The primary conclusion to be drawn from this brief discussion of cultural differences is a simple one. Problems in cross-cultural marketing occur primarily because, being unfamiliar with the customs, laws, values, social norms, etc. of the other culture, one frequently does not even know what questions to ask and is, therefore, frequently taken by surprise. Indeed, it is extremely difficult to learn the character of another culture, especially a culture that is not contiguous with one's own, at a distance, or even from brief experience. There is no substitute for long-term, total emersion in a culture. This is one reason why international firms should, and frequently do, rely heavily on local people in adapting their marketing strategy to local conditions. Therefore, rather than present a large number of examples of the consequences of cultural differences, we shall turn our attention to a brief discussion of the general transferability of marketing strategies across national and cultural boundaries.

Standardization of International Marketing Strategies

Every adaptation of a firm's marketing program to local conditions tends to raise costs and generally complicate the coordination of the firm's activities. With the explosive increase in the number of multinational firms since World War II, marketers have shown increased interest in the question of whether a firm's marketing strategy, especially its advertising strategy, can be standardized across national and cultural boundaries. The answer generally given is a qualified yes (e.g., Buzzell 1968, Sorenson and Wiechmann 1975).

The qualifications are of two types. First, while fundamental aspects of the firm's strategy will often travel well, the firm must be sensitive to the need to adapt details to local conditions. Fatt (1965, 1967), for example, suggests that advertising appeals such as the desire to be beautiful, freedom from pain, and glow of health are universally recognized appeals. These general appeals, however, often need to be modified for optimal effect in specific environments. Beauty, for example, does lie in the eye of the beholder and what is considered beautiful varies across cultures. This, however, is not unlike adaptations that marketers often make within a culture. Recall, for example, the five different lines of cosmetics, and the promotional appeals of each, which Helena Rubenstein markets to women of different ages. Frequently, the transfer of marketing programs across cultural boundaries can be made with adjustments of this magnitude.

The second qualification is that cultures differ substantially in their degree of similarity. In general, the transferability of marketing programs across cultures increases with increasing cultural similarity (Sorenson and Wiechmann 1975). This is important because there is a strong tendency for trade to occur among countries with similar cultures; e.g., within the Common Market, among developed nations.

Many studies have attempted to assess cultural similarity among nations (e.g., Sethi 1971). Published studies have generally addressed broad questions, such as the general market potential and receptivity to various types of market entry by foreigners. The methodology of these studies, however, is directly applicable to a firm's effort to group cultures relative to a specific product or products. First, the relevant dimensions of culture must be identified and measured. Second, cultures are grouped according to their degree of cultural similarity. The grouping procedure may be informal and intuitive or involve the use of mathematical techniques, such as factor and cluster analysis.

Of the many cultural differences of importance to marketers, language warrants special attention. Perhaps one of the most frequent, and easily identified, problems encountered in cross cultural marketing is the literal translation that turns out to have a meaning very different from the one intended. Ricks, Fu, and Arpan (1974, p. 12), for example, report the experience of an unidentified firm which introduced its powerful new detergent into the French-speaking Quebec Province of Canada with the boast, "*les parties de sale.*" The intended meaning was that the new brand was especially useful for the really dirty parts of the wash. Unfortunately, the phrase turned out to be roughly comparable to the American idiom, "private parts" (p. 12), and sales rapidly declined.

A simple procedure for detecting potential language problems is *back-translation* (Brislin 1970, Werner and Campbell 1970). In back-translation a number of translators translate the material into another language, exchange translations, and translate them back into the original language. This process may be repeated several times to counter biases of individual translators and to determine if cumulative distortions of the message occur.

Marketing Concepts and Tools

It is important to recognize that the basic concepts and research tools of marketing generally, and buyer behavior specifically, are as relevant to cross cultural marketing as they are to domestic marketing. In both situations, the firm needs to understand potential buyers and develop an effective marketing mix. In both situations, the market and the optimal marketing strategy are to some extent unknowns, which must be made known through careful research. Of course, in neither situation is success guaranteed. Although the risk of failure in a different culture is usually greater, the rewards are also usually greater.[1] With diligent

---

[1]This statement is essentially a tautology in the sense that the firm will normally only enter high risk markets when it perceives the chance for high returns.

effort the firm can cope with the risks and earn the higher rewards of cross cultural marketing.

SUBCULTURES

The Concept of a Subculture

Within any society it is usually possible to identify subgroups with distinct characteristics. This is especially true of the United States which experienced wave after wave of immigrants (English, Irish, Polish, Italian, etc.) until the 1920s when the free flow of immigration was substantially restricted. Even after this period, however, there has been a steady inflow of immigrants punctuated by occasional mass migrations from various troubled spots around the world; e.g., Cuba, Southeast Asia, Haiti, Mexico.

Both the relative newness of the United States and the continual inflow of immigrants give American society a kind of polyglot character. This is not to deny that there is a dominant American culture, which is largely defined by the core values previously discussed, that is generally recognized if not fully accepted or implemented in precisely the same way by all members of society. What needs to be emphasized is that the American culture is in no sense monolithic. There exist many variations on the basic pattern and some notable deviations. At some point, the divergence becomes sufficiently large to be termed a subculture. Like culture, the term subculture is inherently vague. It is also, like culture, a very useful concept for the marketer.

Acculturation and Assimiliation

It will help in understanding the concept of a subculture to discuss the ideas of acculturation and assimilation. As we know, culture is learned. The *process* of learning a culture is called acculturation. In the United States, acculturation primarily involves learning the norms and values of the middle class. The *process* of acceptance of an outside group by the dominant culture is called assimilation. The word process is emphasized because both acculturation and assimilation occur gradually over time.

The predominant pattern is acculturation followed by assimilation. The two processes, however, are to a large degree independent. At any given time, different new groups may display markedly different degrees of acculturation and assimilation. Indeed, as Berelson and Steiner noted:

> The fact is that people can become acculturated without being assimilated, and they can be assimilated without being acculturated. For example, in the United States it is probably safe to say that the Amish are more assimilated than accultured, whereas the Northern Negro is more accultured than assimilated (1964, pp. 16–17).

American Subcultures

Depending upon how stringent one's definition of a subculture, it is possible to recognize a great many subcultures within American society. Blacks, Hispanics,

American Indians, Eskimos, Aleuts, Jews, Catholics, Muslims, Upper Middle Class, ad infinitum can be, and have been, discussed in terms of subcultures. In fact, some consumer behavior texts even speak of subcultures based on factors such as age and region.

In this section we shall limit our discussion to Blacks and Hispanics. We do this for several reasons. First, the number of subcultures we could conceivably discuss is too large to even be considered. Second, Blacks and Hispanics have been recognized as separate groups both by government and by society at large. Consequently, a large amount of data is available on the characteristics of these two groups. Third, both groups are large both in terms of their numbers and their aggregate buying power. Thus, variations in buying behavior of these two groups are of considerable practical interest to marketers.

Blacks

This discussion should begin by acknowledging that the question of whether Blacks constitute a truly unique subculture or a generally underpriviledged segment of the dominant culture has been vigorously debated. Sturdivant (1973) provided a review of this controversy and it shall not be pursued here. What we can say is that in many dimensions Blacks and Whites do differ significantly in ways that are potentially important to marketers. While noting these differences, we shall also note that there are far more similarities than differences between Blacks and Whites. Sturdivant puts the point this way: "Indeed, the question may be posed as to whether researchers have not been guilty of focusing on a limited number of unique differences rather than the many common characteristics that are shared with the dominant culture," (1973, p. 477).

Table 14.1 presents data on differences between Blacks and Whites on a number of selected demographic and socioeconomic variables. These data are taken from a recent Bureau of the Census report, *The Social and Economic Status of the Black Population in the United States: An Historical View, 1790–1978*. This 271-page report provides a wealth of information on Blacks that is of potential relevance to marketers.

Blacks currently account for approximately 12 percent of the population. They are also, because of a higher fertility rate, increasing as a percentage of the population. As an aside, it is interesting to note that many current consumer behavior books note the higher fertility of Blacks without further comment. Although the fertility rate of Blacks is higher than that of Whites, it is much closer to the current fertility of Whites than the fertility rate of Whites during the peak of the baby boom years. Thus, while the fertility rate of Blacks is relatively high, with all of the marketing consequences that go with population growth, the current fertility rate of Blacks has closely followed the general social trend. This, of course, is an example of Sturdivant's point about focusing on dissimilarities rather than similarities. It is not that the dissimilarities are unimportant, for they frequently are; rather, they should not be exaggerated.

Other data in Table 14.1 reveal that Blacks are, relative to Whites, heavily concentrated in cities, more likely to have a female-headed household, younger, less likely to attend college or be a college graduate, and have significantly lower incomes. Blacks are also less likely to be registered voters; a fact that has been widely noted and condemned by civil rights leaders. Although the exact numbers

Table 14.1
Selected demographic and socioeconomic characteristics of black and white Americans

Variable	Black	White
Total Population (000)***	26,488	188,341
Residential Location		
Metropolitan Areas	75.0%	66.0%
In Central Cities	55	24
Outside Central Cities	20	41
Outside Metropolitan Areas	25	34
Family Structure		
Husband-Wife Household	56.1%	85.9%
Female-Headed Household	39.2	11.5
Male-Headed Household,		
no wife present	4.6	2.5
Total Fertility Rate	2.2	1.8
Median Age		
Male	23.1	29.5
Female	25.5	32.1
College Enrollment of		
Persons 18–24 years		
old**		
Males	20.2%	28.7%
Females	22.2	24.4
Four or More Years of College		
by Persons Age 25–34**	12.0%	29.0%
Males	12.0%	29.0%
Females	11.0	21.0
Income		
Median Family Income	9,563	16,740
Percent $10,000 or Over	47.0%	72.0%
Percent $25,000 or Over	7.0	19.0
Percent Below Poverty Level	28.2	7.0
Percent Registered Voters	58.0%	68.0%

*1976   **1977   ***1980

Source: Derived from U.S. Bureau of the Census, Current Population Reports, Series P–23, no. 80, "The Social and Economic Status of the Black Population in the United States: Historical View, 1790–1978, and *1980 Census of Population and Housing.* Washington, D.C.: U.S. Government Printing Office.

Note: All data are for 1978 unless otherwise noted.

in Table 14.1 may be new information, the general pattern should be one with which the reader is familiar.

A simple calculation from Table 14.1 shows that in 1978 the median income of Black families was approximately 57 percent of the median income of White families.[2] Despite this relative income deprivation, the aggregate income of Blacks is large. How large can be conservatively estimated by multiplying the number of Black families by the median income of Black families: $242 *billion.* Clearly, the marketer cannot afford to ignore Black buyers and must be sensitive to the special needs and purchasing patterns of Blacks.

[2]The relative income of Blacks was actually lower in 1978 than in 1974 (when it was 62 percent). This reflects the historical fact that Blacks normally suffer more from recessions than do Whites. More generally, the poor typically are the most heavily impacted by recessions.

A relatively large number of academic studies examine the similarities and dissimilarities of Black and White buying behavior. Undoubtedly, the number of unpublished propriety studies is far greater. Many studies found differences, sometimes very substantial differences, between Blacks and Whites in the ownership and consumption of a great many products.[3] Tables 14.2, 14.3, and 14.4 present illustrative data. Blacks have also been found to tend to prefer popular brands (e.g., Bauer 1966) and be more brand loyal than Whites (e.g., Larson and Wales 1973). Further, there is evidence that brand preferences differ considerably for Blacks and Whites. A study by Larson (1968), for example, found that Blacks preferred Colgate to Crest ten-to-one while Whites were evenly split. Larson also found that Blacks were far less likely to purchase brands with negative associations, such as Aunt Jemima and Uncle Ben.

In addition to differential product class use and brand preferences, researchers have found a wide range of other differences between the purchasing behavior of Blacks and Whites. It has been found, for example, that Blacks save a higher percentage of their income (Alexis 1962), often pay more for their food (Sexton 1971), shop less by phone (Feldman and Star 1968), do less comparison shopping for food (Sexton 1974), respond more positively to advertising (Tolley and Goett 1971), and listen to radio more often, especially at night and on weekends (Glasser and Metzger 1975). A relatively large number of other specific differences between Blacks and Whites could be cited; however, it will be more profitable to turn the discussion back to a more general level.

The reader may have noticed that many of the references to differences in Black and White buying behavior are dated. This is indeed true and reflects the state of the literature. Perhaps just as important is the fact that many of the frequently reported racial differences are based on very limited data; often a single study in a single geographic area. This is not to suggest that the reported differences are illusory, for the evidence in total does not permit such a judgment. Rather, the reader should treat the above findings as potential hypotheses and suggestive of the nature of the differences in Black and White buying behavior.

So far we have referred to Blacks without further differentiation; and, in fact, most researchers have implicitly made this assumption. Indeed, the conclusion has frequently been drawn that the Black market is more homogeneous than the White market. This is probably true, although it may well primarily reflect the constraints of low income and discrimination. A number of researchers have suggested that many, but certainly not all, of the differences in buying behavior between Blacks and Whites can be attributed to income differences. Sexton (1972), in particular, reviewed the literature and concluded that "as black income levels gradually rise, many of the apparent overall differences between 'black' and 'white' markets will substantially diminish" (p. 39). Rising incomes should increase the heterogeneity of the Black market as it permits an increasing degree of self-expression through greater discretionary consumption.[4]

A study by Barry and Harvey illustrates how the Black market may be segmented. Barry and Harvey found four different segments, which they describe as follows:

---

[3]A good summary of this research is provided by Bauer and Cunningham (1970).

[4]The rise of the Black middle class has been widely noted (e.g., *Time*, June 17, 1974, pp. 19–20).

Table 14.2
Percentage of blacks and whites consuming or owning various household products

Products	Annual Family Income ($)							
	Less than 3,000		3000–5999		6000–7999		8000 or more	
	Whites	Negroes	Whites	Negroes	Whites	Negroes	Whites	Negroes
Food products[a]								
Butter	6.6	23.3	8.0	31.2	7.7	26.9	14.1	45.4
Margarine	58.3	61.6	63.6	72.7	69.8	57.7	69.5	81.8
Frozen vegetables[b]	30.5	31.4	28.0	50.6	39.6	34.6	47.1	54.6
Canned vegetables[c]	20.5	35.6	35.6	44.5	37.9	40.4	40.6	43.2
Dietary soft drinks	7.3	17.4	11.9	23.4	20.8	23.1	25.5	13.6
Nondietary soft drinks	26.5	60.5	55.5	71.4	62.4	23.1	67.1	45.4
Liquor								
All respondents[d]	15.2	26.7	29.7	39.0	39.3	46.2	56.5	54.6
Scotch[e]	3.3	9.3	4.2	22.1	7.7	34.6	19.7	27.3
Bourbon[e]	7.3	15.1	20.3	23.4	29.2	7.7	40.9	40.9
Personal hygiene products[f]								
Shampoo	42.4	41.9	59.3	52.0	74.5	65.4	72.6	50.0
Deodorant	39.7	65.1	56.8	79.2	74.5	92.3	76.6	81.8
Toothpaste	48.3	76.7	75.0	89.6	86.9	88.5	89.1	86.4
Mouthwash	43.7	61.6	58.5	75.3	56.7	88.5	63.5	86.4
Disinfectants	52.3	69.8	56.4	80.5	70.1	61.5	68.6	86.4
Home appliances[g]								
Auto. washing machine	47.4	19.8	57.6	29.9	78.6	50.0	85.5	72.7
Auto. clothes dryer	12.6	5.8	16.5	7.8	34.2	15.4	54.9	27.3
Auto. dishwasher	2.0	—	5.5	—	14.1	3.8	33.8	—
Black-and-white television	87.4	91.8	89.5	98.7	83.7[h]	97.9[h]	—	—
Color television	3.3	0.6	5.7	1.9	24.3[h]	6.2[h]	—	—
Home ownership								
Own home	68.3	39.5	49.4	57.1	70.8	73.0	81.5	77.3

[a]Purchased within the past 7 days.
[b]Includes all types of frozen vegetables.
[c]Includes canned corn, peas, green beans, and tomatoes.
[d]Percentage of total respondents purchasing some alcoholic beverages within past 12 months.
[e]Percentage of Scotch and Bourbon purchases among total respondents.
[f]Purchased within past 30 days.
[g]Percentage "having" in the home.
[h]Last two income classes were combined because of small number of respondents.

Source: Stafford, J.F., Keith Cox, and J.B. Higginbotham, "Some Consumption Pattern Differences Between Urban Whites and Negroes," *Social Science Quarterly,* 49 (December 1968): 626–627. Reprinted by permission of the University of Texas Press, publisher.

Table 14.3
Black and white ownership of selected appliances and automobiles

Appliance	Black	White
Refrigerator	84%	89%
Clothes dryer	47	76
Dishwasher	22	49
Home food freezer	36	44
Kitchen range	78	85
Clothes washing machine	74	86
Television sets		
One or more	99	99
Black and white only	26	20
Color only	19	28
Black and white and color	55	50
Air conditioning (available)	49	64
Room unit	30	35
Central system	19	29
Automobiles		
One or more	91	97
Two automobiles	35	34
Two or more automobiles	56	63
Latest model of automobile owned		
1973 or 1974	25	23
1970–1972	43	48
1969–1969	19	17
1967 or earlier	13	12

•Households are in highest income quartile and have incomes of approximately $15,000 or more.

Source: U.S. Bureau of the Census, *Current Population Reports*, series P-23, no. 54, "Social and Economic Status of the Black Population in the United States" Washington, D.C.: U.S. Government Printing Office, 1974, p. 139.

Negroes—This segment is more closely identified with the white middle class than with other segments of the population. They strive to emulate the white middle class, purchase products with status and have high brand loyalty for some national brands.

Blacks—This segment has recently evolved and is in the process of developing its own set of cultural standards while minimizing the values of white society. Their reference groups consist of other members of this movement, which makes this group transitory in nature. Because of this feature marketers may have a difficult time determining an appropriate strategy for this group.

Afro-Americans—This segment has not only discarded the white middle-class standards but may also be said to be rejecting the established standards of white supremacy. Reference groups and opinion leaders for this segment would be any strong anti-establishment individuals or groups. Marketing to this group could be difficult because of the degree of change occuring in the movement and the possibility of a backlash by appealing to them.

Recent Black Immigrants—This segment may still identify with the society from which it emigrated. Members may try to adapt their consumer behavior to the sophisticated American culture. Reference groups for this segment would be individuals and groups in their own culture. The small size of this market makes it insignificant to marketers (1974, p. 53).

Table 14.4
Purchases and average price paid for selected appliances and automobiles for black and white households: fall 1972 to fall 1973

Average purchase price	Household purchases per 100 households		Average price paid	
	Black	White	Black	White
Clothes washing machine	17	13	$ 239	$ 236
Clothes dryer	11	11	194	197
Dishwasher	1	8	201	246
Refrigerator	9	10	385	376
Home food freezer	6	6	350	248
Kitchen range	9	9	307	312
Room air conditioner	8	7	239	209
Television set				
Black and white	11	8	131	103
Color	15	14	417	434
Automobiles				
New	22	23	4,954	4,409
Used	18	20	2,354	1,858

•Households are in highest income quartile and have incomes of approximately $15,000 or more.

Source: U.S. Bureau of the Census, *Current Population Reports,* Series P-23, no. 54, "The Social and Economic Status of the Black Population in the United States." Washington, D.C.: U.S. Government Printing Office, 1974, p. 139.

Although the above descriptions are quite brief and general, they at least give a "feel" for differing motivational patterns of Blacks and should sensitize the reader to the need to consider the potential profitability of a segmentation strategy. It should be kept in mind, however, that because the Black market is relatively small, successful segmentation strategies will often be more difficult to develop for the Black market than for the White market.

The final issue to be discussed is of both practical and social importance: What is the reaction of White and Black audiences to advertisements with White, Black, or integrated models? Although several early studies suggested the possibility of a White "backlash" to Black or integrated ads (e.g., Cagley and Cardozo 1970; Stafford, Birdwell, and Van Tassel 1970), the overall evidence is positive regarding the use of Black or integrated models.

Whites do not react negatively to Black or integrated models (e.g., Barban 1969, Guest 1970, Solomon and Bush 1977). Blacks generally respond more favorably to Black or integrated models (e.g., Choudbury and Schnid 1974; Szybillo and Jacoby 1974). Although the evidence is limited, a study by Solomon, Bush, and Hair (1976) found no differences in the purchasing behavior of Blacks and Whites to Black, White, or integrated models in a promotional display. Finally, Bush, Hair, and Solomon (1979) provided evidence contradictory to the Cagley and Cardozo study, which is generally regarded as the most serious challenge to the use of Black or integrated models with White audiences. Thus, there appears much to be gained from Black audiences and little chance of loss with White audiences from the use of Black or integrated models.

Hispanics

The second subculture to be considered is the Hispanic subculture. The term Hispanic refers to people of Spanish origin. At various times the Bureau of the Census has used country of birth, country of birth of parents, Spanish surname, and Spanish mother tongue to identify Hispanics.[5] The 1980 census reported slightly over 14.6 million Hispanics. Because of a high fertility rate and heavy immigration, Hispanics are the fastest growing minority in America. Indeed, the Hispanic population has been increasing by approximately *one million* persons per year and it has been estimated that by the year 2030 Hispanics will be the largest minority group in the United States.[6]

Table 14.5 provides data on the Hispanic population. For comparison, data on the Black and White populations are also included in Table 14.5.[7]

A particularly important characteristic of Hispanic families is a generally traditional lifestyle. Families tend to be larger and wives are much less likely to work when compared to both White and Black families. Hispanics are also tightly clustered geographically. Over half of all Hispanics reside in California (4.5 million) and Texas (3.0 million). Another 2.6 million Hispanics reside in New York (1.7 million) and Florida (.9 million). The latter two concentrations are to a large degree made up of Puerto Ricans clustered about New York City and Cubans clustered about Miami. Western Hispanics, by far the largest group, are primarily Mexicans.

There are two distinct reasons why Hispanics constitute a clearly identifiable subculture within the United States. First, there is and has been a continuous inflow of new immigrants that has tended to keep Hispanics in close contact with their cultural heritage. This is in marked contrast to Blacks, who were largely stripped of their cultural heritage when they were forcibly brought to the United States as slaves (Frazier 1966). Second, although most Hispanics are bilingual, the Spanish language has tended to confer a unique identity upon them as well as to separate them from English speaking members of society.[8]

The present and rapidly increasing size of the Hispanic population, along with its extreme geographic concentration, makes this an important market segment. There is, surprisingly, virtually no academic work on the marketing implications of the Hispanic subculture. Trade publications, however, contain a wealth of information on the buying behavior of Hispanics. Although much of this work is anecdotal and unsupported by published research, it illustrates how marketers can improve their performance by recognizing the special characteristics of the Hispanic market.[9]

---

[5]For a detailed discussion of the problems in identifying the Hispanic population, see "Coverage of the Hispanic Population of the United States in the 1970 Census: A Methodological Analysis," *Current Population Reports,* P-23, no. 82. Washington, D.C.: Government Printing Office.

[6]See "The Newest Americans: A Second 'Spanish Invasion'," *U.S. News & World Report,* July 8, 1974.

[7]Total fertility rates are currently unavailable for Hispanics. For this reason "Expected Lifetime Births" has been substituted in Table 14.5. The difference between the two fertility measures is that total fertility is a statistical projection that assumes that each woman will experience the reproductive history of a specific group (e.g., Hispanics), while expected lifetime births is the sum of births to date and future births that women of child bearing age expect. Generally, the two measures follow a similar pattern with total fertility being slightly lower than expected lifetime births.

[8]It is interesting to note that the current debate over bilingual education largely centers around the desirability of allowing a unique subculture with its own language and values to develop within the United States.

[9]An especially interesting source of information on the Hispanic market is the supplement to the April 16, 1981 issue of *Advertising Age.*

Table 14.5
Selected demographic and socioeconomic characteristics of Hispanic, Black, and White Americans

Variable	Hispanic	Black	White
Total Population (000)***	13,244	26,488	188,341
Residential Location			
Metropolitan Areas	84.0%	79.2%	73.3%
In Central Cities	50.3	57.1	25.0
Outside Central Cities	33.7	20.1	48.3
Outside Metropolitan Areas	16.0	20.8	26.7
Family Structure			
Husband-Wife Household	76.5%	55.5%	85.6%
Female-Headed Household	19.2	40.2	11.6
Male-Headed Household,	4.3	4.3	2.8
no wife present			
Expected Lifetime Births****	2.34	2.21	2.02
Median Age	23.2	24.9	31.3
Male	22.7	23.6	30.0
Female	23.8	26.2	32.6
College Enrollment of Persons			
18–24 Years Old**			
Males	24.7%	26.4%	34.0%
Females	19.1	28.8	30.2
Four or More Years of College			
by Persons Age 25–34	9.2%	12.7%	25.4%
Income			
Mean Family Income	13,423	10,216	17,333
Percent $10,000 or Over	64.3%	50.9%	72.7%
Percent $25,000 or Over	18.5	13.6	29.8
Percent Below Poverty Level	19.7	27.6	6.8
Percent Registered Voters	36.3%	60.0%	68.4%

Note: All data are for 1978 unless otherwise noted.
*1976
**1977
***1980
****1981

Source: See Table 14.1 for sources of Black and White data. Hispanic data have been compiled from the following Bureau of the Census documents:
(1) *Current Population Reports,* Series P-20, No. 362, 1981.
(2) *Current Population Reports,* Series P-60, No. 130, 1981.
(3) *Current Population Reports,* Series P-20, No. 371, 1981.
(4) *Current Population Reports,* Series P-20, No. 369, 1982.
(5) *1981 Statistical Abstract of the United States.*

It has been found, for example, that Hispanics spend about 10 percent more for food and visit fast food restaurants more often than non-Spanish speaking buyers (Aguayo 1977). Hispanics are also reported to be highly brand loyal and to be resistent to innovations. Although low income is probably a factor underlying their behavior, it has been suggested that lack of education and language problems may also be involved. Campbell Soup, for example, had great difficulty with the Hispanic market because of lack of familiarity with the *concept* of condensed soup, the absence of a picture on the package illustrating product use, and misreading of soup labels that sometimes lead Hispanic buyers to read a label such as "celery" soup as "cereal" soup (Rothmyer 1975).

Hispanics are reported to frequently complain about pricing techniques such as multiple pricing, simultaneous presence of preprinted and stamped prices, and cents-off labels (Loudon and Della Bitta 1979, p. 159). Part of the reason for this relates to the fact that most Hispanics come to this country poor and are proud that they have made it and can afford to pay the full price (Diaz-Albertini 1979). Part of the reason, however, clearly relates to language difficulties.

The point regarding language raises all of the issues discussed earlier in conjunction with culture and, especially, the technique of back-translation. For example, the literal translation of Coke's "It's the Real Thing" had a somewhat off-color meaning (Aguayo 1977); while a Tang breakfast drink commercial featuring a woman Ph.D. serving Tang to her family had to be changed because it was not believable to the Hispanic audience (Rothmyer 1975).

The basic conclusions to be drawn from our brief discussion of the Hispanic market should by now be familiar. Although Hispanics are *not* always different in their buying behavior, they frequently are and it behooves the marketer to be sensitive to such potential differences and their implications for developing effective marketing strategy. Furthermore, the marketer will often need specialized help in effectively reaching the Hispanic market. Fortunately, many firms, especially certain advertising agencies and the Spanish-language media, specialize in this task. In addition to generally available print media and radio, a number of Hispanic-oriented television stations have emerged in recent years in areas of large Hispanic populations.

SOCIAL CLASS

The final basis for defining subgroups of buyers to be considered is social class. Although Americans have traditionally been reluctant to admit the existence of a class stratified society, social stratification is readily apparent and generally recognized in a variety of implicit and exlicit ways. As shall be seen, there are significant differences among social classes that are of importance to marketers.

The Concept of a Social Class

Social classes represent relatively permanent and homogeneous divisions in society, which differ in levels of prestige and esteem. That is, the social class concept implies a *vertical* stratification of society. Within a social class, individuals *tend* to share common interests, opinions, attitudes, lifestyles, values, and behavior. This occurs for two primary reasons. First, differing levels of education, occupation, job security, income, etc. tend to give each social class a unique position from which it experiences life. Second, general social exchange occurs primarily within social classes. Contacts between social classes tend to be specialized; e.g., doctor-patient, plumber-homeowner. This tends to isolate each social class and to strengthen common opinions, attitudes, values, and behavior.

Although some type of social stratification exists in all societies, the number of strata, the basis for stratification, and the possibility of moving from one stratum to another differ considerably across cultures. At one extreme is the caste system of

India, which has a large number of castes, based on parentage and deeply rooted in religious beliefs, with formal prohibitions against movement and even contact among castes.[10] At an intermediate position in terms of rigidity and formality, the British class system has both formal elements (e.g., the nobility) and informal elements (e.g., language).[11] The class system in the United States tends to be at the other extreme in the sense that it is informal and formally open to movement between social classes. The class system within the United States is primarily based on *source* of income, education, and, especially, occupation. Most discussions of social class in the United States recognize four to six distinct social classes.

Although informal, the American class system is quite real. This is seen, for example, in surveys of occupational prestige that typically show high levels of agreement among people regarding the perceived prestige of a wide range of occupations. Such perceptions tend to be stable over long periods of time. For example, Hawkins, Coney, and Best (1980, p. 155) cite two studies of the "standing" of 90 occupations by the National Opinion Research Center, which correlated at .99 despite a sixteen-year separation between the two studies. Particularly interesting is the fact that young children rate occupations almost identically with older children and adults (Simmons and Rosenberg 1971). This suggests just how deeply ingrained class consciousness is in America.

The American class system is, at least in comparison with most other cultures, relatively open to movement of individuals between social classes. Despite this fact, research shows a high degree of stability in the class structure of the United States and large odds against actual, as opposed to potential, movement between social classes (Hauser, et. al. 1975; Tyree and Hodge 1978). This stability, along with the tendency for interpersonal communication to occur primarily *within* social classes, may account for the attitudinal, value, and behavioral differences that continue to persist among social classes despite the presumed leveling influences of the mass media, and rising education and income levels (cf., Lenski 1966; Nisbett 1968; Rich and Jain 1968; Schaninger 1981).

A proper understanding of the social class concept requires that two points be kept in mind. First, social class is a multidimensional concept. This gives rise to the concepts of "status crystalization" and its counterpart "status incongruence." Persons of crystalized status are consistent in terms of occupation, education, residence, source of income, and other variables that define social class membership. Such persons tend to closely follow social class stereotypes. Status incongruence occurs when there are inconsistencies among the variables that define social class membership; e.g., the English professor who has high education and occupational prestige but relatively low income. Such persons tend to behave in discrepant, nonconforming ways and may be more receptive to social change and product innovation (Schaninger 1981, p. 194).

Second, it is important to remember that the boundaries that define the social classes are somewhat arbitrary (Felson 1975). This is especially important for marketers, since the social class concept, and the scales used to assess social class, have been *developed* largely outside of the marketing context. This, of course,

---

[10]Although outlawed by the British, the caste system continues to operate in India, especially in rural areas.

[11]The play *My Fair Lady* was largely about how a Cockney accent both identified and permanently consigned one to the lower class.

raises all of the issues of borrowing raised in the first chapter of this book. Despite this important caveat, sufficient empirical research links buyer behavior to social class so that there is no doubt about the potential usefulness to marketers of social class as a segmentation variable.

Measuring Social Class

In order to use social class as a segmentation variable, it must be measurable. Over the years, sociologists have developed a variety of techniques for measuring social class. Krech, Crutchfield, and Ballachery (1962, pp. 313–319) divide these techniques into four categories: reputational, sociometric, subjective, and objective. The reputational method involves asking respondents to rate the social position of other persons. This task is easily performed, even by persons who say they are not class conscious. The reputational method was developed by Warner, Meeker, and Eels (1949). Warner is responsible for some of the most important work on social class in America. Sociometric techniques involve assessing interpersonal association to define cliques and social classes. The classic example of sociometric analysis is Hollingshead's (1949) study of Elmstown youth. Because of inherent biases, subjective measures in which subjects rate their own social status have been generally abandoned.

Reputational and sociometric techniques for measuring social class tend to be expensive and are essentially limited to small geographic areas. Marketers generally require measurement techniques that can be economically administered to large numbers of individuals who are geographically dispersed. Multiple-item and single-item objective indices of social class are well suited to the typical requirements of the marketer.

Multiple-item indices of social class involve a system of weights that are applied to two or more indicators of social status. Among the many variables used in such indices are occupation, source of income, house type, dwelling area, property value, education, and expenditures for housing. A large number of specific multiple-item indices of social class have been proposed (e.g., Hollingshead and Redlick 1958, Warner, Meeker, and Eels 1949, Coleman and Rainwater 1978, Carmen 1965, Ellis, Lane, and Oleson 1963). Because they are both well known and are generally accepted the discussion will concentrate on the indices developed by Warner and Hollingshead.

Warner's *Index of Status Characteristics* (ISC) is based on occupation, source of income, house type, and dwelling area. Respondents are sorted into one of seven categories on each scale. The scale values are then multiplied by the following weights:

occupation	4
source of income	3
house type	3
dwelling area	2

and summed to form an overall social status score. Based on the total ISC score Warner defines the following six social classes:

upper upper	(1.4 percent)
lower upper	(1.6 percent)
upper middle	(10.2 percent)
lower middle	(28.1 percent)
upper lower	(32.6 percent)
lower lower	(25.2 percent)

The second major multiple-item index of social class was developed by Hollingshead (Hollingshead and Redlich 1958). This index is based on occupation, dwelling area, and education. A two-factor version of this index has been found to be very satisfactory. Because it is inexpensive and easy to use, this index has been widely employed in buyer behavior studies. The Hollingshead index requires individuals to be assigned to one of seven occupational and educational categories. Occupation is weighted by seven and education by four. Based on the sums of these two weighted variables respondents are assigned to one of five social classes. Further details are presented in Table 14.6.

Table 14.6
Hollingshead two-factor index of social class

A. Occupation scale

Description	Score
Higher executives of large concerns, proprietors, and major professionals	1
Business managers, proprietors of medium-sized businesses, and lesser professionals	2
Administrative personnel, owners of small businesses, and minor professionals	3
Clerical and sales workers, technicians, and owners of little business	4
Skilled manual employees	5
Machine operators and semiskilled employees	6
Unskilled employees	7

B. Educational scale

Description	Score
Professional (M.A., M.S., M.E., M.D., Ph.D., LL.B., and the like)	1
Four-year college graduate (A.B., B.S., B.M.)	2
One to three years college (also business schools)	3
High school graduate	4
Ten to eleven years of school (part high school)	5
Seven to nine years of school	6
Under seven years of school	7

C. Weighting system
[Occupational score × 7] + [Educational score × 4] = Index score

D. Classification system

Class	Range of scores
I	11–17
II	18–31
III	32–47
IV	48–63
V	64–77

Source: August B. Hollingshead and Frederick C. Redlich, *Social Class and Mental Illness.* (New York: Wiley & Sons, 1958. Reprinted with permission.

Single-item indices of social status almost always use one of the components of the multiple-item indices just discussed. Generally education or occupation is used as the single-item index of social status. Both variables have the advantage of simplicity. Education, of course, can be used directly since social status increases with increasing education. Occupation, however, requires conversion to a numerical index of social status. Fortunately, extremely detailed tables of occupational prestige have been published. Siegel (1971), for example, developed such an index for all 435 occupations listed in the Bureau of the Census' *Classified Index of Industries and Occupations.* An excellent reference for indices of occupational prestige, as well as suggestions for eliciting occupational information from respondents, is Hauser and Featherman (1977).

The multiplicity of available indices of social status raises the question of which index to select for a specific study. The best advice on this question is to carefully consider which of the variables used to define social class is likely to be related to the behavior under study. Education, for example, is likely to be closely related to the consumption of a wide range of cultural, intellectually oriented goods and services. This is clearly shown in a study by Dimaggio and Useem (1978), which examined the relationship between seven types of cultural consumption (art museum, theater, classical music, science museum, book reading, cinema, and popular music) and education and income. With the exception of cinema (movies) and popular music, education was more closely related to cultural consumption than income. This was particularly true of classical music where 77 percent of college graduates but only 23 percent of those without a college degree reported listening to classical music within the last twelve months.

In a very similar way, occupation tends to permit and often requires certain types of lifestyles, which makes occupation a particularly good segmentation variable. For example, both the amount and type of business related entertaining vary considerably by occupation. This should tend to make occupation a relevant segmentation variable for a wide range of products; e.g., home furnishings, silver, china, crystal, carpets, draperies, gourmet cookware. Also, both the amount and timing of leisure time varies considerably by occupation, which makes occupation a potentially useful segmentation variable for any buyer behavior study that involves the use of leisure time.

Multiple-item indices of social status are likely to be especially relevant in situations that involve a person's general social prestige. For example, studies of social influence and opinion leadership should probably use a multiple-item index. Multiple-item indices also give the researcher the flexibility to examine the individual components of social class to determine if a single index or some unique combination of variables is best suited for the problem under study.

Social Class Profiles

So far social class has been discussed in quite general terms. Before proceeding to discuss specific relationships between social class and buyer behavior, a brief description or profile of the different social classes will be presented. These profiles will be based on Warner's six-part classification of social classes and are taken primarily from Warner, Meeker, and Eels (1949), Coleman (1960), and Levy (1966).

The *upper upper* class are the elite members of society. Most have inherited wealth and are sufficiently secure in their social position that they may deviate from their class norms when they choose without loss of status. Such persons are active in community and cultural affairs and tend to emphasize breeding and community responsibility. They dress conservatively, spend money as if it were unimportant, avoid ostentatious purchases and displays of wealth, and send their children to the best private schools. Pirie (1960) has suggested that this group tends to emulate the British aristocracy. Constituting less than 2 percent of the market this group is of little importance to the mass marketer.[12]

The *lower upper* class is distinguished from the upper upper class primarily by the fact that their wealth has been earned rather than inherited. This class is the *nouveaux riche.* Being new to wealth they are less secure in their social position. This group tends to display its new wealth and status through ownership of large homes in the best areas, swimming pools, luxury automobiles, expensive jewelry and clothing, and other conspicuous symbols of status. Despite its small size, less than 2 percent, this group constitutes an important market for luxury goods and for innovations that are perceived to convey social status.

The *upper middle* class is composed of successful professional and business people who are strongly career oriented and achievement motivated but lack the wealth and status of the upper classes. Well educated, the *upper middle* class demands high educational performance from their children. The home is of central importance to this group as it is a symbol of their success. Upper middle class families emphasize gracious living, demand high quality and value in the products they purchase, carefully evaluate their purchases, are fashion conscious, and emphasize leisure activities as a counterbalance to their busy professional lives. Women in this group are especially likely to make their purchasing decisions as a means of self-expression. Constituting something over 10 percent of the population, their relatively high incomes make the upper middle class an extremely important market.

The *lower middle* class consists of white-collar workers, small businessmen, and highly paid blue-collar workers. These are the typical Americans who emphasize respectability, a strong work ethic, and close adherence to cultural norms. Although relatively well paid, this group is not strongly career oriented. Unsure of their own tastes, the lower middle class tend to be emulators. They are not innovators. The home is very important and they want it to be neat, presentable, and located in a respectable neighborhood. The home, however, is not a symbol of success. Traditional and family oriented, the lower middle class family works hard at shopping, tends to be price sensitive, and is motivated by pride in a comfortable and well run home. The lower middle class constitutes approximately 28 percent of the population.

The *upper lower* class is composed primarily of blue-collar workers. Also referred to as the working class, this group largely works at routine, uncreative, dull jobs and sees work as a means to an end. Many working class families, especially those who enjoy union wages and security, have a fair amount of

---

[12]The estimates of the sizes of the different social classes most frequently cited are both approximate and dated. Despite this these estimates are probably still relatively good because the *relative* position of individuals does not appear to have changed appreciably since World War II. This situation is clearly evident in U.S. Census Bureau data which show that the distribution of income has remained virtually unchanged since the end of World War II.

discretionary income. This group is especially subject to impulse purchasing as a means of escaping the dull routine of their lives. They also tend to be highly brand loyal. When vacationing they are very likely to visit a relative in another city. Constituting approximately one-third of the population, the upper lower class, along with the lower middle class, form the heart of what is generally referred to as the mass market.

The final group, the *lower lower* class, is composed of persons who are generally unskilled, poorly educated, and socially disadvantaged. They are often perceived by higher status persons as being somewhat disreputable. Upper lower class people, in particular, are especially anxious not to be confused with them. Occupying a marginal position in society, the buying behavior of this group is severely constrained. Despite this, they frequently impulse buy and engage in what Rotzoll (1967) has called "compensatory consumption" aimed at compensating for their bleak present and unpromising future. Thus, expensive cars and color televisions are not uncommon among this group. Poorly informed about alternative choices, the lower lower class often pays too much, buys on credit at high interest rates, and too frequently is stuck with low quality goods because of an inability to make sound value judgments. The lower lower class constitutes 20 to 25 percent of the market.[13]

Social Class Differences in Buying Behavior

The discussion of social class should make it abundantly clear that social class differences in buyer behavior do exist. This section reviews the literature regarding these differences. In evaluating this literature, three points should be kept in mind. First, many of the citations are out of date. This is an accurate reflection of the literature. Fortunately, a recent study by Schaninger (1981) confirmed many of these earlier findings. Second, many of the frequently cited differences in buying behavior are based on a small number of studies that are difficult to compare directly. Third, the results of social class studies are often complex. Thus, the reader should regard the specific studies reviewed here as illustrative and suggestive rather than definitive.

Social class differences have been found for a number of goods and services. Clothing has been widely studied both because it is a highly visible item and casual observation suggests class related differences in the style and quality of clothing (Hoult 1954, Gordon 1957, Ostermeier and Eicher 1966). Schaninger (1981) has found that higher social classes tend to purchase more high priced dresses and men's suits. He notes that this supports earlier work by Coleman (1960) and Levy (1966). Research also suggests that upper and middle class women are more style conscious and interested in fashion than lower class women. They are more likely to read fashion magazines, attend fashion shows, and observe and discuss fashion (Rich and Jain 1968). Closely related to fashion consciousness is the observation

---

[13]An in-depth and fascinating portrait of the marketing system with which the poor must cope and the buying behavior of the poor (roughly equivalent to Warner's lower lower class) is presented in Caplovitz's *The Poor Pay More* (1964). Although dated, and probably somewhat attentuated by subsequent consumer legislation, this book continues to be one of the best references for understanding the buying behavior of the lowest socioeconomic group of consumers.

by Roscoe, LeClaire, and Schiffman (1977) that lower class women dress more for comfort than fashion. Finally, social class has been positively related to the use of makeup (Wells 1972, Schaninger 1981). Schaninger's data, however, are complex and suggest the need to consider income and working status for at least some types of cosmetics.

Social class differences in the emphasis on style, fashion, and comfort have also been found for home decorating and major appliances. A number of researchers have found that the value of furniture owned is directly related to both social class and income (Coleman 1960, Tucker 1964, Levy 1966, Schaninger 1981). Higher social classes tend to use highly styled furniture, art, and sculpture as a means of self-expression. In contrast, lower social classes emphasize comfort, sturdiness, and maintenance (Levy 1966). A feel for the social class differences in home decorating is provided by a study of living room styles by Laumann and House (1970). Using a 53-item checklist and direct observation, Laumann and House found that differences in living room styles could be explained by two basic factors: social status and modern vs. traditional orientation. Figure 14.1 presents a graphic summary of their results.

Social class differences in appliance ownership have also been found. The higher social classes are reported to own more modern appliances, prefer colored appliances, and indicate a greater general willingness to pay for the better things in life (Coleman 1960, Levy 1966, Roscoe, LeClaire, and Schiffman, 1977). Other researchers, however, argued that often, but not always, income provides a better basis for segmenting the appliance market (Myers and Mount 1973, Schaninger 1981). These somewhat contradictory results may be explained by generally rising incomes, widespread diffusion of most major appliances, and inconsistent definitions of both independent and dependent variables.

Another area where there are major differences among social classes is in the use of leisure time. We have already noted differences in reading and cultural events. Tennis, bridge, canasta, swimming, skiing, and ice skating have all been associated with higher social status. In contrast, boxing, hunting, fishing, roller derby, bingo, and bowling are more heavily engaged in by lower social status individuals (Graham 1956, Adams and Butler 1967, Bishop and Ikeda 1970). Researchers have also found that the higher social classes are more likely to participate in solitary or two-person activities and to pursue leisure time activities as a family (Greendorfer 1978). This research provides marketers with insights into both to whom and how they should promote their products.

Many social class differences in food and beverage consumption have also been reported (Levy 1966, Schaninger 1981). Schaninger's data are particularly important because they generally support older studies (Schaninger 1981, p. 198). In general, what these data suggest is that food has more symbolic value to the higher classes and more pragmatic value to the lower social classes. The higher social classes are also more likely to be self-indulgent in their eating and drinking habits.

A number of social class differences in the sources and uses of credit have been reported. The higher social classes rely more on banks and insurance policies, while the lower classes rely more on personal finance companies, credit unions, and friends. While higher social class persons are more likely to possess and use credit cards, there are even stronger differences in the uses to which they put their cards (Mathews and Slocum 1969, Slocum and Mathews 1970, Plummer 1971,

Figure 14.1.
Social status and living room styles

Source: Edward O. Laumann and James S. House, "Living Room Styles and Social Attributes: The Patterning of Material Artifacts in a Modern Urban Community." *Sociology and Social Research*, 54 (April 1970): 326. Reprinted with permission.

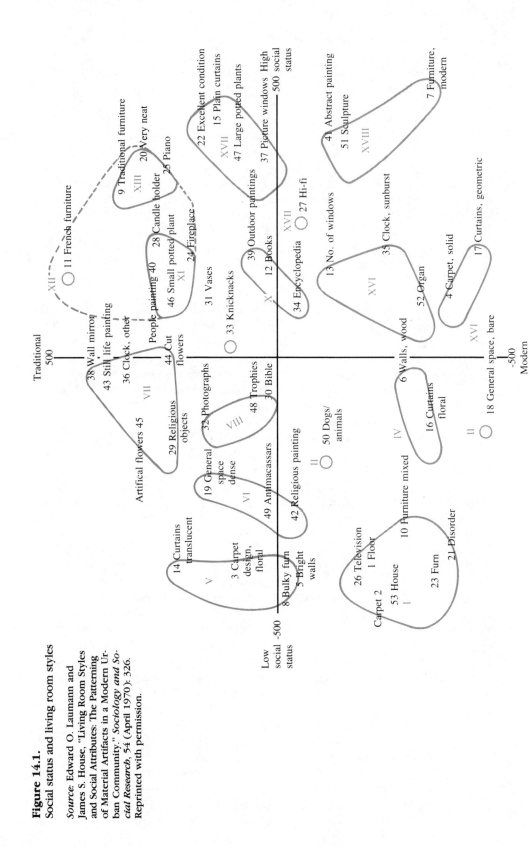

Hawes, Blackwell, and Talarzyk 1977). Higher class persons have more favorable attitudes toward credit cards and are more likely to use their cards as a convenience and for the purchase of luxury goods. In contrast, lower class persons are more likely to use their credit cards as a type of installment loan for the purchase of durable and necessary goods.

In the above discussion we have referred several times to income as a competing and/or complementary variable to social class effects on buyer behavior. The reader may also recall our discussion of over/under- priviledgedness as a basis for explaining automobile purchasing behavior. This taps us into a debate that raged in the late 1960s and early 1970s as to *whether* social class *or* income was the best predictor of buyer behavior (cf., Schaninger 1981). Schaninger argues that the relevant question is not whether but under what conditions social class, income, or some combination of these two variables is likely to be superior. Based on a comprehensive literature review and a wide ranging empirical study, he offers the following guidelines.

1. Social class is superior to income for areas of consumer behavior that do not involve high dollar expenditures, but do reflect underlying lifestyle, value, or homemaker role differences not captured by income. Such differences as importance of quality or quality symbolism, price-rational versus deal-prone orientations, impulsiveness, preferences for active versus passive entertainment, concern with health and body, self-indulgence, immediate gratification, and emphasis on the evening meal are identified by Levy (1966, 1971) across social classes. They are reflected in greater significance for social class in consumption of instant, frozen, and canned convenience foods and beverages and their "prepare from scratch" counterparts; snack foods and sweet beverages; imported and domestic wines; shopping behavior and deal proneness; and evening television exposure.

    Although social class and income are equivalent in predicting value of furniture owned, social class is clearly superior for both method and place of purchase of highly visible, symbolic, and expensive livingroom furniture as suggested by Coleman (1960).

2. Income is generally superior for major kitchen and laundry appliances, products which require substantial expenditures, and, contrary to Coleman's (1960) findings, may no longer serve as symbols of status within class or as status symbols to the upper lower class. Evidently, ability to pay for providing for basic necessities and more visible symbols of status is the important factor in predicting major appliance ownership and feature levels. Income is also superior for soft drinks, mixers, and distilled alcohol when frequency of purchase is examined. Heavier in-home (and thus nonvisible) consumption of such products may reflect ability to pay for these "luxury" items even though they do not require major expenditures.

3. The combination of social class and income is generally superior for product classes that are highly visible, serve as symbols of social class or status within class, and require either moderate or substantial expenditure (clothing and makeup, automobiles, and television sets).

    Although relative income is supported for automobile ownership (and television sets to a lesser degree), status incongruence/inconsistency is also supported for these categories. Support is obtained for a modified version of relative income for several makeup usage items and for higher priced dress purchases.

    Status incongruence/inconsistency is strongly supported for low priced dresses and receives some support for grocery shopping behavior. Lower income upper middle class housewives are more likely to purchase low priced dresses, and lower income upper middle and lower middle class housewives are also more likely to take advantage of grocery pricing promotions than housewives of the same classes in higher income quartiles—indicating a willingness to compromise their social class tendencies to cope with low relative income.

Relative social class is supported for television ownership and for several meat convenience food entrees. For such products, income or ability to buy tends to mask underlying social class tendencies, which become stronger after removal of income.

Finally, and especially noteworthy, is the finding by Hirisch and Peters (1974) that social class effects are more closely associated with the *frequency* of use or purchase than with simple usage/nonusage of a product.

Another aspect of buying behavior that has been related to social class is store choice. Stores, just like goods and services, often project a very distinct image (Levy 1966). In fact, buyers can often identify the social classes to which a store appeals even if they do not shop there (McCann 1957). Good examples of this are Tiffany's, Neiman-Marcus, and Saks Fifth Avenue. Print advertisements, in particular, tend to identify the social class of a store. High class stores typically use delicate line drawings and large amounts of white space; lower class stores tend to use crowded ads with large block print.

There is evidence that buyers tend to shop in stores in which they feel comfortable. This is particularly a problem for lower class women who often feel they are punished by clerks for shopping in higher status stores (Martineau 1958). Martineau, for example, relates the anecdote of one woman who, after waiting some time to be helped, was told "We thought you were a clerk" (p. 121). The reader, no doubt, has had similar experiences; e.g., being in a restaurant where the menu is in French or Spanish, a clothing store without posted prices. Closely related to the issue of comfort is research by Rich and Jain (1968) to indicate that upper class persons are especially attracted by a pleasant store atmosphere and interesting displays. There is also evidence that middle class families are especially sensitive to price differences among stores and most willing to try store brands (Murphy 1978) and to shop at home via mail or telephone (Gillett 1970).

The relationships between social class and store choice vary both over time and products. Both effects are well illustrated by discount stores. Originally discount stores appealed primarily to middle class buyers who were both price sensitive *and* sufficiently self-confident to choose products that were not national brands (Martineau 1957, Ross 1965). Now most discount stores carry a wide range of national brands. In a more recent study, Prasad (1975) found that social class was negatively related to patronage of discount stores for products high in social risk; e.g., clothing and accessories, stereos, china. As hypothesized, Prasad found no effect from economic risk on the relationship between social class and patronage of discount stores. A study by Dardis and Sandler (1971), which found social class negatively related to the purchase of clothing in discount stores, lends further support to Prasad's results.

Finally, a number of studies link social class to information acquisition and the specific media used. Previous chapters frequently observed that individuals with low income and education are less likely to acquire information before purchase

Table 14.7
Prepurchase sources of information for appliances by social class

Source	Lower Class	Middle Class
	%	%
Brochures and leaflets	17.1	26.6
Newspaper and magazine ads	6.7	12.2
Friends, neighbors	2.6	13.7
Test Reports	—	12.2
In-store sources	42.3	15.8
No source specified	34.6	30.2
No answer	0.8	10.1
n =	236	278

Percentages sum to more than 100% because of multiple responses.

Source: Gordon R. Foxall, "Social Factors in Consumer Choice: Replication and Extension." *Journal of Consumer Research*, 2 (June 1975): 62. Reprinted with permission.

and are less likely to receive value from their purchases. These same patterns hold for social class. Data obtained by Foxall (1975), presented in Table 14.7, illustrate social class differences in prepurchase information acquisition. Note especially, the heavy reliance upon in-store sources of information by lower class buyers.

There are also rather major differences in the degree to which different social classes make use of different media. Education, in particular, is strongly related to use of different media. Robinson (1977) found that education is negatively related to television viewing and positively related to listening to radio, reading magazines and books, reading news and analysis magazines, and editorials. Fortunately for the marketer, most media have developed audience profiles that are often extremely detailed.

SUMMARY

As seen in this chapter, large differences exist in the buying behavior of persons grouped by culture, subculture, and social class. Recognition of these differences provides an important basis for the development of effective market segmentation strategies.

Throughout this and the last two chapters, it has been necessary to raise caveats regarding the definitiveness and current validity of the research reviewed. It has been suggested that the reader regard the specific findings cited as illustrative and suggestive of the nature of cultural, subcultural, and social class differences among buyers. What this research should provide to the reader is ideas that must be tested against and adapted to specific marketing situations.

Collective Buying
Behavior

VI

Up to this point, the analysis of buyer behavior has focused on the behavior of the individual buyer. It has, of course, been recognized that buying behavior occurs within a larger social context and that individual buyers sometimes rely heavily upon social cues in making their buying decisons. However, even in the discussion of reference groups, the perspective has been on how individual buyers incorporate social cues into their individual buying decisions.

In this and the next chapter, attention is turned to buyer behavior that is conducted and experienced on a collective basis. Although it is difficult to specify the amount, it is clear that many buying decisions, as well as the actual consumption of goods and services, involve collective actions. This occurs, for example, when two friends *decide* to buy a boat together, to take a joint vacation, or to pool their experience and effort in preserving and sharing the produce from their gardens. The primary collective buying agencies are, of course, the family and business organizations. Because research on collective buyer behavior is largely limited to the family and business organizations, we shall limit our discussion to these two entities.

Most presentations of the topics discussed in the next two chapters are characterized as family or organizational "decision making." The title Collective Buying Behavior has been chosen to reflect the fact that the entire range of involvement, effort, and consciousness is present in family and organizational buying behavior. For important decisions (e.g., buying a new home or factory), the decision-making process may be both elaborate and formally constituted in some type of "family council" or "purchasing committee." Often, however, low involvement and dissonance/attribution processes operate. Families and businesses both purchase many incidental supplies with no more thought or effort than an individual buyer gives to buying new shoelaces. And, both families and business organizations are subject to the exigencies of life that often given rise to dissonance/attribution processes; e.g., leaking plumbing, broken furnaces.

In terms of the overall organization of this text, the next two chapters represent both a shift in focus and a general continuation of the last three chapters. The shift in focus, of course, is from an individual to a collective perspective. However, the text also discusses how structural differences among families and organizations affect buying behavior. This aspect of these two chapters is a continuation of our discussion of how individual and social group differences among buyers present the marketer with opportunities to develop more effective and profitable segmented marketing strategies.

Collective Buying Behavior: Family Buying Behavior

15

Despite dramatic social changes in recent decades, the family remains the basic unit of social organization. Among the many decisions that families make are purchasing and consuming decisions. A basic marketing implication of this fact is that a full and proper understanding of consumer behavior requires knowledge of how the interdependencies of family life affect consumer behavior.

This chapter is organized into three major sections: an analysis of the similarity between family and organizational buying behavior; a discussion on the marketing and ethical implications of research into collective buying behavior, and a review of family buying behavior. The discussion continues in the next chapter, which takes up the topic of organizational buying. As you read this chapter, keep in mind that the first two sections are relevant both to family and organizational buying.

THE SIMILARITY BETWEEN CONSUMER AND ORGANIZATIONAL BUYING BEHAVIOR

The first issue regarding collective buying behavior that must be addressed concerns the degree of similarity between consumer and organizational buying behavior. Consumers, both as individuals and as families, would appear on the surface to be quite different from all other types of purchasers. For example, organizations are commonly presumed to be far more rational buyers than individual consumers and families. Thus, one might presume that organizational buying behavior would require quite different theories and concepts than consumer buying behavior.

In fact, there are a great many similarities between families and organizations. Both are formal, legally sanctioned collectives. Both typically accord members of the group differential authority and responsibility for making specific types of purchasing decisions. Within both families and organizations, the full range of specialized roles may be seen manifested in different individuals; e.g., buyer, user, decision maker, gatekeeper, influencer. Furthermore, both types of groups require balancing collective and individual goals, reliance on a common pool of resources, and recognition that the actions of individual members of the group frequently affect the well-being of other group members. These, and other, shared attributes create the *potential* for substantial conflict in both families and organizations. Thus, both types of groups typically try to establish rules and decision-making strategies that will minimize conflict.

At a more formal level, researchers have generally concluded that there is a high degree of similarity between consumer and organizational buying behavior. Sheth, in a review of the literature on organizational buyer behavior, summarizes this argument very effectively.

> A remarkable degree of parallel research, thought, and discovery exists between organizational and household buying behavior.... Contrary to popular belief, research clearly indicates that organizational buyers are no more rational than consumers in their purchase decisions. The only area where there seem to be some differences is the greater formalization of the buying process as shown by requisition slips, written agreements, formal negotiations with the help of legal departments, and the like in organizational buying as compared to consumer buying behavior. Even more remarkable is the tendency of scholars and researchers to extend the same economic and behavioral theories of choice making to both household and organizational buying behavior (1977, p. 30).

For these reasons, the title chosen for this book is the inclusive *Buyer Behavior* rather than the most popular *Consumer Behavior* or *Consumer and Organizational Buyer Behavior*. This is not to suggest that there are no significant differences in buying behavior between consumers and organizations. Rather, it seems reasonable to assume that these differences are largely matters of degree, and that basic theories and concepts are generally as applicable to organizations as to individual consumers and families. Stated somewhat differently, the differences that exist between consumers and organizations are probably of no greater magnitude than those that exist between different types of consumers. They are also of no lesser importance to the development of effective marketing strategies.

MARKETING AND ETHICAL IMPLICATIONS OF RESEARCH ON COLLECTIVE BUYING BEHAVIOR

Each individual involved in a collective activity brings his or her own unique motivations, preferences, attitudes, and a host of other elements to that activity. Thus, the study of buyer behavior in the first fourteen chapters is clearly relevant to the study of collective buying behavior. Collective buying involves an *additional* set of dynamic factors, factors which are frequently powerful and often subtle, that must be assessed in order to fully understand the complete buying *process*.

At a general level, collective buying has two basic kinds of marketing implications: determination of who makes the buying decision and resolution of internal conflicts. Regarding the first implication, virtually all families and organizations manifest considerable role specialization in who makes specific types of purchasing decisions. This role specialization occurs both across *and* within decisions for different goods and services. In some situations (e.g., home owner's insurance), the entire decision may be delegated to a single individual. In other situations (e.g., automobiles or computers), there may be considerable joint decision making. In joint decision making, there is often considerable variation in interest among decision makers at various stages of the decision process and in various aspects of the final decision. For example, Dad may be more likely to initiate the idea to buy a new car and be more concerned with performance. Once initiated, Mom may be more interested in interior styling, color, and comfort.[1] Similarly, various members of an organization considering a computer purchase may have quite different interests in the cost, speed, and flexibility of various alternatives, as well as the uses to which it will be put.

Determining who decides can affect virtually every aspect of the firm's marketing strategy. To *whom* should the marketing firm target its promotions designed to stimulate initial buying interest? In designing the product or service *whose* preferences should dominate the many specific components of the design of the complete product or service? In pricing the product or service *whose* price sensitivity is most relevant? In assessing the importance of image congruence in brand choice decisions, *whose* self and brand images should be measured? All of these questions require answers to the basic question: Who decides?

---

[1]These particular examples may strike some readers as sexist; however, they reflect typical research findings. More generally, the *tendency* of most research findings on family buying behavior is toward stereotypical male/female roles. Buying roles, however, show considerable variation across families.

Although determining who decides is clearly important, it is often difficult. For unimportant decisions, no one may be able to accurately determine who really decided. For complex decisions, especially where the decision evolved over a long period or where a substantial number of people were involved, it may be difficult or even impossible to accurately reconstruct the decision process. For important decisions, answers to the question who *really* decided may be emotionally charged and ego threatening. For reasons to be subsequently discussed, group members may be unwilling or even unable to answer the question under such conditions. For these reasons, it is especially important for researchers to approach collective buying behavior from a variety of perspectives and methodologies; e.g., direct observation *and* retrospective questions. It is also usually desirable, although typically difficult and expensive, to gather information directly from all parties involved in the buying process.

The second basic type of implication stems from the potential for substantial conflict posed by many collective buying decisions. Although this is probably most obvious in family buying behavior, conflicts among organization members or between personal and organizational objectives are quite common. For example, the sales manager, whose performance is frequently judged on sales revenue rather than profits, can often be motivated by appeals (e.g., faster and more expensive methods to ship goods to customers), which are not necessarily in the best interest of the organization. In another area of quite direct conflict, only recently have most supposedly independent movie critics begun paying any of their own expenses at lavish movie previews thrown by Hollywood.

Conflict among members of a collective buying group presents marketers with opportunities for profit. The most desirable situation is when the marketer devises solutions that resolve the conflict. For example, a faster and more expensive method of shipment may be sufficiently important to organizational buyers that they will actually pay more than the incremental cost. In the area of family buying, different family members may have quite different ideas of what constitutes an "ideal" vacation. Some innovative universities, for example, now offer summer programs featuring a wide range of academic and nonacademic courses, supervised recreation, and proximity to local cultural and recreational events in which different family members may pursue their individual interests together.

Ethical issues may arise when marketers exploit conflicts in ways that fail to resolve, and potentially increase, the conflict. The most frequently cited example of unethical exploitation of family conflict concerns television advertising directed toward young children. Figure 15.1 presents a typical example of such criticisms. In organizational buying, the most blatant example of unethical exploitation of conflict is bribery. Although clearly not the norm in American business, the frequency of news reports of bribery suggests that the use of bribery is all too frequent.[2]

Of course, most ethical problems present more subtle questions where the answer is usually not clear to all those who consider themselves ethical persons. For example, is it ethical to promote home computers to children as sophisticated

---

[2]Interestingly, bribery is the norm in many parts of the world. Indeed, in recent years, the United States Congress has seriously debated whether U. S. laws which prohibit bribery in foreign markets should be amended to allow American business to compete more equally. To date, no such changes in the law have been made.

electronic toys while promoting the same computers to their parents as sophisticated educational tools? The reader can probably supply several arguments on
both sides of this ethical question. Such ethical questions are not resolvable by
logical means unless there is a consensus on the underlying values as well as the
facts. Thus, these brief comments on the ethical implications of better understanding of collective buying behavior is intended to sensitize the reader to the issue
rather than to provide definitive answers. As the discussions of family and organizational buying proceed, keep these underlying ethical implications in mind.

FAMILY BUYING BEHAVIOR

In a comprehensive review of the literature on "Decision Making Within the
Household," Davis (1977) observes that consumer behavior researchers have
historically been preoccupied "with consumers as individual decision makers" (pp.
73–74). The great majority of people, of course, live in multiperson households. In
addition to individual consumption, multiperson households jointly consume a
wide range of products both directly (e.g., meals and television) and indirectly
(e.g., paint and lawnmowers). Furthermore, to the extent that members of a
multiperson household draw on a common pool of resources to satisfy their
individual needs, their purchasing and consuming behaviors will be interdependent.
Clearly, a full understanding of buyer behavior requires an understanding of how
such interdependencies influence the buying process.

There are, of course, a great many types of multiperson households. Because
so much descriptive data is collected by the Bureau of the Census, their definitions
of households' types are especially important. Figure 15.2 presents these definitions.
Table 15.1 presents historical data, including data for 1980, on the number of each
type of household. The remainder of this section limits the discussion to "married
couples" as defined by the Census Bureau; i.e., husband and wife, with or without
children. Our primary reason for limiting our discussion to married couples is that
there has been little research on other types of living arrangements (Davis 1977,
Murphy and Staples 1979).

Although the lack of research on nontraditional living arrangements, particularly unmarried couples and single parent households, is a serious omission there
are many other reasons for focusing attention on married couples. Despite the
increasing number of nontraditional households, most Americans still reside in
married couple households. Specifically, in 1980, 160.5-million or 70.9 percent of
all Americans resided in married couple households. Furthermore, the median
income of married couples was at $21,540 in 1979, more than double the median
income of other types of households. Finally, and somewhat speculatively, it seems
likely that the constraining effects of married life, especially married life with
children, should make prediction of many aspects of buying behavior easier for
married couples than for other types of households. In the remainder of this
discussion, we shall use the term family synonymously with married couple.

The discussion of family buying behavior is divided into five sections. It begins
with a structural analysis of families generally referred to as the family life cycle.
Next, the general environment within which family decisions are made is examined.
This is followed by a discussion of the relative influence of husband and wife on
the family's purchasing decisions. As shall be seen, this is where much of the

Elimination of advertising on children's programs would affect only a small percentage of companies in the United States. Almost all advertising on children's TV falls into one of three categories: 1) toys, 2) edibles, 3) vitamins. TV advertisements for children's vitamins place the manufacturer's profit motive ahead of the real health needs of children. The ads suggest that children are competent to make judgments about their need for medicine. Most pediatricians feel that children who eat an adequate diet do not require vitamin supplements after one year of age. TV ads for vitamins ignore or obscure the very real health hazard to children who ingest too many candy-like pills. Ingestion of a single bottle of children's vitamins with iron added can seriously endanger a child's health. The amount of iron contained in one bottle of vitamin pills can put a four-year-old child into a coma. Yet, these vitamins are sold to children every day on television. . . . [Another] . . . category of advertising directed to children is food, which includes cereal, candy, and snack foods. Even a casual examination of ads for edibles is enough to establish that the aim of these ads is not to lead the child along the pathways to proper nutrition, but rather to cater to his fondness for sugar, to his need to be as big or as strong as his peers, or to his passion for premiums. Parents, who are concerned about what their children eat, try to limit sugar intake and encourage their children to eat fruit or raw vegetables between meals. If advertisers had their way, children's cereal would be sugared, their milk would be syrupped, and their snacks would be candy. . . .

It should also be pointed out that many ads feature standards of performance and enjoyment which are quite unattainable by children. Children can make cookies, but they can not decorate them like a master chef; they can play with target games, but not hit the bull's eye every time; they can manipulate some mechanical toys, but often not as easily as the ads promise. While an adult automatically discounts some of the promise in a commercial, a child does not—and will often blame himself if he cannot measure up to the standards he saw in the commercial. Advertising of toys on television should be confined to adult programs, with the sales message directed to adults.

Advertisements directed at children via TV are unfair because they put additional stress on the parent-child relationship. Dr. John Condry, Professor of Human Development and Psychology, Cornell University, points to the serious consequences of manipulating children to reach parents: "I believe advertisements directed toward children may seriously interfere with family life by creating conflicts between parents and children, by teaching children to be materialistic, and by disrupting attempts to teach the child responsibility." (Testimony to the Federal Trade Commission, November 10, 1971)

Parents resent advertisers who make it more difficult for them to raise responsible children. A study, *Mothers' Attitudes Toward Children's Television Programs and Commercials*, by Daniel Yankelovich, Inc., (March, 1970), found that "there is a great

Figure 15.1
An example of criticisms of television advertising directed at young children
Source: Peggy Charren, "The Child Market," *BAEYC Reports*, 8 (April 1972): 103–109. Reprinted with permission.

research on family decision making has been concentrated. Next, the discussion of husband-wife influence is broadened to a more general analysis of strategies for making family buying decisions. The section concludes with a discussion of children's influence on family buying decisions.

The Family Life Cycle

The essential idea underlying the family life cycle (FLC) concept is that the majority of persons pass through a specific sequence of stages. There will, of deal of hostility and resentment toward most commercials on children's programs. Mothers' complaints center around misrepresentation of the product, manipulation of the child, stresses and strains imposed on low income mothers by the demands created by the commercials and a general unhealthy environment." (p.4) Among the specific findings were the following: The most serious criticisms are directed at those commercials which manipulate or 'use' the child to get the mother to buy a broad variety of products from soap powder to vitamins." (pp. 6, 7). Misrepresentation is another important complaint. Mothers feel that the children are fooled into wanting something due to actual misrepresentation. Examples were given of toys and games which seem large or exciting on television—but then turn out to be very inferior once they are actually bought. This type of misrepresentation leads to frustration, disappointment, tears, etc. *Often the anger is expressed against the mother, not the sponsor.*" (pp. 7, 8, emphasis added). In all income strata, the constant duel of children asking for things and mothers having to say yes or no creates, mothers feel, an unhealthy environment and relationship." (p. 8).

It is unfair to consider children as miniature consumers. At the first National Symposium on Children and Television, held in Boston in 1970. Fred Rogers, of "Misterrogers' Neighborhood," said: "Commercialism bombards us all and all too frequently with messages which say you have to have something besides yourself to get along. You have to have a pill for a headache or a smoke to feel cool or a drink to cope, or, worst of all, a toy to play. Your resources are not enough, so be sure to buy ours. Our children are being raised on messages like this: and what is more, they think we adults condone them."

In the past few years, the amount of TV advertising directed to children has increased. Earlier, ads to children were for child-oriented products—such as toys and cereals. Today, vitamin pills, frozen dinners, bread, gasoline, shoes, and snack foods are all being advertised directly to children, with the clear implication that they should pressure their parents into buying the adult-oriented products. In the next decade we may see advertising directed to children used to promote an even wider and less-child-oriented range of products as a growing number of advertisers realize that you can sell anything to a child through television.

However, the possibility also exists that we may see advertising eliminated from children's television if enough people demonstrate their concern. Consumer groups have alerted the Federal regulatory agencies to the special needs of children, and parents and teachers are becoming more aware of the importance of television in the lives of children. Public pressure is needed to take children's television out of the marketplace, and the public has started to act.

course, be exceptions, and the exact timing of each stage will vary across individuals. Nevertheless, all persons are born into and almost all persons grow up in some type of family. Well over 90 percent of all Americans eventually marry and the vast majority of married couples will have or adopt one or more children. Furthermore, husbands, and often wives, will spend the middle portion of their lives working and raising their children. At some point the children will leave home, eventually to establish their own families, and the couple will retire. Death, of course, completes the cycle.

Since the concept was first introduced by Rowntree in 1903 as a method for

Table 15.1
Households, families, subfamilies, married couples, and unrelated individuals: 1950–1981
(In thousands, except as indicated. As of March. Prior to 1960, excludes Alaska and Hawaii.
Based on Current Population Survey; includes members of Armed Forces living off post or
with their families on post, but excludes all other members of Armed Forces; see text,
pp. 1 and 2. Minus sign (−) denotes decrease. For definition of terms, see text [Figure 15.2].
See also *Historical Statistics, Colonial Times to 1970*, series A 288–319)

Type of Unit	1950	1960	1965[1]	1970[1]	1975	1980[2]	1980[3]	1981	Percent change 1960–1970	Percent change 1970–1981
Households	**43,554**	**52,799**	**57,436**	**63,401**	**71,120**	**79,108**	**80,776**	**82,368**	**20.1**	**29.9**
Family households	38,838	44,905	47,838	51,456	55,563	58,426	59,550	60,309	14.6	17.2
Nonfamily households	4,716	7,895	9,598	11,945	15,557	20,682	21,226	22,059	51.3	84.7
Average size of household	3.37	3.33	3.29	3.14	2.94	2.75	2.76	2.73	(x)	(x)
Families[4]	**39,303**	**45,111**	**47,956**	**51,586**	**55,712**	**58,426**	**59,550**	**60,309**	**14.4**	**16.9**
Married couple[4]	34,440	39,329	41,749	44,755	46,971	48,180	49,112	49,294	13.8	10.1
Male householder[4,5]	1,184	1,275	1,181	1,239	1,499	1,706	1,733	1,933	−2.8	56.0
Female householder[4,5]	3,679	4,507	5,026	5,591	7,242	8,540	8,705	9,082	24.1	62.4
Average size of family	3.54	3.67	3.70	3.58	3.42	3.28	3.29	3.27	(x)	(x)
White families	(NA)	3.61	3.64	3.52	3.36	3.22	3.23	3.20	(x)	(x)
Black families[6]	(NA)	4.39	4.37	4.13	3.90	3.67	3.67	3.66	(x)	(x)
Family households	38,838	44,905	47,838	51,456	55,563	58,426	59,550	60,309	14.6	17.2
Married couple	34,075	39,254	41,689	44,728	46,951	48,180	49,112	49,294	13.9	10.2
With own children under 18	(NA)	(NA)	(NA)	25,532	25,165	24,568	24,961	24,927	(NA)	−2.4
Male householder[5]	1,169	1,228	1,167	1,228	1,485	1,706	1,733	1,933	–	57.4
With own children under 18	(NA)	(NA)	(NA)	341	478	609	616	666	(NA)	95.3
Female householder[5]	3,594	4,422	4,982	5,500	7,127	8,540	8,705	9,082	24.4	65.1
With own children under 18	(NA)	(NA)	(NA)	2,858	4,301	5,340	5,445	5,634	(NA)	97.1
Unrelated subfamilies	465	207	118	130	149	348	360	393	−37.2	202.3
Married couple	365	75	60	27	20	19	20	22	−64.0	(B)

								(B)	(B)
Male reference person[5]	16	47	14	11	14	36	36	36	(B)	(B)
Female reference person[5]	85	85	44	91	115	294	304	334	7.1	267.0
Related subfamilies	**2,402**	**1,514**	**1,293**	**1,150**	**1,349**	**1,115**	**1,150**	**1,236**	**-24.0**	**7.5**
Married couple	1,651	871	729	617	576	567	582	580	-29.2	-6.0
Male reference person[5]	113	115	72	48	69	55	54	78	-58.3	62.5
Female reference person[5]	638	528	492	484	705	494	512	578	-8.3	19.4
Married couples	**36,091**	**40,200**	**42,478**	**45,373**	**47,547**	**48,765**	**49,714**	**49,896**	**12.9**	**10.0**
With own household	34,075	39,254	41,689	44,728	46,951	48,180	49,112	49,294	13.9	10.2
Without own household	2,016	946	789	645	596	585	602	602	-31.8	-6.7
Percent without	5.6	2.4	1.9	1.4	1.3	1.2	1.2	1.2	(x)	(x)
Unrelated Individuals	**9,136**	**11,092**	**12,333**	**14,988**	**19,100**	**25,838**	**26,426**	**27,348**	**35.1**	**82.5**
Nonfamily householder	4,716	7,895	9,598	11,945	15,557	20,682	21,226	22,059	61.3	84.7
Male	1,668	2,716	3,277	4,063	5,912	8,594	8,807	9,279	49.6	128.4
Female	3,048	5,179	6,321	7,882	9,645	12,088	12,419	12,780	52.2	62.1
Secondary individuals	4,420	3,198	2,735	3,043	3,543	5,156	5,200	5,288	-4.8	73.8
Male	2,541	1,746	1,432	1,631	2,087	3,011	3,006	2,942	-6.6	80.4
Female	1,879	1,451	1,303	1,412	1,456	2,145	2,194	2,346	-2.7	66.1

– Represents zero.

B = Not shown; base less than 75,000.

NA = Not available.

X = Not applicable.

[1] Data revised using population controls based on the 1970 census; therefore, figures do not agree with table 61. (The latter used population controls based on the 1960 census.)

[2] Population controls based on 1970 census; see text, p. 2.

[3] Population controls based on 1980 census; see text p. 2.

[4] Beginning 1980, data are not comparable with prior years due to definitional change.

[5] No spouse present.

[6] Through 1965, data are for races other than White.

Source: Bureau of Census, *Statistical Abstracts of the United States, 1981*, Washington, D.C.: U.S. Government Printing Office, 1981, p. 43.

Living arrangements.—Living arrangements may be in households or in group quarters. A "household" comprises all persons who occupy a "housing unit," that is, a house, an apartment or other group of rooms, or a single room that constitutes "separate living quarters." A household includes the related family members and all the unrelated persons, if any, such as lodgers, foster children, wards, or employees who share the housing unit. A person living alone or a group of unrelated persons sharing the same housing unit as partners is also counted as a household. . . .

All persons not living in households are classified as living in group quarters. These individuals may be institutionalized, e.g., under care or custody in juvenile facilities, jails, correctional centers, hospitals, or rest homes; or they may be residents in college dormitories, military barracks, rooming houses, etc. . . .

Householder.—Beginning in 1980, the terms "householder" and "family householder" have been used in the presentation of data that had been previously presented with the designations "head of household" and "head of family". The householder is the first adult household member listed on the questionnaire. The instructions call for listing first the person (or one of the persons) in whose name the home is owned or rented. If a home is owned or rented jointly by a married couple, either the husband or the wife may be listed first. Prior to 1980, the husband was always considered the household head (householder) in married-couple households.

Family.—The term "family" refers to a group of two or more persons related by birth, marriage, or adoption and residing together in a household. A family includes among its members the person or couple who maintains the household.

Subfamily.—Subfamilies are divided into "related" and "unrelated" subfamilies. A related subfamily consists of a married couple and their children, if any, or one parent with one or more never-married children under 18 years old living in a household and related to the person or couple who maintains the household. Members of a related subfamily are also members of the family with whom they live. The number of related subfamilies, therefore, is not included in the number of families. An unrelated subfamily comprises two or more persons such as guests, lodgers, or resident employees who are related to each other, but not to the person or couple who maintains the household in which they live.

Married couple.—A "married couple" is defined as a husband and wife living together in the same household, with or without children and other relatives.

Unrelated individuals.—"Unrelated individuals" refers to persons (other than inmates of institutions) who are not living with any relatives. An unrelated individual may be a nonfamily householder who lives alone or with nonrelatives only, or a secondary individual such as a guest, lodger, or resident employee who is not related to any other persons in the household. Persons in group quarters, except inmates of institutions, are classified as secondary individuals.

Figure 15.2
Bureau of the Census definitions of types of household units and number of each type of household in 1980.

Source: Bureau of Census, *Statistical Abstracts of the United States, 1982.* Washington, D.C.: U.S. Government Printing Office, 1982, p. 4.

studying poverty patterns in England, a number of specific FLCs have been proposed (Murphy and Staples 1979). Table 15.2 presents nine different FLCs which are temporally ordered into foundation, expansion, and refinement eras. Note that over time, there has been a clear tendency to recognize more stages in the FLC.

The primary importance of the FLC to marketers is that distinct lifestyles tend to characterize each stage of the cycle. Furthermore, both specific buying needs and the income available to fulfill those needs varies systematically over the FLC. Figure 15.3 presents a thumbnail sketch of each stage of the FLC using the stages proposed by Wells and Gubar (1966). Read Figure 15.3 carefully and note the specific differences in needs and buying behaviors associated with each stage in the FLC.

Given the number of different FLCs that were proposed, the reader may suspect that there is no general agreement on how the FLC concept should be defined. Indeed, this is a frequent, although not a fatal, criticism of the FLC. More serious is the charge that the FLC ignores many recent demographic changes and, thereby, leaves large numbers of families unaccounted. The demographic changes toward later first marriage, smaller family size (including an increasing number of couples who remain childless by choice), and divorce and remarriage, to cite only a few of the most significant changes, suggest the need to reexamine the FLC concept.

Table 15.2
Alternative views of the family life cycle

Author(s)/stages	Author(s)/stages	Author(s)/stages
Foundation era		
Sorokin, Zimmerman, and Galpin (1931)	Kirkpatrick, Cowles, and Tough (1934)	Loomis (1936)
1. Married couples just starting their independent economic existence 2. Couples with one or more children 3. Couples with one or more adult self-supporting children 4. Couples growing old	1. Preschool family 2. Grade school family 3. High school family 4. All adult family	1. Childless couples of childbearing age 2. Families with children (eldest under 14) 3. Families with oldest child over 14 and under 36 4. Old families
Expansion era		
Bigelow (1942)	Glick (1947)	Duvall and Hill (1948)
1. Establishment 2. Child-bearing and preschool period 3. Elementary school period 4. High school period 5. College 6. Period of recovery 7. Period of retirement	1. First marriage 2. Birth of first child 3. Birth of last child 4. Marriage of first child 5. Marriage of last child 6. Death of husband or wife 7. Death of spouse	1. Childless 2. Expanding (birth of first to last child) 3. School age 4. Stable (birth of last child to launching) 5. Contracting (first launched to last launched) 6. Aging companions (no children at home) 7. One partner deceased

Source: Patrick E. Murphy and William A. Staples, "A Modernized Family Life Cycle." *Journal of Consumer Research,* 6 (June 1979): 13. Reprinted with permission.

Table 15.2 continued

Author(s)/stages	Author(s)/stages	Author(s)/stages

Refinement era

Rodgers (1962)

1. Beginning families (defined as childless couples)
2. Families with infants (all children less than 36 months old)
3. Preschool families
   a. With infants (oldest child 3–6 years; youngest child, birth to 36 months)
   b. All children 3–6 years
4. School-age families
   a. With infants (oldest child, 6–13 years; youngest child, birth to 36 months)
   b. With preschoolers (oldest, 6–13 years; youngest, 3–6 years)
   c. All children 6–13 years
5. Teen-age families
   a. With infants (oldest, 13–20; youngest, birth to 36 months)
   b. With preschoolers (oldest, 13–20; youngest, 3–6)
   c. With school-agers (oldest, 13–20; youngest, 6–13)
   d. All children 13–20 years
6. Young adult families
   a. With infants (oldest, over 20; youngest, birth to 36 months)
   b. With preschoolers (oldest, over 20; youngest, 3–6)
   c. With school-agers (oldest, 13–20; youngest, 6–13)
   d. With teen-agers (oldest, over 20; youngest, 6–13)
   e. All over 20

Rodgers (1962) cont.

7. Launching families
   a. With infants (first child launched; youngest, birth to 36 months)
   b. With preschoolers (first child launched; youngest, 3–6)
   c. With school-agers (first child launched; youngest, 6–13)
   d. With teenagers (first child launched, youngest, 13–20)
   e. With young adults (first child launched; youngest, over 20)
8. Middle years (all children launched to retirement of breadwinner)
9. Aging couple (retirement to death of one spouse)
10. Widowhood (death of first spouse to death of survivor)

Wells and Gubar (1966)

1. Bachelor stage (young single people not living at home)
2. Newly married couples (no children)
3. Full nest I (youngest child under 6)
4. Full next II (youngest child 6 or over)
5. Full nest III (older married couples with dependent children)
6. Empty nest I (no children living at home, head in labor force)
7. Empty nest II (head retired)
8. Solitary survivor (in labor force)
9. Solitary survivor (retired)

Duvall (1971)

1. Married couples (without children)
2. Childbearing families (oldest child under 30 months)
3. Families with pre-school children (oldest, 2½–6)
4. Families with school children (oldest, 6–13)
5. Families with teen-agers (oldest, 13–20)
6. Families as launching centers (first child gone to last child's leaving home)
7. Middle-aged parents (empty nest to retirement)
8. Aging family members (retirement to death of both spouses)

Recently, Murphy and Staples (1979) proposed a "Modernized Family Life Cycle," which incorporates many of the recent demographic changes. Their modernized FLC is presented in Figure 15.4. Note in particular that the modernized FLC provides for cycling between married and divorced stages. The explicit recognition of such cycling does not, however, change the central point that persons in different stages of the FLC tend to have different lifestyles, which have implications for the development of marketing strategy.

The large number of different FLCs raises the question of which specific one should a marketer use. The answer is that there is no inherent reason to prefer any specific FLC for all situations. Each FLC sorts families somewhat differently. The problem for the marketer is to define the stages of the FLC in such a way that the stages coincide with viable and, ideally, nearly optimal, market segments. In this process, it may be desirable to define the stages of the FLC differently from those proposed in Table 15.2 and Figure 15.4. For example, for automobile manufacturers, it might be desirable to identify the FLC stage "oldest child living at home 14 or over," since this is about the age that many children become very interested in their family's automobile purchasing decisions.

A more basic question, of course, is under what conditions is the FLC likely to be especially relevant. This is a difficult question to answer generally. The FLC has been related to everything from the purchase of furniture (Grossack 1964) to the frequency of shopping and the type of stores patronized (Rich and Jain 1968) to the type and amount of energy consumed (Fritzsche 1981). Determining the relevance of the FLC is primarily a matter of intuition and careful research. Fortunately, there are a number of sources of information from which the marketer may get preliminary insights regarding the relevance of the FLC to a specific marketing situation. The U. S. Department of Commerce, especially the Bureau of the Census, is a rich source of such information. Also, many private marketing research firms, such as Axiom Market Research Bureau which publishes *Target Group Index*, provide extensive FLC data. Another excellent source of information is the consumer behavior book by Reynolds and Wells (1977), which is partially organized around the FLC.

The FLC, of course, is an example of how simpler demographic and socioeconomic variables may be combined to form richer measures of individual differences. Thus, the previous discussion of the proper uses of demographic and socioeconomic data is relevant in its entirety to the use of the FLC in the development of effective marketing strategies. Without repeating that discussion, it may be noted that the FLC captures forces that impel buyers in certain directions and creates special needs for the marketer to serve.

One final point which should be made is that it may be desirable to combine the FLC with other types of individual difference measures. This idea may be illustrated with the furniture replacement frequently made by middle age couples. When a couple first marries, their buying needs are high and their income is generally low. Furthermore, children are notoriously hard on furniture. For these, and other reasons, young families tend to buy furniture that is sensible and practical rather than stylish and beautiful (Grossack 1964). Over time family income tends to rise, reaching a peak in late middle age. This is also approximately the time when children become financially independent. Thus, in late middle age many families suddenly find themselves with relatively large amounts of discretionary income and a house full of furniture that is neither stylish nor beautiful. This is why it is not unusual to find couples in late middle age replacing entire rooms or even an entire house with new and expensive furniture, which is both stylish and beautiful. Of course, as we know from the last chapter, furniture tastes vary considerably by social class. Furthermore, many couples in late middle age will not have the discretionary income necessary for general redecorating. Under such circumstances, it may be desirable to identify market segments in terms of FLC, social class, *and* income.

Bachelor Stage
In the bachelor stage of the life cycle, income is relatively low, since most bachelors are just beginning their business careers. Often they live in apartments or share a dwelling unit with others, so that they have few financial burdens for fixed living expenses. As a consequence, their discretionary income is relatively high. Expenditures go, primarily, for personal consumption items—clothing, food, entertainment, dating, vacations, and possibly a car. A few basic furniture items may be acquired, as well as some kitchen equipment. Such purchases are generally made on a nonsystematic basis and tend to be minimal because possessions restrict freedom of movement. Since bachelors are often opinion leaders for fashions, they are a logical market for the apparel industry.

Newly Married Couples
With marriage, both requirements and resources change. The newly married are often better off financially than when they were single because, in many cases, both work. At the same time, however, their household requirements increase. This stage represents a high expenditure period, particularly for durable goods. If neither owned a car before marriage, one is generally acquired. The couple is an important market for major appliances—refrigerators, ranges—and for inexpensive, durable furniture. They also enter the market for home entertainment items, such as phonographic equipment and television sets, with these items often taking priority over other possessions. Since the newly married are not tied down by children, they continue to represent a market for vacations and recreational equipment.

Full Nest I
The arrival of the first child creates major changes in the couple's lives and expenditure patterns. Not only do they lose much of the freedom of activity they had enjoyed, but also—since most wives stop working—they suffer a reduction of income. Their liquid assets are low, since this is a peak period of home buying, and they face mortgage payments and obstetric and pediatric bills. They also become concerned about the future, so that personal insurance costs often increase. During this period, they are interested in new products and are susceptible to advertising. Their purchases include washing machines, dryers, baby furniture, toys, cough medicine, chest rubs, vitamins, and baby foods. It is also in this period that they become most dissatisfied with their income and their inability to accumulate savings.

Full Nest II
During this stage, the family's financial position starts to improve because of progress in the husband's career and because some wives return to work. They are still interested in

Figure 15.3
Illustrative differences in buyer behavior over stages of the family life cycle

Source: Kenneth E. Runyon, *Consumer Behavior,* 2nd edition. (Columbus, Ohio: Charles E. Merrill Publishing Co., 1980), pp. 168–171. Reprinted with permission.

The Environment Within Which Family Decisions Are Made[3]

Before we explicitly consider the interactions among family members in making buying decisions, it will be instructive to examine the environment in which family

[3]This section relies heavily on the analysis of the family decision-making environment provided by Davis (1977, pp. 87–88).

new products but are somewhat less influenced by advertising because they are more experienced buyers. They begin buying larger package sizes and multiple-unit deals and are an active market for a wide variety of food products, household cleaning materials, bicycles, music lessons, and pianos.

Full Nest III
The family's financial position generally continues to improve as the husband's salary increases and more wives work. Some children get part-time jobs and earn some or all of their spending money. They have high average expenditures for durable goods because of replacement buying. They are little influenced by advertising and begin buying expensive, tasteful furniture, unnecessary appliances, second cars, boats, dental services, and magazines. Automobile travel and recreation also take a larger proportion of their incomes.

Empty Nest I
With no children living at home and continued income growth, families in this stage are most satisfied with their financial position and the money they have saved. They are interested in and can afford travel and recreation. There is usually a resurgence in self-education, and hobbies often become an important source of satisfaction. These families are the principle contributors to charitable organizations and an important part of the gift market. Home ownership is at its peak, with major expenditures being made for home improvements and luxuries.

Empty Nest II
With retirement, there is usually a sharp drop in income. The family may keep the home or move to a smaller house or apartment, often in a retirement community where the climate is more benign. Medical costs increase because they suffer more ailments, and there are increased expenditures for ethical and proprietary medicines, medical appliances, and products that aid digestion and sleep.

Solitary Survivor
If the solitary survivors are still in the labor force, income will continue to be high. They will probably sell their homes and continue to spend money for vacations, recreation, and medical treatment and supplies. The retired solitary survivors will have the same medical product needs as the other retired group and will usually suffer a further drop in income. At this stage, they also have special needs for attention, affection, and security.

decisions are made. Davis (1977) notes that "A number of writers have suggested that families, more than other groups, are likely to be 'poor' decision makers. This is owing, in part, to the environment in which families decide, the non-task needs that impinge on all decisions, and the interrelatedness of family decisions" (p. 87). The term "poor" is presumably in quotes to emphasize the fact that it is extremely difficult, especially in a family environment, to objectively define what constitutes a "good" decision.

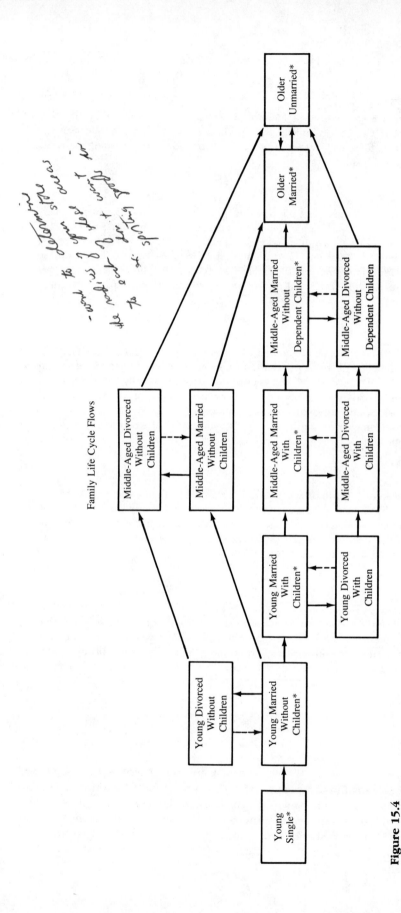

Family Life Cycle Flows

Figure 15.4

A modernized family life cycle

→ Usual Flow

⇢ Recycled Flow

⟶ Traditional Family Flow

*   *

Source: Patrick E. Murphy and William A. Staples, "A Modernized Family Life Cycle." *Journal of Consumer Research*, 6 (June 1979): 17. Reprinted with permission.

Physically, the environment in which family decisions are made is often less than ideal. Families often come together in the early morning and evening hours when energy levels are low. Furthermore, the family environment typically contains many distractions. The demands of meal preparation, the pressures to leave for work on time, the more or less constant demands that young children make on parents, noise emanating from stereos and televisions, and a host of other distractions are often present when family decisions are being made. Although there has been no research on the effects of distraction on family decision making, Davis (1977, p. 87) cites a suggestive laboratory study by Wright (1974), which found that distraction increased the salience of negative information and reduced the number of dimensions on which choice alternatives were evaluated.

Another aspect of the family decision-making environment follows from the fact that all permanent groups have so-called maintenance needs. In the case of family decision making, these needs are especially strong and probably constitute an important goal in many buying decisions. At the very least, Davis (1972) showed that consumers are very aware of group maintenance needs. The proceedings of a symposium on family problem solving (Aldous et al. 1971) contains a number of suggestions as to how maintenance needs can interfere with effective problem solving. Weick (1971), for example, described the intentional masking of expert power within families in the interest of maintaining the legitimate power of specific family members. For example, even if a wife knows more about the stock market than her husband, she may be reluctant to involve herself too forcefully in such decisions because "men are supposed to know more about such things." More generally, Aldous (1971) argues that the emphasis within families "tends to be one of reducing the tension laden situations to an innocuous level rather than submitting the problem to rigorous analysis and assessing the consequences of possible alternative strategies" (p. 267). Although maintenance needs may interfere with the "rational" solution of narrowly defined problems, the maintenance needs of the family are not irrational and clearly have a legitimate claim on any family's resources.

Finally, family decisions are often highly interdependent. Since different family members will tend to have different needs and objectives and since family resources are limited, potential conflict among family members is associated with many purchase decisions. Given the maintenance needs of families, researchers (e.g., Aldous 1971, Weick 1971) have suggested that families are often more solution oriented than problem oriented. That is, it is the appearance of a solution that precipitates choice rather than the careful analysis of the problem that leads logically to the best choice.

Aldous (1971) suggested that the interdependence and resulting conflict characteristic of family decisions leads to a variation of Gresham's Law[4] in which families are more likely to focus on unimportant problems leaving more important

---

[4]Gresham's Law (circa 1559) states "if coins containing metal of different value enjoy equal legal-tender power, then the 'cheapest' ones will be used for payment, the better ones will tend to disappear from circulation—or, to use the usual but not quite correct phrase, that bad money drives out good money." (Schumpeter 1954, p. 343). Variations of Gresham's Law have appeared in a number of contexts. In organizational decision making, for example, it has frequently been observed that less important but more pressing short-run problems are solved while fundamental but less pressing long-run problems are ignored.

problems unresolved or even undefined Some support for this idea is provided by a study by Foote (1974), which found a high proportion of purchases not preceded by plans and a high proportion of unfulfilled plans. The latter point is particularly interesting because family decision-making research has focused on decisions that were actually completed, often using retrospective questioning. Although other factors are involved, Foote's study suggests that conflict is often resolved or avoided by *not* purchasing.

While conflict is presumed to be a common occurence during family decision making, its strength will vary considerably across buying situations and families. Davis (1977) suggests that conflict will be less when one family member is recognized as the legitimate authority for a specific type of decision, when the husband substantially dominates his wife in terms of educational and occupational prestige and income, and when one family member has a relatively high investment in the decision. The distinction between the last two factors is in terms of the potential for and the motivation to exert influence. For example, in a traditional family with children and a nonworking wife, the husband will tend to have potential control over all major financial decisions. However, he may largely cede decision-making responsibility in areas where his wife has high involvement; e.g., kitchen appliances, sewing machines, washers, and dryers.

Burns and Granbois (1977), in a study of automobile purchasing behavior, provide empirical support for Davis' propositions regarding legitimate authority and involvement. They also found high empathy positively associated with the resolution of conflict. Perhaps their most interesting findings are that, for automobile buying, spouses first preferences show a high degree of agreement and that "spouses generally have compatible expectations as to whether a decision should be resolved jointly or falls within one spouse's sphere of decision-making authority" (p. 85). The authors note that these results suggest the existence of less conflict among spouses than is commonly assumed. Given the fact that subjects in this study had been married an average of 15.5 years, their findings may also indicate the learning of each other's preferences and the development of strategies for avoiding or minimizing conflict. Certainly, we need to keep clearly in mind the distinction between potential and actual conflict.

With this background, the next three sections explore the nature and marketing implications of the interdependencies and interactions among family members in making family buying decisions. It should be recognized at the outset of this discussion that there are many ways by which families may reduce or circumvent conflicts without actually resolving the conflict before making a purchase.

Husband-Wife Influence in the Family Decision-Making Process

Probably the most widely studied aspect of family decision making concerns the relative influence of husbands and wives on the buying decision. This type of research is frequently referred to as role structure research because husbands and wives typically play different roles in family decision making. In reality, however, this research has not been conducted from the perspective of role theory. Rather, it has involved attempts to assess the relative influence of husbands and wives on family decision making. This issue has been studied across product classes, for subcomponents of the purchase decision, over stages of the decision process, and in terms of individual differences among families. Tables 15.3 and 15.4 and Figure

Table 15.3
Marital roles in selected automobile and furniture purchase decisions as perceived by husbands

	South Carolina study (n = 350)			Davis study (n = 97)		
	H > W	H = W	W > H	H > W	H = W	W > H
Automobile decisions						
1. When to buy?	69[b]	24	7	68	29	3
2. How much money to spend?	66	29	5	62	37	1
3. What make to buy?	59	31	9	60	32	8
4. What model to buy?[a]	57	32	11	41	50	9
5. What color to buy?[a]	39	32	30	25	50	25
6. Where to buy?	65	29	6	62	35	3
Furniture decisions						
7. What pieces to buy?	14	24	62	3	33	64
8. How much money to spend?	22	38	40	22	47	31
9. Where to buy?[a]	17	35	49	7	53	40
10. When to buy?	16	37	47	16	45	39
11. What style to buy?[a]	12	20	69	2	26	72
12. What color and fabric?[a]	9	20	71	2	16	82

Notation: H > W: Husband has more influence than wife.
　　　　　H = W: Husband and wife have equal influence.
　　　　　W > H: Wife has more influence than husband.
[a]Chi-square analysis indicates a significant difference in response patterns between the two studies at or at less than the .05 level.
[b] Percent of respondents.

Source: F. K. Shuptrine and G. Samuelson, "Dimensions of Marital Roles in Consumer Decision Making: Revisited." *Journal of Marketing Research*, 13 (February 1976): 88. Reprinted by permission of the American Marketing Association.

15.5 present data that illustrate many of the major questions addressed by relative influence studies.

Tables 15.3 and 15.4 present data on the relative influence of husbands and wives, as perceived by each, on six different components of the purchase decision for automobiles and furniture. The data, from an original study by Davis (1970) and a replication by Shuptrine and Samuelson (1976), provide some measure of how relative influence varies over both geographical area and time. Perhaps most striking is the fact that the numbers reported in the two studies are, with a few exceptions, remarkably similar despite being separated by six years and conducted in different regions of the country (South Carolina and Chicago). It is readily apparent that husbands dominate all aspects, except color, of the automobile purchase decision, while wives dominate, except for amount to spend, the furniture purchase decision. Both studies report substantial perceptions of approximately equal influence although wives are more likely to perceive equal influence than husbands. The study by Davis (1970, Chicago) also reported more nearly equal influence. Both studies indicate substantial aggregate agreement between husbands and wives regarding each spouse's relative influence. Davis (1977), however, indicates that agreement within specific couples is lower than aggregate agreement among all husbands vs. all wives.

Table 15.4
Marital roles in selected automobile and furniture purchase decisions as perceived by wives

	South Carolina study (n = 350)			Davis study (n = 97)		
	H > W	**H = W**	**W > H**	**H > W**	**H = W**	**W > H**
Automobile decisions						
1. When to buy?	67[b]	26	7	68	30	2
2. How much money to spend?	67	28	5	62	34	4
3. What make to buy?[a]	62	29	9	50	50	—
4. What model to buy?[a]	57	32	11	47	52	1
5. What color to buy?[a]	37	35	27	25	63	12
6. Where to buy?	64	30	7	59	39	2
Furniture decisions						
7. What pieces to buy?[a]	15	33	53	4	52	44
8. How much money to spend?[a]	25	41	34	17	63	20
9. Where to buy?[a]	18	41	41	6	61	33
10. When to buy?	21	43	37	18	52	30
11. What style to buy?[a]	10	27	63	2	45	53
12. What color and fabric?[a]	7	27	65	2	24	74

Notation: H > W: Husband has more influence than wife.
H = W: Husband and wife have equal influence.
W > H: Wife has more influence than husband.
[a]Chi-square analysis indicates a significant difference in response patterns between the two studies at or at less than the .05 level.
[b]Percent of respondents.

Source: F. K. Shuptrine and G. Samuelson, "Dimensions of Marital Roles in Consumer Decision Making: Revisited." *Journal of Marketing Research*, 13 (February 1976): 89. Reprinted by permission of the American Marketing Association.

Figure 15.5 presents data from a study by Davis and Rigaux (1974) on the relative influence of husbands and wives on the purchase decision for 25 products. The average influence for all couples is plotted against two variables: relative influence and extent of role specialization. The latter variable was used to distinguish situations in which most couples decide jointly from situations in which couples are about evenly split between husband dominate and wife dominant. Because the horizontal axis is scaled in terms of percent of joint decisions the extent of role specialization increases from left to right. The triangular boundary indicates the set of feasible combinations of relative influence and role specialization.

Using a classification system originally suggested by Herbst (1952) and Wolfe (1959), Figure 15.5 was divided into four regions each of which reflects a different pattern of husband-wife decision making. The regions husband dominant and wife dominant should require no further description. Syncratic decisions reflect a high degree of joint decision making. In the autonomic region, there tends to be a high degree of role specialization with husband dominant in some families and wife dominant in others.

The data in Figure 15.5 were averaged over three stages of the decision process: problem recognition, search for information, and final decision. Figures 15.6 and 15.7 present changes in relative influence and role specialization between stages in the decision process. Except for wife dominant products, Figure 15.5 indicates a very definite increase in role specialization as the decision process

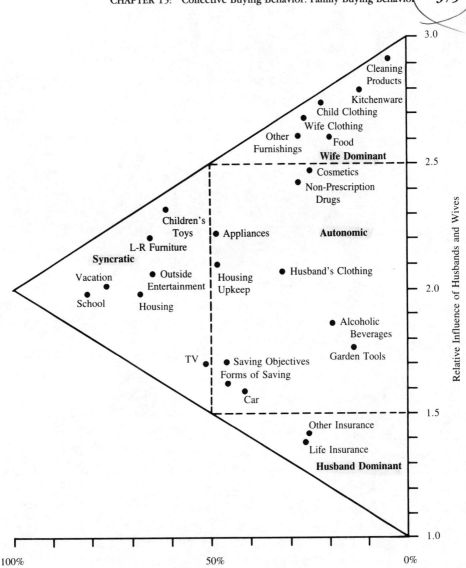

Figure 15.5
Relative influence and extent of role specialization of husbands and wives for 25 purchasing decisions

Source: Harry L. Davis and Benny P. Rigaux, "Perception of Marital Roles in Decision Processes." *Journal of Consumer Research*, 1 (June 1974): 54. Reprinted with permission.

moves from problem recognition to search for information. Figure 15.7 indicates an even stronger reverse trend toward more joint or syncratic decision making as the decision process moves from information search to final decision. These patterns suggest that for many products it may be desirable to target advertising to one spouse more than the other spouse while providing information that appeals to the needs and perceptions of the problem of *both* spouses.

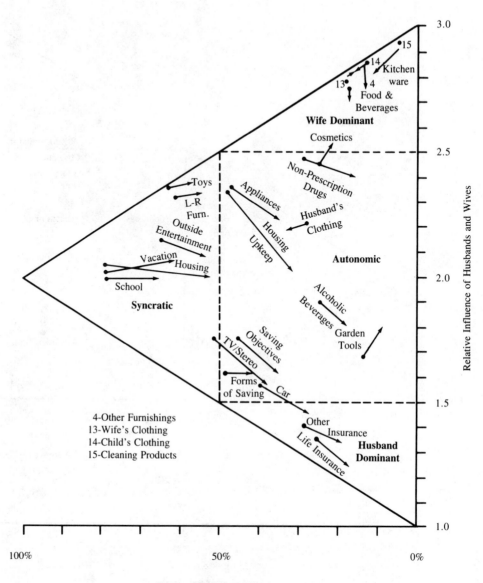

Figure 15.6
Changes in decision-making roles of husbands and wives between problem recognition and search for information

Source: Harry L. Davis and Benny P. Rigaux, "Perception of Marital Roles in Decision Processes." *Journal of Consumer Research,* 1 (June 1974): 56. Reprinted with permission.

A number of additional studies of the relative influence of husbands and wives on purchasing decisions could be cited; however, for a number of reasons, a comprehensive review of these studies would not be particularly fruitful.[5] First,

[5]References to this literature can be found in three recent critical reviews of the family decision-making literature (Davis 1977, Burns and Granbois 1980, Jenkins 1980). These reviews focus on the theoretical and methodological limitations of existing research on family decision making, and are highly recommended references for anyone planning to conduct a study of family decision making.

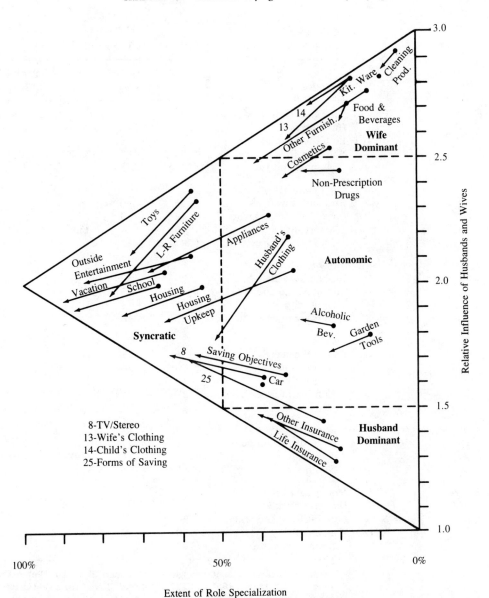

Figure 15.7
Changes in decision-making roles of husbands and wives between search for information and final purchase decision

Source: Harry L. Davis and Benny P. Rigaux, "Perception of Marital Roles in Decision Processes." *Journal of Consumer Research* 1 (June 1974): 57. Reprinted with permission.

much of the literature frequently cited in consumer behavior books is quite dated. Second, the findings regarding husband-wife influence for frequently studied decisions, primarily automobiles and housing, are not consistent across studies (Jenkins 1980, p. 208). Because almost all academic studies of family decision making have employed small samples, been conducted at different times and in different places, and used methods that are not strictly comparable, it is not possible to resolve the inconsistencies across studies in any systematic way. Third, many of the social

Table 15.5
Husband-wife decision-making roles in 1955 and 1973

Decision Area	1955 (%)	1973 (%)	χ^2	Proba-bility
Food and Groceries				
Husband usually	13	10		
Both husband and wife	33	15		
Wife usually	54	75	34.70	<.001
Number of cases	(727)	(248)		
Life Insurance				
Husband usually	43	66		
Both husband and wife	42	30		
Wife usually	15	4	45.03	<.001
Number of cases	(727)	(247)		
Automobile				
Husband usually	70	52		
Both husband and wife	25	45		
Wife usually	5	3	37.19	<.001
Number of cases	(727)	(248)		
Vacation				
Husband usually	18	7		
Both husband and wife	70	84		
Wife usually	12	9	21.80	<.001
Number of cases	(727)	(244)		
House or Apartment				
Husband usually	18	12		
Both husband and wife	58	77		
Wife usually	24	11	31.05	<.001
Number of cases	(727)	(245)		
Money and Bills				
Husband usually	26	27		
Both husband and wife	34	24		
Wife usually	40	49	3.09	n.s.
Number of cases	(727)	(248)		

Source: Isabella C. M. Cunningham and Robert T. Green, "Purchasing Roles in the U. S. Family, 1955 and 1973." *Journal of Marketing,* 38 (October 1974): 63. Reprinted by permission of the American Marketing Association.

changes that occurred in the last three decades (e.g., working wives) could reasonably be expected to affect the relative influence of husbands and wives.

Data, presented in Table 15.5, from a partial replication of a 1955 study by Sharp and Mott (1956) conducted in 1973 by Cunningham and Green (1974), illustrates the potential magnitude of such changes in relative influence over time.[6] Note, in particular, the dramatic increase in syncratic decision making for automo-

[6]Although the authors argue that the two studies are highly comparable, they do acknowledge differences in geography (Detroit vs. Houston) and method of collecting data (interview vs. self-administered mail questionnaire). Thus, the Cunningham and Green study is only a partial replication of the study by Sharp and Mott.

biles and the probably unexpected increases in wife domination of food and groceries decisions and in husband domination of life insurance decisions. The managerial implication that Cunningham and Green draw from their study is very consistent with what is generally known about husband-wife purchasing roles.

> The major implication that these findings offer to marketing management is that it is difficult to generalize the impact that changes in the environment will have on family purchasing patterns. While family decision-making roles have been changing in response to environmental change, all products apparently have not been affected in the same way. Thus, it would be a mistake to base any marketing decisions that are affected by family decision-making patterns on information concerning general role shifts within the family; *product-specific information should be required* (p. 64, emphasis added).

With this limited review of the literature, it is appropriate to ask what, if anything, can be concluded about the relative influence of husbands and wives on purchasing decisions. Perhaps the most basic conclusion is that relative influence varies widely over product classes, for subcomponents or subdivisions of the final purchase decisions, over stages of the decision process, and among families. The clear implication is that to develop effective managerial strategies the marketing manager needs, as Cunningham and Green state, "product-specific information" about the extent and nature of role specialization and interactions among family members in purchasing specific types of products.

Another side of the variability in relative influence of husbands and wives is the inconsistent findings of studies that examined the same type of purchase decision. Given the previous discussions of major social trends and regional differences in lifestyles, the fact that similar studies conducted at different times and in different places yield different results should, if anything, be expected. To turn the point around, it might be a greater surprise to find, as in Tables 15.3 and 15.4, many similarities in relative influence in studies conducted at different times and places. The basic point, however, reinforces the need for product-specific information. It also is a reminder of the need to be sensitive to changing social conditions and to the diversity of patterns of behavior among people.

Another conclusion that is probably warranted is that the degree of interaction between husbands and wives varies considerably over product types. Indeed, because researchers, with a few exceptions such as the study by Davis and Rigaux (1974), typically select products for study because they expect joint decision making, it is easy to overstate the degree of syncratic decision making that actually exists. For example, many husbands are probably totally unaware of many of the ingredients their wives use in cooking.

The data, however, suggest considerable syncratic decision making for expensive products and for products that are consumed jointly. Based on the assumption that extent of information search and degree of family interaction are based on the same determinants, Burns and Granbois hypothesize[7] that the

> Degree of interaction in generic product purchase discussions will vary directly with:

---

[7]The basis for these hypotheses is established in Granbois (1977, especially pp. 261–262).

Number of salient attributes used

Product importance

Interpurchase interval

Availability of information

Degree of differentiation among alternative products

Price

Size of physical bulk

Length of product life

Social conspicousness

Complexity (1980, p. 224)

It has also been frequently reported that syncratic decision making occurs more frequently in middle class families than in either lower or upper class families (Ferber 1977).

There is also some reason to believe that the degree of syncratic decision making has and will continue to increase (cf., Ferber 1973). Cunningham and Green (1974), for example, suggest that a general increase in egalitarianism and increasing participation of wives in activities outside the home may be partially responsible for the reported increase in syncratic decision making. Among these outside activities, of course, is working. The "relative resource contribution" theory suggests that as more working wives directly contribute to family income, they will gain increasing authority to decide how that income is spent. Although Jenkins (1980) suggests the evidence is mixed, a wide range of studies (e.g., Blood and Wolfe 1960, Hempel 1975) have found support for the relative contribution hypothesis. This hypothesis also suggests a possible increase in the number of wife dominant decisions.

The final conclusion to be drawn is that despite substantial variation among couples and an increasing trend toward syncratic decision making, the *general tendencies* observed are, to a large extent, what might be expected in terms of traditional sex role stereotypes. For example, Woodside (1972) concluded that

Husband-dominance is more likely when the product is used manually outside the home (e.g., lawnmowers, gardening supplies) and when the product is mechanically complex (e.g., automobiles).

Wife-dominance is more likely when the product is used inside the house, especially if it relates to decor (e.g., rugs) and when the product is a cleaning supply or appliance (e.g., detergents, washing machines).

To point out these stereotypical trends is not to suggest an innate or permanent subservance of women to men. Rather, it is to suggest that even when legal and economic equality between men and women is achieved, men and women will continue to differ in many ways that the marketer must consider in the construction of effective marketing strategies.

Family Decision-Making Strategies

Although it is common to speak of family decision making a number of reviewers have observed that very little research has actually examined the family decision-making *process* (e.g., Davis 1977, Burns and Granbois 1980). As Burns and Granbois

(1980, p. 221) note, approximately three-fourths of the 38 articles on family purchasing behavior that appeared in major marketing publications during the 1970s focused on the relatively narrow topic of husband-wife role structures. Furthermore, most of these studies focused on the *outcome* of the decision process rather than the decision process itself (Davis 1977, p. 81).

Even those studies that address the decision process, rarely actually observe the decision-making process. Rather, subjects are usually asked to reconstruct the decision process or speculate on their relative influence on various aspects of specific types of decisions. The accuracy of such data is a matter of some dispute. Jenkins (1980, p. 208), for example, cites a study of home buying by Munsinger, Weber, and Hansen (1975), that found a general willingness of husbands and a general reluctance of wives to admit dominance by either spouse. A study of children's influence by Turk and Bell (1972) found from direct observation that children often had considerable influence on family buying decisions despite the fact that self-reports by parents indicated the same children had no power to influence buying decisions. Davis and Rigaux (1977, p. 59), however, suggest that the evidence is mixed making it difficult to draw general conclusions about the direction of self-report biases.

In a few studies (e.g., Burns and Granbois 1977), laboratory simulations of husband-wife decision making for complex decisions such as buying an automobile have been investigated. While there is good reason to believe that such simulations can provide useful insights, the extent to which simulated family decision processes correspond to decision processes in the normal environment in which family decisions are made is unknown.

Although direct research is largely lacking, two writers (Sheth 1974, Davis 1977) offer typologies of general strategies for making family buying decisions. Both writers offer some, primarily indirect, support for their typologies. Furthermore, personal experience and common sense gives each strategy some face validity. Despite these positive points, little is known about how employment of these strategies varies over the many aspects of the family decision-making process or among families. With these caveats in mind, each typology will be briefly discussed. As you read this material, keep in mind that family members often have different goals and perspectives with respect to specific buying decisions and that it is not always necessary for complete agreement to be obtained before a decision is made.

Sheth Model of Family Decision Making

Sheth (1974) developed a model of family decision making that is a variant of the Howard-Sheth model of buyer behavior discussed extensively in Chapter 2. Sheth suggests that conflict, when it arises, may be resolved by one of four strategies: problem solving, persuasion, bargaining, and politics (pp. 32–33). Problem solving is likely to occur when family members agree on buying motives but disagree on specific beliefs. For example, there might be agreement about the desirability of reliability in an automobile but disagreement about which brands are highly reliable. When this happens, family members seek more information and deliberate more on the available information, seek support from credible sources outside the family, and look for new alternatives in an effort to resolve the problem. Sheth argues that problem solving is characteristic of many family decisions.

Sheth argues that persuasion is likely to occur when family members agree on a fundamental level but disagree on specific subgoals. For example, all family members may agree on the need for a new car. However, if the family is heavily in debt or if other needs are more pressing, an effort may be made to persuade the individual who wants to buy a car immediately that now is not a good time. Persuasion involves no attempt to gather new information.

Bargaining is likely to occur when disagreement is not directly reconcilable. For example, some family members may want to vacation at the shore while other family members prefer the mountains. In such situations, concepts of distributive justice or fairness are likely to be involved; e.g., this year we'll visit the shore, next year the mountains. Sheth argues that, because of limited resources and incompatible viewpoints, bargaining is likely to be quite common in family decision making.

Politics is likely to occur in situations where fundamental disagreements about lifestyles extend well beyond specific purchasing decisions. Short of dissolution of the family, politics involves the formation of subgroups within the family designed to isolate the member with whom there is conflict. The high divorce rate today and the fact that sex and money are the most frequently cited marital problems, money being first in most lists, suggest that political solutions are involved in many family decisions. Of course, children are attempting to invoke politics when they pit one parent against another.

Davis Typology of Family Decision Strategies

Davis (1977) developed another typology of family decision strategies, which to some extent overlaps Sheth's typology. He also suggested alternative ways in which certain strategies may be implemented. Table 15.6 presents the typology. Two fundamentally different types of strategies are recognized. Consensus strategies occur when family members generally agree about goals. Accommodation strategies are necessary when there is basic disagreement regarding buying goals.

Davis' typology recognized three types of consensus strategies: role structure, budgets, and problem solving. Role structure strategies involve one family member

Table 15.6
Alternative family decision-making strategies

Goals	Strategy	Ways of implementing
"Consensus"	Role structure	"The Specialist"
(Family members	Budgets	"The Controller"
agree about		"The Expert"
goals)	Problem	"The Better Solution"
	solving	"The Multiple Purchase"
		"The Irresponsible Critic"
"Accommodation"		"Feminine Intuition"
(Family members	Persuasion	"Shopping Together"
disagree about		"Coercion"
goals)		"Coalitions"
		"The Next Purchase"
	Bargaining	"The Impulse Purchase"
		"The Procrastinator"

Source: Harry L. Davis. "Decision Making Within the Household." In *Selected Aspects of Consumer Behavior: A Summary from the Perspective of Different Disciplines*, RANN Program. Washington, D. C.: National Science Foundation, 1977, p. 89.

assuming responsibility for certain decisions. That member becomes a specialist and, thereby, acquires a legitimized right to make certain types of decisions. Closely related to this point is the fact that one of the recurring findings of husband-wife role studies is that joint decision making is greatest in the first few years of marriage (cf., Ferber 1977). Among the many reasons for this pattern, probably the most important is that in the first few years of marriage, each spouse is learning the tastes and preferences of the other spouse. Thus, the role specialist will frequently be implementing the explicit or implicit preferences of other family members.

Budget strategies involve setting rules that limit the range within which decisions are made. Many families apparently use periodic family budget meetings as a vehicle for discussing, if not fully resolving, divergent family needs. Blood (1960) makes the interesting observation that "the process of agreeing on a budget is still liable to plenty of conflict, but, once formulated, a budget tends to divert attention from the hostile antagonist to the operational code" (p. 215). Family budgets may also give each family member an allowance for which he or she is not accountable to other family members.

Davis' problem solving strategy is essentially the same as Sheth's. Problems may be solved by calling upon an expert (e.g., *Consumer Reports* or a person who owns the good in question), by proposing a new solution that is generally agreed to be superior, or by proposing a multiple purchase. Blood (1960) has suggested that the trend toward a second automobile, television set, telephone, etc., helps reduce family tensions as well as create new markets. One of the best examples of an advertisement targeted at resolving family conflict via a multiple purchase is an early Volkswagen ad. The ad showed two neighbors with similar resources and with needs for a car, food freezer, and washer and dryer. One neighbor bought a standard American car. The other neighbor bought a Volkswagen *and* the freezer *and* the washer *and* the dryer.

Davis recognizes two general types of accommodation strategies, each of which may be implemented in a variety of ways. Persuasion strategies involve inducing others to engage in behavior they otherwise would not make. Davis' conception of persuasion strategies is in many ways closer to Sheth's notion of politics. This overlap is especially evident in the coercion (e.g., "you will do what I say!") and in the coalition formation methods of implementation. Shopping together presents a means of coopting the other person by gaining implicit acquiescence to the purchase via the commitment to shop. Feminine intuition may occur in situations where the wife is generally dominated by her husband and she must learn to discern when he is most receptive to new ideas and persuasion. Davis suggests that feminine intuition may have some factual basis and cites the following comment by Turner as support.

> Under the long-standing subordination of women to men, learning to detect and interpret the subtle gestures of the opposite sex accurately has been more adaptive for the woman than for the man. Such learning comes partly from individual discovery during the socialization process, partly from the accumulation of a woman's repertoire of folk techniques for understanding and dealing with men and partly from the selective direction of attention during interaction. (1970, p. 189)

Finally, the irresponsible critic is someone who can put forth ideas freely because he or she does *not* have legitimate authority for the decision in question and will, therefore, not be blamed if the decision does not work out. The "nagging wife" is the stereotypical example of the irresponsible critic. Davis suggests that in extreme cases the husband may become so tired of hearing his nagging wife that he simply cedes responsibility to her whatever the decision. Of course, he (or she) may simply decide to leave.

Davis's concept of bargaining strategies, especially as implemented in the next purchase tradeoff among family members, closely parallels Sheth's. Davis also suggests that bargaining strategies may be implemented by impulse purchase and procrastination. Automobile ads, for example, sometimes portray the husband who drives home in a new car. His wife, of course, is surprised but thrilled and all is well. Procrastination in making an agreed upon purchase provides time for new information or changing circumstances to emerge that will block the purchase of the good in question.

Although there is little research on family decision-making strategies, some reflection should suggest a number of marketing implications beyond those already pointed out. For example, is the role specialist acting primarily upon his or her own motives, preferences, and perceptions or upon those of other family members? Or, are there certain types of products (e.g., flowers, candy, jewelry) where it can be subtly suggested how a woman can use her feminine intuition to get what she wants? The second example should remind the reader of the ethical implications of developing marketing strategies based upon knowledge of family decision making.

Children and Family Decision Making

In the discussion of core American values in an earlier chapter, Americans were noted to be very child centered, at least when compared to other societies. It may, therefore, come as something of a surprise that academic research on children as consumers, and especially as influencing agents in family decision making, is largely of recent origin and is still very limited. It, however, is possible to identify four relatively well defined types of research on children.

Children as Consumers
The first type of research has been conducted by industry and is highly descriptive, tending to focus on specific differences in the consumption of a wide range of goods and services as a function of the age of the child. Chapters 3 and 4 of the consumer behavior text by Reynolds and Wells (1977) contains many illustrative examples. Although this research focuses on children as individual consumers, it can potentially be related to family decision making through the family life cycle concept.

Effects of Advertising
A second type of research has focused on the effects of advertising, especially television advertising, on children of different ages. This line of research has a strong public policy orientation and will be explored in the final chapter's discussion of the public policy implications of buyer behavior research. Much of the impetus for this research has centered around parents' complaints about the negative effects of advertising directed to children, especially young children, and the decade long involvement of the Federal Trade Commission in investigating

industry practices.[8] In terms of the present discussion, it should be noted that one aspect of this research is that advertising may negatively affect family interaction by encouraging children to attempt to influence their parents' purchasing decisions (Ward and Wackman 1972; Reynolds and Wells 1977).

Consumer Socialization

A third type of research has been directed to the consumer socialization process (e.g., Ward 1974; Ward, Wackman, and Wartella 1977; and Moschis and Churchill 1978). "Consumer socialization is the process by which young people develop consumer-related skills, knowledge, and attitudes" (Moschis and Churchill 1978, p. 599). A major issue in socialization research is the extent to which parents attempt to explicitly teach their children consumer skills. On this point, Ward, Wackman, and Wartella offer the following conclusion:

> The most striking impression to emerge from these data is that consumer behavior is not an area in which parents consciously set about training their children to any great extent. The mothers in our sample generally had only a few rather general goals, and typically they said they used only one method to teach their child. The consumer training that does occur in the home is more likely to arise through parents' modeling behaviors for the child or in situations where parents are harassed by children for products, or when parents check on what children do with their allowances.... There seem to be few attempts to plan direct methods of training children to be "good" consumers. (1975, pp. 142–143)

In light of the above conclusion, a disturbing finding by Moschis and Churchill (1978, especially Table 3 and pp. 605–606) is that formal courses in consumer education bear virtually no relationship to the extent of consumer skills. Recently, however, a study by Kourilsky and Murray (1981) demonstrated the feasibility of teaching the use of economic reasoning in making family decisions via experienced-based methods of instruction. The authors report that, in addition to a substantial increase in the use of economic reasoning, both parents and children reported greater satisfaction with the entire family decision-making process.

Children's Influence on Parents

The fourth, and apparently least studied, type of research involves children's attempts to influence their parents' purchasing decisions. Indeed, in their review of the family decision-making literature, Burns and Granbois (1980) were able to locate only three studies in the academic marketing literature that specifically addressed this issue.

A study of parent-child interaction by Atkin (1978) is particularly interesting because it is also one of the few studies of family decision making to employ direct observation. Cereal was selected as the product for study largely on the basis of a study by Ward and Wackman (1972), which found that children frequently make requests for specific brands of cereal.

Figure 15.8 displays Atkin's principal results. Note that the child initiates the selection process 66 percent of the time and that almost half (46 percent) of these

---

[8]In 1978, a Federal Trade Commission Staff report recommended substantial restrictions, including bans on certain types of advertising, on television advertising directed at children. Recently, the FTC abandoned this area of investigation without taking action on the 1978 staff recommendations.

Table 15.7
Children's purchase requests and parent yielding

Products	Frequency of requests[a]				Percentage of yielding[b]			
	5–7 years	8–10 years	11–12 years	Total[b]	5–7 years	8–10 years	11–12 years	Total[b]
Relevant foods								
Breakfast cereal	1.26	1.59	1.97	1.59	88	91	83	87
Snack foods	1.71	2.00	1.71	1.80	52	62	77	63
Candy	1.60	2.09	2.17	1.93	40	28	57	42
Soft drinks	2.00	2.03	2.00	2.01	38	47	54	46
Jell-o	2.54	2.94	2.97	2.80	40	41	26	36
Overall mean	1.82	2.13	2.16	2.03				
Overall percentage					51.6	53.8	59.4	54.8
Less relevant foods								
Bread	3.12	2.91	3.43	3.16	14	28	17	19
Coffee	3.93	3.91	3.97	3.94	2	0	0	1
Pet food	3.29	3.59	3.24	3.36	7	3	11	7
Overall mean	3.45	3.47	3.49	3.49				
Overall percentage					7.6	10.3	9.3	9.0
Durables, for child's use								
Game, toy	1.24	1.63	2.17	1.65	57	59	46	54
Clothing	2.76	2.47	2.29	2.52	21	34	57	37
Bicycle	2.48	2.59	2.77	2.61	7	9	9	8
Hot wheels	2.43	2.41	3.20	2.67	29	19	17	22
Record album	3.36	2.63	2.23	2.78	12	16	46	24
Camera	3.91	3.75	3.71	3.80	2	3	0	2
Overall mean	2.70	2.58	2.73	2.67				
Overall percentage					25.6	28.0	35.0	29.4
Notions, toiletries								
Toothpaste	2.29	2.31	2.60	2.39	36	44	40	39
Bath soap	3.10	2.97	3.46	3.17	9	9	9	9
Shampoo	3.48	3.31	3.03	3.28	17	6	23	16

Aspirin								
Overall mean	3.64	3.78	3.97	3.79	5	6	0	4
Overall percentage	3.13	3.09	3.26	3.16	16.8	16.3	18.0	17.0
Other products								
Automobile	3.55	3.66	3.51	3.57	2	0	0	12
Gasoline brand	3.64	3.63	3.83	3.70	2	0	3	2
Laundry soap	3.69	3.75	3.71	3.72	2	0	3	2
Household cleaner	3.71	3.84	3.74	3.76	2	3	0	2
Overall mean	3.65	3.72	3.70	3.69				
Overall percentage	2.0	.75	1.50	1.75				

[a]On a scale from 1 = often to 4 = never.

[b]5–7 years, $n = 43$; 8–10 years, $n = 32$; 11–12 years, $n = 34$; $N = 109$.

Source: Scott Ward and Daniel B. Wackman, "Children's Purchase Influence Attempts and Parental Yielding," *Journal of Marketing Research*, 9 (August 1972): 317. Reprinted by permission of the American Marketing Association.

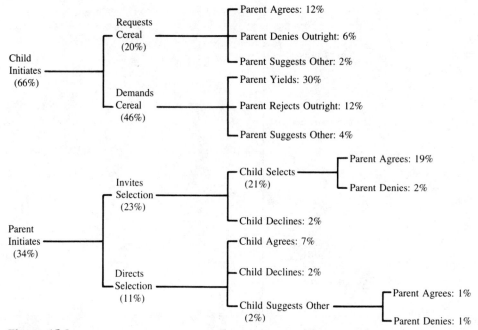

Figure 15.8
Flow of parent-child interaction in breakfast cereal selection

Source: Charles K. Atkin, "Observation of Parent-Child Interaction in Supermarket Decision-Making." *Journal of Marketing*, 42 (October 1978): 43. Reprinted by permission of the American Marketing Association.

initiations take the form of demands. Interestingly, parents are somewhat more likely to yield to a demand than to a request. In cases where the child's request was denied, conflict resulted 65 percent of the time and the child left unhappy 48 percent of the time. Particularly interesting are the observations that approximately one-fourth of the children based their choice primarily on a premium (e.g., a toy) and that in less than 1 percent of all observations was there "explicit mention of either vitamins, minerals or general health value of the product" (p. 43). Finally, citing a different but apparently related study, Atkin reports that the frequency of cereal requests correlated +.46 with the amount of Saturday morning television viewing. Cereals, of course, is one of the principle battlegrounds over which the issue of advertising directed to children has been fought.

Several other studies show that children frequently make, and are often granted, specific brand requests. An early observational study by Wells and LoSciuto (1966), for example, found that three-fourths of the children observed attempted to influence the selection of cereal and in more than one-half of these cases were successful. Reynolds and Wells (1977) cite a large scale 1966 survey by Bruskin Associates, which found that parents frequently allow children age four–twelve to select a wide range of food and nonfood products.

Table 15.7 presents data from a study by Ward and Wackman (1972), that is interesting for a variety of reasons. In addition to collecting data for a variety of products and separating the responses by age of child, the authors also distinguish between the frequency of requests and the percent of yielding to the request.

There are considerable differences both in requests and yielding across products and age of child that are intuitively plausible. Children frequently attempted to influence food purchases. Such attempts, however, decreased with age. The second most requested items were durable goods directly used by the child. Younger children frequently requested games and toys, while older children more often requested clothing and record albums. There was also a general tendency for mothers to yield more frequently to older children. Finally, there was a small, but statistically significant, positive correlation between influence attempts and parental yielding.

The final study of child influence attempts to be cited was conducted by Berey and Pollay (1968). The researchers began with the hypothesis that child-centered mothers would be more likely to yield to their children's requests. They found just the reverse. This suggests that child-centered mothers more closely monitor their children's buying and consuming and that less child-centered mothers may yield as a way of quieting the child and avoiding conflicts. When these findings are coupled with Atkin's finding that children who make "demands" are more likely to be yielded to, the ethical implications of managerial insights gained from family decision-making research are again apparent.

SUMMARY

The most fundamental conclusion to draw from this analysis of research on family buying behavior is that virtually every aspect that has been researched shows a high degree of variability. This variability exists across products, stages in the decision process, subcomponents of the total decision, over time and geography, and across families. Despite the methodological limitations of research on family buying behavior, there is no question that this variability is an accurate reflection of reality.

It is also clear from this review that the focus of research on family buying behavior has been quite narrow. Specifically, research has focused on the relative influence of husbands and wives and has largely ignored the actual processes through which family buying decisions are made and implemented. Given the continuing and intimate nature of the family, the lack of research on the family decision-making process is not really surprising. Nevertheless, it is a factor that those who wish to develop effective marketing strategies cannot ignore.

The most appropriate managerial implication to be drawn from research on family buying behavior is the need for product specific information. Available research provides general insights and hypotheses that must be developed and validated in each specific managerial application. For example, if the product of interest is automobiles, it can reasonably be anticipated that the husband is most likely to initiate the decision-making process, that the husband will be more concerned with mechanical and performance features, that the wife will be more concerned with comfort and interior styling, that teenage children will try and may succeed in influencing the purchase decision, and that middle class wives and wives who work will play a larger role in the final purchase decision. Of course, exactly how these variables operate may vary considerably for decisions regarding luxury foreign and economy domestic automobiles. Nevertheless, they provide a reasonable basis both for designing preliminary marketing strategies and for developing specific research programs to assess the validity of those strategies.

Finally, the point must be reinforced that those who would design optimal marketing strategies based on family buying behavior research may face serious ethical issues. Nowhere is this issue clearer in the review than in research suggesting that television has a strong effect on children's influence attempts and that children who demand rather than request are more likely to be yielded to by parents. The manager, of course, must consider legal constraints as well as the dictates of his or her own conscience when grappling with such ethical issues.

Collective Buying Behavior: Organizational Buying Behavior

16*

As was seen in the last chapter, recognition that much buying behavior is conducted on a collective basis raises a number of new issues, such as who performs
specific buying tasks and how conflicts are resolved when they arise. This chapter
continues the discussion of collective buying behavior by focusing on the buying
behavior of organizational buyers. As suggested in Chapter 15, there are many
similarities between family and organizational buying behavior. Therefore, the
focus here will be on the unique characteristics of organizational buying.

One of these unique characteristics is that organizational buyers buy primarily
to satisfy the demands of *their* customers. Some of these customers are *final*
consumers; most, however, are other organizational buyers. For example, the bread
that you buy at the supermarket has been resold many times in the form of seeds,
fertilizer, grain, flour, and so on. This implies that the vast majority of sales are sales
to organizations rather than final consumers. Thus, organizational buying is of great
importance to the majority of marketers, a fact that often surprises students.

The analysis of organizational buying begins with a brief presentation of
general models of organizational buying behavior. This section provides a general
overview of the concepts that are of special importance in the study of organizational buying. The next section discusses major similarities and differences between organizational and family buying behavior. The third, and final, section
analyzes the processes through which organizational buying decisions are made.
Although this analysis is relevant to virtually all organizational buyers, it focuses on
for-profit organizations that intend to further process the goods and services they
purchase before selling the resulting products to other organizational buyers or
final consumers. Most specifically, our analysis excludes retail merchandisers, who
buy finished goods for direct resale to final consumers, since successful merchandising essentially requires anticipation of the behavior of final consumers.

GENERAL MODELS OF ORGANIZATIONAL BUYING

Researchers have proposed a number of general models of organizational buying
behavior. The uses, strengths, and weaknesses of such models are essentially the
same as those of general models of the behavior of individual consumers. Of necessity,
however, models of organizational buying tend to be both more complex and less
precisely specified because, the behavior of the individuals who make organizational buying decisions must be placed within a larger organizational context.

Task and Nontask Oriented Models

As Webster and Wind (1972a) note, early models of organizational buying tended
to focus on either task variables or nontask variables. Table 16.1 illustrates the
difference between these two types of variables. Although task and nontask variables may conflict, they may also be mutually reinforcing. For example, the nontask
personal value of achievement may cause the organizational buyer to perform the
buying task more effectively; e.g., by securing the lowest price.

*The author is much indebted to Professor Michael Kolchin of Lehigh University, who prepared the
initial draft of this chapter.

Table 16.1
Examples of task and nontask variables

	Task	Nontask
Individual	desire to obtain lowest price	personal values and needs
Social	meetings to set specifications	informal, off-the-job interactions
Organizational	policy regarding local supplier preference	methods of personnel evaluation
Environmental	anticipated changes in prices	political climate in an election year

Source: Frederick E. Webster, Jr. and Yoram Wind, "A General Model for Understanding Organization Buying Behavior." *Journal of Marketing*, 36 (April 1972): 13. Reprinted with the kind permission of the American Marketing Association.

Most task models are essentially microeconomic models that attempt to analyze organizational buying in terms of profit maximization (Johnston 1981). Such models are typically based on highly simplified assumptions; e.g., perfect information and economically rational behavior by both buyer and seller. Although useful for predicting behavior and for improving the decision-making process within the firm, task models generally fail to capture the richness of organizational buying behavior.

Nontask oriented models tend to explain organizational buying behavior in terms of individual differences, such as achievement motivation, interpersonal relationships, and perceptions of risk to the individual making the decision. For example, research suggests that as the level of perceived risk to the individual decision maker increases that person tends to adopt specific strategies, such as becoming more loyal to well-known and highly credible sellers, to reduce the perceived risk (cf., Bauer 1960, Cox 1967a).

As Webster and Wind (1972a) suggest, both task and nontask models tend to be very limited in their perspective on organizational buying behavior. These authors argue that what is required is a more comprehensive model that includes both task and nontask variables in the context of a buyer organizational and environmental framework. More specifically, Webster and Wind state that

> The fundamental assertion of the more comprehensive model to be presented here is that organizational buying is a decision-making process carried out by individuals, in interaction with other people, in the context of a formal organization (p. 13).

Their model will be briefly examined over the next few pages, as will two other general or comprehensive models of organizational buying behavior.

The Webster and Wind Model

As can be seen in Figure 16.1, the Webster and Wind model recognizes four broad categories of variables that influence organizational buying decisions. The environ-

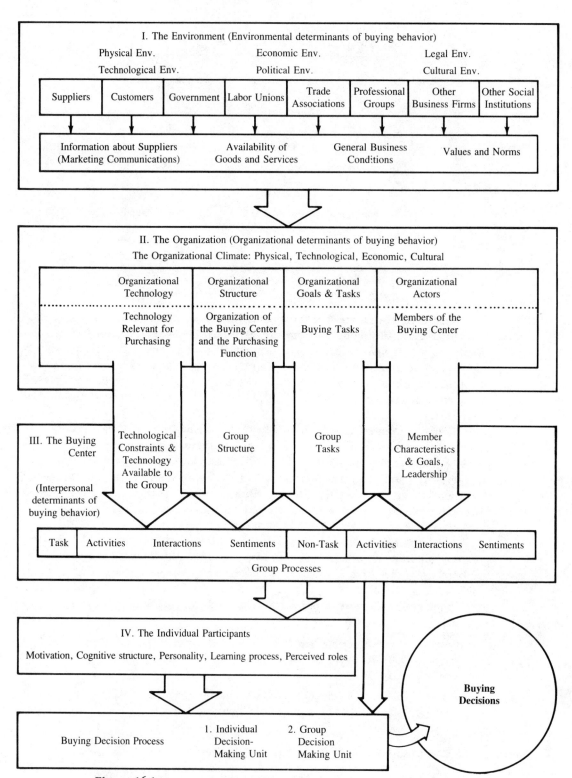

Figure 16.1
The Webster and Wind model of organizational buying behavior

Source: Frederick E. Webster, Jr. and Yoram Wind, "A General Model for Understanding Organizational Buying Behavior," *Journal of Marketing*, 36 (April 1972): 15. Reprinted with the kind permission of the American Marketing Association.

mental variables recognize that organizational buying decisions are influenced by many outside forces, such as government and trade unions, as well as suppliers of goods and services.

The second category of organizational variables recognizes that "Organizational factors cause individual decision makers to act differently than they would if they were functioning alone or in a different organization" (Webster and Wind 1972a, p. 14). Organizational technology, structure, goals and tasks, and people (actors) interact to "define the information, expectations, goals, attitudes, and assumptions used by each of the individual actors in their decision making" (Webster and Wind 1972a, p. 16).

The third category of variables defines what is generally referred to as the buying center. The buying center consists of the subset of organizational members who perform the roles of users, influencers, deciders, gatekeepers, and buyers in the organizational decision-making process. As Webster and Wind note,

> The marketer's problem is to define the locus of buying responsibility within the customer organization, to define the composition of the buying center, and to understand the structure of roles and authority within the buying center (p. 17).

It is important to recognize that the buying center is largely informal and will generally be constituted by different organizational members for different types of decisions.

The fourth, and final, category of variables recognizes that ultimately all organizational behavior is performed by individuals. Thus, a full account of organizational buying behavior must consider individual factors, such as motivation and personality, as these individual difference variables function within the larger context of organizational buying decisions.

As Johnston (1981, pp. 21–22) notes, the Webster and Wind model has a number of limitations. In particular, "The model is loosely constructed and offers no testable propositions" (p. 21). This criticism, however, could be made of most general models of individual *or* organizational buying behavior. Thus, the primary value of the Webster and Wind model is that "it presents the major set of variables ... that marketing personnel should identify in their attempt to understand (organizational) buying behavior" (Webster and Wind 1972b, p. 39).

The Sheth Model

The second general model of organizational buying behavior to be considered was developed by Sheth (1973). Figure 16.2 presents the model. Essentially, the Sheth model is an extremely complex stimulus-response model that attempts to describe and explain every type of buying decision from simple to complex (Bonoma, Zaltman, and Johnston 1977).

The key component of the Sheth model is expectations of buyers about suppliers and brands. These expectations are created on the basis of four factors: background of the individual, the nature and source of information the buyer has acquired, the perceptions the buyer has developed about the supplier and the brand, and the buyer's past experience with a supplier or brand. These expectations are then further influenced by product-specific factors, organizational factors, and situation and environmental factors. Other noteworthy aspects of the Sheth model are its emphasis on the conditions that tend to produce joint decision

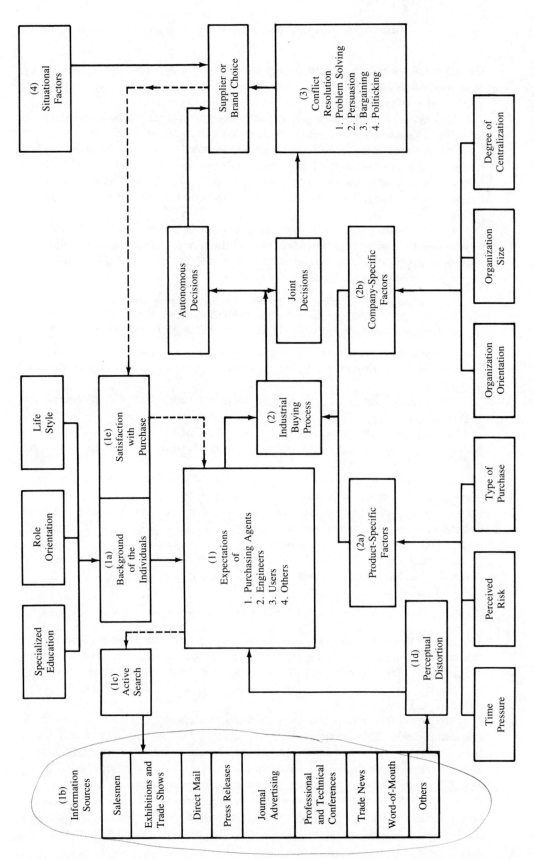

Figure 16.2
The Sheth model of industrial buying behavior

Source: Jagdish N. Sheth, "A Model of Industrial Buyer Behavior," *Journal of Marketing,* 37 (October 1973): 51. Reprinted with the kind permission of the American Marketing Association.

making, the conflict that can arise when group members have different goals and different perceptions of the problem, and that conflict can be resolved in a number of different ways. As the reader can see in Figure 16.2, these methods of conflict resolution are the same ones presented in the last chapter; i.e., problem solving, persuasion, bargaining, and politicking.

The uses and criticisms of the Sheth model closely parallel those of the Webster and Wind model (cf., Johnston 1981, pp. 22–23). In comparison to the Webster and Wind model, the Sheth model attempts to specify the relationships among the variables that affect organizational buying behavior in addition to identifying those influences. As Johnston notes, the Sheth model also "enable(s) one to begin to order the mass of existing literature and complexity of industrial marketing" (1981 p. 23).

The Choffray and Lilien Model

Both the Webster and Wind and the Sheth models are essentially attempts to define the variables that affect organizational buying decisions and to specify the relationships among these variables. While these models suggest many managerial strategies for marketing to organizational buyers, they provide no direct links to the controllable marketing mix variables: product, price, promotion, and distribution. Recently, Choffray and Lilien (1978) developed an industrial market response model, that models the organizational decision-making process in terms of responses to controllable marketing mix variables. The authors also outline a measurement methodology for their model.

Figure 16.3 presents the Choffray and Lilien model. The overall model is composed of four submodels of awareness, acceptance, individual evaluation, and group decision processes. Each submodel is developed in terms of the probability of a specific response to a specific brand (brand a) that is a member of a particular class of products (denoted by A).

For example, awareness is modeled in terms of the probability that brand a will be evoked as a relevant choice alternative; i.e., $P(a = \text{evoked})$. This probability is then specified in terms of such controllable marketing variables as advertising, technical service, and personal selling and external measures, such as communication consumption for each participant in the buying process and specific organizational constraints and requirements. In a similar way, Choffray and Lilien develop submodels of the probability that an evoked brand will be accepted as a feasible alternative, that a feasible brand will be chosen by individual members of the buying center, and that brand a will be the feasible brand that is finally chosen by the decision-making group.

As Johnston (1981, pp. 23–24) notes, the Choffray and Lilien model can be criticized on a number of grounds, such as the assumption that individuals who occupy equivalent positions (e.g., production engineers) use the same product evaluation criteria. Nevertheless, the Choffray and Lilien model is an important development in the effort to construct valid models of organizational buying behavior. It is "the first complex model to be empirically capable of evaluation" (Johnston 1981, p. 23). In this regard, the model recognizes the need to operationally define such important, but generally vague, concepts as the buying center. Finally, the Choffray and Lilien model is another example of rapidly developing technologies for *directly* linking buyer behavior concepts to managerial decisions.

Controllable Variables   Decision Process   External Measures

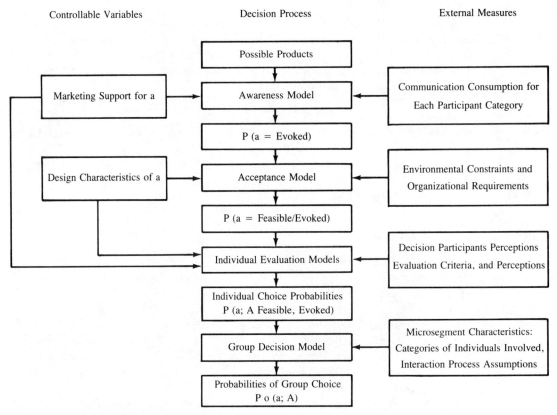

Figure 16.3
Choffray and Lilien industrial market response model

Source: Jean-Marie Choffray and Gary L. Lilien, "Assessing Response to Industrial Marketing Strategy." *Journal of Marketing*, 42 (April 1978): 23. Reprinted with the kind permission of the American Marketing Association.

SIMILARITIES AND DIFFERENCES BETWEEN ORGANIZATIONAL AND CONSUMER BUYING BEHAVIOR

The last chapter briefly discussed a number of ways in which organizational buyers and final consumers are similar. It also stated that "the differences that exist between consumers and organizational buyers are probably of no greater magnitude than those that exist between different types of consumers. They are also of no lesser importance to the development of effective marketing strategies." Having presented an overview of the general models of organizational buying behavior, the similarities and, especially, the differences between consumer and organizational buying behavior may now be more fully developed.

A Caricature of the Organizational Buyer

In the nineteenth century, Elbert Hubbard described the typical organizational buyer as

. . . a man past middle-life, spare, wrinkled, intelligent, cold, passive, noncommittal, with eyes like a codfish, polite in contact, but at the same time, unresponsive, cool, calm, and damnably composed as a concrete post or a Plaster of Paris cat; a human petrification with a heart of feldspar without charm or a sense of humor. Happily they never reproduce and all of them go to hell (cited in Boone and Stevens 1970, p. 48).

While Hubbard's words are those of a nineteenth century man, his portrait of the industrial buyer very likely at least partially coincides with that of many readers. To what extent is this portrait of a cold, calculating, economically rational man an accurate portrayal of the organizational buyer and to what extent is it a gross caricature?

Similarities

The last chapter noted a number of parallels between family and organizational buying; e.g., specialized buying roles and potential conflict among group members. Beyond this, there are two additional types of similarities between consumer and organizational buying behavior.

First, virtually every influence on buyer behavior studied throughout this book has been shown to operate to some extent in organizational buying. For example, Shoaf (1959) in an article titled "Here's Proof—The Industrial Buyer *IS* Human," found that a variety of emotional factors such as longevity of supplier relations, desire to avoid risky decisions, and subjective attitudes become increasingly important in organizational buying as alternative products become more standardized.

Another illustration of the similarities between organizational buyers and final consumers comes from a study of decision-making styles of 132 purchasing agents. Wilson (1971) identified two basic "styles" of decision making and found that the preferred style was related to the personality variable need for certainty. Purchasing agents who followed a so-called normative, or economically rational, decision-making style had a low need for certainty. Purchasing agents who followed a conservative, risk avoiding strategy had a high need for certainty. Interestingly, only 26 percent of the purchasing agents were found to consistently apply a normative style of decision making. Similarly, a variety of studies have reported influences on the organizational buyer such as opinion leadership (Martilla 1971, Schiffman and Gaccione 1974), vendor loyalty (Bubb and van Rest 1974) and word-of-mouth communication (Martilla 1971) that influence organizational buyers in essentially the same ways as they influence consumer decision making.

Second, the theories and concepts that have been successfully used to study consumer buying behavior tend to be applicable to organizational buying behavior as well. For example, the theories of motivation presented in Chapter 6 are as applicable to organizational buyers as to final consumers. Of course, account must be taken of the organizational structure in which the motivations function. This, however, in no way lessens the relevance or value of the theories themselves. In a very similar way, such concepts as the extended Fishbein model may be used to study the attitudes of organizational buyers or diffusion of innovation concepts may be applied as readily to industrial product innovations as to consumer product innovations. Again, the specifics of the situation (e.g., the choice criteria used) must be considered. The theories themselves, however, remain essentially unchanged.

Differences

Although there are many similarities between organizational and consumer buying behavior, there are also important differences. Perhaps the most important of these differences is that organizational buying tends to be much more formalized than consumer buying. Indeed, most medium and large size organizations have formal purchasing departments whose primary job is to insure a continuing flow of needed materials, supplies, and services of adequate quality, reliable availability, and minimum costs. When one considers that in many organizations, especially manufacturing firms, such purchases exceed 50 percent of sales the importance of effective purchasing to the economic well-being of the organization becomes obvious.

This formality of organizational buying is manifested in many ways. The goal structure of organizations is both different in content and more explicit than in consumer buying. Theoretically, of course, organizational buying by profit-making firms is guided by the single, unifying objective of maximizing profits. However, at the level where buying decisions are actually made the goals are likely to be more specific and potentially in conflict; e.g., marketing attempting to insure an adequate supply of finished goods for sale *and* finance trying to minimize inventory carrying costs.

The formality of much organizational buying means that purchasing agents will typically become more knowledgeable of the items they are responsible for purchasing. For the purchasing agent, whose job is at stake, these are high involve-ment decisions that tend to follow a learning hierarchy of decision making. A reflection of this fact is that organizational purchasing requirements are frequently expressed in terms of precise technical product or service specifications. In this regard, Webster (1978) observed that the entire process of organizational buying is more complex for reasons such as

> the influence of formal organization, the large number of persons involved, the complex technical and economic factors that must be considered, the environ-ment in which the firm operates, and the frequently large sums of money involved in the transaction (p. 23).

Pruden (1969) characterized both the buyer and seller as "men-in-the-middle," who must engage in a great deal of communication with each other in order to satisfy their individual and organizational goals. Webster (1978) makes the same point by observing that

> Buyer-seller interdependence is indeed a hallmark of industrial marketing, especially for products used in the customer's operations, as most industrial products are.
>
> The buyer becomes crucially dependent on the supplier—for an assured supply of raw materials, components or subassemblies; for continued supply of maintenance and repair parts and skilled repair service for capital equipment; for efficient order handling, delivery, and, usually, extension of credit terms, etc. One significant result is the fact that the "sale," the actual transaction, is only one point on the time continuum of industrial marketing, albeit a crucially important one and the way most businesses keep score. By contrast, in consumer marketing the buyer-seller relationship often ends with the sale.
>
> In industrial marketing, again, a significant negotiation process is often the

most important regulator of the buyer-seller relationship. Consumer marketing usually lacks this, relying instead on an "arm's length" transaction in a more or less competitive market (p. 25).

Webster also identifies a number of additional distinctions between consumer and organizational marketing that are often given insufficient recognition such as

... that industrial markets often consist of a small number of potential customers; that demand for industrial products is "derived demand"; that customers are often concentrated geographically; that there are tremendous ranges in customer size; that there are fewer sales transactions for much larger dollar amounts, etc. (p. 24).

These, and other, differences mean that quite different marketing strategies will be required even when the same good is being marketed to consumer and organizational buyers. Consider, for example, marketing strategies for selling automobiles to Hertz or Avis as opposed to final consumers.

This brief examination of general models of organizational buying and some of the major similarities and differences between organizational and consumer buying behavior provides a basis for a detailed consideration of the processes through which organizational buying decisions are made, and especially those aspects of the decision-making process that tend to be unique to organizational buyers.

ORGANIZATIONAL BUYING DECISION PROCESSES

The Purchasing Function

Organizations typically assign purchasing responsibilities to specific individuals. Except for relatively small organizations, these purchasing responsibilities and the purchasing agents who perform them are typically organized as a purchasing department. From a systems point of view, purchasing can be thought of as performing the acquisition function of the firm. This function has increasingly been recognized as critical to both the quality and profitability of the firm's products. For this reason, persons who perform the purchasing function have increasingly been recognized as important members of management rather than clerks who simply implement purchase orders.

It is important to recognize that purchasing agents are staff members and rarely have line authority over the other departments for whom they buy (Strauss 1962). Although other organizational members may be required to place orders through the purchasing department, the purchasing department normally cannot order specific purchasing decisions. Rather, it must rely on its "expert" power as a base of influence (Spekman 1979). That is, it must show other departments that its agents are experts on market conditions, product availability, pricing, contracting, and so on to insure that it is able to exert a proper amount of control over the buying process. It is for this reason that purchasing agents tend to be sensitive to and value sincere efforts of industrial salespeople to provide them with information that allows them to perform their job more effectively.

Buying Objectives

Effective strategies for marketing goods and services to organizations require understanding the objectives of the purchasing firm. Organizations, of course, buy in order to satisfy the demands of their customers whether those customers are final consumers or other organizations. This is why the demand of organizations for goods and services is also referred to as derived demand.

The purchasing agent's job is to assist other departments in meeting their individual responsibilities in order to obtain the overall goals of the organization. The purchasing agent's objectives are often characterized as obtaining the right material, at the right price, at the right time. More specifically, Kiser and Rao (1971) suggest that the purchasing agent normally tries to meet the following eight general objectives.

1. Maintaining continuity of supply
2. Avoiding duplication and waste
3. Maintaining standards of quality
4. Procuring at lowest cost
5. Maintaining the company's competitive position
6. Providing information to management
7. Maintaining satisfactory relations with vendors
8. Developing satisfactory relationships with other intraorganizational units.

In essence, the purchasing agent's job is to obtain the goods and services required by the organization at the lowest *total* cost. Total cost goes well beyond the invoice price and includes such things as late deliveries, short counts, poor quality, inventory carrying charges, maintenance of capital equipment, and a host of possible expenses associated with the acquisition of different types of goods and services. Fulfilling these objectives often requires very complex decision-making processes.

The Organizational Buying Process

In order to accomplish their objectives organizational buyers must engage in a number of different types of activities. Robinson, Faris, and Wind (1967, pp. 13–18) state that the organizational buying process is composed of the following eight broad categories of activities or buyphases, as they have been labeled by the authors.

1. Anticipation or recognition of a problem (need) and a general solution
2. Determination of characteristics and quantity of needed items
3. Description of characteristics and quality of needed items
4. Search for qualifications of potential sources
5. Acquisition and analysis of proposals
6. Evaluation of proposals and selection of suppliers
7. Selection of order routine
8. Performance feedback and evaluation.

In performing these activities the purchasing agent assumes the role of master coordinator. Within the organization the various, and often conflicting, needs of different organizational members must be reconciled and put into the form of specific required goods and services. These needs must then be coordinated with what potential sellers are capable of and willing to supply on terms that are acceptable to the buying organization.

As the next section will show, the exact activities that must be performed in conjunction with any specific buying decision depend very much on the characteristics of the buying problem.

Types of Buying Decisions

The types of buying situations faced by organizational buyers can be classified in a variety of ways. For example, buying problems are frequently classified as capital versus noncapital purchases or by degree of technical complexity or by magnitude of expenditure. Table 16.2 presents a very general system for classifying organizational buying situations originally developed by Robinson, Faris, and Wind (1967).

As can be seen in Tale 16.2 three different types of buying situations, or buyclasses, are recognized. These three buyclasses are distinguished in terms of three basic attributes: the newness of the problem, the amount and type of information required, and the number of new alternatives to the buying problem that the decision maker seriously considers. Figure 16.4 illustrates a number of the principle characteristics of each of the three buyclasses.

The buyclasses—straight rebuy, modified rebuy, and new task—closely parallel the consumer decision-making stages of routinized response behavior, limited problem solving, and extensive problem solving, respectively. Although such things as the specific goals and choice criteria will differ, the concepts and many of the empirical findings discussed in Chapters 4–11 in conjunction with consumer decision making transfer quite readily to organizational decision making. For example, research shows many parallels in the adoption processes for innovations for final consumers and organizational decision makers (cf., Baker 1975).

Table 16.2
Types of organizational buying situations

Type of Buying Situation (Buyclass)	Newness of the Problem	Information Requirements	Consideration of New Alternatives
New Task	High	Maximum	Important
Modified Rebuy	Medium	Moderate	Limited
Straight Rebuy	Low	Minimal	None

Source: Patrick J. Robinson, Charles W. Faris and Yoram Wind, *Industrial Buying and Creative Marketing.* Boston: Allyn & Bacon, Inc., 1967, p. 25. Reprinted with permission.

I. New Task
A requirement or problem that has not arisen before

Little or no relevant past buying experience to draw upon

A great deal of information is needed

Must seek out alternative ways of solving the problem and alternative suppliers

Occurs infrequently—but very important to marketers because it sets the pattern for the more routine purchases that will follow

May be anticipated and developed by creative marketing

II. Straight Rebuy
Continuing or recurring requirement, handled on a routine basis

Usually the decision on each separate transaction is made in the purchasing department

Formally or informally, a "list" of acceptable suppliers exists

No supplier not on the "list" is considered

Buyers have much relevant buying experience, and hence little new information is needed

Appears to represent the bulk of the individual purchases within companies

Item purchased, price paid, delivery time, etc., may vary from transaction to transaction, so long as these variations do not cause a new source of supply to be considered

III. Modified Rebuy
May develop from either new task or straight rebuy situations

The requirement is continuing or recurring or it may be expanded to a significantly larger level of operations

The buying alternatives are known, but they are *changed*

Some additional information is needed before the decisions are made

May arise because of outside events, such as an emergency or by the actions of a marketer

May arise internally because of new buying influences, or for potential cost reductions, potential quality improvements or potential service benefits

Marketers who are not active suppliers try to convert the customer's straight rebuys into modified rebuys

---

Figure 16.4
Characteristics of buyclasses

Source: Patrick J. Robinson, Charles W. Faris, and Yoram Wind, *Industrial Buying and Creative Marketing.* Boston: Allyn & Bacon, Inc., 1967, p. 28. Reprinted with permission.

Another classification system, which is more unique to the organizational buying context, was developed by Lehmann and O'Shaughnessy (1974). Specifically, the authors identify the following four types of products: routine order products, procedural problem products, performance problem products, and political problem products. As the name implies, routine order products present no special problems, require essentially no new information except price and availability, and require little decision-making activity beyond placing the order.

For procedural problem products, it is presumed that while the product *will* perform satisfactorily, personnel in the buying organization must be taught how to use the product. As Lehmann and O'Shaughnessy note

> A buyer intent on minimizing problems associated with such a product will favor the supplier whose total offering is perceived as likely to reduce to a minimum the time and difficulty required to learn the product's operation.

Procedural problems tend to be regarded as having a definite end, with some confidence about the outcome, so that long-term goals predominate. Thus, the buyer is likely to give an early buying commitment, although the purchase may be by stages so that training does not outstrip resources. However, it is probable that the choice of supplier will be greatly influenced by the extent to which a supplier can persuade the buyer of the superiority of the service he offers in reducing the time likely to be spent in learning how to operate the product (p. 37).

Performance problem products raise technical issues about whether the product will perform as expected. For such products, the buying organization will seek various kinds of reassurances that the product will perform properly. Lehmann and O'Shaughnessy argue

> ... that the buyer will favor the supplier who can offer appropriate technical service, provide a free trial period, and who appears flexible enough to adjust to the demands of the buyer's company (p. 37).

Performance problem products raise especially serious problems for both buyers and sellers when a failure to perform would disrupt the buyer's basic production schedule.

Political problem products are those that put the requirements of different persons or departments in conflict. For example, large capital outlays frequently raise political problems because of the limited available capital, which restricts other desired expenditures. The issues raised by political products tend to arise from conflicting aspirations and goals, and are difficult to resolve by appeals to "the facts."

The consequences of the distinctions among types of organizational buying processes stem from the fact that organizational buyers go through different specific decision-making processes for different types of buying situations. For example, the degree of effort, the amount of new information required, and the uncertainty that accompanies the whole decision process will vary for straight rebuys, modified rebuys, and new tasks in ways that closely parallel routinized response behavior, limited problem solving, and extensive problem solving. Furthermore, the relative importance of different choice criteria, the number of individuals involved in the decision, and the magnitude and means of resolving conflict will all vary considerably by type of buying situation. Understanding these differences can be of great importance in developing effective marketing strategies. The next three sections examine a number of these differences.

Choice Criteria

A successful marketing strategy for selling to organizational buyers requires a clear understanding of the criteria by which alternative choices are evaluated. As noted earlier, one distinction between organizational and consumer buying is that organizational requirements are much more frequently specified in terms of precise technical and performance specifications. For example, a bottler may require a machine capable of bottling a minimum of 1,500 bottles per minute, with a maximum defect rate of 1 per 1,000 bottles, with normal maintenance and recalibration required no more than once every 168 hours (i.e., once a week), etc. These criteria, of course, will be highly unique to each buying problem.

At a more general level, Lehmann and O'Shaughnessy (1974) compiled a list of seventeen attributes, or choice criteria, typically used to evaluate choice alternatives by organizational buyers. These criteria are presented in Table 16.3. In a study involving 19 major American companies and 26 major British companies, Lehmann and O'Shaughnessy (1974) asked purchasing agents to rate the importance of each attribute for each of four types of buying situations: routine order, procedural problem, performance problem, and political problem products. Table 16.4 presents the results.

Although Table 16.4 is essentially self-explanatory, several points merit further comment. First, there are considerable differences in attribute importance across types of products that are in accord with what one might logically expect. Training offered, for example, is very important only for procedural problem products. Also, price is very important for routine order and political problem products, but only of moderate importance for procedural and performance problem products. In considering the extreme importance of price for political problem products, recall that such products often involve conflict over general budget priorities.

Second, several attributes have relatively similar importance ratings across all four product types. For example, convenience in ordering is rated relatively unimportant. In contrast, flexibility of supplier in adjusting to company needs and reliability of delivery date promised are rated relatively important.

Third, the data are consistent with the unique characteristics of organizational buying, some of which have been previously discussed. The overall pattern of the importance ratings, for example, suggest that frequently organizational buyers are "buying" a supplier as much or even more than a specific product. Similarly, that reliability of delivery is a consistently important attribute reflects the unique problems of organizations. Note also that the mean importance ratings, which have

---

Table 16.3
Seventeen choice criteria of general importance to organizational buying decisions

1. Overall reputation of the supplier
2. Financing terms
3. Supplier's flexibility in adjusting to your company's needs
4. Experience with the supplier in analogous situations
5. Technical service offered
6. Confidence in the salesmen
7. Convenience of placing the order
8. Data on reliability of the product
9. Price
10. Technical specifications
11. Ease of operation or use
12. Preferences of principal user of the product
13. Training offered by the supplier
14. Training time required
15. Reliability of delivery date promised
16. Ease of maintenance
17. Sales service expected after date of purchase

Source: Donald R. Lehmann and John O'Shaughnessy, "Difference in Attribute Importance for Different Industrial Products," *Journal of Marketing*, 38 (April 1974): 38. Reprinted with the kind permission of the American Marketing Association.

Table 16.4
Average importance of choice criteria for routine order, procedural problem, performance

Attribute	Product Type							
	I		II		III		IV	
	Mean	Rank	Mean	Rank	Mean	Rank	Mean	Rank
1. Reputation	4.84[a]	4	5.33	7	5.29	5	5.53	2
	(1.09)		(0.80)		(0.82)		(0.69)	
2. Financing	4.51	9	4.07	16	3.91	16	4.91	13
	(1.39)		(1.29)		(1.31)		(1.24)	
3. Flexibility	5.07	3	5.40	5	5.42	2	5.51	5
	(1.12)		(0.62)		(0.62)		(0.59)	
4. Past experience	4.71	6	4.93	13	5.07	9	5.04	10
	(0.94)		(0.86)		(0.69)		(0.93)	
5. Technical service	4.36	12	5.53	1	5.38	3	5.40	7
	(1.28)		(0.66)		(0.89)		(0.62)	
6. Confidence in salesmen	3.96	14	4.73	15	4.42	15	4.58	16
	(1.35)		(1.23)		(1.20)		(1.20)	
7. Convenience in ordering	3.80	15	3.73	17	3.71	17	4.08	17
	(1.32)		(1.29)		(1.34)		(1.24)	
8. Reliability data	4.47	11	5.16	11	5.33	4	5.53	3
	(1.24)		(1.07)		(0.67)		(0.59)	
9. Price	5.60	2	5.29	8	5.18	8	5.56	1
	(0.62)		(0.70)		(0.94)		(0.69)	
10. Technical specifications	4.73	5	5.22	9	5.27	6	5.42	6
	(1.25)		(0.67)		(0.69)		(0.72)	
11. Ease of use	4.51	10	5.53	2	5.24	7	5.18	8
	(1.29)		(0.59)		(0.80)		(0.83)	
12. Preference of user	4.00	13	4.76	14	4.53	13	4.84	14
	(1.19)		(1.11)		(1.14)		(0.90)	
13. Training offered	3.22	16	5.42	3	4.73	12	5.00	11
	(1.18)		(0.87)		(1.19)		(0.83)	
14. Training required	3.22	17	5.11	12	4.44	14	4.69	15
	(1.22)		(1.23)		(1.22)		(1.02)	
15. Reliability of delivery	5.64	1	5.42	4	5.44	1	5.53	4
	(0.53)		(0.72)		(0.66)		(0.69)	
16. Maintenance	4.60	8	5.20	10	4.82	11	5.00	12
	(1.05)		(0.69)		(0.96)		(0.74)	
17. Sales service	4.64	7	5.36	6	5.07	10	5.09	9
	(1.25)		(0.77)		(0.84)		(0.70)	
Product Type Mean	4.46		5.07		4.90		5.11	

[a]Mean (standard deviation)

Source: Donald R. Lehmann and John O'Shaughnessy, "Difference in Attribute Importance for Different Industrial Products." *Journal of Marketing,* 38 (April 1974): 39. Reprinted with the kind permission of the American Marketing Association.

a maximum value of seven, are all very high. This suggests that organizational buyers tend to be highly involved with *all* types of buying problems, even routine purchases. Recently, Evans (1981), in a study that attempts to specifically assess the level of purchasing agents' involvement with different types of buying problems, collected data that directly support this suggestion. This, of course, reminds us that organizational buying is a job activity, and that organizational buyers are far more likely to follow a learning hierarchy pattern of decision making than is the typical consumer.

Lehmann and O'Shaughnessy (1982) recently reported another study of the relative importance of choice criteria that defines both the choice criteria and buying situations somewhat differently. They begin by defining the following five types of criteria and the key question each raises.

1. *Performance Criteria.*
   These criteria evaluate the extent to which the product is likely to maximize performance in the application(s) envisaged for it.
   Key Question: How well will the product do the job?

2. *Economic Criteria.*
   These criteria evaluate the anticipated cost outlays associated with buying, storing, using, and maintaining the product.
   Key Question: What are the various cost outlays that will be associated with buying and utilizing the product?

3. *Integrative Criteria.*
   These criteria evaluate the willingness of suppliers to cooperate and go beyond minimal standards in providing services to integrate their efforts in accordance with the buyer's requirements.
   Key Question: Is the supplier customer oriented and committed to meeting or exceeding the buyer's expectations?

4. *Adaptive Criteria.*
   These criteria evaluate the extent to which the buying firm may have to adapt its plans to accommodate uncertainty about the capability of the supplier to meet the buyer's requirements for production and delivery.
   Key Question: How certain is the buyer that the supplier can produce and deliver to specification?

5. *Legalistic Criteria.*
   These criteria evaluate the impact on the buying decision of legalistic or quasi-legalistic constraints (e.g., government regulations, company policies and practices, etc.).
   Key Question: What legalistic policy constraints must be borne in mind when buying this product?

Next, they define the following attributes on which products can be dichotomized: standardization (standard vs. nonstandard), make-up (simple vs. complex), application (standard vs. novel), and dollar commitment (low vs. high). Two hundred and twenty purchasing agents were asked to allocate 10 points to reflect the relative importance of the first four choice criteria for eight different combinations of the four product attributes. Table 16.5 presents the data. Lehmann and O'Shaughnessy summarize the data as follows.

> In general, as products become less standard, economic factors decrease in importance and performance criteria become more important. However, adaptive criteria are important for all product-attribute categories except for simple standard products with standard applications. Integrative criteria are generally less important. Additionally, this category shows the least variation over the various product attribute categories (1982 p. 13).

Lehmann and O'Shaughnessy also examined the impact of legal and policy constraints on both the buying criteria and the buying decision itself. They conclude that

Table 16.5

Importance of choice criteria for eight product-attribute categories

Product				Average Points Per Criteria Category			
Product	Make-Up	Application	Dollar Commitment	Economic Criteria	Performance Criteria	Integrative Criteria (Cooperation)	Adaptive Criteria (Capability Certainty)
1. Standard	Simple	Standard	Low	4.89	1.93	1.64	1.54
2. Standard	Complex	Novel	High	2.32	3.76	1.77	2.17
3. Nonstandard	Simple	Novel	High	2.86	3.16	1.59	2.37
4. Nonstandard	Complex	Standard	Low	2.31	3.84	1.76	2.11
5. Standard	Simple	Standard	High	4.40	1.72	1.47	2.42
6. Standard	Complex	Novel	Low	2.36	3.53	1.90	2.32
7. Nonstandard	Simple	Novel	Low	2.84	3.10	1.82	2.25
8. Nonstandard	Complex	Standard	High	2.58	3.56	1.63	2.23
			Mean	3.07	3.08	1.70	2.16

Source: Donald R. Lehmann and John O'Shaughnessy, "Decision Criteria Used in Buying Different Categories of Products." *Journal of Purchasing and Materials Management,* 18 (Spring 1982): 11. Reprinted with permission.

... the role of these constraints becomes more important as the product and its applications become increasingly unique and non-standard. These constraints appear to have the greatest impact for complex products that generate a high dollar expenditure (1982 p. 12).

The two studies of the relative importance of different choice criteria across different types of organizational buying situations conducted by Lehmann and O'Shaughnessy are largely mutually supportive. Together, they provide many important insights into how organizational buyers evaluate choice alternatives. From such understanding the marketer can construct *total* offerings that will be more attractive to potential organizational customers.

The Buying Center

One of the most important problems in developing a marketing strategy for organizational buyers is to identify the individual or individuals who actually make the buying decision. For simple or routine decisions, it is often possible to identify a single individual, typically a purchasing agent, who is responsible for the decision. For new, complex, or important decisions, a number of people may be involved in various aspects of the buying decision. Each of these people will tend to have a unique perspective on the purchasing problem, will tend to emphasize different criteria in evaluating choice alternatives, and will generally carry a different (and often unknown) degree of influence in the final decision.

The last point is particularly important because a consistent research finding is "that there are significant differences in the perceived influence of major participants in the buying process, but that *every* participant or group reports that it is one of the most important and central" (Johnston and Bonoma 1981, p. 144, emphasis added). This suggests that even participants in the buying process often have difficulty identifying who *really* was responsible for the multitude of decisions that culminated in a purchase order. It also reminds us that organizational buyers are not immune to the effects of such human needs as bolstering one's self-image and sense of importance.

In order to better understand the processes through which members of an organization transform organizational needs into specific buying decisions, researchers have developed the concept of the buying center. The buying center is composed of all those members of the organization who participate in the buying process and extends beyond those who are formally charged with implementing the organization's purchasing needs (Robinson, Faris, and Wind 1967). More important, the buying center is *not* a fixed group of individuals. Rather, the composition of the buying center will be constantly changing as a function of the type of purchase and many factors unique to each buying decision.

As Johnston and Bonoma (1981) observe, the buying center has been more discussed than researched. For this reason they have further developed the buying center concept in terms of a communication perspective, which is both more operational and more valuable to marketing managers. Figure 16.5 presents a hypothetical example of the pattern of communications within the buying center for a specific buying problem. Johnston and Bonoma develop the structure of the buying center in terms of five dimensions and attempt to relate these dimensions to several specific measures of organizational structure and attributes of the purchase situation.

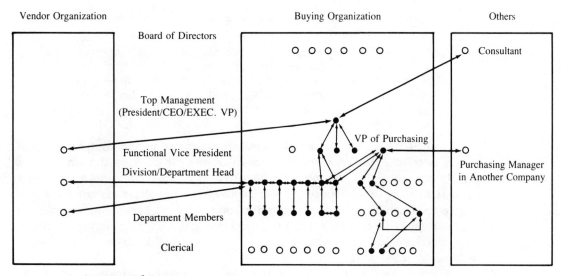

Figure 16.5
A hypothetical example of communication patterns within the buying center

Source: Wesley J. Johnston and Thomas V. Bonoma, "The Buying Center: Structure and Interaction Patterns." *Journal of Marketing*, 45 (Summer 1981): p. 147. Reprinted with the kind permission of the American Marketing Association.

The five dimensions of the structure of the buying center are defined as follows.

- *vertical involvement in the buying center's communications.* This dimension is characterized by the number of levels of the organization's authority hierarchy exerting influence and communicating within the buying center. Six levels of authority were defined for the purpose of this study: ownership (board of directors), top management (CEO, president, executive vice president), policy level management (functional vice presidents, general managers), upper level operating management (e.g., directors, managers), lower level operating management (e.g., supervisors, product managers), and production work/clerical employees.

- *lateral involvement* of different departments and divisions in the buying communications. This dimension can be operationalized as the number of separate departments, divisions, or firm functional areas involved in the purchase decision (see Strauss 1962 on the relevance of lateral involvement).

- *extensivity*, or the total number of individuals involved in the buying communication network. Communication and information processing systems can be described in terms of the number of parts (e.g., people, departments) at work in a system. Schroder et al. (1966) referred to this property as "differentiation." We operationalized buying center extensivity as the total number of individuals involved in the buying process; this measure has been previously shown to correlate positively with decision quality by Schroder.

- *connectedness* of those involved in the buying communication network. This concept and its associated measure indicates the degree to which the members of the buying center are linked with each other by directed communications concerning the purchase. The degree of connectedness can be empirically expressed as a percentage of the total possible connectedness in a particular buying center. Only communications about the purchase under consideration were included in this percentage. Others were disregarded.

- *centrality* of the purchasing manager in the buying communication network. The centrality of the purchasing manager was expressed as the sum of his/her purchase communications, both sent and received, weighted by the total number of individuals in the buying center. Previous studies in psychology found centrality correlated highly with perceived leadership, status, and influence (Shaw 1976) (Johnston and Bonoma 1981, pp. 146–148).

Table 16.6 presents the organizational structure and purchase situation attribute variables that Johnston and Bonoma attempted to relate to the structure of the buying center. For the most part these variables have either *been* previously discussed or are self-explanatory. Conceptually, the centralization variable is "the degree to which authority, responsibility, and power are concentrated within an organization or buying unit" (p. 148). Data was collected for one capital equipment purchase and one industrial service purchase for 31 firms representing a wide range of industries.

Johnston and Bonoma found that the involvement of members of the organization, outside of the purchasing department, increases as the importance and complexity of the purchase increases. This relationship tended to be strongest where the buying process was highly formalized and was more prominent for capital equipment purchases than the purchase of services. They also found that purchases that involved new tasks were accompanied by more lateral involvement across departments than were either straight or modified rebuys.

As the authors acknowledge, their findings are not new. Indeed, a number of these relationships have been suggested in previous sections of this chapter. The primary importance of the Johnston and Bonoma study lies in its demonstration of

Table 16.6
Organizational structure and purchase situation attributes investigated in Johnston and Bonoma study of the buying center

Organizational Structure	Measure
Size	Annual sales in dollars
Complexity	Number of divisions/subsidiaries
Formalization	Percentage of the buying process communication that was written
Centralization	Organization and operation of the purchasing function in the firm (Centralized/Decentralized/Combination)

Purchase Situation Attribute	Measure
Importance	Average of entire buying center's perceived importance (1–10 scale)
Complexity	Time required to complete the buying process
Novelty	Buy grid categorization (New task, modified rebuy, straight rebuy)
Purchase Class	Type of purchase (capital equipment or industrial service)

Source: Wesley J. Johnston and Thomas V. Bonoma, "The Buying Center: Structure and Interaction Patterns." *Journal of Marketing*, 45 (Summer 1981): 149. Reprinted with the kind permission of the American Marketing Association.

a highly operational and very practical method for studying the decision-making processes of organizations. By understanding the flow of communication within a buying organization and the concerns of each member of the buying center, marketers are in a much improved position to develop *total* marketing programs that have strong appeal to the buying organization.

Relative Influence in the Buying Center

It should be obvious that every individual in the buying center does not have the same degree of influence over the purchase decision. Table 16.7, for example, presents data collected by Johnston and Bonoma (1981) identifying the most central individual in the buying center for 62 specific decisions. It is clear from Table 16.7 that the most central individual in the buying center varies greatly over companies and specific purchase decisions. This raises the question of whether it is possible to generally specify the type of individual who is most likely to be highly influential in specific types of purchasing problems.

Each buying organization will tend to have a somewhat unique power structure. One rule, however, tends to be common to most organizations. Specifically, those individuals or organizational units most affected by the decision tend to have the most influence on that decision (Patchen 1974).

Illustrative of this relative influence rule is a study of modified rebuys for three industrial products by Cooley, Jackson, and Ostrom (1978). They had 122 respondents from 26 manufacturing firms allocate 100 points to different departments to reflect the relative power of each department over the buying decisions. Separate allocations were made for the product decision and the supplier decision for each of the three products studied. As expected, engineering dominated the product decision, while purchasing dominated the supplier decision for each of the three product classes.

Cooley, Jackson, and Ostrom (1978) also found that other departments were perceived to have moderate influence over all of the buying decisions studied. This is what one would logically expect for a modified rebuy. In contrast, there is a general tendency for relative influence to be more concentrated for straight rebuys (usually concentrated in the purchasing department) and to be more diffuse for new tasks.

Conflict in Organizational Buying Decisions

The final issue regarding the buying center to be discussed is conflict among individual members of the buying center. Conflict, of course, can arise any time individuals must make a joint decision. In a way that closely parallels family conflict, organizational conflict arises because different members have different objectives, motives, and perspectives regarding specific purchase decisions. In contrast to families, the organizational buying center may be quite large and involve far less face-to-face contact. Indeed, frequently the exact composition of the buying center will be known by few members of the buying center, or even by no one. Also, formal organizations are much more likely than families to establish formal procedures for resolving inevitable buying conflicts. The purchasing department, in particular, generally plays this critical role in larger organizations.

How and why conflict arises is well illustrated by Kiser's (1976, p. 5) descrip-

Table 16.7
The most central individual in the buying center for 62 organizational buying decisions

Company	Capital Equipment		Industrial Services	
Chemical manufacturer	Heat exchanger	Purchasing manager	Construction contract labor	Purchasing manager
Industrial safety products manufacturer	Automatic drilling machine	Engineer VP of manufacturing	Plant janitorial service	Purchasing manager
Steel mill furnace manufacturer	Standby oil heating system	Purchasing manager	Temporary drafting service	Engineer
Steel manufacturer	Coke oven	Purchasing manager	Maintenance repair contract	Buyer
Water transportation & construction co.	Locomotive crane	Purchasing manager	Contract cement work	Purchasing manager
Heating equipment manufacturer	Large industrial press	Engineer	Refuse removal	Purchasing manager
Industrial products distributor	Plasma cutting equipment	VP of operations	Installation of fire prevention system	VP of operations
Specialty steel manufacturer	Hot piercer mill	Purchasing manager	General contracter for asphalt work	Engineer
Machine tooling co.	Vertical boring mill	VP of operations	Fabricating work	Purchasing manager
Specialty steel manufacturer	Steel plate leveler	Manufacturing engineer	Calibration of lab instruments	Purchasing manager
Industrial products distributor	Storage shelving	Director of materials	Refuse removal	Director of materials
Metal and wire manufacturer	Wrapping machine	Division manager	Machinery rigging for shipping	Traffic manager
Aerospace & automotive products manufacturer	Metal working machine tool	Divisional purchasing manager	Technical consultant	Director of purchasing
Paper products manufacturer	Banding system	General manager	Vending machine service	Personnel manager
Steel mill builder	Processing pump	Project manager	Pump installation & start up	Project manager
Refractory	Fork-lift trucks	Plant purchasing manager	Plant security protection	Buyer purchasing manager

Source: Wesley J. Johnston and Thomas V. Bonoma, "The Buying Center: Structure and Interaction Patterns." *Journal of Marketing*, 45 (Summer 1981): 150–151. Reprinted with the kind permission of the American Marketing Association.

tion of the expectations that marketing, design and development, manufacturing, and research and development have regarding product performance. Marketing is interested in enhancing the salability of the finished products, while design and development engineers are more concerned with minimizing the risks or making an error. Manufacturing is especially interested in procuring simple items that

Table 16.7 continued

Company	Capital Equipment		Industrial Services	
Pipe fabricator	Presses	Safety engineer maintenance supervisor	Janitorial service	Buyer purchasing manager
Petroleum products manufacturer	Gasoline storage tank	Buyer	Printing of advertising materials	VP of marketing
Power plant builder	Nuclear load cell	Job-shop order department manager	External building maintenance	Manager of facilities
Steel manufacturer	River tow barge	VP of production	Employee food service	Plant labor relations manager
Mining equipment manufacturer	Executive office desk	Purchasing agent	Training for 1st line supervisors	General manager
Chemical & scientific instrument distributor	Medical instruments	District VP of sales	Management consultant	Senior VP of sales
Electrical parts distributor	Recessed lighting fixtures	Company VP	Architectural services	Executive VP
Cement manufacturer	Fork-lift truck	General manager (VP)	Plant security protection	Assistant plant superintendent
Steel fabricator	Bar stock steel	Materials manager purchasing agent	Typewriter maintenance	Engineer
Construction company	Steel tonnage	Manager of sales	Site survey	Project manager engineer
Steel manufacturer	Galvanized steel processor	Engineer	Slap processing & metal recovery	Divisional VP
Engineering and construction company	Cooling vessel	Job site foreman	Tar sludge removal	Buyer Purchasing manager Divisional VP
Home products manufacturer	Mixing machines	Buyer engineer	Drapery cleaning	Service manager
Electrical parts manufacturer	Resistor	General manager Purchasing manager	Refuse removal	Purchasing manager
Building materials manufacturer	Pump	Engineer	Engineering services	Executive VP

make production as inexpensive and trouble free as possible. Finally, research and development is more interested in technical aspects of the product and whether it will lead to future improvements.

Clearly there is considerable potential for conflict in organizational buying. But, under what circumstances is conflict actually likely to arise and be most intense? Ryan and Holbrook (1982) suggest that conflict is most likely to occur where responsibility for the buying decision is equally shared by two or more decision-making units and where actual responsibility for the decision is not clearly assigned. They also suggest that time available for the decision affects the degree of conflict. Specifically, substantial time pressure tends to force quick resolution of any potential conflict. Ryan and Holbrook (1982), in a study of fleet administrators (persons responsible for corporate automobiles), provide empirical support for effects of shared responsibility and time on conflict.

Assessing conflict within a buying organization can provide marketers with important insights into how to best approach a potential buyer. Pettigrew (1977), for example, shows how a salesman lost a computer sale to a competitor because he failed to recognize that the buying problem was largely political. However, as Ryan and Holbrook (1982) note, questions involving conflict are highly reactive. In particular, they note that the most frequent answer to questions about conflict is "self-protective denial by fleet administrators that any such condition existed in their jobs" (p. 64). Thus, efforts to understand conflict over organizational buying decisions require sensitivity to the intricacies and subtleties of corporate power relationships.

For example, when subjects proved extremely reluctant to admit the existence of conflict, Ryan and Holbrook had subjects identify the five decision areas, from a list of seventeen, that had the greatest likelihood of arousing organizational conflict. The proportion of times a decision was selected was used as an index of its likelihood of conflict. For example, the type of lease (finance, net, or maintenance) was identified as an area of conflict in the automobile leasing decision by only 7 percent of the subjects. In marked contrast, options and size were selected as areas of conflict by approximately two-thirds of the subjects. Understanding such conflicts is clearly an important step in developing a comprehensive marketing strategy for marketing to organizational buyers.

SUMMARY

Throughout the text, it has been maintained that consumer and organizational buying behavior are much more similar than is generally presumed. This chapter emphasized the real and important aspects of buying behavior that tend to be unique to organizational buyers. To a large degree this uniqueness is directly attributable to the formality, size, and goal structure of organizational buyers.

As has been seen, organizations tend to assign responsibility for specific buying decisions to specific organizational members, especially for routine buying tasks. Organizations also more frequently tend to purchase according to precise technical specifications, negotiate prices and other terms, and maintain long-term relationships with suppliers. This, of course, reminds us that organizational buying is a job-related activity. As such, organizational buying is far more likely to follow a learning hierarchy decision-making process than is consumer decision making.

None of the unique aspects of organizational buying requires organizational buyers to precisely follow the rational economic man model of decision making. Organizational buyers continue to be human. As was seen, they frequently are influenced by a variety of "emotional" factors, such as the desire to minimize risk, to enhance their self-image, and to maintain positive interpersonal relations with other individuals both inside and outside the organization.

Public Policy and
Buyer Behavior
Research

VII

Throughout this book our perspective has been that of the marketing manager who intends to use buyer behavior research as a basis for formulating effective marketing strategies. In this final chapter, the potential contributions of buyer behavior research to the development of effective public policies governing marketing practices will be examined.

Public Policy and Buyer Behavior Research

17

The public policy issues that involve buyer behavior are numerous and typically complex. They could easily justify a book of their own. For this reason no attempt will be made at a general survey. Rather, how the development of public policy can benefit from buyer behavior research will be illustrated by examining three specific issues: unit pricing, deceptive advertising, and television advertising targeted at children.

For a number of reasons business people should be aware of the interface between buyer behavior research and public policy. Perhaps most important is the increasing receptiveness of agencies that formulate public policy to including research on buyers in their deliberations. Morgan (1979), for example, recently provided a historical analysis of the role of buyer behavior research in federal court proceedings; while Cohen (1980) described the Federal Trade Commission's (FTC) advertising substantiation program in some detail.[1]

An especially relevant aspect of Cohen's review is that firms can, and have, used buyer behavior research to successfully defend against allegations of deceptive practices. More generally, Cohen suggests that "Consumer research by firms may aid the FTC in developing trade regulation rules[2] that are not unduly restrictive" (p. 32).

Finally, a rather substantial number of people move between business and government policy-making positions. Thus, many business people will, at some time during their careers, be in a position to formulate public policy.

From the perspective of the makers of public policy much can be gained from the systematic incorporation of buyer behavior research into policy decisions. Recently, and rather suddenly, the political environment has become extremely sensitive to the issue of "over-regulation." Much of the expressed concern appears to be addressed to rules and regulations that are perceived to be needless or ineffective. As shall be seen, there is good reason to believe that these concerns are justified. Careful research showing that the need for regulatory policies in an area is real and that the proposed solutions are effective should help raise the currently diminished credibility of public policy makers.

With this general background, the concluding chapter illustrates the implications of buyer behavior research for the development of effective and efficient public policies with research on unit pricing, deceptive advertising, and television advertising targeted at children. However, these topics must be prefaced by a brief discussion of the underlying "values" upon which public policy decisions are made and the implications this has for the role of buyer behavior *research* in the formulation of specific public policies regarding firms' marketing practices.

VALUES, RESEARCH, AND PUBLIC POLICY DECISIONS

Typically, major public policy issues involve complex questions of law, costs and benefits, other facts, and values. Close examination of most, if not all, intense

---

[1]The FTC's advertising substantiation program requires advertisers to acquire proof for any specific claims they intend to make *before* an advertisement is run.

[2]The FTC has two different types of trade regulation rules. Interpretative rules set forth the FTC's general view with respect to unfair or deceptive acts and practices. Substantive rules specify acts and practices that the FTC regards as unfair or deceptive. Violation of substantive rules is subject to all penalties the FTC is authorized to apply (Welch 1980, p. 13).

debates over the desirability of a proposed public policy reveals that differences in values, as well as facts and self-interest, are deeply involved in both the perception of the problem and in proposed "optimal" solutions. For example, the first issue to be considered concerns the provision of unit price information to consumers. It is clear from the record that many advocates of unit pricing believed that consumers had the "right to be informed" to use the phrase from President John F. Kennedy's 1962 "consumer bill of rights."[3] Questions of costs or even whether consumers actually use unit price information were, for many advocates, of secondary concern, if not entirely irrelevant.

Given the central role of values in public policy debates, it is clear that public policy decisions cannot be made on the basis of buyer behavior research alone. To the extent that facts are in dispute, buyer behavior research can help establish the factual basis within which the debate occurs. All too often, public policy debates have been based on opinions masquerading as facts (cf., Feldman 1980). Also, once a public policy decision has been made, buyer behavior research can help determine effective means for implementing the decision. The first public policy issue to be considered provides a particularly good illustration of this role of buyer behavior research.

UNIT PRICING

The issue of unit pricing is particularly interesting for several reasons. First, buyer behavior research provides some relatively clear implications. Second, unit pricing offers a good illustration of how the prior beliefs of policy makers *may* be at considerable variance with what is actually known about buyer behavior. Third, the unit pricing literature suggests that the regulations issued by policy makers *may* also benefit business.

The Problem

Anyone who has ever faced a display of a dozen or so brands, all in different sizes and with different prices, and tried to determine which brand and which size is *really* the best buy should appreciate the basic problem that unit pricing attempts to overcome. In fact, the problem is so severe that even when well educated consumers are specifically instructed to find the most economical package for one or more products and given unlimited time in which to accomplish the task, approximately half of all choices are incorrect (cf., Russo, Krieser, and Miyashita 1975, p. 12). Of course, none of these results should be particularly surprising given our knowledge of the limits on human information processing.

Unit Pricing Laws

As part of a broader movement in the 1960s and 1970s to provide consumers with more information on which to (presumably) make better decisions, a number of

---

[3]The "consumer bill of rights" is not a legal document. Rather, it was a political message that is generally credited with bringing consumer problems into the mainstream of political debate. In addition to the "right to be informed," President Kennedy insisted that American consumers had "the right to safety," "the right to choose," and "the right to be heard."

states passed unit pricing laws.[4] These laws were aimed primarily at supermarkets and generally required the posting of prices by unit of weight, volume, or per hundred count. Supporters of this legislation claimed that the primary beneficiaries of unit pricing would be low income consumers[5] (Isakson and Maurizi 1973).

Despite the hopes of unit pricing supporters, the results in the marketplace were equivocal. Russo, Kriesser, and Miyashita (1975) summarize the effects of unit pricing by stating: "At best, limited effects of unit pricing have been observed; but more often the posting of unit prices caused no significant purchasing changes" (p. 13). Perhaps even more distressing to advocates of unit pricing is the persistent finding that low income consumers are *not* the primary beneficiaries of unit pricing. Rather, and this again should be expected given previous discussions, it is high income, well-educated, and middle class consumers who are the primary beneficiaries of unit pricing (e.g., Monroe and LaPlaca 1972, Isakson and Maurizi 1973).

Two Unit Pricing Experiments

The general failure of laws requiring the posting of unit prices points up a basic bias that many marketers have attributed to makers of consumer policy; specifically, that providing consumers with more factual information will lead to "better" consumer decisions (e.g., Bettman 1979, p. 294). Implicit in this view is the presumption that consumers possess a large capacity for processing information. Policy makers have also given little attention to the format in which information is presented to consumers.

Russo (1977, Russo, Krieser, and Miyashita 1975) has suggested that the lack of use of unit prices can be partially attributed to the format in which the information is typically presented to consumers: a separate tag or label with the price, unit of measure, and price per unit is affixed to each item or to the shelf on which the item is positioned. This arrangement requires the consumer to examine each label separately and to hold information relevant to *at least* one brand in memory for purposes of comparison. For even a small number of brands, this can impose a substantial demand on the consumer's information processing capacity.

Building on these ideas, Russo conducted two experiments designed to increase consumers' use of unit price information. Both experiments involved posting lists of brand, size, and price information for a number of different product classes. Figure 17.1 presents one of these lists. In the first experiment, the effectiveness of unit price lists was compared with unit price labels affixed to the shelf upon which each brand was stored. The second experiment added a condition in which no unit price information was displayed. The primary dependent variables were unit prices actually paid and the market shares of brands for each product class under the different unit price conditions.

Because of the need to control a variety of possible confounding variables, which can arise in this type of research, the actual methodology of the two studies is considerably more complicated than the above description suggests. Fortunately,

---

[4]For an excellent description and analysis of the consumer protection movement, see Feldman (1980).

[5]Congress has considered a federal Price Disclosure Act, which would require unit pricing of packaged consumer goods. At this time, however, no federal legislation requires unit pricing.

List of Unit Prices			List of Unit Prices		
Listed in Order Of Increasing Price Per Quart			Listed in Order Of Increasing Price Per Quart		
Par 48 oz.	54¢	36.0¢ per quart	Brocade 12 oz.	27¢	72.0¢ per quart
Par 32 oz.	38¢	38.0¢ per quart	Supurb 12 oz.	29¢	77.3¢ per quart
Sweetheart 32 oz.	55¢	55.0 ¢ per quart	Ivory 32 oz.	80¢	80.0¢ per quart
Brocade 48 oz.	85¢	56.7 ¢ per quart	Dove 22 oz.	56¢	81.5¢ per quart
Sweetheart 22 oz.	39¢	56.7¢ per quart	Ivory 22 oz.	56¢	81.5¢ per quart
Supurb 32 oz	59¢	59.0¢ per quart	Lux 22 oz.	56¢	81.5¢ per quart
White Magic 32 oz.	59¢	59.0¢ per quart	Palmolive 32 oz.	85¢	85.0¢ per quart
Brocade 32 oz.	63¢	63.0¢ per quart	Ivory 12 oz.	32¢	85.3¢ per quart
Brocade 22 oz.	45¢	65.5¢ per quart	Palmolive 22 oz.	60¢	87.3¢ per quart
Supurb 22 oz.	45¢	65.5¢ per quart	Palmolive 12 oz.	34¢	90.7¢ per quart
White Magic 32 oz.	45¢	65.5¢ per quart			

Figure 17.1
An example of a unit price list

Source: J. Edward Russo, Gene Krieser, and Sally Miyashita, "An Effective Display of Unit Price Information." *Journal of Marketing*, 39 (April 1975): 14. Reprinted with the kind permission of the American Marketing Association.

the results are relatively straightforward. Average prices paid were approximately *1 percent* less with shelf labels than when no unit price information was available. Providing unit prices in organized lists produced a *further* savings of approximately *2 percent*. Given the very thin margins on which supermarkets typically operate a *3 percent* total reduction in average price paid is quite a substantial savings.

Russo also observed that "almost all changes caused by shelf tags were to larger sizes but not to different brands, whereas the lists caused shifts to cheaper brands but not to larger sizes" (p. 201). These patterns of behavior are consistent with research that shows that whether consumers process information by brand or by attribute is strongly affected by the specific format in which that information is made available (Bettman and Kakkar 1977).

The explanation for the above results lies in the fact that shelf labels encourage processing by brand, because finding larger sizes of the same brand is relatively easy and larger sizes normally have lower unit prices. Locating other brands with lower unit prices is considerably more difficult, because of the lack of physical proximity and the need to store brand, as well as unit price, information in memory. Lists of unit prices remove these barriers and encourage processing of information by attribute, i.e., by unit prices across brands.

Benefits and Costs of Unit Pricing

The financial benefits to consumers of unit pricing are clear. It is also likely that lists of unit prices will allow consumers to make choices more quickly and with greater confidence. Russo (1977) reports that unit price lists caused the market share for store brands to increase from 35 percent to 40 percent. Because store brands typically carry a higher profit margin, retailers may actually benefit from unit pricing. Retailers may also benefit from customer goodwill and loyalty created by providing unit price information.

A number of studies have examined the costs of unit pricing. Russo (1977) summarizes these studies by stating that "unit pricing costs retailers a maximum of 10 percent of profits and possibly much less" (p. 193). A number of factors, beyond the shift to store brands, help offset these costs. In particular, unit pricing has been reported to improve inventory control, reduce costly price-marking errors, and reduce stock outages (Coyle 1970, Peterson 1974). The costs of unit pricing should be further reduced as retailers turn increasingly to computerized inventory systems, which can easily and cheaply generate unit price lists. Thus, it may be concluded that public policy makers could have definitely benefited consumers, and possibly benefited retailers, by incorporating research on consumer information processing into the design of unit pricing laws.

DECEPTIVE ADVERTISING

The second example of how buyer behavior research can facilitate public policy formulation concerns deceptive advertising. Although deceptive advertising has been discussed in the marketing literature for years, only recently have attempts been made to bring buyer behavior theory and research directly to bear on the problems of defining, measuring, and correcting deceptive advertising.

The discussion of deceptive advertising begins with a brief discussion of the Federal Trade Commission (FTC) and its historical approach to the problem of deception. What is meant by "deceptive" advertising is next considered, followed by a discussion of research efforts to measure deception. Finally, attempts to counter the effects of deceptive advertising through so-called corrective advertising are examined.

As you read this material keep in mind the question of underlying values. In particular, note how far public policy has evolved from the doctrine of caveat emptor. As shall be seen, an advertisement may be entirely factually correct and still be judged deceptive.

The FTC and Deceptive Advertising

The FTC was established by an act of Congress in 1914 to monitor and take legal action against business practices generally described as unfair. The Wheeler-Lea Amendment of 1938 specifically extended the authority of the FTC to "deceptive acts and practices." This extension had the effect to "sanction the FTC as a consumer agency" (Welch 1980, p. 83).

To understand the issues involved in deceptive advertising requires recognizing that "an administrative agency is held [in its legal standing] to be a body of experts possessing among themselves the expertise necessary to make findings of fact" (Brandt and Preston 1977, p. 59). In the context of the present discussion, this expert standing of the FTC has two major implications. First, the FTC has traditionally focused on the advertisement and its *potential* to deceive. Questions of whether any consumers were actually deceived or injured have largely been ignored (Gardner 1975, Welch 1980). Second, a finding by the FTC that an advertisment is deceptive will normally be treated as a *fact* in any subsequent court challenges to an FTC order. Only in highly unusual circumstances will the courts reverse the FTC on a point of fact (Brandt and Preston 1977, p. 59).

The above statements do not contradict our initial observation that buyer behavior research is increasingly being incorporated into deliberations regarding public policy. For example, Brandt and Preston (1977, p. 59) determined from a comprehensive review that the use of so-called external consumer evidence increased from a scant 3.6 percent for deception cases during the period 1916–1954 to 54.5 percent for deception cases during the period 1970–1973.

The official position of the FTC is that "When [external] evidence is offered to assist the Commission in interpreting advertising representations, it supplements rather than supplants the Commission's expertise" (cited in Brandt and Preston 1977, p. 59). Unofficially, however, Brandt and Preston suggest that

> One suspects the [FTC trial] judge often formulates his opinion on the basis of outside testimony, yet with an eye on the Commissioners' review of his decision maintains, for reasons of propriety, that he has made the determination on his own (1977, p. 59).

In terms of the present discussion, the critical points are (1) there is good reason to believe that evidence gathered directly from consumers, including research sponsored by firms, is playing an increasing role in FTC deception cases, and (2) nothing in the law prohibits the FTC from incorporating buyer behavior research into decisions regarding specific cases or more general trade regulations. In fact, the present reaction against "over-regulation" provides strong incentive for all public policy makers to provide as sound a factual basis as possible for their decisions.

This background on the legal treatment of deceptive advertising lays a foundation for the principal question of how buyer behavior research can help public policy makers formulate more effective policies for detecting and correcting deceptive advertising.

The Concept of Deception

The concept of deception in advertising is not currently well defined. A basic problem is that the word deception means different things in everyday, legal, and behavioral research use. In everyday use, deception implies an intent to deceive or lead another person into error. Legally, however, the FTC has not been required to prove intent for over 30 years (Russo, Metcalf, and Stephens 1981). Indeed, as discussed earlier, the FTC is not required to prove or even raise the question of whether consumers were actually deceived by an advertisement. Behavioral researchers, of course, focus on the effects of an advertisement on consumers.

The legal issue is further clouded by the fact that the FTC has no general definition of what constitutes deception, partially because of the difficulty of defining deception and partially because what *legally* constitutes deception is constantly changing as new cases are brought before the FTC and the courts. Early deception cases frequently involved what Gardner (1975) calls unconscionable lies, e.g., patent medicines that would cure everything from cancer to bad breath. Over the years, such unconscionable lies have decreased markedly and the FTC has become increasingly aware of, and responsive to, the potential of advertising to deceive by implication, association, and the exploitation of existing consumer beliefs (Russo, Metcalf, and Stephens 1981, Shimp and Preston 1981). Table 17.1 presents major principles that are currently used to identify deception. It should be readily apparent from these "principles" that an advertiser may not always be certain whether a given advertisement is *legally* deceptive.

Furthermore, regulatory agencies have the resources to deal with only a very small proportion of the advertisements that are potentially deceptive. This raises a number of interesting questions. For example, a basic approach to defining deception is to rely on consumer judgments. Research suggests that consumers regard many advertisements as deceptive (Feldman 1980, p. 116). However, "it seems clear that consumers who recognize an ad as deceptive are in fact not deceived by it" (Olson and Dover 1978, p. 29). The expenditure of public resources to correct such "deception" is probably not worthwhile.

Another practical aspect of the problem of defining deception concerns whether the market is self-correcting. Product attributes that might be involved in deception can be classified as search, experience, or credence qualities (Nelson 1970, Darby and Karni 1973). Search qualities involve attributes a consumer can discern

Table 17.1
Principles for Identifying Deception

- It has the capacity to deceive.
- The FTC does not have to look further than the ad itself in interpreting meaning.
- When an ad has more than one meaning one of which is false the entire ad can be considered false.
- It is deceptive to combine statement of facts in such a way as to mislead.
- Deception may be implied as well as explicitly stated.
- If an ad may be read in a deceptive way, even though it generally is not misread, it is illegal.

Source: Joe L. Welch, *Marketing Law.* Tulsa, Okla.: PPC Books, 1980, p. 85. Reprinted with permission.

from inspection of the product before purchase. Experience qualities can be assessed only during the consumption of the product. Credence qualities are not readily discernable even after use. For example, for a refrigerator size, durability, and energy efficiency would be search, inexperience, and credence qualities, respectively. The market is likely to be self-correcting for search qualities for durable goods and for search and experience qualities for nondurable goods. Under such circumstances it may be desirable, *if the harm attributable to the deception is not too great*, to let the market discipline deceptive advertisers through the refusal of consumers to purchase or repurchase the offending advertiser's product (Eighmey 1978, pp. 88–89).

Measuring Deceptive Advertising

The review of the legal perspective on deceptive advertising yields two conclusions critical to the present discussion. First, relatively little attention has been given by public policy makers to the actual impact on consumers of advertisements that have been declared deceptive. Second, public policy makers have no established general definition or concept of what constitutes deception.

Recognizing the above limitations, a number of researchers (e.g., Armstrong and Russ 1975, Cohen 1972, Gardner 1975, Dyer and Kuehl 1978) have argued that the cognitive effects of advertising upon consumers can provide the basis for both a conceptual definition of what constitutes deception and an empirical framework for measuring deception. As Olson and Dover note, "these authors seem to have adopted an implicit information-processing perspective in which an ad is considered to contain (or have the potential to impart) false information" (1978, p. 29).

An article by Gardner (1975) has been especially influential in research efforts to define and measure deception in advertising. Gardner began by describing three different types of deception: unconscionable lie, claim-fact discrepancy, and claim-belief interaction. In the first type of deception, a statement is completely false; e.g., claiming a caburetor device will increase gasoline mileage when it will not. A claim-fact discrepancy deception exists when some factual qualification is necessary for the claim to be properly understood and evaluated. For example, a dandruff shampoo might claim to treat a certain type of dandruff without acknowledging that it is a relatively uncommon type. A claim-belief interaction deception occurs when existing beliefs lead consumers to draw incorrect conclusions that are neither stated nor implied in an advertisement. For example, if a manufacturer knew that consumers attributed cleaning power to blue crystals, an advertisement might simply state that the detergent contains blue crystals. Gardner notes that the three types of deception are not entirely independent and suggests that claim-belief interactions are probably involved to some extent in all types of deception.

Gardner argued that while traditional legal approaches were generally adequate for handling unconscionable lies, a different approach, one which explicitly incorporated the consumer, was necessary for handling deceptions arising from claim-fact discrepancies and claim-belief interactions. On the assumption that these types of deception involve attitudes formed on a foundation of false beliefs, Gardner suggested that multi attribute models of attitude (e.g., the Rosenberg and Fishbein models studied extensively in Chapter 8) provided a logical framework for both defining and measuring deception. Gardner also outlined several different procedures for detecting deception.

Several researchers have attempted to develop Gardner's idea that multiattribute models provide a logical and feasible framework for defining and measuring deception. Olson and Dover, in what they described as "essentially an experimental demonstration of a conceptual and operational approach to deceptive advertising research" (1978, p. 31), showed quite clearly that multiattribute models can provide such a framework. Dyer and Kuehl (1978), working more closely within the specific framework suggested by Gardner, and on a real world problem, have demonstrated the potential of the multiattribute model framework for dealing with deception in the real world that is both long standing and, presumably, widely diffused.[6]

Recently, Russo, Metcalf, and Stephens (1981) suggested and experimentally demonstrated a procedure for detecting deception that appears quite general. The procedure involves identifying the *alleged* deception and creating one or more advertisements that correct the deception. Information on beliefs about the product are gathered from three groups of respondents: those shown the original advertisement, those shown the corrected advertisement, and a control group that is shown no advertisement. If the false belief is greater in the group shown the original advertisement than in the control group the advertisement is said to be incrementally misleading; i.e., exposure to the advertisement *increases* the false belief. If this does not occur but the false belief is greater for the group shown the original advertisement than the group shown the corrected advertisement the advertisement is said to be exploitively misleading; i.e., it exploits existing consumer beliefs to create a false belief. Figure 17.2 presents examples of the original and corrected advertisements used in this study.

As Russo, Metcalf, and Stephens (1981, p. 129) acknowledge, their procedure requires that allegedly deceptive claims be verifiably true or false. They leave to future research the task of developing methods for verifying claims that are essentially evaluative or subjective. They do note, however, that claims which are not directly verifiable *may* give rise to specific subclaims that can be subjected to a verifiability criterion. For example, a toothpaste advertisement using a "sex appeal" theme may give rise to a demonstrably false belief that the toothpaste whitens teeth. On the other hand, a person who *believes* that he or she is sexy (or some similar subjective attribute) may actually appear sexy to others. Shimp (1979) and Shimp and Preston (1981) explore the cognitive processes involved in subjective/evaluative advertising claims in some detail. At the present time, however, procedures for assessing the deceptive consequences of evaluative advertising remain undeveloped.

Corrective Advertising

Once an advertisement is determined to be deceptive, an appropriate course of remedial action must be found. The traditional remedies employed by the FTC are consent orders and cease and desist orders. A consent order is an agreement between the FTC and the agency accused of wrongdoing that outlines the offense and proposed remedies. Usually the remedy is to stop the practices to which the

---

[6]Dyer and Kuehl's research was based upon the well-known claim that Listerine mouthwash would help prevent and lessen the severity of colds. The details of this case are presented in the next section.

FTC objects. The consent order represents no admission of guilt and is by far the most common method for reconciling cases brought before the FTC. Should the accused agency fail to enter into a consent order, the FTC may issue a cease and desist order, which becomes the basis for adjudication within the FTC and any subsequent appeals to the federal courts.

The problem with the traditional remedies for deception is that they fail to rectify any unwarranted effects the deception may have had on consumers. Responding to this limitation the FTC, during the 1970s, began developing remedies, generally referred to as corrective advertising and affirmative disclosure, for removing the effects of deceptive advertising on consumers. "The objective of corrective advertising is to change or correct purportedly erroneous beliefs, while the objective of affirmative disclosure is to instill new beliefs" (Jacoby, Nelson, and Hoyer 1982).

Although relatively few cases have been subjected to corrective advertising or affirmative disclosure, the general consensus appears to be that these remedial actions were largely ineffective (e.g., Feldman 1980) or as misleading as the deceptive claims to be corrected (e.g., Jacoby, Nelson, and Hoyer 1982).

At least part of these problems are attributable to the fact that "The difficulty involved in accurately communicating meaning is often underestimated, and regulators would seem to be no exception in this regard" (Jacoby, Nelson, and Hoyer 1982, p. 68). More to the point, regulators apparently failed to address the issues of how consumers would receive and process the information in the proposed remedial advertisements and what effects would result in terms of beliefs, attitudes, and behavior from the corrective and/or affirmative disclosure advertisements.

The issues raised by corrective and affirmative advertising are both new and complex. Thus, it is not surprising that to date research is scarce and largely inconclusive. Nevertheless, the research that has been conducted suggests the potential of buyer behavior research to facilitate the design of and systems for delivering corrective and affirmative disclosure advertisements.

The first study to be discussed is based on FTC affirmative disclosure orders against the makers of Bufferin and Excedrin, which are currently under appeal. According to the FTC, the available evidence is not sufficiently strong to conclusively support either Bufferin's claim that it is a faster pain reliever and gentler on the stomach than plain aspirin or Excedrin's claim that it is a more effective pain reliever than plain aspirin. Expecting a favorable ruling, complaint counsel supplied three possible remedial statements each for Bufferin and Excedrin and suggested the FTC order inclusion of one statement in subsequent advertising. Figure 17.3 presents the proposed remedial statements.

Testifying as an expert witness before the FTC, Jacob Jacoby "expressed the belief that a substantial number of consumers would either be confused as to the intended meaning or would extract some unintended meaning from the proposed remedial statements" (Jacoby, Metcalf, and Stephens 1982, p. 62). Subsequent research by Jacoby, Metcalf, and Stephens (1982) strongly supported Jacoby's expert opinion.

Of somewhat more interest here is the use of previous buyer behavior research by Jacoby, Metcalf, and Stephens (1982) to formulate three specific hypotheses regarding which of the remedial statements would be most effective. Specifically, research showing that comprehension of a message (1) decreases as the number of concepts contained in a message increases, and (2) is less in sentences containing

Figure 17.2
Misleadingly false, legitimate, and corrected claims for selected advertisements

Advertised product and type of claim	Content of claim
Dole bananas	
Misleadingly false	"and there's [sic] only about 85 calories (in a banana)." This number is true only for small bananas. A typical medium-sized banana contains 101 calories.
Legitimate	The central theme of the ad is that a banana and a glass of milk are relatively healthful as a very fast breakfast. The headline reads "the 60-second breakfast from Dole."
Corrected	The corrected ad substituted 101 for 85 in the calorie claim.
Chevy Nova automobile	
Misleadingly false	The bottom of the ad prominently displays a picture of a Chevrolet Nova with a price. The car is shown with white striped tires, wheel covers, and body side molding. The price shown, $3,823, is not the price of the car shown. The actual price is $3,948 a value that can be obtained only by adding three additional prices (white striped tires $44; wheel covers $39; body side molding $42). These latter values are given in the text of the ad.
Legitimate	The ad's theme is that a Chevy Nova is inexpensive, yet rugged enough to be a police car.
Corrected	The boldly printed price at the bottom of the ad is changed from $3,823 to $3,948. Thus, the price shown becomes that of the car shown.
Nature Valley Granola bars	
Misleadingly false	"Nature Valley Granola bars [are] crunchy, wholesome, delicious." According to a proposed Trade Regulation Rule of the FTC the word "wholesome" may connote "nutritious" and cannot be used unless the product satisfies a minimum standard of nutrition (defined in terms of the percent U.S. RDA of the eight nutrients listed on the food label). Granola bars fall far short of the minimum standard.

Note: A complete description of all ten ads can be found in Russo, Metcalf, and Stephens (1981).

Source: J. Edward Russo, Barbara L. Metcalf, and Debra Stephens, "Identifying Misleading Advertising." *Journal of Consumer Research*, 8 (September 1981): 123. Reprinted with the permission of the Journal of Consumer Research.

negation (e.g., "There is real question . . .") were used to postulate which of the remedial statements would be most effective in communicating the intended message, that Bufferin's and Excedrin's claims *may* be true but that the available evidence is insufficient to prove them.

The hypothesis regarding the inferiority of negatively, as opposed to positively,

Figure 17.2 continued

Advertised product and type of claim	Content of claim
Legitimate	The theme of the ad is that Granola bars are a "100 percent natural" snack. They contain "no additives [and] no preservatives." The headline is "Go Natural."
Corrected	The word "wholesome" was removed, eliminating the nutrition claim. This was judged to be an advertiser's likely response. The only alternative permitted by the FTC's proposed rule is the inclusion of a very unflattering table of percent of U.S. RDA.
Carlton cigarettes Misleadingly false	The ad includes a list of alternative "low tar" brands and their mg. of tar per cigarette. This list is shown in the left panel of Exhibit 2. The alternative brands listed are not those lowest in tar. The misleading implied claim is that no other "low tar" brands are nearly as low as Carlton; specifically, that even if one smokes the second lowest brand, one must inhale five times the tar of Carlton.
Legitimate	The ad truthfully claims that Carlton has less than all other brands. This claim is stated in the headline, "Carlton is lowest."
Corrected	The misleading panel is changed to contain the six brands lowest in mg. of tar, in order and without omissions, as shown on the right of Exhibit 2.
Diet Imperial margarine Misleadingly false	The ad states no restriction on the use of Diet Imperial, implying that it can be substituted for regular margarine in any situation. This implied claim is true when margarine is used as a spread, a use pictured in the ad; but it is not true when margarine is used in cooking. As Diet Imperial achieves its caloric reduction by diluting regular margarine with water, there is 50 percent less oil per tablespoon.
Legitimate	The central claim is that Diet Imperial has 50 instead of 100 calories per tablespoon. The headline reads. "Try delicious, new Diet Imperial. Still only half the caories of butter or margarine."
Corrected.	A disclaimer is added, "Do not use in baking."

worded sentences was strongly confirmed. The support for the other hypotheses was mixed and inconclusive. In this regard, however, it should be noted that the remedial statements tested were those proposed *without* benefit of direct application of knowledge gained through buyer behavior research. Whether *more* effective remedial statements can be constructed from such knowledge remains to be

Figure 17.3
Proposed corrective statements for Excedrin
and Bufferin

"For inclusion in Excedrin advertising, the disclosure that:

1. Excedrin has not been proven to be a more effective pain reliever than aspirin; or,
2. It is not known whether Excedrin is a more effective pain reliever than aspirin; or,
3. There is a real question whether Excedrin is a more effective pain reliever than aspirin.

"For inclusion in Bufferin advertising, the disclosure that:

4. Bufferin has not been proven to be a faster pain reliever or gentler to the stomach than aspirin; or,
5. It is not known whether Bufferin is a faster pain reliever or gentler to the stomach than aspirin; or,
6. There is a real question whether Bufferin is a faster pain reliever or gentler to the stomach than aspirin."

determined. The potential for such an application of buyer behavior research, however, is strong and clearly warrants further research addressed to the important issue of developing *effective* corrective and affirmative advertising.

Another case where buyer behavior researchers have investigated the effectiveness of proposed remedial statements concerns the FTC's finding "that Warner-Lambert had falsely claimed that its mouthwash, Listerine, would prevent, cure, and provide relief from colds and sore throats" (Feldman 1980, p. 128). The FTC ordered Warner-Lambert to spend approximately $10-million over a two year period on advertising that contained the following remedial statement: "Contrary to prior advertising, Listerine will not prevent colds or sore throats, or lessen their severity." On appeal the circuit court found that the FTC had authority to order the corrective advertising but removed the words "Contrary to prior advertising" on the grounds that they were "humiliating and unnecessary" (cited in Feldman 1980, p. 128).

Regarding the actual implementation of the FTC's corrective advertising order, as modified by the court, Feldman offers the following observations.

> A problem with the implementation of a policy of corrective advertising is that it requires a knowledge of the precise effects of advertising that so far has been lacking on the part of both advertisers and the FTC....
> Actual observation of the implementation of the order suggests that it was ineffective for two reasons. First, while the corrective statement that Warner-Lambert was required to insert in its Listerine advertising was quite explicit, the manner of its presentation seemed to give it little impact. It was inserted midway in a 30-second commercial showing a comparative test of Listerine versus a competing brand in terms of ability to fight 'onion breath', blending into the overall message so skillfully as to be almost unnoticeable. Second, its impact was undoubtedly reduced by its use in a 'breath freshener' context rather than in the health context in which the original false claims were made (1980, pp. 128, 129).

The Listerine case is of considerable importance both because of the legal precedent it established and the size of the settlement. It is, therefore, not surprising that this case has attracted considerable interest among academic researchers. Of particular interest here is a recent study by Mizerski, Allison, and Calvert (1980). They began by noting that the results of three previous studies (Dyer and Kuehl 1978, Mazis and Adkinson 1976, Sawyer and Semenik 1978) of the corrective statement ordered by the FTC in the Listerine case were contradictory and generally challenged the use of corrective advertising as a remedy for deceptive advertising. In particular, previous studies suggest the corrective statement may be ineffective in reducing the false belief regarding the ability of Listerine to cure colds and sore throats while affecting nontarget beliefs (e.g., that Listerine kills germs). The latter point is important because it is well beyond the remedy's legal bounds and may, therefore, be regarded as *punitive* because it changes a nontarget belief.

Mizerski, Allison, and Calvert (1980) argued that these inconsistencies and generally disappointing results might be largely attributable to methodological limitations of previous studies. In particular, they noted that except for the study by Dyer and Kuehl (1978), the phrase "contrary to prior advertising" was used in the corrective advertisements, the studies were conducted in an experimental, rather than a more realistic, setting, that subjects received only one exposure to the corrective message, and that subjects may have been sensitized to the experimental hypothesis.

The researchers attempted to correct for these limitations by presenting the corrective message to subjects in an ingenious field experiment using a regularly broadcast radio program on a college campus. Experimental subjects were exposed at least four times to a professionally prepared corrected version of an actual Listerine advertisement. Subsequently, data on the following four beliefs were collected for both experimental subjects and control subjects who were not exposed to the corrective advertisement:

1. Listerine is effective for killing germs;
2. Listerine leaves mouth feeling refreshed;
3. Listerine fights colds and sore throats;
4. Listerine has long-lasting effects.

The results of the study show that the corrective advertisement was effective in changing the target belief (belief 3) while leaving the three nontarget beliefs unchanged. The researchers conclude that

> At this point corrective advertising, as it is currently implemented, *appears to be capable* of removing a false belief without harming the offending advertiser or its competition. This conclusion should be welcome news for the FTC and the entire marketplace (pp. 347–348, emphasis added).

Despite the fact that the corrective advertising remedy, as well as specific research on this topic, is quite recent our review should make clear the *potential* of buyer behavior in the design of effective corrective messages and delivery mechanisms.

TELEVISION ADVERTISING TARGETED AT CHILDREN

The "Problem" of Child-Oriented Television Advertising

The post-World War II period witnessed two events that fundamentally changed many firms' marketing strategies for products of interest to children. The first event was mass prosperity, which gave rise to a heretofore unknown level of discretionary buying. This affluence gave children greatly increased opportunities to influence family purchasing decisions. This influence was especially important for products that children consumed themselves. The second event was the mass diffusion of television. Before television ownership was common, advertisers were largely constrained to promoting products consumed by children directly to parents—primarily through the print media. Television provided a highly attractive and intrusive medium through which advertisers could *directly* reach even preliterate children.

Advertisers quickly took advantage of the new medium of television. The result was that advertising on childrens' programs consisted largely of promotions for sugared cereals, candy, over-the-counter drugs and vitamins, toys, and similar products. All of these products have, at various times, been severely criticized as being detrimental to the well-being of children. Furthermore, there is the reasonably well-documented charge that television advertising disrupts family harmony by inducing children to demand products their parents cannot or will not buy. When combined with the widespread presumption that children constitute a special class of consumers whose limited development necessitates special protection from exploitation, a national debate on the need to restrict television advertising targeted at children was inevitable.

This debate was, and continues to be, intense and, at times, acrimonious and even accusatory. Illustrative of the emotions which some have felt are the following charges by Robert Choate made before a 1970 Senate hearing on the food industry generally and the breakfast cereal industry specifically.

> We claim that our children are deliberately being sold the sponsor's less nutritious products; that our children are being programmed to demand sugar and sweetness in every food; and that our children are being countereducated away from nutrition knowledge by being sold products on a nonnutritive basis....
>
> It would seem that the worst cereals are huxtered to the children on a totally antinutritional basis equating sweetness with health and ability, while the very few good cereals are sold to adults in a manner all but defying nutrient cost analysis....

Furthermore,

> they (the cereal manufacturers) are absolutely convinced that, for the prepuberty set, sugar appeal is the counterpart of sex appeal (cited in Feldman 1980, pp. 177, 178).

The issues involved in child-oriented advertising are as complex as they are emotional. Feldman (1980, pp. 175–200) provides a fascinatingly detailed review of the economic, ethical, value, and legal issues involved. Of particular interest here is Feldman's observation that the public policy debate over child-oriented television advertising has been largely conducted without the benefit of specific research on the problem. In fact, considerable research has been conducted on this topic; summaries of which are available in Adler (1977), Adler, et al. (1980), Atkin (1980), Goldberg and Gorn (in press). Two illustrative examples of this research are presented here.

A Study of the Effects of Televised Food Messages on Children

A recent experimental study by Gorn and Goldberg (1982) provides an excellent example of how buyer behavior research can potentially facilitate the development of effective public policy. In addition to establishing new insights into the effects of television advertising on the food preferences and consumption behavior of children, this study further supports several previously established conclusions regarding the effects of television advertising on children. Perhaps even more important is that this well-controlled field experiment was conducted in a summer camp, where the behavior of children could be unobtrusively studied over a two week period.

The subjects in the experiment were 228 children, aged five to eight, attending a fourteen-day camp. Each afternoon the children had a "quiet hour" during which they watched a 30-minute television cartoon show and then had a snack. The physical arrangement of the experiment resulted in approximately 36 children per room watching one of two 26-inch color television sets.

Currently televised shows and advertisements were used. The children were randomly assigned to one of four experimental conditions:

1. Candy commercials: typical Saturday morning 30-second commercials for sweets (candy bars such as Hersheys, Mounds, Almond Joy, Kit-Kat, Three Musketeers, and other highly sugared foods including Kool Aid, M & Ms, Lifesavers, Crackerjacks, and so on)

2. No commercial messages: control programs only; no messages at all

3. Fruit commercials: 30-second messages for oranges, orange juice, apples, grapes, and so on; commercials for yogurt were also included in this condition

4. Public service announcements (PSAs): 30-second messages on the value of moderating one's intake of sugar and eating a balanced variety of foods each day (Gorn and Goldberg 1982, p. 201).

There were 4.5 minutes of advertising distributed in the normal manner through each 30-minute show (except for the control condition).

Following each show the children were offered (1) orange juice or Kool Aid *and* (2) two selections of four foods: two fruits and two candy bars. At the completion of the study, using a rating scale specially designed for use with young children, the seven- and eight-year-old children were asked to respond to the following three questions using the alternative choices "all candy," "mostly candy," "half candy/half fruit," "mostly fruit," "all fruit":

1. The experimenter (name) wanted me to eat . . .

2. The doctor at the camp would like me to eat . . .

3. The camp should buy . . . for the new kids who are coming to camp next week.

and to the slightly modified fourth question

4. The camp should buy Kool Aid (1) . . . orange juice (5) for the new kids coming to camp next week (Gorn and Goldberg 1982, p. 203).

Table 17.2
Proportion of fruit and orange selected in each condition

Condition	Orange Juice	Fruit
Fruit Commercials	.45	.36
PSAs	.40	.35
No message	.35	.33
Candy Commercials	.25	.25

Source: Gerald J. Gorn and Marvin E. Goldberg, "Behavioral Evidence of the Effects of TV Food Messages on Children," *Journal of Consumer Research*, 9 (September 1982): 204.

Table 17.2 presents information on the children's food choices over the course of the experiment. The effect of the advertisements on beverage choice was highly significant, strong, and in the direction initially hypothesized. The 20 percent difference in the selection of orange juice between children exposed to the candy commercials (25 percent) and children exposed to the fruit commercials is particularly striking. The data also support the hypothesis that the commercials would affect the childrens' choice of fruit or candy. An unexpected finding was that the no message condition was just as effective as the fruit and PSA messages in getting children to eat fruit. Analysis of the four postexperimental questions found that the different advertisements produced no demand effects (question 1), strong evidence that children know what they ought to eat (questions 1 and 2), and no effect on children's opinions as to what should be bought for the next group of children (questions 3 and 4).

These results have a number of interesting public policy implications. First, the data lend further credence to the conclusion that advertising of sugared products leads to greater consumption of sugared products (cf., Scammon and Christopher 1981). Second, that the no message condition was as effective as the fruit and PSA messages in getting children to eat fruit lends support to those who would ban entirely the advertising to children of heavily sugared foods. Third, the authors note the occasional airings of public service advertisements emphasizing the need for a balanced diet and argue that "[t]his study suggests that these messages must be aired frequently and continuously if they are to be effective" (p. 204). Fourth, the confirmation of the findings that even very young children know what they *should* eat suggests the strategy of reinforcing this knowledge and using it to alter childrens' food preferences and eating habits.

The final point we should make is that in no case did the selection of "healthy" foods exceed 45 percent. This suggests that those who would create an environment that would lead children away from consumption of heavily sugared foods face a difficult task. In this regard, it must be remembered that television advertising is only one part of the total environment that encourages the consumption of heavily sugared products.

Age Differences in Childrens' Responses to Television Advertising

From the examples of public policy decisions presented so far, it is clear that policy makers have given little thought to how consumers process information or to how specific messages and formats might affect the intended outcome. As seen in previous examples, buyer behavior research has provided some insights regarding these problems. Recently, Roedder (1981) brought together two different lines of research that provide a number of insights into how children process information. Although her synthesis is theoretical, the empirical research on which it is based is sufficiently firm to place some confidence in the public policy implications she draws.

The first line of research is based upon Piaget's theory of cognitive development. The essence of this theory is that children pass through a series of "stages" in which they acquire increasingly sophisticated cognitive structures for mediating their understanding of events and concepts. To recall an earlier example, very young children do not possess a concept of conservation of volume. Thus, when water is transferred between containers of different shapes, these children are likely to conclude that the amount of water in the container has also changed. Somewhat older children, of course, know that this is not true; i.e., they have acquired the cognitive structure of conservation of volume. As Roedder notes, however:

> Piaget's cognitive structures indicate limits on childrens' capacity to process information, but they do not explain how or why children process information within their limits.... As a result, Piaget's theory is silent with respect to the strategies likely to promote processing in young children (pp. 144–145).

Roedder argues that information processing theory can fill this void in Piaget's theory. Specifically, once information has been received, short-term memory (STM) must transfer that information, through the mechanism of rehearsal, to long-term memory (LTM). For that information to be used subsequently, STM must recall the information, through the mechanism of retrieval, from its permanent storage in LTM.[7] However, children of different ages do *not* have the same cognitive structures available to perform these tasks. More specifically,

> The information-processing view interprets age differences in childrens' reactions to television advertising in terms of cognitive abilities to store and retrieve information. The best documented shortcoming of young children is their failure to evoke and utilize cognitive plans for storing and retrieving information (Roedder 1981, p. 145).

Synthesizing research on cognitive development and information processing, Roedder suggests that three types of information processors can be identified by the age of the child.

1. Strategic Processors—these are older children, approximately 11/12 and over, who possess and routinely use the cognitive skills necessary to store and retrieve information.

2. Cued Processors—these are younger children, approximately 7/8 to 10/11, who are capable of using storage and retrieval skills but must be prompted (i.e., cued) to do so.

---

[7]As discussed in conjunction with theories of attention in Chapter 11, Roedder uses the distinction between STM and LTM as a heuristic for summarizing known facts about information processing.

3. Limited Processors—these are very young children, approximately 6/7 and under, who do not possess and, therefore, cannot use storage and retrieval strategies to enhance learning even if cued to do so.[8]

Although the idea of different types of processors has not been submitted to empirical testing as regards television advertising targeted at children, a number of public policy implications are fairly obvious. The first implication is that children characterized as strategic processors do not require special regulatory procedures. These children possess the cognitive skills needed to select, store, and retrieve information necessary to understand advertising messages. Thus, procedures useful for regulating television advertising targeted at adults should be adequate for strategic processors. However, as our discussion of deceptive advertising makes clear, the necessary regulatory procedures are neither simple nor well developed.

For cued processors, the problem is to devise appropriate and effective cues that will prompt children to use the cognitive skills they possess when receiving a television advertisement. For example, the code of the National Association of Broadcasters requires some form of separation (e.g., a briefly blank screen) between the program and advertisement. However, currently almost nothing is known about the relative effectiveness of different separation devices. Another approach, which is especially suitable for PSAs, is to present information attribute by attribute; e.g., cost, taste, nutrition. Such a presentation format not only invites comparisons among brands but also suggests a strategy for retrieving information stored in LTM, which can improve brand comparisons. There is also the possibility of using consumer education, along the lines of research presented in Chapter 15 for teaching economic reasoning to families, to teach cued processors to use their available cognitive skills to evaluate advertising messages.

Past regulatory effort has been largely aimed at children characterized as limited processors. Roedder suggests that

> Because storage and retrieval prompts are unlikely to be effective, strategies other than those described in this paper will have to be pursued to reduce limited processors' difficulties. One approach would be to reduce the need for elaborate processing by reducing the complexity or quantity of product information presented (1981, p. 150).

Another strategy, which is suggested by Gorn and Goldberg's previously discussed finding that no message was equally effective with fruit and PSA advertisements in inducing very young children to eat "healthy" foods, is to simply ban such advertising from television. The current regulatory climate, however, is not conducive to such bans. Furthermore, any attempt to implement such a policy would face a number of practical, ethical, and legal problems.

SUMMARY

This final chapter used three specific examples to illustrate how buyer behavior research can facilitate the construction and implementation of effective public policies governing marketing practices. Research, of course, cannot resolve differ-

---

[8]The ages cited here vary somewhat depending on the task to be performed. For further details, see Roedder (1981).

ences that arise from different values. It can, however, provide a sounder factual basis for debate and insights into effective means for implementing public policy decisions, once they have been made. Buyer behavior research may also be useful for deciding among various policy options *if* the desirability of each option can be stated as a function of one or more unknown facts, such as the percentage of consumers actually using unit price lists.

General interest in the systematic application of buyer behavior research to public policy issues is quite recent. The potential for such application is clearly present, and the rapidly developing marketing literature suggests that public policy research will be one of the major growth areas of buyer behavior research.

The Role of Theory in the Study of Buyer Behavior

Appendix A

Chapter 2 discussed, at an elementary level, some of the most important aspects of theory in the study of buyer behavior. Specifically considered were the abstractive property of theory, the interplay between theory and method in developing an understanding of buyer behavior, and selected aspects of the value of theory.

The purpose of this appendix is to extend that earlier discussion of theory and to develop some previously discussed aspects of theory at a more sophisticated level. It is assumed in the following discussion that the reader has carefully read Chapters 1 and 2. The theory of perceived risk will again be used to facilitate the discussion. The specific theory to be used is illustrated schematically in Figure A.1. The basic components of this theory should be familiar by now: consumers perceive risk in making brand choices and attempt to reduce this risk to tolerable levels.

THEORY AND DATA

The world surrounding us is literally a buzz of stimuli. To make sense of our environment, and to operate effectively within it, we need some type of framework that allows us to select relevant facts and properly interpret those facts. Quite literally, we need a *theory* of how the world is structured and functions.

The following pages discuss formal theory as it applies to the study of buyer behavior. It is important to recognize, especially for those who question the value of theory, that all behavior is guided by theory, however informal and implicit those theories may be. To take a simple example, recall the first time you observed a complicated sport, such as football. Until you learned the rules of the game (i.e., until you learned the theory of how the game was supposed to be played), you probably experienced the unpleasant sensation of watching a kaleidoscope of action with little or no idea of what was *really* going on.

Potentially Observable Data

In Figure A.1, the kaleidoscope of action just referred to is represented by the area to the right of the feathered vertical line. Note carefully the words potentially observable. Not only will the researcher *choose* to ignore most of this potential data in the attempt to build and verify a theory of perceived risk; the sheer mass of such potential data forces a high degree of selectivity in the data selected if any progress is to be made at all.

Assume, in the present case, that all *obviously* irrelevant data is ignored; realizing, of course, that even knowing what is obviously irrelevant requires some prior knowledge or theory. A consumer might be observed reading magazines or watching TV ads, talking with friends or salespeople, carefully reading brand labels, paying for goods, or engaging in, literally, any of thousands of other specific acts. To focus attention on the *relevant* data or facts requires a theory.

Hypothetical Constructs

The essence of theory is contained in the interrelationships among variables. For example, in Figure A.1 perceived risk gives rise to a general class of behaviors that share a characteristic: they all are partially used as strategies for reducing risk to

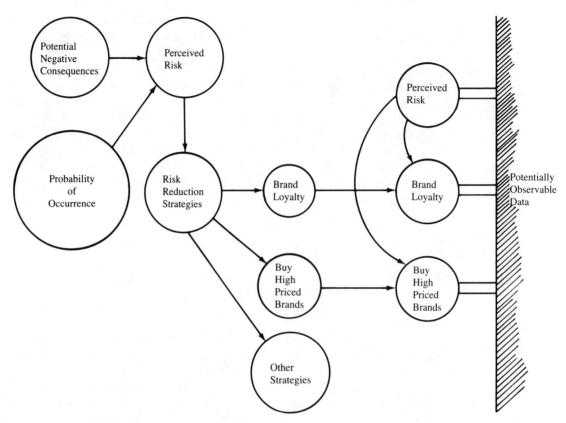

Figure A.1
An example of the relationship between theory and data

tolerable levels. In this sense, hypothetical constructs are the building blocks of theory. But what are hypothetical constructs, and how do they relate to data?

First of all, as discussed in Chapter 2, hypothetical constructs are highly abstract in comparison to the behavioral phenomena they represent. Consider perceived risk. Unless trained in the study of buyer behavior, the average consumer probably has no concept that could accurately be labeled perceived risk as consumer researchers define the term. Rather a consumer remembers that Uncle Ed was seriously injured by a power saw whose blade broke and, therefore, perceives power saws as dangerous. It is the researcher who abstracts out the property of perceived risk. And, because it is so abstract, the perceived risk concept may be used to explain a wide range of behaviors, all of which are highly distinct in their details.

Hypothetical constructs, then, are clearly different from the behaviors they represent. To the extent that they abstract out the essence of behavior, ignoring behavior presumed to be idiosyncratic and therefore not useful for theory building, hypothetical constructs are less than the behaviors they represent. This, of course, is true. But in a more important sense hypothetical constructs are more than the specific behaviors they represent.

What we mean by *more* is difficult to fully define at an elementary level.

Hypothetical constructs are variously said to be rich in meaning, to contain excess meaning, and to have openness in their meaning. To say that hypothetical constructs are rich in meaning and contain excess meaning basically refers to how hypothetical constructs must be translated and narrowed for use in empirical research. Consider, for example, the hypotherical construct *risk reduction strategies.* As one proceeds to the right in Figure A.1, the constructs become more specific. Brand loyalty and buying high priced brands are two specific strategies a consumer might use to reduce risk. Both, however, concern the purchase act itself. Many other risk reduction strategies might be proposed. For example, searching for more brand information. In any empirical study, therefore, the researcher is always forced to greatly narrow his or her concepts. Put another way, hypothetical constructs are always far richer in meaning than the variables that must be worked with at an empirical level. Another element of this perspective is that hypothetical constructs are never completely defined; i.e., they are always open to extension and new interpretation. This "openness of meaning" allows the constant extension and enrichment of the theories and the understanding of buyer behavior.

Rules of Correspondence

One reason theories are so powerful is that their elements can be easily manipulated. That is, they can be used to ask What ... If questions, reasoning out the conclusions without actually having to collect any data. This allows ideas or hypotheses[1] to be generated from theories more easily and quickly than could be done without abstract hypothetical constructs. Hopefully, hypotheses with little merit get quickly weeded out as *logically* implausible. But once what appears to be a good hypothesis has been formulated, it still must be tested to determine if it is correct; i.e., the hypothetical constructs must be connected to potentially observable data.

Such connections are made by rules of correspondence. These rules are indicated by the double lines in Figure A.1, which run from the intervening variables (to be discussed next) to potentially observable data. In the example, the theory of perceived risk is connected to data at three points: perceived risk, brand loyalty, and buying high priced brands. Note carefully that of seven hypothetical constructs only three are connected directly to data. Some (for example, potential negative consequences) are not tied to observable data because they are not relevant to the immediate purpose of the research, which is to study the consequences of the perception of risk rather than to study the underlying factors that cause perceived risk. Others (for example, other risk reduction strategies) are not tied to observable data because what they are is not precisely known even though it is certain that there are ways of reducing risk other than the two strategies specified in Figure A.1.

What rules of correspondence do is specify the procedures whereby numbers are assigned to the behavior under study. For example, perceived risk might be measured by giving consumers a specific definition of perceived risk (e.g., Bettman 1973; Horton 1976) and asking them to rate the level of risk they perceive in different product classes on a 25-point scale. In this case, the rule is quite simple. However, there still must be rules on how to handle cases where the subject

---

[1]A hypothesis is a specific assertion about the world whose truth is to be tested. Hypotheses are discussed in more detail later in this appendix.

scratches out one number and then checks another or makes a mark between two numbers.

In a similar way, rules of correspondence can be developed to assign numbers to brand loyalty and the selection of high price brands. In each case many different choices of rules are possible. Brand loyalty, for example, might be measured by the percent of dollars spent on the brand of a product class for which the most dollars were spent during the last six months. In fact, a definition similar to this is quite common in studies of brand loyalty. As seen in Chapter 5, however, there are many problems with such a definition, besides the obviously arbitrary six-month period. For example, it does not take into account the pattern of purchases for any brand other than the favorite. As shall be seen, many alternative definitions or rules of correspondence for measuring brand loyalty have been proposed to overcome this and other problems.

The rules of correspondence used here as illustrations are relatively simple and straightforward. Often, however, the rules are extremely complex. Examples of such complex rules of correspondence shall be seen subsequently in the study of brand loyalty and attitudes.

Intervening Variables

The outcome of applying the rules of correspondence to data is a set of numbers. These numbers are the intervening variables that are linked directly to the data. In the example, a consumer who gives a rating of 4 to dish detergents on a 25-point scale of perceived risk, indicating low perceived risk, who is 38 percent loyal to her favorite brand, and 90 percent of the time pays less than the median market price for dish detergent.

Two things about intervening variables are very important to understand. First, they stand between the hypothetical constructs and the data. The importance of this is that intervening variables are quite different from both. Second, and intimately related, is that all empirical testing of theory, as specified by hypothetical constructs, is conducted at the level of the intervening variables. In Figure A.1, for example, the theory might be tested by correlating subjects' ratings of perceived risk with their scores on brand loyalty and the purchase of high priced brands. If such tests support the theory, the study should be replicated to make sure that the findings are reliable; e.g., not narrowly confined to a particular group of subjects or products or due to some artifact of the methodology. If such tests do not support the theory, however, the possibility that the intervening variables do not adequately represent the corresponding hypothetical constructs or measure the relevant data must seriously be considered. For example, the subjects may not understand the definition of perceived risk being used or, for some reason, they may be unwilling to admit to perceiving risk when questioned directly. Because there are so many ways in which any one study may fail to adequately link hypothetical constructs with relevant data, an established or promising theory is virtually never abandoned on the basis of one, or even a few, studies. Indeed, because it is so difficult to operate without theory, even repeated empirical failures will often be unable to dislodge an established theory until a new theory comes along to take its place. In terms of the Chapter 1 discussion of the history of buyer behavior research, it seems that despite poor empirical results motivation research remained the dominant theory for many years because there was no adequate theory to displace it.

HYPOTHESES AND LAWS

So far the discussion has centered on how theories help in selecting relevant data or facts, interpreting or giving meaning to observed data, and organizing these individual meanings into a consistent pattern. In this regard, one of the key points of Chapter 2 was that because theories, especially comprehensive theories, of buyer behavior are so primitive, they serve more as blueprints or frameworks for the study of buyer behavior than as general explanations of buyer behavior.

Because buyer behavior theories are so primitive, it is really not possible to test them in any comprehensive sense.[2] Rather, researchers tend to logically derive relatively specific hypotheses from a theory, using the empirical tests of these hypotheses as evidence of the correctness or incorrectness of the theory. In the example, such a hypothesis might be that consumers who report higher levels of perceived risk for a product class will tend to be more brand loyal. A smililar, but conceptually distinct hypothesis, might be that consumers tend to display more brand loyalty for product classes they perceive as higher in risk. To the extent that these hypotheses are consistent with the data they may be offered in support of the theory of perceived risk.

One of the principle objectives of any science is to develop theories that allow specification of hypotheses to be as precise as possible. To attain such precision, generally accepted or standardized procedures for measuring the variables of interest and the proper mathematical functions that link these variables must be developed. When the variables and the relationships among these variables can be consistently measured with such a high degree of accuracy, the hypothesis may be said to have attained the status of a law.

The fact is that there are very few laws of buyer behavior. This, of course, is not unexpected. More important, however, is the question of whether it is even possible in principle to develop such laws. Although this question has not been vigorously addressed recently, it has been in the past and, no doubt, will be again. Many (e.g., Buzzell 1963) have suggested that human behavior is inherently too complex, too dynamic to be reducible to lawful generalizations.

Others, most notably Ehrenberg, take vigorous exception to this position. Ehrenberg (1971), in particular, argues forcefully that laws of buyer behavior can only be developed if researchers carefully select behaviors to study that have potential for lawful generalization rather than wasting their time studying behavior that they do not understand sufficiently *at the time* to have such potential. Ehrenberg then goes on to discuss three instances in which such laws were established.[3] These "laws" are quite narrow in terms of the behavior they de-

---

[2]For a discussion of this point, the reader is referred to Farley and Ring's (1970) effort to develop a comprehensive test of the Howard-Sheth model.

[3]The laws presented by Ehrenberg concern (1) duplication of viewing, i.e., the percentage of people who watch a specific channel during any *two* specific time periods; (2) the relationship between *expressed* intentions to buy and current level of use of a brand; and (3) the purchasing constant 1.4, which says that a buyer who buys a brand in one time period but not the next will purchase 1.4 units of the good in the first time period.

scribe and describe the behavior without really explaining it. Despite this, these laws do demonstrate the potential for developing lawful generalizations of buyer behavior. Only time will tell whether it is in fact possible to reduce most buyer behaviors to lawful generalizations.

FUNCTIONS OF THEORY

Chapter 2 briefly discussed the value or functions of theory. Specifically, it discussed how theories provide a parsimonius description of buyer behavior, provide a basis for predicting and possibly influencing buyer behavior, and provide a framework for integrating a diversity of findings from individual studies of buyer behavior. This final section will briefly discuss two additional functions of theory.

The first of these functions is the generative function of theory. A good theory not only describes the behavior of interest, it is also sufficiently general and open to extension that new hypotheses can be generated. That is, a good theory must be capable of constantly evolving. Such generation of new hypotheses is possible because of the openness of meaning of hypothetical constructs, which was previously discussed, and the everpresent possibility of finding new relationships among existing hypothetical constructs or developing and integrating into the theory entirely new hypothetical constructs.

The second of these functions is the delimiting function of theory. Various aspects of this function of theory have already been discussed. To begin, it should by now be quite clear to the reader that a theory is needed to determine which facts are relevant. A theory tends to focus attention on a very narrow range of the total data potentially available. Of course, this discipline is necessary to keep from being overwhelmed by data. But it must be recognized that by so limiting the inquiry, data may be concealed that with another theory might seem obviously relevant. For example, Chapter 1 noted in some detail how acceptance of an information processing theory of buyer behavior changed the kinds of data that tend to be regarded as relevant to understanding buyer behavior; e.g., the importance of strategies for reducing the complexity of the buying task.

The delimiting function, however, works in a second and more subtle way. Specifically, it imposes a certain meaning on the facts to be collected even before they are collected. For example, those who hold a motivation research theory of behavior are inclined before even beginning a study to *interpret* the existence of brand loyalty as behavior that enhances the consumer's self-image. On the other hand, those who hold an information processing theory of behavior are predisposed to *interpret* the same existence of brand loyalty as a risk reduction strategy or a strategy for simplifying the buying task.

That the same set of facts may be interpreted in different ways that depend intimately on the theory subscribed to may be disconcerting to the reader. However disconcerting, there is no way out of this state of affairs. The reason for this is that, while relations do exist among objects in the real world outside the observer, meaning does not. Meaning exists only within the observer. Of course, with sufficient interchange of ideas different observers may come to share *approximately* the same meaning about the same set of facts. Indeed, this is essentially what happens when different observers subscribe to the same theory of buyer behavior.

Coupling the ideas that different observers who subscribe to different theories may interpret the same facts in quite different ways with the discussion, especially in Chapter 1, of how theories evolve and new theories arise to replace older theories raises an interesting question, and a fitting one on which to conclude this discussion of theory. How can we know if a theory is true? The answer is that we cannot. The reason is quite simple, even if the point is somewhat subtle. To test the truth of a theory requires a standard for comparison that can only be the true theory itself. This is an obviously impossible situation. The ultimate test of a theory then is not and cannot be its truthfulness.[4]

Rather, the ultimate test of a theory is its usefulness. A theory is adopted because it helps us understand and more effectively function in the world. How a theory helps us depends very much on who we are and what we do. For the scholar, it may be sufficient to understand buyer behavior. For the marketing manager, theory is most useful in designing marketing programs that will attract and hold buyers and create profits. For the government regulator, it will be designing and implementing effective consumer policies and regulations.

---

[4]Although, from a philosophical perspective, we can never know with absolute certainty that a theory is true, it is, nevertheless, common to speak of a theory as being true or not true. Indeed, I have followed this practice in this book. More precisely, however, what is generally meant by true is that the theory appears consistent with the known facts and is felt to be useful in the various ways we have discussed in this appendix and Chapter 2.

Stochastic Models of Brand Choice

Appendix B

The concluding section of Chapter 5 discussed two quantitative models of brand choice at a verbal level. The primary goal in this earlier discussion was to illustrate the potential managerial value of such models.. The purpose in this appendix is to extend that discussion by reviewing, at an elementary level, the mathematical structure of several different types of stochastic (i.e., probabilistic) models of brand choice.

The literature on stochastic brand choice models[1], which has been developing for some three decades, is both extensive and complex. No brief discussion of this literature could even begin to do it justice.[2] Thus, this appendix's goals will of necessity be quite modest. Three different models will be discussed. While their mathematical structure will be outlined, no attempt will be made to develop formal proofs. The selection of the specific models to be discussed came from a suggestion by Montgomery (1967), that most stochastic brand choice models develop out of one of three different types of basic stochastic models; zero-order, Markov, and linear learning. The specific goals of this appendix are to acquaint the reader with (1) an example of the basic mathematical structure of each of these three types of stochastic models and (2) the potential managerial usefulness of such models.

THE PROBABILITY DIFFUSION MODEL

The probability diffusion model, developed by Montgomery (1969), is an example of a zero-order stochastic model. In a zero-order model it is assumed that there is no "purchase event feedback." That is, each buyer's probability of buying any brand is assumed *not* to be affected by the buyer's previous purchase history. This, however, does not mean that the probability of purchase must be constant. It merely requires any change factors to be located in the external environment rather than arise from the buyer's prior purchasing experience.

No claim is made that the probability diffusion model actually models the buyer's choice process. Rather, it attempts to model the uncertainty associated with a binary choice. This binary choice is cast in the form of brand A, the brand of interest, and a collective category of all other brand choices, labeled "brand" B. The model is specified at the level of the individual buyer and then aggregated to the level of the market to provide a means for estimating the parameters of the model and empirically evaluating the goodness of fit of the model.

The model begins by assuming that each buyer has some number, N, of hypothetical response elements. Of these elements i are associated with the response "choose brand A" and (N−i) are associated with the response "choose

---

[1]There are actually two quite different types of models discussed in the stochastic choice process literature. The first, which is discussed in this appendix, deals with brand choice on a "purchase occasion." The second, which is not discussed, deals with the timing of purchase. These are referred to as purchase incidence models. A thorough discussion of these, as well as brand choice, models can be found in Massy, Montgomery, and Morrison (1970).

[2]The best sources for current research on stochastic models are *Management Science, Operations Research*, and the *Journal of Marketing Research*. Although somewhat dated, one of the best technical references for stochastic brand choice and purchase incidence models is Massy, Montgomery, and Morrison (1970). A basically nontechnical review of much of the same material is presented in Montgomery and Ryans (1973).

brand B." It is further assumed that on any purchase occasion, t, the probability of purchasing brand A is equal to the proportion of the N elements associated with brand A. Mathematically,

$$Pr[A] = i/N \tag{1}$$

and since there are only two choices

$$Pr[B] = 1 - Pr[A] = (N-i)/N. \tag{2}$$

There is no requirement that buyers have the same probabilities of purchasing brands A and B; i.e., the model is heterogeneous.

At any given time the buyer has i elements associated with response A and $(N-i)$ elements associated with response B. The heart of the probability diffusion model is a mechanism whereby elements associated with response A tend to become associated with response B, and elements associated with response B tend to become associated with response A. Mathematically, the propensities for response elements to change are assumed to be

$$\lambda_i = (\alpha + i\,\gamma)\,(N-i), \text{ for elements associated with B} \tag{3}$$
$$\mu_i = [\beta + (N-i)\,\gamma]\,i, \text{ for elements associated with A} \tag{4}$$

λ_i may be interpreted in the following way. There are $(N-i)$ elements associated with response B. Each of these response elements has a propensity to change to response A that is equal to α plus a quantity that is proportional to the number of elements associated with response A (i.e., $i\gamma$). μ_i may be interpreted in a similar way. The change process specified by equations (3) and (4) is assumed to be common to all buyers. α, β and γ are parameters that must be estimated from empirical data.

Montgomery proceeds to develop the steady state solution and define the behavior of the probability of purchasing brand A over purchase occasions. Although complex, the mathematics are straightforward. Therefore, they will not be presented here. In the steady state (i.e., when the proportion of elements associated with response A(i/N) is constant) the distribution of the probability of purchasing brand A follows a beta distribution with mean $\alpha/(\alpha + \beta)$ and variance $\alpha\beta\gamma/(\alpha + \beta)^2\,(\alpha + \beta + \gamma)$.

More important, the probability of purchasing brand A on any purchase occasion t is

$$Pr[A_t] = P_o e^{-kt} + a(1-e^{-kt}) \tag{5}$$

where $k = \alpha + \beta$, $a = \alpha/(\alpha + \beta)$, e is the base of the naperian logarithms, and P_o is the probability of purchasing brand A at some arbitrary time, $t=0$. Figure B.1 presents equation (5) graphically.[3] As t approaches infinity the probability of purchasing brand A approaches $\alpha/(\alpha + \beta)$ at a rate defined by k. Because the change process itself, including the parameters α, β, and γ, is assumed to be common to all buyers, the parameters a and k define the expected value of the purchase probability and its variance for the market. That is, P_o may be interpreted as an initial market share at some arbitrary time $t=0$ and $a=\alpha/(\alpha + \beta)$ may be

---

[3]Montgomery also proves that $k \geq 0$ and $0 \geq a \geq 1$. It is these restrictions that give the curve in Figure B.1 its general shape.

Figure B.1
Expected value of purchasing
brand A over purchase occasions

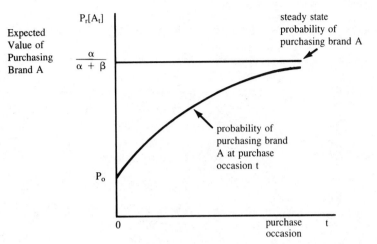

interpreted as the ultimate steady state market share for brand A. Note that although the probability of purchasing brand A is shown increasing it could just as easily be decreasing.

Montgomery shows how the model may be aggregated over buyers and empirically tested. He also applied the model to brand choice data for Crest toothpaste both before and after the endorsement of the American Dental Association in 1960. The probability diffusion model fitted the data remarkably well both in the stable period before and in the transient period after the ADA's endorsement of Crest.

The application to Crest provides an excellent vehicle for discussing both the managerial value of the probability diffusion model and the circumstances under which it is likely to be appropriate. Before the ADA endorsement, the toothpaste market was quite stable in terms of such things as new market entries and major change in firms' marketing strategies for existing brands of toothpaste. In the terminology of Chapter 4, most buyers were probably in a state approximating routinized response behavior; i.e., buyers were fully learned in terms of their purchasing behavior for toothpaste. The ADA's endorsement of Crest presented a major *external* shock to the competitive environment and provided a major opportunity for a change in Crest's promotional strategy. In such circumstances, the probability diffusion model provides a procedure for assessing where the firm is heading in terms of market share and how rapidly this change is likely to take place. Although framed in terms of Crest, note carefully that the model could be applied to any other specific brand to assess the effects of the ADA endorsement. Presumably these effects would be negative for brands other than Crest. Such information is clearly of managerial importance.

FIRST ORDER MARKOV MODEL

Unlike a zero-order brand choice model, a Markov model allows for purchase event feedback. In the simple first order Markov model presented here, the probabilities governing the brand choice process are assumed to be affected *only* by the previous purchase. Such a situation might be expected to be appropriate when buyers forget prior purchases except for the brand currently owned and where the competitive environment is relatively stable.

Three principal issues must be addressed in building a Markov model: order, stationarity, and homogeneity. Most Markov models are first order. It is, however, possible to build higher order processes by defining the relevant states (i.e., the purchase history) of the buyer in terms of sequences of brand purchases on two or more purchase occasions. Stationarity involves the question of whether the probabilities that govern the choice process are allowed to change over time (nonstationary) or are required to be stable (stationary). In a homogeneous model all buyers are required to share the same brand choice probabilities. In a heterogeneous model this is not required.[4] The simple Markov model discussed here is first order, stationary, and homogeneous. For a discussion of more complex Markov models, and references to the literature, the reader is referred to Massy, Montgomery and Morrison (1970).

Table B.1 presents data for three brands that will be used to illustrate the first order Markov model. The first step is to build a matrix of transition probabilities. Part I presents an example of a transition matrix. The rows represent the brand purchased on some arbitrary purchase occasion t and the columns define the brand purchased on the next purchase occasion $t+1$. For example, a person who bought brand A on the last purchase occasion has probabilities of .80, .15, and .05 of purchasing brands A, B, *or* C, respectively, on the next purchase occasion. A different set of probabilities governs the brand choices of buyers who chose brand B or brand C on the previous purchase occasion. This, of course, is precisely what is meant by a first order purchase event feedback. Transition matrices are usually estimated empirically from panel data.

The transition matrix provides information which is of obvious managerial importance. Brand A, for example, is clearly doing a better job of retaining its own customers than either brands B or C. Similarly, brand B is losing far more of its customers to brand C (25 percent) than to brand A (10 percent). The transition matrix also allows the firm to calculate the expected market shares for all brands in designated future periods. Part II of Table B.1 presents the transition matrix recast in the form of market share equations. The letters A, B, and C designate market shares. The subscripts t and $t+1$ indicate the relevant purchase occasion. To see how the market share calculations are made, assume that the market share in time period t are 60 percent, 20 percent, and 20 percent for brands A, B, and C, respectively. Applying the first equation shows that the market share for brand A in $t+1$ is *expected* to be

$$.80(60) + .10(20) + .15(20) = 53 \text{ percent}$$

In a similar way, expected market shares for brands B and C could be calculated. These market shares are 29 percent (brand B) and 18 percent (brand C). This process could be continued indefinitely to trace the evolving market shares for the

---

[4]As noted in Chapter 5, heterogeneity is normally introduced into a brand choice model by assuming that the choice probabilities are distributed over buyers according to some probability distribution. The beta distribution, previously mentioned in the discussion of the probability diffusion model, is frequently used for this purpose because it is very flexible in terms of the specific shapes it can assume. The exact shape of any probability distribution is defined by its parameters, which must be estimated from empirical data.

Table B.1

Illustration of a first order Markov Model

Part I.   *Transition Matrix*

Brand Purchased at Time $t+1$

Brand Purchased at Time t		A	B	C
	A	.80	.15	.05
	B	.10	.65	.25
	C	.15	.35	.50

Note that the transition probabilities must sum to 1 across each row.

Part II.   *Market Share Equations*

$$.80A_t + .10B_t + .15C_t = A_{t+1}$$

$$.15A_t + .65B_t + .35C_t = B_{t+1}$$

$$.05A_t + .25B_t + .50C_t = C_{t+1}$$

Part III.   *Steady State Market Shares*

Brand	Market Share
A	37.2 percent
B	39.4 percent
C	23.4 percent

three brands in this market. For period $t+2$, of course, the market shares for period $t+1$ would be used in the calculations. The reader should try calculating these market shares: they are 48.0 percent (A), 33.1 percent (B), and 18.9 percent (C).

This process of calculating future expected market shares could be continued indefinitely. Eventually a stable situation would be reached in which the market shares for each brand are constant. This stable situation is referred to as the steady state. How long it takes to reach this steady state depends both on the initial market shares *and* the transition matrix. However, the steady state market shares themselves depend *only* on the transition matrix.[5] Calculating the steady state market shares is relatively easy. In the steady state, the market shares are constant. Thus, the subscripts of the market share equations in Part II of Table B.1 may be dropped and the relevant terms consolidated. This yields

$$-.20A + .10B + .15C = 0$$
$$.15A - .35B + .35C = 0$$
$$.05A + .25B - .50C = 0$$

i.e., three equations in three unknowns. Only two of these equations, however, are independent. By progressive substitution, both A and B can be expressed in terms of C; i.e., $A = 1.591C$ and $B = 1.682C$. The solution is obtained by substituting

[5]This assumes that no market share is zero.

these terms into the constraint that the sum of all market shares is 100 percent. The steady state solution is presented in Part III of Table B.1.

A Markov analysis provides information that is clearly important to marketing managers. As a description of the market, it provides much relevant information on the effectiveness of the firm's efforts to retain its own customers and to attract its competitors' customers. The pattern of switching probabilities also gives insight into who the firm's competitors really are; i.e., the higher the transition probabilities between brands the more intense the competition. Indeed, from a managerial perspective, the ease with which a Markov model adapts to the analysis of more than two brands, in contrast to many brand choice models that require creation of an artificial "all other" brand B, is a major advantage of Markov models.

Using a Markov analysis to predict future market shares requires the assumption that the transition matrix is stationary; i.e., does not change over time.[6] Even if the transition matrix is thought to tend to be stable in a stable environment, it will usually be true that the marketing environment, as it is defined by all firms' marketing mixes, will be changing and this will affect the transition matrix. What the transition matrix does show is where market shares are trending, *assuming* a constant transition matrix. In the hypothetical illustration, for example, the market share is expected to fall dramatically for brand A and rise almost as much for brand B. Note the interesting pattern for brand C: the market share first falls to 18 percent and then gradually begins to rise to its steady state value of 23.4 percent. This pattern occurs because such a large percentage of brand C's customers come from brand B (25 percent) and brand B's share of the market is rising over time. The important implication is that brand C's fall in market share is only temporary. Management, of course, will normally attempt to encourage favorable trends and to stop or reverse unfavorable trends. Although beyond the scope of the present discussion, Markov models have been constructed that link the probabilities in the transition matrix to elements in the firm's marketing mix; e.g., price (Telser 1962) and advertising (Lipstein 1965).

LINEAR LEARNING MODEL

The linear learning model, originally proposed by Kuehn (1962), grows out of work on mathematical learning theory by Bush and Mosteller (1955). A basic assumption of this model is that a specific response (e.g., purchasing a brand) tends to increase the probability of making that same response again. This, of course, is equivalent to saying that the response is always positively reinforced, which is likely to be true for many products. Because the probability of purchasing a brand evolves over purchase occasions, this probability incorporates the entire history of prior purchases. In a sense, one might regard its order of purchase event feedback as infinite.

---

[6]Strictly speaking, the transition matrix is assumed to apply to each buyer. In our hypothetical example, this means that any buyer who purchased brand A on purchase occasion t has a .80 probability of purchasing brand A again. It does *not* mean, as is frequently and incorrectly assumed, that 80 percent of brand A's customers will buy brand A again. An important aspect of this point is that Markov analysis has largely developed without an explicit sampling theory. This means we are generally unable to estimate the variance of the model's outputs; e.g., predicted market shares.

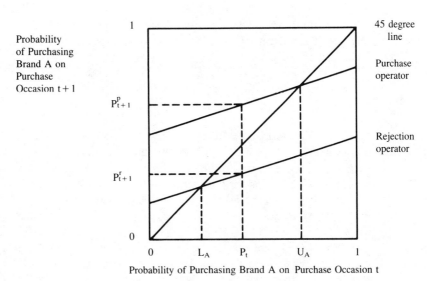

Figure B.2
An illustration of the linear learning model

Figure B.2 illustrates the linear learning model. The horizontal axis measures the probability of purchasing brand A on some purchase occasion t, while the vertical axis measures the same probability on purchase occasion $t+1$. The probability of purchasing brand A on the next purchase occasion depends on two factors: (1) the probability of purchasing brand A on purchase occasion t; and (2) whether brand A or some other brand was purchased on purchase occasion t. If brand A was purchased, the probability of purchasing brand A next time is defined by the so-called purchase operator. If some other brand was purchased, the probability of purchasing brand A is defined by the rejection operator.

Mathematically, the purchase and rejection operators are defined by

$$P^p_{t+1} = \alpha + \beta + \gamma P_t \text{ (purchase operator)} \tag{6}$$
$$P^r_{t+1} = \alpha + \gamma P_t \text{ (rejection operator)} \tag{7}$$

where P_{t+1} is the probability of purchasing brand A on the next purchase occasion, α is the intercept of the rejection operator with the vertical axis, β is the *incremental* height of the purchase operator, and γ is the common slope of both operators. It is further assumed that all buyers share the same operators, i.e., homogeneity is assumed. Implicit in equations (6) and (7) is the assumption that environmental factors (e.g., marketing activities) do not affect the height or slope of the two operators. Most of these assumptions can be relaxed somewhat. This, however, greatly complicates the model and, therefore, shall not be pursued further here. For details the reader is referred to Massy, Montgomery, and Morrison (1970).

Constructing a linear learning model requires estimating the parameters α, β, and γ. Although more difficult than it may appear to the reader with some familiarity with regression analysis, it is possible to estimate these parameters (Massy, Montgomery, and Morrison 1970). Once these estimates are obtained, the probability of buying brand A, and implicitly the probability of buying all other brands, is defined by P_t (probability of purchasing brand A on purchase occasion t) and wnether the purchase or rejection operator is relevant. These effects are illustrated in Figure B.2 where, given P_t, the rejection and purchase operators define P_{t+1}^r and P_{t+1}^p, respectively.

An interesting aspect of the linear learning model is that P_t, P_{t+1}^r, and P_{t+1}^p are all constrained to lie within the following boundaries

$$L_A \leq P_t, P_{t+1}^r, P_{t+1}^p \leq U_A.$$

L_A, the lower boundary, is defined by the intersection of the rejection operator with the 45 degree line in Figure B.2. U_A, the upper boundary, is defined in a similar way with the purchase operator. Psychologically, this implies incomplete learning and repeat purchase behavior that is always less than 100 percent.

The linear learning model has been successfully applied to a number of frequently purchased nondurable goods and to the problem of store choice (Montgomery and Ryans 1973). Haines (1964), in a very innovative study, used a variation of the linear learning model to assess the effects of a firm's marketing mix for a new product on its ultimate market share and the rate at which this stable market share was approached. Because Haines assumed that no directly competitive products were available, he modeled buyers' learning over purchase occasions with the major modification that this learning process was allowed to be affected by the firm's marketing mix. Procedures for incorporating the effects of advertising and other promotional influences into the linear learning model were suggested by Kuehn (1962) and Kuehn and Day (1964).

For a number of reasons, including the difficulty of estimating parameters, the linear learning model has been less popular than either zero-order or Markov models. Despite this lack of popularity, the linear learning model has been successfully applied to both brand and store choice and is clearly capable of providing important managerial insights into the consequences of buyer choice behavior; e.g., the upper and lower limits on market share implied by L_A and U_A in Figure B.2.

Perhaps more important, the linear learning model has been merged with the probability diffusion model to create a new type of model, the dual-effects model (Jones 1970a, 1970b). The dual-effects model incorporates both the external influences of the probability diffusion model and the purchase event feedback of the linear learning model. In applying the dual-effects model to the Crest data, Jones (1970b) concluded that the ADA endorsement had a strong positive influence on buyers, while purchase event feedback was somewhat negative. These results suggest potential problems with product features, such as taste. The dual-effects model represents a significant increase in the state of the art of brand choice modeling. Because of its complexity, however, the dual-effects model will not be pursued further. For additional details on this model, the reader is referred to Jones (1970a, 1970b).

A CONCLUDING NOTE ON THE MANAGERIAL USE OF STOCHASTIC MODELS OF BRAND CHOICE

This appendix and Chapter 5 introduced the reader to stochastic brand choice models. The primary purpose has been to alert the reader to the potential managerial relevance of such models. Although stochastic brand choice models continue to undergo rapid development, they are already developed to a level that justifies their routine use in many situations. Indeed, as seen in Chapter 5, specialized businesses such as the Hendry Corporation have emerged to offer stochastic brand choice model building services to industry.

The reader should realize, however, that the discussion has been limited to relatively simple versions of three types of stochastic models and has largely avoided many of the complexities associated with the actual construction and empirical testing of such models. Knowing which model is most relevant and building such a model requires both substantial technical competence and, frequently, experienced judgment. The reader interested in acquiring these skills is referred to Massy, Montgomery, and Morrison (1970) for a more complete treatment of the technical issues involved in building stochastic brand choice models.

Multidimensional Scaling and Conjoint Measurement

Appendix C

In the last two decades, a powerful technology has developed for measuring perceptions and preferences. This appendix describes two general classes of these multivariate measurement techniques, multidimensional scaling (MDS) and conjoint measurement, which have found widespread acceptance and use among both academic researchers and marketing managers.

MDS and conjoint measurement techniques are mathematically and computationally complex. Fortunately, the basic concepts that underlie both techniques are relatively simple and intuitively understandable. The basic objectives, then, are twofold. First, MDS and conjoint measurement techniques will be described at an elementary level. Second, how these techniques help in the design of effective marketing strategies will be discussed. In particular, MDS and conjoint measurement have found major applications in the areas of market segmentation, product positioning, and in product design decisions and decisions involving other variables in the supporting marketing mix; i.e., price, promotion, and distribution decisions. Also, references to the MDS and conjoint measurement literature, which the interested reader may pursue, will be cited.

For a proper understanding of MDS and conjoint measurement techniques, it is important to recognize that they have been developed almost exclusively for the purpose of predicting, as opposed to explaining, buyer behavior. More specifically, both techniques attempt to "represent" buyers' brand perceptions and perferences in terms of a geometric spatial model. The test of such a model is the extent to which it leads to accurate predictions. There is no *necessary* requirement that each buyer actually make his or her buying decisions based upon calculations in a "mental" geometric space. This argument is, as the reader may recall, precisely the same one as discussed in conjunction with quantitative models of brand switching. The important point, of course, is that MDS and conjoint measurement *have* proven to be very useful research tools for academicians and marketing managers.

Of necessity, this review of attitude measurement techniques will be highly selective. Readers desiring a fuller, but still elementary, discussion of attitude measurement procedures will find Green and Tull (1978, especially Chapter 6) and Tull and Hawkins (1980, especially Chapter 9) excellent references. Readers desiring more in-depth discussions of attitude measurement procedures can consult Torgerson (1958), Scott (1968), Hughes (1971), Kerlinger (1973) and the proceedings of the attitude research meeting held each year under the auspices of the American Marketing Association.

MULTIDIMENSIONAL SCALING

A large number of specific MDS models have been proposed. In general, these specific models can be classified as either perceptual models or preference models. Perceptual models attempt to develop a geometric representation of buyers' perceptions of the attributes they use to identify brands of a product class and to locate the position of each brand within this geometric space. Preference models extend this analysis by developing a geometric representation of the combination of product attributes that each subject desires. Although interest normally centers on the results of the preference analysis, data for a perceptual MDS analysis are normally also collected because preference MDS models rest upon an assumption that all individuals in a given preference analysis share a common perceptual space for the brands under study.

Figure C.1
Illustration of typical MDS output

Source: Adapted from Richard W. Johnson, "Market Segmentation: A Strategic Management Tool." *Journal of Marketing Research*, VIII (February 1971): 16. Reprinted with the kind permission of the American Marketing Association.

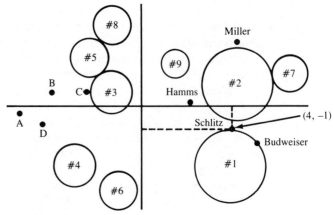

The output of a typical MDS analysis can be seen in Figure C.1. Subsequently, this appendix will examine how such a geometric representation of buyers' perceptions and preferences is constructed. For the moment, Figure C.1 will be used to present some basic terminology.

The brands in Figure C.1 are represented by black dots. Eight brands of beer are present; the four brands on the right are national brands and the four brands on the left, identified as A, B, C, and D, are local brands in the Chicago market. More generally, since MDS techniques are not limited to the analysis of goods and services, it is common to refer to the brands as *objects* that are represented by *points* in the geometric space. As can be seen, the space consists of two *dimensions.* The term attribute is not used to describe the dimensions that are initially output by an MDS analysis because it requires additional analysis to attach interpretive labels to the basic geometric dimensions.

The circles in Figure C.1 represent clusters of *ideal points.* Each subject is assumed to have a preferred level for each product attribute. The preferred levels on each dimension define an ideal brand for each subject, which is called an *ideal point.*[1] In Figure C.1, the ideal points for each subject are not represented directly. Rather, subjects whose ideal points are close have been grouped into more homogeneous clusters. The size of each circle represents the *relative* size of each cluster of ideal points.

Finally, each brand and ideal point can be located on each dimension of the geometric space. The location of a point is given by its *coordinates.* For example, the coordinates of Schlitz beer are $(4, -1)$; i.e., 4 on the horizontal dimension and -1 on the vertical dimension.[2] The specific locations of all brands and ideal points are said to constitute a *configuration* and the total geometric space presented in Figure C.1 is referred to as a perceptual/preference *map.*

[1]Ideal point models assume that buyers prefer a specific value of any attribute. For some attributes this may be a reasonable assumption. For others it probably is not. For example, a car buyer might want a medium size engine but probably desires, all other things equal, as high a MPG as possible. For an introductory discussion of models which handle preferences that cannot be represented by ideal points, see Green and Carmone (1970, Chapter 4).

[2]Actually, the unit of measurement is arbitrary. It is only the *relative* positions of the points that are important. For example, the coordinates of Schlitz beer could be set at $(8, -2)$ without changing the information contained in Figure C.1.

Figure C.2.
Hypothetical example of perceptual map for three brands of
automobiles and two perceptual dimensions

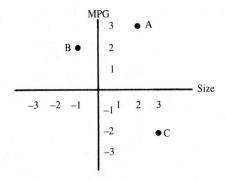

With this background the discussion proceeds to how the perceptual/preference
map in Figure C.1 may be constructed. Because preference MDS analysis presumes
that all subjects in the analysis share a common perceptual map, the discussion
begins with perceptual MDS analysis. This is followed by discussions of preference
models and managerial uses of MDS techniques.

Perceptual MDS models

To understand the principles upon which a MDS analysis of perceptual data is
based, begin by assuming that we know what the perceptual map for a single buyer
looks like. More specifically, assume that a hypothetical buyer's brand perceptions
can be represented by the perceptual map in Figure C.2. This map indicates the
buyer uses two attributes to evaluate three brands of automobiles.[3]

One basic question to ask regarding the data in Figure C.2 is "How *similar* are
the automobiles?" The question requires a measure of similarity. The most frequently used measure of similarity is the Euclidean distance between two objects.
Algebraically, the distance between any two objects i and j is

$$d_{ij} = \left[\sum_{k=1}^{n} (X_{ik} - X_{jk})^2 \right]^{\frac{1}{2}}$$

where

d_{ij} is the distance between any two objects i and j
X_{ik} is the value of object i on dimension k
X_{jk} is the value of object j on dimension k
n   is the number of dimensions or attributes.

From the data in Figure C.2 it is a simple matter to calculate the distance between
any two objects; e.g.,

$$d_{A\,B} = [(2-(-1))^2 + (3-2)^2]^{\frac{1}{2}}$$
$$= (10)^{\frac{1}{2}} = 3.16$$

In a similar way we may calculate $d_{B\,C} = 5.66$ and $d_{A\,C} = 5.10$.

Given the data in Figure C.2, it is clearly a simple matter to calculate the

---

[3]An actual MDS analysis requires more than three objects, as will subsequently be discussed more
fully.

distance between any pair of objects. But what if *only* the distances between the pairs of objects are available. Can Figure C.2 be reconstructed from such data? The answer is yes. Indeed, given interobject distances that are measured without error, it is possible to reproduce any configuration of points, such as Figure C.2, *exactly*.[4] The mathematical calculations are based on matrix algebra techniques, which are beyond the level of this discussion. However, with only three objects and three interobject distances, it is relatively easy to illustrate the principles involved.

Since three points can always be fitted into a two dimensional space, the number of dimensions must be either one or two.[5] If the true space is one dimensional, then the two smaller distances must sum to the larger distance, i.e.,

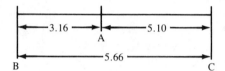

Clearly this is not the case and the conclusion must be that two dimensions are necessary to fit the interobject distances. Given a second dimension, point A may be pulled in an upward direction until a position is found that satisfies all interobject distances;[6] i.e.,

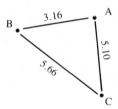

This simple illustration of the principles that allow construction of a perceptual map using only interobject distances forms the preparation for discussing several additional factors, which are necessary to understand how MDS techniques are used in practice.

First, since three objects can *always* be fitted into a two dimensional space, there is no way of knowing if a subject is actually making his or her judgments with more than two attributes. That is, it is necessary to use a larger number of objects in order to have some redundancy in the number of interobject distances

---

[4]To be completely accurate it must be noted that while the *relative* positions of the objects can be reproduced exactly given errorless distances, the orientation of the dimensions is arbitrary; i.e., the dimensions may be rotated clockwise or counter-clockwise without affecting the interobject distances. Therefore, in the output of a MDS analysis the dimensions carry no evaluative labels such as mpg or size. These evaluative labels may be developed by a subjective inspection of the positions of the objects on each dimension or by more sophisticated analytical techniques that are beyond the scope of our presentation (for details see Green and Carmone 1970, especially pp. 57–61).

[5]More generally, n points can always be fitted in a space of n−1 dimensions.

[6]Technically, we have three interobject distances with which to determine or fix six numbers; i.e., the coordinates of each of three points on each of two dimensions. However, we may arbitrarily locate any two objects as long as we maintain the required interobject distance. This fixes four coordinates and uses up one distance, leaving two coordinates to fix and two distances with which to fix them. This is why we can determine *exactly* both the number of dimensions and the *relative* positions of the objects on those dimensions in this simple example.

with which to fix the coordinates of the objects.[7] Shepard (1966) showed, using simulation techniques, that MDS techniques are extremely accurate with as few as eight objects in a two dimensional space. Since marketing applications of MDS techniques typically reveal two or three dimensions, rarely more, ten–twelve objects will normally be sufficient to produce a good MDS solution.

The second factor to be considered is the use of interobject distances as the basic input data into a MDS analysis. As a practical matter, people find it very difficult to evaluate a pair of objects in terms of the distance between them. Various attempts have been made to resolve this problem. However, a major breakthrough by Roger Shepard (1962a and b; 1966) allowed MDS to become an applied, as opposed to largely academic, research tool. Specifically, Shepard demonstrated that the interobject distances may be replaced by a *rank ordering* of the interobject distances with little loss in the accuracy of the MDS analysis. In actual studies, subjects are normally instructed to rank all possible *pairs* of objects from most similar to least similar. Similarity is assumed to be inversely related to the distance between two objects. Although tedious, this task is one that subjects typically find easy to perform.[8] When rank order data is used the analysis is referred to as a nonmetric MDS analysis.[9]

The third factor that must be considered is that the input data, whether they are distances, similarities or some other measure, do contain error. This raises the questions of how to determine the proper number of dimensions of the solution space and how to judge the adequacy of the obtained solution. To do this requires some measure of goodness of fit of the solution; the most common of which are based on Kruskal's measure of stress.

The stress concept can best be explained by briefly discussing how a nonmetric MDS solution is obtained. The first step is to select a space of some dimensionality presumed to be larger than the actual number of dimensions used by subjects. The second step is to place the objects into this space using one of several techniques for developing an initial configuration. Third, a set of distances (d_{ij}) is calculated among all pairs of objects. These distances will not necessarily be in the same rank order as the similarities. Thus, the fourth step is to construct another set of numbers called disparities. The disparities, symbolized by d_{ij}, are chosen to be as close to their corresponding distances as possible, subject to being in the same rank order as the original similarities. Stress is calculated from the distances and disparities using some version of Kruskal's original stress formula; i.e.,

[7]This redundancy occurs because the number of interobject distances expands roughly in proportion to the square of the number of objects—specifically $n(n-1)/2$. If $n = 10$, and the dimensionality of the perceptual space is two, then there are $10(9)/2 = 45$ interobject distances with which to fix the 20 coordinates.

[8]In practice, the rank ordering task is usually broken down into steps. For example, a subject might be asked to first sort the pairs of objects into three to five categories ranging from very similar to very dissimilar and, then, to rank the pairs within each category. For a more complete description of data collection techniques, see Green and Carmone (1970, pp. 53–57).

[9]For technical reasons, it is often desirable to analyze the rank order similarity data as if it were fully metric; i.e., as if the similarities were proportional to the underlying interobject distances. Typically, the results of metric and nonmetric analyses are quite similar (Green and Carmone 1970).

$$\text{Stress} = \left[\frac{\displaystyle\sum_{i \neq j}^{n} (d_{ij} - \hat{d}_{ij})^2}{\displaystyle\sum_{i \neq j}^{n} d_{ij}^2} \right]^{1/2} \cdot$$

Stress takes on values ranging from one to zero, with lower values indicating a better fit. Fifth, the objects are systematically moved to reduce stress. This procedure is repeated until stress fails to fall by a sufficient amount. When this occurs the dimensionality of the solution space is reduced by one and the entire process is repeated.

The dimension of the solution space actually used by the subject is estimated by examining the change in the minimum obtained stress as the dimensionality of the solution space is reduced. Figure C.3 gives an example of an "ideal" stress curve. A clear solution is obtained when the stress curve shows a pronounced kink, indicating that the objects have been forced into a solution space of too few dimensions, and when stress is low. Although somewhat arbitrary, a stress value of .05 or less is frequently regarded as "good." The curve in Figure C.3 is referred to as ideal because there is no guarantee that either a sharp kink or a low stress value will be obtained.

Preference MDS Models

Preference MDS models represent a significant extension of perceptual MDS models. A critical point to understanding preference models is that they rest on the assumption that all subjects in the analysis share the same perceptual map. If this assumption is not met the analysis of preference data will normally be meaningless and possibly misleading. For this reason, similarity data are typically collected along with preference data. Subjects sharing common perceptual maps are then separated into more homogeneous subgroups for preference analysis.

The basic idea upon which preference MDS analysis is based will be illustrated using a single dimension or attribute. The basic principle generalizes directly to any number of dimensions. Assume that some group of individuals perceive four objects as being located on a single dimension in the following positions.[10]

Figure C.3
An example of an "ideal" stress curve

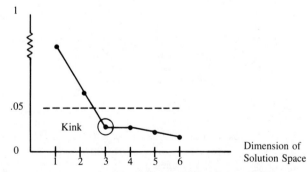

[10]This example is taken from Coombs (1950). It should be noted that the analytical technique, generally known as unfolding, developed by Coombs was superceded by later developments. The basic concept of unfolding, which this example illustrates, is retained in these subsequent techniques for analyzing preference data.

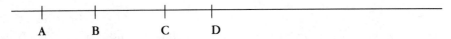

Furthermore, assume that each person has a preferred level for the attribute represented by the dimension. Geometrically this preferred level, which is called an ideal point and symbolized by I, can be placed on the same dimension as the objects; e.g.,

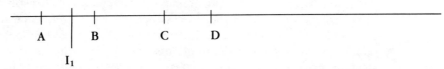

where I_1 is the ideal point for subject 1. Because two different types of data (i.e., objects and ideal points) are embedded in a common geometric space, preference MDS analysis is often referred to as *joint* space analysis.

The preference MDS model assumes that when asked to rank his or her preferences the individual will rank the object closest to his or her ideal point first, the next closest object second, and so on. Another way of looking at the process of rank ordering preferences is to think of the perceptual space as being "folded" at the ideal point; e.g.,

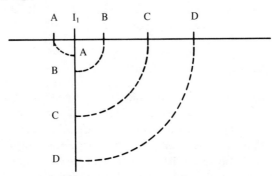

which yields ABCD as the preference ordering for subject 1.

Since all subjects are assumed to share the same perceptual space, the reported rank order of preferences depends *only* on the location of the person's ideal point. For example, if a second subject has an ideal point (I_2) just far enough to the right of I_1 to cause the rank order of preference for objects A and B to be reversed, the rank order for subject 2 would be BACD. By continuing to move the ideal point to the right, it is easy to show that *only* seven distinct rank orders of preferences are possible; i.e.,

I_1	ABCD
I_2	BACD
I_3	BCAD
I_4	CBAD
I_5	CBDA
I_6	CDBA
I_7	DCBA

The basic concept on which preference MDS analysis is based can now be stated. If there were no constraints on the data, it would be possible, given four objects, for 24 rank orders of preferences to emerge. That is, there are 4 ways to choose the most preferred object, 3 ways to choose the next most preferred object, and so on; i.e., $4 \cdot 3 \cdot 2 \cdot 1 = 24$. Because the possible rank order preferences *are* constrained by the fixed positions of the objects in the perceptual space only seven, out of 24 possible, rank orders actually occur. Furthermore, a different set of rank order preferences would occur if the subjects shared a different, but still common, perceptual space.

Given a joint space of objects and ideal points, it is clearly a simple matter to determine a rank order of preference for each subject. The task of a preference MDS analysis is to reverse this process. Specifically, a preference analysis attempts to "unfold" the preferences to recover from the rank order preference data: the number of dimensions of the solution space, the coordinates of the objects in the solution space, and the coordinates of the ideal points. Although difficult, and beyond the scope of this discussion, a number of procedures have been developed for recovering the desired information from the rank order preference data. In order to do this the data must meet *two* basic criteria. First, all subjects must share a common perceptual space. This is why it is normal practice to collect perceptual data and group subjects who share the same perceptual maps into more homogeneous subgroups for preference analysis. Second, subjects must have different ideal points. That is, the rank orders of preferences cannot be the same for all subjects. More succinctly stated, an MDS preference analysis requires *homo*geneous perceptions and *hetero*geneous preferences. Fortunately, abundant evidence indicates that preferences are far more heterogeneous than perceptions.

Managerial Uses of MDS

Although relatively recent and far more complex than our simple examples might suggest, MDS techniques have found widespread acceptance as an applied marketing research tool. To see why, recall the MDS analysis of the Chicago beer market, reproduced here for convenience as Figure C.4. Although how to conduct such an analysis has not been discussed, it is possible to have subjects rate each object in an MDS analysis on a number of unidimensional scales and mathematically fit these scales to the derived MDS solution space to facilitate interpretation of the solution. Figure C.5 presents the results of such an analysis conducted on the Chicago beer market.

Figure C.4
MDS analysis of buyers' perceptions and preferences for eight brands of beer

Source: Richard M. Johnson, "Market Segmentation: A Strategic Management Tool." *Journal of Marketing Research*, VIII (February 1971): 16. Reprinted with the kind permission of the American Marketing Association.

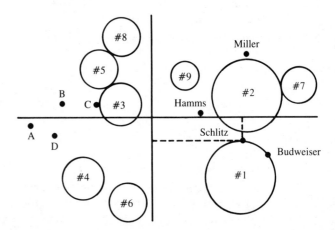

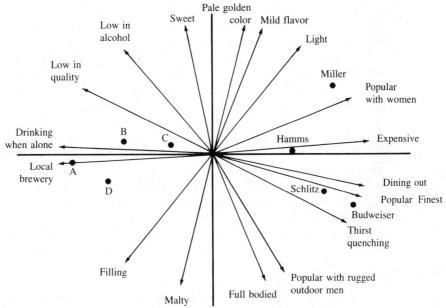

Figure C.5
Interpretation of dimensions in Figure C.4.

Source: Richard M. Johnson, "Market Segmentation: A Strategic Management Tool." *Journal of Marketing Research*, VIII (February 1971): 14. Reprinted with the kind permission of the American Marketing Association.

As Green and Tull (1978, p. 472) note, the most common managerial use of MDS techniques has been as a diagnostic tool to help managers understand how their products are positioned in buyers' minds vis á vis competing brands. This type of analysis is generally referred to as a brand image/brand positioning analysis. On the basis of Figure C.5, for example, Johnson (1971) characterized the horizontal dimension as a popular vs. premium price attribute and the vertical dimension as a relative heaviness dimension. Thus, this analysis suggests that beer brand images are formed largely on the basis of these two attributes. Note that Budweiser and Schlitz are positioned relatively close together, which suggests they are strongly competitive brands, and that both are perceived to be heavy, premium brands. In contrast, Miller is off by itself, as a light, premium beer, which suggests that Miller is not perceived as a close substitute for any of the other seven beers in the analysis. Thus, an analysis of a perceptual map can provide marketing managers with valuable information about the brands with which their brand competes directly and with insights into the attributes that buyers *actually* use to identify and evaluate brands in a given product class.

In a similar way, an analysis of the location of ideal points, and more particularly clusters of ideal points, can provide the marketing manager with insights about market opportunities. A cluster of ideal points is one way of defining a market segment. A cluster of ideal points that coincides with one or more brands (e.g., cluster 1 in Figure C.4) suggests a segment of the market that is being satisfied by existing brands. A cluster of ideal points that is not close to any brand (e.g., cluster 6) suggests a potential new product opportunity. Of course, the possibility that this segment of the market is being satisfied by brands not in the analysis must be examined.

At a more general level, as Green, Carroll, and Goldberg (1981, p. 18) note, virtually all marketing MDS studies have been concerned either directly or indirectly with the relationship between perceptual/preference maps and brand choice. The normal assumption in such studies is that the probability of choosing a brand is inversely related to the distance of a brand from a buyer's ideal point. This idea forms the basis for a number of models that attempt to predict the potential success of new products, partially on the basis of perceptual/preference map data.[11]

Most models that attempt to predict the success of new products on the basis of MDS data require the researcher to specify the characteristics of a contemplated new product. The new product is then located in the perceptual/preference space and brand choice predictions are made on the basis of the position of the new product relative to the position of existing brands and buyers' ideal points. Recently, procedures were proposed for systematically searching the perceptual/preference map for new product concepts, specified in terms of the attributes that define the solution space, which will maximize some objective function such as sales revenue, market share, or profits. Although many conceptual and methodological problems remain to be solved, the potential use of MDS techniques for the formulation of new product concepts is an exciting new development in the field of marketing. For further discussion, and numerous references to the literature regarding the use of MDS techniques in the development of new products, the reader is referred to Green, Carroll, and Goldberg (1981).

CONJOINT MEASUREMENT

Comparison with MDS

The concept of conjoint measurement is closely related to MDS. Both seek to construct geometric representations of buyer perceptions and preferences and to relate brand preference to brand choice. The task of MDS is to *reconstruct*, from perceptual and preference data, a geometric map of buyers' perceptions and ideal points. The task of conjoint measurement is to *relate* buyer preferences to a set of *prespecified* brand attributes. More specifically, the task of conjoint measurement is to determine the contribution of each attribute level to a buyer's preferences. Because preferences are typically very heterogeneous, conjoint measurement is almost always conducted at the level of the individual buyer.

An Example of Conjoint Measurement

As a simple example of conjoint analysis, consider an airline that is interested in how buyer preferences for different airlines relate to the number of stops made en route and the attitudes of flight attendants toward passengers. Assume that management decides that on the route in question two, one, or zero stops are feasible and that passengers normally put flight attendants into one of two categories, warm and friendly or curt and cold. Furthermore, let us assume that a subject could rate his or her preferences with a set of numbers, called utilities, that have interval properties and that higher utilities present a higher level of preference. Table C.1 gives data that can be used to illustrate the conjoint measurement task.

[11]For a more detailed discussion of this use of perceptual/preference maps, the reader is referred to Urban and Hauser (1980, especially Chs. 9 and 10).

Table C.1
Example of conjoint measurement for a single person evaluating airline service on two attributes

Part I. Intervally Scaled Utilities

Number of stops

Attendants	2	1	0
Warm and Friendly	2.60	2.40	2.50
Cold and Curt	.80	1.40	2.30

Part II. Estimated Part-Worths of Utility Function

Number of stops

Attendants	2	1	0	
Warm and Friendly	+.40	.00	−.40	+.50
Cold and Curt	.40	.00	+.40	−.50
	−.30	−.10	+.40	2.00

Part I of Table C.1 gives the utilities for our hypothetical subject for each of the six possible combinations of stops and flight attendant attitudes. The objective of conjoint analysis is to separate the total utility for each of the six combinations into components that represent each level of each attribute (called main effects) and into components that represent the *additional* effect of a specific level of one attribute when combined with a specific level of another attribute (called interaction effects). These components are called part-worths; i.e., each is a *part* of the total *worth* of the utility a subject has for any specific combination of product attributes.

Part II of Table C. 1 gives the part-worths. The procedure used to obtain the part-worths is the analysis of variance. To see how the procedure works note that the average utility for the six attribute combination is 2.00. Furthermore, the average utility for warm and friendly is 2.50 while the average utility for cold and curt is 1.50. Thus the main effects are .50 for warm and friendly and −.50 for cold and curt. The main effects for number of stops (i.e., −.30, −.10, and +.40) are similarly defined. Now if an attempt is made to estimate the utility for the combination of attributes warm and friendly and two stops *only* from the average for all six combinations and the main effects for these two attribute levels, the result would be

$$2.00 + .50 + (−.30) = 2.20.$$

Since the actual utility of 2.60 is .40 above this value, it is clear that there is some extra effect, above the main effects, from the *joint* occurrence of two stops and warm and friendly service. It may be for example, that passengers feel that flight attendants are going out of their way to be warm and friendly *because* of the inconvenience of two stops en route. This is, of course, only a possibility. Additional data would be needed to test this suggestion.

Conjoint Measurement in Practice

As the reader might expect, an actual conjoint measurement study requires a number of modifications and extensions of the simple example given above. First, subjects find it quite difficult to give direct, intervally scaled judgments of utility. Fortunately, such input data are not required to derive intervally scaled part-worths. Although a number of different data collection procedures have been proposed, conjoint measurement studies largely use one of two alternatives: two factor trade-offs or the full profile approach. In the two factor trade-off approach, the subject is asked to rank his or her preference for all possible combinations of the levels of two attributes. This procedure is repeated for all possible pairs of attributes.[12] The full profile data collection procedure is more frequently used. In this approach, a subject is presented with a complete description of each choice alternative. The subject is then asked to rank the alternatives in terms of preference.[13]

A second factor to be contended with in most real studies is that management is typically interested in more than two or three attributes. This presents a problem because the amount of data required from subjects increases very rapidly as the number of attributes and the number of levels per attribute increases. For example, in an actual study of preferences for airlines (Green and Wind 1975), management was interested in eight attributes; four with two levels and four with three levels. In this case, the full profile approach yields

$$2^4 \cdot 3^4 = 2 \cdot 2 \cdot 2 \cdot 2 \cdot 3 \cdot 3 \cdot 3 \cdot 3 = 1296$$

different profiles. A problem of this size is of practical importance but clearly too large for a single subject to provide complete data. Therefore, much of the research on conjoint measurement has focused on ways of reducing subject effort to manageable levels. Among the techniques developed to handle this problem are partitioning the possible profiles into subsets and confining the analysis to main effects (e.g., Green 1974; Green, Carroll, and Carmone 1978; Green, Carroll, and Goldberg 1981).

Third, and finally, the proper procedures for analyzing the input preference data must be considered. There are a number of analytical techniques. The appropriateness of each technique depends partially on the nature of the input data. Furthermore, each technique has certain advantages and disadvantages. Since the details of these techniques are well beyond the scope of our discussion, we shall simply note that the basic concepts are similar to those used for analyzing MDS data and that, in general, the different techniques yield very similar predictions (Green and Srinivasan 1978, p. 114). For further details and references to the technical literature, the reader is referred to Green and Srinivasan (1978, epsecially pp. 112–114).

[12]For a more complete description of the trade-off analysis approach to conjoint measurement, see Johnson 1974.

[13]For a discussion of the relative merit of these two data collection procedures and the circumstances where each is likely to be most effective, see Green and Srinivasan (1978, pp. 107–109).

Figure C.6
Illustration of conjoint measurement analysis of buyer preferences for eight attributes of airline service to Paris

Source: Paul E. Green and Yoram Wind, "New Way to Measure Consumers' Judgments." *Harvard Business Review*, 75 (July–August 1975): 112. Copyright © 1975 by the President and Fellows of Harvard College; all rights reserved. Reprinted by permission of the Harvard Business Review.

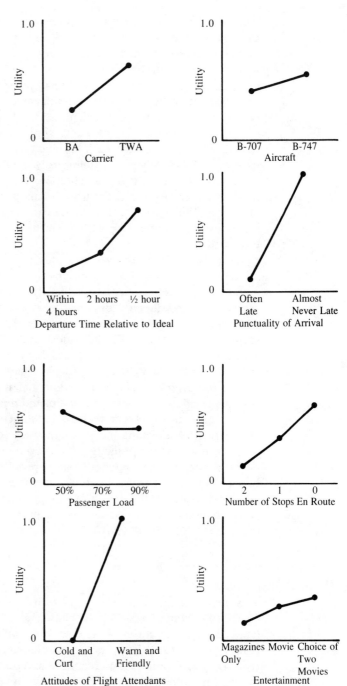

Managerial Uses of Conjoint Measurement

One of the basic uses of conjoint measurement is in analyzing the sensitivity of buyers' preferences to changes in product attributes. For example, in the previously referred to airline study (Green and Wind 1975), management was interested in the effects of eight attributes on buyers' preferences for service to Paris. In particular, management was interested in the cost-effectiveness of replacing B-707s with B-747s. As can be seen from Figure C.6, the analysis suggests that buyers are not particularly sensitive to the type of plane used. More specifically, the analysis suggests that money might be better spent on such things as improved scheduling, entertainment, and flight attendant service.

A particularly important use of conjoint measurement is in the evaluation of new products. In this use, each "profile" represents a potential new product or an existing product. Since a conjoint analysis yields an estimated utility function for each subject it is possible to compute the utility for any proposed or existing product for each subject. From such data it is possible to estimate buyers' brand choices and to aggregate this choice data into market shares. If the researcher has good cost data, potential profits from the contemplated new product can also be estimated.

Since conjoint measurement yields a separate utility function for each subject in the analysis, conjoint measurement also provides a powerful technique for identifying market segments. Specifically, individuals with similar utility functions are grouped together to form market segments. If demographic, socioeconomic, personality-life style or similar types of data have been collected, the market segments defined from the individual utility functions may be further identified. Such data can provide important insights into such things as motivational appeals and relevant media for reaching specific market segments.[14]

In the typical evaluation of potential new products management proposes several specific versions of a contemplated new product, which are then evaluated via conjoint measurement techniques. Recently, procedures were proposed for *systematically* searching the attribute space to identify combinations of attributes that maximize some objective; e.g., revenue, market share, or profit. Although major conceptual and methodological problems exist, Green, Carroll, and Goldberg (1981) report that a number of commercial applications of conjoint measurement techniques in the design of new products have been made. For details, and a generally optimistic assessment for the future of conjoint measurements, see Green, Carroll, and Goldberg (1981).[15]

SUMMARY

This appendix has given the reader an introduction to the recently developed analytical techniques generally known as MDS and conjoint measurement. As emphasized at the outset of the discussion, MDS and conjoint measurement do *not* constitute theories of buyers' perceptions and preferences. Rather, they provide *representations* of buyers' perceptions and preferences that can help the marketing manager make better decisions.

The intention of this appendix is confined to providing the reader with

[14]For further details on the use of conjoint measurement in defining market segments, see Green (1977).

[15]For a number of other potential applications of conjoint measurement techniques, see Green and Rao (1971).

knowledge of the existence and uses of these powerful analytical tools. No attempt has been made to provide a level of knowledge that would allow the reader to actually conduct a MDS or conjoint measurement study. The reader desiring a more detailed knowledge of MDS might begin by consulting Green and Carmone (1970). A more technical introduction to conjoint measurement is presented by Green and Rao (1971). Finally, the more recent references given in this appendix provide good sources of information regarding the technical issues involved in the proper application of MDS and conjoint measurement to buyers' brand perceptions and preferences.

References

Aakers, David A., and John G. Myers (1975). *Advertising Management.* Englewood Cliffs, N.J.: Prentice-Hall.

Abelson, Robert P. (1963). "Computer Simulation of 'Hot Cognitions'." In *Computer Simulation of Personality*, edited by S. Tomkins and S. Mesick. New York: Wiley & Sons.

Achenbaum, Alvin A. (1966). "Knowledge is a Thing Called Measurement." In *Attitude Research at Sea*, edited by Lee Adler and Irving Crespi. New York: American Marketing Association.

Achenbaum, Alvin A. (1972). "Advertising Doesn't Manipulate Consumers." *Journal of Advertising Research*, 12 (April): 3–13.

Adams, Bert N., and James E. Butler (1967). "Occupation Status and Husband-Wife Social Participation." *Social Forces*, 45 (June): 501–507.

Adler, Richard P. (1977). *Research on the Effects of Television Advertising on Children.* Washington, D.C.: National Science Foundation.

Adler, Richard P., Scott Ward, Gerald S. Lesser, Laurence K. Merringoff, Thomas S. Robertson, and John R. Rossiter (1980). *The Effects of Television Advertising on Children: Review and Recommendations.* Lexington, Mass.: Lexington Books.

Aguayo, Joseph M. (1977). "Latinos: Los Que Importan Son Ustedes." *Sales and Marketing Management*, (11 July): 23–29.

Ahmed, Sadrudin A., and Douglas N. Jackson (1979). "Psychographics for Social Policy Decisions: Welfare Assistance." *Journal of Consumer Research*, 5 (March): 229–239.

Aldous, J. (1971). "Framework for the Analysis of Family Problem Solving." In *Family Problem Solving* edited by J. Aldous et al. Hinsdale, Ill.: Dryden Press, 265–281.

Aldous, J., T. Condon, R. Hill, M. Strans, and I. Tillman, eds. (1971). *Family Problem Solving: A Symposium on Theoretical, Methodological, and Substantive Concerns.* Hinsdale, Ill.: Dryden Press.

Alexis, Marcus (1962). "Some Negro-White Differences in Consumption." *American Journal of Economics and Sociology*, 21 (January): 11–28.

Alexis, Marcus, George H. Haines, and Leonard Simon (1968). Consumer Information Processing: The Case of Women's Clothing. In *Proceedings, Fall Conference.* Chicago: American Marketing Association.

Allen, Chris T. (1982). "Self-Perception Based Strategies for Stimulating Energy Conservation." *Journal of Consumer Research*, 8 (March): 381–390.

Andreason, Alan R. (1965). "Attitudes and Customer Behavior: A Decision Model." In *New Research in Marketing*, edited by Lee Preston, 1–16. Berkeley: Institue of Business and Economic Research, University of California.

Andreasen, Alan R., and Peter G. Durkson (1968). "Market Learning of New Residents." *Journal of Marketing Research*, 5 (May): 166–176.

Angelus, Theodore L. (1969). "Why Do Most New Products Fail?" *Advertising Age*, (24 March 1969): 85–86.

Armstrong, Gary M., and Lawrence P. Feldman (1976). "Exposure and Sources of Opinion Leaders." *Journal of Advertising Research*, 11 (August): 21–27.

Armstrong, Gary M., and Frederick A. Russ (1975). "Detecting Deception in Advertising." *MSU Business Topics*, 23 (Spring): 21–31.

Arndt, Johan (1967). "Role of Product-Related Conversations in the Diffusion of a New Product." *Journal of Marketing Research*, 4 (August): 291–295.

Arndt, Johan (1968). "Profiling Consumer Innovators." In *Insights into Consumer Behavior*, edited by J. Arndt, 71–83. Boston: Allyn and Bacon.

Aronson, Elliot (1968). "Dissonance Theory: Progress and Problems." In *Theories of Cognitive Consistency: A Sourcebook*, edited by R. Abelson, et al. Chicago: Rand McNally.

Aronson, Elliot (1969). "Theory of Cognitive Dissonance: A Current Perspective." In *Advances in Experimental Social Psychology*, edited by L. Berkowitz. Vol. 4. New York: Academic Press.

Asch, S. E. (1952). *Social Psychology*. Engelwood Cliffs, N. J.: Prentice-Hall.

Assael, Henry (1974). "Product Classification and the Theory of Consumer Behavior." *Journal of the Academy of Marketing Science*, 2 (Fall): 539–552.

Assael, Henry (1981). *Consumer Behavior and Marketing Action*. Boston: Kent Publishing Company.

Assael, Henry, and George S. Day (1968). "Attitudes and Awareness as Predictors of Market Share." *Journal of Advertising Research*, 8 (December): 3–10.

Atkin, Charles K. (1976). "Children's Social Learning from Television: Research Evidence on Observational Modeling of Product Consumption." In *Advances in Consumer Research*, edited by B. B. Anderson, Vol. III, 513–559. Ann Arbor, Mich.: Association for Consumer Research.

Atkin, Charles K. (1978). "Observation of Parent-Child Interaction in Supermarket Decision-Making." *Journal of Marketing*, 42 (October): 41–45.

Atkin, Charles K. (1980). "Effects of Television Advertising on Children." In *Children and the Faces of Television*, edited by E. L. Palmer and A. Dorr, 287–305. New York: Academic Press.

Axel, H., ed. (1977). *A Guide to Consumer Markets 1976–1977*. The Conference Board 192.

Bagozzi, Richard P. (1975a). "Marketing as Exchange." *Journal of Marketing*, 39 (October): 32–39.

Bagozzi, Richard P. (1975b). "Social Exchange in Marketing." *Journal of the Academy of Marketing Science*, 3 (Fall): 314–327.

Bagozzi, Richard P. (1980). *Causal Models in Marketing*. New York: Wiley & Sons.

Bagozzi, Richard P., and Robert E. Burnkrant (1979). "Attitude Organization and the Attitude-Behavior Relationship." *Journal of Personality and Social Psychology*, 37 (6): 913–929.

Bagozzi, Richard P., Alice M. Tybout, C. Samuel Craig, and Brian Sternthal (1979). "The Construct Validity of the Tripartite Classification of Attitudes." *Journal of Marketing Research*, 16 (February): 88–95.

Bagozzi, Richard P., and M. Frances Van Loo (1978). "Fertility as Consumption: Theories from the Behavioral Sciences." *Journal of Consumer Research*, 4 (March): 199–228.

Baker, Michael J. (1975). *Marketing New Industrial Products*. London: The MacMillan Press, Ltd.

Baker, Michael J., and Gilbert A. Churchill, Jr. (1977). "The Impact of Physically Attractive Models on Advertising Evaluations." *Journal of Marketing Research*, 14 (November): 538–555.

Bandura, Albert (1969). *Principles of Behavior Modification*. New York: Holt, Rinehart & Winston.

Bandura, Albert (1971). *Social Learning Theory*. Morristown, N. J.: General Learning Press.

Bandura, Albert (1977). *Social Learning Theory*. Englewood Cliffs, N. J.: Prentice-Hall.

Bandura, Albert (1978). "The Self System in Reciprocal Determinism." *American Psychologist*, 33 (April): 344–358.

Barban, Arnold M. (1969). "The Dilemma of Integrated Advertising." *Journal of Business*, 42 (October): 447–496.

Barker, Roger G. (1975). "Commentaries on Belk, 'Situational Variables and Consumer Behavior.' " *Journal of Consumer Research*, 2 (December): 165.

Barry, Thomas E., and Michael G. Harvey (1974). "Marketing to Heterogeneous Black Buyers." *California Management Review*, 17 (Winter): 50–57.

Bartels, Robert (1962). *The Development of Marketing Thought.* Homewood, Ill.: Richard D. Irwin, Inc.

Bass, Frank M. (1969). "A New Product Growth Model for Consumer Durables." *Management Science*, 15 (January): 215–227.

Bass, Frank M. (1974), "The Theory of Stochastic Preference and Brand Switching." *Journal of Marketing Research*, 11 (February): 1–20.

Bauer, Raymond A. (1960). "Consumer Behavior as Risk Taking." In *Proceedings of the American Marketing Association*, edited by R. S. Hancock, 389–398. Chicago: American Marketing Association.

Bauer, Raymond A. (1966). "Negro Consumer Behavior." In *On Knowing the Consumer*, edited by Joseph W. Newman, 161–165. New York: Wiley & Sons.

Bauer, Raymond A. (1967). "Source Effect and Persuasibility: A New Look." In *Risk Taking and Information Handling in Consumer Behavior*, edited by D. F. Cox, 23–33, 559–578. Boston: Division of Research, Graduate School of Business Administration, Harvard University.

Bauer, Raymond A. (1970). "Self-Confidence and Persuasibility: One More Time." *Journal of Marketing Research*, 7 (May): 256–258.

Bauer, Raymond A., and Scott M. Cunningham (1970). *Studies in the Negro Market.* Cambridge, Mass.: Marketing Science Institute.

Bauer, Raymond A., and Stephen A. Greyser (1968). *Advertising in America: The Consumer View.* Cambridge, Mass.: Harvard University Press.

Bearden, William O., and Michael J. Etzel (1982). "Reference Group Influence on Product and Brand Purchase Decisions." *Journal of Consumer Research*, 9 (September): 183–194.

Becker, Gary S. (1962). "Irrational Behavior and Economic Theory." *Journal of Political Economy*, 70: 1–13.

Belk, Russell W. (1975a). "Situational Variables and Consumer Behavior." *Journal of Consumer Research*, 2 (December): 157–164.

Belk, Russell (1975b). "Situating the Situation: A Reply to Barker and Wicker." *Journal of Consumer Research*, 2 (December): 235–236.

Belonax, Joseph J., Jr., and Robert A. Mittelstaedt (1978). "Evoked Set Size as a Function of Number of Choice Criteria and Information Variability." In *Advances in Consumer Research*, edited by H. Keith Hunt, 48–51. Ann Arbor, Mich.

Bem, Daryl J. (1965). "An Experimental Analysis of Self-Persuasion." *Journal of Experimental Social Psychology*, 1: 199–218.

Bem, Daryl J. (1967). "Self-Perception: An Alternative Interpretation of Cognitive Dissonance Phenomena." *Psychological Review*, 74: 183–200.

Bem, Daryl J. (1968). "The Epistemological Status of Interpersonal Simulations: A Reply to Jones, Linder, Kiesler, Zanna, and Brehm." *Journal of Experimental Social Psychology*, 4 (July): 270–274.

Bem, Daryl J. (1972). "Self-Perception Theory." In *Advances in Experimental Social Psychology*, edited by L. Berkowitz, Vol. 6, 1–62. New York: Academic Press.

Bem, Daryl J., and H. K. McConnell (1970). "Testing the Self-perception Explanation of Dissonance Phenomena: On the Salience of Premanipulation Attitudes." *Journal of Personality and Social Psychology*, 14 (January): 23–41.

Bennett, Peter D., and Robert M. Mandell (1969). "Prepurchase Information Seeking Behavior of New Car Purchasers—The Learning Hypothesis." *Journal of Marketing Research*, 6 (November): 430–433.

Berelson, Bernard, and G. A. Steiner (1964). *Human Behavior: Shorter Edition.* New York: Harcourt Brace Jovanovich.

Berey, Lewis A., and Richard W. Pollay (1968). "The Influencing Role of the Child in Family Decision-Making." *Journal of Marketing Research*, 5 (February): 70–72.

Berger, Seymour M., and William W. Lambert (1968). "Stimulus-Response Theory in Contemporary Social Psychology." In *The Handbook of Social Psychology*, edited by Gardner Lindzey and Elliot Aronson, 81–178. Reading, Mass.: Addison-Wesley.

Berkowitz, Leonard (1969). "Social Motivation." In *The Handbook of Social Psychology*, edited by Gardner Lindzey and Elliot Aronson, 50–135. Reading, Mass.: Addison-Wesley.

Berlyne, D. E. (1960). *Conflict, Arousal, and Curiosity.* New York: McGraw-Hill.

Berlyne, D. E. (1963). "Motivational Problems Raised by Exploratory and Epistemic Behavior." In *Psychology: A Study of Science*, edited by S. Koch, Vol. 5. New York: McGraw-Hill.

Berlyne, D. E. (1968). "The Motivational Significance of Collative Variables and Conflict." In *Theories of Cognitive Consistency: A Sourcebook*, edited by R. P. Abelson. Skokie, Ill.: Rand McNally.

Berlyne, D. E. (1969). "Laughter, Humor, and Play." In *The Handbook of Social Psychology, 2nd ed.,* edited by Gardner Lindzey and Elliot Aronson, *Vol. III*, 795–852. Reading, Mass.: Addison-Wesley.

Berning, Carol A. Kohn, and Jacob Jacoby (1974). "Patterns of Information Acquisition in New Product Purchases." *Journal of Consumer Research*, 1 (September): 18–22.

Bettinghaus, Erwin P. (1973). *Persuasive Communication.* New York: Holt, Rinehart and Winston, Inc.

Bettman, James R. (1970). "Information Processing Models of Consumer Behavior." *Journal of Marketing Research*, 7 (August): 370–376.

Bettman, James R. (1973). "Perceived Risk and Its Components." *Journal of Marketing Research*, 10 (May): 184–190.

Bettman, James R. (1974), "Toward a Statistics for Consumer Decision Net Models." *Journal of Consumer Research*, 1 (June): 71–80.

Bettman, James R. (1979). *An Information Processing Theory of Consumer Choice.* Reading, Mass.: Addison-Wesley.

Bettman, James R., Noel Capon, and Richard J. Lutz (1975a). "Multiattribute Measurement Models and Multiattribute Attitude Theory: A Test of Construct Validity." *Journal of Consumer Research*, 1 (March): 1–15.

Bettman, James R., Noel Capon, and Richard J. Lutz (1975b). "A Multimethod Approach to Validating Multiattribute Attitude models." In *Advances in Consumer Research*, edited by M. J. Schlinger, Vol. II, 357–374. Chicago: Association of Consumer Research.

Bettman, James R., and Pradeep Kakkar (1977). "Effects of Information Acquisition Strategies." *Journal of Consumer Research*, 3 (March): 233–240.

Bexton, W. H., W. Heron, and T. H. Scott (1954), "Effects of Decreased Variation in the Environment." *Canadian Journal of Psychology*, 8: 70–76.

Birdwell, Al E. (1968). "A Study of the Influence of Image Congruence on Consumer Choice." *Journal of Business*, 41: 76–88.

Bishop, Doyle W., and Massaru Ikeda (1970). "Status and Role Factors in the Leisure Behavior of Different Occupations." *Sociology and Social Research*, 54 (January): 190–208.

Blattberg, Robert C., Thomas Buesing, and Subrata K. Sen (1980). "Segmentation Strategies for New National Brands." *Journal of Marketing*, 44 (Fall): 59–67.

Blood, R. O., Jr. (1960). "Resolving Family Conflicts." *The Journal of Conflict Resolution*, 4 (June): 209–219.

Blood, R. O., Jr., and D. M. Wolfe (1960). *Husbands and Wives: The Dynamics of Married Living*. Glencoe, Ill.: The Free Press.

Bonfield, E. H. (1974). "Attitude, Social Influence, Personal Norms, and Intention Interaction as Related to Brand Purchase Behavior." *Journal of Marketing Research*, 11 (November): 379–389.

Bonoma, Thomas V., Gerald Zaltman, and Wesley J. Johnston (1977). *Industrial Buying Behavior*. Cambridge, Mass.: Marketing Science Institute.

Boone, Louis E., and Robert E. Stevens (1970). "Emotional Motives in the Purchase of Industrial Goods: Historically Considered." *Journal of Purchasing*, 6 (August): 48–53.

Boote, A. S. (1975). "An Exploratory Investigation of the Role of Needs and Personal Values in the Theory of Buyer Behavior." Ph.D. diss., Columbia University.

Bourne, Francis S. (1957). "Group Influence in Marketing." In *Some Applications of Behavioral Research*, edited by R. Likert and S. Hayes, 208–224. Paris: UNESCO.

Bourne, Lyle E., Jr., and Bruce R. Ekstrand (1979). *Psychology: Its Principals and Meanings*, 3rd ed. New York: Holt, Rinehart and Winston.

Bower, Gordon H., John B. Black, and Terrance J. Turner (1979). "Scripts in Memory for Text." *Cognitive Psychology*, 11 (April): 177–220.

Bramel, D. (1968). "Dissonance, Expectation, and the Self," In *Theories of Cognitive Consistence: A Sourcebook*, edited by R. Abelson, et al. Chicago: Rand McNally.

Brandt, Michael T., and Ivan L. Preston (1977). "The Federal Trade Commission's Use of Evidence to Determine Deception." *Journal of Marketing*, 41 (January): 54–62.

Brehm, Jack W., and Arthur R. Cohen (1962). *Explorations in Cognitive Dissonance*. New York: Wiley & Sons.

Brislin, Richard W. (1970). "Back-Translation for Cross-Cultural Research." *Journal of Cross-Cultural Psychology*, 1 (September): 185–216.

Britt, Stewart Henderson, Stephen C. Adams, and Alan S. Miller (1972). "How Many Advertising Exposures Per Day?" *Journal of Advertising Research*, 12 (December): 3–10.

Brody, Robert P., and Scott M. Cunningham (1968). "Personality Variables and the Consumer Decision Process." *Journal of Marketing Research*, 5 (February): 50–57.

Brown, George H. (1952). "Brand Loyalty—Fact or Fiction?" *Advertising Age*, 23 (19 June), 53–55; 23 (30 June), 45–47; 23 (14 July), 54–56; 23 (28 July), 46–48; 23 (11 August), 56–58; 23 (1 September), 76–79.

Bruner, J. S. (1957). "On Perceptual Readiness." *Psychological Review*, 64: 123–152.

Bubb, Peter Lawrence, and David John van Rest (1973). "Loyalty as a Component of the Industrial Buying Decision." *Industrial Marketing Management*, 3: 25–32.

Bucklin, Louis P. (1965). "The Informative Role of Advertising." *Journal of Advertising Research*, 5 (September): 11–15.

Bucklin, Louis P. (1966). "Testing Propensities to Shop." *Journal of Marketing*, 30: 22–27.

Bucklin, Louis P. (1969). "Consumer Search, Role Enactment, and Market Efficiency." *Journal of Business*, 42: 416–438.

Burnett, John J., and Richard L. Oliver (1979). "Fear Appeal Effects in the Field: A Segmentation Approach." *Journal of Marketing Research*, 16 (May): 181–190.

Burnkrant, Robert E., and Alain Cousineau (1975). "Informational and Normative Social Influence in Buyer Behavior." *Journal of Consumer Research*, 2 (December): 206–215.

Burns, Alvin C., and Donald H. Granbois (1977). "Factors Moderating the Resolution of Preference Conflict in Family Automobile Purchasing." *Journal of Marketing Research*, 14 (February): 77–86.

Burns, Alvin C., and Donald H. Granbois (1980). "Advancing the Study of Family Purchase Decision Making." In *Advances in Consumer Research*, edited by J. Olson, 221–226, Vol. VII. Ann Arbor, Mich.: Association for Consumer Research.

Burns, Alvin C., and Mary Carolyn Harrison (1979). "A Test of the Reliability of Psychographics." *Journal of Marketing Research*, 16 (February): 32–38.

Bush, Robert R., and Frederick Mosteller (1955). *Stochastic Models for Learning.* New York: Wiley & Sons.

Bush, Ronald R., Joseph F. Hair, Jr., and Paul J. Solomon (1979). "Consumers' Level of Prejudice and Response to Black Models in Advertisements." *Journal of Marketing Research* 16 (August): 341–345.

Butz, William P., and Michael P. Ward (1979). "Baby Boom and Baby Bust: A New View." *American Demographics*, 1 (September): 11–17.

Buzzell, Robert D. (1968). "Can You Standardize Multinational Marketing." *Harvard Business Review*, 46 (November-December): 102–113.

Cagley, James W., and Richard N. Cardozo (1970). "White Responses to Integrated Advertising." *Journal of Advertising Research*, 10 (April): 35–39.

Calder, Bobby J. (1981). "Cognitive Consistency and Consumer Behavior." In *Perspectives in Consumer Behavior, 3rd ed.,* edited by Harold H. Kassarjian and Thomas S. Robertson, 258–269. Glenview, Ill.: Scott, Foresman and Company.

Calder, Bobby J., and Robert E. Burnkrant (1977). "Interpersonal Influence on Consumer Behavior: An Attribution Theory Approach." *Journal of Consumer Research*, 4 (June): 29–38.

Campbell, Brian M. (1969). "The Existence of Evoked Set and Determinants of its Magnitude in Brand Choice Behavior." Ph.D., diss., Columbia University.

Campbell, Rex R. (1966). "A Suggested Paradigm of the Individual Adoption Process." *Rural Sociology* 31 (December): 458–466.

Caplovitz, David (1964). *The Poor Pay More.* New York: The Free Press.

Carey, J. Ronald, Steven H. Clicque, Barbara A. Leighton, and Frank Milton (1976). "A Test of Positive Reinforcement of Customers." *Journal of Marketing*, 40 (October): 98–100.

Carman, James M. (1965). *The Application of Social Class in Market Segmentation.* Berkeley: Institute of Business and Economic Research, University of California.

Carman, James M. (1970). "Correlates of Brand Loyalty: Some Positive Results." *Journal of Marketing Research* 7 (February): 67–76.

Charren, Peggy (1972). "The Child Market." *BAEYC Reports*, 8 (April): 103–109.

Chase, William G., and Herbert A. Simon (1973). "Perception in Chess." *Cognitive Psychology*, 4 (January): 55–81.

Choffray, Jean-Marie, and Gary L. Lilien (1978). "Assessing Response to Industrial Marketing Strategy." *Journal of Marketing*, 42 (April): 20–31.

Choudbury, P. K., and L. S. Schnid (1974). "Black Models in Advertising to Blacks." *Journal of Advertising Research*, 14 (June): 19–22.

Clarke, Keith, and Russell W. Belk (1979). "The Effects of Product Involvement and Task Definition on Anticipated Consumer Effort." In *Advances in Consumer Research*, edited by W. L. Wilkie, 313–318, Vol. 6. Ann Arbor, Mich.: Association for Consumer Research.

Clarkson, Geoffrey P. E. (1962). *Portfolio Selection: A Stimulation of Trust Investment.* Englewood Cliffs, N. J.: Prentice-Hall.

Claxton, John D., and C. Dennis Anderson (1980). "Energy Information at the Point of Sale: A Field Experiment." In *Advances in Consumer Research*, edited by J. Olson, 277–282, Vol. 7. Ann Arbor, Mich.: Association for Consumer Research.

Claxton, John D., Joseph N. Fry, and Bernard Portis (1974). "A Taxonomy of Prepurchase Information Gathering Patterns." *Journal of Consumer Research*, 1 (December): 35–42.

Cohen, Arthur R. (1962). "An Experiment on Small Rewards for Discrepant Compliance and Attitude Change." In *Explorations in Cognitive Dissonance*, edited by J. W. Brehm and A. R. Cohen, 73–78. New York: Wiley & Sons.

Cohen, Dorothy (1972). "Surrogate Indicators and Deception in Advertising." *Journal of Marketing*, 36 (July): 10–15.

Cohen, Dorothy (1980). "The FTC'S Advertising Substantiation Program." *Journal of Marketing*, 44 (Winter): 26–35.

Cohen, Joel B. (1967). "An Interpersonal Orientation to the Study of Consumer Behavior." *Journal of Marketing Research*, 4 (August): 270–278.

Cohen, Joel B., and Ellen Golden (1972). "Informational Social Influences and Product Evaluation." *Journal of Applied Psychology*, 56 (February): 54–59.

Coleman, Richard P. (1960). "The Significance of Social Stratification in Selling." In *Marketing: A Maturing Discipline*, edited by M. L. Bell, 171–184. Chicago: American Marketing Association.

Coleman, Richard P., and Lee Rainwater (1978). *Social Standing in America: New Dimensions of Class.* New York: Basic Books.

Collins, Allan M., and M. Ross Quillian (1969). "Retrieval Time from Semantic Memory." *Journal of Verbal Learning and Verbal Behavior*, 8 (August): 240–247.

Collins, Barry E. (1969). "Financial Inducements and Attitude Change Produced by Role Players." In *Role Playing, Reward, and Attitude Change*, edited by A. C. Elms. New York: Van Nostrand.

Collins, Barry E., and Bertram H. Raven (1969). "Group Structure: Attraction, Coalitions, Communication, and Power." In *The Handbook of Social Psychology*, edited by G. Lindzey and E. Aronson, 102–204, Vol. Four. Reading, Mass.: Addison-Wesley.

Comstock, George (1978). "The Impact of Television on American Institutions." *Journal of Communication*, 28 (Spring): 12–28.

Cook, S. W., and Claire Selltiz (1964). "A Multiple-Indicator Approach to Attitude Measurement." *Psychological Bulletin*, 62: 36–55.

Cooley, James R., Donald W. Jackson, Jr., and Lonnie L. Ostrom (1978). "Relative Power in Industrial Buying Decisions." *Journal of Purchasing and Materials Management*, 14 (1): 18–20.

Coombs, Clyde H. (1950). "Psychological Scaling Without a Unit of Measurement." *Psychological Review*, 57: 148–158.

Coombs, Clyde H. (1964). *A Theory of Data*. New York: Wiley & Sons.

Cooper, Peter (1970a). "Subjective Economics: Factors in a Psychology of Speaking." In *Pricing Strategy*, edited by Bernard Taylor and Gordon Wills, 112–121. Princeton, N. J.: Brandon/Systems Press.

Cooper, Peter (1970b). "The Begrudging Index and the Subjective Value of Money." In *Pricing Strategy*, edited by Bernard Taylor and Gordon Wills, 122–131. Princeton, N. J.: Brandon/Systems Press.

Copeland, Melvin Thomas (1923). "Relation to Consumers' Buying Habits to Marketing Methods." *Harvard Business Review* 1:282–289.

Copeland, Melvin Thomas (1925). *Principles of Merchandising*. Chicago: A. W. Shaw Company.

Cort, Stanton G., and Luis V. Dominguez (1977). "Cross-Shopping and Retail Growth." *Journal of Marketing Research* 14 (May): 187–192.

Courtney, Alice E., and Sarah Wernick Lockeretz (1971). "A Woman's Place: An Analysis of the Roles Portrayed by Women in Magazine Advertisements." *Journal of Marketing Research*, 8 (February): 92–95.

Cox, Donald F. (1962). "The Measurement of Information Value: A Study in Consumer Decision-Making." In *Emerging Concepts in Marketing*, edited by W. S. Decker, 413–421. Chicago: American Marketing Association.

Cox, Donald F. ed. (1967a). *Risk Taking and Information Handling in Consumer Behavior*. Boston: Division of Research, Graduate School of Business Administration, Harvard University.

Cox, Donald F. (1967b). "Clues for Advertising Strategists." In *Risk Taking and Information Handling in Consumer Behavior*, edited by Donald F. Cox, 112–151. Boston: Division of Research, Graduate School of Business, Harvard University.

Coyle, Joseph S. (1970). "What Cost Dual Pricing?" *Progressive Grocer*, (November): 81.

Craik, Fergus I. M., and Robert S. Lockhart (1972). "Levels of Processing: A Framework for Memory Research." *Journal of Verbal Learning and Verbal Behavior*, 11 (December): 671–684.

Craik, Fergus I. M., and Endel Tulving (1975). "Depth of Processing and the Retention of Words in Episodic Memory." *Journal of Experimental Psychology: General*, 104 (September): 268–294.

Cummings, William H., and M. Venkatesan (1976). "Cognitive Dissonance and Consumer Behavior: A Review of the Evidence." *Journal of Marketing Research*, 13 (August): 303–308.

Cunningham, Isabella C. M., and Robert T. Green (1974). "Purchasing Roles in the U.S. Family, 1955 and 1973." *Journal of Marketing*, 38 (October): 61–64.

Cunningham, Ross M. (1956). "Brand Loyalty—What, Where, How Much?" *Harvard Business Review*, 34 (January–February): 116–128.

Cunningham, Scott M. (1967). "Perceived Risk and Brand Loyalty." In *Risk Taking and Information Handling in Consumer Behavior*, edited by Donald F. Cox, 507–523. Boston: Division of Research, Graduate School of Business Administration, Harvard University.

Danzig, Fred (1971). "Bristol-Myers Turns Out Parade of Clinkers." *Advertising Age*, (2 August): 1, 50.

Darby, Michael R., and Edi Karni (1973). "Free Competition and the Optimal Amount of Fraud." *Journal of Law and Economics*, 16 (April): 67–88.

Darden, William R., and William D. Perreault, Jr. (1975). "A Multivariate Analysis of Media Exposure and Vacation Behavior with Life Style Covariates." *Journal of Consumer Research*, 2 (September): 93–103.

Darden, William R., and William D. Perreault, Jr. (1976). "Identifying Interurban Shoppers: Multiproduct Purchase Patterns and Segmentation Profiles." *Journal of Marketing Research*, 8 (February): 51–60.

Darden, William R., and Fred D. Reynolds (1974). "Backward Profiling of Male Innovators." *Journal of Marketing Research*, 11 (February): 79–85.

Dardis, Rachel, and Marie Sadler (1971). "Shopping Behavior of Discount Store Customers in a Small City." *Journal of Retailing*, 47 (Summer): 60–72.

Davidson, Hugh J. (1976). "Why Most New Consumer Brands Fail." *Harvard Business Review*, 54 (March–April): 117–122.

Davis, Harry L. (1970). "Dimensions of Marital Roles in Consumer Decision Making." *Journal of Marketing Research*, 7 (May): 168–177.

Davis, Harry L. (1972). "Household Decision Making," Working Paper 72-41. Brussels: European Institute for Advanced Studies in Management.

Davis, Harry L. (1977). "Decision Making Within the Household." In *Selected Aspects of Consumer Behavior: A Summary from the Perspectives of Different Disciplines*, RANN Program, 73–99. Washington, D.C.: National Science Foundation.

Davis, Harry L., and Benny P. Rigaux (1974). "Perception of Marital Roles in Decision Processes." *Journal of Consumer Research*, 1 (June): 51–62.

Day, George S. (1969). "A Two Dimensional Concept of Brand Loyalty." *Journal of Advertising Research*, 9 (September): 29–35.

Day, George S. (1973). "Theories of Attitude Structure and Change." In *Consumer Behavior: Theoretical Sources*, edited by Scott Ward and Thomas S. Robertson, 303–353. Englewood Cliffs, N. J.: Prentice-Hall.

Day, George S., and Terry Deutscher (1983). "Attitudinal Predictions of Choices of Major Appliance Brands." *Journal of Marketing Research*, 14 (May): 192–198.

DeLozier, M. Wayne (1976). *The Marketing Communication Process.* New York: McGraw-Hill.

Deslauries, Brian C., and Peter B. Everett (1977). "The Effects of Intermittent and Continuous Token Reinforcement on Bus Ridership." *Journal of Applied Psychology*, 62 (August): 369–375.

Deutsch, M., and H. B. Gerard (1955). "A Study of Normative and Informational Social Influences upon Individual Judgment." *Journal of Abnormal and Social Psychology*, 51:629–636.

Dholakia, Ruby R., and Brian Sternthal (1977). "Highly Credible Sources: Persuasive Facilitators or Persuasive Liabilities?" *Journal of Consumer Research*, 3 (March): 223–232.

Diaz-Albertini, Luiz (1979). "Brand-Loyal Hispanics Need Good Reason for Switching," *Advertising Age*, (16 April 1979): 552–523.

Dimaggio, P., and M. Useem (1978). "Social Class and Arts Consumption." *Theory and Society*, 5 (March).

Dodson, Joe, Alice M. Tybout, and Brian Sternthal (1978). "Impact of Deals and Deal Retraction on Brand Switching." *Journal of Marketing Research*, 15 (February): 72–81.

Dolich, Ira J. (1969). "Congruence Relations Between Self Images and Product Brands." *Journal of Marketing Research*, 6 (February): 80–84.

Dommermuth, William P. (1965). "The Shopping Matrix and Marketing Strategy." *Journal of Marketing Research*, 2:128–132.

Dommermuth, William P., and E. Cundiff (1967). "Shopping Goods, Shopping Centers, and Selling Strategies." *Journal of Marketing*, 31 (October): 32–36.

Donnelly, Jr., James H. (1970). "Social Character and Acceptance of New Products." *Journal of Marketing Research*, 7 (February): 111–113.

Donnelly, Jr., James H., and John M. Ivancevich (1974). A Methodology for Identifying Innovator Characteristics of New Brand Purchasers." *Journal of Marketing Research*, 11 (August): 331–334.

Doob, A., J. Carlsmith, J. Freedmen, T. Landauer, and S. Tom (1969). "Effect of Initial Selling Price on Subsequent Sales." *Journal of Personality and Social Psychology*, 11:345–350.

Douglas, Susan P., and Christine D. Urban (1977). "Life-style Analysis to Profile Women in International Markets." *Journal of Marketing*, 41 (July):46–54.

Duncan, Calvin P., and Richard W. Olshavsky (1982). "External Search: The Role of Consumer Beliefs." *Journal of Marketing Research*, 14 (February): 32–43.

Dyer, Robert F., and Phillip G. Kuehl (1978). "A Longitudinal Study of Corrective Advertising." *Journal of Marketing Research*, 15 (February): 39–48.

Ehrenberg, A.S.C. (1968). Review of *Consumer Decision Processes: Marketing and Advertising Implications*, by Francesco Nicosia. *Journal of Marketing Research*, 5:334.

Ehrenberg, A.S.C. (1971). "Laws in Marketing: A Tailpiece." In *New Essays in Marketing Theory*, edited by George Fisk, 28–39. Boston: Allyn and Bacon, Inc.

Ehrlich, D., I. Guttman, P. Schonbach, and J. Mills (1957). "Postdecision Exposure to Relevant Information." *Journal of Abnormal and Social Psychology*, 54: 98–102.

Ehrlich, Howard J., and Dorothy Lee (1969). "Dogmatism, Learning and Resistance to Change: A Review of a New Paradigm." *Psychological Bulletin*, 71 (April):249–260.

Eighmey, John (1978). "Consumer Research and the Policy Planning of Advertising Regulation." In *The Effect of Information on Consumer and Market Behavior*, edited by A. Mitchell, 86–91. Chicago, Ill.: American Marketing Association.

Ellis, Robert A., Clayton Lane, and Virginia Olesen (1963). "The Index of Class Position: An Improved Intercommunity Measure of Stratification." *American Sociological Review*, 28 (April): 271–277.

Engel, James F., and Roger D. Blackwell (1982). *Consumer Behavior*, 4th ed. Chicago: The Dryden Press.

Engel, James F., Roger D. Blackwell, and David T. Kollat (1978). *Consumer Behavior*, 3rd ed. Hinsdale, Ill.: The Dryden Press.

Engel, James F., David T. Kollat, and Roger D. Blackwell (1969). "Personality Measures and Market Segmentation." *Business Horizons*, (June): 61–70.

Eskin, Gerald J., and John Malec (1976). "A Model for Estimating Sales Potential Prior to Test Market." In *Proceedings of the American Marketing Association*, edited by K. L. Bernhardt, 230–233.

Evans, Franklin B. (1959). "Psychological and Objective Factors in the Prediction of Brand Choice." *Journal of Business*, 32 (October): 340–369.

Evans, Richard H. (1981). "Product Involvement and Industrial Buying." *Journal of Purchasing and Materials Management*, 17 (2):23–28.

Faison, Edmund W. J. (1977). "The Neglected Variety Drive: A Useful Concept for Consumer Behavior," *Journal of Consumer Research*, 4 (December): 172–175.

Farley, John U. (1964a). "Why Does Brand Loyalty Vary Over Products?" *Journal of Marketing Research*, 1 (November): 370–381.

Farley, John U. (1964b). "Brand Loyalty and the Economics of Information," *Journal of Business*, 37 (October): 370–381.

Farley, John U., and L. Winston Ring (1970), "An Empricial Test of the Howard-Sheth Model of Buyer Behavior." *Journal of Marketing Research*, 7 (November): 427–438.

Fatt, Arthur C. (1965). "A Multi-National Approach to International Advertising." *International Executive*, 7 (Winter): 5–6.

Fatt, Arthur C. (1967). "The Danger of 'Local' International Advertising." *Journal of Marketing*, 31 (January): 60–62.

Federal Trade Commission (1967). "Permissible Period of Time During Which New Product May be Described as 'New,'" *Advisory Opinion Digest.* (120) (15 April 1967).

Feldman, Laurence P. (1980). *Consumer Protection: Problems and Prospects.* St. Paul, Minn.: West Publishing Co.

Feldman, Laurence P., and Alvin D. Star (1968). "Racial Factors in Shopping Behavior." In *A New Measure of Responsibility for Marketing*, edited by Keith Cox and Ben Enis. 216–226. Chicago: American Marketing Association.

Felson, Marcus (1975). "A Modern Sociological Approach to the Stratification of Material Lifestyles." In *Advances in Consumer Research*, edited by M. J. Schlinger. Vol. 2. Chicago: Association for Consumer Research.

Ferber, Robert (1955). "Factors Influencing Durable Goods Purchases." In *Consumer Behavior: The Dynamics of Consumer Reactions*, edited by L. H. Clark, 75–112. New York: New York University Press.

Ferber, Robert (1973). "Family Decision-Making and Economic Behavior." In *Family Economic Behavior: Problems and Prospects.* edited by E. B. Sheldon, Philadelphia: J. B. Lippincott Co.

Ferber, Robert (1977). "Applications of Behavioral Theories to the Study of Family Marketing Behavior." In *Behavioral Models for Market Analysis*, edited by F. N. Nicosia and Y. Wind.

Festinger, Leon (1954). "A Theory of Social Comparison Processes." *Human Relations*, 7 (May): 117–140.

Festinger, Leon (1957). *A Theory of Cognitive Dissonance.* Stanford, Calif.: Stanford University Press.

Fishbein, Martin (1967). "Attitude and the Prediction of Behavior." In *Readings in Attitude Theory and Measurement*, edited by Martin Fishbein, 477–492. New York: Wiley & Sons.

Fishbein, Martin, and Icek Ajzen (1974). "Attitudes Toward Objects and Predictors of Single and Multiple Behavioral Criteria." *Psychological Review*, 81:59–74.

Fishbein, Martin and Icek Ajzen (1975). *Belief, Attitude, Intention and Behavior.* Reading, Mass.: Addison-Wesley.

Fiske, D. W., and S. R. Maddi (1961). *Functions of Varied Experience.* Homewood, Ill.: Dorsey Press.

Foote, Nelson (1974). "Unfulfilled Plans and Unplanned Actions." In *Advances in Consumer Research*, vol. 1, edited by S. Ward and P. Wright, 529–531. Urbana, Ill.: Association for Consumer Research.

Ford, Jeffrey, and Elwood Ellis (1980). "A Reexamination of Group Influence on Member Brand Preference." *Journal of Marketing Research*, 12 (February): 125–132.

Fourt, Louis A., and Joseph W. Woodlock (1960). "Early Prediction of Market Success for New Grocery Products." *Journal of Marketing*, 25 (October):31–38.

Foxall, Gordon R. (1975). "Social Factors in Consumer Choice: Replication and Extension." *Journal of Consumer Research*, 2 (June): 60–64.

Frazier, E. F. (1966). *The Negro Family in the United States*, rev. abr. ed. Chicago: University of Chicago Press.

Freedman, J., and P. Sears (1965). "Selective Exposure." *Advances in Social Psychology*, Vol. 2, edited by L. Berkowitz. New York: Academic Press.

Fritzsche, David J. (1981). "An Analysis of Energy Consumption Patterns by Stage of Family Life Cycle." *Journal of Marketing Research*, 18 (May): 227–232.

FTC Staff Report on Television Advertising to Children. Washington, D.C.: Federal Trade Commission (February 1978).

Gabor, Andri, Clive Granger, and Anthony Sowter (1971). "Comments on 'Psychophysics of Prices'." *Journal of Marketing Research*, 8 (May): 251–252.

Gardner, David M. (1975). "Deception in Advertising: A Conceptual Approach." *Journal of Marketing*, 39 (January): 40–46.

Gardner, David M. (1977). "The Role of Price in Consumer Choice." In *Project on Synthesis of Knowledge of Consumer Behavior,* RANN Program, 415–433. Washington, D.C.: National Science Foundation.

Gensch, Dennis H. (1978). "Image Measurement Segmentation." *Journal of Marketing Research*, 15 (August): 384–394.

Gilden, L. Paul (1976). "Sampling Candy Bar Economics." *The New Englander*, 22 (January).

Gillett, Peter L. (1970). "A Profile of Urban In-Home Shoppers." *Journal of Marketing*, 34 (July): 40–45.

Goldberg, Marvin E., and Gerald J. Gorn. In press. "Researching the Effects of TV Advertising on Children: A Methodological Critique." In *Learning From Television: Psychological and Educational Research*, edited by M. Howe. London: Academic Press.

Goffman, Erving (1979). *Gender Advertisements.* New York: Harper Colophon Books.

Golden, Linda L. (1977). "Attribution Theory Implications for Advertisement Claim Credibility." *Journal of Marketing Research*, 14 (February): 115–117.

Gorn, Gerald J., and Marvin E. Goldberg (1982). "Behavioral Evidence of the Effects of TV Food Messages on Children." *Journal of Consumer Research*, 9 (September): 200–205.

Glasser, Gerald J., and Gale D. Metzger (1975). "Radio Usage by Blacks." *Journal of Advertising Research*, 15 (October): 39–45.

Gordon, C. Wayne (1957). *The Social System of the High School.* New York: The Free Press.

Graham, Saxon (1956). "Class and Conservatism in the Adoption of Innovations." *Human Relations*, 9: 91–100.

Granbois, Donald H. (1977). "Shopping Behavior and Preferences." In *Project of Synthesis of Knowledge of Consumer Behavior*, RANN Program, 259–298. Washington, D.C.: National Science Foundation.

Granovetter, M. (1973). "The Strength in Weak Ties." *American Journal of Sociology*, 78 (May): 1360–1380.

Gray, Francine du Plessix (1978). "Friends: A New Kind of Freedom for Women." 1978 Commencement Address delivered at Barnard College, reprinted in *Vogue*, (August 1978): 190, 191, 257.

Gray, Ralph (1978). "Cadillac Finds Youth Market: Couples Earning $40,000-plus." *Advertising Age* 2 (January): 21.

Green, Paul E. (1966). "Consumer Use of Information." In *On Knowing the Consumer*, edited by J. W. Newman, 67–80. New York: Wiley & Sons.

Green, Paul E. (1974). "On the Design of Choice Experiments Involving Multifactor Alternatives." *Journal of Consumer Research*, 1 (September): 61–68.

Green, Paul E. (1977). "A New Approach to Market Segmentation." *Business Horizons*, 20: 61–73.

Green, Paul E., and Frank J. Carmone (1970). *Multidimensional Scaling and Related Techniques in Marketing Analysis.* Boston, Mass.: Allyn and Bacon.

Green, Paul E., J. Douglas Carroll, and Frank J. Carmone (1978). "Some New Types of Fractional Designs for Marketing Experiments." In *Research in Marketing*, edited by J. N. Sheth, Vol. I. Greenwich, Conn.: JAI Press.

Green, Paul E., J. Douglas Carroll, and Stephen M. Goldberg (1981). "A General Approach to Product Design Optimization Via Conjoint Analysis." *Journal of Marketing*, 45 (Summer): 17–37.

Green, Paul E., and Vithala R. Rao (1971). "Conjoint Measurement for Quantifying Judgmental Data." *Journal of Marketing Research*, 8 (August): 355–363.

Green, Paul E., and V. Srinivasan (1978). "Conjoint Analysis in Consumer Research: Issues and Outlook." *Journal of Consumer Research*, 5 (September): 103–123.

Green, Paul E., and Donald S. Tull (1978). *Research for Marketing Decisions*, 4th ed. Englewood Cliffs, N. J.: Prentice-Hall.

Green, Paul E., and Yoram Wind (1975). "New Way to Measure Consumers' Judgments," *Harvard Business Review*, 75 (July–August): 112.

Greendorfer, Susan L. (1978). "Social Class Influence on Female Sport Involvement." *Sex Roles*, 4 (August): 619–625.

Greyser, Stephen A., and Raymond A. Bauer (1966). "Americans and Advertising: Thirty Years of Public Opinion," *Public Opinion Quarterly*, 30: 69–78.

Gronhaug, Kjelf (1973/74), "Some Factors Influencing the Size of the Buyer's Evoked Set." *European Journal of Marketing*, 7: 232–241.

Grossack, Martin H. (1964). *Understanding Consumer Behavior.* Boston: Christopher Publishing House.

Grubb, Edward L., and Gregg Hupp (1968). "Perception of Self, Generalized Stereotypes, and Brand Selection." *Journal of Marketing Research*, 5 (February): 58–63.

Guest, Lester (1944). "A Study of Brand Loyalty," *Journal of Applied Psychology*, 28 (February): 16–27.

Guest, Lester (1955). "Brand Loyalty—Twelve Years Later." *Journal of Applied Psychology*, 39 (December): 405–408.

Guest, Lester (1964). "Brand Loyalty Revisited: A Twenty Year Report." *Journal of Applied Psychology*, 48 (April): 93–97.

Guest, Lester (1970). "How Negro Models Affect Company Image." *Journal of Advertising Research*, 10 (April): 29–33.

Haines, George H. (1964). "A Theory of Market Behavior After Innovation." *Management Science*, 10 (July): 634–658.

Haines, George H. (1974a). "Information and Consumer Behavior." In *Models of Buyer Behavior: Conceptual, Quantitative, and Empirical*, edited by Jagdish N. Sheth, 108–125. New York: Harper & Row.

Haines, George H. (1974b). "Process Models of Consumer Decision Making." In *Buyer/Consumer Information Processing*, edited by G. David Hughes and Michael L. Ray, 89–107. Chapel Hill: University of North Carolina Press.

Haire, Mason (1950). "Projective Techniques in Marketing Research." *Journal of Marketing*, 14 (April): 649–656.

Haley, Russell I., and Peter B. Case (1979). "Testing Thirteen Attitude Scales for Agreement and Brand Discrimination." *Journal of Marketing*, 43 (Fall): 20–32.

Hall, Calvin S., and Gardner Lindzey (1968). "The Relevance of Freudian Psychology and Related Viewpoints for the Social Sciences." In *The Handbook of Social Psychology*, edited by Gardner Lindzey and Elliot Aronson, 2nd ed., Vol. I, 245–319. Reading, Mass.: Addison-Wesley.

Hansen, Fleming (1969). "Consumer Choice Behavior: An Experimental Approach." *Journal of Marketing Research*, 6 (November): 436–443.

Hansen, Fleming (1970a). "Primary Group Influence and Consumer Conformity." In *Marketing Involvement in Society and the Economy*, edited by P. R. McDonald, 300–305. Chicago: American Marketing Association.

Hansen, Fleming (1970b). "Consumer Choice Behavior: An Experimental Approach." *Journal of Marketing Research*, 6 (November): 436–443.

Hansen, Fleming (1972). *Consumer Choice Behavior: A Cognitive Theory.* New York: The Free Press.

Hansen, Fleming (1981). "Hemispheral Lateralization: Implications for Understanding Consumer Behavior." *Journal of Consumer Research*, 8 (June): 23–36.

Hansen, Robert A., and Carol A. Scott (1976). "Comments on Attribution Theory and Advertising Credibility." *Journal of Marketing Research*, 13 (May): 193–197.

Hauser, Robert M., Peter J. Dickinson, Harry P. Travis, and John N. Koffel (1975). "Structural Changes in Occupational Mobility Among Men in the United States." *American Sociological Review*, 40 (October): 585–598.

Hauser, Robert M., and David L. Featherman (1977). *The Process of Stratification.* New York: The Academic Press.

Hawes, Douglass K., Rogert D. Blackwell, and W. Wayne Talarzyk (1977). "Attitudes Towards Use of Credit Cards: Do Men and Women Differ?" *Baylor Business Studies*, 110 (January): 57–71.

Hawkins, Del I., Kenneth A. Coney, and Roger J. Best (1980). *Consumer Behavior: Implications for Marketing Strategy.* Dallas, Texas: Business Publications, Inc.

Heider, Fritz (1944). "Social Perception and Phenomenal Causality." *Psychological Review*, 51: 358–374.

Heider, Fritz (1958). *The Psychology of Interpersonal Relations.* New York: John Wiley and Sons.

Hempel, D. J. (1969). "Search Behavior and Information Utilization in the Home Buying Process." In *Marketing Involvement in Society and the Economy*, edited by P. R. McDonald, 241–249. Chicago: American Marketing Association.

Hempel, Donald J. (1975). "Family Role Structure and Housing Decisions," *Advances in Consumer Research, Vol. II.* Association for Consumer Research.

Henderson, James M., and Richard E. Quandt (1958). *Microeconomic Theory: A Mathematical Approach.* New York: McGraw-Hill.

Henry, Walter A. (1976). "Cultural Values Do Correlate with Consumer Behavior," *Journal of Marketing Research*, 13 (May), 121–127.

Herbst, P. G. (1952). "The Measurement of Family Relationships," *Human Relations*, 5 (February), 3–35.

Herniter, Jerome D. and Victor J. Cook (1978). "A Multidimensional Stochastic Model of Consumer Purchase Behavior," In *Behavioral and Management Science in Marketing*, edited by A. S. Silk and H. J. Davis, 237–268. New York: John Wiley and Sons.

Hess, E. H. (1965). "Attitude and Pupil Size." *Scientific American*, 212: 46–54.

"Hidden Costs." *The Wall Street Journal*, 15 February 1977: 1.

Hill, Winfred F. (1977). *Learning: A Survey of Psychological Interpretations*, 3rd ed. New York: Thomas Y. Crowell Company.

Hirisch, R., and M. Peters (1974). "Selecting the Superior Segmentation Correlate." *Journal of Marketing*, 38 (July): 60–63.

Hirschman, Elizabeth C. (1980). "Innovativeness, Novelty Seeking, and Consumer Creativity." *Journal of Consumer Research*, 7 (December): 283–295.

Hirschman, Elizabeth C., and Morris B. Holbrook (1982). "Hedonic Consumption: Emerging Concepts, Methods and Propositions." *Journal of Marketing*, 46 (Summer): 92–101.

Holbrook, Morris B., and Elizabeth C. Hirschman (1982). "The Experiential Aspects of Consumption: Consumer Fantasies, Feelings, and Fun." *Journal of Consumer Research*, 9 (September): 132–140.

Holbrook, Morris B., and John A. Howard (1977). "Frequently Purchased Nondurable Goods and Services." In *Selected Aspects of Consumer Behavior: A Summary from the Perspective of Different Disciplines*, RANN Program, 189–222. Washington, D.C.: National Science Foundation.

Hollingshead, August B. (1949). *Elmstown's Youth.* New York: Wiley & Sons.

Hollingshead, August B., and Frederick C. Redlick (1958). *Social Class and Mental Illness.* New York: Wiley & Sons.

Holt, E. G. (1931) *Animal Drive and the Learning Process.* New York: Holt, Rinehart and Winston.

Horton, Raymond L. (1973a). "On the Appropriateness of Brand Loyalty and Brand Choice as Dependent Variables in Consumer Personality Studies." *Proceedings of the Southern Marketing Association*, 147–151.

Horton, Raymond L. (1973b). "Personality as a Moderator Variable in the Purchase Decision." Doctoral diss., Indiana University.

Horton, Raymond L. (1974). The Edwards Personal Preference Schedule and Consumer Personality Research." *Journal of Marketing Research*, 11 (August): 335–337.

Horton, Raymond L. (1976). "The Structure of Perceived Risk: Some Further Progress." *Journal of the Academy of Marketing Science,* 4 (Fall): 694–706.

Horton, Raymond L. (1979). "Some Relationships Between Personality and Consumer Decision Making." *Journal of Marketing Research*, 16 (May): 233–246.

Horton, Raymond L. (1983a). "A Study of the Effects of Information on the Size of the Evoked Set." In *Developments in Marketing Science*, Vol. VI. Miami, Fla.: Academy of Marketing Science, 72–77.

Horton, Raymond L. (1983b). "An Experimental Study of the Effects of Number of Available Brands and Attributes on Consumer Information Aquisition." In *Proceedings of the 1983 American Marketing Association Educators Conference*, edited by Patrick Murphy et al., 102–107. Chicago: American Marketing Association.

Horton, Raymond L., Lauren Lieb, and Martin Hewitt (1982). "The Effects of Nudity, Suggestiveness, and Attractiveness on Product Class and Brand Name Recall." In *Developments in Marketing Science*, Vol. V. Miami, Fla.: Academy of Marketing Science, 456–459.

Hoult, Thomas Ford (1954). "Experimental Measurement of Clothing as a Factor in Some Social Ratings of Selected American Men." *American Sociological Review*, 19 (June): 324–325.

Houston, Michael J. (1979). "Consumer Evaluations and Products Information Sources," In *Current Issues and Research in Advertising*, edited by J. H. Leigh and C. R. Martin, Jr., 135–144. Ann Arbor: Graduate School of Business, University of Michigan.

Howard, John A. (1963). *Marketing Management: Analysis and Planning.* Homewood, Ill.: Richard D. Irwin.

Howard, John A. (1973). *Marketing Management: Operating, Strategic, and Administrative,* 3rd ed. Homewood, Ill.: Richard D. Irwin, Inc.

Howard, John A. (1974). "Confidence as Validated Construct." In *Buyer Behavior*, edited by John A. Howard and Lyman E. Ostlund, 426–442. New York: Alfred A. Knopf.

Howard, John A. (1977). *Consumer Behavior: Application of Theory.* New York: McGraw-Hill.

Howard, John A., and Lyman E. Ostlund (1973). "The Model: Current Status of Buyer Behavior Theory." In *Buyer Behavior*, edited by John A. Howard and Lyman E. Ostlund, 3–32. New York: Alfred A. Knopf.

Howard, John A., and Jagdish N. Sheth (1969). *The Theory of Buyer Behavior.* New York: Wiley & Sons.

Hughes, G. David (1971). *Attitude Measurement for Marketing Strategies.* Glenview, Ill.: Scott, Foresman and Company.

Hunt, J. M. (1963): "Motivation Inherent in Information Processing and Action." In *Motivation and Social Interaction—Cognitive Determinants*, edited by O. J. Harvey. New York: The Ronald Press.

Isakson, Hans R., and Alex R. Maurizi (1973). "The Consumer Economics of Unit Pricing." *Journal of Marketing Research*, 10 (August): 277–285.

Jacoby, Jacob (1971). "Personality and Innovation Proneness." *Journal of Marketing Research*, 8 (May): 244–247.

Jacoby, Jacob (1975). "A Brand Loyalty Concept—A Comment on a Comment." *Journal of Marketing Research*, 12 (November): 484–487.

Jacoby, Jacob, and Robert W. Chestnut (1978). *Brand Loyalty: Measurement and Management.* New York: Wiley & Sons.

Jacoby, Jacob, and David B. Kyner (1973). "Brand Loyalty vs. Repeat Purchasing Behavior." *Journal of Marketing Research*, 10 (February): 1–9.

Jacoby, Jacob, Margaret C. Nelson, and Wayne D. Hoyer (1982). "Corrective Advertising and Affirmative Disclosure Statements: Their Potential for Confusing and Misleading the Consumer." *Journal of Marketing*, 46 (Winter): 61–72.

Jacoby, Jacob, George J. Szybillo, and Jacqueline Busato-Schach (1977). "Information Acquisition Behavior in Brand Choice Situations." *Journal of Consumer Research*, 3 (March): 209–216.

Jacoby, Jacob, George J. Szybillo, and Carol Kohn Berning (1977). "Time and Consumer Behavior: An Interdisciplinary Overview." Project on Synthesis of Knowledge of Consumer Behavior, RANN Program, 451–475. Washington, D.C.: National Science Foundation.

Jain, Arun K. (1975). "A Method for Investigating and Representing Implicit Social Class Theory," *Journal of Consumer Research*, 2 (June): 53–59.

Jarvis, Lance P., and James B. Wilcox (1973). "Evoked Set Size—Some Theoretical Foundations and Empirical Evidence." In *Combined Proceedings Fall Conference of the American Marketing Association*, edited by Thomas V. Greer 236–240. Chicago: American Marketing Association.

Jenkins, Roger L. (1980). "Contributions of Theory to the Study of Family Decision-Making." In *Advances in Consumer Research*, edited by J. Olson, Vol. VII, 207–211. Ann Arbor, Mich.: Association for Consumer Research.

Johnson, Eric J., and J. Edward Russo (1978). "The Organization of Product Information in Memory Identified by Recall Times." In *Advances in Consumer Research*, edited by H. Keith Hunt, Vol. V, 79–86. Ann Arbor, Mich.: Association for Consumer Research.

Johnson, Richard M. (1971). "Market Segmentation: A Strategic Management Tool." *Journal of Marketing Research*, 8 (February): 13–18.

Johnson, Richard M. (1974). "Trade-Off Analysis of Consumer Values." *Journal of Marketing Research*, 11 (May): 121–127.

Johnston, Wesley J. (1981). *Patterns in Industrial Buying Behavior.* New York: Praeger Publishers.

Johnston, Wesley J., and Thomas V. Bonoma (1981). "The Buying Center: Structure and Interaction Patterns." *Journal of Marketing*, 45 (Summer): 143–156.

Jones, Edward E., and Keith E. Davis (1965). "From Acts to Dispositions: The Attribution Process in Person Perception." In *Advances in Experimental Social Psychology*, edited by L. Berkowitz, Vol 2. New York: Academic Press.

Jones, Edward E., and Harold B. Gerard (1967). *Social Psychology.* New York: Wiley & Sons, Inc.

Jones, J. Morgan (1970a). "A Dual-Effects Model of Brand Choice." *Journal of Marketing Research*, 7 (November): 458–464.

Jones, J. Morgan (1970b). "A Comparison of Three Models of Brand Choice." *Journal of Marketing Research*, 7 (November): 466–473.

Kahle, Lynn R., and John J. Berman (1979). "Attitudes Cause Behaviors: A Cross-Lagged Panel Analysis." *Journal of Personality and Social Psychology*, 37 (March): 315–321.

Kahneman, D. (1973). *Attention and Effort.* Englewood Cliffs, N. J.: Prentice-Hall.

Kalwani, Manohar U., and Donald G. Morrison (1977). "A Parsimonious Description of the Hendry System." *Management Science*, 23 (January): 467–477.

Kassarjian, Harold H. (1965). "Social Character and Differential Preference for Mass Communication." *Journal of Marketing Research*, 2 (May): 146–153.

Kassarjian, Harold H. (1971). "Personality and Consumer Behavior: A Review." *Journal of Marketing Research*, 8 (November): 409–418.

Kassarjian, Harold H. (1973). "Field Theory in Consumer Behavior." In *Consumer Behavior: Theoretical Sources*, edited by Scott Ward and Thomas S. Robertson, 118–140. Englewood Cliffs, N. J.: Prentice-Hall.

Kassarjian, Harold H. (1978). "Presidential Address, 1977: Anthropomorphism and Parsimony." In *Advances in Consumer Research*, edited by H. Keith Hunt, Vol. 5. Ann Arbor, Mich.: Association for Consumer Research, xii–xiv.

Kassarjian, Harold H. (1982). "Consumer Psychology." *Annual Review of Psychology*, 33: 619–649.

Katona, George (1960). *The Powerful Consumer.* New York: McGraw-Hill.

Katona, George, and Eva Mueller (1955). "A Study of Purchase Decisions." In *Consumer Behavior: The Dynamics of Consumer Reactions*, edited by L. H. Clark, 30–87. New York: New York University Press.

Katz, Daniel (1960). "The Functional Approach to the Study of Attitudes." *Public Opinion Quarterly*, 24 (Summer): 163–204.

Katz, Elihu, and P. F. Lazarfeld (1955). *Personal Influence.* New York: The Free Press.

Katz, Herbert, and Elihu Katz (1956). "Social Relations and Innovations in the Medical Profession: The Epidemiology of a New Drug." *Public Opinion Quarterly*, 19 (Winter): 337–352.

Kelley, Harold H. (1952). "The Two Functions of Reference Groups." In *Readings in Social Psychology*, edited by G. E. Swanson, T. M. Newcomb, and E. C. Hartley, 410–414. New York: Holt.

Kelley, Harold H. (1967). "Attribution Theory in Social Psychology." In *Nebraska Symposium on Motivation*, edited by D. Levine. Lincoln: University of Nebraska Press.

Kelley, Harold H. (1971). *Attribution in Social Interaction.* Morristown, N. J.: General Learning Press.

Kelley, Harold H. (1973). "The Processes of Causal Attribution." *American Psychologist*, 28: 107–128.

Kelly, Robert F. (1967). "Estimating Ultimate Performance Levels of New Retail Outlets." *Journal of Marketing Research*, 4 (February): 13–19.

Kelly, Robert F. (1968). "The Search Component of the Consumer Decision Process—A Theoretic Examination." In *Marketing and the New Science of Planning*, edited by C. King. Chicago: American Marketing Association.

Kelman, Herbert C. (1961). "Processes of Opinion Change." *Public Opinion Quarterly*, 25: 57–78.

Kelman, Herbert C. (1974). "Attitudes Are Alive and Well and Gainfully Employed in the Sphere of Action," *American Psychologist*, 29 (May): 310–324.

Kerlinger, F. N. (1973). *Foundations of Behavioral Research,* 2nd ed. New York: Holt, Rinehart and Winston.

Kernan, Jerome B., William P. Dommermuth, and Montrose S. Sommers (1970). *Promotion: An Introductory Analysis.* New York: McGraw-Hill.

Kiesler, Charles A., Barry E. Collins, and Norman Miller (1969). *Attitude Change: A Critical Analysis of Theoretical Approaches.* New York: Wiley & Sons.

Kimble, Gregory A. (1968). *Hilgard and Marquis' Conditioning and Learning*, 2nd ed. New York: Appleton-Century-Crofts.

King, Charles W., and John O. Summers (1970). "Overlap of Opinion Leadership Across Consumer Product Categories." *Journal of Marketing Research*, 7 (February): 43–50.

Kiser, G. E. (1976). "Elements of Purchasing Strategy." *Journal of Purchasing and Materials Management*, 12 (3): 3–7.

Kiser, G. E., and S. R. G. Rao (1971). "Purchasing Agents Are Obsolete." *Journal of Purchasing*, 7 (May): 5–14.

Klaus, Marshall H., and John H. Kennell (1976). *Maternal-Infant Bonding.* Saint Louis, Mo.: The C. V. Mosby Company.

Kluckhohn, Florence, and Fred Strodtbeck (1961). *Variations in Value Orientation.* Evanston, Ill.: Row, Peterson.

Kotler, Philip (1956). "Behavioral Models for Analyzing Buyers." *Journal of Marketing*, 29 (October): 37–45.

Kotler, Philip (1967). *Marketing Management.* Englewood Cliffs, N. J.: Prentice-Hall.

Kotler, Philip (1971). *Marketing Decision Making: A Model Building Approach.* New York: Holt, Rinehart and Winston.

Kotler, Philip (1972). *Marketing Management*, 2nd ed. Englewood Cliffs, N. J.: Prentice-Hall.

Kotler, Philip (1980). *Marketing Management*, 4th ed. Englewood Cliffs, N. J.: Prentice-Hall.

Kotler, Philip, and Sidney J. Levy (1971). "Demarketing, Yes, Demarketing." *Harvard Business Review*, 49 (November–December): 74–80.

Kourilsky, Marilyn, and Trudy Murray (1981). "The Use of Economic Reasoning to Increase Satisfaction with Family Decision Making." *Journal of Consumer Research*, 8 (September); 183–188.

Krech, David, Richard S. Crutchfield, and Egerton L. Ballachery (1962). *Individual in Society.* New York: McGraw-Hill.

Kroeber, A. L., and C. Kluckhohn (1952). "Culture: A Critical Review of Concepts and Definitions." *Papers Peabody Mus.*, 47 (1).

Kroeber-Riel, Werner (1979). "Activation Research: Psychobiological Approaches in Consumer Research." *Journal of Consumer Research*, 5 (March): 240–250.

Kroeber-Riel, Werner (1980). "Rejoinder." *Journal of Consumer Research*, 7 (June): 96–98.

Krugman, Herbert E. (1965). "The Impact of Television Advertising: Learning Without Involvement." *Public Opinion Quarterly*, 29 (Fall): 349–356.

Krugman, Herbert E. (1979). "Low Involvement Theory in the Light of New Brain Research." In *Attitude Research Plays for High Stakes*, edited by J. C. Maloney and B. Silverman, 16–22. Chicago: American Marketing Association.

Kuehn, Alfred A. (1962a). "How Advertising Performance Depends on Other Marketing Factors." *Journal of Advertising Research*, 2 (March): 2–10.

Kuehn, Alfred A. (1962b). "Consumer Brand Choice as a Learning Process." *Journal of Advertising Research*, 2 (December): 10–17.

Kuehn, Alfred A., and Ralph L. Day (1964). "Probabilistic Models of Consumer Buying Behavior." *Journal of Marketing*, 29 (October): 27–31.

Lancaster, Kelvin (1971). *Consumer Demand: A New Approach.* New York: Columbia University Press.

Lancaster, Kelvin (1977). "Theories of Consumer Choice from Economics: A Critical Survey." In *Project on Synthesis of Knowledge of Consumer Behavior*, RANN Program, 11–31. Washington, D.C.: National Science Foundation.

Lambert, Zarrel V. (1972). "Perceptual Patterns, Information Handling, and Inovativeness." *Journal of Marketing Research* 9 (November): 427–431.

Landon, E. Laird, and D. R. Emery (1975). "Causal Attribution of Consumer Dissatisfaction as a Predictor of Consumer Complaint Action: A Preliminary Report." In *Advances in Consumer Behavior*, edited by J. Schlinger. Vol. 2. Chicago: Association for Consumer Research.

Larson, Carl M. (1968). "Racial Brand Usage and Media Exposure Differentials." In *A New Measure of Responsibility for Marketing*, edited by Keith Cox and Ben Enis, 208–215. Chicago: American Marketing Association.

Larson, Carl M., and Hugh G. Wales (1973). "Brand Preferences of Chicago Blacks." *Journal of Advertising Research,* 13 (August): 15–21.

Lastovicka, John L. (1982). "On the Validation of Lifestyle Traits: A Review and Illustration." *Journal of Marketing Research*, 19 (February): 126–138.

Laumann, Edward O., and James S. House (1970). "Living Room Styles and Social Attributes: The Patterning of Material Artifacts in a Modern Urban Community." *Sociology and Social Research*, 54 (April): 326.

Lavidge, Robert J., and Gary A. Steiner (1961). "A Model of Predictive Measurements of Advertising Effectiveness." *Journal of Marketing*, 25 (October): 59–62.

Lazer, William, and John E. Smallwood (1977). "The Changing Demographics of Women." *Journal of Marketing*, 41 (July): 14–22.

Learner, David B. (1968). "Profit Maximization Through New-Product Marketing Planning and Control." In *Applications of the Sciences in Marketing Management.* edited by F. M. Bass, C. W. King, and E. A. Pessemier, 151–167. New York: Wiley & Sons.

Lehmann, Donald R., William L. Moore, and Terry Elrod (1982). "The Development of Distinct Choice Process Segments Over Time: A Stochastic Modeling Approach." *Journal of Marketing*, 46 (Spring): 48–59.

Lehmann, Donald R., and John O'Shaughnessy (1974). "Difference in Attribute Importance for Different Industrial Products." *Journal of Marketing*, 38 (April): 36–42.

Lehmann, Donald R., and John O'Shaughnessy (1982). "Decision Criteria Used in Buying Different Categories of Products." *Journal of Purchasing and Materials Management*, 18 (1): 9–14.

Lenski, Gerhard E. (1966). *Power and Privileges*. New York: McGraw-Hill.

Leonard-Barton, Dorothy (1981). "Voluntary Simplicity Lifestyles and Energy Conservation." *Journal of Consumer Research*, 8 (December): 243–252.

Levy, Sidney J. (1966). "Social Class and Consumer Behavior." In *On Knowing the Consumer*, edited by J. W. Newman, 146–160. New York: John Wiley & Sons.

Levy, Sidney J. (1971). "Symbolism and Lifestyle." In *Perspectives in Marketing Management*, edited by F. D. Sturdivant. 112–118. Glenview, Ill.: Scott, Foresman and Company.

Linden, Fabian (1977). "Downstairs, Upstairs." *Across the Board*, XIV (October), The Conference Board, Inc.

Lindzey, Gardner, and Elliot Aronson (1969). *The Handbook of Social Psychology*, 2nd ed., Vol. IV. Reading, Mass.: Addison-Wesley.

Lipstein, Benjamin (1965). "A Mathematical Model of Consumer Behavior." *Journal of Marketing Research*, 2 (August): 259–265.

Liu, W. T., and R. W. Duff (1972). "The Strength of Weak Ties." *Public Opinion Quarterly*, 36 (Fall): 361–366.

Locander, William B., and W. Austin Spivey (1978). "A Functional Approach to Attitude Measurement." *Journal of Marketing Research*, 15 (November): 576–587.

Lorenz, Konrad Z. (1952). *King Solomon's Ring*. New York: Crowell.

Lorenz, Konrad Z. (1966). *On Agression*. New York: Harcourt Brace Jovanovich.

Loudon, David L., and Albert J. Della Bitta (1979). *Consumer Behavior: Concepts and Applications*. New York: McGraw-Hill.

Lundstrom, William J., and Donald Sciglimpaglia (1977). "Sex Role Portrayals in Advertising." *Journal of Marketing*, 41 (July): 72–79.

Lunn, J. A. (1974). "Consumer Decision-Process Models," In *Models of Buyer Behavior*, edited by Jagdish N. Sheth, 34–69. New York: Harper & Row.

Lutz, Richard J. (1975). "Changing Brand Attitudes Through Modification of Cognitive Structures." *Journal of Consumer Research*, 1 (March): 49–59.

Lutz, Richard J. (1979). "A Functional Theory Framework for Designing and Pretesting Advertising Themes." In *Attitude Research Plays for High Stakes*, edited by J. C. Maloney and B. Silverman, 37–49. Chicago: American Marketing Association.

Lutz, Richard J., and James R. Bettman (1977). "Multiattribute Models in Marketing: A Bicentennial Review." In *Consumer and Industrial Buying Behavior*, edited by A. G. Woodside, J. N. Sheth, and P. D. Bennett, 137–149. New York: North-Holland.

McAlister, Leigh (1982). "A Dynamic Attribute Satiation Model of Variety Seeking Behavior." *Journal of Consumer Research*, 9 (September): 141–150.

McCall, Suzanne H. (1977). "Meet the 'Workwife'." *Journal of Marketing*, 41 (July): 55–56.

McCann, Charles B. (1957). *Women and Department Store Newspaper Advertising*. Chicago: Social Research, Inc.

McDougall, W. (1908). *Introduction to Social Psychology*. London: Methuen.

McDougall, W. (1923). *Outline of Psychology.* New York: Charles Scribner's Sons.

McEwen, William J. (1978). "Bridging the Information Gap." *Journal of Consumer Research*, 4 (March): 247–251.

McGuire, William J. (1969). "The Nature of Attitudes and Attitude Change." In, *The Handbook of Social Psychology*, 2nd ed., edited by Gardner Lindzey and Elliot Aronson, Vol. III, 136–314. Reading, Mass.: Addison-Wesley.

McGuire, William J. (1976). "The Concept of Attitudes and Their Relations to Behavior." In *Perspectives on Attitude Assessment: Surveys and Their Alternatives*, edited by N. W. Sinaiko and A. Broedling. Champaign, Ill.: Pendleton.

Maddi, S. R. (1968). "The Pursuit of Consistency and Variety." In *Theories of Cognitive Consistency: A Sourcebook*, edited by R. P. Abelson, et al. Skokie, Ill.: Rand McNally.

Maddox, R. Neil, Kjell Gronhaug, Richard D. Homans, and Frederick E. May (1978). "Correlates of Information Gathering and Evoked Set Size for Automobile Purchasers in Norway and U.S." In *Advances in Consumer Research*, edited by H. Keith Hunt, Vol. V, 167–170. Ann Arbor, Mich.: Association for Consumer Research.

Mahajan, Vijay and Eitan Muller (1979). "Innovation Diffusion and New Products Growth Models in Marketing." *Journal of Marketing*, 43 (Fall): 55–68.

Maloney, J. C. (1962). "Curiosity Versus Disbelief in Advertising." *Journal of Advertising Research*, 2: 2–8.

Management of New Products (1968). Chicago: Booz, Allen & Hamilton, Management Consultants.

Mancuso, Joseph R. (1969). "Why Not Create Opinion Leaders for New Product Introduction?" *Journal of Marketing*, 33 (July): 20–25.

March, James G. and Herbert A. Simon (1958). *Organizations.* New York: John Wiley & Sons, Inc.

Marketing News (1978). "Hendry System Gives Marketers Handle on Buyers Prior to New Brand Introduction" (interview with Ben Butler, Jr., president of the Hendry Corporation), American Marketing Association (8 September): 5.

Markin Rom J., Jr. (1974). *Consumer Behavior: A Cognitive Orientation.* New York: Macmillan.

Markin, Rom J. (1977). "Motivation in Buyer Theory," In *Consumer and Industrial Buying Behavior*, edited by Arch G. Woodside, et al. 37–48. New York: North-Holland.

Markin, Rom J., and Chem L. Narayana (1976). "Behavior Control: Are Consumers Beyond Freedom and Dignity?" In *Advances in Consumer Research*, edited by B. B. Anderson, Vol. III, 222–228. Ann Arbor, Mich.: Association of Consumer Research.

Martilla, John A. (1971). "Word-of-Mouth Communication in the Industrial Adoption Process." *Journal of Marketing Research*, 8 (May): 173–178.

Martineau, Pierre (1958). "Social Classes and Spending Behavior." *Journal of Marketing*, 23 (October): 121–129.

Maslow, A. H. (1973a). "Theory of Human Motivation," In *Dominance, Self-esteem, Self-actualization: Germinal Papers of A. H. Maslow*, edited by R. J. Lowry. Monterey, Calif.: Brooks Cole.

Maslow, A. H. (1973b). "Self-actualizing People: A Study of Psychological Health." In *Dominance, Self-esteem, Self-actualization: Germinal Papers of A. H. Maslow*, edited by R. J. Lowry. Monterey, Calif.: Brooks Cole.

Massey, William F. (1969). "Forecasting Demand for New Convenience Products." *Journal of Marketing Research*, 6 (November): 405–412.

Massy, William F., Ronald E. Frank, and Thomas M. Lodahl (1968). *Purchasing Behavior and Personal Attributes.* Philadelphia: University of Pennsylvania Press.

Massy, William F., David B. Montgomery, and Donald G. Morrison (1970). *Stochastic Models of Buying Behavior.* Cambridge, Mass.: M.I.T. Press.

Mathews, H. Lee and John W. Slocum, Jr. (1969). "Social Class and Commercial Bank Credit Card Usage." *Journal of Marketing*, 33 (January): 71–78.

May, Frederick E. and Richard E. Homans (1977). "Evoked Set Size and the Level of Information Processing in Product Comprehension and Choice Criteria." In *Advances in Consumer Research*, edited by William D. Pereault, Jr., Vol. IV, 172–175. Ann Arbor, Mich.: Association for Consumer Research.

Mazis, Michael B., and Janice E. Adkinson (1976). "An Experimental Evaluation of a Proposed Corrective Advertising Remedy." *Journal of Marketing Research*, 13 (May): 173–177.

Mazis, Michael B., Olli T. Ahtola, and R. Eugene Klippel (1975). "A Comparison of Four Multi-Attribute Models in the Prediction of Consumer Attitudes." *Journal of Consumer Research*, 2 (June): 38–52.

Michaels, Peter W. (1973). "Life Style and Magazine Exposure." In *Marketing Education and the Real World and Dynamic Marketing in a Changing World*, Combined Proceedings of the Spring and Fall Conferences of the American Marketing Association, edited by B. W. Becker and H. Becker, 324–331. Chicago: American Marketing Association.

Midgley, David F. (1976). "A Simple Mathematical Model of Innovative Behavior." *Journal of Consumer Research*, 3 (June): 31–41.

Midgley, David F., and Grahame R. Dowling (1978). "Innovativeness: The Concept and Its Measurement." *Journal of Consumer Research*, 4 (March): 229–242.

Milliman, Ronald E. (1982). "Using Background Music to Affect the Behavior of Supermarket Shoppers." *Journal of Marketing*, 46 (Summer): 86–91.

Miniard, Paul W., and Joel B. Cohen (1979). "Isolating Attitudinal and Normative Influences in Behavioral Intentions Models." *Journal of Marketing Research*, 16 (February): 102–110.

Mitchell, Andrew A. (1978). "An Information Processing View of Consumer Behavior." *Proceedings of the American Marketing Association's Education Conference.* Chicago: American Marketing Association, 188–197.

Mitchell, Andrew A. (1979). "Involvement: A Potentially Important Mediator of Consumer Behavior." In *Advances in Consumer Research*, edited by William L. Wilkie, Vol. VI, 191–196. Ann Arbor, Mich.: Association for Consumer Research.

Mitchell, Arnold (1978). *Consumer Values: A Typology.* Menlo Park, Calif.: SRI International.

Mizerski, Richard W., Neil K. Allison, and Stephen Calvert (1980). "A Controlled Field Study of Corrective Advertising Using Multiple Exposures and a Commercial Medium." *Journal of Marketing Research*, 17 (August): 341–348.

Mizerski, Richard W., Linda L. Golden, and Jerome B. Kernan (1979), "The Attribution Process in Consumer Decision Making." *Journal of Consumer Research*, 6 (September): 123–140.

Monroe, Kent B. (1971). "Psychophysics of Price: A Reappraisal." *Journal of Marketing Research*, 8 (May): 248–250.

Monroe, Kent B. (1973). "Buyers' Subjective Perceptions of Price." *Journal of Marketing Research*, 10 (February): 70–80.

Monroe, Kent B., and Peter J. LaPlaca (1972). "What Are the Benefits of Unit Pricing." *Journal of Marketing*, 36 (July): 16–22.

Montgomery, David B. (1967). "Stochastic Modeling of Consumer Behavior." *Industrial Management Review*, 8 (Spring): 31–42.

Montgomery, David. B. (1969). "A Stochastic Response Model with Application to Brand Choice." *Management Science*, 15 (March): 323–337.

Montgomery, David B. and Adrian B. Ryans (1973). "Stochastic Models of Consumer Choice Behavior." In *Consumer Behavior: Theoretical Sources*, edited by Scott Ward and Thomas S. Robertson, 521–576. Engelwood Cliffs, N. J.: Prentice-Hall.

Montgomery, David B., and Alvin J. Silk (1971). "Clusters of Consumer Interests and Opinion Leaders' Spheres of Influence." *Journal of Marketing Research*, 8 (August): 317–321.

Morgan, Fred W. (1979). "The Admissibility of Consumer Surveys as Legal Evidence in Courts." *Journal of Marketing*, 43 (Fall): 33–40.

Morris, Ruby Turner, and Claire Sekulski Bronson (1969). "The Chaos of Competition Indicated by *Consumer Reports*." *Journal of Marketing* 33 (July): 26–34.

Moschis, George P. (1976). "Social Comparison and Informal Group Influence." *Journal of Marketing Research*, 8 (August): 237–244.

Moschis, George P., and Gilbert A. Churchill, Jr. (1978). "Consumer Socialization: A Theoretical and Empirical Analysis." *Journal of Marketing Research*, 15 (November): 599–609.

Munsinger, Gary M., Jean E. Weber, and Richard W. Hansen (1975). "Joint Home Purchasing Decisions by Husbands and Wives." *Journal of Consumer Research*, 1 (March): 60–66.

Murphy, Patrick E. (1978). "The Effect of Social Class on Branch and Price Consciousness for Supermarket Products." *Journal of Retailing*, 54 (Summer): 33–42.

Murphy, Patrick E., and William A. Staples (1979). "A Modernized Family Life Cycle." *Journal of Consumer Research*, 6 (June): 12–22.

Myers, John G. (1967). "Determinants of Private Brand Attitudes." *Journal of Marketing Research*, 4 (February): 73–81.

Myers, James H., and John F. Mount (1973). "More on Social Class vs. Income as Correlates of Buyer Behavior." *Journal of Marketing*, 37 (April): 71–73.

Myers, James H., and William H. Reynolds (1967). *Consumer Behavior and Marketing Management*. New York: Houghton Mifflin.

Myers, James H., and Thomas S. Robertson (1972). "Dimensions of Opinion Leadership." *Journal of Marketing Research*, 9 (February): 41–46.

Nakanishi, Masao (1974). "Decision-Net Models and Human Information Processing." In *Buyer/Consumer Information Processing*, edited by G. David Hughes and Michael L. Ray 75–88. Chapel Hill; University of North Carolina Press.

Narayana, Chem L., and Rom J. Markin (1975), "Consumer Behavior and Product Performance: An Alternative Conceptualization." *Journal of Marketing*, 39: 1–6.

Neisser, Ulric (1967). *Cognitive Psychology*. New York: Appleton-Century Crofts.

Neisser, Ulric (1975). *Cognition and Reality*. San Francisco: W. H. Freeman and Company.

Nelson, Philip (1970). "Information and Consumer Behavior." *Journal of Political Economy*, 78 (March–April): 311–329.

Nelson, Philip (1974). "Advertising is Information." *Journal of Political Economy*, (July–August): 729–754.

Nevers, J. V. (1972). "Extensions of a New Product Growth Model." *Sloan Management Review*, 14 (Fall): 51–62.

Newman, Joseph W. (1977). "Consumer External Search: Amount and Determinants." In *Consumer and Industrial Buying Behavior*, edited by A. G. Woodside, J. N. Sheth, and P. D. Bennett, 79–94. New York: North-Holland.

Newman, Joseph W., and Bradley D. Lockeman (1975). "Measuring Prepurchase Information Seeking." *Journal of Consumer Research*, 2 (December): 216–222.

Newman, Joseph W., and Richard Staelin (1971). "Multivariate Analysis of Differences in Buyer Decision Time." *Journal of Marketing Research*, 8 (May): 192–198.

Newman, Joseph W., and Richard Staelin (1972). "Prepurchase Information Seeking for New Cars and Major Household Appliances." *Journal of Marketing Research*, 9 (August): 249–257.

Newman, Joseph W., and Richard Staelin (1973). "Information Sources of Durable Goods." *Journal of Advertising Research*, 13 (April): 19–29.

Newman, Larry M., and Ira J. Dolich (1979). "An Examination of Ego Involvement as a Modifier of Attitude Change Caused from Product Testing." In *Advances in Consumer Research*, edited by William L. Wilkie, Vol. VI, 180–183. Ann Arbor, Mich.: Association for Consumer Research.

Nicosia, Francesco M. (1966). *Consumer Decision Processes.* New York: Prentice-Hall.

Nisbett, R. A. (1968). "The Decline and Fall of Social Class." In *Tradition and Revolt*, edited by R. A. Nisbett. New York: Random House.

Noerager, Jon P. (1979). "An Assessment of CAD—A Personality Instrument Developed Specifically for Marketing Research." *Journal of Marketing Research*, 16 (February): 53–59.

Nord, Walter R., and J. Paul Peter (1980). "A Behavior Modification Perspective on Marketing." *Journal of Marketing*, 44 (Spring): 36–47.

Norman, Donald A., and Daniel G. Bobrow (1975). "On Data-Limited and Resource-Limited Processes." *Cognitive Psychology*, 7 (January): 44–64.

Olshavsky, Richard W. (1973). "Consumer-Salesman Interaction in Appliance Retailing." *Journal of Marketing Research*, 10 (May): 208–212.

Olshavsky, Richard W., and Donald H. Granbois (1979). "Consumer Decision Making—Fact or Fiction?" *Journal of Consumer Research*, 6 (September): 93–100.

Olshavsky, Richard W., and Donald H. Granbois (1980). "Rejoinder." *Journal of Consumer Research*, 7 (December): 333–334.

Olson, Jerry C. (1979). "Theories of Information Encoding and Storage: Implications for Consumer Research." In *The Effect of Information on Consumer and Market Behavior, Proceedings Series*, edited by Andrew A. Mitchell, 49–60. Chicago: American Marketing Association.

Olson, Jerry C., and Philip A. Dover (1976). "Effects of Expectation Creation and Disconfirmation on Belief Elements of Cognitive Structure." In *Advances in Consumer Research*, edited by B. B. Anderson, Vol. III, 168–175. Cincinnati: Association for Consumer Research.

Olson, Jerry C., and Philip A. Dover (1978). "Cognitive Effects of Deceptive Advertising." *Journal of Marketing Research*, 15 (February): 29–38.

O'Shaughnessy, John, and Michael J. Ryan (1979). "Marketing Science and Technology." In *Conceptual and Theoretical Developments in Marketing*, edited by O. C. Ferrell, et al., 577–589. Chicago: American Marketing Association.

Ostermeier, Arlene Bjorngoard, and Joanne Bubolz Eicher (1966). "Clothing and Appearance as Related to Social Class and Social Acceptance of Adolescent Girls." *Michigan State University Quarterly Bulletin*, 48 (February): 431–436.

Ostlund, Lyman E. (1974). "Perceived Innovation Attributes as Predictors of Innovativeness." *Journal of Consumer Research*, 1 (September): 23–29.

Palda, Kristian S. (1966). "The Hypothesis of a Hierarchy of Effects: A Partial Evaluation." *Journal of Marketing Research*, 3 (February): 13–24.

Parfitt, J. H., and B. J. K. Collins (1968). "Use of Consumer Panels for Brand Share Prediction." *Journal of Marketing Research*, 5 (May): 131–146.

Park, C. Whan, Robert W. Hughes, Vinod Thukral, and Roberto Friedmann (1981). "Consumers' Decision Plans and Subsequent Choice Behavior." *Journal of Marketing*, 45 (Spring): 33–47.

Park, C. Whan, and Richard J. Lutz (1982). "Decision Plans and Consumer Choice Dynamics." *Journal of Marketing Research*, 19 (February): 108–115.

Parsons, Leonard J., and Randall L. Schultz (1976). *Marketing Models and Econometric Research*. New York: Elsevier North-Holland.

Patchen, Martin (1974). "The Locus and Basis of Influence on Organizational Decisions," *Organizational Behavior and Human Performance*, 2 (2), 195–211.

Pernica, Joseph (1974). "The Second Generation of Market Segmentation Studies: An Audit of Buying Motivations," In *Life Style and Psychographics*, edited by W. D. Wells, 279–313. Chicago: American Marketing Association.

Pessemier, Edgar A. (1959). "A New Way to Determine Buying Decisions." *Journal of Marketing*, 24 (October): 41–46.

Peter, J. Paul, and Walter R. Nord (1982). "A Clarification and Extension of Operant Conditioning Principles in Marketing." *Journal of Marketing*, 46 (Summer): 102–107.

Peter, J. Paul, and Michael J. Ryan (1976). "An Investigation of Perceived Risk at the Brand Level." *Journal of Marketing Research*, 13 (May): 184–188.

Peters, William H. (1970). "Relative Occupational Class Income: A Significant Variable in the Marketing of Automobiles." *Journal of Marketing*, 34 (April): 74–77.

Peterson, Esther (1974). "Consumerism as a Retailer's Asset." *Harvard Business Review*, 52 (May–June): 91–101.

Peterson, Robert A., and Roger A. Kerin (1977). "The Female Role in Advertisements: Some Experimental Evidence." *Journal of Marketing*, 41 (October): 59–63.

Petri, Herbert L. (1981). *Motivation: Theory and Research*. Belmont, Calif.: Wordsworth.

Pettigrew. A. M. (1977). "The Industrial Purchasing Decision as a Political Process." *European Journal of Marketing*, 9 (1): 4–19.

Pirie, M. C. (1960). "Marketing and Social Classes: An Anthropologist's View." *Management Review*, 49 (September): 45–48.

Plummer, Joseph T. (1971). "Life Style Patterns and Commercial Bank Credit Card Usage." *Journal of Marketing*, 35 (April): 35–41.

Polli, Roland, and Victor Cook (1969). "Validity of the Product Life Cycle." *Journal of Business*, 42 (October): 385–400.

Postman, L., J. S. Bruner, and E. McGinnies (1948). "Personal Values as Selective Factors in Perception." *Journal of Abnormal and Social Psychology*, 42: 142–152.

Prasad, V. Kanti (1975). Socioeconomic Product Risk and Patronage Preferences of Retail Shoppers." *Journal of Marketing*, 39 (July): 42–47.

Pruden, Henry O. (1969). "The Outside Salesman: Interorganizational Link." *California Management Review*, 12 (2): 57–66.

Rainwater, Lee, Richard P. Coleman, and Gerald Hanel (1959). *Workingman's Wife*. New York: Oceana.

Rao, Tanniru R. (1969). "Consumer's Decision Process: Stochastic Models." *Journal of Marketing Research*, 6 (August): 320–329.

Ray, Michael L. (1973a). "Psychological Theories and Interpretations of Learning." In *Consumer Behavior: Theoretical Sources*, edited by Scott Ward and Thomas S. Robertson, 45–117. Englewood Cliffs, N. J.: Prentice-Hall.

Ray, Michael L. (1973b). "Marketing Communication and the Hierarchy of Effects." Cambridge, Mass.: working paper, Marketing Science Institute.

Ray, Michael L., and Donald A. Dunn (1978). "Local Consumer Information Systems for Services: The Market for Information and Its Effect on the Market." In *The Effect of Information on Consumer and Market Behavior*, edited by Andrew A. Mitchell, Proceedings Series, 92–96. Chicago: American Marketing Association.

Ray, Michael L., and William L. Wilkie (1970). "Fear: The Potential of an Appeal Neglected by Marketing." *Journal of Marketing*, 34 (January): 54–62.

Reingen, Peter H., and Jerome B. Kernan (1977). "Compliance with an Interview Request: A Foot-in-the-Door, Self-Perception Interpretation." *Journal of Marketing Research*, 14 (August): 365–369.

Reingen, Peter H., and Jerome B. Kernan (1979). "More Evidence on Interpersonal Yielding." *Journal of Marketing Research*, 16 (November): 558–593.

Reynolds, Fred D., and William R. Darden (1972). "Intermarket Patronage: A Psychographic Study of Consumer Outshoppers." *Journal of Marketing*, 36 (October): 50–54.

Reynolds, Fred D., and William D. Wells (1977). *Consumer Behavior.* New York: McGraw-Hill.

Reynolds, W. H. (1965). "More Sense about Market Segmentation." *Harvard Business Review*, 43 (September–October): 107–114.

Rich, Stuart U., and Subhash C. Jain (1968). "Social Class and Life Cycle as Predictors of Shopping Behavior." *Journal of Marketing Research*, 5 (February): 41–49.

Ricks, David, Marilyn V. C. Fu, and Jeffrey S. Arpan (1974). *International Business Blunders.* Columbus, Ohio: Grid, Inc.

Reisman, David (1950). *The Lonely Crowd.* New Haven, Conn.: Yale University Press.

Ring, Alexander, Mitchell Shriber, and Raymond L. Horton (1980). "Some Effects of Perceived Risk on Consumer Information Processing." *Journal of the Academy of Marketing Science*, 8 (Summer): 255–263.

Robertson, Thomas S. (1967). "The Process of Innovation and Diffusion of Innovation." *Journal of Marketing*, 31 (January): 14–19.

Robertson, Thomas S. (1971). *Innovative Behavior and Communications.* New York: Holt, Rinehart and Winston.

Robertson, Thomas S. (1974). "A Critical Examination of 'Adoption Process' Models of Consumer Behavior." In *Models of Buyer Behavior*, edited by J. N. Sheth, 271–295. New York: Harper & Row.

Robertson, Thomas S., and James N. Kennedy (1968). "Prediction of Consumer Innovators: Application of Multiple Discriminant Analysis." *Journal of Marketing Research*, 5 (February): 64–69.

Robertson, Thomas S., and James H. Myers (1969). "Personality Correlates of Opinion Leadership and Innovative Buying Behaviors." *Journal of Marketing Research*, 6 (May): 164–168.

Robertson, Thomas S., and John R. Rossiter (1974). "Children and Commercial Persuasion: An Attribution Theory Analysis." *Journal of Consumer Research*, 1 (June): 13–20.

Robertson, Thomas S., and Scott Ward (1973). "Consumer Behavior Research: Promise and Prospects," In *Consumer Behavior: Theoretical Sources*, edited by Thomas S. Robertson and Scott Ward, 3–42. Englewood Cliffs, N. J.: Prentice-Hall.

Robinson, J. P. (1977). *How Americans Use Time.* New York: Praeger, Publishers.

Robinson, Patrick J., Charles W. Faris, and Yoram Wind (1967). *Industrial Buying and Creative Marketing.* Boston: Allyn & Bacon, Inc.

Roedder, Deborah L. (1981). "Age Differences in Children's Responses to Television Advertising: An Information-Processing Approach." *Journal of Consumer Research*, 8 (September): 144–153.

Rogers, Everret M. (1976). "New Product Adoption and Diffusion." In *Selected Aspects of Consumer Behavior: A Summary from the Perspective of Different Disciplines*, RANN Program, 223–238. Washington, D.C.: National Science Foundation.

Rogers, Everett, and Rehka Agarwala-Rogers (1976). *Communication in Organizations.* New York: The Free Press.

Rogers, Everett M., and F. Floyd Shoemaker (1971). *The Communication of Innovations.* New York: Free Press.

Rogers, Everett M., and J. David Stanfield (1968). "Adoption and Diffusion of New Products: Emerging Generalizations and Hypotheses." In *Applications of the Sciences in Marketing Management*, edited by F. M. Bass, C. W. King, and E. A. Pessemier, 227–250. New York: Wiley & Sons.

Rokeach, Milton (1968). *Beliefs, Attitudes, and Values.* San Francisco: Jossey-Bass, Inc.

Rokeach, Milton (1973). *The Nature of Human Values.* New York: The Free Press.

Rokeach, Milton (1979). *Understanding Human Values: Individual and Societal.* New York: The Free Press.

Roscoe, A. Marvin, Jr., Arthur Le Claire, Jr., and Leon G. Schiffman (1977). "Theory and Management Applications of Demographics in Buyer Behavior." In *Consumer and Industrial Buying Behavior*, edited by A. G. Woodside, J. W. Sheth, and P. D. Bennett. New York: North-Holland, 66–76.

Roselius, Ted (1971). "Consumer Rankings of Risk Reduction Methods." *Journal of Marketing*, 35 (January): 56–61.

Rosenberg, Milton J. (1956). "Cognitive Structure and Attitudinal Affect." *Journal of Abnormal and Social Psychology*, 53 (November): 376–382.

Ross, H. Lawrence (1965). "Uptown and Downtown: A Study of Middle-Class Residential Areas." *American Sociological Review*, 30 (2): 255–259.

Rothmyer, Karen (1975). "A Spanish Accent is Very 'In' These Days on Madison Avenue." *The Wall Street Journal*, 24 (January): 1.

Rothschild, Michael L. (1979). "Advertising Strategies for High and Low Involvement Situations." In *Attitude Research Plays for High Stakes*, edited by J. C. Maloney and B. Silverman, 74–93. Chicago: American Marketing Association.

Rothschild, Michael L., and William C. Gaidis (1981). "Behavioral Learning Theory: Its Relevance to Marketing and Promotions." *Journal of Marketing*, 45 (Spring): 70–78.

Rotzoll, Kim B. (1967). "The Effect of Social Stratification on Market Behavior." *Journal of Advertising Research*, 7 (March): 22–27.

Rubenstein, Herbert (1973). "Some Problems of Meaning in Natural Languages." In *Handbook of Communication*, edited by Ithiel de Sola Pool, et al., 27–48. Chicago: Rand McNally.

Runyon, Kenneth E. (1980). *Consumer Behavior*, 2nd ed. Columbus, Ohio: Charles E. Merrill.

Russo, J. Edward (1977). "The Value of Unit Price Information." *Journal of Marketing Research*, 14 (May): 193–201.

Russo, J. Edward, Gene Krieser, and Sally Miyashita (1975). "An Effective Display of Unit Price Information." *Journal of Marketing*, 39 (April): 11–19.

Russo, J. Edward, Barbara L. Metcalf, and Debra Stephens (1981). "Identifying Misleading Advertising." *Journal of Consumer Research*, 8 (September): 119–131.

Ryan, Michael J. (1977). "Programmatic Research Based on Fishbein's Extended Model." In *Consumer and Industrial Buying Behavior*, edited by A. G. Woodside, J. N. Sheth, and P. D. Bennett, 151–166. New York: North-Holland.

Ryan, Michael J. (1980). "Psychobiology and Consumer Research: A Problem of Construct Validity." *Journal of Consumer Research*, 7 (June): 92–96.

Ryan, Michael J., and E. H. Bonfield (1975). "The Fishbein Extended Model and Consumer Behavior." *Journal of Consumer Research*, 2 (September): 118–136.

Ryan, Michael J., and E. H. Bonfield (1980). "Fishbein's Intentions Model: A Test of External and Pragmatic Validity." *Journal of Marketing*, 44 (Spring): 82–95.

Ryan, Michael J., and Morris B. Holbrook (1982). "Decision-Specific Conflict in Organizational Buyer Behavior." *Journal of Marketing*, 46 (Summer): 62–68.

Sarbin, Theodore R., and Vernon L. Allen (1969). "Role Theory." In *The Handbook of Social Psychology* 2nd ed., edited by G. Lindzey and E. Aronson, Vol. I, 488–567. Reading, Mass.: Addison-Wesley.

Sawyer, Alan G. (1977). "Repetition and Affect: Recent Empirical and Theoretical Developments." In *Consumer and Industrial Buying Behavior*, edited by Arch G. Woodside, Jagdish N. Sheth, and Peter D. Bennett, 229–242. New York: North-Holland.

Sawyer, Alan G., and Richard J. Semenik (1978). "Carryover Effects of Corrective Advertising." In *Advances in Consumer Research*, vol. 5, edited by H. K. Hunt, 343–351. Ann Arbor, Mich.: Association for Consumer Research.

Scammon, Debra L. and Carole L. Christopher (1981). "Nutrition Education With Children Via Television: A Review." *Journal of Advertising*, 10 (2): 36–36.

Schachter, S. (1959). *The Psychology of Affiliation: Experimental Studies of the Sources of Gregariousness.* Stanford, Calif.: Stanford University Press.

Schachter, S. (1964). "The Interaction of Cognitive and Physiological Determinants of Emotional State." In *Advances in Experimental Social Psychology*, edited by L. Berkowitz. Vol. 1. New York: Academic Press.

Schachter, S., and J. E. Singer (1962). "Cognitive, Social, and Physiological Determinants of Emotional State." *Psychological Review* 59: 379–399.

Schaninger, Charles M. (1981). "Social Class Versus Income Revisited: An Empirical Investigation." *Journal of Marketing Research*, 18 (May): 192–208.

Schaninger, Charles M., and Donald Sciglimpaglia (1981). "The Influence of Cognitive Personality Traits and Demographics on Consumer Information Acquisition." *Journal of Consumer Research* 8 (September): 208–216.

Schiffman, Leon G., and Vincent Gaccione (1974). "Opinion Leaders in Institutional Markets." *Journal of Marketing*, 38 (April): 49–53.

Schiffman, Leon G., and Leslie Kanuk (1978). *Consumer Behavior.* Englewood Cliffs, N. J.: Prentice-Hall.

Schramm, Wilbur (1955). "How Communication Works," In *The Process and Effects of Mass Communication*, edited by Wilbur Schramm, 3–26. Urbana: University of Illinois Press.

Schroder, H., M. Driver, and S. Streufert (1966). *Human Information Processing.* New York: Holt, Rinehart and Winston.

Schultz, D. P. (1964). "Spontaneous Alteration Behavior in Humans: Implications for Psychological Research." *Psychological Bulletin*, 62: 394–400.

Schumpeter, Joseph A. (1954). *History of Economic Analysis.* New York: Oxford University Press.

Scott, Carol A. (1977). "Modifying Socially-Conscious Behavior: The Foot-in-the-Door Technique." *Journal of Consumer Research*, 4 (December): 156–164.

Scott, William A. (1968). "Attitude Measurement." In *The Handbook of Social Psychology*, 2nd ed., edited by Gardner Lindzey and Elliot Aronson, Vol. II, 204–273. Reading, Mass.: Addison-Wesley.

Sethi, S. Prakash (1971). "Comparative Cluster Analysis for World Markets." *Journal of Marketing Research*, 8 (August): 348–354.

Settle, Robert B. (1972). "Attribution Theory and Acceptance of Information." *Journal of Marketing Research*, 9 (February): 85–88.

Settle, Robert B., and Linda L. Golden (1974). "Attribution Theory and Advertiser Credibility." *Journal of Marketing Research*, 11 (May): 181–185.

Sexton, Donald E., Jr. (1971). "Comparing the Cost of Food to Blacks and to Whites—A Survey." *Journal of Marketing*, 35 (July): 40–46.

Sexton, Donald E., Jr. (1972). "Black Buyer Behavior." *Journal of Marketing*, 36 (October): 36–39.

Sexton, Donald E., Jr. (1974). "Differences in Food Shopping Habits by Areas of Residence, Race, and Income." *Journal of Retailing*, 50 (Spring): 37–48.

Sharp, Harry, and Paul Mott (1956). "Consumer Decisions in the Metropolitan Family." 22 (October): 149–156.

Shaw, Marvin E. (1976). *Group Dynamics: The Psychology of Small Group Behavior*, 2nd ed. New York: McGraw-Hill.

Shepard, R. N. (1962a). "Analysis of Proximities: Multidimensional Scaling With an Unknown Distance Function, Part I." *Psychometrika*, 27: 125–139.

Shepard, R. N. (1962b). "Analysis of Proximities: Multidimensional Scaling With an Unknown Distance Function, Part II." *Psychometrika*, 27.

Shepard, R. N. (1966). Metric Structures in Ordinal Data." *Journal of Mathematical Psychology*, 3: 287–315.

Sherif, M. (1953). "The Concept of Reference Groups in Human Relations," In *Group Relations at the Crossroads*, edited by M. Sherif and M. O. Wilson, 203–231. New York: Harper & Row.

Sherif, M., and C. I. Hovland (1961). *Social Judgment: Assimilation and Contrast Effects in Communication and Attitude Change*. New Haven, Conn.: Yale University Press.

Sherif, C. W., M. Sherif, and R. E. Nebergall (1956). *Attitude and Attitude Change: The Social Judgment—Involvement Approach*. Philadelphia: W. B. Saunders Company.

Sheth, Jagdish N. (1968). "How Adults Learn Brand Preferences." *Journal of Advertising Research*, 8 (September): 25–36.

Sheth, Jagdish N. (1973). "A Model of Industrial Buyer Behavior." *Journal of Marketing*, 37 (October): 50–56.

Sheth, Jagdish N. (1974). "A Theory of Family Buying Decisions." In *Models of Buyer Behavior*, edited by Jagdish N. Sheth, 17–33. New York: Harper & Row, Publishers.

Sheth, Jagdish N. (1977). "Recent Developments in Organizational Buying Behavior," In *Consumer and Industrial Buying Behavior*, edited by A. G. Woodside, J. N. Sheth, and P. D. Bennett, 17–34. New York: North-Holland.

Sheth, Jagdish N. (1979). "The Surpluses and Shortages in Consumer Behavior Theory and Research." *Journal of the Academy of Marketing Science*, 7 (Fall): 414–427.

Sheth, Jagdish N., and W. Wayne Talarzyk (1972). "Perceived Instrumentality and Value Importance as Determinants of Attitudes." *Journal of Marketing Research*, 9 (November): 465–467.

Sheth, Jagdish N., and M. Venkatesan (1968). "Risk Reduction Processes in Repetitive Consumer Behavior." *Journal of Marketing Research*, 5 (August): 307–310.

Shibutani, Tamotsu (1955). "Reference Groups as Perspectives." *American Journal of Sociology*, 60 (May): 562–569.

Shimp, Terence A. (1979). "Social Psychological (Mis)representations, in Advertising." *Journal of Consumer Affairs*, 13 (Summer): 28–40.

Shimp, Terence A., and Ivan L. Preston (1981). "Deceptive and Nondeceptive Consequences of Evaluative Advertising." *Journal of Marketing*, 45 (Winter): 22–31.

Shoaf, F. Robert (1959). "Here's Proof—The Industrial Buyer is Human." *Industrial Marketing*, 44 (May): 126–128.

Shoemaker, Robert W., and F. Robert Shoaf (1975). "Behavior Changes in the Trial of New Products." *Journal of Consumer Research*, 2 (September): 104–109.

Shuptrine, F. K., and G. Samuelson (1976). "Dimensions of Marital Roles in Consumer Decision Making: Revisited." *Journal of Marketing Research*, 13 (February); 87–91.

Siegel, P. M. (1971). *Prestige in the American Occupational Structure.* Unpublished diss., University of Chicago.

Silk, Alvin J., and Glen L. Urban (1978). "Pre-Test-Market Evalution of New Packaged Goods: A Model and Measurement Methodology." *Journal of Marketing Research*, 15 (May): 171–191.

Simmons, Robert G., and Morris Rosenberg (1971). "Functions of Children's Perceptions of the Stratification System." *American Sociological Review*, 36 (April): 235–249.

Simon, Herbert A. (1969). *The Sciences of the Artificial.* Cambridge, Mass.: The M.I.T. Press.

Simon, Herbert A. and Kevin Gilmartin (1973). "A Simulation of Memory for Chess Positions." *Cognitive Psychology*, 5 (July): 29–46.

Skinner, B. F. (1953). *Science and Human Behavior.* New York: Macmillan.

Skinner, B. F. (1969). *Contingencies of Reinforcement: A Theoretical Analysis.* New York: Appleton-Century-Crofts.

Skinner B. F. (1971). *Beyond Freedom and Dignity.* New York: Bantam/Vintage Book.

Slocum, John W., Jr. and H. Lee Mathews (1970). "Social Class and Income as Indicators of Consumer Credit Behavior." *Journal of Marketing*, 34 (April): 69–74.

Smith, Robert E., and Shelby D. Hunt (1978). "Attributional Processes and Effects in Promotional Situations." *Journal of Consumer Research,* 5 (December): 149–158.

Smith, Wendell R. (1956). "Product Differentiation and Market Segmentation as Alternative Marketing Strategies." *Journal of Marketing*, 21 (July): 3–8.

Solomon, Paul J., and Ronald F. Bush (1977). "Effects of Black Models in Television Advertising on Product Choice Behavior." In *Contemporary Marketing Thought*, edited by B. A. Greenberg and D. N. Bellenger, 19–22. Chicago: American Marketing Association.

Solomon, Paul J., Ronald F. Bush, and Joseph F. Hair, Jr. (1976). "White and Black Consumer Sales Response to Black Models." *Journal of Marketing Research*, 13 (November): 431–434.

Sorenson, Ralph Z., and Ulrich E. Wiechmann (1975). "How Multinationals View Marketing Standardization." *Harvard Business Review*, 53 (May–June): 38–56.

Sparkman, Richard M., Jr. and William B. Locander (1980). "Attribution Theory and Advertising Effectiveness." *Journal of Consumer Research*, 7 (December): 219–224.

Spekman, Robert E. (1979). "Influence and Information: An Exploratory Investigation of the Boundary Role Person's Basis of Power." *Academy of Management Journal*, 22 (1): 104–117.

Staats, A. W. (1975). *Social Behaviorism.* Homewood, Ill.: The Dorsey Press.

Stafford, James E. (1966). "Effects of Group Influence on Consumer Brand Preferences." *Journal of Marketing Research*, 3 (February): 68–75.

Stafford, James E., Al E. Birdwell, and Charles E. Van Tassel (1970). "Integrated Advertising—White Backlash?" *Journal of Advertising Research*, 10 (April): 15–20.

Stafford, James E., and A. Benton Cocanougher (1977). "Reference Group Theory." In *Selected Aspects of Consumer Behavior*, RANN Program, 361–379. Washington, D. C.: National Science Foundation.

Stafford, James E., Keith Cox, and J. B. Higginbotham (1968). "Some Consumption Pattern Differences Between Urban Whites and Negroes." *Social Science Quarterly*, 49 (December): 626–627.

Steadman, Major (1969). "How Sexy Advertisements Affect Brand Recall." *Journal of Advertising Research*, 9 (February): 15–19.

Stefflre, Volney E. (1968). "Market Structure Studies: New Products for Old Markets and New Markets (Foreign) for Old Products." In *Application of the Sciences in Marketing Management*, edited by F. M. Bass, C. S. King, and E. A. Pessemier. New York: Wiley & Sons.

Sternthal, Brian, and C. Samuel Craig (1973). "Humor in Advertising." *Journal of Marketing*, 37 (October): 12–18.

Sternthal, Brian, and C. Samuel Craig (1974). "Fear Appeals: Revisited and Revised." *Journal of Consumer Research*, 1 (December): 22–34.

Stigler, George J. (1961). "The Economics of Information." *Journal of Political Economy*, 69 (June): 213–225.

Stockwell, E. G. (1976). *The Methods and Materials of Demography.* New York: The Academic Press.

Stone, L. Joseph, and Joseph Church (1979). *Childhood and Adolescence*, 4th ed. New York: Random House.

Strauss, George (1962). "Tactics of Lateral Relationships: The Purchasing Agent." *Administrative Science Quarterly*, 7 (2): 161–186.

Sturdivant, Frederick D. (1973). "Subculture Theory: Poverty, Minorities, and Marketing." In *Consumer Behavior: Theoretical Sources*, edited by S. Ward and T. S. Robertson, 469–520. Englewood Cliffs, N. J.: Prentice-Hall.

Summers, John O. (1970). "The Identity of Women's Clothing Fashion Opinion Leaders." *Journal of Marketing Research*, 7 (May): 178–185.

Summers, John O. (1971). "New Product Interpersonal Communications." In *Combined Proceedings of the American Marketing Association*, edited by F. C. Allvine, 428–433. Chicago: American Marketing Association.

Summers, John O. (1972). "Media Exposure Patterns of Consumer Innovators." *Journal of Marketing*, 36 (January): 43–49.

Swinth, Robert L., Jack E. Gaumnitz, and Carlos Rodriguez (1975). "Decision Making Processes: Using Discrimination Nets for Security Selection." *Decision Sciences*, 6: 439–448.

Szybillo, George J., and Jacob Jacoby (1974). "Effects of Different Levels of Integration on Advertising Preference and Intention to Purchase." *Journal of Applied Psychology*, 59 (3): 274–280.

Tarpey, Lawrence X., Sr. (1974). "A Brand Loyalty Concept—A Comment." *Journal of Marketing Research*, 11 (May): 214–217.

Tarpey, Lawrence X., Sr. (1975). "Brand Loyalty Revisited: A Commentary." *Journal of Marketing Research*, 12 (November): 488–491.

Teel, Jesse E., William O. Bearden, and Richard M. Durand (1979). "Psychographics of Radio and Television Audiences." *Journal of Advertising Research*, 19 (April): 53–56.

Telser, L. G. (1962). "The Demand for Branded Goods as Estimated from Consumer Panel Data." *Review of Economics and Statistics*, 44 (August): 330–334.

Thorelli, Hans B., Helmut Becker, and Jack Engledow (1975). *The Information Seekers.* Cambridge, Mass.: Bellinger Publishing Co.

Tigert, Douglas, and Behrooz Farivar (1981). "The Bass New Product Growth Model: A Sensitivity Analysis for a High Technology Product." *Journal of Marketing*, 45 (Fall): 81–90.

Tinbergern, N. (1951). *The Study of Instinct.* London: Oxford.

Toffler, Alvin (1970). *Future Shock.* Random House.

Tolley, Stuart and John J. Goett (1971). "Reactions to Blacks in Newspapers." *Journal of Advertising Research*, 11 (April): 11–17.

"Toilet Tissues: Softness, Strength, or Price?" (1977). *Consumer Reports*, 42 (April): 466–468.

Torgerson, Warren S. (1958). *Theory and Methods of Scaling.* New York: Wiley & Sons.

Tucker, W. T. (1964). *The Social Context of Economic Behavior.* New York: Holt, Rinehart and Winston.

Tull, Donald S., and Del I. Hawkins (1980). *Marketing Research.* New York: Macmillan.

Tulving, Endel (1972). "Episodic and Semantic Memory." In *Organization of Memory*, edited by Endel Tulving and W. Donaldson. New York: Academic Press.

Turk, J. L., and N. W. Bell (1972). "Measuring Power in Families." *Journal of Marriage and the Family*, 34 (May): 215–222.

Turner, R. H. (1970). *Family Interaction.* New York: Wiley & Sons.

Tybout, Alice M. (1978). "Relative Effectiveness of Three Behavioral Influence Strategies as Supplements to Persuasion in a Marketing Context." *Journal of Marketing Research*, 15 (May): 229–242.

Tyree, Andrea, and Robert W. Hodge (1978). "Five Empirical Landmarks." *Social Forces*, 56 (March): 761–769.

Udel, John G. (1965). "Can Attitude Measurement Predict Consumer Behavior." *Journal of Marketing*, 29 (October): 46–50.

Urban, Glen L. (1970). "SPRINTER Mod III: A Model for the Analysis of New Frequently Purchased Consumer Goods." *Operations Research*, 18 (September–October): 805–853.

Urban, Glen L., and John R. Hauser (1980). *Design and Marketing of New Products.* Englewood Cliffs, N. J.: Prentice-Hall.

Urban, Glen L., and Richard Karash (1971). "Evolutionary Model Building." *Journal of Marketing Research*, 8 (February): 62–66.

Ursic, Michael (1980). " 'Consumer Decision Making—Fact or Fiction?' Comment." *Journal of Consumer Research*, 7 (December): 331–333.

Valle, Valerie A., and Melanie Wallendorf (1977). "Consumer Attributions of the Cause of Their Product Satisfaction and Dissatisfaction," In *Consumer Satisfaction, Dissatisfaction and Complaining Behavior*, edited by Ralph L. Day, 26–30. Bloomington: Indiana University.

Veblen, Thorstein (1899). *The Theory of the Leisure Class.* New York: Macmillan.

Venkatesan, M. (1966). "Experimental Study of Consumer Behavior Conformity and Independence." *Journal of Marketing Research*, 3 (November): 384–387.

Vinson, Donald E., and J. Michael Munson (1976). "Personal Values: An Approach to Market Segmentation." In *Marketing: 1776–1976 and Beyond*, edited by K. L. Bernhardt, 313–317. Chicago: American Marketing Association.

Ward, Scott (1974). "Consumer Socialization." *Journal of Consumer Research*, 1 (September): 1–14.

Ward, Scott, and Daniel B. Wackman (1972). "Children's Purchase Influence Attempts and Parental Yielding." *Journal of Marketing Research*, 9 (August): 316–319.

Ward, Scott, Daniel B. Wackman, and Ellen Wartella (1975). *Children Learning to Buy: The Development of Consumer Information Processing Skills.* Cambridge, Mass: The Marketing Service Institute.

Ward, Scott, Daniel B. Wackman, and Ellen Wartella (1977). *How Children Learn to Buy.* Sage Publications.

Warner, W. Lloyd, Marchia Meeker, and Kenneth Eels (1949). *Social Class in America: A Manual of Procedure for the Measurement of Social Status.* Chicago: Science Research Associates.

Wason, P. C., and P. N. Johnson-Laird (1972). *Psychology of Reasoning.* Cambridge, Mass.: Harvard University Press.

Webster, Frederick E., Jr. (1978). "Management Science in Industrial Marketing." *Journal of Marketing*, 42 (January), 21–27.

Webster, Frederick E., Jr., and Frederick von Pechmann (1970). "A Replication of the 'Shopping List' Study." *Journal of Marketing*, 34: 61–63.

Webster, Frederick E., Jr., and Yoram Wind (1972a). "A General Model for Understanding Organizational Buying Behavior." *Journal of Marketing*, 36 (April): 12–19.

Webster, Frederick E., Jr., and Yoram Wind (1972b). *Organizational Buying Behavior.* Englewood Cliffs, N. J.: Prentice-Hall.

Weick, K. E. (1971). "Group Processes, Family Processes, and Problem Solving." In *Family Problem Solving*, edited by J. Aldous, et al., 265–281. Hinsdale, Ill.: Dryden Press.

Welch, Joe L. (1980). *Marketing Law.* Tulsa, Okla.: PPC Books.

Wells, William D. (1972). "Seven Questions About Lifestyle and Psychographics." In *Combined Proceedings of the American Marketing Association*, edited by B. W. Becker and H. Becker. Chicago: American Marketing Association.

Wells, William D., and Stephen C. Cosmas (1977). "Life Styles." In *Selected Aspects of Consumer Behavior: A Summary from the Perspectives of Different Disciplines*, RANN Program, 299–316. Washington, D.C.: National Science Foundation.

Wells, William D., and George Gubar (1966). "Life Cycle Concept in Marketing Research." *Journal of Marketing Research*, 23 (November): 355–363.

Wells, William D., and Leanard LoSciuto (1966). "Direct Observation of Purchasing Behavior." *Journal of Marketing Research*, 3 (August): 227–233.

Werner, Osward, and Donald T. Campbell (1970). "Translating, Working Through Interpreters, and the Problems of Decentering." In *A Handbook of Method in Cultural Anthropology*, edited by R. Naroll and R. Cohen, 398–420. Garden City, N.Y.: The Natural History Press.

Wicker, Allan W. (1975). "Commentaries on Belk, 'Situational Variables and Consumer Behavior'." *Journal of Consumer Research*, 2 (December): 165–167.

Wilkie, William L., and Edgar A. Pessemier (1973). "Issues in Marketing's Use of Multi-Attribute Attitude Models." *Journal of Marketing Research*, 10 (November): 428–441.

Wilson, David T. (1971). "Industrial Buyers' Decision-Making Styles." *Journal of Marketing Research*, 8 (November): 433–436.

Wilson, David T., H. Lee Mathews, and James W. Harvey (1975). "An Empirical Test of the Fishbein Behavioral Intention Model." *Journal of Consumer Research*, 1 (March): 39–48.

Wind, Yoram (1977). "Brand Loyalty and Vulnerability," In *Consumer and Industrial Buying Behavior*, edited by Arch G. Woodside, Jagdish N. Sheth, and Peter D. Bennett, 313–319. New York: Elsevier-North Holland.

Wind, Yoram (1978). "Issues and Advances in Segmentation Research." *Journal of Marketing Research*, 15 (August): 317–337.

Wingfield, Arthur, and Dennis L. Byrnes (1981). *The Psychology of Human Memory.* New York: Academic Press.

Witt, Robert E. (1969). "Informal Social Group Influence on Consumer Brand Choice." *Journal of Marketing Research*, 6 (November): 473–476.

Witt, Robert E., and Grady D. Bruce (1972). "Group Influence and Brand Choice Congruence." *Journal of Marketing Research*, 9 (November): 440–443.

Woodside, Arch (1972). "Dominance and Conflict in Family Purchasing Decisions." In *Proceedings of the Third Annual Association for Consumer Research Conference*, edited by M. Venkatesan, 650–659. Chicago: Association for Consumer Research.

Wolfe, D. M. (1959). "Power and Authority in the Family." In *Studies in Social Power*, edited by D. Cartwright. Ann Arbor: University of Michigan Press.

Wright, Peter L. (1974). "The Harrassed Decision Makers: Time Pressures, Distractions, and the Use of Evidence." *Journal of Applied Psychology*, 59 (October): 555–561.

Wright, Peter L., and Frederic Barbour (1977). "Phased Decision Strategies: Sequels to an Initial Screening." In *North-Holland/TIMS Studies in the Management Sciences*, edited by Martin K. Starr and Milan Zeleny, Vol. 6, *Multiple Criteria Decision Making*, 91–109. Amsterdam: North Holland.

Wrightsman, Lawrence S., and Fillmore H. Sanford (1975). *Psychology: A Scientific Study of Behavior*, Monterey, Calif.: Brooks/Cole.

Yavas, Ugur, and Glen Riecken (1982) "Extensions of King and Summers' Opinion Leadership Scale: A Reliability Study." *Journal of Marketing Research*, 19 (February): 154–155.

Zajonc, Robert B. (1960). "The Concepts of Balance, Congruity, and Dissonance." *Public Opinion Quarterly*, 24: 280–296.

Zajonc, Robert B. (1965). "Social Facilitation." *Science*, 149: 269–274.

Zajonc, Robert B. (1980). "Feeling and Thinking: Preferences Need No Inferences." *American Psychologist*, 35 (February): 151–175.

Zajonc, Robert B., and Hazel Markus (1982). "Affective and Cognitive Factors in Preferences." *Journal of Consumer Research*, 9 (September): 123–131.

Zaltman, Gerald, Charistian R. A. Pinson, and Reinhard Angelman (1973). *Methatheory and Consumer Research.* New York: Holt, Rinehart and Winston, Inc.

Zaltman, Gerald, and Ronald Stiff (1973). "Theories of Diffusion." In *Consumer Behavior: Theoretical Sources*, edited by S. Ward and T. S. Robertson, 416–468. Englewood Cliffs, N. J.: Prentice-Hall.

Zaltman, Gerald, and Melanie Wallendorf (1979). *Consumer Behavior: Basic Findings and Management Implications.* New York: Wiley & Sons.

Zielski, Hubert A. (1959). "The Remembering and Forgetting of Advertising." *Journal of Marketing*, 23 (January): 239–243.

Zimbardo, Philip G. (1979). *Essentials of Psychology and Life*, 10th ed. Glenview, Ill.: Scott, Foresman and Company.

Author Index

Subject Index